Contents

The maps and town plans in this guide are based upon the Ordnance Survey of Great Britain with the permission of the Controller of Her Majesty's Stationery Office. Crown Copyright reserved.

PRINCIPAL SIGHTS

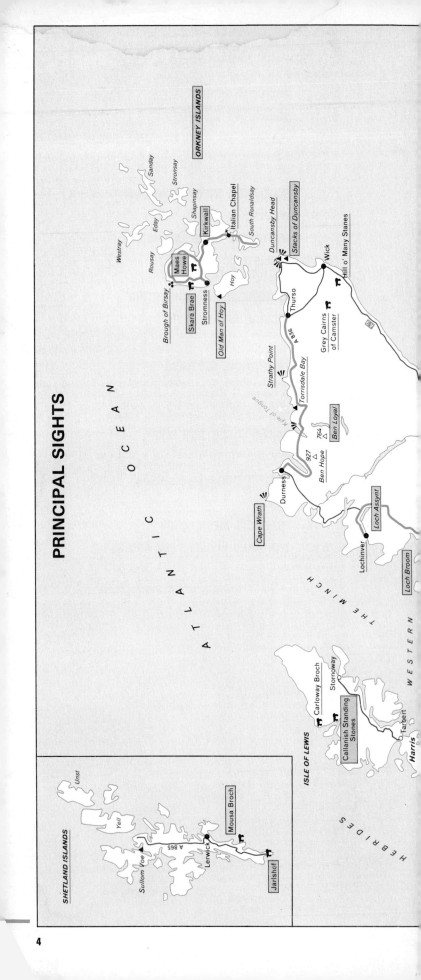

ATLANTIC OCEAN

ORKNEY ISLANDS

Westray
Rousay
Eday
Sanday
Stronsay
Shapinsay

Kirkwall
Italian Chapel
South Ronaldsay

Maes Howe
Brough of Birsay
Skara Brae
Stromness
Hoy
Old Man of Hoy

Duncansby Head
Stacks of Duncansby
Wick
Hill o' Many Stanes

Thurso
B 836
Grey Cairns of Camster

Strathy Point

Torrisdale Bay
Kyle of Tongue
Ben Loyal
764

Ben Hope
927

Durness
Cape Wrath

Loch Assynt
Lochinver
Loch Broom

THE MINCH

WESTERN HEBRIDES

ISLE OF LEWIS

Carloway Broch
Stornoway
Callanish Standing Stones
Tarbert
Harris

SHETLAND ISLANDS

Unst
Yell
Sullom Voe
A 965
Lerwick
Mousa Broch
Jarlshof

4

PLANNING YOUR HOLIDAY
AND LEISURE TIME

The various Michelin publications are complementary and specifically designed to be used in conjunction with one another, as all are cross-referenced.

Accommodation. – The **Michelin Red Guide Great Britain and Ireland** recommends and classifies a selection of hotels and restaurants, based on regular on the spot enquiries and visits. The establishments are classified according to the standard of comfort of their amenities. Those noted for a pleasant setting and decor, a particularly quiet or secluded site, a warm welcome and those with a special mention for the cuisine are distinguished by specific symbols.

The town plans indicate the exact location of the listed hotels and restaurants, major through routes, important public buildings, tourist information centres (🖪) and the principal historic buildings and other tourist sights.

Other information given under the individual town headings includes, STD dialling codes, early closing days (ECD) when shops shut at midday, ferry links and frequencies, airport and terminal addresses and cross-references to the appropriate Michelin guide and map.

Touring. – The **Michelin Map 401** at a scale of 1 : 400 000 covers the whole of Scotland. The existence of a town plan and the inclusion of a hotel and restaurant in the Red Guide are indicated on the map by a red frame and red underlining respectively. In addition to a wealth of motoring information, tourist details include golf courses where visitors are welcome, scenic routes, long distance footpaths, pleasure boat harbours, National Forest Parks and country parks.

Tourist Information Centres. – National, regional and local centres denoted by 🖪 are open during the summer months, and some for longer, from 10am to 6pm as a general rule. Tourist information points have a series of boards giving information on the immediate area. For the seasonal centres the Red Guide Great Britain and Ireland gives the months of opening. In addition to the usual range of services the various centres offer a local booking service for accommodation (small fee charged). Some also offer a Book-a-bed-ahead service (deposit required).

National Trust for Scotland Visitor Centres. – The **National Trust for Scotland** (NTS) is a separate organization from the National Trust, covering England, Wales and Northern Ireland. The two bodies share the same objectives : "to promote the preservation of this heritage of fine buildings, beautiful landscape and historic places, and to encourage public enjoyment of them." A reciprocal arrangement exists whereby members of one body are admitted free to the properties of the other.

The Scottish organization has established **NTS Visitor Centres** throughout the country (Bannockburn, Ben Lawers, Culloden, Glencoe, Killiecrankie ...). The purpose of these, in addition to serving the property on which they are situated, is to help the visitor take the fullest advantage of the facilities in that area.

The address and phone number of the NTS headquarters are listed in the Practical Information Chapter at the end of the guide.

Historic Buildings and Monuments Directorate. – The Directorate administers all sites in the care of the Secretary of State for Scotland. An annual membership card gives free access to 330 sites across the country. Such sites are denoted in the Times and Charges Chapter at the end of the guide by the initials HBM after the admission price. The hours for manned sites are standard, although some may have particular days off. Unmanned sites are open most days and there is no admission charge.

ACCESS TO SCOTLAND'S WIDE OPEN SPACES

In the absence of a system of national parks the Countryside Commission for Scotland has created an alternative, where both landscape conservation and public access for recreation are successfully combined. The country park is the most common element in the Scottish park system.

Country Parks. – These areas are primarily for outdoor recreation and are often situated near large towns.

Some like Culzean Country Park are on NTS properties. See Michelin map 401 for their distribution.

National Nature Reserves. – Nature conservation is the main aim of these reserves established by the Nature Conservancy Council. In general visitors are welcome and amenities include visitor centres, nature trails and observation hides. Most reserves have a warden. The reserves provide the visitor with a good chance of seeing wildlife. In some cases there are certain restrictions.

National Forest Parks. – The Forestry Commission, Scotland's largest landowner, created forest parks in areas of scenic attraction. Timber growing is the main activity but recreation is encouraged. In addition to designated forest drives and marked walks and trails there are picnic sites, camping and caravan sites and visitor centres. The four in Scotland are Glenmore, Queen Elizabeth, Argyll and Galloway Forest Parks. The Michelin map 401 gives their location. Other Forestry Commission properties are open to the public on foot and are well equipped with recreational facilities.

Long distance footpaths. – At present Scotland has three long distance footpaths waymarked by the thistle symbol. The Countryside Commission for Scotland publishes official guides and route maps (H.M.S.O.) giving full details of routes and scenery. These are available at bookshops and some tourist information centres. Each route has a ranger service to help and advise.

West Highland Way. – This runs 95 miles from Milngavie on the outskirts of Glasgow, north to Fort William. The route follows the eastern shore of Loch Lomond, crosses the remote Rannoch Moor and the mountains of Lochaber, passing Ben Nevis on the way. Guide and map available.

Speyside Way. – Of the 60 miles from Tugnet on Spey Bay to Glenmore Lodge, east of Aviemore, only the northern 30 miles to Ballindalloch are completed. The Speyside Way passes through varied countryside as it follows the river from the coast to the Cairngorms. Leaflets available.

Southern Upland Way. – This 212 mile coast to coast footpath joins Portpatrick in the west to Cockburnspath in the east. Some of the longer stretches are arduous, covering remote hill country. Guide and map available.

The thistle sign which waymarks the Scottish long distance footpaths.

SPORTS AND OUTDOOR ACTIVITIES

The Practical Information Chapter at the end of the guide lists the addresses of the relevant organizations and associations.

Angling. – Scotland provides excellent fishing. Salmon, sea trout and brown trout abound in the many lochs and rivers. Permits are available from private owners and local angling associations. For further information apply locally to an information office or a fishing tackle dealer.

Sea angling. – The waters around the Scottish coast provide ample opportunities for sea anglers to test their skills. Some of the main centres include Eyemouth, Arbroath, Stonehaven, Kippford, Ullapool, Shetland ... where there is a ready availability of boats for hire. Sea angling festivals are regular features in some resorts.

Sailing. – In a land where sea and freshwater lochs abound, sailing is well catered for. The western seaboard with its many isles and sheltered water is a safe playground. Many sailing centres have local regattas. Some of the main centres are Largs, Tobermory, Lamlash Bay, Oban (Kilmelford) Crammond Port, Aberdour, Helensburgh, Crinan, Tarbert. Inland, sailing facilities are good on Loch Earn, Loch Lomond and Loch Morlich. Cruising yachts can be hired on the western seaboard and the Caledonian Canal.

Mountaineering and hillwalking. – Scotland provides ideal country for hillwalking, mountaineering and rock climbing. Many Scottish peaks lie within easy reach of a public road but some areas in the Cairngorms, Skye and Knoydart are very remote. The relatively low altitude of most peaks, only four are over 4 000ft, is deceptive as rapid weather changes make them hazardous. All climbers should be aware of the potential dangers and be properly equipped. Winter may present an entirely different picture from spring and summer.
Some of the principal climbing centres include Arran, Skye, Ben Nevis, Glencoe and the Cairngorms. The western and northern Highlands provide some remoter ranges and peaks. The more popular, Bens Nevis and Lomond, have well marked footpaths. The Scottish Mountaineering Club publishes a series of specialized guide books which are available from climbing shops and good booksellers.

Golf. – As the alleged home of golf Scotland provides a wealth of possibilities for golfers. Apart from the world famous courses at St Andrews, Turnberry, Carnoustie, Muirfield or Dornoch, public and many private courses welcome visitors. See the current Red Guide Great Britain and Ireland for those open to visitors.

Pony trekking and riding. – A wide choice of centres throughout Scotland welcome the beginner or the experienced rider for a day, or longer holiday spells. Trekking and trail riding are good ways of discovering the countryside.

Skiing. – The main centres include Cairngorm in Speyside, Glenshee north of Blairgowrie and off the Lecht road.

Water sports. – Lochs Morlich and Earn are two of the more important inland sites.

Times and charges for admission to sights described in the guide are listed at the end of the guide.

The sights are listed alphabetically in this section either under the place – town, village or area – in which they are situated or under their proper name.

Every sight for which there are times and charges is indicated by the initials tc in the margin in the main part of the guide.

Introduction
to the tour

Scotland is a country of infinite variety and contrasts where one image conjures up another of placid lochs and magnificent mountain scenery, of beautiful islands and spectacular clifflines, of bleak and desolate moors and rich pastoral landscapes, of austere castles, rugged ruins and villages of vernacular charm.

Discover the Scotland of the past, through the many prehistoric sites, a rich heritage of clans and chieftains, feuds and fighting and the traditions with all the colour and pageantry of the games and gatherings.

A hundred thousand welcomes. Ceud Mìle Fàilte.

(Baker/Vloo)

Kilchurn Castle – Loch Awe

13

SCOTLAND'S SCENIC SPLENDOUR

A few facts. – Scotland has an area of 30 414 sq miles (England 50 362 sq miles) including the numerous fringing islands. Deeply penetrated by the Atlantic on the west and by the North Sea on the east, most places are within 60 miles of the sea. There are 787 islands (under one quarter are inhabited) and 6 214 miles of coastline. The resident population in 1981 was estimated at 5 117 146 giving an average density of 171 per square mile. 98 % of Scotland is classified as countryside.

A country of contrasts. – Although generally recognized as a mountainous country the infinite variety of landscapes is one of Scotland's major tourist assets. The country is traditionally divided into three areas, the Southern Uplands, Central Lowlands or Midland Valley and the Highlands.

Southern Uplands. – Here the hills are lower and more rounded than their northern counterparts. In the southwest the smoothly rounded forms of the Galloway hills are dominated by the more rugged granitic masses of the Merrick (2 764ft-843m), Criffel (1 886ft-569m) and Cairnsmore of Fleet (2 331ft-711m). Both the **Clyde** and **Tweed** have their sources in the vicinity of the lead bearing Lowther Hills. The Nith, Annan and Esk drain southwards to the Solway Firth. Hill country continues eastwards with the **Moorfoot** and **Lammermuir Hills** which demarcate the **Southern Upland Fault**. To the south the fertile Tweed basin, with the rich arable farmland of the Merse, is fringed by the Cheviot Hills, acting as a frontier barrier.

Central Lowlands. – The **Highland Boundary Fault** extending from Stonehaven to Helensburgh and Southern Upland Fault delimit this lower lying rift valley. Neither low lying nor a rift valley, the area has little land below 400ft and is not without its own hill masses, the **Campsie Fells, Kilpatrick Hills, Ochils** and **Sidlaws.**
The Lothian plains fringing the Firth of Forth and stretching to the sea at Dunbar are interrupted on the southern outskirts of Edinburgh by the Pentland Hills. Lowland continues along the carselands of the Forth up through Strathearn to the Tay and the rich Carse of Gowrie, overlooked by the **Sidlaw Hills.**To the north the

14

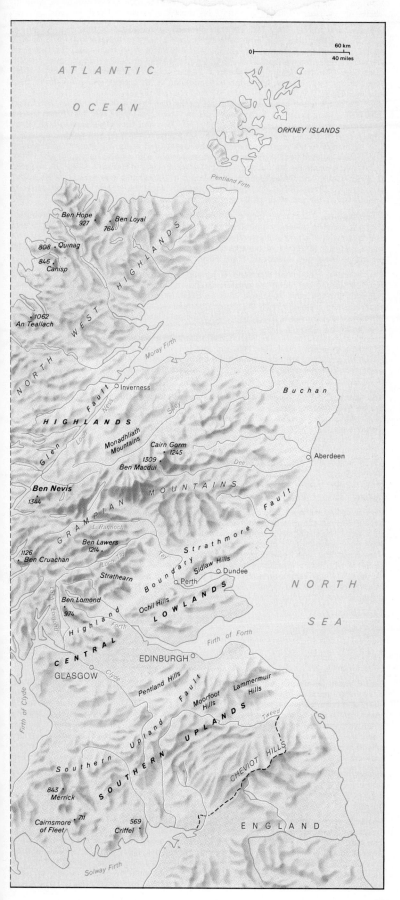

ATLANTIC

OCEAN

ORKNEY ISLANDS

Pentland Firth

Ben Hope
927
Ben Loyal
764

808 Quinag

846
Canisp

1062
An Teallach

NORTH WEST HIGHLANDS

Moray Firth

Inverness

Buchan

HIGHLANDS

Glen

Loch Ness

Spey

Monadhliath
Mountains

Cairn Gorm
1245

1309
Ben Macdui

Dee

Aberdeen

Ben Nevis
1344

GRAMPIAN MOUNTAINS

Fault

L. Rannoch

Ben Lawers
1214

Strathmore

1126
Ben Cruachan

Loch Tay

Tay

Boundary

Sidlaw Hills

Dundee

Strathearn

Perth

NORTH

Ben Lomond
974

Ochil Hills

LOWLANDS

SEA

Loch Lomond

Highland

Forth

CENTRAL

Firth of Forth

GLASGOW

EDINBURGH

Firth of Clyde

Clyde

Pentland Hills

Fault

Moorfoot
Hills

Lammermuir
Hills

Upland

SOUTHERN UPLANDS

Tweed

Southern

CHEVIOT HILLS

843
Merrick

Cairnsmore
of Fleet

711

569
Criffel

ENGLAND

Solway Firth

0   60 km
0   40 miles

fertile sweep of **Strathmore** passes northeastwards, to become beyond Brechin the more restricted **Howe of the Mearns.** The minor relief features of Dumbarton, Stirling and Edinburgh Castle Rocks, North Berwick and the Bass Rock are associated with volcanic activity.

Highlands. – Altitudes are low by Alpine standards but much of this area lies above 2 000ft. The **Great Glen Fault,** stretching from Loch Linnhe to the Moray Firth, acts as a divide between the Grampian Mountains and the North West Highlands. The **Cairngorms** are an extensive tract of land above 3 500ft punctuated by peaks rising to over 4 000ft **(Cairn Gorm** 4 084ft-1 245m ; **Ben Macdui** 4 296ft-1 309m and **Braeriach** 4 248ft-1 295m). West of the Spey are the Monadhliath Mountains, a featureless rolling upland of peat and moorland.

Here are to be found some of the highest peaks **(Ben Nevis** 4 406ft-1 344m, **Ben Lawers** 3 984ft-1 214m) finest sea lochs **(Lochs Fyne** and **Long)** and freshwater ones **(Lochs Lomond, Katrine, Awe** and **Tay)** and great rivers (Spey, Tay, Dee and Don). The Buchan and Moray Firth (Laigh of Moray) lowlands fringe the mountains to the east and north.

The Highlands to the north and west of the Great Glen are a wilder and more remote area where isolated peaks rise above a plateau surface with an average height of 2 000ft. Outstanding examples are the spectacular Torridon peaks of **Suilven** (2 399ft-731m) **Canisp** (2 779ft-846m) and **Quinag** (2 653- 808m), and in Sutherland **Bens Hope** (3 042ft-927m) and **Loyal** (2 504ft-764m). The indented western coastline where sea lochs separate peninsulas, is fringed offshore by the **Inner** and **Outer Hebrides.**

The coastline. – Scotland's long coastline is deeply indented and largely rocky, although the east coast is generally smoother and straighter. The coastline is one of impressive cliff faces with offshore arches and stacks as at Hoy in Orkney, Cape Wrath and St Abb's Head, or great stretches of dune-backed sandy beaches, the asset of such east coast resorts as Montrose, Aberdeen, Fraserburgh and Nairn.

The islands. – Mainland Scotland is fringed by approximately 787 islands with the Hebrides strung out along the western seaboard, as the largest group (500). The Inner Hebrides include such evocative isles as Skye, Mull, Iona, Jura and Islay. The Minch separates the mainland from the Outer Hebrides, an archipelago stretching 140 miles from the Butt of Lewis to Barra Head. The principal islands in the Firth of Clyde are Arran, Bute and the Cumbraes. Beyond the Pentland Firth in the north are two important clusters of isles and islets, the Orkney Islands comprising 90 in all and further north the Shetland Islands, a group of about 100. Fair Isle, St Kilda and Rockall are isolated outliers of this island fringe. Many are now uninhabited but it was on these distant isles that the Norse and Gaelic cultures resisted the longest. Today each one has a jealously guarded character of its own.

The Munros. – A large percentage of Scotland lies above 800ft and hills and mountains are an ever present aspect of the landscape. In 1891 Sir Hugh Munro drew up tables of all the Scottish peaks over 3 000ft. With perfected surveying techniques the total includes some 280. Many climbers make Munro-bagging a lifetime task or the object of a day's outing in the hills.

Heights in the guide have been given in both feet and metres to facilitate correlation with the Michelin map**401**. The table below gives a few conversions to help as a ready reckoner.

feet	100	200	300	500	800	1000	2000	3000	4000
metres	30	61	91	152	244	305	610	910	1219

Conservation policy. – The difficult task of reconciling the increasing demand for public access and recreation with the conservation of the countryside and in particular the areas of outstanding scenic value is met in Scotland – in the absence of a National Park system – by the cooperation of numerous bodies. Agreements ensure the conservation of our scenic heritage with its wildlife. The National Trust for Scotland owns and administers some of Scotland's most important mountain areas – Balmacara-Kintail, Glencoe and Torridon – where ranger-naturalists meet the need for public access to the countryside. The visitor centres and rangers provide information, expert advice, illustrated talks and a programme of guided walks in summer.

GARDENS

Somewhat surprisingly for its northern latitude, gardens whether historically or horticulturally, are an important part of Scotland's heritage.

Gulf Stream Gardens. – For the foreign visitor these are pehaps the most unexpected. In secluded spots all along Scotland's Atlantic seaboad are to be found gardens where a profusion of tropical and sub-tropical plants flourish. The outstanding example is Osgood Mackenzie's woodland garden at Inverewe, in its perfect Highland setting. Moving southwards others include Carae Woodland Garden, the Younger Botanic Gardens, Benmore and the Logan Botanic Gardens, to name only a few open at all times. A wider selection of private gardens are open on specified dates under Scotland's Gardens Scheme *(see the Practical Information Chapter, at the end of the guide).*

Particular Plant Collections. – In addition to the specialized collections of some of the Botanic Gardens (rhododendrons at Edinburgh) certain of the National Trust properties are known for their specialization. Brodie Castle and Threave Garden excel in daffodils, Inverewe in a wide variety of exotics and Branklyn in alpines and peat garden plants.

Gardens with a difference. – The formal gardens at Pitmedden, Edzell and Drummond Castle reflect the spread of Renaissance ideas from the continent and in particular France. The garden at Castle Kennedy was the result of a move away from the too formal but without the informality of the late Romantic Movement. Many gardens simply adorned an ancestral home as at Brodick, Falkland, Kellie and Tyninghame. Crathes Castle has its linked but intimate enclosures, which are distinguished by colour, season or plant species. The topiary at Earlshall remains a rare example in Scotland.

WILDLIFE

Scotland is endowed with a rich natural heritage of wildlife, vegetation and land. It was nominated a priority area, as one of the great wildlife regions of the world, by the World Conservation Strategy in 1980. Man has been largely responsible for destroying certain habitats (deforestation and in particular the loss of the native pinewoods) and the extinction of the fauna. The first to suffer were the larger animals – reindeer, elk, brown bear and wild boar – which are extinct in Scotland in the wild state. The tide is turning and active cooperation between government bodies and specialised organizations is now responsible for the successful conservation of this heritage of habitats and wildlife.

The **Nature Conservancy Council** (f 1949) establishes reserves to safeguard certain wildlife communities, as on Rhum for the deer, North Rona for the grey seal, St-Kilda for its seabird colony, Ben Lawers for its important Arctic-alpine flora and Beinn Eighe with its remnant of the native pinewoods.

The **Scottish Wildlife Trust** was founded in 1964 to combat the increasing dangers to Scotland's wildlife. The SWT wildlife reserves number 65 many of which are sites of national or international importance for nature conservation. The Loch of the Lowes *(qv)* one of the osprey's regular nesting sites and St Abb's Head *(qv)* with its famous breeding seabirds are two sites which are managed in conjunction with the NTS. Not all reserves are open to the public and access to others may be restricted to avoid undue disturbance.

Discovering Scotland's Wildlife. – The beauty of a landscape or site can be heightened by the rewarding experience of seeing an osprey, golden eagle, secretive pine marten, a dainty stepping ptarmigan or that acrobat the capercaillie.

Of Scotland's **birds of prey** the most majestic but elusive is the golden eagle which is still to be found on Skye, the Outer Hebrides and on the mainland in the Aviemore area, Deeside and North West Highlands, often in the former territory of the sea eagle. The fish eating osprey is once again to be seen in Scotland, which is a major European stronghold for that other raptor the hen harrier with its aerial acrobatics and unusual ground nesting habits. Both the peregrine falcon with its high powered dive and buzzards are quite common sightings in the Highlands. Of the better known **game birds** the capercaillie (reintroduced

(Tom Weir)

Capercaillie

*c*1770), the biggest of the grouse family has increased in number with the spread of forestry plantations. Red grouse thrive on the heather moors, with black grouse or blackcocks on forest edges and moors. The latter indulge in ferocious looking mock battles at the lek or traditional display areas. The ptarmigan, the fourth member of the grouse family with its successful white camouflage prefers the mountain tops. This is also the habitat of that colourful bird but reluctant flyer the dotterel and the elusive snow bunting. The offshore islands (Bass Rock, Ailsa Craig, St Kilda ...) and cliffs of Scotland are the haunts of a wide variety of **sea birds** from the comical puffin with its burrowing habits, to the ledge dwellers, the guillemots and kittiwakes, razorbills, fulmars and other members of the gull family. The Bass Rock *(qv)*, which is one of the easier gannetries to visit, gave the gannet its scientific name *Sula bassana*. Excursions from Anstruther take visitors to the Isle of May which is usually thronged with seabirds.

The early mammal population counted elks, northern lynx, brown bear, beaver, reindeer wild boar, ponies, white cattle with black points (still found in some parks today) and the wolf. With re-afforestation Scotland has become the last British stronghold of otters on the west coast, wildcats, and the secretive pine marten. The fox is a newcomer to the north eastern coastal lowlands and badgers have recolonised most of the mainland. Some of these can now be seen in the Highland Wildlife Park near Kincraig in Speyside or Edinburgh Zoo. Rare breeds such as the Soay sheep from the St Kilda group of islands are part of the museum of farming life at Pitmedden Garden. Those scene stealers, the shaggy Highland cattle pasture the parklands of Scotland's castles. The rarer white cattle with black points are still to be seen at Drumlanrig.

FOLLOW THE COUNTRY CODE

Guard against all risk of fire.
Fasten all gates.
Keep dogs under proper control.
Keep to the paths across farmland.
Avoid damaging fences, hedges and walls.
Leave no litter.
Safeguard water supplies.
Protect wildlife, wild plants and trees.
Go carefully on country roads.
Respect the life of the countryside.

HISTORICAL TABLE AND NOTES

Prehistoric Period : early migrations

4000-2500 BC	Neolithic settlers arrive by the Atlantic route
2000-1000 BC	Bronze Age agriculturalists arrive from the continent
800 BC-400 AD	Iron Age peoples from central Europe

The Romans 1C AD - 4C AD

55,54 BC	Caesar invades Britain ; conquest begins 43 AD
71-84 AD	Romans push north into Caledonia ; Agricola establishes a line of forts between the Clyde and Forth
84	Mons Graupius : Agricola defeats the Caledonian tribes
142 - c145	Building of turf rampart, the 39 mile long Antonine Wall
end 4C	Power of Rome wanes

Dark Ages 4C - 11C : merging of kingdoms into medieval Scotland

397	St Ninian establishes a Christian mission at Whithorn
563	St Columba and his companions land on Iona. The Celtic Church evolves in isolation until the Synod of Whitby (663/4) when certain Celtic usages were abandoned to conform with the practices of Rome
8C	Beginning of Norse raids. The Western Isles remain under Norse domination until 1266, the Orkney and Shetland Islands until 1468-9
843	Kenneth MacAlpine obtains the Pictish throne unifying the Picts and the Scots

Medieval Scotland

1034	Strathclyde becomes part of the Scottish Kingdom
1058-93	Malcolm III ; His second queen Margaret introduces the Catholic Church
1124-53	David I last of the Margaretsons, reorganizes the church, settles monastic orders and creates royal burghs, all of which increase the monarchy's prestige
1249-86	Alexander III the last Canmore king ; brief period of peace and prosperity
1263	Battle of Largs
1290	Margaret the Maid of Norway dies

The Wars of Independence

1296	Edward's choice, John Balliol, abdicates during the first of the Hammer of the Scots punitive conquering campaigns in Scotland 1296, 1298, 1303 and 1307
1297	Wallace wins the Battle of Stirling Bridge ; Falkirk the following year is a defeat
1306-29	Robert the Bruce ; kills the Comyn ; is crowned at Scone then starts the long campaign to free Scotland
1314	Battle of Bannockburn
1320	**Declaration of Arbroath** ; Treaty of Northampton (1328) recognizes Scotland's Independence

The Stewarts (later Stuarts)

1406-37	James I ; James takes the reins of power in 1424 after 18 years in English captivity
1410	Teaching began at St Andrews University ; founded 1412 ; Papal Bull 1413
1411	Battle of Harlaw
1437-60	Accession of James II following the assassination of his father at Perth
1440	Black Dinner
1451	Founding of Glasgow University
1455	Fall of the Black Douglases
1460-88	Accession of James III following the death of James II at the siege of Roxburgh
1468-9	Orkney and Shetland Islands pass to Scotland as the dowry of Margaret of Denmark
1488-1513	Accession of James IV following his father's death after Sauchieburn
1493	Forfeiture of the Lordship of the Isles
1495	Founding of Aberdeen's first University (King's College) ; Marischal 1593
1513-42	Death of James IV at the Battle of Flodden ; Accession of James V
1542-67	Mary Queen of Scots
1544-7	Rough Wooing or Hertford's invasions
1548	The five year old Mary is sent to France for safety and affianced to the French Dauphin
1559	Riot at Perth
1560	**Reformation** ; death of Mary's French husband, François II
1561	Mary returns to Scotland as an 18 year old widow ; 4 years later she marries her cousin, Henry Stewart, Lord Darnley
1567	Murder of Darnley ; Bothwell becomes Mary's third husband ; she abdicates, and flees to England after the Battle of Langside (1568) ; executed after 19 years in captivity (1587)

(Photo Lauros-Giraudon)

Mary Queen of Scots, Musée Carnavalet

The Stuarts and the Commonwealth

1567-1625	James VI of Scotland and I of England
1582	Raid of Ruthven
1600	Gowrie Conspiracy
1603	**Union of the Crowns** with the accession of James VI to the throne of England
1625-49	Charles I ; Scottish coronation ceremony in Edinburgh (1633)
1638	National Covenant ; Glasgow General Assembly abolishes Episcopacy
1643	The Solemn League and Covenant
1645	Montrose loses the Battle of Philiphaugh
1650	Execution of Montrose following that of Charles I the previous year
1651	Cromwellian occupation, the **Commonwealth**
1660	Monck and his regiment set out from Coldstream on the long march south to London on 1 January 1660 which leads to the Restoration
1660-85	Charles II
1661	Restoration of Episcopacy
1685-8	Accession of James VII : Monmouth Rebellion 1685
1688	James VII flees the country in late December
1689	William and Mary are offered the crown ; **Battle of Killiecrankie**
1692	Massacre of Glencoe
1702-14	Queen Anne
1707	**Union of the Parliaments**

House of Hanover

1714-27	Accession of George I
1715	Jacobite Rising, Battle of Sheriffmuir
1719	Jacobite Rising in Glen Shiel
1727-60	George II
1745	Jacobite Rising ; The Year of the Prince opens with the raising of the standard at Glenfinnan
1746	**Battle of Culloden**
1747-82	Proscription Act
1760-1820	George III
1790	Opening of Forth-Clyde Canal
1803-22	Building of the Caledonian Canal
1822	George IV State Visit
1843	The Disruption
1871-8	Tay Railway Bridge ; disaster the following year
1883-90	Forth Railway Bridge
1886	Crofters Act
1906-13	Home Rule Bills
1928	National Party of Scotland formed ; SNP founded in 1934
1951	Stolen Stone of Destiny found in Arbroath
1964	Opening of the Forth Road Bridge ; Tay Bridge opens 2 years later
1964-1970s	Discovery and development of major oil and natural gas fields in the North Sea with the subsequent growth of the North Sea Oil Industry
1974-5	Reorganization of local government ; the old counties and burghs were abolished to be replaced by 9 regions and island areas *(see map p 3)* with a secondary tier of districts
1979	Referendum on proposed Assembly failed to produce the necessary 40%

HISTORICAL NOTES

Kingdom of the Western Isles. – The early Scottish nation owed much to its western territories. The royal line descended from the Dalriadic royal house with the accession of Kenneth MacAlpine as king of Alba, the territory north of the Forth and Clyde. Scottish kings had their ancient burial place, Reilig Oran, on Iona and the nation took its name from the western kingdom of the Scots.

During the Dark Ages the territory of Scotland was occupied by the Britons of Strathclyde, the Scots of Dalriada, the Angles of Northumbria and the Picts of the north. In the 8 and 9C the first Norse raiders arrived by sea. These were followed by peaceful settlers in search of new lands who occupied the western isles which they called 'Sudreyiar' or southern isles. Gradually the isles became independent territories over which the Dalriadic kings had no power. The kingdoms of the Picts and Scots merged, under the Scot Kenneth MacAlpine, to form Alba later to become Scotia, while the western fringes remained under Norse sway.

In 1098 by the Treaty of Tarbert King Edgar, the son of Malcom Canmore, ceded to **Magnus Barefoot,** King of Norway (1093-1103) "all the islands around which a boat could sail". Magnus included Kintyre having had his galley dragged across the isthmus. On the death of Magnus the native ruler of Argyll, **Somerled** (d 1164) seized power and assumed the kingship of the Isles and briefly of Man, under the tutelage of Norway. Somerled died in 1164 fighting the Scots. Alexander II (1214-49) set out on a campaign to curb Norse rule but he died on Kerrera. It was his son Alexander III (1249-86) who following the **Battle of Largs** *(qv)* against King Haakon IV negotiated the Treaty of Perth in 1266 returning the Western Isles to Scotland. Orkney and Shetland remained Norse until 1468-9.

It was a Macdonald descendant of Somerled, Donald of Islay (d 1386) who assumed the title Lord of the Isles. There were four lords before James IV annexed the title in 1493. This title is still borne by the Prince of Wales.

The Wars of Independence (1296-1330). – On the death of the Maid of Norway, the direct heir to the throne in 1290, Edward I was instrumental in choosing from amongst the various **Competitors** the ultimate successor. In 1292 John Balliol, later known as Toom Tabard, became king and the vassal of Edward. Following Balliol's 1296 treaty with the French, Edward set out for the north on the first of several pacification campaigns. Strongholds fell one by one from Dunbar to Kildrummy Castle and thus started several decades of intermittent warfare.

These years of struggle for independence from English overlordship, helped to forge a national identity. Heroes were born. The unknown knight **William Wallace** (1270-1305) rallied the resistance in the early stages achieving victory at Stirling Bridge (1277). He assumed the Guardianship in the name of Balliol. Wallace was captured in 1305 and taken to London where he was executed.

The next to rally the opposition was **Robert The Bruce** (1274-1329) grandson of one of the original Competitors and therefore with a legitimate claim to the throne. Following the killing of John Comyn, who was the son of another Competitor, Bruce had himself crowned at Scone (1306). The struggle was long and hard where victory and defeat alternated, and Border raid and counter raid succeeded one another. The name of the Black Douglas, Sir James Douglas (1286-1330) one of Bruce's faithful lieutenants became legendary in the tales of Border raiding.

Slowly Bruce forced the submission of the varying fiefs and even achieved the allegiance of Angus Og, natural son of the 4th Lord of the Isles. The victory at Bannockburn (1314) was crucial in achieving independence but formal recognition only came eight years after the **Declaration of Arbroath** (1320) with the signing of the Treaty of Northampton.

Covenanters and the Covenanting Period. – In the largely Protestant Scotland of the 17C James VI attempted to achieve a situation similar to that in England by re-establishing Episcopacy. This implied royal control of the church through the bishops appointed by the Crown. His son Charles I aroused strong Presbyterian opposition with the forced introduction of the *Scottish Prayer Book,* an event made famous by the stool throwing episode in St Giles.

By February of 1638 the **National Covenant** or Solemn Agreement was drawn up, which pledged the signatories to defend the crown and true religion. Later in the same year a Covenanter-packed General Assembly at Glasgow abolished Episcopacy, in spite of having been dissolved itself. The Covenanters, under Archibald Campbell 8th Earl of Argyll, took up arms and thus began the First Bishops War (1639).

In 1643 the **Solemn League and Covenant** united the Covenanters and English parliamentary cause against Charles I. Many like the Marquess of Montrose were torn between their loyalty to the King and Covenant. In 1644 Montrose pledged to win back Scotland for the King. At the end of a year of campaigning with a largely Highland army he was master of Scotland. Defeat came at the **Battle of Philiphaugh** (1645) and Montrose was forced into exile. In England the struggle led to the execution of Charles I (1649).

The Covenanters were quick to offer Charles II the throne on his acceptance of the Covenant. Montrose on another rallying expedition was captured and executed. Cromwell marched north defeating the Covenanters army at **Dunbar** (1650) and Scotland became an occupied country (1651-60) and part of the Commonwealth.

On the **Restoration** of Charles II, made possible by Monck's march on the capital, the king rejected his promise and restored Episcopacy (1661). The 1st Duke of Lauderdale ruled Scotland and the Covenanters suffered severe persecution. Field preachers, often "outed ministers", held out of door meetings or conventicles. Risings such as the 1666 Pentland Rising and the 1679 one were quashed respectively at **Rullion Green** by Tam Dalyell and **Bothwell Bridge** *(p 49)*. The Test Act of 1681 barring Covenanters and Catholics from holding certain offices only confirmed their defiance. The years around 1685 were known as the Killing Times and the people responsible for the persecution such as the then Lord Advocate, Sir George Mackenzie and the military commander John Graham of Claverhouse, Viscount Dundee, earned the sobriquet of "bluidy".

The death of Charles II and the prospect of a new line of openly Catholic monarchs, with the accession of his brother James VII, inspired the ill-fated **Monmouth Rebellion** led by Charles II's natural son. The two landings, one in western Scotland under the 9th Earl of Argyll and the second in western England under Monmouth both failed *(see Michelin Green Guide England : The West Country)*.

The Protestant Mary and William were invited to rule (1689). Viscount Dundee rallied the Jacobites or those faithful to King James VII who had already fled the country. The initial victory at Killiecrankie 1689 cost the life of their leader and the Highland army was later crushed at Dunkeld. The 1690 Act established for good the Presbyterian Church of Scotland.

The Jacobite Risings (1715 and 1745). – These attempts to restore the Stuarts to their throne reflected in some measure the discontent of post Union (1707) Scotland. In the late 17C Viscount Dundee had already rallied Highland support for the deposed James VII. John 11th Earl of Mar raised the standard at Braemar in the summer of 1715. The rising ended at the indecisive Battle of **Sheriffmuir**. James VIII or **the Old Pretender** (1688-1766) arrived too late and lacked the charisma of his son. His departure by boat from Montrose was furtive and final. Following this, General George Wade set out to pacify the Highlands with a programme of road and bridge building to facilitate military access.

A generation later the 1745 rising was led by **Charles Edward Stuart** or **Bonnie Prince Charlie** (1720-88) born 5 years after the first rising. After landing near Arisaig the 24 year old prince raised his standard at Glenfinnan and with an essentially Highland army won an initial victory at Prestonpans where he routed the government troops under Sir John Cope. The Prince held court at Holyroodhouse before setting out for the south. At Derby his military advisers counselled retreat which ended in the defeat of **Culloden** (1746). For 5 months the Prince wandered the Highlands and Hebrides as a hunted fugitive with £ 30 000 on his head. Shortly after Flora Macdonald enabled his flight from the Outer Hebrides. The prince embarked for lifelong exile.

The aftermath rather than the failure of the '45 was tragic for the Highlands : Highlanders were disarmed, their national dress proscribed and chieftains deprived of their rights of heritable justice. Economic and social change was accelerated.

PREHISTORIC MONUMENTS AND DARK AGE SCULPTURE

In prehistoric times seafaring invasions left a rich legacy of monuments and ancient sites.

Neolithic (4400BC-2000BC). – The settlers arriving by the western coastal route colonized the coastal areas and valleys. Skara Brae is the best such example where the local stone slabs have been used in every conceivable way. They practised collective burials in chambered tombs, which either took the form of a galleried grave or passage grave. Orkney is rich in examples as at Unston and Maes Howe, that outstanding site no doubt the tomb of some notable. Other sites on the mainland include the Clava Cairns near Inverness, the Grey Cairns of Camster near Wick and Cairn Holy I and II in the southwest.

The Bronze Age (2000BC-1000BC). – The Beaker people were continental agriculturalists who buried their dead in individual cists or graves. They erected the round cairns, stone circles and alignments as at Callanish, Ring of Brodgar, Hill o'Many Stones and Cairnpapple.

Iron Age (800BC-400AD). – This period left the largest group of monuments. These include the hill forts and settlements (Traprain, Eildon Hill North, White Caterthun and Dunadd), crannogs or lake dwellings, earth houses or souterrains (Rennibister, Tealing) and wheelhouses (Jarlshof). This period is also marked by the brochs. These hollow round towers of drystone masonry are unique to Scotland. The outstanding broch, Mousa in the Shetland Islands, dates from 1 to 2C AD. Some claim that the broch builders were the ancestors of the Picts.

Roman Scotland. – Although the conquest of Caledonia was never fully accomplished the Romans left a considerable heritage from their two main periods of occupation. The initial one (c80-c100), which started with Julius Agricola's push northwards, is notable for marching camps along the route of penetration (Dere Street), the victory at Mons Graupius *(qv)* against the native tribes in 84 AD and a chain of forts across the Forth-Clyde isthmus built prior to the general's return to Rome and retirement. In the first half of the 2C AD the Tyne-Solway line marked the northern frontier of the Roman province of Britain.
The second period followed the death in 138 of the Emperor Hadrian (builder of the wall in the 120s), when his successor Antoninus Pius, advanced the frontier to its earlier limits. In 142-c145 the turf **Antonine Wall** was built with walkway and ditch, along the Forth-Clyde line. Forts were placed at regular intervals along the wall. By the mid-160s both the wall and forts were definitively abandoned.
The southern regions continued to be patrolled, although they were no longer occupied. The relative peace was disturbed by Pictish incursions (305 and 364) and by 368 Rome was no longer a power in Scotland, although Britain remained a part of the Empire for another 40 years.

Britons. – The Barbarian invasions of Britain forced the Britons to take refuge in the barren mountains and moorlands of Cornwall, Wales, and even beyond Hadrian's Wall in southwest Scotland. It was at Whithorn, in the native kingdom of Strathclyde with its main fortress at Dumbarton *(qv)*, that the Romano-Briton St Ninian established the first Christian community in the late 4C. The **Latinus Stone** AD 450 *(p 204)* and a group of three other 5-6C tombstones at Kirkmadrine *(qv)* are a few of the rare examples of this period.

Anglo-Saxons. – The monumental **Anglian crosses** with their sculptured figures and patterns of vine scroll are the rich artistic heritage of the Northumbrian Kingdom. The 7C **Ruthwell Cross** is an outstanding example, where rich figure sculpture is accompanied by patterns of vine scroll intertwined with birds and animals, mingling Anglian and Celtic influences.

Scots. – The characteristic monument of this people of Irish descent was the **free standing cross** with ring of glory, spiral patterns and high bosses. St Martin's Cross (8C) on Iona is one of the better examples. The Scots brought with them their Celtic ornamental tradition which they applied to stonecarving, metalwork and mss illumination. The tradition was continued to some extent in the art of the Picts and the influence is also clearly seen in the works of the 14-16C school of West Highland Sculpture *(see over)*.

Picts. – In the Pictish Kingdom of the east and north, a flowering of this native culture produced the **Pictish Symbol Stones**. These incised and carved boulders and stones portray animal symbols (boar, fish, goose, snake and bull as at Burghead, *illustration p 103*) or purely abstract symbols (mirror and comb, double-disc and Z-rod, crescent and V-rod, snake and Z-rod). Their symbolism remains a mystery but the vigorous pictorial scenes tell us much about the daily life of the Picts. Later monuments, the cross-slabs, included a cross and interlace, with symbols on the reverse as on the Aberlemno churchyard stone *(illustration p 51)*. This art died out once the Scots had become rulers of Pictland c 843AD.
Sueno's Stone near Forres *(qv)* remains a unique monument closely covered with sculpture of intertwined foliage and beasts and the serried ranks of troops on the shaft.

Snake and Z-rod   Crescent and V-rod   Double disc and Z-rod

ECCLESIASTICAL ARCHITECTURE

Celtic foundations. – Of the earliest Christian communities at Whithorn and Iona there remain conjectural foundations of St Ninian's *Candida Casa* and the supposed site of Columba's cell. Sadly these western seaboards were harried by the Vikings and the monastic settlements plundered and fired. Mainland Scotland retains two of the earliest buildings erected by the Celtic clergy, the round towers of Brechin and Abernethy. Dating from the late 10C to early 11C these refuges or belfries are outliers of an Irish tradition. Although tangible remains are few, the Christian faith was an important unifying factor in Dark Age Scotland.

Anglo-Norman period. – Scotland of the mid-11C with its Celtic and Norse influences was soon to undergo a new and gradual Anglo-Norman colonization. It was the west and north, the strongholds of the old cultures, that resisted the new imprint.

The 11 and 12C were a time of church reorganization and all building efforts were concentrated on ecclesiastical works. Queen Margaret and her sons were the principal promotors. David I's church at Dunfermline has in the nave (12C) one of the most outstanding examples of Norman art. The parish churches of Leuchars and Dalmeny are equally well preserved examples of this period.

Gothic. – Early monastic foundations included Arbroath, Dryburgh, Dundrennan, Holyrood and Jedburgh. Many spanned the 12 and 13C and are early Gothic in style. Outstanding 13C Gothic buildings include Elgin, Dunblane and Glasgow Cathedrals where the lancet window, pointed arch and vaulting are triumphant. War and strife brought building to a standstill and wreaked much havoc on existing buildings. Melrose Abbey rebuilt in the 14C is in the pure Gothic tradition.

Prosperity returned to the burghs in the 15C and the great burghal churches were an expression of renewed wealth and civic pride. (Holy Rude, Stirling; St John's, Perth; St Nicolas, Aberdeen and St Mary's, Haddington). The period also saw the flourishing of collegiate churches built by the baronial class (Dunglass, Seton, Tullibardine, Crichton and Dalkeith). The style was truly Scottish, with a martial influence where buttresses were stepped, towers crenellated, and roofs stone slabbed. Some of the loveliest churches date from this last Gothic phase, such as Tullibardine and Kirk o'Steil.

The late Gothic King's College Chapel in Old Aberdeen still has a splendid crown spire *(illustration p 33)* as does St Giles in Edinburgh. Others collapsed (Linlithgow) or were never built (Haddington).

In the west, Celtic traditions persisted in the 14-16C with the flourishing of a school of **West Highland Sculpture**. The tomb slabs of unrivalled craftsmanship portray the Hebridean potentates, their martial panoply, claymores, galleys and Celtic patterns (Kilmory Knap, Kilmartin and Iona). The sculptured crosses, notably at Kilmartin and Kilmory Knap, have moving depictions of Christ Crucified.

Tomb slabs – Kilmory Knap

Also of the period is the elaborate monument (1528) of the 8th Chief of Macleod (d1546) in the small church of Rodil on Harris. Finished prior to his death the carvings represent a castle – some say Dunvegan – a galley and a variety of other subjects.

Post-Reformation. – After the Reformation many churches suffered through neglect during the protracted struggle for ownership – but few were destroyed. Most were modified to meet the needs of the Reformed Church by being subdivided, rearranged and divested of all ornament. Although generally lacking in decorative detail the churches of the Reformed faith have some interesting features well worth looking for.

Laird's loft. – A gallery reserved for a particular family or an incorporated guild in the towns. At Abercorn the Hopetoun Loft includes a suite of rooms and burial vault. The front of the gallery was often emblazoned with a painted or sculpted armorial crest as at Yester and Abercorn.

Aisle. – In a Scottish church this is an area separated from the nave or choir by an arcade. They usually served as private or memorial chapels (The Binns Aisle, Abercorn).

Church furnishings. – Little pre-Reformation woodwork remains other than at St Machar's and King's College, both in Aberdeen, and at Dunblane. All have examples of vigorously carved panels and stalls. The enclosed or box pews and bench ends were often carved as at Cullen Auld Kirk. Other interesting items include a few remaining hourglasses as sermon timers, baptismal brackets (Pencaitland) and jougs (Garvald) on the walls.

Sacrament house. – Common in the Episcopalian northeast, the sacrament house is a highly ornate wall recess for the sacrament and holy vessels. Cullen and Deskford Churches have two of the better examples.

For a pleasant stroll in a town look for the pedestrian streets indicated on the town plans.

SECULAR ARCHITECTURE

CASTLES

The earliest predecessors of the Scottish castle were the enigmatic stone built **brochs** of the 1C AD. These were truly defensive structures which already adhered to the premises of verticality. The outstanding example is at Mousa in Shetland.

The feudalisation of Scotland was marked by the introduction of the Norman motte and bailey castles. Several imposing earthen mounds or mottes remain at Duffus, Inverurie and Invernochty. The earliest stone built castles had a stone curtain wall, as a replacement for the wooden palisade, as seen at Rothesay, Sween and Dunstaffnage.

Medieval period. – Later constructions combined towers and curtain walls. 13C works include the masterly masonwork and skilfully devised defensive systems of Dirleton, Kildrummy and Caerlaverock. During the Wars of Independence Edward altered a few strongholds including Kildrummy, giving it a Harlech type gatehouse. From then on the gatehouse replaced the keep as place of strength.

In 14C Scotland weak kings and a disunited Kingdom encouraged turbulent and ambitious feudal lords to build fortified fortresses. Limited means favoured the tower house where sheer height and thickness of wall were its principal defences. The entrance at first floor level gave access to the principal apartment. Above, a single chamber at each level was served by a turnpike, which rose to the rooftop cap-house. Early examples include Drum, Threave, Castle Campbell and Craigmillar. The tradition continued with Cardoness and Newark where wings or jambs were added to increase floor space and more attention was accorded to decorative details inside. The quelling of the Douglas revolt in 1455 marked the end of baronial conflict and the Crown took over as the main builder from 1480 to 1560. The impact of the European Renaissance was limited to the royal works at Stirling, Falkland and Linlithgow.

Post Reformation. – Following the redistribution of church lands, property and monies (in Scotland the Crown did not take all) the gentry had the means to build. The tower house was adapted to conform to new ideas and ways of life, becoming less austere and more decorative. The problem of restricted space was overcome by ingeniously combining several towers to give the characteristic L or Z plans (Claypotts, Menzies, Elcho and Glenbuchat). Corbelling played an important role in the change from square to circle and the wall head became a profusion of architectural features, turrets, garrets, gables, rich in contrivance (Kellie Castle).

The tower house reached its apotheosis in the late 16 and early 17C in the Grampian area, where a local school of architecture flourished. These **baronial** masterpieces - Craigievar, Crathes, Fyvie and Castle Fraser - all show a skilful handling of traditional features and a concentration on the skyline.

The 17C saw the infiltration of foreign influences as at Crichton with its Italianate façade, Edzell with its pleasance, at Huntly Castle, the Earl's Palace in Kirkwall and the inner courtyard façade of Caerlaverock. With extensions and additions many tower houses became courtyard in plan (Craigmillar, Crichton and Castle Campbell).

Two early 17C buildings, Drumlanrig and George Heriot's Hospital, Edinburgh are Scottish in character in so far as the roofline interest is maintained and towers still play a dominant role. Both display a strong tendency to façade decoration.

The Restoration brought a new series of royal works, designed by the Architect Royal **Sir William Bruce,** (c1630-1710). Bruce excelled in the classical style which he used for the courtyard at Holyroodhouse Palace (1671), the now demolished Parliament House, Hopetoun House and his own home, Kinross House. One of the first professional architects, he was nicknamed "Kit Wren of Scotland". Bruce enlarged and remodelled the main front of the Duke of Lauderdale's principal Scottish seat, Thirlestane Castle. Bruce's successor as surveyor to the king in Scotland in 1683 was **James Smith** (c1644-1731). Smith refitted the Chapel Royal and converted the old palace at Hamilton and the castle at Dalkeith into two fashionable residences. Dalkeith House was in the best tradition of Palladianism.

Georgian. – Apart from Smith the main exponent of this style in the early 18C was **William Adam** (d1748) father of a family of famous architects. "Old Stone and Lime" dominated the period between the two Jacobite Risings. His better known works are Hopetoun House, the more modest sized Dun House, Haddo House and Duff House, a medieval castle in baroque finery. Of the sons **Robert Adam** (1728-92) was the most famous and creator of the Adam style. With his brothers he finished Hopetoun after the death of his father. Following 4 years of travel in Europe in the entourage of Charles Hope and a period when he worked on a series of London mansions (Osterley, Syon and Kenwood), Adam returned to Scotland. From this period we have Mellerstain a house of homely proportions with all the refinement of his neo-classical interiors. Altogether more grandiose and typical of his later castle style are Culzean, Seton and Airthrey Castles.

19C. – The Romantic movement was accompanied by a revival of medieval styles, as at Scone Palace, Abbotsford and Dalmeny House. David Bryce and Gillespie Graham both revived the baronial style in the Victorian period, notably at Blair and Brodick Castles respectively. Balmoral Castle is the best known example of the Scottish neo-baronial style. These imitations generally lacked the vigour and sculptural qualities of their 17C predecessors.

20C. – At the close of the century **Charles Rennie Mackintosh** (1868-1928) revived the Scottish vernacular tradition in his design for the Glasgow School of Art. Mackintosh followed this early design in the art nouveau style with Hill House in Helensburgh, a work which even today, some 80 years later, still seems modern. Another exponent of the distinctly Scottish style was **Sir Robert Lorimer** with his many restorations (Earlshall and Dunrobin Castles) and creations (Thistle Chapel in St Giles and the National War Memorial in Edinburgh Castle). On the castle scene the 20C has been one of loss either by direct demolition, dereliction or neglect. The current trend is however in favour of restoration and even conversion to modern day homes.

INTERIOR DECORATION

The bare stone walls of castles and tower houses were rarely hung with expensive tapestries but at times panelled and painted.

Decorative painting. – This art form was prevalent in the late 16C and early 17C at a time when Scotland's main trading links were with Scandinavia and the Low Countries. Undoubtedly influenced by such contacts, it is no coincidence that the remaining examples are mainly on or near the east coast.

Dry powder colour mixed with blue size or the **tempera technique** was most frequently used to decorate board and beam ceilings and panelling, then in vogue. Decorative painting was less expensive than the more usual hangings and the decorative painters were active in covering the ceilings and panelling of newly built houses of the period, notably those belonging to the wealthy merchants (Provost Skene in Aberdeen, Sir George Bruce in Culross and Gladstone's Land, Edinburgh) or in extensions as at Alexander Seton's Pinkie House.

Although most of the painted decoration was executed by local craftsmen, with centres in both Aberdeen and Edinburgh, it is often difficult to attribute any one name to a work. Painters active at the time included **James** and **John Workman, John Anderson**, Robert Telfer and Mungo Hanginschaw.

The designs included fruit and floral patterns, arabesques, Biblical scenes and quotations, or imagery from classical sources, in bright colours lightening the interiors. The more outstanding examples include those at Crathes Castle (allegorical with texts and proverbs, the Nine Heroes : *illustration p 57*), Huntingtower Castle (oldest at 1540, with knotwork patterns, conventional foliage, fruit scrolls...) and the ceiling from Rossend Castle now in the National Museum of Antiquities (an emblematic ceiling). Others exist at Culross, Falkland and Holyroodhouse Palaces, Earlshall Castle and Traquair.

Although the technique itself was to be superseded by plasterwork the origins of Scottish painting are rooted in this tradition. George Jamesone, the first Scottish portraitist of any note, was apprenticed to John Anderson, and his family tree for Sir Colin Campbell of Glenorchy shows many similarities.

Plasterwork ceilings. – In England the Elizabethan period introduced plasterwork ceilings with their ornate strapwork. In Scotland the early 17C saw the introduction of ornate plaster ceilings as at Craigievar (1625), Glamis (1621), Muchalls (1624), and The Binns (1630). The ceilings were often accompanied by magnificent heraldic achievements (Craigievar and Muchalls) or elaborate fireplaces (Glamis). This art evolved and was adapted by Sir William Bruce for the classical interiors of Holyroodhouse and Thirlestane. The series at the latter include the magnificent Lauderdale eagles.

All this is only a step away from the delicately detailed neo-classical designs of Robert Adam (Mellerstain, Culzean and Hopetoun House).

BURGHS

While several towns (Haddington, Elgin and Old Edinburgh) retain their medieval layouts, relatively few medieval buildings exist, in part due to their timber construction. As a rule the main street linked the castle and church and was the site of the market and tolbooth. Pends and wynds led off to closes with burgess plots extending back to the town wall pierced by gates or ports.

The burghs tended to lavish funds on such symbols of civic authority and pride as the tolbooth and mercat cross, with the result that the townscapes of today are still enhanced by some fine examples.

Market cross. – Known in Scotland as mercat crosses, these provided the focal point of the burgh, where goods for sale were presented, proclamations made and public punishment executed. Of the larger platform type the outstanding example is at Aberdeen, where a series of royal portrait medallions adorn the platform. Others are topped by the royal unicorn (Edinburgh, Cockburnspath). The rare pre-Reformation cross at Banff figures the Crucifixion and the Virgin and Child.

(After Aberdeen Tourist Board Photo)

Aberdeen – Mercat Cross

Tolbooth. – Originally for collecting taxes, the booths gradually came to embody civic authority and house the council chamber, court and prison. Today they represent one of the most attractive elements of Scottish townscapes. Kelso and Haddington have handsomely elegant buildings reflecting periods of agricultural prosperity. Tolbooths incorporated a tower (Glasgow, Aberdeen and Stirling) which was often adjoined by a later range of buildings.

Fine examples exist at Linlithgow, Crail, Culross, Dumfries and Old Aberdeen while vernacular versions remain in Kirkcudbright, North Berwick, and the Canongate, Edinburgh. The most renowned of all was Edinburgh's now vanished Heart of Midlothian, as popularized by Scott's novel.

Tron. – Now a rare feature the public weigh beam was once a common sight. Both Culross and the village of Stenton still have examples.

DOVECOTS

Dovecots (doocots in Scotland) are a familiar and attractive sight in rural Scotland and are found in their greatest number in the rich farming areas of the Lothians, Fife, Angus and Moray where grain growing predominated.

Origins and purpose. – Although the Romans had pigeon houses *(Columbariums)* it was probably the Normans who introduced pigeon farming to Britain. In times when salted and dried meat was the winter staple, pigeons were appreciated as a source of fresh meat. Pigeons had the added advantage of fending for themselves. The earliest examples of pigeon farming were associated with monastic establishments as at Crossraguel and Melrose Abbeys and date from the 15 and 16C. At the time laws were harsh on those destroying the houses or killing the birds.

Boath

Design. – Most are stone built, some of rubblework covered with harling, others of ashlar. They vary in type from the fairly common beehive as at Phantassie, Craigmillar, Dirleton and Aberdour Castles to the more typically Scottish lectern of Tantallon Castle and Tealing. Others were cylindrical (Lady Kitty's Garden, Haddington). The majority were freestanding, although nesting boxes were incorporated into towers of certain castles (Hailes, Rothesay and Huntingtower) or even a church belfry (Aberlady, Stenton and Torphichen). 18 and 19C versions were built as part of farm buildings.

Phantassie

Utilitarian features include the entrance of flight holes usually facing south, string courses or projecting ledges – to deter rats – which doubled as alighting ledges and ventilation holes.

Ornamental features included weathervanes, crow steps, sundials and even dated armorial panels. Inside the stone or wooden nestholes were either square or rectangular with a potence providing access. Some dovecots true to Scottish castle building traditions remain unfailingly Scottish with moats and turrets or a corbelled and crow stepped tower.

Tealing

GLOSSARY

Aisle – *see p 22*

Barmkin – outer enclosing wall

Box pew – enclosed pew

Broch – *see p 183*

Cap-house – small chamber at the head of turnpike stairs serving as guardroom

Close – courtyard or passage leading to other buildings

Crow steps – stepped gable ends

Donjon – castle's main tower or keep

Doocot – dovecot

Forestair – external stair

Gait or Gate – street leading to...

Garth – cloisters or garden

Harling – wall plastered with roughcast. Often painted or with colour incorporated

Laird's loft – *see p 22*

Laird's lug – listening post or spy hole

Land – tenement

Marriage lintel – dated lintel inscribed with couple's initials

Pend – covered passageway

Port – town gateway

Skewputt – gable's corner stone

Tolbooth – *see opposite*

Turnpike – spiral stair

Tower house – fortified house

Wynd – subsidiary street

Yett – wrought iron gate usually at the main doorway.

(By permission of Lord Rosslyn)
Apprentice Pillar

TRADITIONAL SCOTLAND

CLANS

Clann in Gaelic means children or family. All owed loyalty to the head of the family or the chief. In return for their allegiance he acted as leader, protector and dispenser of justice. Castle pit prisons, gallows hills, beheading pits are common features in clan territories. The ties of kinship created a powerful social unit which flourished north of the Highland Line where Scottish monarchs found it hard to assert their authority. There the Lord of the Isles ruled as an independent monarch. As late as 1411 with the Battle of Harlaw the monarchy was threatened by combined clan action. Clan ties ran deep and rivalries and feuds, often for land or cattle, were common. Scott popularized the Campbell MacGregor feud in *Rob Roy*. The late 17C was marked by the Massacre of Glen Coe *(p 122)*. The mainly catholic clans pinned their hopes on the "King over the water" and the Jacobite risings were based on clan support. Sweeping changes followed the Battle of Culloden (1746) with the passing of the Act of Proscription (1747-82). The wearing of tartan in any form and carrying of arms were banned and heritable jurisdictions abolished. This was the destruction of the clan system and the death knell came with the clearances of the early 19C.

The battles and feuds, loyalty and traditions live on in legends and literature. Today Clan Societies and Associations are active organizations, both in Scotland and abroad. Some of them finance museums (Macpherson at Newtonmore, Donnachaid north of Blair Atholl), others undertake the restoration of clan seats (Menzies Castle) or building of clan centres (Clan Donald Centre, Armadale Skye).

TARTANS

The colourful clothing material, tartan, now so symbolic of Scotland has ancient origins while clan tartans are an invention of the early 19C. In the Highlands a coarse woollen cloth (*tartaine* in French) was dyed using vegetable plant sources (bracken for yellow ; blaeberries for blue, whin bark or broom for green). Originally patterns or setts corresponded to the district in which a particular weaver with his distinctive pattern operated. In early portraits it is common to see a variety of patterns being worn at one time. Some of the best examples are Francis Cote's splendidly defiant *Pryse Campbell, 18th Thane of Cawdor (illustration p 55)*, *The MacDonald Boys* (*c*1750) in Comrie Museum, Raeburn's series of Highland chiefs including *Macnab* and J Michael Wright's 17C *Highland Chieftain* at Holyroodhouse Palace.

The repeal of the Proscription Act (1782) led to the commercialization of tartans and standardization on a clan basis and a more rigid observation of clan or family tartans. The first tartan pattern books appeared at this time. George IV's 1822 visit when the monarch wore a kilt, initiated the tartan boom of the 19C, a vogue continued by Queen Victoria and Albert with their interest in all things Highland.

Colours. – Any given sett or pattern may be woven in modern, ancient or reproduction colours. With the introduction of aniline dyes in the 19C the colours became bright and harsh and were termed '**modern**'. Post World War I an attempt was made, again using chemical dyes, to achieve the softer shades of the natural dyes. These were defined as '**ancient**' and created a certain amount of confusion on the tartan scene as some tartans, like the Old Stewart or Old Munro already had "old" as part of their title. More recent developments include the invention of '**reproduction**' and '**muted**' colours.

The introduction in the 19C of synthetic dyes gave vivid colours and the kilt began to lose its camouflage quality on the hills. **Hunting tartans** were created where the bright red backgrounds were replaced by green, blue or brown. The **dress tartan** was another innovation of the period. The clan tartan was given a white ground and used for men's evening dress.

A tartan exists for every occasion be it everyday, hunting or evening wear. The most common form is the kilt which constitutes the principal item of Highland dress. By the 16C a belted plaid *(feileadh mor)* was in use for everyday wear. The little kilt *(feileadh beag)* developed from this and was popular in the 18C. A proper kilt may use as much as 8 yards of tartan. Both the Museum of Scottish Tartans in Comrie run by the Scottish Tartans Society and the National Museum of Antiquities, Edinburgh have costume displays. The former has registered as many as 1 600 tartans or setts.

HERALDIC DISPLAYS

The clan system created a strong sense of belonging to a family, which was often proudly proclaimed by some heraldic device. Chiefs like the monarch, the Chief of Chiefs, have their own coat of arms. It is an offence for anyone else to misappropriate them. Even heirs are required to register a "difference" mark with the **Lord Lyon King of Arms**, who regulates all Scottish armorial matters and adjudicates upon chiefships of clans. Members of a clan may adopt the clansmen's badge consisting of the crest encircled by a strap with a buckle and a motto. It is interesting to note that when heraldry was no longer used for identification in warfare it was perpetuated as a decorative symbol in architecture on furniture and clothes.

The monarch and ecclesiastics led the way with their seals. The arms of James IV on a buttress of the west front of King's College Chapel Aberdeen are dated 1504 and are among the earliest. Most of the Scottish heraldic devices are already in evidence, the lion rampant on the shield, the crest, a crowned lion front on, the two unicorn supporters and the thistle below the shield. Kings emblazoned their castles and palaces (Falkland, Holyroodhouse Palace) bishops their palaces (Glasgow, Spynie) and even bridges (Guardbridge). The nobility and lairds followed suit. Intricate carved **armorial panels** proudly proclaimed that they held their lands directly from the king. Huntly Castle has a splendid heraldic doorway where the arms of the Ist Marquess are surmounted by those of James VI, impaled with those of his queen, with the Scottish unicorn and Danish wyvern as supporters. Inside, one of the second floor chimneypieces, dated 1606 only three years after the Union of the Crowns shows the adjusted royal arms of the United Kingdom with two quarters for Scotland and the unicorn in place. The even more prominently displayed armorial frontispiece at Castle Fraser is of a slightly later date, 1618. Armorial displays also featured in some interiors as at Craigievar where the great hall has an impressive chimneypiece, which when appropriately tinctured must have provided a splash of colour to Danzig Willie's interior. Muchalls, The Binns and Glamis have other plasterwork armorials dating from this period. Painted **heraldic ceilings** were also popular. The black and white one at Earlshall (1617-20) aligns the arms of various Scottish nobles while the ceiling of St Mary's Church, near Aberfeldy incorporates the heraldic devices of Stewart landlords. The outstanding 16C oak heraldic ceiling in St Machar's Cathedral, Aberdeen, portrays the European scene around 1520.

Carved armorials are found on church stalls and pulpits (King's College, Aberdeen), the lofts and galleries of titled families (Abercorn and Gifford) and of incorporated trades. The colourful Thistle Chapel is a modern example. Mercat crosses (Aberdeen) and city gateways were similarly adorned. Armorials were also used as decorative motifs on glass, porcelain and silverware, tiles, stained glass, tapestries, jewellery and furniture (the Kinghorne bed).

TRACING YOUR ANCESTORS

Before applying for professional help eliminate any home sources of information that you may have to hand. Check out old letters, diaries, albums and newspaper cuttings and books with inscriptions, including the family Bible or school prizes. Ensure that research has not already been done on the family with a visit to the **National Library of Scotland** in Edinburgh. Birth, marriage and death certificates from 1855 onwards, Census Returns from 1801 and Parish Registers pre-1855 may be consulted in the **General Register Office**. The **Scottish Record Office** holds property records (Sasines and Deeds Registers) and will furnish names of researchers experienced in using such documents. For those with titled or eminent ancestors *Burke's* and *Debrett's Peerages,* the *Dictionary of National Biography* and *Who's Who* are useful sources. The names of professional geneologists can be obtained from the Scots Ancestry Research Society which also furnishes the addresses of Clan Associations.

BAGPIPES

Now generally acknowledged as the national musical instrument, bagpipes are of uncertain origin. Already in use in 14C Scotland they developed from the original one drone instrument to the modern example of three drones, chanter and blow stick (mouthpiece). Bagpipe music is unquestionably a Scottish art be it the *ceol mor* (big or great music) or *ceol beag* (small or light music). The latter, more recent and common, covers the lighter music for marching and dancing (strathspeys and reels). The older or classical music of the bagpipes is known as Piobairochd (Pibroch).

Many towns, police departments and Highland regiments have pipe bands which muster for Highland Gatherings and visitor entertainment. The best known are the Muirhead and Shotts, Dykehead, Glasgow and Edinburgh City Police Bands.

Clan chiefs usually maintained a personal piper. This tradition has given such legendary piping families as the hereditary MacCrimmons of the MacLeods and the MacArthurs. The earliest piping competitions were held at the annual Falkirk Tryst in 1781 at a time when a Highlander could still be penalised for wearing the kilt or playing that warlike instrument, the bagpipes. The Northern Meeting Piping Competitions, Inverness and the Argyllshire Gathering, Oban, are the venues for today's piping competitions *(pp 28 and 212).*

GAELIC

Spoken Gaelic. – Although on the decline there were 79 307 speakers in 1981 representing 1.6 % of the resident population. The majority of Gaelic speakers are bilingual. As a living language Gaelic continues to flourish in the North West Highlands, the Hebrides where 76 % of the population are Gaelic speakers and Skye (58 %). Outside these regions Glasgow has a pocket of Gaelic speakers.

One of the oldest European languages and a Celtic one, Scottish Gaelic is akin to the Irish version. The Gaeldom culture has given much that is distinctive to Scotland (tartans, kilt, bagpipes, music ...). An Comunn Gaidhealach (f 1891) with its headquarters in Inverness promotes the use of Gaelic, its literature and music and organizes an annual festival, the **Mod** of Gaelic song and poetry *(p 212).*

SCOTTISH CRAFTS

Craftsmen offer a wide variety of quality objects, which make perfect souvenirs of a visit to Scotland. Of the many traditional Scottish crafts the best known is the **knitwear** of Fair Isle and Shetland. These include the natural colours of Shetland sweaters, the extremely fine lace shawls and the complicated multicoloured patterned Fair Isle jerseys. **Harris tweed,** woven exclusively on handlooms in the Outer Hebrides is a quality product well meriting its high reputation. **Tartans** *(p 26)* are nearly all machine woven but **kiltmaking** has remained a handicraft. Both **glassmaking** and **engraving** are thriving crafts today. The best known products, other than cut crystal, are the engraving and handblown paperweights, in particular the delightful **millefiori.** Jewellery making includes the setting of semi-precious stones such as the Cairngorm or Tay pearls. Both serpentine and granite are employed for various ornaments and objects (paperweights, penholders ...) and granite is used for the polished curling stones. The straw backed and hooded **Orkney chairs,** white fleecy **sheepskin rugs** and **leather** and hornwork articles (cutlery handles and buttons) are also popular.

Both individual craftsmen and larger firms usually welcome visitors to their workshops and showrooms. For further information apply to the local tourist information centres or the **Scottish Craft Centre,** Edinburgh which organizes exhibitions of craft work. Further north in the village of Beauly, 12 miles west of Inverness, **Highland Craftpoint** has an exhibition, audiovisual programme, demonstrations and workshop tours.

GHOSTS AND GHOSTLY HAPPENINGS

For the intrepid the following places are the haunt of a ghostly form : Glamis Castle : the grey or white lady in the chapel ; The Binns : General Tam on his white horse ; Barnbougle Castle : a dog in search of his master ; Ben Macdui : the big grey man of Ben Macdui ; Fyvie Castle : the phantom trumpeter and green lady ; Craigievar : the Gordon who fell foul of Red John ; Skye : the phantom kilted army and Austin car.

HIGHLAND GAMES AND GATHERINGS

Visitors are well advised to attend one of these colourful occasions where dancing, piping and sporting events are all integral parts of the programme. As early as the 11C contests in the arts of war were organized to permit clan chiefs to choose their footrunners and bodyguards from the winners.

Following the repeal of the Proscription Act, Highland Societies were formed to ensure the survival of traditional dances and music. Today these events are popular with locals and visitors alike. Of particular interest and charm are those of the Grampian and Highland areas.

Traditional events include dancing, piping, athletics and the never failing attraction of massed pipe bands. The heavy events include putting the shot, throwing the hammer and tossing the caber as straight as possible and not as far as possible.

The map shows a selection of Highland Games, Gatherings and Common Ridings. The background colour indicates the month, and for certain games the principal attraction is also given.

(Serrailler/Rapho)

Tossing the caber

COMMON RIDING FESTIVALS

These festivals are common to the Border towns and recall the unsettled times of the Middle Ages when raids and reiving were common. Ride outs were organized to control the burgh boundaries. Today the ridings often figure as the main events in a week long programme of festivities and are a source of colour and pageantry for the visitor.

CALENDAR OF EVENTS

The main events have been listed in the Practical Information chapter at the end of the guide.

In addition to the events listed in the calendar there are many more of a more local appeal which may interest the visitor. Most agricultural shows provide a good afternoon's entertainment while sheep dog trials can also be a source of enjoyment. Sporting events have been omitted from the calendar but for the enthusiast the traditional rugby (Triple Crown, Border Sevens) and football matches, golf championships etc. are all of high entertainment value. For further details contact the Local Tourist Information Centres.

Traditional dates

25 January. – Burns Night. The birthday of the national poet Robert Burns (1759-96) is celebrated the world over by Burns Suppers.

12 August. – The Glorious Twelfth marks the opening of the grouse shooting season.

WHISKY THE WATER OF LIFE

Today the word whisky conjures up a seemingly endless variety on the shelves of supermarkets (whisky, whiskey, bourbon ...) while Scotch Whisky is synonymous with a quality product, which possesses an unrivalled international reputation.

The highly competitive whisky industry is Scotland's biggest export earner (£900 million a year) and one of the government's main sources of revenue (foreign earnings and excise taxes and duty)

A troubled past. – Undoubtedly among the earliest distillers of whisky, the Scots have played a major part in the perfection of this art. In the 15C monks were distilling a spirit and soon after it became an everyday domestic occupation. The Union of 1707 brought exorbitant taxation, including the 1713 malt tax. Distilling went underground and smuggling became a way of life. From the illicit stills on the hillsides the spirit was transported along a smugglers trail from Speyside to Perth over 140 miles of hill country. Excisemen became the scourge of the Highlands. A succession of new laws in the early 19C did nothing to halt illicit distilling until the 1824 Act. The latter sanctioned distillation on payment of a licence fee and duty per gallon produced. Many distilleries were founded after this date including Glenlivet 1824, Fettercairn 1824, and Talisker 1830. Whisky production developed rapidly in the 1880s as the replacement spirit for gin and brandy, which was highly taxed and becoming increasingly scarce due to the failure of the vine crop. Blending produced a more palatable drink which rapidly achieved universal success. Although blended whiskies still dominate the market the subtler and finer qualities of a single malt are gaining recognition.

Malt whisky. – The original spirit was a malt or straight unblended product of a single malt whisky. What makes a good whisky? The quality and subtle differences in character depends essentially on a combination of certain factors : barley not always home grown, water filtered through peat or over granite, equipment such as the shape of the still and the experience and skill of the stillmen. The 116 single malts are classified into Highland, Lowland or Islay.

Blended whisky. – Grain whisky is made from a malted barley and other cereals. The blends are a mixture of a lighter grain with a malt in secret proportions. Blended varieties are subdivided into two categories : de luxe and standard.

Whisky making. – The germination of barley steeped in water turns the starch into sugar. The grain is then kiln dried over a peat fire. Mashing comprises the mixing of the crushed and dried barley with warm water. The remaining barley husks or draff is used as cattle fodder. Yeast is added to the sugary suspension (wort) in vast vats to convert the sugar into alcohol and carbon dioxide. The wash passes into vast copper pot stills. Two distillations are common to produce the high proof distillate before it is matured in oak barrels in Scotland for a minimum of three years.

Around 50 distilleries welcome visitors and guided tours invariably end with a traditional dram. Speyside is the home of a Whisky Trail *(p 70)*. Since 1979, recession has left the trade with a surplus and few distilleries now operate at full capacity, so enquire locally if you wish to see the whisky making process from barley to bottle.

SCOTTISH FARE

Scottish cooking is characterized by the excellence and quality of the natural products from river, moor, sea and farm.

Soups. – These number **Cock-a-Leekie** using fowl, cut leeks and prunes ; **Scots** or **Barley Broth,** a vegetable and barley soup ; **Game Soup** ; **Partan Bree** a crab soup and **Cullen Skink** made with smoked haddock.

Fish. – Of the many varieties of fish, pride of place goes to the **salmon** be it farmed or wild from the famous fisheries of the Tay, Spey or Tweed. Served fresh or smoked, it is a luxury dish. **Trout** and **salmon- trout** with their delicately pink flesh are equally appreciated. Breakfast menus often feature the **Arbroath Smokie** - a small salted and smoked haddock ; the **Finnan Haddie**, a salted haddock dried on the beach prior to smoking over a peat fire and the **kipper** a split, salted and smoked herring.

Game. – The hills and moors provide a variety of game. The best known are the superb **red grouse** and **venison**. Like salmon the raw material is either farmed or wild.

Meat. – With such first class beef cattle as the Aberdeen Angus and Galloway and home bred sheep, it is hardly surprising that the quality of Scotch **beef** and **mutton** is unsurpassed.

Desserts. – Succulent **soft fruits** (strawberries, raspberries and blackcurrants) ripened slowly in mild sunshine make an excellent sweet. Other creamsweets like **Cranachan** often incorporate one of the soft fruits. **Atholl Brose** is a secret mixture of honey, oatmeal, malt whisky and cream.

Cheeses. – Although not of international repute, Scotland possesses several home-made cheeses. Both the **Dunlop** cheese from Orkney, Arran and Islay and the **Scottish Cheddar** are hard cheeses. **Caboc** is a rich double cream cheese rolled in oatmeal while **Crowdie** is similar to a cottage cheese.

Breakfast and tea-time. – These two particularly Scottish meals provide the chance to taste porridge, a smokie or kipper, a rasher of Ayrshire bacon, oatcakes, an Aberdeen buttery or a softie.

Tea-time specialities include shortbread and Dundee cake to mention only two of the many teabreads.

Preserves. – Heather honey or Scottish made jam and marmalade make ideal presents to take home.

Taste of Scotland. – For those eager to sample some of the above, the Scottish Tourist Board publishes a booklet entitled "Taste of Scotland" listing hotels and restaurants which offer the best Scottish fare. Listed establishments are identified by the "stockpot" sign.

KEY

Sights

★★★ **Worth a journey**
★★ **Worth a detour**
★ **Interesting**

Sightseeing route

with departure point

Castle, historic house

Ruins

Lighthouse

Wayside cross

Panorama – View

Viewing table

Dam – Windmill

Ecclesiastical building

Building

Fort – Fountain

Ramparts – Tower – Gate

Fountain – Statue, monument

Gardens, parks, woods

Miscellaneous sights

A Z B Letters giving the location of a place on the town plan

---

Motorway

Complete interchange

Limited interchange

Major through road

Stepped street – Footpath

Pedestrian street

Unsuitable for traffic

Tramway

Headroom (given when less than 4.30m)

Load limit of a bridge

Swing bridge

Station – Coach station

Airport

Ferry services :

} Passengers and cars

Passengers only

Main post office (with poste restante)

Tourist information centre

Car park

Hospital

Covered market

Shopping centre

Barracks

Synagogue

Cemetery

Stadium – Racecourse

Outdoor or indoor swimming pool

Pleasure boat harbour

Skating rink – Golf course

Water tower – Factory or power station

Telecommunications tower or mast

MICHELIN maps and town plans are north orientated.
Main shopping streets are printed in a different colour in the list of streets.

C County Council Offices

H Town Hall

M Museum

T Theatre

POL Police

U University, colleges

tc Times and charges for admission are listed at the end of the guide.

Additional Signs

Prehistoric site

Gardens

Safari park

SIGHTS

listed alphabetically

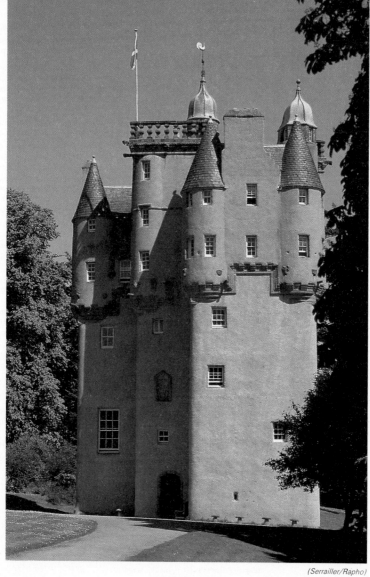

(Serrailler/Rapho)

Craigievar Castle

tc Abbotsford, a fantasy in stone, is typical of **Sir Walter Scott (1771-1832)** the man who did so much to romanticize and popularize all things Scottish. Here there are souvenirs of the man, his friends and contemporaries, his literary works, and his cherished collection.

The Wizard of the North. – Born 15 August 1771, the youngest of thirteen children of an Edinburgh solicitor, his earliest contacts with the region began at Sandyknowe, his grandfather's farm *(p 139)*. At the age of eight he attended Edinburgh High School and then the university where he qualified as an advocate. In 1799 he became sheriff-depute of Selkirkshire. To be nearer his work he acquired a property at Ashiestiel in 1804 and then in 1812 the small farm house of Cartleyhole which he renamed Abbotsford.

(Hinous/Top)

Sir Walter Scott by Raeburn

Scott's narrative poems, *The Lay of the Last Minstrel, Marmion* and *The Lady of the Lake* were written before coming to Abbotsford, as were his Scottish novels : *Waverley* (1814), *Guy Mannering* (1815), *The Antiquary* and *Old Mortality* (1816), *Rob Roy* (1818), *The Heart of Midlothian* (1818), *The Bride of Lammermoor, Ivanhoe* (1820), *A Legend of Montrose* (1819) and *Redgauntlet* (1824). The literary reputation of Scott is largely based on these novels where he shows a genius for character and a masterful handling of Scots dialogue.

"Conundrum Castle... this romance of a house". – Scott lavished much thought and effort on the building of his beloved Abbotsford, which was to house his collection of "gabions", a word he invented to cover "curiosities of small intrinsic value". They often related some part of Scotland's chequered history.

Study. – The small book-lined room is almost entirely occupied by the massive writing desk and is adjoined by a "speak-a-bit" turret room.

Library. – The moulded ceiling is a copy of Rosslyn Chapel *(qv)*. The Chantrey bust of Scott is dated 1820, the year George IV knighted the author. The showcase in the bow window contains many of the treasured "gabions" : Rob Roy's purse, Napoleon I's cloak clasp, Burns' tumbler... The painting on the easel records the one and only meeting between Burns and the 16 year old Scott. This took place in Sciennes House, home of Professor Adam Fergusson, the father of one of Scott's school friends at the High School. Also present in the assembled company were Joseph Black, Adam Smith, John Hume and James Hutton.

Drawing Room. – The paintings include portraits of Scott's mother and father and, over the fireplace, Henry Raeburn's *Portrait of Sir Walter* with Camp at his feet. In one of the wall alcoves (to the right of the fireplace) is the silver urn which Byron gave to Scott. It also figures in the Sciennes House painting.

Armoury. – A smoking corridor in Scott's time, the items on display include a Highland broadsword with basket hilt by Andrea Farara, Rob Roy souvenirs, a Landseer painting of *Ginger,* the companion portrait of his master is in the National Portrait Gallery, and a still life of the Regalia of Scotland, a reminder that Scott was instrumental in their rediscovery. The miniatures include one of Bonnie Prince Charlie and John Graham of Claverhouse. Scott was one of the first to break away from the Bluidy Clavers view.

Dining Room. – It was here, where he could command a view of the Tweed to the last, that Scott died on 21 September 1832. His death was undoubtedly precipitated by the burden of overwork in his last years (1826-32). Following a financial crisis in 1826 Scott produced a phenomenal three novels a year, in an age when there were no mechanical aids.

Entrance Hall. – Panelling from Dunfermline Abbey's Church is surmounted by arms of the Border families, while the fireplace and statues are copied from details in Melrose Abbey. Other souvenirs include people and events prominent in Scottish history.

South Court. – Note the door from the Heart of Midlothian, Edinburgh's Old Tolbooth.

Chapel. – Along with the neighbouring wing it is a 19C addition. Ghirlandaio's *Madonna and Child* dominates the altar.

Michelin map **401** *is the map to use for Scotland.*

Michelin map **402** *for the Lake District and Northern England.*

Michelin map **403** *for the West Country.*

Michelin map **404** *for South East England,*
the Midlands and East Anglia.

Michelin map **405** *for Ireland.*

The "Granite City" lies between the Don and the Dee, backed by a rich agricultural hinterland and facing the North Sea which has given her a new role, that of Offshore Capital of Europe.

HISTORICAL NOTES

Twin burghs. – The present city developed from two separate fishing villages on the Dee and Don. By the 12C Old Aberdeen was the seat of an episcopal see with an ever increasing secular community outside its cathedral precincts. The cathedral city acquired burgh status and in the late 15C Bishop Elphinstone founded a university. The second distinct burgh grew up around the king's castle (13C) to become an active trading centre based on coastwise and Baltic trade. While the Reformation brought ruin and stagnation to Old Aberdeen, the city centre continued to prosper, acquired its own university (f1593) and by the late 17C had started to break out of its medieval bounds.

The Granite City. – Following Edinburgh and Perth, Aberdeen implemented its own plan for expansion with the laying out of Union and King Streets (1801). The native architect **Archibald Simpson** (1790-1847) was responsible for giving the city much of its present character by his masterly use of Aberdeen granite as a building material. He gave to his buildings, of fully dressed granite, a simplicity and dignity fully in keeping with the nature of the stone. The streets were lined with dignified public buildings (Medical Hall, 29 King Street 1818-20, Assembly Rooms now the Music Hall, Union Street 1822) and imaginative private ventures, the Athenaeum and a successful design for the Clydesdale Bank at the Union and King Street corner site. His rival John Smith was also responsible for some fine buildings at the time.

Maritime Past. – The tradition of shipbuilding has always been strong in Aberdeen as the yards produced vessels for whaling and line fishing. Then came that age of international fame, the **clipper ship era** when the city's boatyards specialized in fast sailing ships. With the legendary and graceful tea clippers, *Stornoway, Chrysolite* and *Cairngorm*, Britain gained supremacy in the China tea trade. Wooden clippers gave way to composite built vessels and finally iron in the 1870s. Sail yielded to steam. Throughout, the local shipbuilding industry remained to the fore and continues today as an important aspect of the city's economy, although now geared to the oil industry.
The earliest fisheries included whaling (1752-1860s) and line fishing. Aberdeen became a fishing port with the herring boom (1875-96) and by 1900 had converted to trawling and remains Scotland's premier white fishing port. The recent decline in trawling has in some way been counteracted by the increase in oil activities.

★★OLD ABERDEEN *time : 3 hours*

Old Aberdeen became a burgh of barony in 1489 under the patronage of the bishops and retained its separate burghal identity until 1891.
Today, the quarter stretching from King's College Chapel to St Machar's Cathedral, is part of a conservation area where the old burgh's essential character has been well retained. The medieval streets - College Bounds **(6)**, High Street, Don Street and the Chanonry - are now bordered by a variety of single and double storey cottages, and some more substantial detached mansions, a happy mix.

From King's College Chapel to the Brig o'Balgownie

★King's College Chapel (X). – Of the university founded in 1495 by **Bishop Elphinstone** *tc* (1431-1514) the beautiful chapel, in its campus setting, is the only original building. The chapel in the Flamboyant Gothic style (1500- 5) is famous for its attractive Renaissance **crown spire★★★** of great deli-cacy. It was restored in the 17C following storm damage. The bronze **monument** in front of the chapel is a 19C tribute to the founder. The tinctured arms on the but-tresses of the west front are those of the sovereign James IV, his Queen Margaret Tudor, the founder Bishop Elphinstone, and a royal bastard, Archibald of St Andrews.

Inside is an extremely rare ensemble of **medieval fittings★★★** : rood screen, canopied stalls, pulpit and desk all richly and vigorously carved. The plain Tournoi mar-ble tomb is that of the founder's and the plaque is to the first principal Hector Boece (*c*1465-1536).

The square Cromwell Tower in the nor-theast corner of the quadrangle was designed in 1658 to serve originally as student lodgings.

Old Town House (X). – Now a branch library this attractive 18C Georgian town house stands astride the High Street. The Old Aberdeen coat of arms above the door belonged to an earlier building.

(After Aberdeen Tourist Board Photo)
King's College Chapel – the crown spire

The Chanonry (X). – The layout of this once walled precinct is still apparent. Within this area were grouped dependent residences, from the Bishop's Palace to the manses of the secular canons and dwellings of the choir chaplains. *tc* On the left are the university's Cruickshank Botanic Gardens.

★★St Machar's Cathedral (X). – The *tc* twin spires of St Machar's have long been one of Old Aberdeen's most famous landmarks. Its highly individual style – so very Scottish – reflects the nature of the granite building material. Dating from the 14 and 15C the present edifice overlooks the haughlands of the Don. According to legend the original Celtic (*c*580) settlement was established by St Machar slightly to the west so as to overlook the "crook" of the Don and comply with instructions from St Columba. When the bishopric was transferred from Mortlach, now Dufftown, to St Machar's in 1131 a programme of rebuilding was undertaken. The present building is the nave as finally completed in the 15C.

College Bounds ...... X 6	Regent Walk .... X 22
Elphinstone Road .... X 10	School Road .... X 24
Harrow Road .... X 16	Tillydrone Avenue .... X 26

Exterior. – The **west front★★★**, the cathedral's most distinctive feature is immediately impressive for the austerity and strength of its unusual design, where the role of the doorway is reduced to a minimum.

Buttressed and crenellated towers, topped by tapering sandstone spires flank the majestic seven light window. The whole is void of decorative details.

Move round past the south porch (*entrance*) to the east end. The church was truncated at the transept crossing when the choir was demolished at the Reformation and further shortened in 1688 when the central tower and spire collapsed, destroying the transepts. Here are to be found the **tombs** of two of the bishop builders : in the north transept that of Bishop Henry Leighton (1422-40) – his effigy is inside the cathedral – and in the south, now glazed over, that of Bishop Gavin Dunbar (1518-32).

Interior. – *Take binoculars to examine the heraldic ceiling. Enter by the south porch.* A majestically simple but effective interior is the setting for this 16C **heraldic ceiling★★★** attributed to the enterprising Bishop Gavin Dunbar. The flat, coffered oak ceiling is decorated with 48 brightly tinctured coats of arms arranged in three rows of sixteen each running from east to west. Ingeniously designed this unique ceiling presents a vision of the European scene around 1520 and a strong assertion of Scottish nationalism. The central axis representing the Holy Church, until then the traditional unifying force in Europe, is headed by the arms of Pope Leo X followed by other ecclesiastical arms. The absence of York and Trondheim is significant. On the right are the King of Scots (closed crown) and his nobles while on the left, headed by the Holy Roman Emperor, are the other Kings of Christendom. The King of England comes fourth after his fellow monarchs of France, Scotland's traditional ally, and Spain!

The stained glass is all modern. Note the west window with cusped round arches and the Bishops Window (third from east end in the south aisle) 1913 an early example of Douglas Strachan's work showing the three great builder bishops.

★Brig o'Balgownie. – *Approach via Don Street.*

This early 14C bridge, one of Aberdeen's most important medieval buildings, is set astride the Don. The single span bridge with its pointed Gothic arch has cobbled approaches and a defensive kink at the south end.

Further downstream is the **Bridge of Don,** by Aberdeen's first city architect, John Smith with modifications by Thomas Telford (1827-30). The cost of building was financed by its illustrious neighbour's 17C maintenance fund.

THE HARBOUR (Z)

Development. – The recorded history of Aberdeen harbour dates back to 1136. The prosperity of Aberdeen has always been closely dependent on its port, from the earliest fishing settlement on the Dee to the subsequent flourishing medieval royal burgh trading with Baltic ports. Even in the second half of the 18C when trade was still seaborne the harbour improvements were the expression of the industrial progress of the time. Then followed the fishing boom with Aberdeen becoming the centre for steam powered trawling. Another boom came with the exploration and exploitation activities in the North Sea oilfields in the 1970s. Aberdeen became the **Offshore Capital of Europe** and the harbour the largest offshore support harbour in Europe.

A programme of modernization has increased the berthage, improved handling facilities and capacity so that ships of up to approx 18 000 tons can now be unloaded. The port's turnover has an annual total of 2 1/2 million tons making this Britain's number 3 port overall. The breakdown of the annual figure is 50 % for oil and oil related industries ; 10 % fishing.

In addition an average of 60 000 passengers pass through the port yearly.

Port Activities. – Fishing, one of the city's traditional industries, has shifted its emphasis from inshore to herring and finally to the white fishery. As one of the bigger ports Aberdeen flourished with the introduction of steam powered trawlers and today the international fishing fleet which operates out of the harbour is a highly modern one with sophisticated tracking gear and navigational aids.

tc The recently modernized **fish market** makes a fascinating visit when in full swing with a crowd of white coated buyers, merchants and fishermen milling around the stacked boxes brimming over with fish of all kinds. Onshore processing industries include freezing, canning and smoking.

Although no **oil** comes ashore in Aberdeen, oil-related industries account for half the harbour's revenue. Aberdeen, as Europe's chief marine support base, has attracted the major oil companies (Amoco, Chevron, Shell, Texaco and Total) with their own private bases and three other multi-user bases shared by other oil companies. There are extensive engineering construction firms, supply industries and other specialized servicing, trading and medical facilities.

Shipbuilding has flourished since the golden era (1850s-60s) of the tea clippers. The introduction of steam heralded the period of trawlers, tugs and dredgers while the development of the North Sea oil industry brought conversion to the buildng of oil supply and fishery protection vessels.

CITY CENTRE

★Maritime Museum (Z M). – *Provost Ross's House, Shiprow.*

tc The museum is housed in two 16C town houses bordering Shiprow, one of the medieval thoroughfares winding up from the harbour. Provost Ross's House was owned by a succession of wealthy merchants, provosts and landed gentry.

First floor. – These galleries retrace the early development of the harbour from John Smeaton's original north pier (1781) through successive fishing booms (Arctic whaling and herring) to today's oil port. Model boats include such pre-steam favourites as the Zulus, Fifies and Scaffies.

Second floor. – The history of shipbuilding is traced from the earliest small sailing vessels. In the 1850s the city was famed for its fast sailing vessels, the clippers. The slender hulled *Chrysolite* and *Cairngorm* raced along as they plied the routes to Australia and the Far East. *Stornoway* was the first of a generation of purpose built tea clippers. Composite wood and iron vessels had a short-lived reign in the 1860s before iron built ships took over. The North Sea Oil and Gas Gallery is a vivid evocation of the most recent chapter in Aberdeen's maritime saga. Here the pioneering high technology of self-contained production platforms and offshore drilling rigs is represented by the scale model of the Murchison Platform. The authenticity is such that the company reserves the right to have access to the model at any time for simulating conditions in case of an emergency.

Castlegate. (Y) – The gait or way to the castle on Castle Hill (marked by two high-rise blocks behind the Salvation Army Citadel) was the medieval market place. Near the paved area known as the "plainstones" stands the mannie fountain (1706), a reminder of Aberdeen's first piped water supply.

Marischal Street (YZ), leading to the harbour, was laid out 1767-8 on the site of the former tenement of the Earls Marischal. The new street was given a uniform design of three storeys and an attic. In the middle of the Castlegate is the splendid **mercat cross★★** (Y) dating from 1686 *(illustration p 24).* The unicorn surmounts the cross which rises from the roof of an arcaded structure. The decoration includes a frieze of oval panels containing 10 portraits of the royal Stuarts from James I to James VII and the series is completed by the royal and Aberdeen coats of arms.

Looking northwards along King Street (Y) the integrated design of the various buildings was the result of collaboration between John Smith and Archibald Simpson. On the

tc north side of Castle Street the 19C **Town House** (Y H) dominates all. Rising from behind this relatively recent façade is the **tower** of the 17C tolbooth, which is best viewed from the opposite side of Castle Street.

★Provost Skene's House (Y) – This 17C town house is named after a wealthy

tc merchant and onetime provost of the town, **Sir George Skene** (1619- 1707). His portrait by Medina hangs in the 17C bedroom. Although title deeds go as far back as 1545 the house acquired its present form under the ownership of Skene. Following restoration in the 1950s a series of tastefully furnished period rooms were created. Note in particular such original features as plasterwork ceilings (Cromwellian, Restoration and 17C bedroom), panelling (1732, Regency) and stone flagging (Georgian Dining Room). Outstanding however is the **Chapel** or Painted Gallery with its 16C **painted ceiling★★**. This form of decorative art was common in Scotland between 1580 and 1630 *(p 24).* These particular paintings are unique for their religious theme and more so when we consider that Aberdeen was noted for its Episcopalian sympathies. New Testament scenes – The Annunciation, Adoration of the Shepherds, The Resurection (centre), The Crucifixion, and The Burial – are portrayed within a geometrical framework.

★Marischal College (Y). – The undoubtedly striking, but controversial, granite facade (1905) overlooking Broad Street was the latest extension to Marischal College. In 1593 George Keith, 5th Earl Marischal *(p 80)* founded a college in the buildings of Greyfriars Monastery, appropriated following the Reformation. Marischal was to be the counterpart of King's – older by a century – and for over two and a half centuries the two universities coexisted, a situation unique in Britain. Rebuilt in 1740, these buildings were in turn replaced by Archibald Simpson's work (1837-44) which bordered the three inner sides of the quadrangle. Following amalgamation with King's in 1860 a later benefaction (1891) permitted the building of the Mitchell Tower (235ft) and the Mitchell Hall now used for examination and graduation purposes. The houses

ABERDEEN
CITY CENTRE

bordering the northeast side of Broad Street were swept away and today's frontage was built (1905) incorporating Greyfriars Church at the far end.

The Hall and Portrait Gallery *(at the far end of the quadrangle)* are open to the public *tc* as is the **Anthropological Museum.**

tc **St Nicholas Kirk (Y).** – *Enter from Correction Wynd and the south transept.* The once vast medieval burgh church was divided into two at the Reformation. The transepts now serve as a vestibule. In Drum's Aisle or south transept are the reclining figures of the Irvines of Drum Castle *(qv)* and a tablet to Edward Raban, master printer to the city and universities in the 17C. At the far end in Collison's Aisle is the effigy of Provost Davidson who fell at Harlaw.

West Church. – The church was rebuilt *c*1752 by the Aberdonian architect, James Gibbs (1682-1754) the designer of St-Martin-in-the-Fields, London. This gift to his native city was his last major church commission. The interior has dark oak pews and galleries with a splendid canopied "Council Loft".

East Church. – Originally designed by Archibald Simpson (1835-7) the church was *tc* restored by William Smith after fire damage in 1875. Steps lead to the 15C St Mary's Chapel, along with the transepts the only medieval parts. The central roof boss depicts the legend of St Nicholas.

The Gothic spire (1876) has a carillon of 48 bells (summer concerts).

tc **James Dun's House (Y A).** – This late 18C house takes its name form its builder James Dun (1708-89) rector of the Old Grammar School which stood nearby and was attended by Byron. The museum houses permanent displays and special exhibitions.

★★Art Gallery (Y). – The permanent collection in pleasant well lit surroundings has a *tc* strong emphasis on contemporary art.

The sculpture court and adjoining rooms contain the larger works of sculpture, while additional pieces are also on display throughout the first floor rooms. Foreign sculptors (Degas, Rodin and Zadkine) and British (Hepworth, Moore and Butler) are represented by a variety of techniques and materials, with a strong emphasis on the 20C.

At the top of the stairs turn left to visit the rooms in numerical order, 1 to 6.

The painting section on the first floor has a well represented **Scottish collection. William McTaggart** (1835-1910) provided a turning point on the 19C Scottish scene, when he broke with the grandeur of the Romantics and commercial sentimentalism of the *genre* artists, in his search for realism. Inspired by nature his works portray a clarity and vitality achieving his own personal "impressionist" style *(A Ground Swell*-1). Appropriately the works alongside include canvases by some of the Glasgow Boys *(qv)*, a late 19C group, which strived for naturalism in landscape painting. Outstanding is Lavery's *The Tennis Party* (1), but note also the works by James Guthrie.

The **Macdonald Collection**★★ of British artists' portraits (2) numbers 92, many of which are self-portraits. This unique series is a highly revealing survey of the art world in the 19C. It includes the patron himself, Alexander Macdonald.

Other works in room 2 include those of the versatile **William Dyce** (1806- 64) another Aberdonian. More thoroughly international in his art, Dyce's *Ferryman* and *Titian's First Essay in Colour* are first and foremost figure compositions with the landscape playing a secondary role. They also show his care for detail and naturalism in outdoor scenes, as does *A Scene in Arran* where the figures are reduced to a minor role while the treatment of landscape anticipates the Pre-Raphaelites.

Room 3 presents some of the earliest Scottish portraitists including a *self-portrait* by Aberdeen's own **George Jamesone** (1588-1644), *Mrs Janet Shairp* by Allan Ramsay (1713-84) who so excelled in his delicate treatment of women and works by Raeburn (1756-1823) portraitist and King's Limner to George IV.

A selection of French Impressionists can be seen in the 19C foreign gallery (4). The 20C British section (6) includes works by Paul Nash, Stanley Spencer, Ben Nicholson, the Scottish Colourist, Peploe *(still life)*, William MacTaggart *(Cornfield Pontarmé)* and Joan Eardley.

ADDITIONAL SIGHTS

Parks and Gardens. – As a city that has been 9 times winner of the Britain in Bloom competition, Aberdeen's parks and gardens are justly worthy of a mention. Take the time to visit at least one be it **Union Terrace Gardens** (**YZ** – off Union Street) with their celebrated floral displays including Aberdeen's coat of arms, the Winter Gardens in **Duthie Park**, the Rose Garden and Maze at **Hazlehead,** the delightful **Johnston Gardens** and the university's **Cruickshank Botanic Gardens** (X).

EXCURSIONS

★★**Deeside.** – *Description p 64.*

★★**Grampian Castles.** – The accompanying map shows those castles described in the guide. All are easily reached from Aberdeen. In addition to those described in the guide there are other castles which are open to the public by appointment only. Enquire locally for further details.

Aberdeen's hinterland is particularly rich in castles with examples from all periods. These include the earliest Norman motte and bailey to the formidable strongholds (Kildrummy) which were the centres of government in the troubled Middle Ages. The golden age of castle building (16-17C) is well represented. In this far from rich area, stability engendered prosperity and encouraged lairds to build castles worthy of their newly acquired status or wealth. A flourishing native school produced the baronial style. Master masons skilfully worked the local stone creating a native tradition which displayed an artistry unparalleled elsewhere.

The Travellers' Friends
Great Britain and Ireland:

Michelin Red Guide for hotels and restaurants.
Michelin Map **986** *14 miles to 1 inch.*
Michelin Maps **401** **402** **403** **404** **405** *6.3 miles to 1 inch.*

★ ABERDOUR (Fife)   Pop 1 576

Michelin map 401 fold 31 – K 15

Aberdour, a small resort on the Fife shore of the Forth estuary, is famous for its castle and silver sands, which make it a popular destination for day outings.

★ABERDOUR CASTLE *time : 1/2 hour*

tc **Seat of the Earls of Morton.** – Initially granted by Robert the Bruce to his nephew, Thomas Randolph, Earl of Moray *c*1325, it passed to William Douglas in 1342 who also acquired the lands of Dalkeith. The latter became the principal seat of this branch of the Douglas family. James 4th, Lord Dalkeith was created Earl of Morton prior to his marriage with James I's daughter Joanna. **Regent Morton**, James Douglas, 4th Earl of Morton (1516-81) inherited Aberdour in 1548. This Scottish lord, active in the overthrow of Mary Queen of Scots is remembered for his iron rule as Regent (1572-8) during James VI's minority when he achieved peace in a time of religious strife. Forced to resign the regency in 1578 he was tried, convicted and beheaded in 1581 for complicity in the murder of Darnley 14 years earlier. **William, 6th Earl** (d 1648) and Lord Treasurer of Scotland was obliged to sell the lands of Dalkeith in 1642 *(p 63)* and in consequence Aberdour became the principal Morton family seat. Extensions and improvements followed. By 1725 the castle was abandoned in favour of nearby Aberdour House.

Buildings. – Today the castle consists of the original 14C west tower, which was rebuilt in its upper part in the 15C. A rectangular extension was added in the 16C to the southeast. This is distinguished by Renaissance decoration on the windows overlooking the courtyard. The internal layout was innovative in that a corridor served the rooms on both levels. The L-shaped extension to the east was built for William, 6th Earl and contained a picture gallery on the first floor. In accordance with the fashion of the time this was in all probability panelled with a painted timber ceiling.

Gardens. – To the east is the walled garden which was once a typical 17C formal garden. It became a bowling green and its lawn is now fringed with herbaceous borders. The pediment over the kirk lane entrance, displays the monogram of the 6th Earl and his wife and the date 1632. The sloping ground to the south of the castle was once laid out as formal terraces, with a dovecot and orchard beyond. The late 16C terrace gardens are at present being reinstated. It is interesting to note that two of the family's near relations in the late 16C early 17C included the owners of other famous gardens, namely Edzell and Glamis.

St Fillans Parish Church. – *South of the walled garden.*
Under its immense and gently pitched roof the nave and chancel are 12C Norman with a square east end. The church served as a place of worship until 1790, and then lay empty as a roofless ruin until its restoration in 1926 to serve as the parish church.

Silver Sands. – The vast sandy beach is a popular spot for a day outing.

EXCURSION

tc **Boat trip to Inchcolm Island.** – During the summer months a ferry plies between West Sands and Inchcolm. Sailings are subject to weather and tides.
Inchcolm Island. – *Description p 186.*

★ ABERFELDY (Tayside)   Pop 1 537

Michelin map 401 fold 23 – I 14

Aberfeldy is a small Perthshire town pleasantly set in Strath Tay seven miles east of the loch. The town is busy with holidaymakers in summer.

General Wade's Bridge. – This elegant five arched bridge adorned with obelisks was built, some say to designs of William Adam, by General Wade to carry his military road north from Crieff to Dalwhinnie.

The Black Watch Monument. – The kilted figure, dressed in a uniform of the time, commemorates the formation of the Black Watch Regiment in 1739 *(p 171)* by the amalgamation of six Independent Companies. The monument marks the site of the first parade.

EXCURSIONS

tc **Castle Menzies.** – *1 1/2 miles to the west. Leave by the B846 crossing General Wade's Bridge. Take the second entrance.*
This 16C Z-plan castle was the chief seat of the Menzies until 50 years ago when the main line died out. In 1959 the Menzies Clan Society took over and restoration has been in progress since 1971. Although much remains to be done, photographs and the visit give some idea, of the work involved and that already accomplished. There are two fine plasterwork ceilings.

tc **St Mary's Church.** – *2 miles northeast of Aberfeldy, signposted off the A827. Take the farm road up to Pitcairn Farm. Electric time switch; handboards available.*
The 16C church, a low unassuming whitewashed edifice, stands behind the farm buildings. Inside is an extraordinary 17C **painted ceiling★** (covers only half of the roof). The elaborate design includes heraldic devices of local Stewart landowners, Biblical texts, the Evangelists all interspersed with vases, fruit, flowers and cherubs. The colours are clear but the figure drawing is crude in comparison with the assurance of the heraldic and other geometric designs.

38

ALFORD (Grampian)

Michelin map **401** fold 20 – L 12

This market town is set in the Howe of Alford, a rich arable basin encircled by hills, notably the Correen Hills to the northwest and Bennachie to the northeast. This was the birthplace of the poet **Charles Murray** (1864-1941) who spent much of his life in South Africa, and was known for his poetry in the Doric.

tc **Grampian Transport Museum.** – *Beside the main car park.*
The main section evokes the transport (cars, cycles and carriages) history of the North East amidst a variety of side exhibits. Look out for the "sociable safety cycle" which was anything but safe and The Craigievar Express, a local postman's 19C steam tricycle. Built in 1895 to help with the delivery round, this mainly wooden steam vehicle is capable of doing at least 10mph.

tc **Alford Valley Railway Museum.** – The station now houses a small museum describing the arrival of the railway and its effect on 19C rural Donside. The Alford Valley Railway operates steam and diesel locomotives between the terminus and two local country parks.

EXCURSIONS

★★★**Craigievar Castle.** – *Description p 56.*

Upper Donside. – *28miles from Alford to Corgarff.*
This excursion follows the Don Valley through the changing scenery of its upper reaches.

> *Leave Alford by the A 944 which follows the river closely to break through the hill rim. Turn left to take the A 97, the Tomintoul road.*

tc In the grounds of Kildrummy Castle Hotel *(take the hotel entrance)* an attractive **alpine garden** has been laid out in a former quarry.

★**Kildrummy Castle.** – *Description p 140.*

Five miles further on is Glenbuchat Castle, in a strategic site, commanding both the Don and Water of Buchat valleys.

tc **Glenbuchat Castle.** – This characteristic Z-shaped castle was built in 1590 by a Gordon laird. This was the home of the "Old Glenbuchat" that hero of the '15 and '45 rebellions who so plagued the dreams of George III.

Bellabeg. – On Games Day in August this tiny village is the scene of a 160 year old tradition, the **March of the Men of Lonach** *(p 28)*. The Men of Lonach, traditionally Forbeses and Wallaces, resplendently attired in full Highland dress with pikes aloft, march proudly through the strath to the scene of the Gathering in the park at Bellabeg.

Beyond the confluence of the Water of Nochty and the Don is the ditch encircled grassy mound, the **Doune of Invernochty**. This was the chief stronghold in the province of Mar, prior to the building of Kildrummy Castle *(qv)*. The remains of the curtain and two buildings are examples of Norman work.

(Scottish Tourist Board)
The Men of Lonach

tc **Corgarff Castle.** – Corgarff is strategically placed at the head of the Don, at a fording point controlling the route to Speyside via the Lecht Pass. The 16C tower house, a hunting seat of the Earls of Mar, was transformed after the '45 as a garrison post for government troops when low wings and a star shaped curtain were added. Abandoned at the beginning of the 19C it was garrisoned again between 1827 and 1831 in an effort to prevent whisky smuggling.

★ ARBROATH (Tayside)

Michelin map **401** fold 24 – M 14

The holiday resort and fishing port of Arbroath on the Angus coast, is known for the lovely ruins of its Abbey Church and its smoked haddocks or "smokies".

★THE ABBEY *time : 1/2 hour*

tc On his release from captivity **William the Lion** (1143-1214) founded a priory in 1178 in memory of his childhood friend Thomas à Becket who had been cruelly murdered in Canterbury Cathedral eight years previously. William died before the abbey was consecrated and was buried in front of the high altar. By 1233 the building was finished and in 1285 the establishment was accorded abbey status and was colonized by Tironensian monks from Kelso. The abbey's most historic moment was the drawing up and signing of the **Declaration of Arbroath** on 6 April 1320 during the Wars of

Independence. In all probability penned by the abbot of the time, Bernard de Linton, this eloquent declaration of Scotland's independence was despatched to the exiled Pope John XXII in Avignon.

A wealthy establishment – the Abbot of Aberbrothock was a highly influential person in the realm – the abbey flourished until 1606 when it became a temporal lordship. Thereafter neglect led to decay.

The abbey once again became national news in 1951 when the "stolen" Stone of Destiny *(p 180)* turned up on the altar.

Buildings. – In the words of Dr Johnson "these fragments of magnificence" give some idea of the onetime splendour of this monastery.

The cobbled precinct is overlooked to the right by a range which has as centrepiece the **gatehouse** controlling access to the abbey. Ahead the west front is flanked by buttressed square towers. The round headed arch of the doorway supports a tribune with above the lower half of a massive rose window. The remains of the abbey church include the south wall of the nave and a glorious **south transept** with two lines of arcading pointing upwards to the triforium. Above are lancets and the great O window which once served as a beacon for ships at sea. The flat east end has more arcading surmounted by a trio of great lancets. A plaque marks William the Lion's burial spot. The 15C **sacristy**, off the south aisle of the chancel, is a beautifully proportioned, rib-vaulted chamber. It was in all probability here that the monks kept the **Monymusk Reliquary** known as the Brecbennoch of St Columba *(p 97)* the custody of which had been given to the monks by William the Lion. The reliquary was solemnly borne into battle with the Scottish army.

Now, standing apart, the late 15 early 16C **Abbots House** is a pleasing dwelling in the vernacular tradition, despite many alterations. Note in particular the street front. The house serves as a museum and noteworthy features include the headless effigy of the founder and one of Thomas à Becket.

ADDITIONAL SIGHTS

tc **Signal Tower Museum.** – *Ladyloan.*
Subjects of interest covered by this local museum include the Signal Tower itself and the construction of the Bellrock lighthouse on the Inchcape reef. The rock was given its name when the abbot of Aberbrothock is said to have set a bell on the reef.

★St Vigeans. – *Access from the A 92.*
This hamlet on the outskirts of the town is composed of a circular arrangement of
tc cottages curving round the church on a knoll. The **museum** has an important collection of early Christian monuments *(p 21)*. Pictish art is well exemplified by the carved symbol stone the Drosten Stone (no1) with cross and animals on the obverse and symbols on the reverse. On the red sandstone cross slab (no 7) decipher the Biblical figures. The coffin shaped recumbent stones are well decorated. No 8 sports a fantastic bird on the side.

★★ ARRAN, Isle of (Strathclyde) Pop 3 576
Michelin map **401** folds 30 and 34 – DE 16 and 17
Access : see the current Michelin Red Guide Great Britain and Ireland.

Arran, the largest of the Clyde islands, with an area of 165 sq miles measures 20 miles long and 10 miles wide. "Scotland in miniature" the island is cut in two by the Highland Boundary Fault. An island of contrasts the mountainous northern part, with Goat Fell (2 866ft-874m) the highest peak, has deep valleys and moorland while the southern half has more typically Lowland scenery. Around the coast, sheltered sandy bays, rugged cliffs and small creeks alternate. Sheltered by the arm of the Kintyre Peninsula the island has a particularly mild climate.

Prehistory. – The heritage of prehistoric times is particularly rich with the island set on the main migration route up the western seaboard. The long cairn collective tombs of the Neolithic agriculturalists, standing stone circles of the Bronze Age (Machrie Moor) and forts of the Iron Age are all to be found on Arran.

Arran today. – The economy is essentially based on agriculture with large sheep runs on the moorland areas and arable farming or dairying restricted to the improved areas of valleys and coastal fringes. Forestry is on the increase on the east coast but the main industry is undoubtedly tourism, exploiting the isle's natural assets : scenic beauty and its changelessness. Facilities for the visitor include golf, cycle and boat hiring, pony trekking, rock climbing, hill and ridge walking, fishing, sea angling, yachting, water skiing and fine sandy beaches with safe bathing.

★★BRODICK CASTLE *time : 3/4 hour*

tc On approaching the isle by steamer one of the first things you can pick out against the towering backdrop of Goat Fell is the red sandstone mass of Brodick Castle, overlooking the bay. In a grand yet homely setting are displayed noteworthy silver, porcelain and painting collections, the heirlooms of Hamilton generations. Added to this are the splendours and beauty of an outstanding rhododendron garden.

The castle. – A stronghold from earliest times, the castle soon became royal and from 1503 Hamilton property, when the 2nd Lord Hamilton inherited the earldom of Arran. Following the 2nd Duke's death at Worcester (1652), Cromwellian troops occupied the castle and extended it westwards. In 1844, a further extension, complete with a four storey tower, all in the baronial style, was made by the ageing Gillespie Graham (1776-1855).

Interior. – In the Hall and first floor staircase landing we meet many of those responsible for the Brodick we see today. Busts portray William the IIth Duke and Princess Marie of Baden who decided to make Brodick their home and for whom Gillespie designed the 19C extensions and decorations, and their son the 12th Duke, gambler, racing man and collector of the many sport-

ing items. Portraits on the landing show the 10th Duke and his Duchess, Susan Beckford *(qv)* who assembled so many of the exquisite treasures now on display. The first and more intimate suite of rooms were those of the Duchess of Montrose, heiress of the 12th Duke ,who made it her life's work to preserve the house and its collections which are now in the care of the National Trust for Scotland. The dressing room provides the setting for the fan collection, two lovely 18C marquetry pieces one Dutch and one English (Boudoir) and Gainsborough landscape sketches (Boudoir). The Boudoir Landing introduces the Beckford link, with the great man portrayed on his deathbed (Willes Maddox) and a Turner watercolour of his home Fonthill Abbey *(see Michelin Green Guide, The*

(National Trust for Scotland)
Silver Thistle Cup – Edinburgh 1692

West Country). David Tenier's *The Temptations of St Anthony* to the left of the cabinet, well rewards a careful study. The cabinet itself is a treasure trove of exquisite objets d'art : ivories, porcelain, glass... The set of late 18C Blackamoor stools are Venetian. In the Drawing Room the richness of the gilded heraldic ceiling matches that of the contents. Noteworthy paintings include two small Watteau's, a Clouet portrait and the late Duchess of Montrose by de Laszlo. A pair of goose tureens, masterpieces of late 18C Chinese art (Chien Lung) grace the 18C Italian commodes between the windows. On display in the two following rooms, part of the Cromwellian extension, are many of the sporting pictures including that master of the art, Herring's *Dirtiest Derby* (1844) and Reinagle's *A Prize Fight* and items from Brodick's magnificent silver collection. Note in particular a pair of 17C Scottish thistle cups and the wall sconces.

tc **Gardens.** – The slope down to Brodick Bay is the setting for another of Brodick's gems, justly of international repute, the two beautiful gardens. Firstly comes the colour and formality of the 1710 walled garden with beyond the 65 acre **woodland garden** a creation of the late Duchess and her son-in-law, and now considered one of the finest **rhododendron** gardens of its kind *(main display April to mid-June).* The gardens form part of Brodick Country Park which provides many facilities for visitors including a ranger service.

TOUR OF THE ISLE

56 miles – about 1/2 day, not including visiting time

Fill up with petrol before setting out as there are few petrol pumps. The visit can be done in either direction or in two trips by taking the String Road between Brodick and Blackwaterfoot to cut across the waist of the island (10 miles).

This mainly coastal route gives a good view of the island and its diversity of scenery from the moors, glens and mountains of the north to the more pastoral landscapes and rocky cliff coastline of the south.

Brodick. – Pop 630. Brodick, with its great stretch of sandy beach and many hotels and boarding houses is the isle's largest and most popular resort and the port of call for the ferry.

tc **Rosaburn Heritage Museum.** – *One mile out of Brodick on the Lochranza road.*
Visit the blacksmith's shop, milk house, cottage furnished in late 19C and early 20C styles and exhibition area with displays of local social history, geology and archaeology. The last mentioned is a must for those who intend visiting the isle's many prehistoric sites. Note the Bronze Age cist 3 500 years old.

Paths lead to the Castle (1 mile) and Goat Fell (3 miles).
Take the Lochranza road to the right.

★★Brodick Castle. – *Entrance for visitors with cars. Walkers should take the path indicated above. See above for description of the castle.*

Corrie. – Pop 188. This former fishing hamlet consisting of a line of whitewashed cottages makes a convenient starting point for ridge walkers and mountaineers.

Sannox Bay. – Another sheltered sandy stretch.

The road moves inland, up Glen Sannox climbing to higher, bleaker moorland scenery in the shadow of the surrounding peaks and crests. Once over the watershed the road drops steeply towards Lochranza.

Lochranza. – Pop 283. Once an active herring fishing village and port of call for the Clyde steamers this rather scattered community has many a holiday home. The roofless
tc ruin of 16C **Lochranza Castle** stands on a spit jutting out into the sheltered haven of Loch Ranza. In summer a ferry operates between Lochranza and Claonaig on the Kintyre Peninsula.

Once round the point the view extends over Kilbrannan Sound to the Kintyre coast. The road becomes more twisting but remains close to the shore. Beyond is the shingle beach of Catacol Bay. Farming country appears again in the vicinity of Dougarie.

Machrie Moor Stone Circles. – *1 1/2 miles inland off the road.* The relatively flat land of the moor backed by the mountains makes an impressive setting for the intriguing remnants of these stone circles. The five circles, all fragmentary, were the work of a Bronze Age people who supplanted the Neolithic culture. Their exact purpose remains unsure, sepulchral or ritualistic? Four of the five had associated short cist burials and in two cases accompanying food vessels, which have been attributed to the period 1650- 1500 BC (Stonehenge *c*2800-1550 BC). The stones of differing dimensions are variously of granite or Old Red Standstone.

Blackwaterfoot at the mouth of a valley of the same name, overlooks Drumadoon Bay. The road continues in corniche fashion, high above the shore before moving inland as it swings round the southern end of the isle. Looming on the horizon is the rounded shape of **Ailsa Craig**, otherwise known as "Paddy's milestone". The islet is famed for its granite, in particular the blue hone, so favoured for the making of curling stones.

Kilmory. – The creamery produces Arran Dunlop cheese.

Just offshore lies Pladda with its lighthouse.

Whiting Bay. – Pop 352. With ample facilities for the visitor, this is another popular resort.

Holy Island comes into view, before the road rounds to Lamlash Bay affording a classic view of Brodick Castle on the north shore of Brodick Bay dominated by Goat Fell.

Lamlash Bay. – The supposed anchorage for King Haakon and his Viking fleet prior to the Battle of Largs in 1263, is now the headquarters of Arran Yacht Club.

★ AVIEMORE (Highland) — Pop 1 570

Michelin map 401 fold 19 – I 12

Set in the Spey valley on the western fringes of the Cairngorms *(qv)* Aviemore with skiing in winter and a range of summer activities is Scotland's premier all year resort. The building of the ultra-modern Aviemore Centre in the mid-1960s transformed this small village, which had grown up around the railway station, into a bustling centre offering day and night entertainment and indoor and outdoor sports and pastimes. Curling is one of the games played in the indoor ice rink.

In the **Highland Craft Village** visitors can see craftsmen at work : silversmith, glass blower, candlemaker...

Aviemore is the venue for **Scotland's Whisky Festival** *(p 212).*

Places with a blue underlining are important centres for outdoor activities

EXCURSIONS

tc ① **Strathspey Railway.** – The sounds and smells on this 5 mile journey between Aviemore and Boat of Garten are evocative reminders of times not so distant.

② **Excursion to the north.** – *34 miles. Leave Aviemore by the B 970.*

★★★Panorama from Cairn Gorm. – *Description p 53.*

Return to Coylumbridge and take the B 970 to the right.

tc **Osprey Hide.** – *Off the B 970. Access to the Royal Society for the Protection of Birds' hide within the sanctuary area, is by a clearly marked path only. 5 min walk. The hide is equipped with binoculars and telescopes.*

After an absence of 40 years the osprey returned to breed in Britain choosing a nest site by Loch Garten, within the ancient Abernethy pine forest. Operation osprey was started to give total protection during the breeding season, and the area round the tree-top eyrie was declared a bird sanctuary. In 1975 the nesting area and surrounding woodland, loch and moor was declared a nature reserve with open access to visitors.

Return to Boat of Garten and continue to the A 95,then branch off to the B 9153 and Carrbridge.

tc **Landmark Visitor Centre.** – The **Highlander★** film and "Man in the Highlands" exhibition are an excellent introduction to the distinct cultural and physical unit that is the Scottish Highlands.

Return to Aviemore by the B 9153.

③ **Excursion to the south.** – *16 miles. Leave Aviemore to the south to take the A 9.*

★**Highland Wildlife Park.** – See at close quarters Scotland's wildlife past and present. The
tc initial drive-through area includes herds of free ranging European bison, Red deer, wild horses, Soay sheep from St Kilda, Ibex (wild goat) and shaggy Highland cattle. In the walk-about section are wild cats, badgers, polecats, pine martens, beavers, golden eagles, snowy owls, wolves, grouse and capercaillie, a true native of the pine forests.

Take the A9 and branch off to Kingussie.

tc **Highland Folk Museum, Kingussie.** – The initial exhibitions in the reception building are an introduction to Highland life, clothes, in particular tartans and Highland dress and musical instruments. The open-air section includes a **black house** typical of the Western Isles with its vegetable enclosure, lazy beds, the **clack mill** and a turf walled building. An agricultural section shows the tools and techniques of what was essentially a mode of subsistence farming, with beyond, a display of domestic tools, crafts and furniture.

Leave Kingussie by the B970.

tc **Ruthven Barracks.** – The ruins of these 18C barracks stand on a mound rising out of the flat Spey valley floor. Following the 1715 Jacobite rising this was one of four infantry barracks built for law and order purposes and in particular to command the new military road. Ruthven fell to a second Jacobite attack in 1746 when it was burnt. The ruined main blocks face each other across a central courtyard with, beyond the wall, a stable block.

Return to Kingussie before continuing southwards to Newtonmore.

tc **Clan Macpherson Museum, Newtonmore.** – This well known pony trekking centre is the home of the Clan Macpherson Museum. Included amongst the relics of people and events associated with this clan and its chieftains is the black chanter used at the clan combat in Perth *(p 171).*

AYR (Strathclyde) Pop 47 896

Michelin map ⓘ fold 34 – G 17
See the town plan in the current Michelin Red Guide Great Britain and Ireland.

(Burns Cottage, Alloway)
Robert Burns

Ayr, the leading holiday resort on the Firth of Clyde coast makes a good centre for exploring Burns country. This lively resort boasts a wealth of modern facilities including a vast expanse of sandy beach backed by its esplanade, several delightful parks, traditional amusements and Scotland's premier racecourse. The latter is the venue for the Scottish Grand National *(p 212)* and the Ayr Gold Cup.

The town grew up around a castle, although remains of its historic past are rare, to become the principal centre of Carrick, later an earldom. By the 16 and 17C the town was the busiest port on the west coast, just ahead of Glasgow for size.

Trade was essentially with France until the late 17C when the West Indian and North American markets opened up. The railway age brought new life to Ayr, with the holidaymakers and commuting businessmen. The many substantial houses date from this era.

Today this lively market town with its excellent shopping centre, has a thriving tourist trade dependant on its amenities as a seaside resort, the proximity of the international airport at Prestwick, the reputation of nearby golfing centres (Turnberry, Troon) and its role as hub of the Burns country.

SIGHTS

Auld Brig. – This 13C bridge, immortalized by Burns, is said to have been financed by two sisters who lost their fiances, drowned while trying to ford the river in spate. The narrow cobbled bridge remains firm while its rival collapsed in the storm of 1870.

tc **Tam o'Shanter Museum.** – *230 High Street.*
A tavern in Burns time this is now a museum of Burnsiana. It was from here that Tam set out on his famous ride one stormy night *(p 44).*

EXCURSIONS

★Alloway. – *3 miles to the south by the B 7024.*
Alloway is famed world wide as the birthplace of Scotland's bard **Robert Burns** (1759-96).

★Burns Cottage and Museum. – This roadside cottage built by William Burnes is where his
tc eldest son Robert was born on 25 January 1759. The but, ben and byre evoke the
spartan living conditions of the 18C. The museum has a most extensive collection
of Burns' manuscripts, letters, documents and other relics.

Continue along the main road.

tc **Land o'Burns.** – This visitor centre makes
a good starting point for any excursion
into Burns country. An audiovisual
presentation introduces the southwest
and gives the life and times of Burns
showing 18C Ayrshire, prior to the
agricultural revolution. Facilities include an exhibition area, shop, garden
and picnic site.

Beyond, on the far side of the main
road, stands **Alloway Kirk,** where William
Burnes is buried and where the hapless Tam emboldened by "bold John
Barleycorn" saw an "unco sight!
Warlocks and witches in a dance".
From here he was chased by "the
hellish legion" till he reached the
nearby 13C **Brig o'Doon** where poor Meg
lost her tail in Burns' racing narrative
poem *Tam o'Shanter.*
Standing in a pleasant garden setting
tc the **Burns Monument** *(see cottage museum)* overlooks the River Doon and the
Brig.

Mauchline. – *10 miles northeast of
Ayr.*
Further landmarks and associations
with Burns and his works.

*The A 758 and then the B 730 lead
to the village of Tarbolton.*

Tarbolton. – Pop 4 300. At the time (1777-84) when Burns' father farmed nearby Lochlea
Farm, Tarbolton was a muslin and silk weavers' village. Here Robert and some friends
tc started a debating society in 1780 in a building today known as the **Bachelors Club.**
Downstairs the early 19C kitchen adjoins the byre, while above (outside stairs) is the
hall where the debating club met. Burns' relics include his masonic belongings.

Return to the A 758 and continue to Mauchline.

Mauchline. – Pop 4 500. Following the death of Burns' father the family moved to
Mossgiel Farm. Mauchline was where Burns met and eventually married a local girl,
Jean Armour, by whom he had nine children. On returning from his triumphant visit
to Edinburgh in 1788 Burns leased an upper room in a Castle Street house, now the
tc **Burns House Museum,** for Jean and his children. Wed later in the year they all moved
to Ellisland Farm *(p 73).* In addition to the Jean Armour Room upstairs the museum
has books, letters, documents and several personal items (watch, walking stick) with
downstairs a folk section including 19C Mauchline ware and Cumnock pottery. The
house next door *(now the curators, not open to the public)* was the home of Dr
Mackenzie who furnished Burns with a letter of introduction to Henry Mackenzie, editor
of *The Lounger* in Edinburgh.
In the churchyard are four of Burns' children and other local worthies *(The Jolly
Beggars)* who frequented Poosie Nansie's (on far side of the churchyard) and figured
largely in his poetry of the period *(The Mauchline Lady, Mary Morrison, The Holy Fair,
Holy Willie's Prayer, Address to the Deil).*

Kirkoswald. – *13 miles south of Ayr by the A 77.*

tc **Crossraguel Abbey.** – *2 miles beyond Maybole.*
This, Scotland's second Cluniac monastery and filial of Paisley was founded in 1244
by Duncan, Earl of Carrick. Patronage came from the Bruces and early Stewart
monarchs, no doubt in part due to the proximity of their residence at Turnberry. The
abbey achieved the height of its influence in the 15C when much rebuilding was done
following the destruction of the Wars of Independence. The extensive ruins are
arranged around several courts. The **church,** lacking both aisles and transepts, has a
15C choir terminated by a three sided apse, a common French feature. Also of the
15C are the attractive **chapterhouse** with beautiful groined vaulting and abbot's sedilia
and the formidable fortified **gatehouse.** Alongside the abbot's house is a 16C **tower house**
in the best secular tradition, surprising in a monastic establishment. Only the
foundations remain of a second unusual feature, the row of **corrodiars** – self-contained
lodgings – for retired monastic officers, ecclesiastics or even benefactors.

Continue on the A 77 to Kirkoswald.

tc **Kirkoswald.** – Pop 320. This village boasts the thatched and limewashed **Souter Johnnie's
Cottage** home of the cobbler that "ancient, trusty, drouthy, cronie" of Tam o'Shanter
the central figure in Burns poem of the same name. Burns had met the real life figures,
a cobbler and farmer, John Davidson and Douglas Graham of this rollicking narrative,
during his 1775 summer stay at Kirkoswald when he came to study under the local

dominie, Hugh Roger. In addition to the two rooms and cobbler's workshop are the original set of life-size figures by James Thom in the garden. The sculptures depict Souter Johnnie, Tam the innkeeper and his wife

> "The landlady and Tam grew gracious
> Wi' secret favours, sweet and precious :
> The Souter tauld his queerest stories ;
> The landlord's laugh was ready chorus :"

Both the real life characters are buried in the local churchyard.

Prestwick. – Pop 13 437. *4 miles north of Ayr.*
The town is known for its international airport and its top-class golf course. It was on the Prestwick course in 1860 that the very first golf open was played for a Challenge Belt. The following year the competition was declared "open to all the world" and was won by Tom Morris *(p 177).*

★ BANFF (Grampian)   Pop 3 723

Michelin map **401** fold 16 – M 10

Set at the mouth of the River Deveron, Banff is a distinguished small town with a wealth of 18C buildings. This rich heritage dates from the time when Banff was a winter seat for wealthy local land-owners. A royal burgh as early as the 12C, the town had at one time both a castle and a monastery.

tc **★Duff House.** – This country mansion with its impressive **baroque exterior★** was designed (*c*1735) by William Adam for his patron the 1st Earl of Fife *(p 102).* Only the central block was completed before the earl and architect were embroiled in a lengthy lawsuit. The gutted interior is being restored. The vestibule and private dining room are now resplendent with delicate plasterwork ceilings.

Upper and Lower Towns. – The following description takes in some of the more attractive 18C buildings in Banff.

Low Street. – Of particular interest are the 18C Carmelite House, the only reminder of the onetime monastery, and the **town house (H)** with its unusual steeple. On the plainstones in front is the rare pre-Reformation **mercat cross★**. The 16C finial depicts the Crucifixion on one side with the Virgin and Child on the reverse.

High Shore. – Numbers 1 to 5 on the left are an attractive group of 18C buildings. The doorway of no3, with its straight headed pediment and grotesque, contrasts with the more vernacular inn with its pend.

Boyndie Street (5). – On the north are two more examples of 18C town houses. The first Boyndie House (**A**) has a date stone and curvilinear gable.

BANFF

0   100 m
         100 yards

Back Path 2
Bellevue Road 3
Boyndie Street 5
Boyndie Street West ... 6
Carmelite Street 7
Gallowhill Street 9
Reid Street 10
Strait Path 12
Water Path 13

High Street. – On the west side is another series nos 47 to 41 (**B**) of two storeyed 18C buildings with further along on the other side Abercrombie Tower House (**D**), an attractive rubblework mid-18C town house. At the south end are more 18C houses, nos 5 to 1 (**E**) with the Old Banff Academy beyond.

EXCURSION

Fishing villages. – 15 mile drive through farming country to former fishing villages with some fine coastal scenery.

Leave by the Fraserburgh road the A 98 and once over the Deveron turn left to Macduff.

Macduff. – Pop 3 894. Facing Banff across the river Deveron, Macduff was renamed in the 18C by the 1st Earl of Fife when he built the harbour. Today the town still boasts an active fishing fleet, fish market and boat building yards due in large part to its deep water harbour and the silting up of the Banff one. Another attraction is the open-air swimming pool at Tarlair, amidst the rocks.

Gardenstown. – Pop 823. A winding narrow road leads down to this village which is terraced on the cliffs of the south side of Gamrie Bay. The small harbour is still the base for lobster boats.

Crovie. – Pop 95. On the east of Gamrie Bay the cottages of this tiny picturesque village stand, gables on to the sea, only a path's width from the shore.
The rocky headland, **Troup Head** *(no access)* with its 300ft cliffs is a prominent landmark on this coastal stretch.

Pennan. – Pop 92. Hairpin bends and steep gradients lead down to this attractive village of white painted cottages with their gable ends on to the rocky shore. Pennan figures as Ferness in Bill Forsyth's film *Local Hero.*

★ BIGGAR (Strathclyde)   Pop 1 931

Michelin map 401 fold 35 – J 17

This small but attractive market centre with its pleasantly wide main street serves an area of marvellously varied scenery of hills, moors, glens and farmland.

SIGHTS

★Gladstone Court Museum. – *North Back Road.*
tc This unusual museum, laid out as a shop-lined street, presents an authentic record of life a century ago. The original and entertaining presentation of various commercial premises passes from schoolroom to bank, ironmonger's to bootmaker's, telephone exchange to photographer's studio and druggist shop.

★Greenhill Covenanting Museum. – The displays and relics in this relocated 17C
tc farmhouse, evoke the **Covenanting Times** (17C) a period of religious persecution *(p 20).* The imposed use of the Book of Common Prayer (copy upstairs) in St Giles, precipitated the signing of the National Covenant 1638 (copy of Biggar's documents at the head of the stairs) when Covenanters pledged to defend the Presbyterian form of church government and worship. The result was strife between Covenanters and Royalists which was to continue until the 1680s. The southwest with its strong Covenanting faction is rich in memories of "outed" ministers, illegal open-air conventicles, martyrs and skirmishes.

EXCURSION

Broughton. – Pop 220. *7 miles from Biggar by the B 7016.*
Broughton is a tidy and colourful village with well tended gardens, the Beechgrove
tc Garden being an outstanding example. The **John Buchan Centre**, in the old church, is a tribute to the author and statesman, **John Buchan** (1875-1940) who as Ist Baron Tweedsmuir was Governor-General of Canada between 1935 and 1940. Having spent carefree childhood holidays in the area, Buchan remained a Borderer at heart and his
tc novels often had a Border setting. On a hillslope above the village, **Broughton Place** (gallery : paintings, prints and crafts) by Basil Spence (1930s), stands on the site of the home of 'Mr Evidence' Murray secretary to Prince Charles Edward Stuart.

The BINNS (Lothian)

Michelin map 401 fold 31 – J 16 – 15 miles west of Edinburgh

tc The home of the Dalyell family stands on a hilltop site commanding a good view of the Firth of Forth. The Jamesone portrait in the Business Room shows Thomas Dalyell an Edinburgh butter merchant who made his fortune in London with James VI and who on his return to Scotland in 1612 purchased this property. In 1630 he enlarged and redecorated the house and the many ciphers found throughout are those of Thomas and his wife. His son **Thomas Dalyell** (1599- 1685) better known as **General Tam** is the colourful family personality who dominates the house's history. A military man and staunch Royalist, on the execution of Charles I (1649) he swore never to cut his hair or beard until the monarchy was restored. Following capture at the Battle of Worcester (1651) and imprisonment in the Tower of London, Tam eventually made his way to Russia where he served the Czar in a military capacity. With Charles II's Restoration in 1660 he returned to command the king's forces in Scotland and proved to be an unrelenting opponent of the Covenanters, defeating their forces at Rullion Green. Tam was also responsible for the forming of a new regiment **The Royal Scots Greys**, holding the first muster at The Binns in 1681. Eventual amalgamation with the 3rd Carabiniers created the new cavalry, the Royal Scots Dragoon Guards.

Interior. – Despite successive alterations and additions the present house retains much that dates from the 1630 reconstruction. Of particular interest are the **plasterwork ceilings★** dated 1630 in the Drawing Room or High Hall and the King's Room. They are among the earliest examples of this kind of work in Scotland. Amidst the many mementoes of General Tam, his Russian boots and sword, huge comb and 1611 "Great She Bible", there are other family and regimental souvenirs. In the Dining Room there is Allan Ramsay's well known portrait of *Christian Shairp* and a portrait of General Tam after the Restoration!

IN THE VICINITY

Abercorn Parish Church. – *3 miles east of the Binns.*
In the small hamlet of Abercorn the old church (refitted 1579, restored 1838) has a particularly fine example of a laird's loft. The **Hopetoun Loft★★** is unusual in that Sir William Bruce when he fitted it out in 1707-8 included a suite of rooms comprising a retiring room with a burial vault underneath. The panelled loft, not unlike a theatre box, is decorated with Alexander Eizat's carvings and Richard Wiatt's highly colourful Hope coat of arms. Alongside is the Binns Aisle of the Dalyell family.

BLAIR ATHOLL (Tayside)

Michelin map 401 fold 23 – I 13

Blair Atholl is the last place of any size on the Great North Road, prior to following Wade's highway through Glen Garry and the Pass of Drumochter to Speyside. The village was removed from the vicinity of its main attraction, Blair Castle, in the 18C.

tc **The Mill.** – *150 yards from the village centre.*
In this corn mill (rebuilt following a fire in 1981), you can follow the different stages of milling from hopper room to basement.

tc **Atholl Country Collection.** – *The Old School.*
This small but well presented local museum gives an insight into life in Atholl of yesteryear. Exhibits range from a domestic interior to agricultural implements and tools of such rapidly disappearing craftsmen as blacksmiths and wheelwrights.

EXCURSION

*★Falls of Bruar.** – *3 miles to the west. Riverside paths on both sides and two bridges allow the visitor to go up one side and down the other.*
Both paths afford good **views** of the rushing water and deep pools as the Bruar Water follows its channel through solid rock.

tc **Clan Donnachaidh Museum.** – The museum tells the clan story and that of its chiefs who descend from the Celtic earls of Atholl. Among the early chiefs was Stout Duncan whose contribution at the Battle of Bannockburn proved decisive. From his great grandson, Robert came the surname Robertson. Clan Donnachaidh includes the septs Robertson, Duncan, Reid and other associated families. Also illustrated are clan country, the work of the Clan Society and prominent clansmen and women, both at home and overseas.

★★ BLAIR CASTLE (Tayside)

Michelin map 401 fold 23 – I 13

tc The white form of Blair bristling with turrets, crow stepped gables, chimneys and crenellated parapets, stands against forested slopes in a site of much strategic importance commanding a route into the Central Highlands. The castle, the family and the nation's history are closely interwoven and a visit to Blair with its many treasures brings to life all three.

Kingdom, earldom, dukedom. – The original ancient province or kingdom of Atholl had its main stronghold at Logierait. Cumming's Tower was built on the present site in 1269 and it became the seat of the Atholl earldom, eventually dukedom, held successively by the Stewart and Murray families. The castle has been considerably altered over the years. The Murrays were given the castle in 1629. It was in the lifetime of the royalist 1st Duke that Montrose raised the king's standard at Blair (1644). This act of rebellion was paid for by a Cromwellian occupation in 1652. In the early 18C further troubles ensued as the Hanoverian 1st Duke, John Murray, had several Jacobite sons. Four members of the family raised regiments of Athollmen in the '15 rising. In 1745 it was one of the former, **Lord George Murray** (1694-1760) an able military tactician, who became Bonnie Prince Charlie's lieutenant general and subsequently laid siege to his own home (1746). Following the '45 the 2nd Duke made many improvements on the estate, including the larch plantings – and transformed the castle into a Georgian mansion house. In the 19C Sir David Bryce rebaronialized the castle, creating what we see today.

The Atholl Highlanders. – The Duke retains the only private army in the British Isles, known as the Atholl Highlanders. The eighty strong army composed mainly of estate workers, still fulfills certain ceremonial duties. It is the sole survivor of the clan system of pre-army days, when the king relied on each chief to bring out his clan forces in order to raise an army. The annual parade is on the last Sunday in May.

TOUR *1 1/2 hours*

The rooms are numbered 1 to 32 and all portraits are cross referenced to genealogical tables displayed in each room. Outstanding are the 18C interiors, enhanced by furniture of the same period, the Clayton plasterwork, a variety of family portraits, fine arms and porcelain collections and interesting special subject exhibitions (Stewarts, Jacobites...).

GROUND FLOOR (Rooms 1-4)

Stewart Room (1). – Stewart relics, 16 and 17C furniture and portraits depicting *Mary Queen of Scots*, her son *James VI* and a matching double portrait of her parents, *James V and Mary of Guise*.

Earl John's Room (2). – Note in particular one of four original copies of the National Covenant (1638) ; the 17C bed and lovely walnut chairs and portraits of *John, the Royalist 1st Earl,* his son the *2nd Earl* and his wife *Lady Amelia Stanley* (Lely) and the *Marquess of Montrose.*

The Picture Staircase (4). – The 2nd Duke employed Thomas Clayton for over nine years on the interior decoration, during his alterations on the castle. The stucco ceiling is an example of his work. Between panels and frames of stucco decoration hang the portraits of the 2nd Duke's grandparents, *John, the 2nd Earl* as Julius Caesar (Jacob de Wet) and *Lady Amelia Stanley* (Lely), a full length one of his father *John, the 1st Duke* (John Murray) with Dunkeld House in the background, and one of himself.

FIRST FLOOR (Rooms 5-10)

Small Drawing Room (5). – An elegant Georgian room with an unusual set of mahogany chairs (1756) decorated with a fish scale pattern by William Gordon.

Tea Room (6). – Fine frieze, fireplace and overmantel and Gerard Honthorst portraits of *Elizabeth, the Winter Queen* and her son *Prince Rupert* (copies) and three of her daughters, cousins of Lady Amelia. The 18C china cabinets are Chippendale and Sheraton. Note the two tea tables.

The Dining Room (7). – Pale green walls and elaborate white stucco work set off Thomas Bardwell's ceiling medallions of the *Four Seasons* and the landscapes of Atholl estate beauty spots.

Blue Bedroom (9). – Part of the Cumming's Tower. There is a delightful portrait of the 7th Duke's wife, that Victorian beauty *Louisa Moncrieffe,* who had six children, none of whom had an heir!

SECOND FLOOR (Rooms 11-24)

Fourth Duke's Corridor (11). – Here is the work by David Allan, painted shortly after the 1782 act ending the proscription on Highland dress, showing the *4th Duke*, resplendently attired, with his family. He was known as "The Planting Duke" for the many larch plantations he created.

Book Room (12). – Some of the books in the library belonged to Lord George Murray during his exile in Holland.

Derby Dressing Room (13). – The unusual wood is broom and the cabinet was the work of Sandeman of Perth.

Derby Room (14). – Portraits include the 2nd Duke's daughters and his nephew, who eventually became the husband of the second daughter and thus 3rd Duke. A tale in itself!

Drawing Room (16). – The crimson damask wall hangings of this sumptuous apartment, set off the all-white coved and compartmented Clayton ceiling. Above the fireplace the Johann Zoffany conversation piece of the *3rd Duke and family* is flanked by portraits of the *4th Duke* (Hoppner), the boy in green in the former, and his wife. The settees and chairs are Chipchase (1783) and the gilt frames of the pier-glasses are by George Cole.

Tullibardine Room (17). – Note the famous portrait of *Lord George Murray* in Highland dress and other Jacobite mementoes.

Tapestry Room (18). – This, the top floor of Cumming's Tower, is hung with Brussels tapestries entitled *Atalanta and Meleager*. The magnificent state bed (1700) with Spitalfields silk hangings originally came from the 1st Duke's suite at Holyroodhouse Palace.

GROUND FLOOR (Rooms 25-32)

Terrace Room (25). – Note in particular the 18C Doune pistols *(qv)* by famous gunsmiths T Cadell and Alexander Campbell. Made entirely of metal, richly engraved, they have the very characteristic ramshorn butts and fluted breech end.

Ballroom (30). – A 19C addition, the walls are decorated with arms, antlers, and portraits. Note in particular Henry Raeburn's work of *Neil Gow,* that legendary fiddler to the 2nd, 3rd and 4th Dukes ;

China Room (31). – Very varied and rich collection of English, continental and oriental fine china.

Grounds. – The walk via Diana's Grove and over the Banvie Burn, passing towering larches, planted in the 18C, leads to the ruins of St Bride's where John Graham of Claverhouse, Viscount Dundee (1643-89) found his last resting place following his death at the Battle of Killiecrankie *(qv).*

★ BOTHWELL CASTLE (Strathclyde)

Michelin map **401** fold 31 – H 16

tc The ruins of this, the most outstanding 13C fortress, remain impressive in their commanding site high above the Clyde valley. This castle, of roughly the same period as Edward I's Welsh strongholds, is one of a group in Scotland (Kildrummy, Tantallon and Dirleton) showing a decided European influence in defensive design and layout.

A much disputed stronghold. – Built in the late 13C by a member of the Moravia family, the castle figured largely in the Wars of Independence. It fell into English hands in 1301 and on being retaken in 1314 after Bannockburn it suffered a first dismantling. The castle was repaired during a second period of English occupation when Edward III made it his headquarters in 1336. By the next year the Scots were again in command and under the "scorched earth" policy Bothwell was again dismantled. The castle lay in ruin until it passed by marriage to **Archibald the Grim,** the 3rd Earl of Douglas in 1362 who made this his chief residence. The late 14C and early 15C saw further additions and embellishments. Following the Douglas forfeiture of 1445 the castle passed through several hands before becoming the property of Patrick Hepburn, Lord Hailes, who exchanged it for Hermitage with the Red or 5th Earl of Douglas.

Castle ruins. – The first impression on seeing this red sandstone ruin, all towers and curtain walls, is one of sheer size and yet only part of the original 13C plan was executed. The initial frontage was to have been a gatehouse flanked by drum towers with curtain walls receding to the present construction. Take the stairs in the northeast tower to reach the courtyard enclosure. At the far end, the oldest and most impressive part, the 13C circular **keep** or donjon designed to serve as the last bastion of defence, shows "masterly design and stonework". The keep itself is protected by a moat on the courtyard side, with the drawbridge giving access to the doorway, sheltering behind a beak construction. Walled up following partial dismantling, three storeys and a fighting level rise above the

basement. The tower communicates with the 13C prison tower and postern in the south curtain wall. In the southeast corner the early 15C chapel, marked at first floor level by two pointed windows, communicates with the other great four storey tower, also 15C. Beyond against the east curtain wall, above cellars, is the great hall with its succession of elegant windows.

Walk round the outside to appreciate the setting, the site, the dimensions and the fine masonry of the 13C parts.

IN THE VICINITY

Bothwell. – Pop 4 840. The town grew up in the shadow of its great castle at an important bridging point on the Clyde. Bothwell developed rapidly in the 19C when
tc it was favoured by wealthy Glasgow merchants. The **choir** of the parish church belongs to the collegiate church founded in 1398 by Archibald the Grim, the 3rd Earl of Douglas. A good example of the Decorated Gothic style it has a unique stone slab roof. The 3rd Earl is said to be buried with his lady, Joanna Moray the Bothwell heiress, in front of the communion table.

A memorial beside Bothwell Bridge (north bank) commemorates the **battle** of 1679 when the Covenanters suffered their worst defeat. 400 were killed and 1200 taken prisoner. Many of the latter were imprisoned for several months in Greyfriars Churchyard, Edinburgh.

tc **The David Livingstone Centre, Blantyre.** – *1 mile from Main Street via Blantyre Mill Road and a footbridge over the Clyde.*

The late 18C mill tenement, Shuttle Row, now a **David Livingstone Museum★**, vividly presents the missionary cum explorer, his life, work and achievements. This extraordinary man (1813-73) was born in one of these single room family homes which in their time were considered to be model accommodation. Like his father he worked in the local cotton mill, as a piecer then spinner. The young David attended evening classes locally and then medical classes at Anderson's Institution, Glasgow in winter, where he met his lifelong friend and benefactor Paraffin Young. A man of strong religious beliefs he set out as a medical missionary but soon embarked on the travels which were to make his name as an explorer. On his three great pioneering journeys through the "dark continent", he made the first ever west-east crossing, discovered the Victoria Falls and Lake Nyasa now Lake Malawi. On his death shortly after his famous encounter with Stanley, the great man's body was carried back to the coast, a journey of over 1500 miles, before finding its final resting place in Westminster Abbey. Pilkington Jackson's wood carving *The Last Journey* is a moving tribute to both Livingstone and his faithful African followers.

★★ BOWHILL (Borders)

Michelin map **401** fold 35 – L 17 – 3 miles west of Selkirk

tc On high ground between the Yarrow and Ettrick Waters, Bowhill with its many treasures, including some exceptional paintings, is the Border home of the Scotts of Buccleuch.

The Scotts of Buccleuch. – The estate was formerly part of the ancient Ettrick Forest which Robert the Bruce granted to the Douglas family in 1322. It then reverted to the Crown in 1450 for about a hundred years before finally becoming the property of the Scott family. Walter Scott, the **Bold Buccleuch** of the Border raids was knighted by Queen Elizabeth who is said to have declared "With ten thousand such men our brethren in Scotland might shake the firmest throne in Europe". His granddaughter **Anne** married **James, Duke of Monmouth** the eldest natural son of King Charles II and Lucy Walter. Created Duchess in her own right, Anne retired to live in Dalkeith Palace *(qv)* on the execution of her husband following his unsuccessful rebellion against James VII.

Henry, the 3rd Duke married Lady Elizabeth Montagu, heiress to Boughton thus uniting the Scott and Montagu families and it was later in 1810 on Old Q's death that Henry inherited the estates and titles of the Douglases of Drumlanrig giving the present name, Montagu Douglas Scott.

BOWHILL★★

TOUR *1 hour*

Entrance Hall. – Added during 19C alterations, the hall is hung with portraits of four Huntsmen of the Buccleuch Hounds, whose service totals 160 years.

Gallery Hall. – Rising through two storeys, the upper walls are hung with four 17C Mortlake tapestries, while an impressive array of family portraits overlooks the BQ monogrammed English carpet in the Savonnerie manner and fine French furniture including the Aubusson covered canape and chairs. Most of the portraits are by the Van Dyck school although *Lady Anne Scott* is by Peter Lely. The children are William II Prince of Orange and Henrietta Mary Stuart, sister of Charles II.

Scott Room. – Here are a collection of portraits and mementoes of Sir Walter Scott. They include Henry Raeburn's (1808) *Sir Walter Scott and Camp* with Hermitage Castle in the background and David Wilkie's *King George IV* in Highland dress, whose state visit to Scotland in 1822 was stage managed by Scott and started the vogue for Highland dress. Scott mementoes include the manuscript of *The Lay of the Last Minstrel* which was dedicated to Harriet, the 4th Duke's wife. Other items recall the poet James Hogg, the Ettrick Shepherd a friend of both Scott and the Duke.

Monmouth Room. – Although never consecrated this room was built as the chapel, and now contains a variety of Monmouth relics from his Dutch cradle, saddlery as Master of the Horse, execution shirt and coral teething ring. The young Monmouth is portrayed with the latter, in a painting by Mytens. The wall opposite the doorway is hung with Lely's majestic portrait of *Monmouth* wearing the robes of a Knight of the Garter, and Kneller's fine family group showing Monmouth's wife, the *Duchess Anne with their two sons James and Henry.*

Italian Room. – Originally the billiard room, it was renamed after the Italian masterpieces including Francesco Guardi's (1712-93) scenes of his native Venice. There are two delightful 18C Dutch marquetry tables.

Dining Room. – The highlight of this more sober yet extremely handsome room, in both proportion and detail, is undoubtedly the collection of paintings in particular the family portraits. On either side of the fireplace are two enchanting portraits by Reynolds of "Winter", Lady Caroline Scott and her brother Charles, Earl of Dalkeith **"The Pink Boy"**. Also included in the array are the children's parents the *3rd Duke of Buccleuch* by Gainsborough his wife, *Elizabeth Montagu* by Reynolds and her mother, *Mary Duchess of Montagu* again by Gainsborough. The Canaletto, on the end wall, shows the London mansion, Montagu House, which stood roughly on the present site of the Welsh Office or Gwydyr House.

Morning Room. – Part of the 18C house, the Chinese painted wallpaper is 17C.

Drawing Room. – Resplendently rich under an attractively patterned ceiling and cornice highlighted with gold are the red carpet, red silk brocade wall hangings now faded to a pink, and Aubusson covered chairs and settees by the greatest French craftsmen. The paintings include Vernet landscapes. Between the two Boulle glazed cabinets with Sevres and Meissen porcelain is Reynolds' appealing portrait of *Elizabeth*, the Montagu heiress with her daughter Lady Mary Scott and various family pets. Between the Claude landscapes is an early Kneller portrait of *James, Duke of Monmouth*. The highlight is the only Leonardo da Vinci in a private collection, *The Madonna with the Yarn-Winder.*

Library. – The centrepiece is the white marble fireplace emblazoned with the A for Duchess Anne, originally from Dalkeith Palace, with above, her portrait by William Wissing. The other portraits, above the bookcases, are by Bradwell, Thomas, Wissing, Lely, Lawrence, Beechey, Kneller and even Landseer.

Primrose Room. – The impressive **collection of miniatures**, includes works by such masters as Samuel Cooper, John Hoskins, Laurence and Nicholas Hilliard and Peter and Isaac Oliver. Pick out Cooper's unfinished one of Cromwell and the two Holbeins (Catherine Howard).

Main Staircase and Hall. – Here are arrayed a series of more recent family portraits.

*The **Maps, Red Guides and Green Guides** are complementary publications. Use them together.*

BRECHIN (Tayside)   Pop 7 674
Michelin map **401** fold 24 – M 13

On the banks of the River South Esk this small cathedral city developed around its original Celtic monastery at a convenient fording point. The city is known for its Round Tower and Cathedral.

★Round Tower. – *View the tower from the churchyard.*
The Round Tower is one of two of the Irish type in Scotland. Dating from *c*1000 the 106ft structure (the spire is 14C) was originally free standing and may well have served as a belfry, look out and place of refuge. The narrow **doorway** six feet above the ground is noteworthy for the carvings of ecclesiastics on the jambs and a Crucifixion above.

Cathedral. – In the mid-12C David I was responsible for making the Celtic settlement the seat of a bishopric. Although the present church had its beginnings in the 13C it has been much altered since. The west doorway is however a good example of 13C work. The square tower alongside is 13-15C. Inside, note in particular two early sculptured stones (St Mary Stone and Albar Stone), both good examples of Pictish art. The stained glass is by such 20C masters as Douglas Strachan (War Memorial Window), Herbert Hendrie, Gordon Webster and William Wilson.

EXCURSIONS

★The Aberlemno Stones. – *6 miles to the*
tc southwest. Leave Brechin by the Forfar road
the A 935 and once past the castle gates turn
sharp left to take the B 9134. The stones are
boarded up in winter.

The gently climbing road offers splendid views
northwards over Strathmore and the winding
South Esk, away to the ramparts of the
Highland rim.

The village has four **Pictish sculptured stones★**
dating from the 7-9C AD. Of the roadside
stones, the one nearest to the village hall, bears
a cross with flanking angels and on the reverse
a hunting scene with Pictish symbols *(p 21)*.
Other examples of these enigmatic symbols are
discernible on the roadside face of the eastern
stone. A road to the left leads to the churchyard
with its **stone★**, another outstanding example
of this Dark Age art form. On one side a cross
with intricate interlacing is flanked by intertwined beasts while on the second a battle
scene evolves full of vigour and movement.

Pictish Symbol Stone – Aberlemno

★Cairn o'Mount Road. – *31 miles from Brechin*
to Banchory allow 1 hour for the drive,
excluding the visits.

This scenic run follows one of the most popular passages over the hills to Deeside.
This historic pass was the main route north from Strathmore to Mar and Moray beyond.
Not all who travelled the pass were drovers and whisky smugglers. Royalty and their
armies also marched this way. Macbeth fled north to his final defeat, even Edward
I negotiated it twice, however, seasoned veterans such as Montrose and Bonnie
Dundee were more at ease in such difficult terrain.

Leave Brechin by the B 9667 to join the A 94 the main Aberdeen road then turn
left almost immediately to Edzell.

Nearby is Stracathro where Edward I's chosen Claimant, John Balliol, submitted his
crown and kingdom to the warrior Bishop of Durham.

Edzell and Castle. – *Descriptions pp 158 and 102.*

Take the Fettercairn road (B 966) out of Edzell.

★Glen Esk. – *Description p 158.*

Continue along the foothills to Fettercairn.

Fettercairn. – Pop 312. This red sandstone village has a certain charm, with its imposing
arch to commemorate Queen Victoria's 1861 visit, and picturesque square.

Take the Cairn o'Mount road.

tc **Fasque.** – Built 1820-8, Fasque, offers an insight into gracious living of Victorian times
and in particular into the life of **W.E. Gladstone** (1809-98) statesman and four times Prime
Minister. The well appointed "below stairs" and public rooms aptly reveal life in those
days. The main feature of the house is the **oval staircase**. Twin flights rise to meet at
the central landing which itself leads off into a series of matching oval-shaped halls
linked by corridors.
Fasque estate includes a commercial deer farm and part of the herd may sometimes
be seen in the enclosure in front of the house.

Continue round the foothills.

Away to the right a green mound is all that remains of Kincardine Castle, a royal
residence. The foothills were part of the King's Deer Park and some slopes are still
marked by the remains of the Deer Dykes.
The road then follows a glen up to the Clatterin Brig. Keep left to climb rapidly through
moorland to the **Cairn o'Mount** (1488ft – 454m). There is a splendid **view★★** from near
the top over the Howe of the Mearns, a lowland tract of fertile farming country,
stretching away to the sea.
The road then descends to Deeside through hill and at times forested countryside
with several narrow bridges over the Water of Dye and steep gradients to negotiate.

Cross the Water of Feugh at the village of Strachan (pronounced Struan) then turn
right to follow the B974 to Banchory.

Bridge of Feugh. – *Description p 64.*

Cross the Dee to reach Banchory.

White Caterthun. – *5 miles to the northwest. Leave Brechin to the north towards*
Menmuir.
Two Iron Age hill forts stand either side of the road. The **White Caterthun** *(400 yds by*
a grassy track to the left) is the nearer and better. Two massive but ruined stone walls
enclose a two acre site on the hill top. Beyond are vestiges of outer ramparts.

The times indicated in this guide
when given with the distance allow one to enjoy the scenery
when given for sightseeing are intended to give an idea of
the possible length or brevity of a visit.

★ BRODIE CASTLE (Grampian)

Michelin map 401 fold 15 – I 11 – 8 miles west of Forres

tc The castle has been the seat of the Brodies since the mid-11C when the land came into the family. The 12th Brodie built a Z-plan tower house in 1567. Additions in the 17C and again in 1824 give us the house we see today, still the home of the 25th Brodie of Brodie.
Brodie is also known for its famous collection of Brodie daffodils to be seen in spring.

Interior. – Interiors of various periods are the setting for a splendid collection of paintings *(hand boards in each room give details of the pictures)* and some exquisite timepieces and French furniture. The contrast is striking as one passes from the starkness of the Guard Chamber, one of the original towers, then across the Entrance Hall once the kitchen, to the 19C Library an extension by William Burn, the noted country house architect. On the way upstairs note the Guido Reni and Paul Van Somer's *Henry, Prince of Wales* (d1612) eldest brother of Charles I. The Dining Room, part of the 17C extension, has an amazingly ornate plasterwork ceiling of uncertain date, which was painted brown in the 19C. Under the gaze of family portraits the table is set with a Chinese export armorial service. The Blue Sitting Room's early 17C plasterwork ceiling incorporates the thistle and rose motifs.
The Red Drawing Room once the High Hall gathers together the 17C Dutch and Flemish works (Gerard Dou, Mytens). The 19C Drawing Room with its delicately decorative compartment ceiling, is hung with a variety of interesting canvases : the Van Dyck of *Charles I* and Romney's portrait (a copy) of *Jane, Duchess of Gordon with her son George* who as 5th Duke of Gordon married Elizabeth Brodie. Much of the French furniture came through Elizabeth in particular two exquisite pieces : the ingenious Louis XV bed table and the Hedouin bureau plat.
The Best Bedroom has 18C lacquer furniture. The William and Mary twin domed cabinet doubles as a secretaire, with secret compartments. In the rooms beyond there is a changing selection from the art collection which includes Scottish works by Peploe, Gillies and MacTaggart and 18 and 19C English watercolours.

★ CAERLAVEROCK CASTLE (Dumfries and Galloway)

Michelin map 401 fold 39 – J19 – 9 miles southeast of Dumfries

tc The substantial and highly attractive ruins of Caerlaverock (Lark's nest) girt by a moat and earthen ramparts stand in a pleasant green setting on the north shore of the Solway Firth. This outwardly formidable medieval fortress has an inner façade of great refinement and charm, an early example of the Scottish Renaissance style. These and other features make this an important Scottish castle.
This, the second castle on the site, was built in the late 13C (1290-1300). The defences were soon put to the test by Edward I's famous siege of 1300 recounted in Walter of Exeter's poem, *Le Siège de Karlaverock*. By then the principal seat of the Maxwells, alterations were made in the following centuries the most important being the Renaissance façade of 1634, the work of the Philosopher Ist Earl of Nithsdale. Following a Protestant attack during the Covenanting wars the castle was abandoned for Terregles and then Traquair *(qv)* and subsequently fell into disrepair.
Triangular in shape the great keep **gatehouse** stands impressively at the apex with tall curtain walls receding to towers at the further extremities, all with 15C machicolations. Inside the courtyard the splendid **Renaissance façade**★★ of the Nithsdale Building (1634) shows both a symmetry of design and refinement of execution. The main elements, triangular or semicircular window and door pediments, are enriched with heraldic or mythological carvings. There is a family resemblance with Drumlanrig's entrance front.

★★ The CAIRNGORMS (Highland and Grampian)

Michelin map 401 fold 19 – I and J 12 – Local map p 42

This granitic mountain range between the Spey valley and Braemar is an area of wild and dramatic scenery. Lying mainly above 3 000ft the highest point is Ben Macdui (4 296ft-1 309m) although three other peaks top the 4 000ft mark namely Braeriach (4 248ft-1 295m) Cairn Toul (4 241ft-1 258m) and Cairn Gorm (4 084ft- 1 245m). Monadh Ruadh meaning Red Mountains was their ancient name to distinguish them from the Grey Mountains or Monadhliath to the west of the Spey valley. The summits have been planed down by glacial erosion to form flat plateaux while glaciers have gouged the trough of Loch Avon and the river Dee. The mountain mass is split in a north south direction by the great cleft of the Lairig Ghru, continued by the Dee valley. Braeriach is the main feature to the west of this divide with Ben Macdui, Scotland's second highest peak to the east. The slopes and corries of the latter are the haunt of that ghostly figure, the Great Grey Man.

Flora and fauna. – The severe climate of these high altitude plateaux and summits, so often windswept, allows only an Arctic-Alpine flora to flourish. Lichen, heather and moss serve as background to the brilliant splashes of colour provided by the starry saxifrage and moss campion. These windswept tracts are the domain of such elusive creatures as the snow bunting, dotterel and ptarmigan. The objectives of the **Cairngorms National Nature Reserve**, designated in 1954, are to protect the scientific, scenic and wilderness values of its 64 000 acres.

Mountaineering and hill walking. – No motorable roads traverse these wild and awesome mountains and their very remoteness makes them all the more attractive to the mountaineer or hill walker. To the inexperienced and ill-equipped they are treacherous due to rapid weather changes bringing conditions sometimes Arctic in severity. Obey the mountain code and always leave a note of your route and expected time of return with someone responsible. Proper clothing and mountain equipment are essential. The Scottish Mountaineering Club publishes a series of District Guide Books in this case, *the Climber's Guide to the Cairngorms. See the chapter on Practical Information at the end of the guide.*

Skiing. – The northern and western slopes of Cairn Gorm *(see below)* provide Scotland's number one ski area. The ski slopes are within easy reach of all Spey valley towns and villages. The main access road passes Loch Morlich (Glen More Forest Park) before dividing to serve the two distinct skiing corries, Coire Cas and Coire na Ciste. Chairlifts, in two stages, and numerous ski tows transport the skiers to the various ski runs ranging from easy to difficult. There is also some skiing off the Lecht Road on the eastern side of the Cairngorms.

★★★PANORAMA FROM CAIRN GORM

tc For the non hill walker or skier the chairlift provides an ideal way of discovering something of the character and austere beauty of this mountainous mass.

The already good view from the car park unfolds still further as you rise to the top of the second stage. From the terminal, near the Ptarmigan Restaurant at 3 600ft, there is an extensive **view★★★** westwards of the Spey valley where it widens into a basin with Loch Morlich below in the foreground and Aviemore beyond. A path leads up another 500ft to the summit of **Cairn Gorm** (4 084ft-1 245m) which affords a wonderful **panorama★★★** in all directions well beyond the Cairngorm mountains.

★ CALLANDER (Central)   Pop 1 768

Michelin map **401** fold 27 – H 15

Known to millions as the Tannochbrae of *Dr Finlay's Casebook*, Callander is a busy summer resort on the banks of the River Teith. Astride one of the principal routes into the Highlands the town was built on Drummond lands confiscated after the 18C Jacobite risings. Its popularity has grown ever since, due in large part to its proximity to the Trossachs.

EXCURSIONS

★★★The Trossachs. – *Description p 197*

Lochearnhead. – *21 miles by the A 84, a busy trunk road.*

Beyond the village of Kilmahog the Highlands are heralded by the Pass of Leny.

Falls of Leny. – *5 min walk from the Leny Woods Walk (FC) car park.*

In this wooded gorge the waters of the Leny cascade over rocks at the Pass of Leny, to join the River Teith. Spates bring the salmon leaping upstream on their way to the spawning grounds in Loch Lubnaig.

Above the pass the valley opens out, displaying a characteristically glaciated form. The four mile long Loch Lubnaig is overlooked on the left by the towering form of **Ben Ledi** (2 873ft-879m). **Meall Mor** rises straight ahead at the point where the loch curves westwards. The plantations of Strathyre Forest cover both flanks of the valley.

Strathyre. – Pop 223 The hamlet of Strathyre, at the head of Loch Lubnaig, is the centre for the Foresty Commission's activities in the vicinity.

Beyond the Balquhidder turn off, the road continues to Lochearnhead *(p 60)*.

Rob Roy Country. – *Leave Callander by the A 84 following the above itinerary. Turn left at Kingshouse. Inverlochlarig is 11 1/2 miles from the main road. The road is single track with passing places.*

This valley provides a pleasant change from the bustle of the main road. The scenery is wilder but less dramatic. The area was the home ground of **Rob Roy MacGregor** (1671-1734) in his later years. Rob, a member of the Children of the Mist branch of Clan Gregor, was a noted freebooter, whose exploits were made famous by Sir Walter Scott in his novel *Rob Roy* (1818).

Balquhidder. – The railed enclosure in the churchyard marks the resting place of Rob Roy MacGregor, his wife Helen and two of their sons.

Loch Voil. – This peaceful stretch of water is overlooked to the north by the rounded outlines of the Braes of Balquhidder and further back Ben More (3 852ft-1 174m) with lower forest clad slopes to the south.

Inverlochlarig. – At the road end, one mile above the head of Loch Doine, is the site of Rob Roy's house where he died. Rob moved here from Glen Gyle, the latter being too near for comfort to the recently established garrison at Inversnaid. This is the departure point for several hill walks with paths leading north to Glen Dochart, Ben More and west to Glen Falloch.

CASTLE DOUGLAS (Dumfries and Galloway)   Pop 3 331

Michelin map **401** fold 39 – I 19

Spaciously laid out to the north of Carlingwark Loch, this inland market town with its important auction mart serves the local farming industry. The settlement assumed its present name and gridiron street plan in the late 18C. It was named, not after the Threave Douglases, but a local merchant, Sir William Douglas (1745-1809) who, with the fortune he had made in the West Indies, bought local estates and established a cotton industry in the town. Another local notable was the antiquarian Joseph Train who supplied Sir Walter Scott with so much information for his novels.

CASTLE DOUGLAS

EXCURSION

Threave Garden and Castle. – *2 miles. Leave Castle Douglas to the southwest by the A75.*

★★**Threave Garden.** – The estate of 4 farms, 120 acres of woodland, the mansion and 65
tc acres of house policies, were presented to the National Trust for Scotland in 1948.
Opened in 1960 the Threave School of Gardening welcomes 8 students annually for
a two year course on all aspects of theoretical and pratical gardening. The Victorian
mansion serves as hotel and school and the 60 acre garden has evolved from the
students practical work.
Beautifully kept the garden with its rich variety of flowers, plants, shrubs and trees
is a sheer delight with something for everyone. The main sections are roses *(June
and July)*, peat, rock, heather gardens, herbaceous borders, walled garden, glasshouses, patio, arboretum and woodland walk a mass of daffodils in April.

*Back to the main road and half a mile further on, a farm road to the right leads
to the car park.*

★**Threave Castle.** – *10 min walk from car park ; ring the bell for ferry.*
tc Ruined but still impressively grim on its island site in the Dee, Threave is a symbol
of the turbulence and insecurity which reigned in medieval Scotland. This tower house
was the stronghold of that most powerful and noble house, the **Black Douglases**. Rising
four storeys above its cellars, it was built in the late 14C by **Archibald the Grim**, 3rd Earl
of Douglas (1330-1400). As part of a campaign against the Douglas ascendancy James
II is said to have besieged the castle in 1455. Additional defences – the outer wall
and towers – were built following Flodden in 1513. The castle was dismantled in 1640
when it fell into the hands of the Covenanters, again after a prolonged siege.

★ CASTLE FRASER (Grampian)

Michelin map 401 fold 20 – M 12 – 15 miles west of Aberdeen – Local map p 37

tc Castle Fraser the grandest of Midmar Castles is a typical product of that period of
castle building (1560-1636) when native genius reached its apogee. The local masons
while adhering to the traditional form of the tower house displayed a highly individual
treatment of decorative detail.

The builders. – The present building was started in 1575 and the project completed
with the addition of the two courtyard wings in 1636. Two **Fraser** lairds were concerned,
Michael the 6th and Andrew the 7th, and members of both the northeast's most notable
families of master masons, the **Bells** and **Leipers**. The castle remained Fraser property
until the early 20C when the new purchasers embarked on a programme of restoration,
before the final donation to the National Trust for Scotland in 1976.

TOUR *3/4 hour*

★★**Exterior.** – The glory of Castle Fraser is its elevations. Here bare lower walls contrast
with the flourish of decorative detail at roof level while harling sets off the sculptured
granite work. Approaching from the car park the layout of this Z-plan castle becomes
apparent. The central block, distinguished by a magnificent heraldic achievement, is
adjoined by towers, one round and one square (Michael Tower) at diagonally opposite
corners. The two storey service wings, flanking the courtyard, serve to emphasize the
height of the main buildings.
Above the stepped and highly decorative corbelling a variety of traditional features
– turrets, conical roofs, crowstepped gables, chimney stacks, decorative dormers and
gargoyles – are deployed to achieve a harmonious composition. The pleasing
combination of such features is the essential charm of this local style and a testimony
to the talent and skill of the master masons. The lantern and balustrade are essentially
Renaissance features but the decorative effect as a whole is Scotland's unique
contribution to Renaissance architecture.

Pass round to the main entrance on the south side.

Interior. – The visit is arranged to include those rooms which have been restored.
Of particular note are the Great Hall and the suite of rooms in the Round Tower reserved
for the laird's family.
The rooftop balustraded area *(101 steps)* affords a view of the surrounding farmland
and of the walled garden.

★ CAWDOR CASTLE (Highland)

Michelin map 401 fold 15 – I 11 – 14 miles east of Inverness.

tc Cawdor is the title that Shakespeare's witches promised to Macbeth and the castle
is reputed to be the place where Duncan was murdered. The Thanes of Cawdor built
the castle, and lived in it from the late 14C.

Legend and reality. – Legend has it that the then Thane of Cawdor had a dream in
which he was given instructions to choose the site of his new castle. He was to send
a donkey laden with gold into the selected area and to build on the spot where the
donkey halted for the night. The donkey lay down under a hawthorn tree! Carbon-14
dating gives the date of the tree as being approximately 1372.

Exterior. – On approaching the castle from the drawbridge side, the central tower
is the 14C keep with the 17C wings to the right. Later additions and transformations
created the castle of today.

Interior. – In the Drawing Room, the original great hall, note Francis Cote's portrait of Pryse Campbell, 18th Thane of Cawdor, resplendently attired in an assortment of tartans. This ardent Jacobite defied all by having himself portrayed thus in 1762, during the period of Proscription of Highland dress. The painting also helps to prove that the idea of one clan one sett, was in reality a concept of the 19C. Emma Hamilton, a friend of John 1st Lord Cawdor and his wife, is portrayed by Romney. The Tapestry Bedroom is so named after the set of 17C Flemish tapestries depicting events from the life of Noah. The imposing 17C Venetian four poster retains its original velvet hangings. The Yellow Room is a good example of Jacobean design. The centre window of the Tower Sitting Room was the original, and only, entrance to the castle in the 14C, served by removable wooden steps. The fine set of 17C Bruges tapestries are after designs by Rubens. For the

(The Earl Cawdor, Cawdor Castle)
Pryse Campbell

thorn tree legend see above. Antwerp tapestries grace the front stairs while the Dining Room has English panels (*c*1690) showing scenes from Cervantes' *Don Quixote* and a most unusual carved stone fireplace.

The gardens to the south and west are well worth a visit.

COCKBURNSPATH (Borders)   Pop 280

Michelin map **401** fold 32 – M 16

This pleasant village of "Copath" just off the A 1 was the birthplace of **John Broadwood** (1732-1812) a cabinet maker by trade and co-founder of the famous piano making company. In the 1880s the village became the centre of a painter's colony with artists from the **Glasgow School** *(qv)* notably James Guthrie, EA Walton and Joseph Crawhall. The 212 mile coast to coast long distance footpath, the Southern Upland Way *(p 12)* links this village to Portpatrick on the west coast.

Mercat Cross. – The cross was built in 1503 to celebrate the marriage of James IV to Princess Margaret Tudor, to whom he presented the lands of Cockburnspath as a dowry. The weathered finial portrays the thistle and the rose.

Church. – The otherwise plain church has an unusual pre-Reformation round tower at the west end. The upper part is 19C. Other typical features include the corner buttresses, one with a sundial, stone slab roofing to the Arnott vault at the east end and a laird's loft inside.

EXCURSIONS

Pease Bay. – *1 mile. Follow the A 1 to Cove then turn right into the local road.*
The excellent sandy beach is backed by Red Sandstone cliffs. Further round the coast to the east is Siccar Point, the site of **James Hutton's** unconformity.

tc **Dunglass Collegiate Church.** – *1 mile to the northwest. Access turn left off the A 1 at the signpost to Bilsdean. Once over the bridge turn left into the grounds of Dunglass House. Follow the drive taking first fork to the right, park at the roadside.* The beautiful setting of grass and trees enhances the mellow tones and attractively weathered forms of the stonework. Founded in 1450 by Sir Alexander Hume, the original building consisted of nave and choir only, to which were soon added the tower and transepts. Despite its use as a stable in the 18C, this late Gothic building retains its charm and some attractive decorative sculptural work and is a good example of a 15C ecclesiastical building, (square east end, stone slab roofing, corner buttresses).

COLDSTREAM (Borders)   Pop 1 649

Michelin map **401** fold 36 – N 17

The name of this small border town on the busy Morpeth-Edinburgh route, instantly evokes the famous Guard Regiment, the **Coldstream Guards** or The Lilywhites. The town developed at a fording point on the banks of the Tweed, at the confluence of the Leet. Heavy traffic makes the narrow and winding main street hazardous. Down nearer the river the old town centre – Market Square, Duke and Leet Streets – offers a more peaceful scene.

tc **Coldstream Museum.** – *14 Market Square.*
Small local museum with an excellent section on the Coldstream Guards where uniforms, medals, flags, buttons and Jacob the Goose, the only ranked fowl in the British Army, tell the story and traditions of the regiment.
George Monck (1608-70) as Commander-in-Chief, was given the task by Cromwell of policing Scotland's east coast for nine years. In 1659 Monck and his regiment came to rest in Coldstream for several months, during which time the General lived in a

house on the present site of the museum. The locals affectionately nicknamed Monck's mainly "Geordie" troops, the Coldstreamers. It was from here on 1 January 1660 that Monck and his regiment set out on their famous march to London which resulted in the Restoration of Charles II. Although formed in 1650 it was 1670 before the regiment was officially named the Coldstream Guards, after Monck's death. The regiment was originally part of Cromwell's Model Army, explaining the crownless tunic buttons.

EXCURSIONS

★Kirk o'Steil. – *7 miles to the northeast by the A 6112 then the B 6437.*
In the small Tweedside village of Lady Kirk stands the beautifully time worn church, **Kirk o'Steil,** built in 1500 by **James IV** following a vow made when in danger of drowning in the Tweed. Built entirely of stone - even to the now replaced benches – to avoid destruction "by fire or water", the masonry is of mellow red sandstone and the roofing of overlapping ashlar slabs. The exterior, typical of the late Gothic style, has staged and pinnacled buttresses with three sided east end and transept terminations. Restored on several occasions, William Adam was responsible for the upper part of the tower, the lower storeys of which served as the priest's lodging. From a squint in the back wall, the priest surveyed the altar.

Just visible above the trees across the river are the ruins of the once great Norham Castle where in 1291 the Hammer of the Scots, Edward I, come to arbitrate between the thirteen **Competitors** to the Scottish throne. Among the claimants were Robert Bruce and the eventual successor Balliol. James IV captured this fortress with the aid of **Mons Meg** prior to Flodden *(see below).*

Flodden Field. – *Battlefield in England 4 miles to the southeast of Coldstream. Follow the A 697 through Cornhill-on-Tweed to the village of Branxton.*
The plain cross on the brow of Branxton Moor commemorates the **Battle of Flodden Field** when on 9 September 1513, James IV fell with the flower of Scottish knighthood. James IV's forray against the English was in support of the French, to honour the previous year's renewal of the Auld Alliance. The slaughter was great and the battle figures largely in ballads and novels, to name only two Sir Walter Scott's *Marmion* and Jane Elliot's *The Flowers of the Forest*. The massacre was felt throughout Scotland and even today the tragedy is commemorated, as in Selkirk's Common Riding ceremony *(p 28)* and the Fletcher statue.

tc **The Hirsel.** – *West of Coldstream on the A 697.*
Seat of the Earls of Home, the present owner, Sir Alec Douglas-Home, the 14th earl relinquished his title in 1963 to become Prime Minister. The estate has several nature trails, the Hirsel lake (a sanctuary for wild fowl) and Dundock Wood *(car park off the A 697)* bright with colour in late May and early June, at the height of the rhododendron and azalea season. The Homestead has a museum cum information centre.

★★★ CRAIGIEVAR CASTLE (Grampian)

Michelin map **401** fold 20 – L 12 – 26 miles west of Aberdeen – Local map p 37

tc Set in a peaceful Donside setting, Craigievar, that masterpiece and work of art is the crowning glory of a local school of castle building. This traditional Scottish tower house rises gracefully to a glorious cluster, where native and foreign influences are skilfully blended.

Danzig Willie. – The lands, including an incomplete castle, were purchased in 1610 by a successful Aberdeen merchant, **Willie Forbes** (d 1627) who had made his money in the Danzig trade. With his new found wealth he financed the castle's construction allowing the master mason free rein to express his ingenuity and skill. Since then Danzig Willie's descendants have occupied the castle right down to 1963 when it was given to the National Trust for Scotland.

TOUR *3/4 hour*

Exterior. – *Illustration p 31.* The glory of this six-storey L-plan tower house is its **elevations,** all different and all worthy of close attention. The composition as a whole displays an assurance and apparent simplicity belying the complexity and ingenuity of construction. Take the time and trouble to examine one by one the wallhead decoration of each elevation where conical roofed turrets, crow stepped gables, dormers, chimney stacks, balustrade, ogee shaped cupolas jostle for position in a composition of infinite variety, activity and humour. These inimitable skylines are the essence of the Scottish baronial style. The decorative detailing of the wallhead contrasts sharply with the starker lower walls. The upward movement, the soft tones of harling, the almost sculptural form accentuated by bull nosed corners, are all part of the beauty of this most compelling of Scottish tower houses.

Interior. – To climb the turnpike stairs and explore the many rooms of Craigievar is to take a step back into history. The visit brings to life the charm and intimacy of the domestic interiors and the homely lifestyle of an early 17C laird.

Main floor. – Little has changed since the Great Hall was terminated in 1625. The medieval type vault is covered by a plasterwork ceiling with ornate pendants and medallion portraits – quite the latest in interior decoration of the time. Panelling with neo-classical details covers the lower part of the walls and matches the screens, another medieval feature to be retained. Above the fireplace is a splendid **heraldic achievement**, that of the United Kingdom. The carpeting is the Forbes tartan. The Ladies Withdrawing Room with its Memel panelling and low ornate plaster ceiling is a pleasantly intimate chamber.

First floor. – In the White Bedroom with another fine ceiling, are family portraits by the Aberdonian, George Jamesone, of *Danzig Willie,* his elder brother *Bishop Patrick Forbes of Aberdeen* and the 2nd baronet *Red Sir John.* On the way out note the laird's lug.

Second floor. – Beyond the box bed, now converted into a bathroom, is the Queen's Room with its magnificent canopied bed and Scottish panelling. Above the fireplace are two early (1788) Raeburns of the *5th baronet* and *his wife*, which were commissioned for the modest sum of 16 guineas.

Third floor. – The Blue Room is the haunt of a Gordon, who fell foul of Red John. The two families were arch rivals. Even the turret ceilings have ornate plasterwork. In the neighbouring Nursery look for the passage disguised as a cupboard.

Fourth floor. – The Long Room, a noble apartment, may well have been where the courts of barony were held. The assembled documents include the 15C charter of the original Mortimer owners and the transfer one dated 1610 when the property passed to Danzig Willie. The secret staircase takes you down to the Great Hall.

★★ CRATHES CASTLE (Grampian)

Michelin map 🔢 fold 20 – M 12 – 15 miles west of Aberdeen – Local map p 37

The 16C tower house of Crathes Castle is an impressive example of the traditional architectural style enhanced by a series of delightful gardens. The interiors include some outstanding painted ceilings and some particularly fine early vernacular furniture. In short the ideal place to see the home and lifestyle of a 16-17C Scottish laird.

Burnetts of Leys. – The Saxon Burnard moved first from England, then the Borders before settling in the area, on land that had been granted to an ancestor by Robert the Bruce following Bannockburn. The original family seat was an island stronghold in the Loch of Leys (now drained) to the north of Banchory. The 9th laird **Alexander Burnett** (1549-56) undertook the building of a new mansion in 1553 but it fell to his great grandson another **Alexander, 12th laird** to finish the building. Some of the finest pieces of furniture belonged to Alexander and his wife Katherine Gordon. The property passed from Burnett laird to Burnett laird with little alteration or addition until the 15th laird, Sir Thomas who built the Queen Anne wing to accommodate his family of twenty-one. It was the last or 25th laird and his wife who created the glorious gardens we see today and donated the property to the National Trust for Scotland in 1951.

★★THE CASTLE *time : 1 hour*

tc **Exterior.** – Although not achieving the harmony of Craigievar *(qv)* the eventful skyline still has a variety and quality of decorative detail making it one of the best examples of this local style. Note the series of coats of arms and examine closely the **yett** now remounted outside. The ingenious construction is typically Scottish. The unique system of interwoven bars reversed in diagonally opposite corners gave great strength to the yett.

Interior. – The tour starts with three vaulted kitchen chambers where family documents are on display and passes by the prison hole. Upstairs the barrel vaulted **Hall** has armorial paintings on the window embrasures and three unusual stone pendants. Above the fireplace is the family's most prized heirloom, the delicate **Horn of Leys,** the original token to tenure (1322) given by Robert the Bruce. The motif is found throughout the castle. The Jamesone (1588-1644) family portraits include the builder, his wife and perhaps the most well known family member, Bishop Burnet, author of *A History of My Own Times* and adviser to William of Orange. Note on the great marriage chest the portraits of Alexander and his wife.

In the **Bedroom** with its original half tree trunk floorboards hangs a Kneller portrait of the Bishop, or busybody, as William called him. Next comes one of the lovely painted ceilings in the **Room of the Nine Nobles** (1602). As was usual the composition was drawn in black and then colourfully infilled. This bright and lively form of decoration was common on the East Coast no doubt influenced by trading contacts with Scandinavia where similar techniques flourished. Plasterwork ceilings superseded this form of decoration. The Crathes examples are some of the best in existence (restored). The figures of the Nine Nobles (Hector, Alexander the Great, Julius Caesar, Joshua, David, Judas, Maccabeus, King Arthur, Charlemagne and Godfrey de Bouillon) are portrayed on the ceiling boards with Biblical quotations on the sides of the beams. Due to the foreignness of their costumes it is

(Clive Friend/Woodmansterne)

Nine Nobles Room Ceiling – detail

supposed that they were copied from a continental source, as were the garden sculptures at Edzell *(p 102)*. Beside the 1641 inlaid bed with its colourful crewel work hangings are two lovely carved chairs, dated 1597 with the initials of Alexander and Katherine. The **Green Lady's Room,** a haunted chamber, has another decorative ceiling where the figures (ceiling boards) and decorative patterns (underside of beams) bear no relation to the maxims and Biblical quotations (sides of beams). Stairs again lead upwards. The **Long Gallery,** running the entire width of the house is unique for its oak panelled roof decorated with armorials and the horn. Take the chance to look out over the gardens from this good vantage point. Downstairs in the **Laird's Bedroom** is the outstanding oak bed (1594) resplendent with carved heads of Alexander and Katherine, their heraldic devices and colourful crewel work. Down again. The **Muses Room** boasts another vividly painted ceiling showing the nine muses and Seven Virtues. The tapestry is a William Morris commission (1881). Look for the mouse trademark on the stool by Robert Thompson (1876-1955) who was known for his church furnishings.

★★★THE GARDENS

tc Full of variety and beauty the gardens at Crathes were the lifetime achievement of the late Sir James and Lady Burnett. The whole is composed of a series of distinct and separate gardens where the visitor is lured on by yet another secluded enclosure beyond. The shape, colour, design and fragrance defy description but here the expert gardener and amateur alike will be enthralled by the display. The yew hedges dating from 1702 separate the Pool Garden (yellows, reds and purples) from the formal Fountain (blues) and Rose Gardens. In the lower area a double herbaceous border separates the Camel and Trough Gardens with beyond the White and June borders and a recent Golden Garden as a memorial to Lady Burnett.
Woodland walks offer the chance to discover the natural life of the Crathes estate. Well signposted they start from the shop and vary from 1 to 5 miles in length.

*The towns and sights described are shown **in black on** the maps.*

CRICHTON CASTLE (Lothian)

Michelin map **401** fold 31 – L 16 – 10 miles southeast of Edinburgh
2 1/4 miles from the A 68 signposted. Car park beside the church.

tc In an isolated setting the imposing ruins of Crichton Castle stand high above the eastern bank of the Tyne. This was the seat of Sir William Crichton (d 1454) Chancellor of Scotland in the reign of James II and more infamously instigator of the "Black Dinner" (1440) in Edinburgh Castle when the Douglas brothers were murdered. The castle was forfeited on a least three occasions once to Sir John Ramsay, another of James III's favourites, then to Patrick Hepburn, Lord Hailes and also to Francis Stewart "a cultured ruffian" who was responsible for the outstanding feature of this castle, the Italianate north range.

Buildings. – 15 and 16C extensions and alterations have transformed the original late 14C tower house into the complex residence, enclosing a courtyard, which we see today. The most striking feature is undoubtedly the **Italianate courtyard range★** with its distinctive diamond bosses. Dating from 1591 this was the work of the much travelled Francis Stewart, 5th Earl of Bothwell and the bane of his kin, James VI. Crichton is unique as there are few examples of such a distinct foreign influence in the 16C architecture of Scotland.
The late 14C **tower house** with pit prison, kitchen and hall above is on the east side adjoined to the south by a keep-gatehouse added by the Lord Chancellor. The three floors include basement cellars, large hall with hooded fireplace and upper hall. The west wing also with three storeys is adjoined to the south by a six storey tower. The late 16C north wing has the striking inner elevation, a seven bay arcade with diamond rustication above. Alongside is a straight stair rich with Renaissance motifs leading to the parlour, dining room and bed chambers above.
The unusual outhouse nearby is probably 16C.

Crichton Parish Church. – This building is one of the many collegiate churches founded by the Scottish baronial class in the 15C. In this case it was Sir William Crichton in 1449 and although incomplete as it lacks a nave it is a typical T-kirk with square east end, battlemented tower and saddleback transept roof with bell-cote.

★ CRIEFF (Tayside)   Pop 5 603

Michelin map **401** fold 27 – I 14

The pleasant holiday resort of Crieff is well situated on a hillside overlooking the fertile sweep of Strathearn. On the Highland rim, with fine scenery all around, Crieff makes an ideal touring centre.
With the convergence on Crieff of routes from the north it was, prior to 1770, a centre of the cattle trade and one of the great cattle trysts. The 17C cross dates from the period when the town was known as Drummond. Burnt down by the Jacobites after the 1715 rising it was rebuilt by the Crown Commissioners and by the end of the 18C it was a resort in a small way. The railway arrived in 1856 and by the late 19C Crieff Hydro was flourishing. The face of Crieff today testifies to its Victorian popularity as a spa.
The **Crieff Highland Gathering** *(p 28)* with the official Scottish Heavyweight Championship is always a popular event.

SIGHTS

tc **Crieff Visitors Centre.** – *Muthill Road.*
Visitors are able to visit two craft firms and watch the manufacture of hand painted ware, featuring the thistle, heather and bluebells (Buchan's Thistle Pottery) and of millefiori glass (Perthshire Paperweights).

tc **Stuart Strathearn.** – *Muthill Road.*
Follow the stages in the manufacture of hand-made crystal ware.

tc **Glenturret Distillery.** – *1/4 mile outside Crieff on the Comrie road the A 85.*
On the banks of the Turret, the distillery established in 1775 (making it the oldest in Scotland) still employs traditional methods to produce its famous product.

EXCURSIONS

★Drummond Castle Gardens. – *2 miles south of Crieff.*
tc The Drummond family seat, consisting of a 1491 tower and later buildings is set high on a rocky eminence. Laid out below in a series of terraces, the **formal gardens** are in the form of St Andrew's Cross. Against the background of lawns and gravel areas, boxwood hedging and the many shaped and pruned trees and bushes present a medley of greens and shapes and provide the detailed patterns. Roses and other beds of flowers add the colour.

★Excursion in Strathearn. – *15 miles round tour. Take the Dunblane road out of Crieff, the A 822.*

★Drummond Castle Gardens. – *Description above.*

Muthill. – Pop 581. This Strathearn village, destroyed in 1715 after Sheriffmuir, is dominated by its 70ft high 12C **tower** one of a group in the area. Formerly free standing, the saddlebacked and crow stepped tower is now embedded in the west end of the ruined 15C church. The east end shelters two recumbent Drummond effigies.

Continuing on the main A 822 road, cross the Machany Water, before branching left to take the A 823. Signposts indicate Tullibardine Chapel to the left.

★Tullibardine Chapel. – This highly attractive red sandstone church stands on its own in
tc the middle of rich agricultural land, sheltered by a couple of gnarled and windswept trees. Sir David Murray of the now vanished Tullibardine Castle, founded this cruciform church in 1446. Enlarged *c*1500 it has survived unaltered ever since. The chapel is a good example of Scottish late Gothic architecture at its most lovely with such characteristic features as rubble stonework, armorial skewputts and crow stepped gables.

Return to the A 823, at the road junction turn left to take the A 824 in the direction of Auchterarder.

Nearby, standing in spacious grounds, is the famous Gleneagles Hotel, a name synonomous with gracious living and first-rate golf (four courses).

Auchterarder. – Pop 2 446. This small but long Strathearn town has a rich historic past. From favourite hunting seat in the 11C, it became the chief burgh of the important earldom of Strathearn. The town was destroyed in 1715 following the Jacobite retreat after Sheriffmuir.

Almost out of Auchterader turn left into the B 8062, continue towards the Earn, cross the Machany Water and just before Kinkell Bridge, branch left into a local road which leads to Strathallan Airfield.

★Strathallan Aero Park. – *There is usually a flying display in summer.*
tc Arranged around a collection of aicraft including a Lancaster Bomber, Lysander and Fairy Battle are side exhibits dealing with many aspects of aviation. Outside a De Havilland Comet, presenting a cockpit in all its complexity, stands alongside a legendary "shack" the aircraft which has seen over 30 years of squadron service.

Take the B 8062 to cross the Earn and continue for approximately 3 miles.

tc **Innerpeffray Library and Chapel.** – *1 mile down a side road to the buildings perched on an eminence, overlooking the Earn.*
The **library** was founded in 1691 by David Drummond, 3rd Lord Madderty, which makes it one of the earliest public libraries in Scotland. A descendant, Robert Hay Drummond, Archbishop of York, added to the collection and built the present building in the late 18C. Noteworthy amongst the many valuable historical items in the book-lined room are Montrose's pocket Bible ; copies of the Breeches and Treacle Bibles ; a chain Bible ; an 18C accounts book appropriately named "Waste Book" and an early lending ledger. The adjoining **chapel** was built in 1508, on the site of a former place of worship. Inside this long, low building is a pre-Reformation stone altar. The upper chamber above the west end was the original home of the library.

The B 8062 leads back into Crieff.

★Upper Strathearn. – *20 miles to Lochearnhead by the A 85. Take the Comrie road, A 85 out of Crieff to the northwest.*

tc **Comrie.** – Pop 1 119. This small but busy tourist centre has the **Museum of Scottish Tartans★** *(Drummond Street)* with an authoritative and wide ranging collection of tartans and Highland dress.

Continue along the north bank of the Earn.

St Fillans. – Pop 160. An attractive village set at the east end of Loch Earn, it is supposedly named after the Celtic saint of the same name.
Roads follow both sides of the loch : that to the north is the faster main road with numerous stopping places and notable views of the lofty summits of Ben Vorlich to the south ; the southern road is narrower and hillier and less well provided with stopping places. For the following, take the north road.

★★Loch Earn. – A typical Highland loch, flanked by majestic mountains. The waters have become a favourite venue for water sports.

Lochearnhead. – Pop 175. Sailing and water skiing centre for Loch Earn.

The Smaa Glen. – *Crieff to Dunkeld via the Smaa Glen : 22 miles. Leave Crieff by the A 85 then branch left to take the A 822.*
This route follows General Wade's Military Road and in so doing leaves behind the open Perthshire countryside to penetrate into the Highland rim.

Smaa Glen. – This narrow V-shaped valley with steep scree covered slopes is a popular beauty spot. There is easy access to the banks of the boulder strewn course of the River Almond.
At the northern end of the glen, between the road and the river, a huge boulder known as Ossian's Stone, is said to have marked the grave of the 3C Gaelic bard, Ossian.
Once over the river the road then rises to cross moorland countryside before descending into Glen Quaich at Amulree, and continuing along the banks of the River Braan to Dunkeld.

Fowlis Wester. – *5 miles east of Crieff by the Perth road the A 85.*
In the village centre is a 10ft high Pictish cross-slab with a cross on one side and pictorial scenes, including horsemen, on the other. Inside the 13C St Bean's Church is a richly carved Pictish stone.

Ardoch Roman Fort. – *10 miles south of Crieff by the A 822. Park in the village of Braco and then walk back to the site at the northern end of the village. From the main road you arrive at the west gate of the fort.*
The fort was built during the short period (AD 81-90) of Roman occupation north of the Clyde-Forth line. A Roman road ran from here to a second fort at Inchtuthil north of Perth. The earthworks are especially impressive on the north and east sides. Beyond is an annexe and overlapping marching camps (only parts are visible).

CULLEN (Grampian)   Pop 1 207

Michelin map **401** fold 16 – L 10

The town is divided into two parts, the spacious upper town and the seatown down by the harbour. Cullen is a popular Moray Firth resort with a splendid stretch of sandy beach to the west, interrupted by isolated rocks known as the Three Kings.
A well known local dish is **Cullen Skink,** a fish broth with smoked haddock.

Seatown. – This labyrinth of cottages, yards and lanes, so typical of local fishing communities, lies down on the seashore between the beach and harbour. Note the loft windows used for drawing up nets to dry.

Upper town. – In marked contrast to the former there is a spacious square and broad main street. The village was laid out in 1822 at a distance from the Earl of Seafield's mansion, Cullen House (*not open to the public*). The mercat cross dating from 1696 originally stood in front of the Auld Kirk.

★Cullen Auld Kirk. – *1/2 mile from the Square, signposted off*
tc the main street.
This 16C church marks the site of the former burgh. On entering, on the wall opposite, note the well preserved 16C **sacrament house★** and an elaborate **sculptured tomb** to Alexander Ogilvie and his wife, who figure in the medallions. The marble monument beyond commemorates the Chancellor Earl of Seafield, one of the Scottish Commissioners who negotiated the Treaty of Union (1707), and who concluded with "There's ane end of ane auld sang!". The laird's loft, opposite, incorporates some finely carved **panels★** no doubt originally from other pews.

Laird's loft-
carved panel

EXCURSIONS

Deskford Church. – *4 miles inland from Cullen, signposted 1/2 mile to the left off the B 9018.*
The feature of interest in this roofless church is the richly wrought **sacrament house★** dated 1551. Donated by Alexander Ogilvie there is a strong family resemblance with the one at Cullen. Above the aumbry for the Blessed Sacrament, angels hold aloft the monstrance while below is an emblazoned and dated inscription naming the donor. The whole is encircled by a grape vine scroll.

★Portsoy. – *6 1/2 miles east of Cullen. Leave to the east by the A 98.*
Once level with Sandend known for its sandy beach, take the local road to the right.

Fordyce. – Pop 145. This charming village is built around its 16C tower house, an attractive example of the Scottish baronial style. In the nearby churchyard stand a tower and belfry, the remains of a medieval church. Of the two 16C recessed tombs one has the recumbent effigy of a knight in armour.
Return to the main road.

★Portsoy. – Pop 1720. The old seatown, with some attractive 17C buildings, clusters round the two harbours, the older of which has vertically coursed stonework. Versailles and other fine European palaces are decorated with Portsoy marble. This local vein of green or red serpentine is still worked for ornaments or souvenirs, in a workshop overlooking the harbour.

Culross (pronounced Cuross) is an attractive small Scottish burgh of the 16 and 17C on the north shore of the Firth of Forth. A programme of restoration has ensured the preservation of its essential charm, a wealth of Scottish vernacular architecture.

16-17C industrial royal burgh. – Legend has it that this was the landing place and subsequent birthplace of St Kentigern (Mungo of Glasgow) following his mother's flight from Traprain in Lothian. The 13C saw the founding of a Cistercian house high on the hill, beside the then main road. In the 16C coal mining, salt panning and trade with the Low Countries were the principal activities. The port of Sandhaven was a flourishing one and the ensuing prosperity was followed by royal burgh status in 1588, accorded by James VI.

The golden age continued until the end of the 17C, the decline setting in with the growth of trans-Atlantic trade and developing industrial centres in the west and central belt. Forgotten for almost 200 years the village's renaissance was triggered off by the purchase of The Palace in 1932 by the National Trust for Scotland only shortly after its own foundation in 1931. An extensive restoration programme has since followed, and in 1981 to mark The Trust's Golden Jubilee, Culross was twinned with Veere in the Netherlands, recreating a link of the past. The village as it stands gives a glimpse of an East Coast burgh of the 16 and 17C.

Vernacular architecture. – The visitor may enjoy the details and richness of Scottish domestic architecture with a walk through Culross : white or pale colour washed harling or rubble stonework, dressed stone window and door trims, red pantiles with the occasional glass one, half or pedimented dormer windows, gable ends, crow stepping, skewputts, decorative finials, inscribed or dated lintels and forestairs.

★★THE PALACE *time : 3/4 hour*

tc Built between 1597 and 1611 by George Bruce, the Palace is a monument to both a period and a man. James VI's reign (1578-1625) was a time of economic change when merchants such as Bruce, Danzig Willie Forbes and Provost Skene of Aberdeen acquired wealth from trade, which financed the construction of substantial dwellings (The Palace, Craigievar Castle and Provost Skene's House). The man, **Sir George Bruce** (d1625) was an enterprising merchant, a burgessman at the height of the burgh's prosperity, with interests in the local coal mines, salt panning and foreign trade.

Despite the fact that many of the materials (pantiles, Baltic pine, Dutch floor tiles and glass) were obtained by Baltic barter, the buildings are a superb example of 16 and 17C domestic architecture. The interior provides an insight into the domestic surroundings of a prosperous merchant of the period. Rooms are small with Memel pine panelling for warmth and have interesting examples of the decorative painting typical of the late 16C and early 17C *(p 24)*. Surprisingly twenty-one fires burned coal rather than logs as elsewhere, perhaps only natural for a coalmine owner.

West wing. – To the left of the main courtyard is the earliest building with George Bruce's initials and the date 1597 on one of the dormer pediments. The initial lodging was later extended to the north and to the south with the creation of the Long Gallery. On the ground floor the Nomad's Room for passing travellers has a painted ceiling (1620 *not restored*) with beyond, one of the rooms of the domestic quarters paved with perforated Dutch tiles. In the northern extension alongside the inner court, the kitchen and bakery are stone vaulted and flagged, with the wine cellar across the passage.

Outside stairs give access to the first floor where the Long Gallery *(explanatory noticeboards)* is now subdivided. The term "palace" (it was neither royal nor episcopal) may come from the word *palatium* meaning long hall which was a typical feature of Elizabethan or Jacobean houses in the south. The Lady's Drawing Room at the south end, is panelled with Baltic pine while the Sun Room beyond, derives its name from the tempera paintings. Commanding a view of the port, the Business Room where Bruce received his captains, has half shuttered and half glazed windows - a window tax dodge. In the adjoining fireproof Strong Room, glazed Dutch tiles pave the floor and wall safes and iron doors ensure security.

On the second floor in the West Bedroom the insertion of the occasional glass pantile is again a window tax dodge. The second panelled room has the **Allegory ceiling**, a fine example of decorative painting, on the pine barrel vaulting. The remaining 16 Biblical scenes have been the object of six years of restoration work.

North wing. – A separate building, this extension dates fom 1611 and the initials S.G.B. commemorate Sir George's knighthood. The three storey building has a stables, byre and hay loft on the ground floor with additional apartments above.

The rooms are panelled and both ceiling and wall paintings can be deciphered although faint : in one first floor room the painting depicts the Judgement Steps of King Solomon while in the other rooms there are more 380 year old paintings depicting heraldic devices, fruit and geometrical patterns.

★★★THE VILLAGE *time : 1 hour (excluding visits)*

Moving away from The Palace along the Sandhaven **(5)** note, on the left, the sundial **(A)** at first floor level on the gable end with the **tron** *(p 25)* in front, then look up the close to see the Tron Shop with its forestair.

tc **Tolbooth (H)**. – *National Trust for Scotland Visitors Centre.*

The Sandhaven is dominated by the stone and slate Tolbooth which contrasts with the white harling and red pantiles all around. Built in 1625, with the tower dating from 1783, the edifice has a strong Flemish influence. On the first floor one chamber serves as information centre while the second was the original council chamber. Engravings, albums and other historical documents give some idea of life in Culross in earlier centuries.

The Back Causeway (2) is a cobbled way with a central line of paving stones slightly higher than the rest. Known as the "crown o'the causie" it was reserved for local notables. Note the corbelled tower of the Study.

★**The Study.** – This delightful example of 17C Scottish burgh architecture dates from 1610. It is said that Bishop Leighton of Dunblane used it as a theological study centre on his occasional pastoral visits to the burgh in the late 17C. Inside, the main room has a restored 17C painted ceiling and original 1633 panelling. The marriage cupboard is Norwegian and the imposing portrait by Jamesone is of the town's merchant hero George Bruce. Directly opposite, is the **oldest house** (B) in Culross with in front of its gable end a replica of the original 1588 **mercat cross.**

On the left on Tanhouse Brae (6), a former **Sea Captain's House** (D), has a window lintel with a Greek inscription : "God provides and will provide".

The wall plaque on the **Butcher's House** (E), displays the tools of the occupant's trade. The road climbs up to the present parish church and remains of the abbey, however on the way take the opportunity of gaps in the wall to admire the view across the Forth and have a glimpse of Abbey House (*private*). Built in 1608, for Sir George Bruce's brother, the style is a complete contrast to The Palace (1597 and 1611) and was probably one of Scotland's earliest classical mansions.

tc **Culross Abbey.** – Of the abbey founded in 1217 by Malcolm, Earl of Fife, little remains. There are some similarities with Inchcolm.

tc **Parish Church.** – This occupies the monks' choir of the former Cistercian Abbey. In the Bruce vault off the north transept, stands Sir George Bruce's **funeral monument** – with alabaster effigies of Sir George, his wife and 8 children – a type unusual in Scotland. The churchyard has some interesting tomb stones.

Go downhill again to the square, noting the 17C **Nunnery** (G) in Wee Causeway (8) marked by its forestair and statue, and pass the **Ark** (K) a onetime seamen's hostel then **Bishop Leighton's House** (L).

St Mungo's Chapel. – *Dunfermline road, slightly out of Culross.*

The scant ruins mark the supposed spot where the disowned Thenew was cast ashore and the birthplace of her son, the future St Mungo or Kentigern. The first Archbishop of Glasgow, Robert Blacader, built a chapel in 1503 to commemorate the city's patron saint *(p 113)*.

★ **CULZEAN CASTLE** (Strathclyde)

Michelin map **401** fold 34 – F 17 – 12 miles southwest of Ayr

Culzean (pronounced Cullane) Castle, in its dramatic clifftop setting★★★, provides another testimony to "the taste and skill of Mr Adam".

Always a Kennedy property, Culzean took precedence over Dunure the traditional family seat when Sir Thomas the 9th Earl of Cassillis inherited in 1744. An improving laird he did much to better the estate but it was his bachelor brother, David the 10th Earl (d 1792) who commissioned **Robert Adam** (1728-92) to transform the old castle. The work was executed in three stages. Initially there was the conversion of the tower house, then the creation of a magnificent suite of rooms on the seaward side with the construction of the oval staircase as the final project. Of Adam's castle houses of the 1780s this is perhaps the most spectacular. A confirmed classicist, the exteriors have, nevertheless, medieval touches in the mock battlements and arrow slits. The seaward front with the great drum tower is by far the most imposing. Additions were made in the 19C and in 1945 the property passed to the National Trust for Scotland which has undertaken an extensive restoration programme.

tc **Castle.** – The Adam interiors throughout characterize "The Age of Elegance". Delicately patterned ceilings – concentric or compartmental – with Antonio Zucchi paintings as focal points, are echoed in equally detailed friezes, overdoors, chimney pieces and furniture.

The centrepiece of the house and an Adam masterpiece is the **Oval Staircase**★★ as it rises soberly elegant through three tiers of columns. An impression of movement is created by the interplay of curving lines, the spiralling serried ranks of delicate ironwork balusters and the upward soaring of the superimposed orders. Outstanding on the first floor is **The Saloon**, the epitome of disciplined 18C elegance, which contrasts so strikingly with the wildness of the seascape framed by the windows. Adam designed furnishings include the carpet (a copy of the original said to have been made locally), mirrors, wall sconces and a pair of semicircular side tables curved to fit.

Also of interest are the armour display (Armoury), two Alexander Nasmyth (1758-1840) works featuring the castle (Picture Room) and the Eisenhower Exhibition.

tc **Culzean Country Park.** – The donation to the Trust included the 565 acre estate, which in 1970 was designated Scotland's first country park. The Adam designed home farm serves as reception and information centre. A series of walks enable the visitor to discover the seashore, the walled garden with its herbaceous border *(best in July and August)*, Swan Lake, the 19C Camellia House, Orangery and terrace garden.

DALKEITH (Lothian)   Pop 11 253

Michelin map **401** fold 31 – K 16 – 6 miles from Edinburgh.

Originally a baronial burgh under the Douglases, Dalkeith situated between the Rivers North Esk and South Esk, is the converging point of two main roads the A 68 and A 7. Busy with through traffic Dalkeith with its modern town centre retains various historic buildings.

tc **St Nicholas Buccleuch Church.** – *High Street.*
Sir James Douglas was responsible for the rebuilding of the church which became collegiate in 1406 and it was James Douglas, 1st Earl of Morton who extended it in 1477 and was probably responsible for the Scottish late Gothic choir. The east end was abandoned in 1590 while the nave and transepts were remodelled as the parish church in the mid-19C. Inside the roofless choir is the 16C **Morton Monument** to James Douglas, 1st Earl of Morton and his wife Princess Joanna. It shows the badly worn effigies in civilian dress with lions at their feet.
The High Street broadens out and is overlooked by the 17C tolbooth.

tc **Dalkeith House Country Park.** – *Entrance at end of High Street. No cars allowed inside the grounds.*
The country park comprises the park and woodlands of Dalkeith House, part of the Buccleuch estate, and is traversed at this point by both the Rivers North Esk and South Esk. Amenities include two numbered nature trails and an adventure woodland play area and picnic sites. From the trail there is a good view of **Dalkeith House** (*not open to the public*), the 1708 reconstruction of the old Douglas castle. Purchased in 1642 from the Earls of Morton by the 2nd Earl of Buccleuch, it was for Duchess Anne, that James Smith built the present edifice. This is one of the great mansions in the Dutch Palladian manner. The architect had come directly from the construction of Hamilton Palace to Dalkeith. Also along the trail can be seen Robert Adam's **Montagu Bridge** (1792) with its single semicircular arch bestriding the North Esk. The trail is worth following if only to see the two works mentioned above.
The former palace chapel, **St Mary's**, just inside the entrance gates, was built in 1842 by William Burn and David Bryce. The unaisled edifice has a double hammerbeam roof, some lovely heraldic Minton tiles, before the choir, and poppyhead pew ends.

EXCURSION

tc **Newbattle Abbey.** – *1 mile to the south of Dalkeith. This is now a residential adult college.*
On the west bank of the River South Esk stands the building which incorporates what remains of the Cistercian abbey founded by **David I** in 1140 as a daughter house of Melrose. The monks were the first to work the local coal seams and subsequently exploit the coal for the salt panning industry and were to the fore in husbandry techniques. Their industriousness rapidly made this one of the most powerful abbeys. At the Reformation the abbot, Mark Kerr, became temporal lord and the converted monastic buildings became part of an 18C house, one of the Kerr family seats.

★ DALMENY (Lothian)   Pop 319

Michelin map **401** fold 31 – J 16

The renown of this charming village, set around several large greens, is its 12C parish church, one of the finest examples of Norman architecture.

★**St Cuthbert's Church.** – Set near the pilgrim route north to Dunfermline, which has another Norman work, there is some evidence to believe that the same masons worked at both places. The simple plan is clearly discernible from outside : a stout western tower, a 20C Lorimer addition, abuts the long nave which in turn is prolonged by the shorter chancel and semicircular apse. Above the string course, round headed and narrow windows are framed by chevron recessed orders but the jewel of the exterior is the superb **Norman south doorway**★★, originally the main entrance. Tall, narrow and round headed without its carved tympanum, the recessed orders are intricately carved showing fabulous animals from the Bestiary, figures and heads. Above is a panel of interlaced arches falling onto twinned columns.

Interior. – Seen from the west end the two decreasing arches focus attention on the high altar. The handsome arches of the chancel and apse have orders of chevron mouldings while the moulded ribs of the chancel and apse vaulting spring from a series of **carved corbels** in the form of monstrous heads. The Rosebery Aisle built in 1671 was remodelled in the 19C. The family arms are carved on the panel.

Carved corbel

★DALMENY HOUSE

2 miles to the east of the village.

tc Sir Archibald Primrose (1616-79) purchased the estate in 1662. His son was created the 1st Earl of Rosebery in 1703 and the then family seat was Barnbougle Castle on the Forth shore. Archibald, 4th Earl of Rosebery (1783-1868) commissioned William Wilkins to build the Gothic revival house we see today. **Archibald, 5th Earl** (1847-1929) succeeded Gladstone as Liberal Prime Minister (1894-5) and was the last politician to head a government from the House of Lords. Archibald married Hannah, the daughter of Baron Meyer de Rothschild of Mentmore. Harry the 6th Earl (1882-1974) like his father was a great racing man and a Member of the Jockey Club, who bred 2 Derby winners from his Mentmore Stud. One is commemorated by a work on the entrance lawn by E. Boehm. On the death of the 6th Earl, the son put Mentmore up for sale. Although some of the best of the 18C French furniture came north to Dalmeny, the rest was sold in the great Mentmore sale of 1977.

Interior. – The family portraits in the hall include the *4th Earl of Rosebery*, the builder of the house, by Raeburn and *the PM* by Millais. The set of five Madrid tapestries are after designs by Goya. The library has a painting by Stubbs and lotus leaf furniture custom made by Wilkins. The Grecian interior of the drawing room is the setting for the Rothschild collection of 18C French furniture and tapestries. The carpet is Savonnerie while some pieces of furniture have the interlaced I's or dauphin stamp on them. In the corridor are 16 and 17C pieces of Scottish furniture overlooked by the portrait of *An Old Man* attributed to Rembrandt. The Napoleon Room was the work of the 5th Earl, a great historical collector who wrote Napoleon's biography. One of David's coronation sketches is here. Reynolds and Gainsborough portraits in the Dining Room portray such personalities as *Dr Johnson, Edward Gibbon, William Pitt the Younger* and *Henry Dundas, the first Viscount Melville.*

The Old Private Apartments, a suite of five rooms, include the 6th Earl's Sitting Room with the famous rose and primrose racing colours amidst other racing mementoes. The Boudoir contains more of the Mentmore collection of furniture. Also on display is the porcelain collection, rich in Sevres and Vincennes pieces, and Rothschild family portraits.

★★ DEESIDE (Grampian)

Michelin map **401** folds 19 and 20 – J, K, L, M and N 12

The Dee, a splendid salmon river, flows from its source 4 000ft up on the Cairngorm plateau at the Wells of Dee through the Lairig Ghru and then due east to the sea at Aberdeen. Scenically attractive with its many fine castles and its royal associations which have earned it the title of "Royal Deeside", the valley is popular and busy in summer. There are many opportunities to explore the neighbouring hills and glens. Always enquire locally before setting out and be suitably dressed and equipped.

From Aberdeen to Linn o'Dee by the North Deeside Road

64 miles – allow at least a day

★★**Aberdeen.** – *Description p 33.*

Leave Aberdeen by the A 93.

First come the western suburbs of Cults, Bieldside, Milltimber and Peterculter before open countryside is reached.

tc **Drum Castle.** – Robert the Bruce granted the lands to his armour bearer William de Irwin and the castle has remained in the same family until 1976 when it was donated to the National Trust for Scotland. The massive rectangular **tower**, dating from the 13C, has as its main defensive features its sheer height and massiveness. The walls taper from 12ft at the base to 6ft near the parapet and are rounded at the corners. External stairs lead up to the first floor entrance and the interior which was divided by timber roofs into three vaulted chambers. Ninety steps in all including a ladder, lead to the battlements. In addition to the tower there is the Jacobean wing with attractively furnished rooms and a 17C family chapel in the grounds.

The A 957 to the left, otherwise known as the Slug Road, leads to Stonehaven. 14 miles.

★★**Crathes Castle.** – *Description p 57.*

Banchory. – Pop 5 320. Banchory, Deeside's largest community, although mainly residential has two thriving industrial enterprises, a sawmill and a lavender factory *(open to the public)*. The South Deeside Road branches off to the left forking from the Cairn o'Mount road (B974) to Fettercairn. At the **Bridge of Feugh** the Water of Feugh negotiates a narrow gorge giving spectacular falls and the chance for salmon to display their leaping abilities.

★★★**Craigievar Castle.** – *8 miles to the north, description p 56*

Aboyne. – Pop 1 900. This popular summer centre is set around a large green, the venue for the **Highland Games** *(p 28)*. Part of the traditional pageantry is the ceremonial entry of the Cock o'the North, Chief of clan Gordon attended by his chieftains.

The Muir of Dinnet (National Nature Reserve) is the terminal moraine of the Deeside glacier with the twin lochs to the north, Kinord and Davan in kettle hole basins. The **Burn o'Vat** *(2 miles from the main road)* is a popular picnic site. The more enclosed valley marks the beginning of the upper reaches and the change to Highland scenery begins with the Cambus o'May defile. Ahead is the rounded form of Craigendarroch, pinpointing the site of Ballater.

(BTA)

Deeside

Ballater. – Pop 1 238. This dignified little town developed as a watering place in the 18C and became the railway terminal in 1863 *(now closed)*. Today it is a lively resort in summer with the **Highland Games** *(p 28)* and its unique hill race up to Craig Coillich. The stretch between Ballater and Braemar is scenically the most attractive.

Crathie Church. – Attended by the Royal Family this is the fifth on the site. In the churchyard is a memorial to John Brown, Queen Victoria's manservant.

tc **Balmoral Castle.** – *Car park to the left of the main road.* Royal summer residence. The exhibition in the ballroom gives an insight into a century of royal life on Deeside.

> *The road now follows the alignment of the Old Military Road. Cross the Dee at the Invercauld Bridge which replaces Telford's one downstream.*

tc **Braemar Castle.** – Standing back from the roadside this L-plan tower house was built in 1628 by the Earl of Mar as a hunting seat. Burned by Farquharson of Inverey, ancestor of the present owners, the castle was rebuilt and strengthened with a star shaped curtain wall and crenellations to serve as a military post for Hanoverian troops after the '45. Traditional features of interest include a fine yett and a pit prison.

Braemar. – Pop 400. This scattered village is a busy summer resort in fine mountain scenery. The two original villages grew up at a strategic convergent point of the routes from the south via the Cairnwell Pass, from Atholl by Glen Tilt (of marble fame) and from Speyside via Glen Feshie. The **Braemar Highland Gathering** *(p 28)* is a highly popular event attended by members of the Royal Family.

> *Take the secondary road out following the south bank of the Dee as it winds in its flood plain.*

★**Linn o'Dee.** – This famous beauty spot is where the placid river suddenly tumbles through a narrow channel to drop into rocky pools. Salmon may be seen leaping here.

> *There is no road right round, the motorist must backtrack to Braemar.*

★ DIRLETON (Lothian) Pop 740

Michelin map **401** fold 32 – L 15 – 7 miles west of North Berwick

A village full of charm, where highly individualistic 17 and 18C cottages and houses enhanced by well tended gardens, stand round two greens. The early 17C church, modernized inside, has at its gate the session house and the traditional group of two storey school house, adjoined by the schoolroom. However the renown of the village is its castle, which dates back to the 13C, and in fact predated the establishment of the village and church. The latter was at Gullane till encroaching sand precipitated the move and necessitated the construction in 1612 of the present building.

★**Dirleton Castle.** – In the mainstream of Scottish history the stronghold was owned
tc at different times by the de Vaux family, the Halyburtons and the luckless Ruthvens *(p 172)*. It suffered a similar fate to the neighbouring castle of Tantallon when it was besieged by Commonwealth soldiers in 1650.

Rising up out of a rocky mound, the castle is adjoined by attractive **gardens**. The **13C part**, to the left of the entrance, includes three towers, surrounding a lesser courtyard. The two storey round tower contains two apartments, the lower one with window slits and the upper one or Lord's Chamber with windows and stone benches, a great hooded fireplace and ante-chamber. The 16C **Ruthven Lodging** built to the north against the 13C part, overlooks the main courtyard and has the refinement of moulded string courses, square headed windows and round loopholes under the former. The eastern wing, the late 14C and 15C **Halyburton Range** was built around the 13C curtain wall linking the two 13C towers now reduced to their bases. This was the main entrance with its murder hole, guardroom to the right and portcullis chamber above. From the courtyard, doors lead into the bakehouse, vaults and chapel at the far end with above the great hall, an impressive apartment with buffet, dais and great alcoved windows. Beyond is the chapel and priest's room.

In the far corner of the garden is a beehive shaped dovecot.

DOLLAR (Central)

Michelin map **401** fold 27 – I 15

The fame of this largely residential Hillfoots' town is twofold, its Academy and nearby Castle Campbell.

Dollar Academy. – This imposing building is now a co-educational school with boarding houses. The building of the academy was financed by a bequest from John McNabb (1732-1802) a native of Dollar who made his fortune as a shipowner in London. In 1818 William Playfair designed this Grecian style building with a columned and pedimented portico and slightly advanced wings with engaged columns.

★Castle Campbell. – *1 1/4 miles from the main street up Dollar Glen. The road up tc is narrow and winding with a limited number of parking places, thereafter it is a 5 minute walk to the castle.*
Castle Campbell has a dramatic site★★★, on a promontory, with burn filled clefts on either side, dominating Dollar Glen and Dollar with the Ochil Hills as a backdrop. Originally known as Castle Gloom the lands and property passed by marriage to the Campbell family *(p 130)*. The builder of the tower house was **Colin Campbell, 1st Earl of Argyll** (d 1493) and Lord High Chancellor to James IV. The castle was adopted as the Campbell lowland seat conveniently close to the various royal residences. Alterations and extensions in the 16 and 17C included the creation of an enclosed courtyard and additional domestic ranges and gardens. The Campbell family was staunchly Presbyterian and legend has it that John Knox visited the castle and preached here in 1556. The knoll named John Knox's Pulpit is a reminder of this event. The personal animosity between Archibald, 8th Earl of Argyll (1607-61) and the Marquess of Montrose no doubt made the estate a target for ravaging raids during Montrose's campaign of 1645 but it is doubtful if the castle was attacked. Damage more probably came nine years later during General Monck's campaign and by the late 19C the castle was in a considerable state of disrepair.

Castle buildings. – The main part is the late 15C four storey **tower house** which rises to an overhanging parapet. Prior to the construction of the turnpike stair, access was by a stair in the thickness of the wall or by an outside stair or ladder to first floor level. The vaulted great hall with its massive fireplace has a vaulted cellar below and two chambers above. The topmost room is noteworthy for its ribbed barrel vault and two unusual grotesque masks. The parapet walk (*84 steps from the courtyard*) provides an excellent view★ away over Dollar to the Forth valley and Pentlands in the distance. The courtyard buildings include the 16C south range with three storeys and the **east range.** The latter, late 16 or early 17C in date, linked the old and new parts and displays more decorative features such as moulded string courses and twinned windows above the loggia. A pend through the south range leads to the gardens which are contemporary with the east range.

★ DORNOCH (Highland)

Michelin map **401** fold 11 – H 10

Away from the bustle of the main road north, the A 9, Dornoch set around its cathedral, has a certain quiet charm. This former royal burgh with its miles of sandy beaches and famous championship golf course is a popular family resort.

Dornoch Cathedral. – In the early 13C the then bishop of Caithness, **Gilbert de Moravia** (1222-45) made Dornoch his episcopal seat and set about building a cathedral. The site had been occupied by a Celtic community since the 6C. The cathedral has, however, been much altered since the 13C. From the outside the rather squat church is dominated by its square tower and broach spire. The interior, although of modest proportions, has a fine sense of dignity enhanced by the original 13C stonework. At the west end are the damaged effigy of Sir Richard de Moravia, brother of the founder. The church has a good selection of stained glass by 19C and 20C master glaziers (Christopher Whall, Morris...)
The hotel opposite the cathedral incorporates the tower of what was the 16C Bishop's Palace.

EXCURSION

Dunrobin Castle. – *12 miles to the north.*
Rejoin the A 9 which takes you slowly down towards Loch Fleet with views across the estuary to Golspie pinpointed by Chantrey's statue of the 1st Duke of Sutherland on Ben Vraggie. The Mound, Telford's artificial embankment (1815-6) carries the A 9 across the head of the loch. The Fleet Nature Reserve covering this estuarine basin provides feeding and roosting grounds for migrant waders and wildfowl in winter.

Golspie. – Pop 1 374. The furnishings of St Andrew's Church include the finely carved **Sutherland loft** (1739) and a canopied pulpit.

tc **Dunrobin Castle.** – Dunrobin Castle, ancestral seat of the earls and dukes of Sutherland, stands in an impressive terrace site overlooking the sea. 19 and 20C additions surround the original 1400 tower. The 2nd Duke called in Charles Barry, architect of the Houses of Parliament, to remodel the interior in the 1850s. Barry's interiors were gutted by fire and in the early 20C Robert Lorimer was responsible for the redecoration. The principal rooms are the setting for a fine collection of paintings. Family portraits include works by masters such as Jamesone, Allan Ramsay (admire the delicate finery of Mary Maxwell mother of the Duchess–Countess) Reynolds, Hoppner and Lawrence. There are two portraits by Jamesone's pupil, John Michael Wright and in the Drawing Room two Canaletto's of the Doge's Palace side by side with 18C Mortlake tapestries.
A good overall view of the formal gardens can be had from the terrace.

DOUGLAS (Strathclyde) Pop 1 733

Michelin map 401 fold 35 – I 17

The narrow winding streets and wynds of Douglas, follow the medieval pattern.

tc **St Bride's Church.** – Beside the octagonal bell tower, with a clock supposedly gifted by Mary Queen of Scots, stands the **choir**, all that remains of 14C St Bride's. As the burial place of the Douglas family, the house that rivalled in strength and wealth the early Stewarts during the 14 and 15C, there are some interesting medieval **tombs**. On the left is the "Good Sir James" killed in battle with the Moors while on his way to the Holy Land with Bruce's heart, beyond the 5th Earl of Douglas, 2nd Duke of Touraine and Marshal of France reclines under a crocketed ogee arch. On the far side the effigies of "James the Gross", the 7th Earl and his Duchess Beatrice are accompanied by their ten children, many of whom including the 8th and 9th Earls perished in or following the 1455 feud with King James II.

The churchyard affords a good view down over the Douglas Water with away to the right the parkland of the ancestral seat of the senior branch of the family. Here in their home territory of Douglasdale, stood Douglas Castle, known also as Douglas Larder. Razed by its then owner the "Good Sir James", rebuilt by the English it was the one and only Duke of Douglas who undertook to build a mansion to outrival the Duke of Argyll's at Inveraray. Of this ambitious scheme only one wing was built which was itself destroyed in 1937 due to mining subsidence.

★ DOUNE (Central) Pop 3 977

Michelin map 401 fold 27 – H 15

Strategically set on one of the main routes into the Central Highlands this neat little burgh, famed in the past for its pistol making and cattle and sheep fairs, is now known for its impressive castle.

(Glasgow Art Gallery & Museum)

Scroll butt pistol by Patrick Buchanan of Glasgow, about 1725

Doune or Highland Pistols. – In the 17C and 18C the village was renowned for the manufacture of fine pistols. Prominent gunsmith families included the Caddells, Campbells, Christies and Murdochs. The trade originated in the mid-17C and catered mainly for the Highland cattle drovers. Of a high quality and entirely of metal, Doune pistols are recognisible by their shape and decoration. With a ram's horn butt, fluted breech, flared muzzles and rich embellishment they lacked a safety catch and were manufactured in pairs for left or right hand use.

The 1747 Proscription Act prohibiting the wearing of Highland dress and the carrying of arms, destroyed the traditional market. By the early 19C revival of Highland dress, mass production had taken over.

★**Doune Castle.** – *Access by car from the A 820.*

tc Standing apart from the village this formidable castle overlooks the Ardoch Burn and River Teith. It was built in the late 14C by the Regents, Robert Duke of Albany and his son Murdoch. On the latter's execution it passed to the Crown and was used as a dower house by successive Dowager Queens before becoming the property of the Earl of Moray branch of the Stewarts. The most notable was **James Stewart** (1568-92) who became the 2nd Earl of Moray or "Bonny Earl of Moray" by marriage to Regent Moray's heiress, Elizabeth.

> "O lang lang will his lady
> Look ower the Castle Doune
> Ere she sees the Earl o'Moray
> Come sounding through the town."

The key to the defence of this 14C fortified castle is the keep-gatehouse. Although primarily concerned with the creation of a secure and easily defended lordly residence it was unusual for its period in that consideration was also given to the provision of practical living quarters.

The 95ft high **keep-gatehouse** rises through four storeys and is flanked to the right by the range of buildings containing the halls. The well defended portal gives onto a vaulted passage flanked by prison, guardroom and cellars. The latter and the well chamber have hatches allowing victuals to be hoisted upstairs in the eventuality of a siege. Curtain walls with wall walks enclose the **courtyard** on three sides while the keep-gatehouse, adjoining range and second tower form the fourth.

A well defended outside staircase, compare to the second one, climbs to the first floor lord's hall. The portcullis was operated from one of the window embrasures here.

Stairs beside the double fireplace lead down to the lord's private chamber with escape hatch, and up to the solar and other apartments of the keep-gatehouse, a truly self contained and secure unit. From the courtyard take the second outside staircase up to the retainers hall where the soldiers were garrisoned. From here access is gained to the impressive **kitchen** area in the second tower, which contained the royal apartments or guest rooms on the upper floors.

EXCURSION

★**Doune Motor Museum.** – *1 mile to the northwest of Doune off the A 84.*

tc This is an interesting private collection of 40 magnificent machines, many pioneers of the road and all roadworthy, over the period 1905– 66. Side by side in the serried ranks of gleaming chrome and paintwork are such evocative names as Rolls Royce, Bugatti, Lagonda, Bentley... It includes the second oldest Rolls Royce made in 1905 before the formation of the company the following year. The first purchase was a 1934 Hispano-Suiza and its 1924 predecessor with separate instrumentation for the rear quarters. Each car has its own story and all are a part of motoring history.
Associated with the museum are the Doune Hill Climbs *(p 212)* on a special course laid out on the estate.

★★ DRUMLANRIG CASTLE (Dumfries and Galloway)

Michelin map ⬛ fold 39 – I 18 – 18 miles northwest of Dumfries

tc Drumlanrig with its theatrical skyline makes an arresting picture in its splendid setting. The interiors are graced by a superb collection of priceless family treasures.

A Douglas seat. – As early as the 14C this was the site of a Douglas stronghold and son succeeded father until the late 18C. **William 3rd Earl and 1st Duke of Queensberry** (1637-97) a man of high position under the Stuarts, and of an artistic nature, built in 1679-91 a mansion worthy of his status. The Duke, appalled by the total cost, spent only one night in his palace before returning to the ancestral seat at Sanquhar, where he bitterly inscribed on the cover of his account book "The Deil pike out his een wha looks herein". His son **James 2nd Duke** (1672-1711) was better known as the Union Duke for his part in negotiating the Treaty of Union (1707). Since both his grandsons predeceased their father,

(Hinous/C de A/Edimedia)
Drumlanrig Castle

Old Q inherited in 1778 and bled his Scottish estates with his profligate life in London (Wordsworth nicknamed him Degenerate Douglas). Through Jane Douglas, a sister of the 2nd Duke and heiress in her own right, her grandson Henry Scott 3rd Duke of Buccleuch inherited in 1810 as 5th Duke. It was he in turn who married the Montagu heiress from Boughton uniting the Douglas, Montagu and Scott families.
Built around a courtyard the square towers quartering the structure are as reminiscent of the native tradition as the main façade with its terraces, horseshoe staircase and dramatic turreted skyline is a departure from such. There is a strong family resemblance with George Heriot's School in Edinburgh, yet the architect is a matter of conjecture. The whole is rich in sculptural detail, not least the entrance breast with its ducal crown aloft. The inner courtyard has turret staircases at each corner.

TOUR *1 hour*

To be found throughout the house are a superb collection of paintings including Old Masters and family portraits, a varied selection of clocks and fine French furniture, mainly 17C and 18C from the workshops of such master cabinet makers as Charles Cressent (1685-1768), Pierre II Migeon (1701-58) and Pierre Roussel. The Winged Heart on plasterwork ceilings, ironwork, wall hangings, wood carvings and picture frames is a constant reminder that Drumlanrig is a Douglas seat.

Ground floor. – In the **Hall** Thomas Hudson's (1701-79) works of *Charles 3rd Duke and His Grace's family group* show a directness typical of 18C portraiture. In the **Parlour** it is interesting to compare the Kneller and Reynolds portraits of the two heiresses responsible for uniting the Montagu, Douglas and Scott families, namely *Lady Jane Douglas* and *Lady Elizabeth Montagu*. The slender Joseph Knibb grandmother clock is a rare pre-1680 piece. The splendid oak staircase with its barley sugar banisters rises in three flights from the **Staircase Hall,** where the highlights are a series of Old Masters in particular Rembrandt's *Old Woman Reading* (1655). Rembrandt, that 17C master of the portrait, has created an atmosphere and attitude of calm introspection, where all the dramatic intensity is focused on the glow of light which suffuses the carefully delineated facial features. Compare with the infinitely more detailed portraits by Holbein (16C), *Sir Nicholas Carew* and Joost van Cleef. In the gloriously oak panelled **Dining Room,** carved panels attributed to Grinling Gibbons alternate with 17C silver sconces and family portraits. *William lst Duke,* the builder of the castle in peer's robes (Kneller), is next to *Old Q* as an 18 year- old (Ramsay) and his heir *Henry the 5th Duke* (1746-1812), and there are two of *Monmouth* (Kneller and Huysmans) one of which is with his mother Lucy Walter. Here also is Thomas Hudson's delicate portrait of *Alice Duchess of Buccleuch.*

First floor. – Both **Bonnie Prince Charlie's Bedroom** and the **Ante-Room** are hung with 17C Brussels tapestries and graced by fine pieces of furniture ; a Roussel commode, a Marot set of high back chairs, Charles II stools, a Saunier parquetry and ormolu mount commode and a 17C Flemish ebony cabinet. In the **Drawing Room,** another nobly proportioned apartment, amidst a selection of very fine pieces of French furniture, is a particularly outstanding **cabinet★** commissioned in 1675 for Versailles, which is portrayed on the central plaque. Louis XIV gifted this to Charles II his uncle by marriage. The portraits include a series of full lengths : *King James VI* and his Queen, *Anne of Denmark* (Jameson, the stance is similar to both the de Critz and Adam Colone portraits) with their grandson, *Charles II,* between them and *Francis 2nd Duke of Buccleuch* by Ramsay. From the **staircase gallery** the superb 1680 **silver chandelier** is seen to its best advantage. On the panelled walls are magnificent Chippendale sconces and full length portraits : *William and Mary, Queen Anne* and her consort *Prince George,* all contemporaries of the Union Duke who as High Commissioner presented Queen Anne with the Treaty of the Union (1707). In recognition he was given an English dukedom. In the **Principal Bedroom,** are canvases by two 18C artists Gainsborough and Hudson, of *Mary Duchess of Montagu* and *Kitty Duchess of Queensberry.* Katherine Hyde better known as Duchess Kitty, wife of the 3rd Duke, was the patroness to John Gay, the 18C poet and dramatist.

★★ **DRYBURGH ABBEY** (Borders)

Michelin map **401** fold 36 – M 17 – 5 miles southeast of Melrose

tc Majestic and evocative the extensive ruins of Dryburgh Abbey stand in a splendid, secluded **setting★★★** on a sheltered meander of the Tweed. The mellow red tones of the Dryburgh stone amidst the green swards of well tended grass and majestic old trees, makes this one of the most attractive of the Border abbeys.
Founded in the 12C Dryburgh Abbey was the first Scottish home of the Order of Premonstratensians and daughter house of Alnwick. Building began in 1150 and the abbey led a peaceful and prosperous existence tending its lands. The Wars of Independence and subsequent Border troubles resulted in destruction and fire damage on at least three occasions 1322, 1385 and 1544, the latter also included the razing of the town of Dryburgh. The religious life of the abbey ended at the beginning of the 17C. It was then inhabited by the commendators or their descendants which explains why the conventual buildings have been so well preserved.

DRYBURGH ABBEY

TOUR *3/4 hour*

Abbey Church. – Little remains of the mainly 12 and 13C church, dedicated to St Mary. The west front robbed of its facing is pierced by a 15C round arched and recessed doorway, devoid of capitals, and adorned by square, conventionalised leaf motifs. Inside only the south wall of the six bay nave with aisles remains.

Transepts. – Like the east end, they are late 12 and early 13C and are in the First Pointed style, best seen in the north transept and its eastern chapels. The main arcade with pointed arches is surmounted by a compressed middle section with cusped circular lights opening onto the interior while the clerestory arcade, taller again, is one storey of triple lancets. The north transept and eastern chapel with moulded, ribbed vaulting and carved bosses are the resting places of Field Marshal Earl Haig (1) and Sir Walter Scott (2).
The south transept has the remains of a night stair leading to the first floor canons' dormitory and a door to the library and vestry. The great window in the upper part of the transept gable is partly blocked where the roof of the dormitory abutted.

Conventual buildings. – One of the best preserved groups in Scotland, they are laid out on the middle and lower levels, around the cloister, with two storeys on the east.

Cloister. – The east range is the best preserved.

East Processional Doorway. – This is an attractive example of late 12C work, still round headed with dissimilar capitals and dog-tooth ornament.
On the left the aumbry (3) or book alcove is complete with shelf grooves. The first door leads to the library and vestry (4), a barrel vaulted chamber later adopted as a family vault by the Earls of Buchan, while the parlour beyond is the Erskine vault (5).

Chapter house. – Similar to the east processional doorway, the doorway with its flanking openings makes an attractive unit. Stairs lead down to the barrel vaulted chamber, with its stone bench and attractive interlaced arcading on the east wall.
Next comes the day stair which gave access to the dormitory and treasury. Ahead the doorway leads down steps to the lowest level where a door on the left opens onto the warminghouse (calefactory) with two central pillars. The original fireplace was in the east wall as in the novices day room across the passage.

Dormitory. – *Access was by the night stair from the south transept.* Extending the full length of the eastern range it was altered following fire damage and in the 16C when dwelling rooms were made.

Frater and subcroft. – Lying on the south side of the cloister are two barrel vaulted chambers which were surmounted by the refectory. The most outstanding feature is the **wheel window** (6) in the west gable.
The west wall of the cloister has a lavatory (7), a recess for hand washing before meals.

Gatehouse. – To the south of the frater on the far side of the water channel is this 15C gatehouse which was at one time connected to the main building by a covered bridge.

DUFFTOWN (Grampian)   Pop 1 680

Michelin map 401 fold 15 – K 11

The rhyming couplet "Rome was built on seven hills Dufftown stands on seven stills" is still valid today as Dufftown is capital of the malt whisky industry. This trim little town was laid out in 1817 by James Duff 4th Earl of Fife, initially to give employment after the Napoleonic Wars. The first of numerous distilleries was established in 1823 with the industry growing from strength to strength until the present recession.
At the intersection of the main streets stands the Clock Tower (tourist information centre) with the clock which is said to have hanged the famous freebooter MacPherson.

Mortlach Church. – St Moluag of Lismore established one of the earliest places of Christian worship *c*566 down by the Dullan Water. Mortlach then became the seat of a bishopric until 1131 when it was transferred to Old Aberdeen *(qv)*. Today this historic church although much altered has examples of stained glass by Cottier and Douglas Strachan and an interesting Pictish symbol stone, the Elephant Stone, in the vestibule. The Battle Stone in the graveyard is said to commemorate Malcolm II's victory (1010) over the Danes. In thanksgiving he extended the church by three spears length.

★**Glenfiddich Distillery.** – The film and tour provide an excellent introduction to the history of this family firm founded in 1886 and the art of malt whisky distilling through all the stages from malting to bottling *(see p 29)* The angel's dram provides an appetiser to the final sampling of the water of life.

Balvenie Castle. – *Behind Glenfiddich Distillery.*
Set on a strategic route from Donside to Moray this now ruined courtyard castle was successively the seat of Comyns, Douglases and Stewarts. The initial structure with its massive curtain wall and moat dated from the period of Comyn ownership in the late 13C and early 14C. In the mid-16C the 4th Earl of Atholl, a Stewart, built a Renaissance dwelling. The latter, along the entrance front, is clearly distinguished by richer architectural ornament : carved armorial panels, mouldings and corbellings.

EXCURSION

Whisky Trail. – This 70 mile long signposted tour takes in six malt whisky distilleries crossing in the process peaceful and unspoilt hills and glens. Allow an hour for the conducted tour at each distillery. Confirm the official opening times given at the end of the guide by phone or at one of the tourist information centres. Leaflets describing the trail in several languages are available from the latter. In some instances children under eight are not admitted to production areas. Enquire locally for other distilleries which welcome visitors.

★Glenfiddich Distillery. – *Description opposite.*

> *Leave Dufftown by the B 9009 following Glen Rinnes past the foot of Ben Rinnes (2 759ft-840m). Turn left onto the B 9008.*

Tomintoul. – Pop 340. This planned village lies at a height of 1160ft on the northern edge of the Cairngorm plateau. The village was set on the military road which was pushed northwards from Corgarff to Grantown and hence to Fort George in 1754.

> *Taking the Grantown road out, branch right onto the B 9136 following Strath Avon, overlooked to the left by the Hills of Cromdale.*

tc Glenlivet Distillery. – Just off the B 9136.

> *The B 9008 leads to the Spey valley and junction with the A 95. Turn right and follow the A 95 to beyond Marypark.*

tc Glenfarclas Distillery. – Off the A 95.

> *Return to Marypark to cross the Spey and take the B 9102 to the right.*

tc Tamdhu Distillery. – Off the B 9102.

> *Continue to Craigellachie on the far bank of the Spey. Branch left onto the A 941 to reach Rothes.*

tc Glen Grant Distillery. – Rothes.

> *Follow the B 9015 then turn right to cross the Spey by the B 9103 and continue via the A 95 to Keith.*

Keith. – Pop 4 660. Set astride the river Isla, at the heart of a rich farming area, Keith is famous for the Keith Agricultural Show. John Ogilvie (1579-1615) Scotland's only recent saint (canonized 1976) was born in the town. Newmill to the north, claims as its son the press baron James Gordon Bennet (1795-1872) founder of the *New York Herald,* the first completely independent newspaper.

tc Strathisla Distillery. – Keith.

> *The B 9014 goes up Strath Isla and back to Dufftown.*

★ DUMFRIES (Dumfries and Galloway)   Pop 29 382

Michelin map **401** fold 39 – J 18

Known as the "Queen of the South" the attractive and bustling town of Dumfries has long been the southwest's most important town. Today this busy tourist centre makes a good departure point for sightseeing excursions into the surrounding area. Farming remains the number one industry with diversification provided by the administrative services of the regional headquarters and some manufacturing.

The town has important historical associations with the national bard **Robert Burns** *(p 44)* and **Robert the Bruce**, as it was here he slew Scotland's co-guardian thus opening the second stage of the Wars of Independence.

SIGHTS

> *The town has a fairly complex one-way system and it is advisable to visit on foot.*

Burns Mausoleum (B). – To the right behind the prominent red sandstone church, rebuilt in 1745, is the mausoleum where Burns, his wife Jean Armour and several of their children are buried. A plan (to the right of the church) indicates where some of Burns' associates and friends are laid to rest.

tc Burns' House (B). – Burns spent the last three years of his life in this house, which now serves as a museum. The ground floor room, on the left, has examples of the poet's abundant correspondence. The small upstairs room with writing desk and chair retains the window pane engraved with the bard's name.

★Midsteeple (B). – This imposing building makes a striking focal point for the High Street. The rather angular outline is relieved by the detailed delicacy of the matching pierced balustrades and wrought ironwork of the forestairs' railings. The family resemblance with Stirling's Tolbooth *(p 190)* is not unexpected since the mason, Tobias Bauchop, had worked under Sir William Bruce on the Stirling project prior to erecting the Midsteeple in 1707 to serve as a prison and courthouse. The royal coat of arms emblazons the front as does a standard measurement of the Ell *(p 79)* and a plan of the town in Burns' day.

Burns Statue (B). – At the north end of the High Street, the 1882 statue commemorates Dumfries' most famous citizen. A wall plaque on the buildings to the west of the statue marks the site of Greyfriars Monastery where the Bruce and followers killed the Red Comyn in 1306.

Dervorgilla Bridge (A). – This narrow six arch bridge with pointed cutwaters, replaced in the 15C the original wooden structure built by Dervorgilla.

tc Old Bridge House (A M¹). – This 17C house, a onetime barrelmaker's premises, an inn and dwelling house is now a branch museum designed to bring to life different aspects of town life in the past.

tc Dumfries Museum (A M²). – A converted 18C windmill and later extensions, house the local collections : geology, archaeology and history with a special section on historic Dumfries. The mill has displays of early Christian stones (basement), country life (first floor) and the origins of the museum which started life as an Astronomical Observatory in 1836. The 8-inch telescope, which still exists ; was used to observe Halley's Comet (July 1836). The **Camera Obscura** on the top floor of the windmill affords good views of Dumfries in clear weather.

SCO 6

DUMFRIES

High Street .... B

Annan Road .... B 2
Assembly Street .... B 3
Castle Street .... AB 5
Church Crescent .... B 6
Craigs Road .... B 7
David Street .... A 9

tc **Lincluden College.** – *Take the A76 Glasgow road out and then College Street.*
The ruins, mostly 15C, were part of a collegiate foundation established by Archibald
the Grim, 3rd Earl of Douglas. The college was in fact predated by a 12C Benedictine
nunnery. The choir although roofless retains some particularly fine sculpture including
the profusely decorated early 15C **tomb★** of the 4th Earl's wife, Princess Margaret, a
daughter of Robert III, and a series of armorial shields.
Adjoining is the outline of a knot garden overlooked by a Norman motte.

EXCURSIONS

★Sweetheart Abbey. – *8 miles. Leave Dumfries to the southwest by New Abbey Road,
the A710 (A). Shambellie House is signposted to the right just before the village of
New Abbey.*

tc **Shambellie House Museum of Costume.** – *Outstation of the Royal Scottish Museum.*
The house was designed in the Scottish baronial style by David Bryce and its
trouble-fraught construction resulted in an abundant and acrimonious correspondence
between the architect and laird. In 1977 Charles Stewart donated both his house and
rich **costume collection★** to the Royal Scottish Museum. It is intended that the initial
experimental displays will be small (3 rooms only and approximately 20 costumes)
and without theme or period. Tastefully redecorated rooms serve as backdrop to a
small selection of delightfully presented costumes.

★Sweetheart Abbey. – *1/4 mile further on in the village of New Abbey.*
tc The community which grew up around the abbey was given the prefix new to
distinguish it from Dundrennan. The beauty and charm of Sweetheart's ruins derive
principally from the colourful contrast of the red standstone and green of the
surrounding lawns. Founded in 1273 by **Dervorgilla**, wife of John Balliol, and colonized
from nearby Dundrennan, Sweetheart was the last Cistercian foundation in Scotland.
The whole is enclosed by a rare precinct wall which was originally interrupted by two
gateways. With the claustral buildings gone the chief interest of the ruins is the
completeness of its **church.** Corbels on the west front indicate the former presence
of an entrance porch, above which are a reconstructed and now partially infilled west
window. Inside directly above the great striding arches of the six bay nave is an
interesting clerestory. Triple openings on the inside are paralleled outside by
semicircular arches filled with five graded lancets. On the stout tower above the
crossing note the rows of masks and heads supporting the battlements. The foundress
Dervorgilla was laid to rest in the presbytery, along with the casket containing the
embalmed heart of her husband – thus explaining the unusual name.
Scott's novel *The Abbot* features Gilbert Brown the last and most famous of
Sweetheart's incumbents in view of his tenacious stand to retain his benefice after
the Reformation. He was greatly encouraged by Maxwell aid and protection.

Ruthwell. – *16 miles. Leave Dumfries to the southeast by the B 725* (B).
The road runs along the east bank of the Nith through dairying country.

Glencaple. – Pop 270. Once a busy port where emigrants set sail for the New World and where Burns worked as an exciseman, it is now a harbour for pleasure craft and dormitory village for Dumfries.

The road continues to follow the estuary, dangerous at this point for its flast flowing tides and quicksands. Criffel (1866ft-569m) looms large on the far side.

★Caerlaverock Castle. – *Description p 52*

Follow the B 725 to Bankend, where it turns to the right.

Burns during his last illness came to Brow Well to take the waters and indulge in sea bathing in an effort to regain his health, but all to no avail.

tc **Ruthwell.** – In this linear village, a small cottage, now the **Duncan Savings Bank Musem,** is where the Rev Dr Henry Duncan founded in 1810 the first savings bank, the forerunner of today's movement.

Take the local road going inland to the church, standing on its own.

★Ruthwell Cross. – Well displayed within this country church is the outstanding example
tc of early Christian art, the 7C Ruthwell Cross. The vivid and realistic sculpture on the shafts of this preaching Cross tell the story of the Life and Passion of Christ. **North side** (top to bottom) : Two Evangelists ; John the Baptist ; Christ Glorified ; Breaking Bread in the Desert and Flight into Egypt. **South side** : the Archer, The Visitation ; Washing the Saviour's Feet ; Healing the Man Born Blind ; The Annunciation and Crucifixion. The artistic skill and craftsmanship of the 7C sculptor is most evident in the vine tracery intertwined with birds and other creatures. The margins are inscribed with Runic characters. The many vicissitudes of the Cross included its demolition on the orders of the General Assembly in 1642 and removal to the churchyard in 1780. During the 19C the Rev Dr Henry Duncan repieced the monument prior to its final installation in the church in 1887.

tc **Ellisland Farm.** – *6 miles. Leave Dumfries by the A 76.*
After leaving Mauchline *(qv)*, Burns leased the farm in June 1788 and moved into the rebuilt house with Jean Armour in December of that year. He introduced new farming methods but the soil was poor and his first crops failed. He accepted a part-time appointment in the Excise in the district but in 1791, on being offered promotion he gave up farming and moved to Dumfries as a full-time exciseman. His first house was in the Wee Vennel, now Bank Street. It was at Ellisland, on the banks of the Nith, that Burns wrote what many consider to be his greatest work *Tam o'Shanter (p 44).* One room of the farmhouse, which is still lived in, has a display of Burns' relics with documents concerning family, patrons and friends. In the granary there is an exhibition of 18C farming methods.

tc **Rammerscales.** – *8 miles from Dumfries by the A 709 to Lochmaben then the B 7020 to the south.*
Rammerscales was built in the early 1760s by Czarist Russia's first ever Royal Physician **Dr James Mounsey** (1700-73) on his sudden return to his native country. Court intrigue made the doctor fearful for his life to the extent that he organized and attended his own funeral, before retiring to live in the countryside. Another of the doctor's exploits was the introduction of True Rhubard seeds to Britain (commemorative medal). Set high on a wooded hillside there are superb views from the front of the house across the Annan valley. Family home of the Bell Macdonalds since 1789 Rammerscales is particularly interesting for the **collection of 20C art** including works by British artists (Victor Pasmore, John Piper, Joan Eardley, Lowry, Wyndham Lewis and Barbara Hepworth) and foreign artists (Vuillard, Hartung).
The essential charm is that in homely surroundings are to be found in close succession a Hepworth sculpture, a tapestry with that unmistakable Lurçat look about it, and that compelling canvas of Joan Eardley's wild seascape at Catterline...

Glenkiln. – *10 miles. Leave Dumfries by the Stranraer road the A 75* (A) *and after 7 1/2 miles turn right in the direction of Shawhead. In the latter turn right then almost immediately left and left again at the Glenkiln signpost.*
The natural beauty of the wild landscapes around Glenkiln Reservoir *(private property, view from roadside)* make a perfect backdrop to **sculptures★** by Henry Moore *(King and Queen)* Epstein, Rodin... In Moore's own words "Nature, trees, clouds are nothing geometric or harsh."

Solway Coast from Dumfries to Dalbeattie. – *18 miles. This coastal drive can be done in either direction taking the A 710.*
The itinerary passes through unspoilt countryside with picturesque villages nestling around sandy bays and rocky coves and offers good views across the Solway Firth.

(Wolfgang Meier/ZEFA)

King and Queen

New Abbey. – Pop 400. The village is famous for Sweetheart Abbey *(qv)*. Nearby is Shambellie House Museum of Costume *(qv)*.

Further on the road skirts the looming granitic mass of Criffel (1 866ft - 569m).

Arbigland. – *2 miles off the main road from Kirkbean.*

On the estate is the birthplace of **John Paul Jones** (1747-92) hero of the American Navy.

Sandyhills. – The bay as its name indicates is a vast expanse of sandy beach.

In this granitic countryside, rocky fingers push out into the Firth. At Colvend a road branches left to the coast.

Rockcliffe. – Pop 110. Holiday village set round a rocky bay looking out across to Rough Island, a NTS bird sanctuary *(no admission)*. From here Jubilee Path (NTS) leads round the coast to Kippford.

★**Kippford.** – Pop 170. Overlooking the Urr estuary the jetties of this well known sailing centre are lined with pleasure boats.

DUNBAR (Lothian)   Pop 6 035

Michelin map **401** fold 32 – M 15

This east coast holiday resort and day excursion centre takes its name from the once powerful stronghold, around which the town grew up.

Battles of Dunbar. – On the main east coast road and in the path of invading armies, the immediate area was the site of two important battles, both Scottish defeats. In the opening stages of the Wars of Independence, Edward I on his first Scottish campaign sacked Berwick and then inflicted a defeat on the Scots army near Spott (1296). The 1650 Battle was part of Cromwell's campaign to subdue Scotland. The Covenanting General David Leslie with a numerically superior army, abandoned a strong position on Doon Hill to fall prey to Cromwell's army under General Monck *(p 55)*.

SIGHTS

Parish Church (Z). – This red sandstone building with its prominent tower was the work of Gillespie Graham in 1821 to replace the 10th Earl of Dunbar's collegiate church of 1342. Inside is the imposing marble and alabaster **monument** to George Home (1556-1611), firm favourite of James VI, who made "Dodie" Earl of Dunbar (second creation) in 1605. Dunbar controlled state affairs in Scotland and was the King's right hand man for pushing through Episcopacy. The highly intricate monument shows the life-size figure of the earl, kneeling in his Garter Robes, surrounded by men in armour.

★**Tolbooth** (Z H). – *Tourist Information Centre.* This attractive 17C tolbooth with its steepled octagonal tower and crow stepped gable is built of red rubblework sandstone.

★**John Muir's Birthplace** (Y M). *tc* – The top flat was the home for 11 years of **John Muir** (1838-1914) the pioneer geologist, explorer, naturalist and conservationist *par excellence*, who was responsible for the creation of America's National Park system. The flat where

DUNBAR

Abbey Road .... Z 2	Custom House Square Y 6
Bayswell Road ...... Y 3	Silver Street .... Z 9
Castle Gate .... Y 5	Victoria Place .... Y 12
	Victoria Street ...... Y 13
	West Port .... Z 14
	Woodbush .... Z 16

he lived with his six brothers and sisters before emigrating to the States, is appropriately furnished, while one of the rooms is used for an audiovisual presentation of the man, his life and work. For long unknown in Scotland, such place names as the Great Glacier, Alaska, Yosemite and Sequoia National Parks are for Americans synonymous with the name of this great man.

Lauderdale House (Y). – *Council property.* This impressive red sandstone mansion dominates the north end of the High Street. In the late 18C the Earl of Lauderdale *(qv)* commissioned Robert Adam to make alterations to the original building. The High Street front is highly characteristic of this confirmed classicist with such Adam features as balustrades, sphinx, fluted and paterae friezes. The south front is dominated by Adam's semicircular portico entrance.

Dunbar Castle (Y). – The ruins, jagged and red, of what was once, strategically, one of the most important castles in the Middle Ages, rises above the waters of the harbour. Much fought over it was the stout defence by Black Agnes, Countess of March and

Dunbar against Salisbury, that stands out most clearly in the castle's history. The orders to demolish came from the Scots Parliament in the same year that Mary Queen of Scots visited it with Darnley (1567).

The harbour (Y). – The **New** or **Victoria Harbour** was opened in 1842 to accommodate the growing number of trading and fishing vessels. However the arrival of the railway 4 years later, saw a decline in the port's activities. The pantiled, dormer windowed house (**Y B**) on the right makes an attractive point of comparison for Basil Spence's block (**Y A**) between the harbours. The **Old Harbour** with its cobbled quays and rubble walls was built by Cromwell in 1650.

★ DUNBLANE (Central)   Pop 4 497

Michelin map 🔢 fold 27 – I 15

This mainly residential town, on the Allan Water, is grouped around its lovely 13C Gothic cathedral in its close setting, a rare feature in Scotland.

★★Dunblane Cathedral. – Although already an ecclesiastical centre in Celtic times, it
tc was David I who created the bishopic *c*1150. The cathedral led a peaceful existence and numbered among its bishops, Clement (1233-58), the builder of the cathedral and that rare ecclesiastic **Robert Leighton** (1611- 84), an enlightened conciliator during the religious strife of the 17C. Leighton sorely regretted leaving Dunblane when translated to Glasgow *c*1671. Despite 15C alterations, neglect following the Reformation but no pillaging and finally several 19 and 20C restorations, it is a fine example of 13C Gothic architecture.
Adjoining the nave on the south side to the left of the entrance is a 12C **tower** which belonged to the early Celtic building. The upper storeys and parapet are later additions. Continue round to the west end overlooking the Allan Water where the masterful design of the **west front★★** combines a deeply recessed doorway with a tall triplet of lancets and Ruskin's small vesica above, all framed by two buttresses.

Interior. – This 210ft long building passes from nave to choir uninterrupted by transepts or crossing. The initial impressions are of simplicity, height and soaring lines (mostly achieved by the predominance of the pointed arch). Built after the Lady Chapel, the pointed arcades of the eight bay nave descend onto clustered columns and are surmounted by a double clerestory where window tracery is repeated inside the gallery. This device is copied at the west end, where the great window shows the Tree of Jesse (1906). Below are two sets of the canopied 15C **Chisholm stalls** deeply and vigorously carved with a wealth of detail. Note in particular the misericords. Like the nave, the wooden barrel vaulted roof with tinctured armorials, has also been restored (19C). Around the pulpit are carved figures of St Blane, who gave his name to the town, King David I, Bishops Clement and Leighton and John Knox while those on the screen depict Biblical personages.
The glory of the building is the **choir** with its great feeling of height emphasized by soaring lancets in the south and east sides. Level with the high altar are the early 15C **Ochiltree stalls,** showing a similar verve of execution. The present stalls and organ case were designed by Robert Lorimer during his 1914 restoration of the choir. Three stone slabs in the floor mark the burial places of the Drummond sisters, allegedly poisoned in 1501 to prevent Margaret the eldest from becoming James IV's Queen in preference to Henry VIII's sister, Margaret Tudor. The effigy in the north wall tomb recess is said to be that of Clement, the bishop builder. The oldest part, the **Lady Chapel** opening off the north side of the choir, has ribbed vaulting with carved bosses. The memorial windows, panelling and flooring are all 20C.

The precincts. – Happily the peaceful air of former times remains. The Dean's House
tc (1624) contains the **cathedral museum** concerning both town and cathedral. Of particular interest are the notes on the great Bishop Leighton, the three Bishop Chisholms and a very good collection of communion tokens, the predecessors of today's cards. Within the manse grounds is a 1687 building, the home of Bishop Leighton's personal **library**. From the northeast corner there is a lovely view along the north side of the cathedral.

DUNDEE (Tayside)   Pop 182 204

Michelin map 🔢 fold 27 – L 14
See the town plan in the current Michelin Red Guide Great Britain and Ireland

Dundee enjoys a nigh perfect situation on the northern shore of the Tay with the Sidlaw Hills as a backdrop. Prosperity accrued from the three j's, jam, jute and journalism. This busy seaport, university town and capital of Tayside Region now has a much wider variety of industries. The town is still known today for its Dundee or rich fruit cakes and its jams, in particular marmalade.
Dundee was home to **James Chalmers** (1823-53) who is now generally acknowledged as the inventor of the adhesive postage stamp. Others with a claim to fame include Desperate Dan, Denis the Menace, Korky the Kat and Our Wullie, comic characters from the Thomson publishing empire.

Premier whaling port. – Hull was Britain's chief whaling port from 1810 until the mid-1840s when Peterhead and then Dundee (1860s) took over with a new generation of steamers for the whale and seal fishery in the far north. The fleet spent 8 months away from March to October. Crews were local but there was a tradition of hiring seamen from Lerwick or Stromness as oarsmen for the whaleboats. The oil found a ready market in the burgeoning jute mills where it was used to soften the raw jute fibres. Whaling continued until World War I. The museum in Broughty Castle has a section on whaling : ships models, whaling gear, paintings and prints.

SIGHTS

tc **McManus Galleries.** – *Albert Square.*

Art Galleries. – *Upstairs.* The gallery has good collections of Victorian paintings (John "Spanish" Phillip, Millais, McCulloch and Rosetti) and the Scottish Colourist School.

Museum. – *Downstairs.* Currently being redeveloped as a local history museum there is a trade and industry gallery covering shipping, textiles and transport. Other exhibits include some fine Pictish symbol stones and the interiors of a shop and pub.

tc **Barrack Street Museum.** – *Barrack Street.*

Presently being developed as a natural history museum with local wildlife displays.

St Mary's. – Of the City Churches the Old Steeple is all that remains of the original 14-15C parish kirk. Like many other churches it was subdivided after the Reformation. St Mary's, occupying the east end, has some fine stained glass by Burne-Jones, Morris (east end and north aisle) and a lovely Gethsemane scene (south aisle).

tc **Tay Road Bridge.** – This 1.4 mile long bridge with its 42 spans carries two carriageways each way and a central walkway. The bridge was opened 2 years after its Forth counterpart in 1966.

Tay Railway Bridge. – To replace the world's first train ferry (1850) the Tay's tidal estuary was bridged (1871-8) by a metallic structure just short of two miles long. A daring enterprise at the time, disaster struck on a stormy winter night of December 1879. The bridge gave way and a train plunged into icy waters. 75 died. The designer civil engineer Thomas Bouch died shortly afterwards greatly affected and ruined by the tragedy. His lifetime dream was fulfilled only 10 years later when both the Forth and Tay were bridged.

★The Frigate Unicorn. – *Victoria Dock. Continuous restoration work.*

tc This 46-gun frigate was commissioned by the Royal Navy in 1824, 19 years after Trafalgar. Today visitors may explore the Captain's Quarters and the main gundeck where the 18 pounder cannon required nine men a piece to man them. The gunners ate and slept on the same deck as their cannon. The deck above has the 'Seats of Easement' and gun ports. On the quarter deck were the 32 pounder Carronades, nicknamed "smashers". In the officers cabins is an exhibition on the Royal Navy.

Dundee Law. – *A road leads right up to the War Memorial.*

This volcanic plug (571ft-174m) affords a circular **panorama** of Dundee and the surrounding countryside. Spread out below is Dundee with the Tay Bridges stretching across to Fife. Visible to the north are Bens Vorlich, Lawers and Macdui.

tc **Mills Observatory.** – *Balgay Park. Follow the signposts to the top.*

This public observatory has on the ground floor, exhibits on astronomy and space exploration. The terrace with its telescope and binoculars affords a view of the far side of the Tay. The main telescope *(access only with a member of staff)* is operational on clear evenings in winter.

EXCURSIONS

Tayside seaside resorts. – *Leave Dundee by the A930.*

On the way to what is now a city suburb pass the substantial villas built by the 19C jute barons.

Broughty Ferry. – As the name suggests this former fishing settlement became the ferry
tc terminus and Dundee's own seaside resort. The restored 15C fort contains **Broughty Castle Museum** with displays on local and military history, seashore wildlife and an
tc interesting section on whaling. On the northern outskirts of Broughty Ferry is **Claypotts Castle.** This perfect example of a 16C Z-plan tower house has round towers at diagonally opposite corners of the rectangular centrepiece. Note the strategically positioned gun-loops at ground level and the change from round to square by means of corbelling at roof level. The castle belonged to the Grahams of Claverhouse but was forfeited after the Battle of Killiecrankie.

Return to the A930 to reach Monifieth.

Monifieth. – This coastal town is another resort with good golfing and extensive sands.

Carnoustie. – Pop 8 817. This coastal resort boasts a championship golf course with the reputation for being one of the toughest.

★Arbroath. – *Description p 39.*

At Inverkeilor on the A92 take the local road to Lunan.

Lunan Bay. – The 4 mile stretch of sandy beach is overlooked by the jagged ruins of Red Castle, a 15C building. William the Lion is said to have occupied the earlier stronghold on the site during the building of Arbroath Abbey.

Montrose. – *Description p 157.*

Tealing. – *5 miles north of Dundee by the Forfar road the A929.*

Beside a farm steading is a 16C **dovecot** *(illustration p 25)* and beyond an **earth house**. The latter consists of a long curving passage, now roofless, leading to an inner chamber. Dating from Pictish times the earth house may have served as a dwelling place, a refuge, food store or shelter for the animals.

The Angus Glens. – The Eastern Highlands are dissected by several glens (Shee, Isla, Prosen, Clova and Esk) which wind their way from their sources on the peaty Mounth to Strathmore, then the sea. Some give access by hill tracks to Deeside but all are dead-ends for those in cars. They provide attractive scenery which becomes quite grand in their upper reaches. The runs may start from any of the Strathmore towns or villages, Brechin, Forfar, Kirriemuir and even Dundee.

Michelin map **401** fold 31 – J 15

Onetime capital of Scotland the "auld grey town" figures largely in Scottish history mainly in association with its great abbey and royal palace. From earliest times it was a thriving industrial centre with coal mining and later linen weaving and the tradition is maintained today with a variety of new industries.

HISTORICAL NOTES

Margaret and Malcolm. – In the 11C **Malcolm III** or Canmore (c1031-93) offered hospitality in his Dunfermline Tower to the English heir to the throne, Edgar Atheling and his family, on their flight from William the Conqueror and the Norman Conquest (1066). Edgar's sister **Princess Margaret** (c1045-93), a devout Catholic, married in 1070 the Scottish King and was largely responsible for introducing the religious ideas of the Roman Catholic church which were gradually to supplant the Celtic church. Together with her husband she founded the church in 1072. Of Queen Margaret's sons who reigned, Edgar, Alexander I and David I, it was Alexander who proclaimed the town a royal burgh between 1124 and 1127 and David I (c1084-1153) who founded the Benedictine abbey. The town prospered as the abbey grew in importance. Following the untimely deaths of Alexander III and Margaret of Norway, Edward I, during his tour as mediator in the struggle for succession, visited the town and on his departure in 1304 the monastic buildings were a smouldering ruin. **Robert the Bruce** (1274-1329), that great national hero, helped with the reconstruction and is buried in the abbey. His heart is in Melrose Abbey.

Royal Palace. – The guest house was refurbished for James V's French wife but it was James VI who gave the abbey and palace to his **Queen, Anne of Denmark.** Once more Dunfermline was the home of royalty and three royal children were born here : Elizabeth known as the Winter Queen, the ill fated Charles I and Robert who died in infancy. With the Union of the Crowns (1603) the court departed to London. James VI subsequently made two fleeting visits to the town as did Charles I in 1633, and his 20 year old son, Charles II to sign the Dunfermline Declaration.

Dunfermline damask. – Dunfermline was one of the main centres of Scotland's foremost industry, linen making. The industry grew from a hand loom cottage tradition. With the specialization in damask the intricacy and quality of the work favoured the hand loom which in consequence lasted longer here. It was well into the 19C (1877) before power looms supplanted the hand loom locally. The town's limits extended as factories sprang up to meet both home and foreign markets with fine table linen. World War I reconversions, shrinking markets and competition from new fabrics resulted in the decline of the industry to the present day situation where only one factory still produces linen. For more of the history, techniques and to see samples visit the local museum *(p 78)*.

Famous citizens. – Although not a native of Dunfermline, one of the greatest 15C poets (makars) **Robert Henryson** (1430-1506) came here to reside in his capacity as schoolmaster. Dunfermline with its influential abbey and royal residence was a meeting place for great minds. In some respects his *Testament of Cresseid* shows a strong Chaucerian influence while on the other hand his humorous version of *Aesop's Fables* and *Robin and Makyne* herald Burns.

The philanthropist and steel baron **Andrew Carnegie** (1835-1919) was born in Dunfermline the son of a handloom weaver. In 1848 the family emigrated to America and young Andrew passed from bobbin boy, telegraphic messenger to working in the railroads before dealing in iron and then the new steel industry. By 1881 he was the foremost steel baron in the USA and in 1901 following the sale of his steel companies he retired and set about spending his fortune in public benefactions. His many gifts to his home town included the Carnegie Baths, the Library, the Lauder Technical School and Pittencrieff Park.

★DUNFERMLINE ABBEY *time: 1/2 hour*

tc The original Celtic church was replaced and dedicated to the Holy Trinity by Malcolm Canmore and Queen Margaret in 1072, when no doubt a religious community was founded. Their son David I accorded it abbatial status in 1128 and rebuilt the monastic church (1128-50) and it was he who brought Geoffrey, the Prior, from Canterbury to head the Benedictine community. The abbey with its extensive lands, property, coal pits, salt pans and ferry dues accrued enormous wealth and its prestige was enhanced by the fact it was a royal establishment and became the Westminster Abbey of Scotland where 22 royal persons were buried. The 13C saw the addition at the east end, of St Margaret's Chapel with the translation of the remains of Malcolm and his consort. The abbey was damaged by fire by Edward I and although restored by Robert the Bruce it never attained its former glory. It was during the 14C that a new royal residence was built adjoining the guest house. At the Reformation the leadership of the community passed into commendators hands, and the abbey declined. No longer used as a place of worship the east end fell into ruins and only following the collapse of the central tower was the east end rebuilt (1818-21).

★★**Abbey Church : Norman nave.** – The nave part of David I's 1128-50 church, was restored by William Schaw, Master of Works to Anne of Denmark. The north porch, northwest tower, west front and unusually massive buttresses are all his work.

The interior presents one of Scotland's finest Norman naves with close affinities to both Durham and St Magnus's, Kirkwall, where simple massive forms and round headed arches predominate. Great cylindrical pillars, four of which have chevron and spiral motifs, separate the seven bay nave from the aisles and support semicircular arches. Marked on the floor are the outlines (blue on the plan) of the original Celtic church and Queen Margaret's 1072 Church of the Holy Trinity.

77

Of the various monuments note **William Schaw's** (1) (1550-1602), near the north porch, erected by Queen Anne to the memory of her Chamberlain and Master of Works who so ably restored parts of the building in the 16 and 17C, and the Renaissance one (2) to Robert Pitcairn (1520-84), Commendator from 1560-84, with above on the panels of the vaulting, 16C paintings.

Abbey Church : East end or parish church. – The east end was rebuilt from 1818 to 1821 and now serves as parish church. A memorial brass (3) marks the tomb of Robert the Bruce (1274-1329) Scotland's hero. The new royal pew (4) commemorates the abbey's 900th Anniversary in 1972.

Leave the building by the nave and the East Processional Door (5), a well preserved example of Norman work.

Chapel of St Margaret. – Foundations only remain of the building which once enclosed St Margaret's Shrine a popular pilgrimage centre. The cemetery affords a good **view** of the Forth in the direction of Edinburgh.

Monastic buildings. – Of the once great ensemble of abbatial buildings which extended to the south of the abbey church there remain four walls of the refectory, with chambers below, joined by the gatehouse bestriding the pend to the kitchen and former royal palace.

Royal Palace. – In the 14C a new royal palace was built adjacent to the 13C guest house. A single wall remains to recall the splendour of this building which is best seen from Pittencrieff Park. Charles I and his sister the Winter Queen or Elizabeth of Bohemia were both born here.

Abbot's House. – *Maygate. Not open to the public.*

This characteristic building with its crow steps, turrets and gables was the home of the post-Reformation Commendator, Robert Pitcairn.

ADDITIONAL SIGHTS

Pittencrieff Park. – Known locally as "The Glen" this highly attractive and well-kept park, in the heart of Dunfermline was another of Andrew Carnegie's gifts to his native town. In addition to the varied facilities provided (nature trail, aviary, pets corner, model
tc traffic area, paddling pools, floral hall and formal garden), 17C **Pittencrieff House** has local history and costume galleries. The plasterwork ceilings were the work of Robert Lorimer during an early 20C renovation.

A rocky eminence overlooking the Tower Burn is capped by the scant remains of Malcolm Canmore's Tower made famous by a couplet from the *Ballad of Sir Patrick Spens*

    "The King sits in Dunfermline toon
    Drinking the Bluid-red wine..."

This was undoubtedly where Malcolm welcomed the Saxon princess his future Queen and where her many children were born.

tc **Andrew Carnegie Birthplace.** – *Moodie Street.*

On the left is the cottage where Andrew Carnegie (1835-1919) was born, arranged as a typical weaver's home, while the adjoining Memorial Hall houses exhibitions illustrating the great philanthropist's life and work *(p 77)*. The many trusts and endowments are too numerous to name but ranged from The Peace Palace in the Hague, through the Carnegie Institute of Pittsburgh, a library building in Toxteth, one of 660 in the United Kingdom, to his Hero Funds in both Europe and America.

tc **Dunfermline District Museum.** – *Viewfield.*

In addition to local collections there is an interesting display on **Dunfermline linen** weaving and damask in particular covering looms, weaving tools and patterns...

EXCURSIONS

Oakley. – Pop 3 480. *5 miles west of Dunfermline by the A 907, branch off to the south at Comrie.*
In the heart of coalmining country, is the small mining community of Oakley which grew in the 1930s and 1940s with the sinking of Comrie Mine and subsequent arrival of many Roman Catholic miners from the ailing Lanarkshire coalfields. The Church of the Most Holy Name (1956-8), a white harled building, standing alone on a small hill, has a unique series of **stained glass windows** in the chipped glass technique by the famous French glass worker, **Gabriel Loire** from Chartres. Highly colourful, even in the poorest light, the smaller round windows (south wall) show scenes from the Life of Christ. On the intervening wall spaces of the nave are *Stations of the Cross* in carved and painted wood blocks, also by Gabriel Loire.

tc **Loch Leven Castle.** – *12 miles north of Dunfermline by the M 90. Ferry service from Kinross.*
This island stronghold comprises a 14C tower house and 16C curtain wall. Access to the tower was originally gained by the round headed opening at the 2nd floor level. This Douglas fortress was the place of emprisonment of Mary Queen of Scots from 17 June 1567 until her escape on 2 May 1568. Following defeat at Langside Mary fled Scotland, never to return.

★ DUNKELD (Tayside)   Pop 273
Michelin map 401 fold 23 – J 14

In reality a cathedral city, the particular charm of this modest village on the north bank of the Tay, is its cathedral and attractive precinct.

Metropolitan See. – As early as 700 AD this was the site of a monastic establishment which was to become for a brief spell the kingdom's principal ecclesiastic centre under Kenneth MacAlpine in the 9C AD (AD 843). Confirmed during the reign of Alexander I, the bishopric was held by such historic figures as William Sinclair and the scholar poet, Gavin Douglas (1474-1522). The settlement which developed around the majestic cathedral (14-16C) never grew to any proportion. By 1650 the cathedral itself was a ruin and in 1689 the village was burnt to the ground in the aftermath of Killiecrankie when the Cameronian regiment held out against the remainder of Dundee's Jacobite Highlander army.

The tales of Beatrix Potter. – It was during her many childhood holidays in the area that Beatrix Potter (1866-1943) created the lovable characters (Peter Rabbit, Jemima Puddleduck...) which have so enthralled generations of children.

SIGHTS

tc **Dunkeld Cathedral.** – In an admirable riverside setting surrounded by tree shaded lawns, the cathedral is divided into two distinct parts, a roofless ruined nave and the choir.

Choir. – Begun in 1315 by Robert the Bruce's "own bishop" William Sinclair, building continued until 1400. In 1600 the choir of the ruined cathedral was renovated to serve as parish church. There have been several restorations since.
Inside recumbent effigies portray, Bishop Sinclair (headless), and the Wolf of Badenoch in an impressive suit of armour. The 15C chapter house serves as Atholl mausoleum and houses a small museum on local church and social history . At the choir's west end is a copy of the 1611 Great SHE Bible.

Nave. – *Restricted access during restoration work.*
The nave dating from the 15C was begun by Robert Cardeny whose mitred effigy lies in the Chapel of St Ninian (south aisle). Others buried here include Colonel Cleland, leader of the Cameronians, and Count Rohenstadt, the last of the Stuart line. The windows of the triforium level are unusual. The late Gothic tower (1469-1501) was the last addition. Inside are two mural paintings while the platform offers a good view.

Behind the cathedral is one of the first larches imported from the Tyrol in 1738 by the Duke of Atholl.
From the grounds can be seen Telford's bridge (1809) the predecessor of which was built by Alexander Mylne, canon at Dunkeld, Abbot of Cambuskenneth, first President of the College of Justice *(p 92)* and ancestor of the family of master masons.
The imposing cathedral gates (1730) came from Dunkeld House (now a hotel), once the Atholl ducal seat.

★**Cathedral Street.** – Like The Cross this was rebuilt to the original street plan after the destruction of 1689. Many of the 17C houses were derelict by the 1950s. An extensive restoration programme, by the National Trust for Scotland and the local authority, has recaptured the 17-18C aspect of these streets providing an attractive approach to the cathedral.
Cathedral Street is lined with houses where the characteristic door and window trims set off the pale coloured harling, and pends interrupt the succession. **No 19**, Dean's House was where **Gavin Douglas** (1474-1522) the poet and scholar of the Scottish Renaissance was consecrated Bishop of Dunkeld in 1516. Apart from his politicizing for the Douglas faction, Douglas is remembered for his translation of Virgil's *Aeneid* into Scots.

The Cross. – Bordering this square are the National Trust for Scotland's Ell Shop
tc named after the ell or weaver's measure fixed to one of its walls and the **Scottish Horse Regimental Museum.** The displays recount the half century life span of this regiment, founded during the Boer War.

EXCURSIONS

tc **Loch of the Lowes Nature Reserve.** – *2 miles out of Dunkeld by the A 923.*
Access is limited to the south shore, visitor centre and observation hide. The 242 acre
reserve covers the freshwater Loch of the Lowes and its fringing woodland and has
a consequently rich flora and fauna.
The tree-top eyrie a pair of ospreys, one of only two nests open to the public, can
be observed from the hide *(binoculars are provided)*.

The Hermitage. – *2 miles west of Dunkeld, off the A 9.*
A woodland walk along the banks of the River Braan. Built in 1758, the **Hermitage**, was
a famous 18C beauty spot and is portrayed in one of Charles Stewart's landscapes
in the Dining Room at Blair Castle. It overlooks the Falls of Braan, where this Highland
torrent rushes through the cleft and under the bridge. Further on is Ossian's Cave,
another folly of the same period as the Hermitage.

★★ DUNNOTTAR CASTLE (Grampian)

Michelin map **401** fold 20 – N 13 – 2 miles south of Stonehaven – Local map p 37

tc The extensive ruins of Dunnottar are impressively set in an almost inaccessible
promontory site★★★ with sheer cliffs on three sides. Added to the drama of this site
is the interest of its two principal historical events.
*The visit may be unsuitable for the elderly or disabled as there are many steep and
uneven steps.*

Early religious site. – Legend has it that St Ninian founded an early Christian
settlement on the crag in the 5C. By 1276 Bishop Wishart of St Andrews consecrated
a stone building which was destroyed 20 years later. In the late 14C Sir William Keith
erected the present keep and in so doing was excommunicated for building on
consecrated ground. From then on Dunnottar served as the principal seat of the Keiths,
Hereditary Earls Marischal of Scotland and as such, Wardens of the Regalia.

Fortified stronghold to resplendent residence. – Always valued as a place of
strength the stronghold was the last castle to remain in Royalist hands during the
Commonwealth. As such it was the natural hiding place for the **Royal Regalia** and other
royal papers. During the 8-month siege in 1651-2 by Cromwell's troops the regalia
was audaciously smuggled out to be hidden under the floorboards of nearby Old
Kinneff Church *(p 192)* where it remained in security until the Restoration.
The second event of importance, although more inglorious, was the incarceration of
Covenanter prisoners in 1685 following the failure of the Monmouth and Duke of Argyll
Rebellions. 122 men and 45 women were kept for 2 months in Whigs Vault. Very
few survived. Refusal to sign the oath meant shipment to the American colonies.
In 1715 the estates were forfeited following the 10th Earl's participation in the rising
(p 173) The castle then gradually fell into disrepair only to be retrieved in the 20C
by a programme of dedicated restoration.

The buildings. – The approach to the flat topped promontory is well guarded by the
fortified **gatehouse** and an intricate system of steps and pends. Having visited this then
move up to the L-shaped **keep**, a traditional Scottish tower house. From cap-house level
there is a good view of the rest of the castle and its audacious site. A store, smithy
and stables were added in an adjoining wing to the east to provide additional
accommodation. The nearby detached **Waterton's Lodging**, with its enclosed garden area,
is a 17C construction. Beyond, arranged around a quadrangle, are the decidedly more
commodious and comfortable **buildings of the 16 and 17C**, a direct contrast to the keep.
These are attributed to **George the 5th Earl** (1553-1623) the founder of Marischal
College.The plan is unusual although the detail is traditional. Note on the west range
how the chimneys are almost Elizabethan! The west wing, dating from the last quarter
of the 16C, has on the ground floor, seven independant chambers each with fireplace,
window and door, with above the gallery or ballroom. On the north side cellars and
a fine kitchen occupy the basement and a staircase with straight flights gives access
to the dining room and recently restored drawing room. Beyond on the very point
is the last extension, the Marischal's Suite (1645) with the infamous Whigs Vault
underneath. The east wing contained a bakery and brewhouse with additional
partments above. The fourth side of the quadrangle consists of the 16C chapel.

DUNS (Borders)   Pop 2 308

Michelin map **401** fold 32 – M 16

This quiet market town and onetime county town now serves the important farming
area of the **Merse.**
The **Duns Summer Festival Week** *(p 28)* with the Reiver and his mounted followers as the
main participants provides a series of varied events.

The Merse. – The rich arable area of the lower Tweed basin is a succession of well
maintained estates and large arable farms. Always to the forefront of agriculture in
Scotland the area boasted such 18C improvers as Dawson of Frogden, Logan of
Fishwick, Elliot of Minto and even the eminent geologist James Hutton farmed at
Bonkyl northeast of Duns. The legacy of such enlightened landowners includes **planned
villages** such as Swinton, and the very imposing **formal steadings** built on a courtyard plan
with an arched entrance as the centrepiece of a symmetrical façade often
accompanied by a row of matching cottages. Farming is mixed, with prime beef and
milk production accompanying cash crops such as wheat, barley, potatoes, fruit and
field vegetables. This is large scale farming with a high degree of mechanisation.

SIGHTS

tc **Jim Clark Memorial Room.** – *44 Newton Street.*
Trophies in all shapes and forms – including a brick from The Brickyard (Indianapolis) – tell the story of **Jim Clark's** (1936-58) racing career. A farmer by occupation Jim was the youngest ever World Champion at 27 and his record of seven Grand Prix wins in one year, at a time when there were fewer such races, was only equalled in 1984. He died tragically in an accident on the Hockenheim track in Germany in 1968.

Public Park. – *Main entrance off Station Road.*
In these attractive gardens are the mercat cross and an unusual bronze statue by Frank Tritchler to commemorate **John Duns Scotus** (1266-1308) Franciscan, medieval philosopher, scholar and native of Duns.

Duns Law. – *713ft-218 m. Access from Duns Castle Avenue. Take the path signposted to the right, 30 mins Rtn, which leads through woods to a wicket gate, then up through the field to the summit.*
On the site of an early fort is the **Covenanter's Stone** recalling the time when General Sir Alexander Leslie and his Covenanting army encamped here in 1639 ready to oppose Charles I waiting at Berwick. The view extends from the Lammermuirs in the north, round to East Coldinghamshire and then south over the Merse to the Cheviots. On the way down, before going through the gate, move round to the left to the brow of the hill which affords a view of Duns. The town was originally sited on the flank of Duns Law *(signposted The Bruntons)* before being moved to its present site in the late 16C, following several English attacks.

Turn right once back at the avenue.

The cairn in front of the lodge of Duns Castle *(private)* indicates the birthplace of John Duns Scotus, the Subtle Doctor.

EXCURSIONS

★Foulden. – *10 miles. Leave Duns by the Berwick road the A 6105.*

★Manderston. – *Description p 153*

The main road continues round the estate wall to Edrom. Continue for 3 miles then branch off to the upper part of Chirnside.

Chirnside. – Pop 1 290. This long straggling village on a ridge offers views of the Merse with the Cheviots as a backdrop. The main street has a memorial to Jim Clark *(see above)* who is buried in the churchyard.

★Foulden. – Pop 130. An attractive line of varied cottages, again with views of the Merse, make up this village which is known for its two storeyed **tithe barn** *(not open to the public)* at the roadside beside the church. Rare in Scotland, the building was used for storing tithes paid in kind to the parish church.

tc **Polwarth Church.** – *4 miles to southwest of Duns by the A 6105.*
The now non-existant village became widely known as a result of Allan Ramsay's poem. A local road leads to the **church** where Grizel Hume *(p 154)* from nearby Redbraes Castle, the former seat of the Humes of Polwarth, took food to her Covenanter father Sir Patrick Hume, 1st Earl of Marchmont, concealed in the church vault in 1684.
Rebuilt in 1703 by Sir Patrick Hume, the T-form church has several interesting features, 3 separate doors (now blocked up) for the congregation, the minister and the laird, the crowned orange of the east gable representing the Marchmont arms accorded by the Prince of Orange and the finial above the tower which bears the arms of Sir Patrick.

DURNESS (Highland)   Pop 327

Michelin map **401** fold 2 – F 8

This small north coast village, once a crofting community, now thrives as a stopping off place for those rounding the northwest corner of Scotland.

Smoo Cave. – An outcrop of well jointed limestones in the Durness vicinity accounts for the presence of this cave and the sandy beaches. The waters of the Allt Smoo plunge down a sink hole to reappear at the mouth of the outer cave. The two inner caves are accessible only to equipped potholers.

tc **Balnakeil Craft Village.** – *1 mile to the west by a local road.*
This former radar station is now occupied by a community of craftspeople. The visitor centre (exhibition area, tea and snacks) and workshops are open to the public. This is a chance to watch craftsmen at work : ceramics, jewelcraft, weaving, bookbinding and leatherwork.

EXCURSION

★★★Cape Wrath. – *By ferry and minibus. The ferry leaves from Keoldale slipway*
tc *1 1/2 miles south of Durness.* The bus takes 40 mins for the 11 1/2 mile trip through bleak moorland country, now MOD territory, to the lighthouse. This exposed cape offers a variety of vantage points affording outstanding views★★ of churning seas and superb coastal scenery especially eastwards.

Respect the life of the countryside
Go carefully on country roads
Protect wildlife, plants and trees.

★★ The EAST NEUK (Fife)

Michelin map **401** fold 28 – L and M 15

The East Neuk or corner, one of the main attractions of Fife, is a stretch of coastline dotted with a series of delightful fishing villages, each clustered around its harbour. The villages are a joy to discover with their wealth of vernacular architecture.

The golden fringe. – As early as the 11C Fife was the very hub of the nation, with Dunfermline as the political and St Andrews as the ecclesiastical centres. The villages flourished as active trading ports with the Hanseatic League and the Low Countries. King James VI described Fife as "a beggar's mantle with a fringe of gold". It was the royal burghs along the coast, with their profitable activities of trading, fishing and smuggling which were the "fringe of gold". With the development of the trans-Atlantic routes, the villages concentrated on fishing.

Era of the China Tea Clippers. – In those heroic days of China tea trade prior to the Suez Canal every day counted. Two masters of these magnificent vessels came from East Neuk ports, Captain Alexander Rodger (1802-77) and Captain Keay. The latter was skipper of the *Ariel* which held the all time sailing ship record of 83 days from Gravesend to Hong Kong. He is also famous for his race with Rodger's *Taeping*.

★★ CRAIL   Pop 1 075

This busy resort is the most attractive burgh. The older heart of the burgh is clustered down by the harbour while the upper town is altogether more spacious.

★**Upper Crail.** – Standing alone in a prominent position overlooking the spacious market place, the **tolbooth** (1598), a tiered tower, is graced by an attractively shaped belfry. The weather vane, a gilded capon (dried haddock), is a reminder that capons were *tc* the town's staple export. Behind the tolbooth at nos 62-64 is a small **museum** which gives an insight into the burgh's history, its main buildings and activities. The tree-lined Marketgate is bordered by elegant two and three storey dwellings. Of particular note are nos 30 and 44 on the south side and Auld House (16C) and Kirkmay House (early 19C) opposite. The "Blue Stone" on the left is said to have been thrown by the devil from the Isle of May in an attempt to destroy the church.

Take Kirk Wynd to pass the 16C circular dovecot, the sole remains of a priory. Follow the path round to Castle Walk which skirts the few remains of what was a royal stronghold. Amongst the landmarks visible *(viewfinder)* across the Forth are St Abb's Head, the Bass Rock, Tantallon Castle, Isle of May...

★★**Old Centre.** – Sloping down to the harbour, **Shoregate** is bordered by an attractive group of cottages (nos 22-28). Crab and lobster boats still use the **inner harbour** with its attractive stonework. On the waterfront is the three storey **Customs House** (no 35). Note the boat carving on the pend lintel. The adjoining group of buildings surround a paved courtyard. On the way up note no 32 Castle Street and the delightful 18C no 1 Rose Wynd with its forestair and attractive door surround.

(Scottish Tourist Board)

Crail harbour

ANSTRUTHER   Pop 3 037

This linear settlement includes the once independent communities of Cellardyke, Anstruther Easter and Anstruther Wester. There is still some creel-fishing (for lobster and crab) and white-fish activity from Anstruther, but most of the fishermen now operate from Pittenweem, a mile to the west, which is home to the East Neuk fishing fleet of trawlers, seiners and creel boats.

★★**Scottish Fisheries Museum.** – Housed in a group of 16-19C buildings on three sides *tc* of a cobbled courtyard, the exhibits recount the history of Scottish fisheries and the life of fisherfolk. New galleries are shortly to be opened, which will illustrate modern developments in the catching, processing and marketing of fish.

West Room and West Gallery : "The Days of Sail", illustrated by paintings, model boats, tableaux of life-size figures at work, fishing gear, dioramas of fishing methods.

Marine Aquarium : fish and shellfish of Scottish waters.

Long Gallery : pictorial map of Scotland's fishing communities ; ancillary trades tableau showing women gutting and packing herring ; coopers making barrels, etc.

Whaling Corridor : illustrating a once important sector of Scotland's industry.

Ship's Loft : "The Days of Steam", devoted to the era of the steam drifter. Paintings, models, original mural, examples of gear and fishing techniques.

Courtyard Gallery : examples of heavier items of machinery.

Courtyard : actual small fishing boats, nets, anchors ; fully-equipped wheelhouse.

Abbot's Lodging : this 16C building, once the property of the monks from Balmerino, has been renovated as an east coast fisherman's home at the turn of the century, a period of prosperity due to the herring fishery. Above the family room is the net loft. Other exhibits in the harbour include the North Carr Lightship and a *Fifie*.

tc **Boat trips to the Isle of May.** – Created a nature reserve in 1956 the island has an important breeding population of seabirds (puffins, kittiwakes, guillemots, shags, eider ducks, razorbills and fulmars). Scotland's first lighthouse, dating from the 1630s is still visible alongside its 19C successor. The beacon consisted of coals burning in the rooftop grate.

PITTENWEEM
Pop 1 650

This burgh is once again on two levels. **Kellie Lodge** *(private)* in the High Street is the 16C town house of the Earls of Kellie from Kellie Castle *(qv)*. Corbelled, pantiled *tc* and crow stepped it is an excellent example of the vernacular style. **St Fillan's Cave** and Holy Well is said to have been the sanctuary of the 7C Christian missionary Fillan. Take one of the six wynds down to the harbour which is today, Fife's busiest fishing port. Of particular interest on the waterfront are **The Gyles** at the east end and no 18 East Shore, a three storeyed building with its Dutch style gable.

ST MONANCE
Pop 1 270

The village is tightly packed around its small harbour. Wynds and closes lead off into the usual maze of lanes, back alleys and yards, a smuggler's paradise. The **church**, standing on an eminence, was probably begun in the 11C by Queen Margaret. A large part of it is 13C and the choir was rebuilt by King David II in 1346. Inside look for, the hanging ship, the coats of arms and the painted panel from the laird's loft.

ECCLEFECHAN (Dumfries and Galloway)
Pop 880

Michelin map **401** fold 39 – K 18

The village of Ecclefechan is famous as the birthplace of **Thomas Carlyle** (1795-1881), essayist, historian, social reformer and literary figure of his age. Following his stern Calvinistic upbringing and local schooling the 13 year old Carlyle attended Edinburgh University. The early years of married life with Jane Welsh were spent at Craigenputtock, a nearby Dumfriesshire farm where he worked on *Sartor Resartus*. Drawn by the literary world of London they moved south in 1834 to settle in Cheyne Row *(see the Michelin Green Guide London)*. Eloquent as a speaker with ideas to put over, Carlyle the reformer and moraliser greatly influenced the Victorians. Denouncing materialism he vehemently advocated the need for faith, hardwork and leadership. On Jane's death he became a virtual recluse ever more embittered, tormented and despairing. His many varied publications included historical works on *The French Revolution*, *Oliver Cromwell* and *Frederick the Great*.

tc **Arched House.** – *Main Street*.
Carlyle, the eldest of a large second family, was born the year before Burns died in this 18C house built by his father. Two of the rooms are refurbishded in the 19C domestic style with some family belongings, while the room above the pend has photographs, mss and other documents highlighting the author's life and work. The 1875 testimonial for his eightieth birthday celebrations was signed by the most prominent literary men of the day.

Churchyard. – The "Sage of Chelsea" refused a place in Westminster Abbey in order to be buried alongside his mother. Also in the churchyard is Dr Archibald Arnott who attended Napoleon on St. Helena.
Carlyle is commemorated in a statue by Boehm at the north end of the village.

EXCURSIONS

Merkland Cross. – *Off the south going carriageway of the A 74 after Kirtlebridge.* This is a 15C floriated wayside cross.

Gretna Green. – Pop 2 809. *7 1/2 miles to the southeast.*
Gretna is widely known for its elopements and smithy marriages although no longer legal. Following an 18C Bill to end clandestine marriages in England the number of runaway weddings increased as Scottish marriage law only required a declaration before witnesses. The marriage trade continued to flourish in spite of an 1857 Act requiring 21 days residence in Scotland, until an Act of Parliament discontinued the pratice in 1940. The Old Blacksmith's Shop has relics of this past trade.

Michelin map 401 fold 31 ; inset folds 33 and 37 – K 16

Edinburgh the capital of Scotland is a beautiful city, open and green, attractively set on a series of volcanic hills. The city boasts a rich historic past and two contrasting towns – the Old and New. A wealth of tourist sights, rich museum collections and its prestigious arts festival are all reasons to visit this charming city.

Viewpoints and vistas. – One of the most attractive features of the central area is the number of spectacular vistas, which are for ever opening up to delight the visitor. In addition to the viewpoints afforded by such prominent landmarks as the Scott and Nelson Monuments, the volcanic hills (Calton, Arthur's Seat, Castle Rock, Blackford, Costorphine...) provide ideal vantage points.

tc **Visiting Edinburgh.** – It is best to do so on foot, particularly in the Old Town. For a general view of the city take one of the conducted coach tours, varying in length from 1 to 4 hours, which leave from Waverley Bridge, just off Princes Street. There are at least three departures each day throughout the year except Christmas. For further information on tours and touristcards or freedom tickets apply to the Transport Information Centre on Waverley Bridge or in writing to Lothian Region Transport head office.

★★★**The Edinburgh International Festival**. – This prestigious annual festival *(3 week*
tc event in August : p 212) provides a quality programme of performances in all art forms. Since its inception in 1947 highlights of the Festival's history have included such specially commissionned works as T.S. Eliot's *The Cocktail Party* (1948), Peter Maxwell Davies's opera *The Lighthouse* (1980) and the world premiere of *Mörder, Hoffnung*
tc der Frauen by the Ballet Rambert (1983). The ever-popular **Military Tattoo** provides a spectacle rich in colour, tradition, music and excitement under the floodlights of the Castle Esplanade. The capacity audience of 9 000 is entertained by a cast of
tc approximately 600. Also part of Festival time is **The Fringe** with its 700 plus productions covering a wide range of entertainment. Often avant-garde or just plain eccentric, The Fringe spills out onto the streets and squares of Edinburgh which become the stage for a variety of entertainers from buskers and jugglers to musicians and mime artists.
tc The sister Edinburgh **Folk Festival** another annual event *(p 212)* dates from 1979. The entertainments include concerts, lectures and workshops.
When visiting Edinburgh, during the Festival it is advisable to reserve accommodation in advance. Many museums, galleries and houses extend their opening hours and organize special exhibitions during festival time. Enquire at the Tourist Information
tc Centre, Waverley Market.

The plan below gives the location of Edinburgh's main recital and concert halls, theatres, multi-purpose auditoriums and halls, serving as venues for Festival events. The official organizations and clubs are also indicated. For the exact addresses and the telephone numbers of the latter, consult the chapter on Practical Information at the end of the guide.

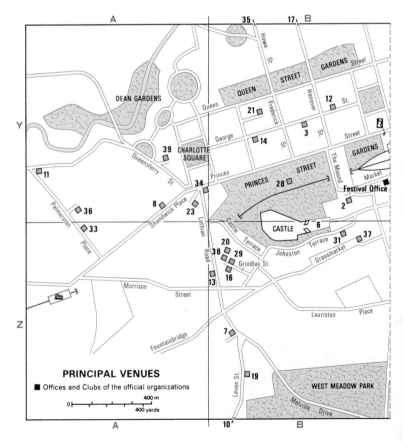

PRINCIPAL VENUES

■ Offices and Clubs of the official organizations

0　　　400 m
　　　400 yards

HISTORICAL NOTES

The Castle Rock no doubt proved to be a secure refuge for the earliest settlers, although the Romans preferred the attractions of Cramond. The name may in fact be derived from the Northumbrian King Edwin (Edwinesburg – Edwin's fortress) although he actually died before his people captured the site in 638. As a residence the Castle Rock site was associated with **Malcolm Canmore** and his **Queen Margaret**. Their son **David I** gave great preferment to the settlement by founding the Abbey of Holy Rood and the building of a small chapel to commemorate his mother. During the Wars of Independence the strategic importance of the castle simultaneously afforded protection to the growing burgh and increased its vulnerability to English attacks.

Medieval Golden Age. – The first town wall dated from 1450. With the early Stewarts, Edinburgh slowly assumed the roles of royal residence, seat of government and capital. Already an important religious centre with the abbey and St Giles, 15C Edinburgh gained two collegiate churches, Kirk o'Field (1450) outside the wall and Holy Trinity (1462), which stood on the site of Waverley Station. Court patronage included the foundation of a College of Surgeons (1505) and the introduction of printing (1507). Some of the earliest works printed were those of the court poet William Dunbar (1460-1520) and Gavin Douglas (1475-1522), both of whom used vernacular to good effect, and belonged to a group of poets known as the Makars.

This Golden Age ended with Flodden when the host of Scots dead included the King and Edinburgh's provost. In haste the town started to build the **Flodden Wall** although only completed in 1560 this was to define the limits of the Ancient Royalty for over two centuries confining expansion upwards in the characteristic tenements (lands) of as many as 10 and 12 storeys.

Mary Queen of Scots and the Reformation. – Two years after the proclamation of the infant Mary's accession, Henry VIII's army set out on the **"rough wooing"**, creating havoc and destruction in the south and east of the country. Mary was sent to France for safety. Already the Roman Catholic church, wealthier than the Crown, was under attack and the ideas of the Reformation being receptively received. The **Reformation** (1560) and return of the Catholic Mary Queen of Scots, a year later, made Edinburgh during her short reign the stage for warring factions, Protestant and Roman Catholic, pro-French and pro-English. Renewed patronage of the arts came with the reign of Mary's son, James VI. With the departure of James and his court after the **Union of the Crowns** (1603) some citizens prospered in the south like "Jinglin Geordie" *(p 94)*, but Edinburgh lost much of its pageantry and cultural activity.

Religious strife. – Relative peace ensued until Charles I, following his 1633 coronation at Holyrood, pushed through episcopacy – a policy inherited from his father. **The National Covenant** was drawn up in 1638 and signed in Greyfriars Church. The signatories swore loyalty to the King but fervently opposed his religious policy. A year later, following the General Assembly of Glasgow, episcopacy was abolished. Covenanters took the Castle. By 1641 Charles had conceded to the Covenanters (defendants of the Reformed Faith) but the outbreak of Civil War brought a pact with the English Parliamentarians, the **Solemn League and Covenant** (1643). Montrose's brilliant royalist campaign ended with defeat at Philiphaugh (1645) and the final outcome of Marston Moor was the king's execution (1649).

Cromwell defeated the Scots at Dunbar (1650) and Montrose was executed. His troops entered Edinburgh and the palace and other buildings served as barracks, some like Holyroodhouse suffered through fire. The Commonwealth was a period of uneasy peace in Edinburgh and much was the rejoicing at the Restoration in spite of the fact it brought the re-introduction of the episcopal system and persecution of the Covenanters. Slowly the Covenanting opposition was eradicated. Many of the prisoners were either executed in the Grassmarket or kept prisoner in Greyfriars Churchyard *(p 94)*.

In the late 17C Edinburgh flourished as a legal and medical centre. The failure of the Darien scheme gave rise to anti-English feelings which were exacerbated by the Union Debates. The activities of both factions were closely followed by Daniel Defoe in his role of government spy. In 1707 Edinburgh lost its Parliament when the politicians headed south. The legal profession took over Parliament Hall and began to dominate Edinburgh society.

Of the two Jacobite rebellions the '45 saw the return of a brief period of glory to Holyroodhouse with the installation of the Prince's court at the palace. Many in Edinburgh, were like the poet Allan Ramsay who by his departure from the city showed his preference for the peaceful option.

The Enlightenment. – In late 18C Edinburgh a circle of great men flourished: Lords of Session Lord Kames, Lord Monbuddo and Lord Hailes, Hugh Blair, historian William Robertson, philosophers David Hume and Dugald Stewart, economist Adam Smith, geologist James Hutton, chemist Joseph Black and architect Robert Adam. Clubs and societies prospered and it was in such a climate of intellectual ferment that plans were put forward for a civic project of great boldness and imagination.

Georgian Edinburgh. – Old Edinburgh on its ridge was squalid and overcrowded. The earliest moves out were made to George Square in the south before plans for the New Town were drawn up, approved, enacted and accepted socially. The project was encouraged by the early establishment of public buildings in the new area ; Theatre Royal (1767-8), Register House (1774-1822), Physicians Hall (1775-7) and the Assembly Rooms (1784-7). Attractive as the elegant streets and squares were, it was to the markets, wynds and closes, taverns and clubs of the Old Town that many still went to earn their livelihood and spend their moments of leisure.

Spanning the two phases of the enlightenment was Henry Mackenzie author of *A Man of Feeling*. The second period was dominated by the figures of Scott, Lord Cockburn and Francis Jeffrey. This was the age of the literary magazines, both Whig and Tory *(Edinburgh Review* and *Blackwood's Magazine)*, their contributors (Francis Jeffrey, Lockhart, Christopher North, James Hogg and the young Thomas Carlyle) and the publishers and book sellers (Constable, Chambers, Creech). Raeburn the portraitist and architects such as Robert Reid, Hamilton, Playfair and Gillespie Graham contributed to the making of Athenian Edinburgh.

The interwar years. – The 1920-30s period was one of a Scots Literary Renaissance centred on such literary figures as Hugh MacDiarmid *(Carotid Cornucopions)*, Lewis Spence, Neil Gunn, Edwin Muir, Helen Cruickshank, and such haunts as the Abbotsford (Rose St) and the Café Royal. This cultural stirring was reinforced by the launching of the Festival in 1947.

★★THE CASTLE (AYZ) *time : 1 1/2 hours*

tc The castle is impressive from all sides perched on its strategic **site★★★** on Castle Rock. As the familiar silhouette of the castle figures prominently on the skyline of most views of the city, the castle's role has been of paramount importance throughout the city's history.

Royal residence to military fortress. – As early as the 11C the buildings atop Castle Rock were favoured as a residence by royalty, in particular by Margaret the queen of Malcolm III and her sons. She in fact died here in 1093 shortly after hearing of the loss of both her liege lord and eldest son at Alnwick. The castle subsequently alternated between Scottish and English forces and in 1313 suffered demolition by the Scots. In the late 14C Bruce's son, David II, built a tower, of which there are no visible remains, on the site of the Half Moon Battery. The infamous **Black Dinner** of 1440 resulted in the execution of the two young Douglas brothers in the presence of their 10 year old sovereign James II in an attempt to quell Douglas power. James II was born, crowned, married and buried in Edinburgh but it was his son James III who formally recongnized the city as his capital.

In the 16C Regent Morton did much to strengthen the castle's defences which suffered again during Sir William Kirkcaldy of Grange's stout defence (1573) in the name of Mary Queen of Scots. The end result was prompt execution for Grange and repairs and rebuilding to the castle. In the 1650s Cromwell's troops took over and thus began the castle's new role as a garrison. The 18C saw two Jacobite attacks, the last by Bonnie Prince Charlie in person from his headquarters at the other end of the Royal Mile. The buildings we see today are basically those which have resulted from the castle's role as a military garrison in recent centuries.

Esplanade. – Created as a spacious parade ground in the 18C the esplanade is the setting for the Festival's most popular event, the **Military Tattoo** *(p 84)*, when the floodlit castle acts as backdrop. Before entering note two of the castle's most imposing features from amongst the tiers of buildings, the appropriately named Half Moon Battery and the Palace Block towering up behind to the left.

Gatehouse. – Beyond the ditch, started in the 1650s by Cromwell's troops, is the gatehouse, built as a suitably imposing entrance in the 19C. Two national heroes, Bruce (1) and Wallace (2) flank the entrance. Once through, the massive walls of the Half Moon Battery loom up ahead. These demarcate the line of the original outer defences. A plaque (3) on the left, commemorates Kirkcaldy of Grange's stoic defence of 1573.

Portcullis Gate. – The lower part dating from Regent Morton's 1570s fortifications has decorative features including Morton's coat of arms while the upper part is a 19C addition.

Further up, the two batteries, Argyle and Mill's Mount, both afford excellent **views**★★ of Princes Street and the New Town. The daily **one o'clock salute** (4) is fired from the upper battery.

Following the signs round to the left, on the right is the Governor's House (1742), with adjoining wings for the Master Gunner and Store-Keeper. The imposing building behind, is the 1790s New Barracks for the castle garrison.

tc **Royal Scots Regimental Museum.** – The Royal Regiment is the oldest and most senior regiment of the British Army. Raised on the 28th March 1633 the unit originally served under King Louis XIII of France where it earned the nickname of "Pontius Pilate's Bodyguard.". Definitively recalled to Britain in 1676, two rooms of exhibits recount the regiment's subsequent history, Corunna, Waterloo, Alma, Sebastopol, Marne... There is an impressive display of medals.

Military Prison. – These cells were built in the 1840s.

French Prisons (5). – Two levels of great vaulted chambers, situated under the Crown Square buildings, housed French and American prisoners in the 18 and 19C. In the end chamber stands the 500 year old siege cannon, **Mons Meg** resplendent in a new coat of paint. Commissioned by the Duke of Burgundy and forged in 1449 at Mons in Flanders it was given eight years later to his nephew James II who lost his life due to his enthusiasm for guns *(p 140)*. During an eventful career Mons Meg is said to have served at Crookston (1489), Dumbarton (1489) and Norham Castles (1497) and even of having spent time in The Tower. Sir Walter Scott petitioned for its return and in 1829 the huge medieval cannon was returned to Edinburgh.

Foog's Gate. – The original entrance to the upper area of the castle was by stairs climbing from beside the Portcullis Gate. With the levelling off of the rest of the Rock, this new entrance was built on the west side.

St Margaret's Chapel. – The small rectangular building on the left incorporates remnants of the castle's oldest structure, and perhaps even Edinburgh's. This 12C chapel is dedicated to Malcolm III's Queen Margaret *(p 77)*. Once englobed by other buildings it served various purposes until the mid-19C when its original role was revealed and restoration ensued. Inside, the chancel arch is Norman in inspiration with its cushion capitals and chevron decoration.

The terrace in front offers an extensive **panorama**★★★ of northern Edinburgh, in particular Princes Street and the gardens, with the geometric pattern of the New Town spreading away beyond.

Half Moon Battery. – The battery was built following the 1573 siege, which saw the destruction of David II's tower house. From here visitors can readily appreciate the superb strategic importance of the original tower with its command of castle approaches and entrance.

The heart of the medieval fortress and onetime royal residence is marked by Crown Square. Of the four buildings overlooking the square today only the southern and eastern ranges are of historic interest.

Scottish National War Memorial. – *North side.* In the 1920s **Robert Lorimer** *(qv)* undertook the task of converting a mid-18C building into Scotland's War Memorial. The exterior, with a strong family resemblance to the palace part of Stirling Castle, is in harmony with the earlier buildings.

The interior achieves a suitable atmosphere of dignity and reverence to honour those who served. War-time scenes are the subject of the attractive stained glass roundels by Douglas Strachan.

Scottish United Services Museum (6). – *West side. East gallery in Palace Block.* This section of the museum houses displays of uniforms, medals, badges, Colours and weapons illustrating the history of the Scottish regiments of the British Army.

Great Hall. – *South side.* The hall built in the late 15C for James IV succeeded a series of earlier buildings. Intended for great occasions, the chief attraction of this spacious apartment is the **hammerbeam roof**★★ which can be fully appreciated since the 19C restoration. Boards and beams are attractively painted and reward inspection.

Palace Block. – *East side.* Dating from the 15C, this range contained the royal apartments, overlooking the old town. The interior was remodelled for James VI's only return visit to Scotland in 1617.

Enter by the door nearest the Great Hall range. A room on the right has Jacobite relics. Straight ahead Queen Mary's Room is hung with family portraits of her son James VI, her grandson Charles I with Henrietta Maria, and great grandson Charles II. The adjoining small **chamber**, with its panelling and timber ceiling, is the room where James VI was born in 1566. The decoration dates from the 1617 refurbishing.

Once in the square again the doorway in the staircase tower leads to the Crown Chamber on the first floor where the **Honours of Scotland**★★★ are displayed. Following the Union of Parliaments in 1707 they were sealed up in this chamber and it was on Sir Walter Scott's initiative that they were rediscovered. Although of unknown age the pearl and gem encrusted **crown** is Britain's only pre-Restoration crown to have escaped being melted down by Cromwell. The **sceptre** and **sword** were gifts from two Popes to the Renaissance prince, James IV, the former from the Borgia Pope, Alexander VI (1492-1503) and the latter from his successor Pope Julius II (1503-13) that great patron of the arts.

The other rooms *(East Gallery)* contain further displays on the Royal Navy, Royal Air Force, Scotland's sole cavalry regiment, the Royal Scots Greys *(p 46)* and the yeomanry regiments. Note the model of the pride of James IV's navy, the magnificent **Great Michael** (1507-11). Rival to Henry's *Great Harry* (1512), like most of the Scottish fleet she set sail in 1513 to support the French King facing the threat of the Holy League. She was eventually sold to Louis XII.

★★THE ABBEY AND PALACE OF HOLYROODHOUSE (BY)

tc At the east end of the Royal Mile stands the Palace of Holyroodhouse, the Queen's official residence in Scotland, adjoined by the ruined nave of the abbey. In the background are the green slopes and rocky crags of Holyrood Park rising to Arthur's Seat.

The Holy Rood. – Legend has it that **David I**, while out hunting, was thrown from his mount and wounded by a stag. In a defensive gesture he made to grasp the animal's antlers only to find he was holding a crucifix, the animal having made off into the forest. In recognition David founded the Augustinian Abbey of Holy Rood in 1128 and granted to the canons the right to their own burgh, Canongate.

The medieval abbey prospered and benefited from royal patronage in the 15C from the Stewart Kings. James II was born, married and buried here and broke with the Scone tradition to be crowned here. His three successors were all married here. It was during this period that the guest house was used as a royal residence in preference to the castle. James IV intent on making Edinburgh his capital started transforming the guest house accommodation into a palace by building the present northwest tower.

Work continued after his death at Flodden (1513). The abbey buildings suffered damage in 1544, were despoiled at the Reformation and burnt in 1650 when Cromwell's troops were quartered there. A moment of glory in the interval was the coronation of Charles I in 1633. From then on the nave served as parish church for the Canongate until 1688, when the congregation was dislodged by James VII who intended converting it into a Chapel Royal and the headquarters of the Order of the Thistle.

Royal palace. – Although Charles II never set foot in the palace he commissioned **Sir William Bruce** (1630-1710) the Architect Royal to draw up designs. The architect had been instrumental – acting as an envoy – in Charles II's restoration. Bruce may have been influenced by designs for Whitehall done by Inigo Jones, as the final result is a handsome example of the Palladian style.

Bruce and his master mason **Robert Mylne** (1633-1710), created a masterpiece of elegance, particularly in the courtyard elevations. They cleverly retained the 16C northwest tower counterbalancing it with a second.

Royal residents. – Following Mary Queen of Scots six year stay, the next royal occupant was James Duke of York (future James VII) from 1679 to 1682 in his capacity as Commissioner for his brother Charles II. With Bonnie Prince Charlie there was a brief period of royal receptions when he made Holyroodhouse his headquarters prior to his ultimate defeat at Culloden. George IV held a levee in 1822 and there were two periods of occupation by a French royal, firstly as Comte d'Artois having fled the Revolution and secondly as the exiled Charles X after his abdication in 1830. Since the reign of Queen Victoria the palace has again been favoured as a royal residence.

THE PALACE *time : 1 hour*

Exterior. – The fountain is a 19C copy of the Linlithgow one. The entrance front was the last part of the palace to be rebuilt as it had originally been intended to retain the front built by James IV. Counterbalancing the towers is the elaborate entrance. Flanked by columns, the door is surmounted by carved stonework incorporating the Scottish coat of arms (note the unicorn supporters), a broken pediment, a cupola and crown. The inner court elevations are an outstanding example of classic Renaissance of the Stuart Period and one of Scotland's earliest examples. The superimposed orders, general proportions, arcades and pediment are applied in the purest classical manner achieving a composition of restraint, symmetry and elegance.

Interior. – The decoration of the State Apartments remains lavish as designed by Sir William Bruce in true Restoration style. Highly intricate decorative plasterwork ceilings, lavishly carved woodwork (doors, doorcases, picture frames and swags) and inset canvases were all integral parts of the decor and all of a very high standard of craftsmanship. The seven outstanding **plasterwork ceilings★★★** in high relief represent 10 years labour by the "gentlemen modellers" **John Halbert** and **George Dunsterfield**. These craftsmen had previously worked at Ham House, the London home of the Lauderdales *(p 146)* patrons and relatives of Bruce, and at Windsor for Charles II.

The impressive Grand Staircase leads up past Her Majesty's portrait by Her Limner, David Donaldson. Other than the ceilings the most notable features of the **State Apartments** are : in the Adam style Dining Room *A Highland Chieftain (c*1680) by John Michael Wright, contemporary of Lely the pre-eminent Restoration painter. It is interesting as a costume piece. In the Throne Room, redecorated in the 1920s, are royal portraits of *George IV in Highland Dress* by Wilkie, the brothers Charles II and James VII, the palace's first royal guest, with their respective queens. Carved door surrounds and 18C Brussels tapestries can be seen in the Evening Drawing Room. Finest of all is the Morning Drawing Room sumptuously decorated with a Jacob de Wet medallion above the fireplace and 17C French tapestries. The King's Suite was on the east side, overlooking the famous Privy Garden of formal design on the site of the demolished cloister.

In the King's Chamber is a magnificent Red Bed (1672) and ceiling with a de Wet medallion resembling the one in the Vine Room at Kellie Castle. Note the pairs of animals 'looking down'. The Gallery walls are lined with many imaginary and a few real portraits of Scottish Kings from 6C Fergus to James VII. Jacob de Wet completed the portraits in two years.

The **Historic Apartments** in the 16C round tower consist of similar suites on two floors. These were refurbished *c*1672 when floor and ceiling levels were adjusted to correspond to the Bruce additions. There are many Mary Queen of Scots associations. The lobby has 17C Mortlake tapestries from the workshop founded by her son James VI. Upstairs are two exquisite **16C coffered ceilings** the first adorned with painted designs. The small chamber adjoining the Bedchamber is closely associated with the murder of Mary's Italian secretary, Rizzio in 1566. His body was found in the outer chamber (brass plaque marks the spot). Paintings depict Mary's 2nd husband **Henry Lord Darnley** (1546-67) as a 17 year old youth with his brother. A second work shows his mourning family, including his son James VI, after Darnley's murder at Kirk o'Field. On the way downstairs note Medina's portrait of the palace architect, Sir William Bruce.

THE ABBEY *time : 1/4 hour*

tc The roofless nave is all that remains of this once great abbey. Dating mainly from the late 12C and early 13C there are some finely sculpted details. Compare the interlaced round headed blind arcading of the 12C in the north aisle with the pointed 13C work opposite. The south elevation is an attractive fragment of 13C design. Queen Victoria rebuilt the royal burial vault following its destruction on the departure of the Roman Catholic James VII. The remains of David II, James II, James V and Lord Darnley are interred here.

Of the west front the remaining flanking tower, recessed pointed doorway and different levels of arcading give some impression of what the whole must have looked like. Note the medallion portraits.

HOLYROOD PARK

Holyrood Park the largest area of open ground within the city is dominated by Arthur's Seat (823ft-251m) and the Salisbury Crags, both volcanic features. It was the 18C geologist **James Hutton** who gleaned evidence from the immense sill to support his theory of magmatic intrusion. A path from the car park on the Queen's Road, within the park, leads up to **Arthur's Seat** *(time : 1/2 hour)* which affords a tremendous **panorama★★** of the Edinburgh area.

Beyond Dunsapie lies the charming village of **Duddingston** in an attractive setting between park and loch (bird sanctuary). The 12C church has some good Norman features. The Rev Thomson, landscape artist, named his studio Edinburgh so that in the case of an unwanted interruption the reply was always 'the Reverend was in Edinburgh'. Bonnie Prince Charlie spent the night here prior to his victory at the Battle of Prestonpans.

★★ROYAL MILE from Castle to Palace

time : allow a day including castle and palace

The principal thoroughfare of the Old Town runs from the castle, in its strategic site, down the ridge to the abbey and palace. The Royal Mile is in fact a succession of four streets, Castle Hill, the Lawnmarket, the High Street and the Canongate. Daniel Defoe wrote in the early 18C, "this is, perhaps, the largest, longest, and finest street for buildings and number of inhabitants, not in Britain only, but in the world". Although blighted in places by dereliction and renewal, the few original buildings which remain give some idea of what medieval Edinburgh must have looked like.

Plaques on the pends record the famous and infamous occupants and historic events associated with the closes.

Ramsay Gardens on the left incorporate **Ramsay Lodge (BY A)** built in the 18C by the poet Allan Ramsay (1686-1758), father of the portrait painter of the same name *(p 194)*.

tc **Outlook Tower and Camera Obscura (BY B)**. – From its rooftop position in the Outlook Tower the **camera obscura** presents a fascinating view of the city. Exhibitions on the intermediate floors deal with holography, pin-hole photography and space photography.

The Church of Scotland General Assembly Hall (**BY D**) stands on the site of what was Mary of Guise's Palace (destroyed 1861).

Enter Mylne's Court (**BY 40**), a 1970s reconstruction, to have some idea of what a court looked like once a narrow burgess strip had been built over. The narrow approach passages from the main street are known as closes or wynds with a pend at the entrance.

★**Gladstone's Land (BY)**. – This narrow
tc six storey tenement (land) is typical of 17C Edinburgh when all building was upwards. The property was acquired in 1617 by a merchant burgess, Thomas Gledstanes who rebuilt and extended out towards the street. Fully restored by the National Trust for Scotland, the premises behind the pavement arcade, as in the past, are arranged as a shop with living quarters on the other floors. The first floor is a good example of a 17C town house. Of particular note are the original gaily **painted ceilings** *(p 24)* and fine pieces of 17C furniture : carved Scottish bed and Dutch chests.

(After National Trust for Scotland Photo)
Gladstone's Land

tc **Lady Stair's House (BY M¹)**. – *Down the close of the same name.*
Built in 1622, this town house takes its name from an occupant of the late 18C, the widow of John Dalrymple, 1st Earl of Stair. Much altered internally the house is used to display mss, relics and other memorabilia of three of Scotland's greatest literary figures Robert Burns (1759-96), Sir Walter Scott (1771-1832) and R. L. Stevenson (1850-94).

In Riddle's Court (**BYZ 47**) go through to the second courtyard which is overlooked on the south side by Bailie MacMorran's House (**BYZ E**). It was here that the burgesses of Edinburgh laid on a banquet in 1598 for James VI and Anne of Denmark.

★★**St Giles' Cathedral (BY)**. – The present High Kirk of Edinburgh is probably the 3rd
tc church on this site. The first dating from the 9C was replaced by a Norman structure in 1126 of which remain the four piers supporting the tower. This was burnt down by the English in 1385 following which the present building was raised. Alterations and restorations have radically changed the character of the 15C church. The Reformation brought troubled times to St Giles, when the many altars and idols, including the precious relic and statue of St Giles, were swept away, the latter into the Nor'Loch. For a short spell Catholic clergy and the Lords of the Congregation shared the church before the return of **Knox** as minister in 1560. Shortly after began his period of confrontation with Mary Queen of Scots. As the capital's principal church it served

as meeting place for Parliament and the General Assembly and witnessed many great state occasions such as James VI's farewell to his Scottish subjects and over 200 years later, George IV's 1822 state visit.

The Jenny Geddes stool throwing incident, although much disputed historically, preceded the signing of the National Covenant *(p 94, see the Linlithgow copy in the Chepman Aisle)* and the ensuing religious strife. At this time, during Episcopacy, the church enjoyed a brief spell of cathedral status (1637-88).

Exterior. – Seen from the west the church is dominated by the square tower raising aloft the delicate **crown spire★★★** (1495) a most distinctive feature of Edinburgh's skyline. The imperial, or eight arched design, differentiates it from that of King's College, Aberdeen. The

Parliament Square

Thistle Chapel

CHANCEL

Preston Aisle

Chapel of Youth

Chepman Aisle

High Street

Royal Mile

□ TRANSEPT

Organ

St Eloi's Chapel

Moray Aisle

NAVE

Albany Aisle

Bookshop

Parliament Square

ST GILES

0 1   5 m
         20 feet

church's exterior lost much of its original character when it was entirely refaced during a 19C restoration.

Interior. – The original cruciform shape has been lost with the addition of laird's aisles and side chapels. Although spared the systematic restoration of the exterior, details, and in particular monuments, provide the main points of interest inside.

Start in the northwest corner and move in a clockwise direction.

The flowing style and strong glowing colours of the north aisle window (1) characterize the work of the Pre-Raphaelites, Burne-Jones and William Morris. The Albany Aisle with its Gothic vaulting was built in expiation for the murder of the Duke of Rothesay *(p 105)* in 1402. The bay beyond contains the imposing 19C marble monument (2) to the 8th Earl and 1st Marquess of Argyll (1607-61) who was executed at the mercat cross only days after the body of his arch rival the Marquess of Montrose had been rehabilitated and interred on the far side of the church. The heraldic window decorated with coats of arms of leading Covenanters is a reminder of the earl's Covenanting beliefs. Move back into the transept crossing to admire Douglas Strachan's great north window (3) a glow of blue above the carved stone screen. From here also admire the attractive 15C rib and groin vaulting of the chancel and compare it with that of the nave which is slightly later.

In the southeast corner stands Pittendrigh MacGillivray's statue of **John Knox** (1512-72) (4) reformer and minister of St Giles. In 1911 Robert Lorimer designed the **Thistle Chapel** in the Flamboyant Gothic style for the most Noble Order of the Thistle founded by James VII in 1687. Some claim it was a revival of an even older foundation. Under a fan vaulted ceiling and its multitude of carved bosses, some tinctured and many heraldic, are the richly carved stalls and canopies for the sovereign and 16 knights. It is a lavishly impressive display of 20C craftsmanship. Above are helmets, crests and banners with knights' arms on the stall backs.

Beyond the Preston Aisle with the royal pew (5) is the side chapel known as the Chepman Aisle in memory of the man who introduced printing into Scotland in the reign of James IV (1488-1513). The aisle is the final resting place of the **Marquess of Montrose** (1612-50) (6) Covenanter turned Royalist whose fame rests on his brilliant 1644-5 campaign. He suffered an ignomious fate at the hands of his protagonist Argyll. The Restoration meant rehabilitation for Montrose and a traitor's execution for Argyll. The bay beyond the organ has a 19C marble monument (7) to James Stewart, Earl of Moray (1531-70) with an original 16C brass. Half-brother to Mary Queen of Scots and Regent for her son, Moray was murdered in Linlithgow *(qv)* in 1570. The Noel Paton window (8) relates the tale and shows Knox preaching at the funeral service of one of his strongest supporters.

The low relief (9) at the end of the Moray Aisle portrays Robert Louis Stevenson (1850-94) offspring of a family of engineers who achieved fame as an author.

The imposing buildings overlooking West Parliament Square are The Lothian Regional Chambers (**BY C**) (1816-8) by Robert Reid of New Town fame, adjoined by the slightly earlier Signet Library (1810-2). Near the Boehm statue of the 5th Duke of Buccleuch in Garter Robes is a heart shape set into the cobbles. This marks the site of the old tolbooth (1466-1817) made famous by Scott in *The Heart of Midlothian*. United under one roof were council room, court house and prison until 1817 when all was swept away. The later day successors, Parliament Hall, Sheriff Court and City Chambers all stand nearby.

tc **Parliament Hall** (BYZ).
– Behind the imposing Georgian facade is the 17C Parliament Hall decreed by Charles I and designed by his master mason **John Mylne.** Where the Scottish Parliament met from 1639 to 1707 lawyers now pace under the carved and gilded **hammerbeam roof** and the gaze of their august predecessors : Duncan Forbes (Roubiliac) ; Sir Adam Cockburn (Brodie) ; Scott ; 1st Viscount Melville (Chantrey) and his nephew, Robert Dundas (also Chantrey) ; Viscount Stair (Aikman) author of *Stairs Institutes* (1681) and his contemporary Sir George Mackenzie, known as "Bluidy Mackenzie" in Covenanting history, but best remembered for his standard work on Scottish law and as founder of the Advocate's Library, today Scotland's National Library ; and Lord Monbuddo that 18C eccentric.

It was Lord Cockburn who said 'The old building exhibited some respectable turrets, some ornamental windows and doors and a handsome balustrade'. The great stained glass window depicts the inauguration of the College of Justice. In the foreground is the Lord Chancellor Gavin Dunbar with Alexander Mylne, Abbot of Cambuskenneth and the first President with the Papal Bull before James V and his assembled court.

This part of Parliament Square to the south of St Giles is dominated by Edinburgh's oldest statue, an equestrian one of the Merry Monarch (1685). Further round at the east end is the **mercat cross**, the onetime hub of Edinburgh life. This was where merchants and traders congregated to transact business and was also the scene of celebrations, demonstrations, executions and royal proclamations. The present 19C structure incorporates the shaft of the 16C cross.

City Chambers (BY H). – The Royal Exchange was built in 1753 to replace the mercat cross as a meeting place. It now houses the administrative services of Edinburgh District Council. The front, facing Cockburn Street, is eleven storeys high. The screen at pavement level shelters the City's Stone of Remembrance.

★Wax Museum (BY M²). – The museum with its collection of over 150 wax figures
tc occupies the 1766 New Assembly Rooms. Here one can meet Scotland's famous figures from all walks of life, relive dramatic historical moments and be beguiled by well loved characters in Never Never Land... from Mr Toad, natty in goggles and gaiters, to Peter Pan and Peter Rabbit.

The first edition of *Encyclopaedia Britannica* was printed between 1768-71 in Anchor Close (BY 2). The original compilers were William Smellie, Colin Macfarquhar and Andrew Bell and their solution became the model for later English language encyclopaedias. The *Encyclopaedia Britannica* still bears a thistle on the covers.

Tron Kirk (BY). – John Mylne built this church prior to undertaking Parliament Hall. The spire is a 19C replacement. This is the traditional gathering place of Hogmanay revellers.

EDINBURGH

tc **Museum of Childhood (BY M³).** – Anything and everything to do with childhood is the theme of this unique museum. Displays include toys, costumes, books, dolls and games. Children discover while parents reminisce.

Across the street 15C Mowbray House (**BY F**) was the studio of the portraitist **George Jamesone** (1588-1644).

tc **John Knox House (BY G).** – This picturesque town house was probably built prior to 1490. The armorial panel on the west wall is that of the goldsmith, James Mossman, whose father was responsible for redesigning the Scottish crown. The **John Knox** connection is now much contested but the house and its exhibits provide an insight into the man, his beliefs and Scotland during the Reformation. The main room on the second floor has a painted ceiling (1600).

The junction with St Mary's and Jeffrey Streets marks the site of the Netherbow Port. The gateway was demolished in 1764. Beyond was the independent burgh of **Canongate** (**BY**) (gait or way of the canons) where the nobility, ambassadors and other royal officers built residences in close proximity to the royal palace of Holyroodhouse. Few of these mansions remain.

The gateway with pyramidal posts and adjoining gable ended building with first floor balcony are all that remain of **Moray House (BY J)**, now better known as a College of Education. Tradition has it rightly or wrongly, that it was in the summer house of this residence that the Treaty of Union of 1707 was signed.

tc **★Canongate Tolbooth (BY)**. – Tolbooth for the independent burgh of Canongate, this building with its turreted steeple was built in 1591 and is a good example of 16C architecture. The original council chamber on the first floor has a tartan collection or temporary exhibitions. Below in the former cell area is a **Brass Rubbing Centre.**

Canongate Church (BY). – This church was built in 1688 for the displaced congregation of Holyrood Abbey when James VII decided to convert the nave into a Chapel Royal for the most Ancient Order of The Thistle. Above the curvilinear south front is a stag's head bearing a cross, a reminder of the founding legend of Holyrood Abbey. Inside, the royal pew and those of officers of the Royal Household are indicated by coats of arms. Interesting memorials in the churchyard include that of Adam Smith and the young Edinburgh poet Robert Fergusson, whose tombstone was paid for by Burns. Another Burns connection is the plaque to Clarinda (east wall).

tc **Huntly House (BY M⁴)**. – These three 16C mansions now contain the main city museum of local history. Some of the rooms (9-11) have 18C Memel panelling. The Edinburgh silver collection (9-10) contains some particularly fine 18C pieces. The museum has an original parchment of the National Covenant.

tc **Acheson House (BY)**. – This 17C courtyard mansion now serves as Scottish Craft Centre and showcase for the works of contemporary Scottish craftsmen.

SOUTH OF THE ROYAL MILE
Royal Mile to George Heriot's School

★Victoria Street (BZ 57). – Descending in a curve to the Grassmarket this street is lined with an attractive series of boutiques. At the bottom on the left **The Traverse Theatre Club (BZ T¹)** has won a reputation for experimental drama in an intimate atmosphere.

Grassmarket (BZ). – The railed enclosure marks the site of the gallows where Captain Porteous was hanged (1736) and over a hundred Covenanters were martyred. At the southwest corner West Port (**AZ**) marks the city's western gate. It was from a close nearby that the bodysnatchers Burke and Hare operated.

Cowgate (BZ). – Although outside the original town wall this was a fashionable quarter in the 16C. It is now a forlorn underpass.
Curving upwards Candlemaker Row (**BZ 9**) rejoins George IV Bridge, passing the **statue** of Greyfriars Bobby on the left, at the top.

tc **Greyfriars Church and Churchyard (BZ)**. – The 1612 church built on the site of a 15C Franciscan friary has been much altered. The church is known in history as the place where the **National Covenant** (1638) was signed. The churchyard memorials include the Martyrs Monument (northeast wall) to the Covenanters taken at Bothwell Brig (1679) and imprisoned here for five months and the grave over which the faithful Skye terrier stood watch for fourteen years.

Take Forrest Road to Lauriston Place. During the daytime when the gate is open the churchyard extension offers a short cut to George Heriot's.

George Heriot's School (BZ). – *Walk round the outside and into the courtyard.*
This great Edinburgh school was endowed by **George Heriot** (1563-1624) goldsmith to James VI who nicknamed him "Jinglin Geordie". On his death Heriot bequeathed the fortune he had made in London to the city fathers, for the education of "fatherless bairns of Edinburgh freemen". Construction was begun by William Wallace in 1628 but completion was delayed until 1659 when used as a hospital by Cromwell's troops. The symmetrical courtyard building is a good example of an early Renaissance building with abundant decorative stone carving and strapwork. The clock tower and statue of Geordie overlooking the courtyard are the work of Robert Mylne (1693).

A fragment of the **Flodden Wall (BZ)** can be seen to the west of the school, at the head of the Vennel. Opposite is the 1879 Royal Infirmary.

To reach George Square take Meadow Walk past Rowand Anderson's Medical School (BZ U¹).

UNIVERSITY CAMPUS
George Square to Chambers Street

George Square (BZ). – Laid out in the 1760s this was the first major residential development outside the Old Town. Distinguished residents included Scott (no 25 west side) and the Duchess of Gordon. The west side is the only complete example of the vernacular classical style. The remaining sides are occupied by the university : library (**BZ U²** 1967) by Basil Spence ; David Hume Tower (**BZ U³** 1963) for the Faculty of Social Sciences and the Science Faculty in Appleton Tower (**BZ U⁴** 1966).

The Meadows (AB Z). – Beyond the Royalty this once fashionable place of promenade was part of the Burgh Muir. Here Scottish armies rallied and the town council held wappinschaws where arms were paraded.
Leave by Charles Street. The round building on the far side of the pedestrian precinct, Bristo Square is Rowand Anderson's Victorian McEwan Hall (**BZ U⁵**). The Student Centre (**BZ U⁶**) is the home of the Fringe Club during the Festival.

Old University (BZ). – The Old College was founded in 1581 and occupied premises within Kirk o'Field Collegiate Church (f 1450) outside the city walls. It was here that Lord Darnley met his death. In 1789 **Robert Adam** provided a grandiose design for a double courtyard building. Only the main front with impressive entrance overlooking South Bridge is his work. Playfair modified the design to one courtyard and completed the surrounding ranges. The **Talbot Rice Art Gallery** *(enter from southwest corner, first floor)* occupies Playfair's Georgian gallery, the original home of the Industrial Museum. *(p 95)*. The permanent Torrie Collection alternates with travelling exhibitions.

Chambers Street (BZ 12). – Mid-Victorian slum clearance at the instigation of Lord Provost Chambers obliterated Adam, Argyle and Brown Squares, when South Bridge and George IV Bridge were linked by this splendid thoroughfare. The north range of Old College and the Royal Scottish Museum occupy the south side. Opposite is the Adam Theatre (BZ T²), followed by the University Staff Club (nos 9-15 – BZ U⁷) remodelled in the 1950s by Basil Spence. The latter houses the Festival Club. Beyond is **Heriot Watt University** (no 23 – BZ). The original institute was founded in 1821 and renamed as a memorial to James Watt. With the demolition of Adam Square the institute took up premises at no 23. A second name change followed in 1885, Heriot Watt College, with a status change to that of university in 1965. The campus is at Riccarton Estate, south of the city limits.

★★Royal Scottish Museum (BZ). – One of the legacies of the 1851 Great Exhibition
tc was the proliferation of many museums and art galleries throughout Britain. Funds were allocated to Edinburgh in 1854 for the foundation of the Industrial Museum. Capt Fowke R.E. of Albert Hall fame designed the building. The elaborate Venetian Renaissance style façade contrasts with the interior, in particular the **Main Hall** so spacious and full of light. It is a masterpiece of Victorian cast iron and plate glass construction. The museum was renamed on two occasions due to the increasing variety of the collections. Both the arts and sciences are covered. Working models, recorded commentaries and push buttons add to the fun. All the galleries are numbered. The lefthand column gives the contents while the righthand one highlights important items or special displays.

Ground Floor

Asiatic sculpture; publications (Main Hall 1, 3, 4) Early power (20) Power and Transport (21)

Industrial water wheel (1862); Wylam Dilly (1813); Stephenson's Rocket and Locomotion (models); Pilcher's Hawk Glider; James Watt and steam engine.

Shipping (22): sail and steam to nuclear power; clipper ships of China Tea Trade; Scottish fishing craft

Great Michael (1513) A'Bataviase Eeuw (1719); Cutty Sark; Fifie, Zulu and Skaffie

Victorian Engineering (18): harnessing of steam, steamships, railways and steam power

Portable steam engine

British Birds (13) and Animals (12) Mammals (10, 11 and 8) Evolution (7): exhibition on five floors on vertebrate evolution.

Methods of taxidermy; 78ft long Blue Whale Skeleton Physical Background of Life (1); Fishes and Amphibians (2), Reptiles (level 3), Mammals (4)

First Floor

Evolution: New Mineral Hall; Foreign Birds (8); Fish (11); Biology (10); Children's Nature Gallery (13); Insects (12)

Moa (extinct); seashore diorama (13)

European sculpture decorative arts (2) Costume and textiles (17, 18) Coins Navigation and Bridges (22)

Closed Constantly changing displays Closed The Bell Rock and Eddystone Lighthouses (models)

Timepieces, weights and measures (21) Ancient Egypt (20) European decorative arts: art and sculpture (3, 6); arms and armour (5); metalwork (4).

Dioramas of Egyptian life 16C German altarpiece; Fountaine Sword; Lennoxlove Toilet Service

Second Floor

Chinese Art (3): porcelain, bronzes
European glass and ceramics (2)
Middle and Far Eastern Art (4)
Minerals and Gems (7)
Scottish Minerals (8)
Osteology (9); Fossils (10); Geology (11); Zoology (12); Invertebrates (13)
Modern Life (21)
Primitive Art of Africa, the Pacific and North America (20).

★★NEW TOWN 1767-1830

When the decision had been taken to extend the Royalty of Edinburgh, the competition organized and won by an unknown architect, **James Craig** (*c*1740-95) and the North Bridge was thrown across the valley, the development of Edinburgh's New Town proceeded apace. Entirely residential at the outstart – business and commerce were to remain in the Old Town centred on the Royal Exchange – the winning plan had a gridiron layout in which vistas and focal points played an important role. The plan was adhered to, giving a succession of splendid squares and elegant streets. Initially strict architectural uniformity was lacking, although by 1782 a series of regulations had been established concerning the number of storeys, width of façade... The success was immediate and people were quick to follow the example of Hume and Lord Cockburn in taking up residence.

Development continued with a variety of extensions, notably to the north with the Second New Town, northwest with the Moray Estate and also the west and east. The New Town with its unique quality, its many gardens and green spaces, is one of the finest town planning ventures. The guardian of the 766 acres of the splendours of Georgian Edinburgh is the **New Town Conservation Committee** (*13A Dundas Street* – AY **21**). When exploring Georgian Edinburgh look for the many decorative details which give the New Town so much of its character. The cast iron work In particular shows great variety of design (Heriot Row and Abercromby Place). Stretches of balcony spanning the frontages (Windsor Street and Atholl Crescent) alternate with window guards ; the serried ranks of railings crested with finials are punctuated by lamp standards, brackets and extinguishers or link horns (Charlotte Square, York Place and Melville Street).

Charlotte Square to the east end of Princes Street

★★★**Charlotte Square** (AY). – Following allegations of piecemeal development of the New Town scheme in its early stages, **Robert Adam** was commissioned in 1971 to design what is now the New Town's most splendid square. Elegant frontages of a unified design frame the garden with a central equestrian statue of **Prince Albert** by Steell. The **north side** is a grand civic achievement where the vertical lines of the advanced central and end blocks are counterbalanced by the rusticated ground floor. The lines of straight headed windows, round headed doorway fanlights and occasional Venetian windows are happily juxtapositioned. Note the wrought iron railings, lamp holders, extinguishers and foot scrapers. The centrepiece (AY K) comprises the headquarters of the National Trust for Scotland (no 5), Bute House (no 6) the official residence of the Secretary of State for Scotland and no 7, **The Georgian House**★. The lower floors have been entirely refurbished by the NTS as a typical Georgian home of the period 1790 to 1810. Some of the delights include the cheese waggon, rare wine rinsing glasses, lovely Scottish sideboard, moreen hangings, tea table and well equipped kitchen and wine cellar. An introduction to Georgian Edinburgh is provided in one of the basement rooms *(12 minute tape and slide programme)*.

(BTA)

Charlotte Square – north side

On the west side, St George's Church (1811-4) by Robert Reid provides the focal point for George Street and is now converted into the Scottish Record Office annexe, **West Register House** (AY L). There is a permanent historical exhibition inside.
Famous residents included Lord Cockburn at no 14, Lord Lister (no 9) and Douglas Haig (no 24).

George Street (AB Y). – The principal street of Craig's plan is closed at either end by Charlotte and St Andrew Squares. Half a mile in length and 115ft wide, many of the houses of this originally residential street are now converted into banks, offices and shops. Statues punctuate the street intersections – Dr Chalmers by Steell at Castle Street ; Pitt by Chantrey at Frederick Street and George IV also by Chantrey at Hanover Street – each of which have good views away to the Forth or down to Princes Street Gardens with the Castle and Old Town as backdrop. Note in particular the **view** surveyed by George IV from his pedestal, with the successive landmarks perfectly positioned : Royal Scottish Academy, National Gallery, Assembly Hall and spire of the Tolbooth Kirk.
Towards the east end are the **Assembly Rooms** (no 54 - AY) built in 1784. The pedimented portico was a later addition, Edinburgh's fifth such institution, but the first in the New Town. Paradoxically it was the more spacious apartments of the New Town dwellings which caused the demise of the rooms as a centre for regular social gatherings. Started in 1784 they were opened 3 years later during Burns' first visit to the capital. It was here that Scott proclaimed his authorship of the *Waverley Novels*. This fine suite of rooms, with the Music Hall behind, is a magnificent setting for public functions.
St Andrew and St George Church (BY) (1785) with its towering spire was intended to close the George Street vista at the St Andrew Square end, but Dundas beat the planners to it. The church was the scene of the 1843 Disruption when a group of ministers led by Dr Chalmers walked out of the church over the issue of patronage, and formed the Free Church of Scotland.

Queen Street Museums (BY M⁵). – In the best Victorian tradition a munificent donation by the proprietor of *The Scotsman* provided a building for the illustration of Scottish history. Rowand Anderson designed an Italianate Gothic, statue decorated building to house the portrait collection founded in 1882. In 1890-1 the Antiquarian Society moved in from its premises in the Mound.

★National Portrait Gallery. – *To the right of the entrance hall*. The initial aim was to "illustrate
tc Scottish history by likeness of the chief actors in it". Notwithstanding, many of the
portraits of persons of historic interest are masterpieces of portraiture. Scottish
exponents of this tradition include the 16C George Jamesone *(self-portrait)*, John
Michael Wright, the 18C masters, Ramsay *(David Hume* the companion portrait to the
one of J. J. Rousseau) and Raeburn *(Scott)*. In addition there are canvases by Wissing,
Lely, Gainsborough, Lawrence... Some of the chief actors portrayed are royalty *(Mary
Queen of Scots, Lord Darnley, James VI, Charles I, Elizabeth of Bohemia and James
VII)* ; statesmen formal and fine *(1st Earl of Dunfermline and Duke of Lauderdale)* ;
18 to 19C politicians *(Kier Hardie, Ramsay MacDonald* and *W.E. Gladstone)* ; literary
figures *(Drummond of Hawthornden, Burns, Scott, Byron, Carlyle, Stevenson and
Barrie)*.

★★National Museum of Antiquities of Scotland. – *To the left of entrance hall*. The museum was
tc originally founded in 1780 to show the whole history of Scottish life and culture. There
is a strong emphasis on archaeology.

Ground floor : Historical Gallery and Dark Age Sculpture. – The **Dark Age Sculpture Collection**
(AD 650-900) astonishes for the vigour and artistic quality of such early works, unique
to Scotland. Of the Pictish Symbol Stones no 25 displays symbols and three
magnificent warriors while no 18 is one of the Burghead bulls. Next chronologically
are the Anglian sculptured crosses more completely covered with carving like no 28
with its decorative borders, symbols and hunting scene. Displayed in the following
bay are the early 16C delicately carved low relief Montrose panels, which formed part
of Patrick Paniter's (James IV's Secretary) pew. Compare with the three Stirling Head
medallions *(p 188)* also 16C which hang on the entrance wall. Note in case 7 the
famous **Monymusk Reliquary** which was borne into battle with the Scottish army, while
alongside are the most delicately worked 14C **St Fillian's Crozier** and 9C Bell. Beyond
are the Highland Arms and Armour - note the Doune pistols *(qv)* cases 30 and 31 - a
collection of 16-19C Scottish silver representing Edinburgh and other areas and a
small costume section at the far end. In the main part is the 1561 *Maiden*, an early
version of the guillotine, as well as collections of coins, communion tokens and
beggars' badges.

First floor : Prehistoric and Viking Antiquities. – The displays include finds from such
well-known sites as the Neolithic settlement of Skara Brae submerged by windblown
sand some 4500 years ago, and Jarlshof which was continuously occupied from
Bronze Age times to the 17C. Treasures include splendid silverware such as the Pictish
pieces from St Ninian's Isle, the 8C Hunterston Brooch and the Viking Skaill hoard.

Second floor : Romans in Scotland. – This attractive display touches on all aspects of
Roman life and demonstrates the high level of skills and organization. Note the
refinement of the silver pieces of the 5C Traprain Treasure.

St Andrew Square (BY). – Here **Henry Dundas**, Viscount Melville, better known as King
Harry the Ninth for his management of Scottish affairs between 1782 and 1805, still
dominates from his 150ft high fluted column. The square, the home of banks and
insurance companies, has none of the unified elegance of its counterpart, Charlotte
Square, but has individual buildings of charm and splendour. On the north side nos
21 to 26 are examples of the vernacular classical style of the first phase of New Town
development.

Buchan House (nos 21, 22 – **BY**) perpetuates the name of the eccentric 11th Earl of
Buchan (1742-1829), founder of the Society of Antiquaries and regular correspondent
of George III whom he addressed as Cousin.

No 26 (BY N), with its elegant touches, was by Adam's chief rival Sir William Chambers
who was also responsible for the magnificent mansion on the east side. **Dundas House★**
(BY) was built 1772-4 for Sir Laurence Dundas on what was originally intended to
be a church site. Well set back, this three storey mansion is adorned with a projecting
three bay pilastered, emblazoned, pedimented central section and an attractive frieze
at roof level. Step inside to see the splendours of the original entrance hall where
capitals and roof bosses are highlighted in gold leaf. The building was purchased by
the Royal Bank of Scotland in 1825 and the domed banking hall was added in 1858.
In front of the bank stands the soldier 4th Earl of Hopetoun and his horse. Of the two
symmetrical pavilions flanking the mansion, no 35 to the north, was on its building
in 1768, the earliest house in the square. The facade of no 38, another bank, is
strikingly ornate with Corinthian columns rising through two floors and each crowned
by a statue. The philosopher David Hume (1711-76) was among the first of Edinburgh's
notables to move in 1771 to a New Town house in St David Street, named after him.
West Register Street leads past the literary pub **Café Royal (BY)** with its oyster bar, to
New Register House (BY P) fronted by fine wrought iron gates and crowned gateposts,
indicating the offices of the Court of Lord Lyon with his Heralds and Pursuivants.
The Lord Lyon King of Arms regulates all Scottish armorial matters, adjudicates upon
Chiefship of clans, conducts and executes Royal Proclamations and state and public
ceremonials of all descriptions in Scotland.

The east end of Princes Street is now dominated by Robert Adam's splendid frontage
tc of **General Register House (BY Q)** (1774-1822) headquarters of the Scottish Record Office.
With the projecting pedimented portico and end pavilions crowned by cupolas it makes
a suitably gracious focal point for North Bridge. Changing exhibitions in the front hall.
Look through into the splendid domed hall with its characteristic Adam motifs.

At pavement level Steell's equestrian **statue of Wellington** shows him astride a Buccleuch
stand in and not Copenhagen.

The **General Post Office (BY)** stands on the site of the Theatre Royal built in 1768, as
one of the first buildings in the New Town development. During its heyday when Scott
was a trustee, famous names such as Sarah Siddons and John Kemble performed
here. The theatre closed in 1859 and was burnt down in 1946. Opposite is the North
British (BY) with its famous clock tower landmark, and clock reputedly two minutes
fast.

PRINCES STREET AND GARDENS

Princes Street (ABY). – Edinburgh's prime shopping street was originally totally residential. Single sided the street marked the southern extension of the New Town. The 1770s town houses were modest but appreciated for the open view across the valley, which later became a private garden for residents. Following the laying of the railway 1845-6 commercial development slowly took over. Today Victorian and modern shops and hotels stand side by side. A few like Jenners are a reminder of the opulent emporiums and establishments that once lined the street.

Princes Street Gardens (ABY). – The Nor'Loch Valley was infilled during New Town excavation work and later laid out as private gardens for residents. Lord Cockburn was the instigator of the Act of Parliament which safeguarded the south side of Princes Street from further development. With the coming of the railways, shops and hotels replaced houses and in 1876 the gardens were opened to the public. Today the gardens with their greenery, welcome benches and many monuments provide a pleasant respite from the milling crowd in Princes Street.

★**Scott Monument** (BY). – This pinnacled monument dominating Princes Street is one of
tc Edinburgh's most familiar landmarks. Following Scott's death in 1832 a successful public appeal was launched. Much controversy ensued as to the site and nature of the monument, however the foundation stone was laid in 1840. The 200ft tall neo-Gothic spire was designed by a joiner and draughtsman, **George Meikle Kemp,** who died before its completion. Steell's Carrara marble statue of Scott and Maida is accompanied by 64 statuettes of characters from his novels (in the niches) and the heads of 16 Scottish poets (on the capitals). The monument immediately became a major attraction. For the agile four viewing platforms *(287 steps to the top by narrow stairs)* give good **views★** of central Edinburgh. The small first floor room has a display on the designer and the construction.

Dividing Princes Street Gardens into East and West, are two imposing classical buildings on the left the National Gallery and the Royal Scottish Academy.

★★★**National Gallery of Scotland** (BY). – The nucleus of the Gallery's work was formed
tc by the Royal Institution's collection, later expanded by bequests and purchasing. To house the works Playfair designed (1850-7) the imposing classical building we see today.

The permanent display of European painting, exhibited in chronological order, presents a number of first class works. The underground wing groups Scottish art from 1600 to 1900.

> *Start your visit to the gallery with the Eye Opener (gallery 6 at the far end), an audiovisual show introducing the Gallery, its collection and masterpieces.*

Gallery 7. – Early Italian works include one of Raphael's madonna series *(The Bridgewater Madonna)* painted in Florence, and an excellent example of High Renaissance portraiture by his contemporary Andrea del Sarto *(portrait of the artist's friend).*

Gallery 8. – Titian displays the virtuosity of his talent in a religious composition *The Three Ages of Man.*

Gallery 9. – The two large panels of the *Trinity Altarpiece* by Van der Goes are a unique example of pre-Reformation art, commissioned for the Collegiate Church of the Holy Trinity. Open, the panels represent James III and Margaret of Denmark with patron saints. Closed, you see, the first provost Sir Edward Bonkil and the Holy Trinity.

Gallery 10. – Richness of colour characterizes the Venetian, Bassano's *Adoration of the Kings* and Tintoretto's *(The Deposition of Christ).* Some of the forcefulness and drama of the latter's style passed to his pupil, El Greco, represented here by *The Saviour of the World.* The colouring, elongation and spiritual power typical of his later style are all in evidence. Although an early work, the kitchen scene *An Old Woman Cooking Eggs* demonstrates the competence of Velazquez's art.

Gallery 11. – The Antwerp portraitist Quentin Massys sets off his *Portrait of a Notary* against a delightfully detailed background.

Gallery 12. – Compare the two 17C Flemish religious scenes, Rubens' *Feast of Herod* a spontaneous, colourful and realistic work, with that of his pupil Van Dyck *(St Sebastian bound for Martyrdom).* Of particular interest is the latter's *The Lomellini Family,* an early group portrait, where the sombre interior of a Genoese palace is the background for some superb detailing in the armour and girls' dresses. Domestic interiors were the favourite subject of 17C Dutch painters with Vermeer's *Christ in the House of Mary and Martha* as an example.

Gallery 13. – The idealized landscapes of Claude greatly influenced British artists.

Gallery 14. – *Upstairs.* Reserve Collection.

Gallery 15. – *Temporary display unit.*

Gallery 16. – In passing note Avercamp's animated winter scene and the *Interior of St Bavo's Church* by that master of the art, Pieter Saenredam. The portraits of Frans Hals display a vitality and realism which make them second only to those of Rembrandt represented by his *self-portrait.* Typical of his late portraits the attitude is one of calmness and introspection with his use of chiaroscuro focusing attention on the face.

Gallery 17. – The theme of this octagon is that of painters in 18C Rome, thereby bringing together portraits by Scotland's Allan Ramsay, including the delightful *Painter's Wife* and one of his friend J.J. Rousseau (a companion to the one of Hume in the National Portrait Gallery) and Raeburn *(Macdonell of Glengarry)*; there is also the Italian Pompeo Batoni who painted so many of Scotland's Grand Tourists. Another Scotsman, Gavin Hamilton, although resident in Rome was a pioneer in neo-classicism.

Gallery 18. – The fluid skill and vitality of Gainsborough's *The Hon. Mrs Graham* makes a direct contrast with Reynold's more academic *Ladies Waldegrave.* Constable *(Vale of Dedham)* and Turner landscapes are accompanied by C.E. Church's *Niagara Falls.*

Take the stairs up to galleries 19 to 23.

Gallery 19. – Poussin's *Seven Sacraments* are classical compositions combining landscape and figures.

Gallery 20. – Watteau's *Fêtes Vénitiennes* is a detailed masterpiece of this genre.

Gallery 21. – The realism of Courbet's everyday scenes *(View of Ornans with Church Tower)* and the romanticism of Corot's landscapes are precursors to the Impressionists.

Gallery 22. – The canvases of Renoir *(La Promenade)*, Monet *(Haystacks* and *Poplars on the Epte)*, Sisley and Pissarro demonstrate a preoccupation with the play of light.

Gallery 23. – *The Vision after the Sermon* and *Three Tahitians* are typical examples of Gauguin's exotic subjects and painting technique. Also characteristic of van Gogh's very personal style of vigorous and bright colours is the *Olive Trees.*

Take the stairs beyond gallery 7 down to the new underground wing. Turn right on entering.

Galleries 1 to 5. – Scottish painting from 1600 to 1900. Portraiture dominates the early works from Jamesone and Aikman to Ramsay's superbly delicate portraits of women *(see also gallery 17)*. Beyond are numerous examples of Raeburn's works including a *self portrait* and *The Reverend Robert Walker Skating on Duddingston Loch.* David Wilkie knew great popularity in his time for his realistic Scottish scenes, *Distraining for Rent, The Letter of Introduction* and his first work *Pitlessie Fair.* William Dyce precursor of the Pre-Raphaelites specialized in religious scenes and landscapes while Noel Paton produced his fairy scenes. McTaggart in reaction to Victorian conventions excelled in landscapes where bold and vigorous brushwork and a feeling for light gave a realistic approach, unique for the period *(The Storm* and *The Young Fishers)*. The follow up movement was the **Glasgow School** to which Guthrie and E. A. Hornel both belonged.

tc **Royal Scottish Academy** (BY R). – The Academy was custom built by William Playfair in 1826 to grace the north end of the Mound and counterbalance the Bank of Scotland's imposing building at the south end. From her perch above the portico, Steell's Queen Victoria looks up Hanover Street towards her uncle, George IV. The initial rivalry between Institution and Academy ended when the latter became royal in 1838. The Royal Scottish Academy, composed of 60 members of whom 30 are Academicians and the others associates, organizes exhibitions throughout the year, notably the Annual Exhibition (April to July) largely of the works of members and in August the Festival Exhibition.

The Mound (BY). – The drained Nor'Loch area was initially crossed by stepping stones laid by an enterprising Lawnmarket clothier as a short cut for his New Town clients. Later excavated earth from New Town building sites was used to build up the Mound (1781-1805) we see today.

Beyond in West Princes Street Gardens is the **floral clock** (BY S) composed of 20 000 annuals, the bandstand, a centre for a full programme of open-air entertainments in summer, statues of the poet Allan Ramsay (east end) and the discoverer of chloroform Sir James Y. Simpson.

CALTON HILL

At the east end of Princes Street rises Calton Hill (328ft-100m) with that familiar skyline of classical monuments which gave rise to the name, Edinburgh's acropolis. Another remnant of volcanic activity, the 22 acres of Calton Hill were left undeveloped when the New Town was being built. The James Craig Observatory (BY V) was the initial building and development continued after 1815 when the ravine to the east of Princes Street had been crossed by Regent Bridge. The flanking porticoes and classical façades of **Waterloo Place** (BY) provide a formal entry, framing Calton Hill in the distance. On the right, **St Andrew's House** (BY W), onetime administrative centre of Scotland, stands on the site of two prisons, built to relieve the Old Tolbooth.

Calton Hill (BY). – *Access by stairs from Waterloo Place (Regent Road) or by a narrow road, suitable for cars, leading off to the left opposite St Andrew's House.*
The most striking monument is the 12 columned portico of the **National Monument** (BY) to commemorate Scots who died in the Napoleonic Wars. Intended as a replica of the Parthenon, construction was stopped by lack of funds. The next in a clockwise *tc* direction and tallest is **Nelson's Monument** (BY) a 106ft tall, tiered circular tower to the victor of Trafalgar. The viewing gallery *(143 steps)* provides a magnificent **panorama**★★★ of Edinburgh : up Princes Street, from the castle down the spine of the Royal Mile past the Canongate Church, to Holyroodhouse with the park and Arthur's Seat in the background. The circular Greek temple (BY X) is Playfair's monument to Dugald Stewart, Professor of Moral Philosophy. The walled enclosure (BY V) has at its south-west corner James Craig's 18C Old Observatory which was subsequently replaced by Playfair's building (1818) in the centre, itself superseded by a new Observatory on Blackford Hill *(p 101)*. At the southeast corner is another Playfair monument to his uncle, the mathematician and natural philosopher, John Playfair.

Regent Road (BY). – The **Royal High School** (BY) with its imposing columned, pedimented and porticoed facade was designed by a former pupil Thomas Hamilton from 1825 to 29. It was refurbished internally for the proposed Scottish Assembly. The oval debating chamber is now used by Scottish MPs when debating Scottish affairs.
Beyond, to the right of the road, is the Greek temple (BY Y) to Robert Burns by the architect of the Royal High School.
Branch left to follow the contour of Calton Hill and the elegant sweep of **Regent** (1825), **Calton** (1820s-1860) and **Royal Terraces** (1821-60). Designed by William Playfair as a residential area, here also are many of the attractive architectural and ironwork features typical of the New Town *(p 95)*. The communal garden *(private)* behind was laid out by Joseph Paxton.

NORTHERN AND WESTERN EDINBURGH

★★★Royal Botanic Garden. – *1 mile from the city centre by Broughton Street* (BY 6).
tc Car parking available near the west gate in Arboretum Road.

The 70 acres of the Royal Botanic Garden are a refreshing haven for those weary of the city bustle. A delight to observe, a pleasure to stroll through and treasure trove for the initiated.

Origins. – In the late 17C when Edinburgh was emerging as a centre for medical studies, a physic garden was established (1670) by Dr Robert Sibbald, first Professor of Medicine at Edinburgh University and Dr Robert Balfour another eminent physician. The original plot was situated near Holyrood Abbey. In 1676 these gentlemen acquired land near Trinity Hospital – on the present site of Waverley Station – appointing James Sutherland as Intendant. An intermediary move to Leith Walk followed before the final one in *c*1820 to a mere 14 acres on the present site. A later extension included Inverleith House and its policies.

Today. – The garden, glasshouses and herbarium, with its vast collection of preserved plant specimens, are the working basis for research, the main role of the garden. Edinburgh's specialization in rhododendrons owes much to such dedicated collectors as George Forrest.

Garden and buildings. – The **rhododendrons** are a major attraction. The modernistic Exhibition Plant Houses (1967) provide unimpeded interiors where winding paths lead through a series of landscaped presentations, a pleasant alternative to serried ranks of pots so normally associated with glasshouses. The Exhibition Hall is devoted to changing displays on various aspects of botany. The Tropical (1834) and Temperate (1858) Palm Houses have an altogether more traditional and imposing architectural style. High in the centre of the gardens stands 18C **Inverleith House** onetime repository for the collection of modern art *(see below)*. From beyond the lawn a view indicator pinpoints Edinburgh's well known landmarks.

★★Edinburgh Zoo. – *3 miles from the city centre, on the main Edinburgh – Glasgow road, the A8.*
tc The 80-acre Scottish National Zoological Park is attractively set on the south slope of Corstorphine Hill. Barless and sometimes glassless enclosures for many of the species allow the visitor better views of the animals and their antics. The tables are turned as the orangutans and chimpanzees from their pole-top perch and climbing apparatus have grandstand views of the public. The famous Edinburgh penguin collection (a colony of 30 Kings and 100 Gentoes) is the number one attraction with their daily **Penguin Parade.** In addition to the usual animals, make a point of looking for some of the native species : the wild cat, shy pine martens or golden eagle.

The **view** from the hilltop (510ft – 155m ; *view indicator)* shows the sprawl of Edinburgh and from the Pentlands to the south right round to the mountains of Loch Lomond.

tc **Lauriston Castle.** – *5 miles from the city centre by the A90 and Cramond Road South.*
The 16C tower house was built by Sir Archiblad Napier, father of the inventor of Logarithms. **John Law** (1671-1729) financier and France's Comptroller General of Finances spent some of his early years here. Greatly extended in the 19C and refurbished in the early 20C the house today is an example of a gracious Edwardian home. Of particular interest are some of the very fine pieces of furniture (18C English and continental and 20C reproductions), the unusual wool "mosaics" and collection of Blue John ware. Tapestries and a large collection of prints adorn the walls. Do not miss the cases of James Tassie's (1735-99) casts of his famous intaglios.

★Scottish Agricultural Museum. – *Ingliston. Leave by Queensferry Road in the*
tc direction of the Forth Bridge ; then branch left to follow signposts to the airport and Ingliston. On arriving at the ground the museum is to the left.

The museum gives an informative and well documented account of Scotland's rural past. On the ground floor the seasonal activities from ploughing to harvesting are presented using a combination of exhibits, backed up by explanatory texts and photographs. In sharp contrast to the sophisticated machinery of today, the implements of the past like the Shetland delling spade, the back harrow, the sickle and scythe are reminders of the sheer physical labour involved in farming of earlier times. Other exhibits evoke scenes which are now a thing of the past : the teams of working horses, the harvests with binders, stooks and cornyards of neatly thatched stacks and the activity of the travelling mill. The authentic details of the house interiors, in particular the bothy, are noteworthy.

tc **St Mary's Cathedral.** – *Enter from Palmerston Place.*
The cathedral was built for the Episcopalian diocese of Edinburgh by George Gilbert Scott in the 1870s. Vast and ambitious, even for the Victorians, the cathedral stands as a testament of faith. The exterior is dominated by the three spires. The two west front ones are later (1917) additions. Inside the quality of Victorian craftsmanship is evident everywhere. Note the pelican lectern, the Robert Lorimer designed rood and the reredos of the high altar. The latter by the architect's son J. Aldrid Scott depicts in the side niches Saints Margaret and Columba, two leading influences in the early Scottish Church.

tc **Scottish National Gallery of Modern Art.** – *Belford Road.*
The Scottish National Gallery of Modern Art is situated in large wooded grounds, on the western edge of the New Town, which provide a fine setting for sculptures by Bourdelle, Epstein, Hepworth, Moore and Rickey. The Gallery is housed in an imposing neo-classical building, the former John Watson's School. The collection has two emphases: international and Scottish art of the twentieth century. If not fully comprehensive in its international collection, it does nevertheless have fine examples of most of the main artists and movements: the Nabis and Fauvism (Vuillard, Bonnard, Matisse, Derain, Rouault), German Expressionism (Kirchner, Nolde, Jawlensky, Kokoschka, Dix), Cubism

and its derivatives (Braque, Picasso, Léger, Delaunay, Lipchitz), Russian Primitivism and Abstract Art (Gontcharova, Larionov, Popova), Dada and Surrealism (Man Ray, Ernst, Miró, Arp, Giacometti, Magritte), Abstraction (Moholy-Nagy, Mondrian, Schwitters, Nicholson), School of Paris (de Staël, Balthus, Dubuffet, Soulages, Riopelle, Tápies, Appel, Picasso), Nouveau Réalisme (César, Arman, Tinguely), St. Ives School (Nicholson, Hepworth, Lanyon, Hilton), Pop Art (Lichtenstein, Hockney, Hamilton, Paolozzi, Tilson, Kitaj), Minimal Art (Lewitt, Judd, Flavin). The Scottish Collection is rich and comprehensive. It has particularly good holdings of the work of the Scottish Colourists (Peploe, Cadell, Hunter, Fergusson) and the Edinburgh School (Gillies, Maxwell, MacTaggart and Redpath).

SOUTHERN SUBURBS

tc **The Royal Observatory** (Visitor Centre). – *3 miles from the city centre by the A7.*
The observatory was transferred to Blackford Hill in 1896 to escape "the smokiness of the air" of Calton Hill. The **visitor centre** introduces the public to the observatory's three major projects : the Schmidt telescope in Australia, the Infrared telescope in Hawaii and the work of COSMOS the observatory's high speed measuring machine. The **West Tower** is occupied by an 0.4m Schmidt telescope *(no longer in active use)* while boards on the walls of the tower describe the role of the UK 1.2m Schmidt telescope in Australia which is used for photographic observations of large areas of the sky.
The flat roof beyond provides a good **view★** of urban Edinburgh from the Bass Rock in the east, away to Fife and the Lomond Hills on the horizon. Calton Hill, the original observatory site is diminutive but distinguishable.
The exhibition in the **Main Gallery** covers the history of astronomy including the role of Scotland's own James Gregory *(qv)*, the development of techniques and the observatory's role today. The latter includes participation in projects such as the Space Telescope to be launched in the late 1980s and the observatory's 3.8m. Infrared Telescope on the summit of an extinct volcano in Hawaii where the dry and cloud free conditions are ideal. Installed in the **second tower** is the 36-inch telescope (1930) which ranks as Scotland's largest.

★Craigmillar Castle. – *3 miles to the southeast by St Leonard's Street* (BZ) *and the A68.*
tc Dramatically set on an eminence, Craigmillar is impressive for its show of strength and seeming impregnability. The 14C tower house rises massively above two successive curtain walls. The outer wall encloses a courtyard in front, and gardens on either side, in all a total area of 1 1/4 acres. The inner curtain built in 1427 is quartered with round towers, pierced by gunloops and topped by attractive oversailing machicolated parapets. Above the inner gate is the Preston family coat of arms. Straight ahead stands the L-shaped **tower house**, now flanked by and linked to the later east (15C) and west ranges (16-17C). The **Great Hall** at first floor level is a grand apartment with a magnificent hooded fireplace and three windows with stone benches lining the embrasures. Climb to the top to get a view down over the other buildings and fully appreciate the strategic excellence of the layout.
Note the dovecot in the northeast corner of the outer wall and the P-shaped fish pond in the field to the south.
It was here that Mary Queen of Scots sought refuge after the murder of Rizzio *(p 89)* and here that the treacherous plot for the murder of Darnley was conceived.

tc **Hillend Ski Centre.** – *Off the A 702.*
On the north slopes of the Pentland Hills, the centre opened in 1965. The artificial ski slopes operate throughout the year and cater for skiers of all abilities. Visitors can take the ski lift up to the top station *(view indicator and binoculars)* which offers a magnificent **panorama★★** of Edinburgh and its southern suburbs with, on the horizon, Ben Lomond, round to Cockenzie Power Station, North Berwick Law, Traprain and the Cheviots.

tc **Castlelaw Hill Fort.** – *Take the road to the left up to Castlelaw farm and the car park. The fort is on a Ministry of Defence Range, obey instructions given by flag or lamps.*
The fort consisting of concentric banks and ditches is set on the summit of Castle Knowe on the south easterly slopes of the Pentland Hills. The earth house built into the inner ditch consists of a 56ft gallery with a beehive chamber off to the right, 11ft in diameter. The floors are of rock while the walls are faced with masonry.

tc **Malleny House Gardens.** – *Balerno off the A 70.*
Situated on the southern bank of the Water of Leith, the 17C house stands on the site of a royal hunting lodge and has an an elegant early 19C wing to the east. There is an attractive woodland garden.

Suggestions for a day out or an afternoon's excursion from Edinburgh. For other ideas consult the map of Principal Sights in the introduction.

Castles and stately homes: *The Binns; Blackness Castle; Crichton Castle; Dalmeny House★; Hopetoun House★★ and Linlithgow Palace★★.*

Churches and chapels: *Abercorn Parish Church; Dalmeny Parish Church; Rosslyn Chapel★★ and Seton Collegiate Church.*

Attractive villages: *Culross★★★; Dirleton★; Tyninghame★; Stenton★; Garvald and Gifford★.*

★ EDZELL CASTLE (Tayside)

Michelin map 401 fold 24 – L 13 – 1 1/4 miles west of Edzell

tc The attractive ruin of Edzell Castle, seat of the Crawford Lindsays, is unique for its pleasance or formal walled garden. Summer is the best time to visit when the flowers are in bloom.

Castle. – The present entrance leads to the cobbled courtyard of the late 16C mansion. Now in ruins this extension was never completed. Go through the pond straight ahead to survey what was the original entrance front. To the right is the early 16C tower house a traditional L-shaped building with decorative corbelling. The rest of the west front is made up of the later 16C extension. The great hall in the tower house affords a good bird's-eye-view of the pleasance.

★★★**The Pleasance.** – The formal walled garden, one of Scotland's unique sights, was created in 1604 by **Sir David Lindsay** (c1550-1610) builder of the courtyard mansion. The garden is a product of Renaissance ideas which flourished during that time of peace. The educated and much travelled Sir David Lindsay, a man of taste, was no doubt influenced by what he had seen abroad. He created a remarkable work displaying great elegance and refinement which is without parallel in Scotland. Initially the impression is one of a blaze of colour when the roses of the flower beds and the blue and white lobelia of the wall boxes are in bloom, with the rich red of the walls as background. The heraldic and symbolic **sculpture** on the walls reward a closer inspection. Between the wall boxes representing the Lindsay colours and arms are sculptured panels portraying the Planetary Deities (east wall), Liberal Arts (south wall) and Cardinal Virtues (west wall). Neatly clipped box hedges spell out the Lindsay motto "Dum spiro spero". The design is completed in the southwest corner by a bath house, a luxury in 17C Scotland, and in the opposite corner by a summer house. On the first floor of the latter are some carved wooden panels, which came from the tower house.

★ ELGIN (Grampian)   Pop 16 407

Michelin map 401 fold 15 – K 11

Set in the rich agricultural Laich of Moray, the attractive town of Elgin stands on the banks of the Lossie. The town is the administrative centre for the Moray district. The medieval plan has been preserved and the main street links its famous cathedral to the former site of the castle, the two mainstays of a medieval burgh.

★ELGIN CATHEDRAL (B) time: 1/2 hour

tc Elgin Cathedral is claimed by many to have been the most beautiful. Today the biscuit coloured ruins still stand, majestic, evocative and rich in style, characteristic of the 13C, that period of intensive church building.
The creation of the diocese dated back to 1120 when territorially it extended over the ancient province of Moray. The Celtic churches of Birnie, Kinneddar and Spynie had served as episcopal seats prior to the final move in 1224 to the Church of the Holy Trinity at Elgin. Following fire damage in 1270 a scheme of enlargement was undertaken comprising the completion of double aisles to the nave, the extension of the choir and the addition of a chapter house. Both the town and the cathedral suffered ignominious destruction in 1390 at the hands of the **Wolf of Badenoch** otherwise known as Alexander Stewart, the second son of King Robert II. Although duly repaired the cathedral suffered gradual deterioration after the Reformation. This was in part due to the fact that it was no longer in use as a place of worship and also due to the protracted struggle over the ownership of church property after the Reformation. In 1711 the collapse of the central tower wreaked much damage and the ruins became a quarry for building materials. Conservation began in the early 19C by the determined efforts of one man.

The buildings. – Between the buttressed twin towers of the west front is a deeply recessed portal with large windows above. Intricate vine and acorn carving frames the doorways. On the internal face is an attractive arcade marking the passageway between the towers at first floor level. This feature is also found at Arbroath. The view of the town from the top of the south tower *(134 steps)* is screened by the trees of Cooper Park, although the Duke can be seen on his column on Lady Hill. The transepts are the oldest parts. The two figures in the south aisle originally adorned the outer walls of the central tower. The east end is an impressive arrangement of two rows of five lancets crowned by a rose window. Note the unusual spire-like terminations of the piers of the choir. The octagonal 13C **chapter house**★★ was reconstructed in the 15C when it was provided with elaborately rich vaulting and carved bosses. The stone benching is discontinued for the five canopied seats.
Standing within the former cathedral precincts are **Pann's Port** (B), a former gateway and in the corner of Cooper Park, the ruins of one of the manses, miscalled the **Bishop's Lodging** (B).

ADDITIONAL SIGHTS

Wynds and pends link the main thoroughfare to streets to the north and south.

tc **Elgin Museum** (B M). – This purpose built Italianate building (1843) houses the local history museum. Items of particular interest are the local fossil fish and reptiles and incised Pictish stones, especially the **Burghead Bulls**.

Braco's Banking House (B A). – Marked by street level arcades, this was the banking house of William Duff of Dipple. His son William Duff of Braco and later Earl of Fife invested the accumulated fortune in the building of Duff House *(p 45)*.

The Tower (A). – At the widening of the street on the right is a 17C tower house, now a hotel.

St Giles (A). – This handsome church designed in the classical style by the Aberdonian, Archibald Simpson is greatly enhanced by its mid-street site. The steepled tower and fluted columned portico dominate the main façades.

Lady Hill (A). – The mound at the far end of the High Street was the site of the medieval castle. Today it is dominated by the monument (**A B**) to the last Duke of Gordon (d 1836) with his Grace above.

EXCURSIONS

Laich of Moray. – *Leave Elgin by the Lossiemouth road, the A 941.*

tc **Spynie Palace.** – *View from the outside only.*
Early in the 13C this was the episcopal seat of the Bishops of Moray and continued to be their residence even once the place of worship had been transferred to Elgin. Bishop David Stewart (1462-76) responded to the excommunicated Earl of Huntly's threat to pluck him out of his "pigeon-holes" by building much of what we see today. Davie's tower is a six storey keep with 9 foot thick walls. This nest served well as a retreat after the Reformation for Bishop Patrick Hepburn the last Catholic incumbent. Here he continued his profligate life until 1573.

> *Turn left onto the B 9135 and left again in the direction of Duffus to skirt the southern edge of the airfield. Take the farm road to the left signposted Duffus Castle.*

tc **Duffus Castle.** – A good example of a motte and bailey castle, rising abruptly out of the flat, fertile Laich of Moray. The 12C motte hill crowned by an early 14C stone keep is separated from the extensive outer bailey by a deep ditch. The whole is encircled by an outer ditch. Part of the tower has subsided due to its superimposition on an artificial mound. This was the early seat of the de Moravia family.

Burghead. – Pop 1 475. Set on a rocky promontory, overlooking the great sandy sweep of Burghead Bay, this village was the site of an early fort. It was occupied if not built by the Picts and the locality is particularly famous for the 7-8C Pictish stones, the **Burghead Bulls** *(p 102)*. Another remarkable sight

tc is the **Burghead Well** *(King Street)*. Steps lead down to a path encircled pool in a vaulted chamber. The origin and purpose of this structure are uncertain.

(After wood engraving by Derek Riley)

Burghead Bull

tc **Pluscarden Abbey.** – *6 miles southwest of Elgin.*
The pastoral Black Burn Valley is the setting for this relatively recent community of Benedictines. A priory was founded in 1230 by Alexander II for the Valliscaulian Order and was one of only three Scottish houses *(p 133)*. In 1494 the Priory was transferred to the Benedictines of Dunfermline. Later, under the Commendators and during the 16C religious upheavals, came decline and deterioration. In 1948 a new Benedictine community from Prinknash Abbey in England was established to restore monastic life. Pluscarden became an abbey in 1974. Visitors are welcome to see restoration work already accomplished : church choir, transepts, and monastic buildings.

A busy fishing port and popular holiday resort, Eyemouth stands on the Berwickshire coast at the mouth of the Eye Water. The Herring Queen Festival week *(p 212)* is one of the highlights of the summer season.

SIGHTS

tc **★Eyemouth Museum.** – Displays give you glimpses of rural life (farming, water milling, wheelwrighting and blacksmithing). The attractive presentations touch on all aspects of the fisherfolks' lives : their homes and customs, the fish, the boats, gear and tackle and the ancillary crafts. The **Eyemouth Tapestry**, rich in symbolism commemorates the Great Fishing Disaster (1881), and tells the story of the tragedy.

Harbour. – The presence of many brightly painted boats lining the quayside and the busy **fish market** testify to the importance of fishing to the town. Ever since the 12C fishing has been the main activity in Eyemouth. In 1881, on Black Friday, 14th October, 189 men were lost in the Great East Coast Fishing Disaster ; 129 of those men came from Eyemouth. 19 boats were lost, almost half the fishing fleet of that time.

Old fishing village. – Despite recent developments the old fishing area still retains certain of the characteristics described by the Rev Daniel McIver : "instead of rows of houses, we have clusters of houses, instead of gables facing gables, we have gables facing fronts and fronts facing back courts". Smuggling reached its height in the 18C and Eyemouth was an important centre in the illicit trade in wines, spirits, tea and tobacco.

Grunsgreen Mansion. – The solitary mansion on the south side of the harbour was once notorious as a smuggling centre. There is reputed to be an opening from the cellars under the forecourt to a slipway into the harbour. This former smugglers haunt was once owned by Robert Logan of Restalrig, laird of Fast Castle (d1606) who was implicated in the Gowrie Conspiracy *(qv)*. His body was exhumed tried and pronounced guilty seven years after his death.

EXCURSIONS

The coast north of Eyemouth. – *10 miles from Eyemouth. Leave by the A 1107.*

tc **Coldingham.** – Pop 520. This inland village is best known for its **priory** which was founded in 1098 by King Edgar for Benedictine monks. The present parish church occupies the choir of a 12-13C building.

In Coldingham take, the B 6438 to the right.

St Abb's. – The church high on the clifftop pinpoints this attractive fishing village clustered round its harbour. Walks in the area include the clifftop path south to the sandy beach of Coldingham Bay and north to St Abb's Head *(see below)*.

tc **★★St Abb's Head.** – *National Nature Reserve. Access road signposted to the left, off the B 6438, just before entering St Abb's.*

200 acres in extent, the reserve covers a variety of habitats – coastal grassland, sandy and rocky shores and cliffs – and includes the man made Mire Loch and the well known landmark, **St Abb's Head**. The cliffs, some of the finest on the eastern seaboard, rise to over 300ft and provide a myriad of nesting ledges for seabirds (guillemots, razorbills, puffins, fulmars and gulls). The spectacle of entire cliff faces alive with diving, swooping birds to a background of piercing cries is a fascinating sight. The knoll beside the lighthouse affords **views★** of the coastline south to Hairy Ness and north to Fast Castle's headland – with, on a clear day, views of the Bass Rock and Fife coast on the horizon. The reserve is a sanctuary for migrating birds in spring and autumn.

Return to the A 1107 and head towards Dunbar.

Fast Castle. – *2.3 miles off the A 1107 signposted. The surfaced road leads to Dowlaw Farm. Leave the car beyond the farm cottages. 15 mins walk down to castle ruins along a path, steep and stony in places. Care is needed on cliffs.*

Once through the gate the clifftop site affords a good **view** westwards of the coastline with ever decreasing red sandstone cliffs, the Torness Nuclear Plant construction site, the Dunbar cement works and on the horizon Berwick Law and the Bass Rock. All the way along, the path offers views of nesting seabirds on cliff ledges. The few jagged remains of **Fast Castle** are perched in an audacious **site★★** on a rocky crag high above the sea, where castle wall and cliff face confound. Impregnable this stronghold dating from the 16C *(excavations are in progress to determine even earlier origins)* belonged first to the Homes and then Logan of Restalrig, a member of the Gowrie Conspiracy. The castle figures as Wolf's Crag in Scott's *The Bride of Lammermoor* and is supposedly the hiding place of a treasure of gold.

Burnmouth. – Pop 290. *2 miles south of Eyemouth.*
On a rocky coastline, the original fishing village and harbour set below the cliffs make an attractive group. Steep narrow road down, sound horn at the corner.

Join us in our never ending task of keeping up to date.
Send us your comments and suggestions, please.

Michelin Tyre Public Limited Company,
Tourism Department,
DAVY HOUSE – Lyon Road – HARROW
MIDDLESEX HA1 2 DQ.

The Dutch engraver, John Slezer's description of Falkand in the 17C "a pretty little Town... a stately Palace" sums up the town of today. Tucked away at the foot of the Lomond Hills, safe from the depredations of war and strife so endemic to Scottish history, Falkland has retained the peaceful charm of a royal burgh of yesteryear.

Fife, the centre of the royal kingdom. – The original castle belonged to the Macduffs, the Earls of Fife and its early history was marked by the mysterious death in 1402 of David, Duke of Rothesay, heir to Robert III, while staying with his uncle, Robert of Fife *(p 67)*. David's brother, James I, on his release from imprisonment in England in 1424, set out to restore the power of the monarchy. His revenge was total and in the following year the Albanys were beheaded. Their property, including Falkland, passed to the Crown. James II gifted the castle to Mary of Gueldres in 1451 and followed this in 1458 by raising the town to a royal burgh and the castle to a palace.

Royal residence (15-16C). – The hunting seat of Falkland became one of the Stewarts favourite royal palaces. James II built an extension, the north range which originally contained the Great Hall and it was here that Margaret of Anjou and her son took refuge when Henry VI was imprisoned. The future James III (1451- 1488) spent his childhood here but his troubled reign with nobles and brothers alike, ended with his murder at Sauchieburn.

James IV (1473-1513), a typical monarch of the Renaissance, re-established royal authority, and with his Queen, Margaret Tudor entertained a splendid court. Royal patronage was extended to the poet **William Dunbar** (1465-1530) who dedicated *The Thistle and the Rose* to his royal patrons. James, who loved to hunt in the Falkland Forest and hawk on the Lomond Hills, built the south range. Other royal hunting lodges of the period included Hampton Court 1515 and Chambord 1519.

James V (1512-42) made extensive alterations in preparation for his marriage, initially to Magdalene, daughter of François I and after her untimely death, to Mary of Guise in 1538. French workmen prepared the palace for a French bride. The result was the Renaissance ornament on the courtyard façade of the south range. A radical departure from the Gothic of the time this stylistic flourish was in fact the earliest of its kind in Britain. James' two sons died as infants and it was to Mary Queen of Scots that the throne went when her father died heartbroken at the age of 30.

Mary came to hunt occasionally, and her son James VI visited on his 1617 royal progress as did her grandson, Charles I and great-grandson, Charles II. It was the latter who presented the Scots Guards with their Colours here in 1650. Abandoned the palace fell into a state of disrepair. In the late 19C the Hereditary Keeper carried out restoration work and the palace, although still royal property is now under the guardianship of the National Trust for Scotland.

★**THE PALACE OF FALKLAND** time : 3/4 hour

Before entering examine the street front of the south range.

tc **South Range : street front.** – Built by James IV this consists of two very distinct parts : on the extreme left is the twin-towered gatehouse completed in its present form in 1541. Inside are the private apartments of the Constable, Captain and Keeper. The corbelled parapet, cable moulding and gargoyles link this with the range to the east where massive buttresses are adorned with canopied niches. The statues are the work of Peter the Flemishman (1538). The street front is a good example of Scottish Gothic.

Enter by the East Port (3) and the National Trust for Scotland visitors centre.

South Range. – On the ground floor one of the vaulted cellars has items relating to the palace and burgh. Upstairs the Tapestry Gallery is hung with 17C Flemish tapestries depicting scenes of the chase and lined along the window wall with replicas of 16 and 17C pieces of furniture. The 19C heraldic glass shows sovereigns and consorts closely associated with the palace.

The outstanding features of the 16C interior of the **Chapel Royal** are the oak screen between chapel and ante-chapel and the painted ceiling redecorated for Charles I's 1633 visit.

The **Drawing Room**, part of the private quarters of the Keeper of the Palace, was restored by the Marquess of Bute in the 1890s. The oak ceiling is emblazoned with the coats of arms of the Stuart Kings and the different keepers of the palace. The paintings include James VII and Mary Queen of Scots, Charles II and Catharine of Braganza.

Take the turnpike down one level to the first floor of the East Range.

East Range. – This was built at the same time as the south one, to contain the royal apartments with the king's suite on the first floor and queen's above. This level affords a good view of the delightful courtyard front of the south range, so different from the Gothic street front. The Renaissance influence is most evident in the buttresses embellished with engaged pilasters and pronounced mouldings and the sets of paired medallions. The latter are not unlike Wolsey's terracotta medallions at Hampton Court and the Stirling Heads *(p 188)*. The ideas of this showpiece façade for the earlier Gothic range, were developed in the more elaborate designs of Stirling's Palace Block. Alas the experiment was confined to royal works and the style had no permanent effect on Scottish architecture.

The **King's Bed Chamber** in the cross house projecting from this range (rebuilt 19C) has been restored. The windows have shutter boards below and leaded glass above and the painted ceiling is resplendent with the monograms of James V and Mary of Guise. The Golden Bed of Brahan is of early 17C Dutch workmanship. James V died here in 1542 several days after learning of the birth of his daughter Mary Queen of Scots, when he pronounced "It came wi' a lass, and will gang wi' a lass".

FALKLAND★

★Gardens. – The foundations of the North Range and Round Tower of the original Macduff stronghold can be seen in the gardens. Replanted since its service as a potato field in the World War II effort, the gardens, ablaze with colour, include shrubs, herbaceous borders and a more formal garden. Beyond is the 1539 **Royal Tennis Court,** built eight years after Henry VIII's one at Hampton Court.

★THE VILLAGE *time : 1/2 hour*

Take the time to stroll around Falkland to discover good vernacular architecture and something of the court officials, royal servants and tradesmen who resided in the village. Of particular interest are the many **lintel and marriage stones.**

Great efforts have been made to preserve the original character of the burgh. Conservation Area status and the National Trust for Scotland's Little Houses Improvement Scheme have been responsible for the implementation of a restoration and renovation programme, and the subsequent injection of life into the community.

On the south side of the High Street, 17C **Moncreif House** sports a thatch of Tay reeds, a marriage lintel and inscribed panel proclaiming the builder's loyalty to his monarch. The hotel **(A)** next door features further panels, and beyond Back Wynd stands the stepled town hall **(H)** (1801) adorned with a sculptured panel of the burgh arms. On the far side of the street next to the Palace is **Key House (B)** with its lintel dated 1713 with a neighbour,

FALKLAND	
	East Port 3
	High Street 5
	Horsemarket 6
Brunton Street 2	Parliament Square 8

the harled and red pantiled 18C **St Andrew's House (D)**. The Bruce Fountain **(E)** is 19C. Cross Wynd is lined by a row of single storey cottages, interrupted by the cobbled Parliament Square **(8)**. Glance up Horsemarket **(6)** to see the building with forestairs. Dominating Brunton Street **(2)** is the imposing three storeyed **Brunton House** (1712) home of the Royal Falconers. Back to the main street, the birthplace **(F)** of the "Lion of the Covenant", **Richard Cameron** (1648-80) is marked by another inscribed lintel. A staunch Covenanter, following a period of exile, he headed the extremist Covenanting group, the Cameronians, the nucleus of which was later to form the regiment of the same name.

★ FLOORS CASTLE (Borders)

Michelin map 🔢 fold 36 - M17 - On the outskirts of Kelso

tc The highly distinctive pinnacled silhouette of Floors in its superb terraced site overlooking the Tweed is best seen from Kelso Bridge.

"A Kingdom for Oberon and Titana". – **Robert Ker of Cessford**, one of King James VI's courtiers obtained the former Kelso Abbey lands and was created 1st Earl of Roxburghe in 1616. **John, 5th Earl** (d1740) an active promoter of the Act of Union (1707) and the Squadrone Secretary of State under Walpole, was created a duke for his services to the Crown and it was during his lifetime that the house was built (1721) to **William Adam's** designs. John's grandson the 3rd duke, and discerning bibliophile, assembled the famous Roxburghe library which the 5th Duke (1736-1823) sold in 1812. Dispersed amongst other stately homes, Chatsworth, Althorp, Blenheim, it was the antiquarian event of the time. The various purchasers grouped together to form the **Roxburghe Club** with a view to publishing volumes in facsimile so that each member would eventually have a complete collection.

William Playfair was engaged by the 21 year old **James, 6th Duke** (1816-79) to enlarge and embellish Adam's original building. The result was the exterior we see today.

TOUR *1 hour*

Exterior. – On the north front. Adam's original castellated main block quartered by towers rises through three storeys and is flanked by Playfair's additions of wings at right angles, linked at ground level to the main building. The wings again quartered by taller towers repeat the pattern of the central block. The dramatic roofscape of cupolas, chimneys, battlements and turrets links and unifies the whole. On the river front the dominance of the central Adam building is counterbalanced by the asymmetry of the wings.

Interior. – Many of the rooms were remodelled by **Duchess May**, the American wife (1876-1937) of the 8th Duke, to accommodate her outstanding collection of tapestries and fine furniture.

Entrance Hall. – Of the paintings hanging in this pleasantly proportioned room with ceiling and fireplace attributed to William Adam, note Raeburn's seated portrait of *Sir James Innes, 5th Duke of Roxburghe.* Successful claimant to the Roxburghe peerage in 1805 he was obliged to sell the famous library to pay the lawsuit.

106

Ante-Room. – The 15C Brussels tapestry, *Day of Pentecost and the Descent of The Holy Ghost* is the highlight of this room. The windows look down over green terraces to the river and the mound on the far bank, the onetime site of Roxburgh Castle.

Sitting Room. – The picture dated 1809 by William Wilson shows Floors as built by William Adam prior to Playfair's alterations. Again looking out the windows, a holly tree marks the spot where James II was killed in 1460 by an exploding cannon while laying siege to Roxburgh Castle.

Drawing Room. – The room was altered to accommodate Duchess May's handsome set of six 17C Brussels tapestries, *The Triumph of the Gods.* The Louis XV gilt chairs and settee are covered with Beauvais tapestry depicting La Fontaine's Fables.

Needle Room. – A small room with rich red wall hangings and fine French furniture, it is said to resemble a room in Versailles. Beside the Nattier, Ramsay and Hogarth portraits is one of *Duchess May.*

Ballroom. – The 17C Gobelins tapestries and dark panelling are the background for some fine pieces of French furniture, Chinese porcelain and portraits including two of *John, 3rd Duke of Roxburghe* by Hoppner and Gilbert Stuart. This was the duke who having taken a vow of celibacy, devoted his lifetime to enlarging his library.

Bird Room. – This small Gothic room was designed by Playfair to house a collection of stuffed birds which is dominated by the great bustard.

Gallery. – A variety of mementoes and documents are displayed including a letter from Mary Queen of Scots to her warden of the Eastern Marches, the Laird of Cessford. Above the staircase is a full-length portrait of *Duchess May* aged twenty. Her husband the *8th Duke,* is in the adjoining painting of a group of Knights of the Thistle.

FOCHABERS (Grampian)   Pop 1 480

Michelin map **401** fold 15 – K11

This attractive 18C planned village has a grid layout with main streets intersecting at a central square. The streets are lined by Georgian one and two storey houses, while the square is dominated by the elegant porticoed parish church with its stone spire. The original village known as Bog o'Gight stood in the policies of Gordon Castle and was demolished by the 4th Duke to make way for a grandiose mansion which was in turn partially demolished.

EXCURSIONS

tc **Tugnet Ice House.** – *Turn right before crossing the Spey and continue to the end of the road.*
This former ice house contains an interesting exhibition on the commercial fisheries of the Spey, their methods, tackle and boats. Built in 1630 and in use until 1968, it stored ice used in the transportation of salmon to the markets. The lower three miles of the Spey are still fished between II February and 26 August.

Speyside Way. – Tugnet is the northern limit of this long distance footpath *(p 12).*

tc **Baxters.** – *Over the Spey.*
This fourth generation family firm produces quality foods, in particular soups, sauces and jams. Following a 15 minute introductory film the guided tour of the factory premises gives an insight into factory methods and ends up in the original **grocer's shop** of a hundred years ago.

FORRES (Grampian)   Pop 8 950

Michelin map **401** fold 15 – J 11

This royal and ancient burgh is situated in the low lying area south of Findhorn Bay. Both the tolbooth and mercat cross are 19C.

tc **Falconer Museum.** – *Tolbooth Street. Tourist information centre in the vestibule.*
Small local museum. Look for the man trap for poachers.

★★**Sueno's Stone.** – *This sculptured stone stands on the outskirts of Forres, close to the Findhorn road the B 9011.*
Another legacy of the mystery shrouded Picts, this 20ft high sandstone cross slab is superbly carved on all sides. Dating in all probability from the 9C, the purpose of this stone, which has no parallel in Scotland, remains uncertain. Three sides including the one with the wheel cross are decorative. The fourth, the most spectacular, is narrative, depicting from top to bottom horsemen, armed warriors and headless corpses. The theory is that this outstanding piece of craftsmanship represents a commemorative funerary monument for some important historic event, probably a battle.

EXCURSIONS

Findhorn area. – *Findhorn is 6 miles by the B 9011.*

Kinloss. – Pop 2 860. Originally the religious centre of the area with an abbey founded in 1150 by David I, the village is now best known for its RAF base for Nimrods and as a mountain rescue base.

Findhorn. – Pop 670. The village of Findhorn, the third on the site, overlooks the tidal bay of the same name. This small resort is a noted water sports centre and has a fine stretch of sandy beach.

tc **Culbin Forest.** – To the west of Findhorn Bay lies an extensive area of dunes, the famous Culbin Sands. Originally held by marram grass the effects were devastating when the grass was widely removed for thatching in the 17C. Fertile land and the village of Culbin were covered by sand. In 1922 the Forestry Commission started afforestation with Corsican pine and the Culbin Forest, a site of special scientific interest, is one of three plantations to stabilize this sandy coast. Beyond the forest and sands is a shingle ridge. The Bar, created by wave action shelters salt-marshes which are a haven for bird-life.

★ FORT WILLIAM (Highland)   Pop 4 214

Michelin map **401** fold 22 – E 13

Fort William lies on the shore of Loch Linnhe in the shadow of Britain's highest mountain, Ben Nevis. As the main town of the Lochaber District, Fort William is ideally situated at the converging point of various routes. The town developed around a succession of strategically sited strongholds and forts at the southern end of the Great Glen. In summer the town is crowded with holidaymakers as Fort William makes an ideal touring centre from which to discover the beauty of the surrounding countryside. Highlights of the tourist calendar are the Ben Nevis Race and the Glen Nevis River Race.

SIGHTS

tc **West Highland Museum.** – *Cameron Square.*
This local museum covers a wide variety of topics. Of particular interest are those dealing with the local industries, the Caledonian Canal, Ben Nevis (all room 2), the former fort (room 3) and Jacobite relics (room 5) including "The Secret Portrait".

tc **Ben Nevis Exhibition.** – *West end of the main street, incorporated within the Scottish Crafts Exhibition.*
A small but fascinating exhibit touching on all aspects of the mountain : the hill race and records, the water tunnel, ascent by car, tourist path and climbing recommendations. This makes an ideal introduction for those intending to make the ascent.

EXCURSIONS

★★**Ben Nevis.** – *4 miles to the southeast. Start of the footpath : from the road along the north side of the River Nevis or from beside the golf course. Access by tourists' footpath : 4/5 hour ascent and 3 hour descent by a well marked path.*
This snow capped granite mass at 4406ft – 1344m Britain's highest mountain but not a shapely one. The Ben is extremely popular with climbers and walkers. Prospective climbers should be suitably clad (boots or strong shoes and waterproofs) and equipped (whistle, map and food). The summit with its war memorial was once the site of an hotel (closed in 1915) and an observatory (1883-1904).
Legend has it that if the snow ever leaves the summit the ownership of Ben Nevis will revert to the Crown.

★★**The Road to the Isles.** – *46 miles.*
This scenic route, often very busy, passes through country rich in historical associations, to the town of Mallaig, one of the ferry ports for Skye and other Inner Hebridean isles.

Leave Fort William by the Inverness road, the A 82 passing on the way the ruins of Inverlochy Castle (closed, unsafe). Turn left to Mallaig taking the A 830 crossing the canal.

Neptune's Staircase. – Banavie. This flight of eight locks was designed by Telford as part of the Caledonian Canal *(qv)* to raise the water level 64ft in 500yds.
From Corpach, with its paper mill (pulping operations ceased in 1980), there are magnificent **views**★★ backwards to Ben Nevis. The road then follows the northern shore of Loch Eil, the continuation of Loch Linnhe.

★**Glenfinnan.** – *NTS Visitors Centre with historical display and recorded commentary on*
tc *the events of 1745 and 46.*
In this glorious setting at the head of **Loch Shiel** stands the 1815 monument to commemorate those who died while following Prince Charles Edward Stuart in the 1745 rising. Here, five days after landing at nearby Loch nan Uamh the standard was raised before a 1300 strong army of Highlanders. The Year of the Prince ended fourteen months later when he left for France from near the same spot. Start with the visitor centre where the exhibition and recorded commentary introduce the principal figures and events of the period.
From the top of the tower *(61 steps with an awkward trap door exit to viewing area)* there is a splendid view of Loch Shiel penetrating deeply into Moidart and framed by mountains, and northwards over the many spanned railway viaduct.

The **Glenfinnan Gathering and Highland Games** held annually on the Saturday in August nearest to the anniversary, is an occasion for the clansmen to meet again.

Beyond Glenfinnan the road and railway part company to go one either side of landlocked Loch Eilt. After the Lochailort turn off, the road passes the head of the sea loch, Loch Ailort, before rising to cross the neck of the Ardnish peninsula.

The road rejoins Loch nan Uamh, providing a seaward **view**★ of the Sound of Arisaig. Down on the foreshore of the north side a **cairn** marks the spot where Prince Charles Edward Stuart came ashore on 19 July 1745 with his faithful companions, the Seven Men of Moidart.

The road then follows Beasdale valley, crosses to Borrodale valley then over the neck of Arisaig Peninsula.

(BTA)

Glenfinnan towards Loch Shiel

★**Arisaig.** – Pop 177. This scattered community looks over the **Sound of Arisaig.** Cruises
tc leave from the pier for Rhum, Eigg and Muck.

Beyond Arisaig, where the road rejoins the coast, the shore although rocky is interrupted by a series of sandy bays, the most famous being the **Silver Sands of Morar★**, known for their pure white silica sand.

Morar. – Pop 290. The village lies at the entrance to Loch Morar the deepest inland loch (over 1000ft deep) with its monster Morag, sister to Nessie.

★**Mallaig.** – Pop 903. The houses spill down the slopes overlooking the bay, sheltered by two headlands. Mallaig an active fishing port with an important fish market is also the terminal for the Skye ferry.

★**Glen Nevis.** – *Signposted from the roundabout at the northern end of the town.*
The road follows the south bank of the River Nevis for 10 miles round the foot of the Ben but provides no views of the summit. The upper stretches of the river are the scene of the very popular Glen Nevis Race. There is plenty of access to the river.

★ GALLOWAY FOREST PARK (Strathclyde, Dumfries and Galloway)

Michelin map **401** folds 38 and 39 – G and H18

The name of the ancient kingdom of Galloway, which formerly covered Wigtown, Kirkcudbright and Carrick lives on today in this Forest Park centred on the Galloway hill country. Within its boundaries is some of the finest scenery of the Southern Uplands where wooded mountains and hills are dotted with lochs and streams.

Forestry. – Although the land was acquired in 1920 the park was not designated until 1943. Forestry now accounts for 60 % of the total area (163 000 acres) and with the afforestation programme now completed the future work entails the replacement of mature plantations.

Coniferous trees are best suited to the peaty soils, with the **Sitka spruce** now replacing such early favourites as Scots pine – the native conifer – European larch and Lodgepole pine. Although forestry work is now highly mechanised, the industry still provides employment for approximately 200.

Wildlife. – In Galloway as elsewhere the reappearance of forests has provided habitats suitable for many a once endangered species such as the golden eagle and the hen harrier. The wildlife is rich and visitors have the chance of seeing any one of the following, red and roe deer, wild goats, foxes, otters, pine marten, wild cat, red squirrel, kestrel, buzzards, sparrowhawks and blackcock with their leks – such display areas are usually in forest fringes.

Amenities. – Visitors are welcome and a wide variety of activities – climbing, hill walking, fishing, camping, swimming and motoring – are permitted within the limits of the park. Descriptive leaflets are available for the various forest trails within the park.

★ QUEEN'S WAY
from New Galloway to Newton Stewart

19 miles – about 1/2 day

This route, renamed in 1977 on the occasion of the Queen's Silver Jubilee, provides a glimpse of the landscapes typical to the southern part of the Forest Park. The route winds through an area of great natural beauty, and a series of other points of interest, all well signposted, add to the interest of the run. Whether in bright sunshine or poorer weather conditions, the scenery can be enchantingly beautiful or menacingly dramatic but is always worthwhile.

New Galloway. – Pop 290. Attractive village at the north end of Loch Ken. It was laid out by the 6th Viscount Kenmure, Sir John Gordon (1559-1634), a Gordon of Lochinvar who had his seat at nearby Kenmure Castle (*now a ruin, not open to the public*).

Take the A712.

The road climbs with the wooded slopes of Bennan Forest on the left, where some of the earliest plantings were done.

Bruce's Stone. – *Short walk from the car park or can be reached on foot from the Deer Museum.*

Here on Raploch Moss (now flooded) in 1307 **Robert the Bruce** (1274-1329) achieved a victory over an English force. This battle was Bruce's first in his campaign to wrest Scotland's independence from Edward I, the Hammer of The Scots.

Clatteringshaws Loch. – This lovely loch in its mountain setting is a man-made creation. As part of the Galloway Hydro Electric Project this reservoir was designed to act as a seasonal storage being depleted in summer and replenished in winter. Water is piped from the reservoir to the Glenlee Power Station to the east.

Galloway Deer Museum. – This interpretative centre describes the Forest Park and its wildlife, in particular the deer.

Just after the road passes the Clatteringshaws Dam, a signpost to the left indicates the Raider's Road.

tc **Raider's Road.** – *10 mile long unsurfaced, but carworthy, forestry track.*

The route through forested countryside gives access to some delightful picnic and bathing spots on the Black Water of Dee. Look out for the life size otter statue.

Red Deer Park. – Highly destructive to plantations, a herd of 35-40 deer roam this large enclosure.

Wild Goat Park. – A 150 acre park centred on the crags of Craigdews supports a flourishing herd of wild goats native to Galloway.

Up on the right is **Murray's Monument**, an obelisk to the memory of a local shepherd's son, Alexander Murray (1774/5-1813) who in his short lifetime rose to become Professor of Oriental Languages at Edinburgh University. Murray was born at nearby Dunkitterick.

The road continues to Newton Stewart running through plantations of the Kirroughtree Forest and passing on the left the mass of Cairnsmore of Fleet (2331ft-711m).

Newton Stewart. – Pop 3 210. Pleasant and busy market town on the banks of the Cree famed for its excellent salmon fishing. As a holiday centre Newton Stewart is a good starting point for exploring the scenically attractive Galloway hills, in particular the
tc Galloway Forest Park. The small local **museum** (*York Road*) depicts life in another age through rural and domestic items.

★ GLAMIS (Tayside)   Pop 240

Michelin map **401** fold 23 – K 14

Set in the rich agricultural countryside of Strathmore this attractive village stands on the periphery of Glamis Castle policies.

★Angus Folk Museum. – *Kirkwynd Cottages.*

tc An attractive row of 19C cottages, houses an outstanding folk collection which depicts rural life of days goneby. In the domestic section (start at the far end) the 19C manse parlour is followed by a dairy, laundry and schoolroom. The next bay recalls the importance in Angus of such cottage industries as spinning and weaving. Beyond the kitchen, room seven has a box bed and baby shelf! A wealth of written and photographic records and the nursery terminate this section.

Across the road the agricultural section has displays of implements large and small, many of local manufacture. Inside many agricultural developments are well explained and the life of farm servants, the bothies and the feeing or hiring markets are well illustrated.

EXCURSION

★★Meigle Museum. – Pop 375. *7 miles west of Glamis.*

The former village school, behind the church on the knoll, houses an outstanding
tc collection of red sandstone **Early Christian monuments★★** (7-10C AD) all found in the vicinity. Cross-slabs, recumbent gravestones and a variety of fragments vividly illustrate the life and art of the Picts.

Although the exact purpose of the monuments remains obscure the carving everywhere is full of spirit and vitality and shows a high degree of skill. The stones are all numbered. Subject matter includes the enigmatic Pictish symbols (Z-rod 1 ; V-rod 4 ; mirror 1 ; comb ; "elephant" 4 ; double disc 3 and crescent 4) ; Celtic type crosses with associated complex interlace, fretwork, spiral and key patterns ; pictoral scenes (Daniel in the Lion's Den 2) ; fabulous animals and human figures (26). These monuments are the unique record of Pictish customs, dress, weapons, and tools. Particularly successful are the equestrian groups (26, 2, 3, 4 and 11) always so full of movement.

Michelin map **401** *is the map to use for Scotland.*
Michelin map **402** *for the lake District and Northern England.*
Michelin map **403** *for the West Country.*
Michelin map **404** *for South East England,*
                        the Midlands and East Anglia.
Michelin map **405** *for Ireland.*

★★ GLAMIS CASTLE (Tayside)

Michelin map 401 fold 23 – K 14 – 12 miles north of Dundee

tc Set in the rich agricultural Vale of Strathmore, Glamis Castle is the epitomy of a Scottish castle with the added interest of many royal connections, literary associations and a ghost in residence. Glamis is the venue for the **Scottish Transport Extravaganza**, an annual event *(p 212).*

Originally a hunting lodge, Glamis has been the seat of the same family since 1372. In 1376 the Chamberlain of Scotland, Sir John Lyon married Joanna the widowed daughter of Robert II. In spite of loyal service to both king and state the family fell out of favour during the reign of James V, in connection with his campaign against the house of Douglas. The 6th Lord Glamis had married a Douglas, sister to the Earl of Angus, who had fled the country. Following her husband's death and after a long period of imprisonment during which the sovereign occupied the castle, James V had Lady Glamis burnt as a witch. Her ladyship's ghost, is said to haunt the castle.

TOUR *1 1/2 hours*

Exterior. – When seen from the end of the tree-lined avenue, the castle is grandly impressive. Its central part rises upwards bristling with towers, turrets, conical roofs and chimneys, with windows seemingly placed at random. Once nearer, the full extent of this rambling red sandstone pile becomes apparent. The 15C L-shaped core has been added to and altered through the centuries, giving the present building.

(Jeremy Marks/Woodmansterne)

Glamis Castle

Interior. – Interiors of various periods, family and other portraits and a variety of interesting items highlight the guided tour. The west wing was destroyed by fire in 1800 and in the rebuilding, the **Dining Room** was given its ornate plaster ceiling. Family portraits include Queen Elizabeth, the Queen Mother's grandparents and brothers. Jacobean furniture, armour and weapons are displayed in the stone vaulted **Crypt**, the main hall of the original tower. This opens onto the great circular staircase, a later addition, the central shaft of which served as an early heating system. The Crypt level is the supposed position of the secret room where an earl and his cronies are still playing cards to this day, blocked in by the Devil for infringing the Sabbath. The splendour of the **Drawing Room** is enhanced by a beautiful vaulted ceiling with **plasterwork decoration** (1621) and a magnificent fireplace (possibly by Inigo Jones) built to commemorate the 1603 Union of the English and Scottish Crowns. Notable among the portraits are the family group showing Patrick 3rd Earl, strangely attired against the background of the castle and grounds previous to landscaping by Capability Brown and double sided wood portraits of the *9th Lord Glamis*, Privy Councillor to James VI, and his secretary, *Boswell* by the school of François Clouet. The Kneller portrait of *Viscount Dundee* is a reminder that Claverhouse Castle *(no visible remains)*, the principal seat of John Graham of Claverhouse, now lies within Glamis estate. The **Chapel's** panelling is decorated with 17C paintings depicting the Twelve Apostles and 15 scenes from the Bible. The paintings are by **Jacob de Wet** (1695-1754) a Dutch artist who also worked at Blair, Kellie and Holyroodhouse. The intriguing feature is the painting showing Christ wearing a hat. The chapel is the haunt of the Grey Lady *(see above)*. The 20C ceiling of the **Library** makes a good comparison with the 17C one in the drawing room. The finely worked (17C) tapestries were woven at the Mortlake factory founded by James VI and *The Fruit Market* is a combined composition by Rubens and Frans Snyders. Delicately worked hangings, a plaster ceiling and coat of arms, unusual fireplace and armorial porcelain are the chief points of interest in **King Malcolm's Room.** The most notable features of the **Royal Apartments** arranged for the Duke and Duchess of York are the hangings of the four poster bed embroidered by Lady Strathmore and the Kinghorne Bed (1606) made for Patrick Ist Earl. **Duncan's Hall,** the oldest part, has literary associations with Shakespeare's *Macbeth* written during the reign of James VI. Here also are a pair of portraits of the castle's royal occupants during the 6th Lady Glamis' imprisonment *(see above).*

The Grounds. – Statues of James VI and his son Charles I flank the end of the drive. Beyond a fine spreading chestnut tree is the delightful **Italian Garden.**

Michelin map 🔲 fold 31 and inset folds 37 and 41 – H 16
See the plan of built up area in the current Michelin Red Guide Great Britain and Ireland.

Scotland's most populous city, with its long established tradition as an important industrial centre and major port, is acquiring a growing reputation as a flourishing cultural centre.

HISTORICAL NOTES

"Dear green place". – Although not the capital, Glasgow was part of the British Kingdom of Strathclyde which was bordered to the north by the Picts, to the northwest by the Scots and south by the Angles of Northumbria. St Mungo came to this embattled kingdom in the mid-6C. Proclaimed bishop he set his wooden church on the banks of the Molendinar Burn. The fish and ring in the Glasgow coat of arms refer to a St Mungo legend when he saved an unfaithful wife from the wrath of her royal husband. A short period of Northumbrian rule in the 7C was followed by incorporation in 1034 into the kingdom of Alba created earlier by the unification of the Pictish and Scottish held territories. The 12C saw the consecration of the see and the new cathedral of Glasgow. Medieval Glasgow developed around its cathedral and its importance increased with the foundation in 1451 of Scotland's second university *(p 116)* and the elevation to archbishopric in 1492.
In the religious troubles of the 17C, Glasgow was the scene of the General Assembly responsible for abolishing Episcopacy in Scotland. The town remained a strong supporter of the Covenanting cause – but the restoration of Episcopacy brought renewed repression for the Covenanters.
By the 17C trade with the American colonies via Port Glasgow was a feature of Glasgow's commerce. When the obstacles occasioned by the Navigation Acts were eventually overcome by the Union of 1707 this particular trade flourished and early fortunes were made in sugar and rum.

Sugar, tobacco and textiles. – Glasgow's growing prosperity in the early 18C depended largely on the tobacco trade (1715 to 1770s). The outward cargoes of locally manufactured goods were paid for by the return loads of tobacco, which was then re-exported to the continent. The merchants known as **Tobacco Lords** – a restricted group – played an important role in Glasgow's economic and social life. With their traditional outfits of scarlet cloaks and black suits they provided a colourful scene on the plainstones, their exclusive trading patch in front of the Tontine Hotel at Glasgow Cross *(p 116)*. Today's street names, Jamaica, Virginia, Glassford, Dunlop, Miller and Buchan are reminders of this flourishing activity and its merchant families. The American War of Independence caused the eventual decline in the tobacco trade but many of the merchants had invested their accumulated wealth in other emergent industries (banking, textiles, coal mining and iron manufacturing) which were to take over later.

Second City. – Cotton manufacturing in particular was responsible for a large increase in the city's population. This trend continued with the impetus of the Industrial Revolution which brought in its wake the centralization of heavy industries (coal, iron, and steel) in the Glasgow area. Improved communications – building of the Forth-Clyde and Monkland Canals, arrival of the railways and deepening of the Clyde which was made navigable up to Broomielaw – also played an important role in a greater expansion.
Once established as an area of heavy industry the emphasis moved to shipbuilding with the development of iron ships and screw propulsion. Some of the world's greatest liners were Clyde built. The prosperity engendered by the Industrial Revolution gave Glasgow its solidly prosperous Victorian face, when it was the workshop of the Empire and came second only to London. This title was lost to Birmingham in 1951.

The Glasgow School. – Commercial prosperity begat a new generation of business men interested in art, some making bequests (Mitchell) and others (McLellan, Burrell, Sir William Maxwell Stirling) collecting, advised by art collectors like Alexander Reid. Out of this cultural activity a movement, sometimes known as **The Glasgow Boys**, emerged in the last quarter of the 19C partly as a protest against the traditions embodied by the Academicians of Edinburgh and the Victorian artistic conventions. The leading members were **WY MacGregor** father of the group, **James Guthrie, George Henry, EA Hornel** and **John Lavery**. The artists sought to achieve realism as an alternative to the prevalent romanticism, sentimentality and staidness. Masterpieces inlude *Galloway Landscape* (Henry, Kelvingrove), *Carse of Lecropt* (MacGregor, Hunterian) *The Tennis Party* (Lavery, Aberdeen). In many ways the group was the equivalent of the contemporary Hague and Barbizon Schools. This ferment of artistic activity nurtured the development of an Art Nouveau movement in the 1890s. The most brilliant exponent was the architect and decorator **Charles Rennie Mackintosh** who along with H McNair and the Macdonald sisters were responsible for a rebirth in fine and applied arts.

Cultural centre, second to none. – Glasgow provides a home for **Scottish Opera** and **Scottish Ballet** in a lavishly refurbished Theatre Royal (1975) and a rehearsal and recording base for the **Scottish National Orchestra** in the SNO centre, Henry Wood Hall. The town patrons an annual **International Folk Festival** *(p 212)*.
With the opening of the Burell Collection Glasgow has added to its collection of artistic gems. It is a jewel *hors pair*. The art lover is torn between the Old Masters of Kelvingrove, the Spanish works at Pollok House, the Whistler and Mackintosh heritages at the Hunterian Art Gallery and the Impressionist holdings of Kelvingrove and Burrell.

Sightseeing in Glasgow. – Since Glasgow's main sights are well scattered out, it is advisable to use public transport. The underground stations are indicated on the map on page 115. City bus tours leave from St Enoch Square. For further information *tc* and advance bookings contact the Travel Centre or the Tourist Information Centre.

★★★CATHEDRAL (DY – *plan p 119*)

tc This imposing Gothic building today stands hemmed in by the Royal Infirmary with the Necropolis behind. The best **view**★ of the cathedral as a whole is from John Knox's stance high up in the Necropolis where the verticality of the composition is best appreciated. This is the fourth church on the site beside the Molendinar Burn, where **St Mungo** built his original wooden church in the 7C. Built chiefly in the 13 and 14C with construction progressing from the east end to the nave, it was the 15C before the cathedral took on its final appearance with the reconstruction of the chapter house and addition of the Blacader Aisle, central tower and stone spire, and the now demolished west front towers. Unusual features of the plan are the non-projecting transepts and two storeyed east end.

Interior. – There is a satisfying impression of unity, although building spanned a period of 300 years. Here the pointed arch reigns supreme.

Nave. – Stylistically later than the choir the elevation with its richly moulded and pointed arches, ever more numerous at each level, rises to the timber roof. The 15C stone screen or pulpitum, unique in Scotland, marks the change in level from nave to choir. The figures around the altars represent the seven deadly sins.

Choir. – The choir and the lower church both dating from the mid-13C are of the finest First Pointed style. The great beauty derives from a combination of harmonious elevations and finely worked details. Note in particular the varied and vigorously worked foliate capitals and corbels and gaily tinctured bosses of the ambulatory vaulting, behind the high altar. The triple lancets of the clerestory are echoed in the design of the east window. Four chapels open out of the ambulatory beyond. From the northernmost chapel a door leads through to the upper chapter room, reconstructed in the 15C. It was there that the medieval university held its classes.

Lower Church. – *Access via stairs to north of the pulpitum.* Here is another Gothic glory where light and shade plays effectively amidst a multitude of piers and pointed arches. This lower area was conceived to enshrine the **tomb of St Mungo,** Glasgow's patron saint. A cordoned off area marks the site. The central panel of the St Kentigern Tapestry (1979) represents the Church and combines the symbols of St Mungo. On the south panel are the ring and salmon of the St Mungo legend *(p 112).* The tapestry was woven by the Edinburgh Dovecot Studios to the designs of Robert Stewart. The Chapel of the Blessed Virgin is the area immediately to the east, distinguished by its elaborate net vaulting with intricately carved bosses. Beyond, the ambulatory is flanked by a series of chapels.
The mid-13C lower chapter room was remodelled at the time of Bishop William Lauder (1408-25). The bishop's arms figure on the canopy. The 15C ribbed vaulting sports heraldic roof bosses including the arms of James I.

Blacader Aisle. – Projecting from the south transept this last addition to the church was designed as a two storey extension by Glasgow's first Archbishop, Robert Blacader. Only the existing or lower part was finished. The late Gothic style with its fully developed ribbed vaulting gives an effect of richness. Look for the carved boss recalling the legend of the hermit Fergus, who was found near to death by St Mungo. The next day the body was placed on a cart yoked to two bulls with the intention of burying the hermit where they stopped. Some say this chapel marks the site.

★★★THE BURRELL COLLECTION (AX M⁵ – *plan p 115*)

tc A visit to the Burrell Collection is a must in order to appreciate the collector for his achievement, the collection for its scope and depth and the imaginative and unashamedly modern building for its accomplished accommodation and enhancement of the treasures.

The collection. – It is important to bear in mind that the Collection was amassed by one man, essentially for his own pleasure. Burrell started buying for the collection only once it had been handed over to public ownership. In about 80 years of collecting, with resources far below those of the millionaire class such as Frick, Hearst and Mellon, Burrell showed taste, insight, discernment and determination in his pursuit and acquisition of the more than 8 000 items. He had strong personal preferences for the medieval glass and tapestries, Chinese ceramics and 19C French paintings. In his latter years he made a determined effort to increase the comprehensiveness of the collection with a view to it becoming public.

The collecter. – Characteristically this very private man, **Sir William Burrell** (1861-1958) maintained that "the Collection and not the collecter is the important thing". William joined the family shipowning firm at the early age of 14 and by 40 he and his brother had made their fortunes. After the final sale of the fleet during World War I he spent the rest of his life amassing his vast art collection which he housed in his Glasgow home at 8 Great Western Terrace and then in his baronial mansion, Hutton Castle. From 1911 Burrell kept a full record of his activities in 28 school jotters known as the Purchase Books. Aged 82 he bequeathed his treasures to his native city with strict conditions for housing the collection : "in a rural setting far removed from the atmospheric pollution of urban conurbations, not less than 16 miles from the Royal Exchange".

The building. – In 1983 almost forty years later and after years of indecision, delays, disappointments, propositions and counter-propositions the Collection found a permanent home and was finally on display to the public. The thoroughly modern custom-built building of warm red sandstone, light wood and walls of glass in its parkland setting with a woodland backdrop, successfully enhances the varied items of the collection. The result fulfills Burrell's own wishes "as simple as possible" to house the "fine contents".

VISIT *time : 1 1/2 hours*

For those with little time to spare the major works are located on the accompanying plan, try not to get side-tracked ! As only parts of the Collection can be shown at any one time, certain sections may change periodically.

Ancient Civilizations. – The 2C AD **Warwick Vase** (1), the centrepiece of the courtyard, is an 18C marble reconstruction incorporating some of the original fragments found at Hadrian's Villa, Tivoli, The work is a recent Trustees' acquisition. Compare the balance, proportion and naturalism of the Egyptian items, designed for eternity, with the later Greek works often having motifs derived from the Near East. The skill of the Greek vase painter is well displayed in the 4C BC bell krater from Lucana in red figure earthenware.

The noble phorphory **Head of Zeus or Poseidon** (2), a 4C AD Roman copy of a Greek bronze, shows as much realism as the mosaic cockerel also Roman of IC BC. The Mesopotamian terracotta lion head of the Isin-Larsa period (*c* 2020-1600 BC) probably belonged to a protective figure in a temple.

THE BURRELL COLLECTION
(GROUND FLOOR)

Oriental Art. – Burrell had a particular fondness for Chinese ceramics, bronzes, jades and this wide ranging section has items from the 3rd millennium BC to the 19C. The charming earthenware watchdog with its intricate harness is an example of one of the earliest pieces from the Han Dynasty (3C BC - 3C AD). The camel, horse and attendant and tomb figures are 8C Tang Dynasty. These earthenware objects all display green, amber and cream lead glazes.

Set against the woodland backdrop is the serenely seated figure of a **lohan** (3) or disciple of Buddha. Almost life-size this Ming Dynasty (1366-1644) figure dated 1484, is a masterpiece of enamel biscuit ware. The superbly decorated underglaze red-decoration **ewer** (4) is of the late 14C Ming period. The decorative scheme includes two cartouches filled with a lotus scroll of five flowers, varyingly open and shut. The full range and beauty of the ceramics, bronzes and jades can be appreciated by following the porcelain corridor.

Medieval and Post-Medieval European Art. – The tapestry and stained glass sections are the highlights of this department. Admire the group of tapestries, in particular the 15C Tournai **Peasants Hunting Rabbits with Ferrets** (5) so alive with amazing and amusing details, and the 16C *Flight of the Heron*.

The stained glass bay, where the smaller gems are assembled, rewards a close inspection. The 12C fragment from the then Abbey Church of St Denis figures the **Prophet Jeremiah** (6). The Romanesque bronze, the **Temple Pyx** (7), shows three sleeping warriors.

GLASGOW

Paintings, Drawings and Bronzes.

Of the early works, Giovanni Bellini introduces a delightful touch to this often portrayed subject, the **Virgin and Child** (8), with the child dangling a flower by a thread. Burrell gathered together a notable holding of 19C French works (Géricault, Delacroix, Courbet, Daumier...). Degas is well represented by examples of his two favourite subjects, dancers and horses. The pastel **Jockeys in the Rain** (9) shows a strong sense of movement. In the 17-18C period room are a selection of portraits, *Portrait of a Gentleman* (Frans Hals) at £ 14 500 the most expensive item in the original collection, the youthful Rembrandt **Self-Portrait** (10) and Hogarth's *Mrs Ann Lloyd*. One of the final rooms is devoted to works by the Maris brothers, members of the Hague School, a movement contemporary with the Glasgow Boys.

Hutton Castle Rooms.

Burrell stipulated that the Hall, Drawing and Dining Rooms from Hutton Castle should be incorporated in the gallery. Arranged around the courtyard they are furnished with fine panelling, tapestries, medieval fireplaces, antique furniture, precious carpets and stained glass.

MEDIEVAL GLASGOW
Cathedral Square to Glasgow Green *(Plan p 119)*

The main road from the cathedral to the bridgehead followed this route to Glasgow Cross then branched to the right via Bridgegate.

Cathedral Square (DY) – Prior to the Reformation this was the very heart of the ecclesiastical city. Cathedral, Bishop's Castle and canons' manses overlooked this focal point. The Bishop's Castle (a stone in the Royal Infirmary forecourt marks the site) was destroyed to make way for the Adam brothers' 1792 Royal Infirmary building. The present **Royal Infirmary** (DY) is a 20C replacement. It was in a ward of the original one that **Sir Joseph Lister** (1827-1912) pioneered the use of carbolic acid as an antiseptic in the treatment of wounds.

tc **Provand's Lordship** (DY). – Provand's Lordship, a former prebendal manse dating from 1471, and the cathedral are the only survivors of the medieval town. The two lower floors are furnished with 16 - 20C pieces.

Necropolis (DY). – Behind the cathedral on the far bank of the Molendinar Burn, is the formal burial garden dating from 1833. Pathways bordered by elaborate tombs lead up to the highest point commanded by John Knox atop his column (DY A). There is a good **view★** of the cathedral and Glasgow away to the southwest.

The statues in the square include one of the missionary explorer David Livingstone (DY B) *(p 49)* and an equestrian statue (DY D) of King William of Orange.

High Street (CDYZ). – A plaque (DY F) on the disused goods yard opposite College Street marks the site of Old College *(see below)* from 1632 to 1870 and the original Hunterian Museum prior to their transfer to Gilmorehill.

At 215 High Street (DY E), the former British Linen Bank building is still crowned by the figure of Pallas, goddess of wisdom and weaving. The stained glass above the door portrays a flax boat.

Glasgow Cross (CZ). – Until Victorian times the Cross at the junction of High Street Saltmarket, Gallowgate and Trongate was the heart of Glasgow. Defoe much admired the Cross set as it was at the centre of a prosperous commercial area known as the "Golden Acre". The **Tolbooth Steeple★** (CZ), in the middle of the street is a striking reminder of this former elegance. The seven storey tower was originally adjoined by the elegant tolbooth and then the Tontine Hotel *(p 112)*. The actual **mercat cross** (CZ) is a 1929 replica.

Bridgegate (CZ). – This now rather dismal street was once a fashionable main thoroughfare to the city's first stone bridge built in 1345. The **steeple** (CZ), rising out of derelict warehouses is all that remains of the 1659 Merchants Hall (demolished 1818), the business and social meeting place for Glasgow's merchants. The steeple rising in tiers to a height of 164ft served as a lookout for cargoes coming up the Clyde. The Ship of Trade in full sail symbolizes the origins of Glasgow's trade. A new Merchants House was built in 1877 in George Square *(p 118)*.

The Saltmarket took over as the main thoroughfare in the 19C.

Glasgow Green (CDZ). – On the north bank of the Clyde this park is one of Glasgow's most historic sites. Successively or simultaneously it was a place of common grazing, bleaching, public hangings, military reviews and parades, merry making at Glasgow Fair and above all of public meetings and free speech. Alternating between fashionable and disreputable it has always been most fiercely defended against encroachment and today lies within the GEAR (Glasgow Eastern Area Renewal Scheme) revitalisation programme. Monuments on the Green include the now sadly abandoned Doulton Fountain (CZ G) – a remarkable piece of pottery figuring Queen Victoria – one to Nelson (DZ J) and the nearby stone (DZ K) commemorating the spot where James Watt, while out on a Sunday walk, worked out his improvement to the steam engine.

tc **People's Palace** (DZ M¹). – *Enter by Morris Place.*

The People's Palace museum and winter gardens were opened in 1898 as a cultural centre for the east end. Now a local and social history museum, the exhibits recount the story of Glasgow from earliest times to the present. There is an exotic plant display in the winter gardens.

Templeton Business Centre (DZ). – Built in 1889 this highly unusual, colourful and richly decorated Dogo's Palace originally housed a carpet factory.

tc **The Barras** (DZ). – A weekend market. An assortment of goods at bargain prices, colourful characters and street entertainment are some of the attractions of a visit to the Barras. Refurbishment and pedestrian precincts have followed in the wake of a renewal programme.

GLASGOW UNIVERSITY AREA *(Plan p 115)*

Bishop William Turnbull founded the university in 1451 and the first classes were held in the cathedral. The early university was greatly dependent on the church and the Bishops and Archbishops of Glasgow held the office of Chancellor until 1642. The university then acquired properties in the High Street which were used until 1632 when the **Old College** a handsome building arranged around a double quadrangle was built. The High Street premises were abandoned and destroyed in 1870 when the university moved to the present site on the estate of Gilmorehill in the west end of the city. The consequent imposing edifice remains the focal point of a complex of new (Adam Smith, Boyd Orr and Hetherington Buildings, Hunterian Art Gallery and Library) and refurbished buildings throughout the local streets. Today eight faculties (Arts, Divinity, Engineering, Law, Medicine, Science, Social and Veterinary Medicine) welcome a student population of over 10 000.

Gilmorehill Building. – This massive Gothic Revival building, the oldest of the university's present buildings, was designed by George Gilbert Scott. Originally incomplete due to a lack of funds, it was Scott's son, John Oldrid, who completed the design with Bute Hall (1882) and the tower (1887). The main façade overlooks Kelvingrove Park. In Professors' Square at the west end of the main building, is the **Lion and Unicorn Staircase** from the Old College. Both the staircase, and Pearce Lodge which faces University Avenue, are reconstructed from the Old College buildings.

tc **Hunterian Museum** (AV M⁶). – *Main building, East Quadrangle, First Floor enter from University Avenue side.*

William Hunter (1718-83), successful medical practitioner, anatomist and pioneer obstetrician, was also a great collector, investing in coins, mss, paintings, minerals, ethnographical, anatomical and zoological specimens. Hunter bequeathed all to the university and in 1807 a Hunterian Museum was opened to house the priceless treasure amassed in his London home. His brother John's collection formed the nucleus of a second Hunterian Museum, now in the Royal College of Surgeons, London *(see the Michelin Green Guide London)*. Today William's treasured items are divided between the museum and the art gallery.

Museum. – The first gallery presents a historical introduction to the university and its many famous sons. The Hunter **coin and medal collection★**, once said to be second only to the French Royal Collection is exhibited in a purpose built gallery. A chronological presentation from a collection of over 30000 items traces the development of coinage from ancient times to the present. The earliest Scottish coinage appeared in 1136 and by the late 12C early 13C there were no fewer than sixteen mints, the greatest number ever. No coins have been minted in Scotland since the closure of the Edinburgh Mint in the 18C following the Treaty of Union. Note the rare example of Scotland's first gold coin issued *c*1357 by David II and one of James V's bonnet pieces (1539) using Scottish gold. The

(The University of Glasgow)
Scottish James V ducat of 1540

endpiece of the collection is the 1984 pound coin with the Scottish design on the reverse. Exhibits in the main hall, beyond, cover material from Captain Cook's voyages, a pleasant display on the Romans in Scotland, early civilizations and British prehistory. The upper gallery is devoted to geology and archaeology. Do not miss recent finds, the Bearsden Shark and the only evidence of a Scottish dinosaur.

★★**Hunterian Art Gallery** (AV M²). – The 1980 building provides a permanent home
tc for the university's art collection which is particularly noted for the Whistler works, 19 and 20C Scottish art and the Mackintosh wing. Outstanding amongst the Old Masters are Rembrandt's *The Entombment* (1) and Rubens *Head of an Old Man* (1). Alongside canvases by the portraitists Raeburn *(Mrs Hay of Spot,* 2), Ramsay (the founder William Hunter, 2), Romney and Reynolds, are several Stubbs and Chardins. Pride of place is given to the **Whistler Collection★★★** (4, 5 and 6) an important holding of works by **James McNeill Whistler** (1834-1903) covering most periods of his career. Examples of his portraiture work include the striking group of full-lengths *(Pink and Silver-The Pretty Scamp ; Red and Black – The Fan* and *Pink and Gold – The Tulip ;* all in 4). A master in the art of etching, the French, Thames and Venetian sets demonstrate his stylistic development.

The remaining galleries present 19 and 20C Scottish art together with some French Impressionists. Breaking away from the conventions of Victorian art, William Mc Taggart (1835-1910) developed his own bold style with vigorous brushwork and a sensitive approach to light *(The Sound of Jura,* 3). He was a precursor of the late 19C group, the Glasgow Boys, which originated as a response to the staidness of the Edinburgh art establishment and whose common denominator was realism. Acknowledged father of the group was W. McGregor *(Carse of Lecropt),* while other members included Hornel, Guthrie, Henry, Walton and Lavery (7 and 10).

Pringle's townscapes *(Tollcross* 10) with their individualistic style, herald the Scottish Colourists (8), namely Fergusson, Peploe, Cadell and Hunter. The modern section includes another atmospheric canvas by Joan Eardley *(Salmon Nets and the Sea* 1960).

★★★**Mackintosh Wing**. – The wing is a reconstruction of the architect designer **Charles Rennie Mackintosh's** (1868-1928) Glasgow home. The domestic interiors with highly distinctive decorative schemes are good examples of Mackintosh's pioneering work in modern architecture and design. Functional, with a restraint and purity of line, painted white woodwork is relieved by decorative motifs. The furnishings include decorative plaques by his wife, Margaret Macdonald.

The top floor exhibition gallery displays selections from the many drawings, watercolours and sketches in the Mackintosh collection.

★★**Art Gallery and Museum Kelvingrove** (AV M³). – Officially opened in 1902 this
tc imposing red sandstone building in Kelvingrove Park was partly financed from the profits of the 1888 International Exhibition on the same site. The nucleus of the permanent collection was formed by the McLellan Bequest (1854) and ever since prominent citizens and captains of industry such as Graham-Gilbert, James Donald and William McInnes have generously continued to bequeath their art treasures, making this one of the outstanding civic collections. The visitor should make a particular effort to visit the first floor galleries.

Ground floor. – The sections of particular interest on this floor are the Scottish Natural History display (east court), the attractively presented European arms and armour (west court) and Scottish weapons, as well as Neolithic, Bronze, Iron Age and Roman material. The Glasgow Style gallery displays the work of Charles Rennie Mackintosh and his Glasgow contemporaries.

First floor. – The upper galleries are devoted to fine and decorative arts particularly glass, silver, ceramics and jewellery.

ITALIAN : Giorgione's *The Adulteress brought before Christ* is accompanied by the fragment *Head of a Man. The Baptism in the Jordan* is a good example of Salvator Rosa's work. There are also fine works by Filippino Lippi, Paris Bordone, Domenichino and Guardi.

DUTCH AND FLEMISH : the gallery has a particularly good holding of 17C paintings. Major works include Jacob Jordaens' *The Fruit Seller,* Van Orley's *Virgin and Child* and a combined composition by Rubens and Bruegel the Elder, *Nature Adorned by the Graces.* Rembrandt is represented by *A Man in Armour* and the earlier still-life *The Carcase of an Ox.* Alongside are notable landscapes by Jacob van Ruisdael and still-lifes by Kalf.

FRENCH : there is a strong emphasis on 19C and early 20C works. Open-air painters of the Barbizon School such as Millet, Daubigny and Harpignies were the forerunners of the Impressionists. Millet's *Going to Work* is a major canvas of this period. Fantin-Latour is represented by several works including *Chrysanthemums* and Courbet by a major still-life *Flower in a basket*. Beyond, compare the various Impressionist works by Monet *(Vétheuil)*, Pissarro, Renoir and Sisley. The Van Gogh portrait of the famous Glasgow art dealer *Alexander Reid* (1887) was painted when the artist and dealer shared rooms in Paris. Reid was responsible for promoting the Impressionists in Scotland and many of the collection's works came through his hands. The bronze of Reid by Benno Schotz was done a year before the sitter died (1927). Other contemporaries of Van Gogh were Cézanne and Gauguin. Later movements are represented by Vuillard *(Mother and Child)* and the Nabis, Braque and Picasso, the Cubists, Derain *(Blackfriars)*, Matisse and the Fauves.

BRITISH : the regal full-length of *Archibald 3rd Duke of Argyll* and the *Dowager Countess of Stafford* show the range of the 18C portraitist Allan Ramsay. Works by Raeburn (*Mr and Mrs Campbell* and the so Scottish *Mrs Anne Campbell of Park*) hang alongside those by Reynolds and Romney. Famous sitters include *Mary Queen of Scots* (unknown artist) and *Robert Burns* (Alexander Nasmyth).

David Wilkie and the Faed brothers excelled in historical and domestic scenes while the awesome grandeur of Scottish scenery was well captured by Horatio McCulloch (*Glencoe*). The Pre-Raphaelites (Burne-Jones, Ford Madox Brown and Rossetti) combine symbolism and a liking for sharp detail. The works of William McTaggart with free bold brushwork and feeling for light, break from the traditions of his time. *Dawn at sea - homewards* is an excellent example of his best work, with that very luminous quality.

The modern works continue to display a preoccupation with colour.

The last room is devoted to the Glasgow Boys *(qv)*. One of the leading works is Henry's *A Galloway Landscape*. The Henry-Hornel compositions show a distinctively Japanese flavour *(p 142)*. Lavery depicts the Glasgow International Exhibition of 1888 which helped to pay for the museum. Intermingled are the colourful canvases of the Scottish Colourists, a generation later (Peploe, Hunter, Cadell and Fergusson).

The two attractive Normandy landscapes are examples of the highly distinctive work of John Q.Pringle.

tc **Botanic Gardens** (AV). – The gardens are renowned for their collection of orchids, begonias and tree ferns. The Kibble Palace, which houses the tree ferns and plants from temperate areas is a unique example of a Victorian iron conservatory. The Main Range contains the tropical and economic plants.

What to look for in Glasgow's museums and art galleries:

Old Masters: Art Gallery and Museum Kelvingrove
Whistler Collection: Hunterian Art Gallery
Mackintosh works: Hunterian Art Gallery, Glasgow School of Art
Spanish Paintings: Pollok House
Impressionists: Art Gallery and Museum Kelvingrove, the Burrell Collection
Glasgow School: Hunterian Art Gallery, Art Gallery and Museum Kelvingrove

CENTRAL GLASGOW *(Plan p 119)*

George Square (CY). – Today the heart of Glasgow, the busy square with attractive floral displays in summer and Christmas decorations in winter, is lined by imposing 19C buildings. Development of the square and adjoining streets began in 1782 and by the beginning of the 19C it had become the city's hotel centre. The initial steps towards a change in character came with the building of the Merchant's House closely followed by the Post Office and City Chambers.

On the north and adjacent to Queen Street Station, is the only hotel to remain, the North British. The **Merchant's House** (f 1869, CY) on the west side, and today the home of the Glasgow Chamber of Commerce, is denoted by the Ship of Trade aloft, a replica of the one in Bridgegate *(p 116)*. On the south are the Post Office buildings. Occupying *tc* all the east side are the **City Chambers★** (CY C) another of Glasgow's magnificent Victorian buildings, a heritage from the time when Glasgow was the second city of the Empire. Inside grandeur and opulence reign supreme, particularly in the loggia, council and banqueting halls.

Sir Walter Scott on the central column dominates a series of famous men : (clockwise) Peel, Gladstone, Lord Clyde, John Moore, Watt...

tc **Hutchesons' Hall** (CY). – *NTS Visitors Centre*. The "hospital" of the original endowment of 1639 for 11 old men and 12 orphan boys was demolished when Hutcheson Street was opened up. The replacement institutional headquarters (1802-5) were designed by David Hamilton to provide the focal point for one of the new thoroughfares of the Merchant City. Statues of the two founding Hutcheson brothers were removed from the original building to occupy niches on the main frontage.Two of Glasgow's best known public schools originate from the early endowment. Hutchesons' Hall is now the Glasgow offices, visitors centre and shop of the National Trust for Scotland.

tc **Royal Exchange** (CY). – Now one of Glasgow's public lending libraries, this elegant building started life in the 1770s as Glasgow's most splendid mansion, the home of the Tobacco Lord, **William Cunninghame**. In the early 18C it became the Royal Exchange to replace the merchants premises in the Tontine Hotel *(p 116)* which had become too cramped. Extensions included a great hall to the rear and an entrance portico as endpiece to Ingram Street. In 1949 the premises were taken over again to house the library of another 18C merchant, **Stirling**. The great hall now the lending department, has a magnificent coffered ceiling.

★**Glasgow School of Art** (BV B). – Charles Rennie Mackintosh designed this major
tc landmark in the history of European architecture when he was only 28. The building
was completed in two stages, 1897-9 and 1907-9 and almost 90 years later it remains
highly functional while also housing one of the largest collections of Mackintosh
furniture, designs and paintings. Of particular interest is the Library, an architectural
tour de force with its three storey high windows and suspended ceiling and
Mackintosh's most original and celebrated interior. Visitors can also see his
decorative stained glass, metalwork, light fittings etc in the Board Room, Director's Room and
the Furniture Gallery, which contains furniture designed for the School, Miss Cranston's
Tea Rooms and "Windyhill".

tc **The Tenement House** (BV A). – This tenement flat consists of two rooms, kitchen
and bathroom and evokes tenement life in the 19C. The original fittings include the
box-beds, gas lamps and coal fired ranges with coal bin. The housing demands of
Glasgow's ever increasing population were met by building tenements. They ranged
from the humble single-end to the grander and highly desirable residences of the West
End. Community life centred on the close and back court. Privacy and neighbourliness
were both possible.

SOUTH OF THE CLYDE *(Plan p 115)*

★★**Museum of Transport** (BX M⁴). – Opened in 1964, the museum is housed in an old
tc tramway depot. The comprehensive collections cover all forms of transport, excepting
aviation. Take plenty of time and be prepared to be side-tracked and delighted by
this fascinating collection.

Trams and trolley buses. – A raised catwalk allows visitors to inspect the upper decks
of the vintage tramcars which were so much part of Glasgow's street scene from 1872
to 1962. These are arranged in chronological order : no 543 the horse-drawn one,
no 1 089, the 1926 single-deck car and no 1 392 of the type nicknamed the Cunarder
because of its comfort, the last tram ever built in the UK (1952). This extremely popular
collection was the nucleus around which the museum was established. The trolley-bus
is an example from the fleet which operated in Glasgow from 1949 to 1967.

(Glasgow Art Gallery & Museum)
1906 Arroll Johnston 18hp production model of the TT winner of 1905 (Museum of Transport)

Motor cars. – The emphasis is on **Scottish built cars★★★** with examples from manufacturers such as Argyll, Albion and Arrol-Johnston, who were all well to the fore in the car industry of the early 20C. The great traditions of Scottish car manufacturing are represented here by the 1902 Argyll Light Car, the 1906 Arrol-Johnston TT Model 18, fast and powerful for its time and the Argyll Voiturette. The 1963 Hillman Imp, IMP 1 was the first Scottish built car after a lapse of 30 years.

Fire vehicles. – This section (behind the Scottish cars) covers a range of fire fighting equipment from the earliest used by insurance companies, those powered by steam to the most modern Leyland Firemaster.

Bicycles and motor cycles. – Follow the development of the bicycle from the replica of MacMillan's 1839 bicycle (on the wall) through boneshakers, sociables, tricycles to the gleaming lightweight road racers and fun cycles of today. The motor cycle section has early examples of British designed machines from the time when British makers dominated the industry.

Railway locomotives. – Most of the seven items on display are from the former Scottish railway companies. There is also a fascinating model railway, a spell-binder for many.

Subway. – Since the 1970s modernization of the Glasgow subway system, the reconstruction of Merkland Street Station is a cherished reminder of days gone by. One of the trains is a cable train from 1898 while the second is an electric powered one from the 1950s.

★★★The Clyde Room of Ship Models. – This beautifully presented collection displays the products of the Scottish shipyards through the ages and in particular those of the Clyde. Side by side are sailing ships (the fully rigged *Cutty Sark),* Clyde River Steamers *(Comet, Columba* and other well loved excursion steamers), cross channel steamers often Denny products, ocean-going passenger liners *(The Queens)*, warships (HMS *Hood)* and yachts including the Czar Alexander II's circular and unsinkable model.

★Pollok House (AX D). – *3 miles southwest of the city centre. The Burrell Collection*
tc (p 113) is in the grounds of Pollok House.
The highlight of this 18C mansion, set in spacious parkland, is a superb collection of paintings acquired by the connoisseur and collector **Sir William Stirling Maxwell** (1818-78). A pioneer authority on the Spanish School of painting, Sir William's enlightened acquisitions form a most representative collection, which today is displayed in a setting of elegant and tastefully furnished rooms.

★★The paintings. – The most memorable pictures in the collection are two superb portraits by El Greco (main corridor). There is also Tristan's *Adoration of the Magi*, Alonso Cano's *Adam and Eve*, Murillo's *Madonna and Child with St John* (all three in the Billiard Room), Goya's series of etchings *Los Disparates* (Dining Room Corridor) and works by William Blake (Cedar Room). In addition there are canvases by Sanchez Coello, Spanish Court Painter, Morales, del Piombo, Jordaens, Mengs, Kneller, Hogarth, Knox and Nasmyth. The Maxwell family portraits hang in the Entrance Hall, a late 19C addition.

EXCURSIONS

★★★The Trossachs. – *Description p 197.*

★★Loch Lomond. – *Description p 152.*

tc **The Clyde Estuary by boat.** – During July and August the paddle steamer *Waverley* visits the Firth of Clyde resorts with departures from Glasgow, Helensburgh, Dunoon, Rothesay, Largs, Millport and Ayr. In the 19C a succession of paddle steamers sailed the Clyde taking Glaswegians "doon the watter" for the day. The Waverley, the last of these famous Clyde paddle steamers, plies her home waters in the high season. The day or half day cruises are an excellent way of discovering the attractive Clyde estuary and its many resorts. For descriptions of the individual sights see below.

★The Clyde Estuary : north shore to Dunoon via the Cowal Peninsula. – *77 miles, 2 hours excluding visiting times. Leave Glasgow by Great Western Road and the A 82. Branch off to the left in the direction of Dumbarton and Helensburgh.*

The distillery and bonded warehouses on the left are guarded by a flock of geese, after the Roman fashion.

tc **Dumbarton Castle.** – The castle has a strategic **site★** perched on the basaltic plug, Dumbarton Rock (240ft-73m). The rock was once the capital of the independent Kingdom of Strathclyde (incorporated into Scotland 1034), a royal seat, and then in medieval times a much disputed stronghold The remaining fortifications are mainly 18C. Steps *(278 from the Governor's House)* lead up to the viewing table on White Tower summit and then to the Magazine on the second summit (*an additional 8 1 steps*). From the former viewpoint there is a vast **panorama** of the Clyde estuary and surrounding area. In 1548 the five year old Mary Queen of Scots left Dumbarton for a new life in France. There, Mary spent the next fourteen years, with the children of Henri II and Catherine de'Medici.

Cardross. – Pop 1890. It was in the vicinity of this village that Robert the Bruce died in 1329.

★Hill House, Helensburgh. – *Upper Colquhoun Street.*

tc On a hillside overlooking the Clyde stands what is considered to be the best example of Mackintosh's domestic architecture. The house was built in 1902-4 as a family home for the Glasgow publisher Walter W Blackie. Designed as a whole by Mackintosh who lavished the utmost care on the tiniest detail. Everything bears the indelible stamp of his genius. Every space corridor, hall, bed or seating alcove was nobly proportioned in itself as well as being part of a harmonious whole. Predominantly white or dark surfaces were highlighted by inset coloured glass gesso plaster panels, delicate light fittings or stencilled patterns.

The monument on the seafront commemorates **Henry Bell** (1767-1830), the designer of the first steamboat *The Comet,* which operated on the Clyde between 1812-20.

The road follows the eastern shores of Gare Loch and Loch Long, favourite waters for sailing. The villages along their banks are good sailing centres (Rhu, Garelochhead, Kilcreggan and Arrochar).

Arrochar. – Pop 450. This village at the head of Loch Long is a favoured climbing centre nestling at the foot of the Arrochar Alps, Bens Ime, Vane and Arthur or the Cobbler all of which are over 3000ft-914m.

The next part of the itinerary goes through the **Argyll Forest Park**, the first of its kind to be established in 1935. The forest park covers a hundred square miles of scenic territory on the Cowal Peninsula between Lochs Fyne and Long. A variety of forest roads and recreational facilities are open to the public.

The forested valley sides of Glen Croe are overlooked by the slopes of Ben Arthur, more popularly known as the Cobbler (2891ft-881m).

The Rest and be Thankful. – 860ft-262m. This windy pass is the main gateway to Argyll. It was named from a stone seat, which has now vanished, but once carried this inscription.

Once through Glen Kinglas branch left by the A815 towards Dunoon.

The road has good views of Loch Fyne, over to Inveraray on the opposite bank.

At Strachur continue on the A815 which goes inland, following the shores of land locked Loch Eck to cross to the opposite side of the Cowal Peninsula.

tc **Younger Botanic Garden, Benmore.** – *Outstation of the Royal Botanic Garden, Edinburgh.* This woodland garden in its attractive mountain setting, is renowned for its rhododendron and azalea collection. The main flowering season is from the end of April to early June.

Dunoon. – Pop 9 718. This popular seaside resort on the Firth of Clyde is the setting each August for the **Cowal Highland Gathering** *(p 28)* and the Pipe Band Championship. The town makes a good centre for touring the Cowal Peninsula and visiting other Clyde resorts by steamer during the high season. Car ferries to Gourock offer a short cut out or an alternative return route.

The Clyde Estuary : south shore to Rothesay using the car ferry. – *3 1 miles 1 hour excluding visiting times and ferry. Leave Glasgow by the M8 in the direction of Greenock.*

Port Glasgow. – Pop 22 876. The town of New Port of Glasgow grew up around the port and harbour facilities built in the 17C by the burgesses of Glasgow, to handle the trade which up until then had passed via the Ayrshire ports. Port Glasgow is still an active shipbuilding centre. Down on the waterfront amidst warehouses and *tc* shipyards, stands a 16C mansion, **Newark Castle.** It was actually on land bought from a 17C owner that the new port was established. A 15C gatehouse and tower house are linked by 16C buildings to form ranges on three sides of a courtyard. The interest of the exterior is at roof level with the interplay between corbelled turrets, crow stepped gables, ornamented dormers and tall chimneys. The detailing on the courtyard fronts is concentrated on the pediments and door surround. Inside, the stairs rise in straight flights to the first floor where the hall has a splendid Renaissance fireplace and in two of the apartments there are remains of 16C painted ceilings.

Greenock. – Pop 69 502. This important shipbuilding centre was the birthplace of **James Watt** (1736-1819) a pioneer in the development of the steam engine. Lyle Hill, behind the town, provides an excellent vantage point, affording a wide **view★★** of the Clyde estuary from Helensburgh right round to Dunoon. Nearby is the memorial, in the form of a Lorraine Cross and anchor combined, to the Free French Naval Forces who lost their lives 1940-5.

Gourock. – Pop 10 922. A continuation of Greenock, this Clyde resort is the railway and ferry terminal for Dunoon.

Wemyss Bay. – Pop 1 513. Mainland railhead for Rothesay.

tc **Rothesay.** – Pop 5 108. Another of the Clyde resorts, Rothesay is Bute's only town. The imposing waterfront dates from Rothesay's heyday as a spa. The safe waters of Rothesay Bay are a base for Clyde yachtsmen. **Rothesay Castle** is an early example of a castle of enclosure. The great circular curtain wall is encircled by a water filled moat and quartered by four round towers, two of which are reduced to their foundations. One has been partially transformed into a dovecot. The forework addition contains the great hall and in the courtyard there is a ruined chapel.

tc **Glasgow Zoological Gardens.** – *6 miles from the city centre by London Road and the A74 the Carlisle road.*
This medium sized zoo is known for its work in the breeding of reptiles.

★★ GLEN COE (Highland and Strathclyde)

Michelin map **401** fold 22 – E 13

This splendid glen with its stark and grandiose mountain scenery lies on the principal tourist route from Glasgow to the north. Awe inspiring in sunshine the glen is all the more dramatically memorable in menacing weather. For the purposes of the guide this heading includes the area from the village of Glencoe to the desolation of Rannoch Moor, although the glen proper is a much more limited section 11 miles long.

The Massacre of Glen Coe. – In the Highlands loyalties ran deep to the Stuart cause and when James VII's short reign (1685-8) ended in flight the clans were reluctant to renounce the cause. After the Convention had offered the Scottish crown to William and Mary (March 1689), John Graham of Claverhouse rallied the Highlanders. Despite victory at Killlecrankie (27 July 1689 ; *p 174*) where they lost their leader, Dundee, all ended a month later in defeat at Dunkeld. William proposed a pardon to all clans willing to take an oath of allegiance by 1 January 1692. **Maclain chief of the MacDonalds of Glencoe** arrived in Fort William belatedly but, within the deadline, only to be sent to Inveraray where he finally took the oath on the 6 January. At the beginning of February a force of 120 men, under Campbell of Glenlyon, was billeted on the MacDonalds and for twelve days all cohabited peacefully. Treachery struck on the 13th with the slaughter of their hosts and the burning of their homes. Forty MacDonalds including Maclain were killed and many more subsequently perished of exposure. An official enquiry confirmed that although the king had given orders, his Scottish Minister, the Master of Stair, undoubtedly exceeded them. Murder was common but "Murder under Trust" was a heinous crime.
Although the glen may be visited in either direction the most dramatic way is to come from the Rannoch Moor end.

SIGHTS

Rannoch Moor. – This endless expanse of desolate moorland lies at a mean height of 1000ft-305m. No road disturbs its isolation. In glacial times it was from an ice sheet centred here that the glaciers flowed westwards gouging the great U-shaped valleys of Glenc Coe and Etive.

Meall à Bhuiridh. – 3 636ft-1 108m. To the south of the A 82 and Kingshouse rises the Hill of the Roaring Stags, noted for its ski runs on the slopes of the White Corries. Although mainly a weekend ski centre the snow cover is usually good.

Glen Etive. – This 10 mile long glacial valley pushes southwards to the even longer sea loch of the same name, which reaches the open sea north of Oban.

Buachaille Etive Mór. – 3 345ft-1 022m. On the left rises the conically shaped Big Herdsman of Etive guarding the entrance to the glen. The mountain offers challenges to the rock climber. Away to the right is the zig-zag of the Devil's Staircase, a series of hairpin bends on the old military road leading over to Kinlochleven. To the right, a flat topped rock, the Study, is said to pinpoint the head of Glen Coe.
From this point there are good views of the Three Sisters on the left.
The road enters the Pass of Glencoe passing the waterfall, and descends slowly towards the valley floor between great rock walls on either side rising to over 3000ft.

The Three Sisters. – These are outliers of the great nine peaked **Bidean nam Bian** (Peak of the Bens) with a highest point of 3766ft-1 141m. The Sisters lie from east to west Beinn Fhada (The Long Mountain), Gearr Aonach (The Short Ridge) and Aonach Dubh (The Black Ridge). Between the first two, although not visible from the glen, is Coire Gabhail (Hidden Valley) where the MacDonalds hid plundered cattle.

Aonach Eagach. – On the right is the great unbroken flank of this serrated ridge (The Notched Heights) which continues for three miles offering the challenge of its ridge walk.
Loch Achtriochtan lies on the flat valley floor.

tc **Glen Coe Centre.** – *NTS Visitors Centre.* The centre provides a good introduction, historical and geological, to the glen and its immediate area. Guided walks are available and a ranger will help with advice on hill walking and climbing in the vicinity. Be guided by those who know the hills. Do not overestimate your capacity.
On the right is Signal Rock used in clan times to warn all in case of danger.

tc **Glencoe.** – Pop 315. On the shores of Loch Leven the village has a small museum, **Glencoe and North Lorn Folk Museum** (main street). Note the glassware engraved with the white rose of the Jacobites, examples of Lochaber axes – some were still in use in 1745 – and the exhibit on the local slate industry.

If you are puzzled by an abbreviation or a symbol in the text or on the maps, look at the key on p 30.

★ The GREAT GLEN (Highland)

Michelin map 401 folds 15, 18, 19 and 22 – E and F 13, F and G 12, G and H 11

The geological fault of the Great Glen slices across the Highlands. From Loch Linnhe in the south a series of freshwater lochs linked by stretches of the Caledonian Canal lead northwards to the Moray Firth. This natural communications corridor divides the Central and Northern Highlands. Loch Ness with its resident monster provides the major tourist attraction.

HISTORICAL AND GEOGRAPHICAL NOTES

Natural avenue. – From earliest times this route was used to penetrate inland. Columba went north to visit the Pictish King Brude at Inverness. Bruce appreciated the importance of its strongholds for repelling attacks or incursions by the Lord of the Isles and other recalcitrant northern chieftains. In the 18C Wade exploited this natural line of communication, when he proposed a military road network linking the key garrison posts at Fort William, Fort Augustus and Inverness. Today the glen is one of the busiest tourist routes to the north.

Caledonian Canal. – This feat of civil engineering was built between 1803 and 1822 to connect the North Sea and Atlantic Ocean and save vessels the treacherous waters of the Pentland Firth and the long haul round Cape Wrath. Initially proposed and surveyed by James Watt the work was later supervised by **Thomas Telford** (1757-1834). Of the total length of 60 miles, lochs account for 38 miles while the remaining 22 were man-made. Twenty nine locks were required to deal with the varying levels of the lochs. The most spectacular series, known as **Neptune's Staircase**, is at Banavie near Fort William.

tc **Boat trips.** – The canal is used principally by pleasure craft and is operated by the British Waterways Board. Enquire locally about cruiser operators : some offer monster hunting systems as an option. Several companies operate cruises on Loch Ness with departures from Inverness and Fort Augustus. For full details apply to the local tourist information centres.

Nessie. – The initial sighting was made in the 8C by a monk. Despite various expeditions some highly equipped with submarines, helicopters and sonar electronic cameras, Loch Ness has failed to reveal its secret (the true identity of Nessie). The Loch Ness Monster Exhibition at Drumnadrochit provides an excellent introduction to the Nessie enigma. The tradition is hardly surprising in a country where the kelpie or water-horse was common in the tales and legends of the past.

Fort William to Inverness 65 *miles – about 1/1/2 hours*

The main lochside road the A82 between Fort William and Inverness is a very busy one and delays at the swing bridges can cause nose to tail driving. A slower road on the east side of the glen follows Wade's 18C military road.

Leave Fort William (p 108) by the A82.

Spean Bridge. – Pop 235. Small village at the junction of Glen Spean leading to Aviemore and the Spey Valley.

Follow the A82.

Commando Memorial. – The monument, to the left of the road, is a memorial to all Commandos who lost their lives in World War II. The site marks their training ground. On a clear day Ben Nevis can be seen away to the left.

Loch Lochy. – Just under 10 miles long the loch narrows towards its head. The hill slopes of the lochsides are blanketed with forests.

Laggan Locks. – Take the chance to go off the road and watch the many boats negotiate the locks between Loch Lochy (93ft) and Loch Oich (106ft).

The road crosses to the west side.

Loch Oich. – This straight, narrow and relatively shallow loch required considerable dredging during the construction of the canal.

Fort Augustus. – Pop 575. This busy little town at the southern end of Loch Ness sits astride the Caledonian Canal and its several locks. It becomes a bottleneck for traffic with the swing bridge.

tc The **Great Glen Exhibition** recounts by means of exhibits and a film the history of the
tc Great Glen from the vitrified forts of Pictish times to the present day. **Fort Augustus Abbey** stands on the site of Wade's 18C fort at the south end of Loch Ness. In 1867 the property was presented to the Benedictine Order and monks from one of the few remaining Scottish monastic foundations in Germany settled in Fort Augustus. The community of Benedictine monks continues its educational role with the running of a Catholic secondary school. The Abbey Church is an interesting 20C achievement.

★★**Loch Ness.** – The pleasantly pastoral aspect with its forested sides and various settlements, lacks the rugged grandeur of some of the north western lochs. The narrow and 23 mile long loch has a maximum depth of 754ft. These dark waters are the home of the elusive Nessie. It was here that the racing motorist John Cobb (d 1952) lost his life in an attempt to beat the water speed record. A roadside memorial commemorates his attempt. The village of Foyers on the far side was the site of an aluminium smelter which closed in 1967.

There are few glimpses of the loch prior to Drummadrochit due to the tree screen.

tc **Urquhart Castle.** – *Fairly steep path and stairs down to the castle.* The ruins are strategically set on a rocky promontory jutting forth into Loch Ness. The castle was one of a chain of strongholds garrisoning the Great Glen, a fact which gave it a turbulent history. Seen from the roadside the various parts are easy to distinguish. The gatehouse on the landward side gives access to a double bailey courtyard. To the right the Norman motte is encircled by walls. On the seaward side, beyond the water gate are the basements of a domestic range and on the left the four storeyed tower house. From the viewing platform (*50 steps*) there are good **views** of the castle's layout and up and down Loch Ness.

There is a good **view** of the northern part of Loch Ness as the road descends to Drumnadrochit.

tc **Drumnadrochit.** – Pop 359. This lochside village is acquiring a growing reputation for its **Loch Ness Monster Exhibition★**. Visit the exhibition, examine the evidence, and judge for yourself. Accompanying a scale model of the loch in the first room are some of the monster's photographs with explanations and scientific judgements. The section beyond covers the various exploration vessels and latest techniques (sonar traces and computer enhancement by NASA) employed in an attempt to solve the mystery.

The final stretch of lochside road provides some good views of the loch.

★ HADDINGTON (Lothian) Pop 8 139

Michelin map **401** fold 32 – L16

Haddington is a handsome market town where the triangular street plan testifies to its medieval origins. The many 18C town houses are witness to the prosperity occasioned by the agricultural improvements of the period. Set on the banks of the Tyne the town serves the outlying agricultural area.

HISTORICAL NOTES

The 12C town grew up around the royal palace in which Alexander II was born in 1198. Royal patronage was extended to the town itself, created a royal burgh by David I, who was responsible for the establishment of two monastic communities. To allow the royal burgh to exercise its foreign trading privileges, Aberlady five miles to the north, was designated as the town's port. The insecurity which followed the Wars of Independence, led to a decline in trade. However, by the 16C this was Scotland's fourth largest town. The Reformation saw the dispersal of the wealth and destruction of the monastic houses while ensuing strife led to the building of a town wall (*c*1604).

The 18C, Haddington's golden age, was the direct result of increasing prosperity created by the agricultural improvements. East Lothian always to the fore in agriculture, witnessed many changes in the first half of the 18C due to the endeavours of improvers such as Fletcher and John Cockburn of Ormiston.

Church Street .... B 2
Lodge Street .... A 3
Newton Port .... AB 6
The Sands .... B 7
Victoria Terrace ...... B 10

TOWN CENTRE

The original market place of this royal burgh was the triangle formed by Market, Hardgate, High and Court Streets. The burgesses built gable ended houses onto this market place with long riggs leading back to the town wall and pends leading off. In the 16C, back to back housing was built in the middle, giving the present layout. The houses themselves were often refronted, in other cases new fenestration was fitted into a chimney gable end. The streets are lined with some rubblework buildings, some harled and painted, but all with a certain harmony of colour since the 1962 conservation programme. Remark the variety of wrought iron shop signs.

★High Street (AB) – The south side has a continuous line of frontages of varying heights, style and colour topped by roofs varyingly pitched, interrupted only by closes. The mercat cross (B) with the Haddington goat is a 19C replacement. Note in particular no 27 with the decorative chimney, no 31 with the roll skewputts of the dormer window and nos 43 and 45 with the stair turret rising through three storeys.

Lodge Street (A 3). – A continuation of High Street, this short street mingles markedly contrasting styles. **Carlyle House** (A A) a misnomer, with its highly ornate Italian palace style façade of the 18C is all the more striking for its direct contrast to the adjoining vernacular house (A B) and its attractive Venetian window. The intervening pend leads to the chidhood home (A) of Jane Welsh, wife of Thomas Carlyle the "Sage of Chelsea" *(p 83).*

Town House (A H). – This splendidly dignified William Adam building (1748), with pediment and pilasters framing a Venetian window, befitted the civic dignity of a town prospering from the agricultural revolution. The steeple was a Gillespie Graham addition in 1831.

Court Street (A). – Leading to the west port, this tree-lined street is bordered on the north side by splendid town mansions, such as the late 18C Bank of Scotland (A). Opposite are the 1854 Corn Exchange (A D) and William Burn's Gothic Council Buildings on the onetime site of the royal palace.

Market Street (AB). – Late 18 and early 19C three to four storey buildings line the north or original side of the triangle. Some gable ends were replaced by new front elevations. Survivals include no 32 with its chimney gable. **Mitchell's Close** (AB) on the north side, (restored 1967) is more typical of the 17C pattern with rubble masonry, pantiles, inset dormers, crow steps, turnpike stairs - a charming vernacular ensemble.

Hardgate (B). – The most striking building is the white harled **Kinloch House** (B) with its Dutch style gable, a good example of an 18C laird's town house. The custom stone (B) in front of the George Hotel marks the spot where customs dues were paid in medieval times.

RIVERSIDE

Church Street (B 2). – On the right is a charming three storey building, the Old Grammar School (B E) and library, combining the rigour of the Georgian style and the mellowness of the rubblework and its decorative patterns. The church opposite stands on the site of the original Lamp of the Lothian, which belonged to the Franciscan friary founded in 1138 by Ada, wife of Prince Henry. No 20 with its goat sculpture has a corbelled corner leading to the Sands (B 7) and down to the riverside.
The sturdily solid 16C **Nungate Bridge** (B) with pointed cutwaters, offers a good view upstream of St Mary's Church in its riverside setting. The far bank was the site of the Cistercian Abbey from which it took its name.
The walled garden known as Lady Kitty's Garden (B), has in one corner a cylindrical **dovecot** *(now an interpretative centre).* This was the practising ground for archery and bowling in the Middle Ages.

tc **St Mary's Parish Church** (B). – The dimensions of this church are enhanced by its unencumbered setting in a spacious churchyard. The first church built 1134 was rebuilt as a great burgh church in the late 14C early 15C and made a collegiate church in 1540. With successive floods and raids the fabric deteriorated and by the Restoration it was no longer used as a place of worship. Extensive alterations were made to the nave from 1808 to 1811 while the choir was restored in 1971-3. The dimensions are 206ft in length and 113ft at the transepts. The truncated crossing tower once carried a crown steeple. The original east end with its red stone, gabled buttresses differs from the grey stone and more highly decorative fleuronned buttress pinnacles and parapet of the nave of the early 19C alterations.
Restored to some of its original glory, the nave's 19C plaster vaulting replaces the original timber roof while the choir was covered with fibreglass vaulting.
The south window of the south transept is by Burne-Jones – cleverly altered to fit a taller window (1895). In the former sacristy is the 17C marble **Lauderdale Monument** figuring the recumbent alabaster effigies of John Maitland 1st Lord Thirlestane his wife Jane Fleming, their son John 1st Earl of Lauderdale and his countess Isabella Seton. In the floor of the choir is the commemorative slab by Thomas Carlyle *(qv)* to his wife Jane Welsh who was a native of Haddington.

Poldrate Mill (B). – Restored to serve as an arts community centre this 18C corn mill retains its undershot water wheel. The water mill, storehouses, barns and millers' cottages are all in attractive biscuit coloured stone.

Sidegate (B).– The most notable building is the early 17C **Haddington House** (B). The street-side entrance was a later addition, the original one being under the turret stair on the garden side. St Mary's Pleasance (B) has been recreated as a traditional 17C Scottish garden.

EXCURSION

★★Northern foothills of the Lammermuir Hills. – This rolling countryside conceals a fascinating series of villages each with a special charm. Pantiles and the attractive red sandstone are two of the essential contributing factors.

Take the A 6093 out of Haddington.

Pencaitland. – Pop 978. Easter and Wester Pencaitland, a double village divided by the River Tyne, has a parish **church** with some unusual features. The earliest part is the 13C Winton Aisle – once installed with a laird's loft – now adjoined by the 17C Saltoun Aisle with attractive 16-17C oak pew fronts. The finely carved 17C pulpit has a baptismal bracket. The octagonal portion of the tower once served as a dovecot. Note the three sundials on the buttress of the south side. The tombstones have some lively depictions of the tools of the trade of the defunct. Watch houses to prevent body snatching stand at each gateway.

On the outskirts of Pencaitland turn right onto the B 6355.

East Saltoun. – This linear village, with its imposing Gothic church and a line of handsome model cottages was the work of enterprising landowners, the Fletchers of Saltoun Hall. **Andrew Fletcher** (1655-1716), the great patriot, worked tirelessly against the 1707 Union of the Parliaments. His brother Henry established weaving enterprises and also the first pot barley mill with the help of James Meikle who brought the technique back from Holland. The Industrial Revolution caused the decline of such small enterprises.

Continue to Gifford.

★**Gifford.** – Pop 663. This late 17 and early 18C estate village was resited, before the enclosing of the park, and rebuilding of Yester House. Less homogeneous than some of the other foothill villages, the main street goes from the church down to the mercat cross then turns at right angles to follow the magnificent avenue of limes leading up to Yester House *(private)*, onetime home of the Hays of Tweeddale.

The T-shaped **church** dating from 1710 has a laird's loft adorned by the Tweeddale armorial crest. On the 17C carved pulpit there is a baptismal bracket.

A monument in the churchyard and plaque on the manse wall opposite, commemorate **John Witherspoon** (1723-94), the First Moderator of the Presbyterian Church, President of Princetown University and only clergyman signatory of the American Declaration of Independence.

The village is in Edinburgh's commuter belt, and is popular for day outings.

Leave by the B 6355 and shortly afterwards branch left onto the B 6370. Take a local road to the right to reach the village of Garvald.

Garvald. – Pop 50. Another attractive village with red sandstone cottages, many of which date from the 1780s when rebuilding followed a disastrous flood. The church, close by the Papana Water, has "jougs" hanging on the west wall.

★**Stenton.** – Pop 145. A linear village running between the west green overlooked by the old schoolhouse and adjoining one storey schoolroom, and the east green puntuated by a now rare feature, the **tron** - for weighing wool. In the churchyard the 16C crow stepped and saddlebacked tower, with a dovecot in its upper section, marks the site of the former church which was replaced in 1828 by William Burn's Gothic parish church. At the eastern end of the village, by the roadside, is a 16C Rood Well.

Backtrack to take the local road to East Linton, then turn left onto the A1. Without going into the village take the local road which follows the south bank of the River Tyne.

tc **Hailes Castle.** – This ruined stronghold, which takes full advantage of the rocky outcrop overlooking the River Tyne, was owned at one time by the Hepburns, in particular James, the 4th Earl of Bothwell. It is said that Bothwell and Mary Queen of Scots rested here on route for Dunbar Castle in April 1567. A later proprietor was David Dalrymple the Law Lord also known as Lord Hailes. An enlightened landowner, he was famous for the long leases he accorded his East Lothian tenants.

The central section and lower part of the riverside curtain wall belong to the original 13C work. The 14C additions to the west, including tower and stout curtain wall round to the entrance, also include a pit prison, vaulted basement and living quarters above. Further buildings were added between the two towers in the 15C, the remains include a bakehouse with chapel above.

To the south, the volcanic outcrop of **Traprain Law** (784ft-239m) rises abruptly from surrounding farmland. A good defensive site of early date it was in all probability the capital of the British tribe the Votadini. The Law is famous for the **Treasure of Traprain**, a hoard of Roman silver plate, buried *(p* 5C AD, rediscovered in 1919 and now in the National Museum of Antiquities *(p 97).*

Follow the local road back to Haddington

★ HADDO HOUSE (Grampian)

Michelin map 401 fold 16 – N 11 – 26 miles northwest of Aberdeen – Local map p 37

tc Haddo House, an 18C mansion, stands in Grampian's castle country. Set in lovely wooded grounds, now a country park, it is the ancestral seat of the Gordon Earls of Aberdeen and renowned as the home of the Haddo House Choral and Operatic Society.

Gordons. – The history of the house is inextricably that of the Gordon Earls of Aberdeen. The Methlick estate was acquired by a Gordon in 1469. **William, 2nd Earl of Aberdeen** (1679-1745) commissionned William Adam to design a mansion house to replace the earlier family seat destroyed by Covenanters in reprisal for Sir John Gordon's Royalist sympathies. Adam achieved a house of symmetry and dignity in keeping with the precepts of Palladianism.

The house was an expression of the prosperity engendered by the agricultural improvements. Alas the next incumbent, George, appropriately named the "wicked earl" dispersed the wealth. A man of great energy he established three mistresses in residences as far apart as Fraserburgh and Wiscombe Park in Devon,and maintained their offspring, all at the cost of Haddo. His heir that noble youth in Pompeo Batoni's painting (staircase) died in a riding accident. With William Pitt the Younger and Henry Dundas, Viscount Melville as his guardians, it was hardly surprising that **George Hamilton Gordon, 4th Earl** (1784-1860) rose to high office as Prime Minister (1852-5) of a coalition government at the time of the Crimean War. A man of many talents, he nevertheless devoted much time to the improvement of the estate, landscaping the parkland and repairing the house which was by then derelict. Of his three sons, two inherited, the eldest, the "Sailor Earl" and the youngest. The latter **John Campbell Gordon, 7th Earl** (1847-1934) with his wife Ishbel – affectionately known as **We Twa** – embarked on a programme of alterations and refurbishment. A ground floor entrance replaced the original first floor one, the terrace was extended the full length of the central block and a chapel was added. Inside all was modernized and redecorated in the Adam Revival style. Today the house is in the care of the National Trust for Scotland, with the south wing as a private residence for the Gordon family.

Haddo House Choral and Operatic Society. – Originally a community centre, the custom built wooden hall serves as home for various productions (concerts, opera and drama) which attract many visiting artists of international repute. The society was founded by the late 4th Marquess and Lady Aberdeen who as a professional musician herself, remains the motivating force.

THE HOUSE *time : 1 hour*

Interior. – The interior of this Palladian country house was entirely transformed when the 1st Marquess employed the London firm of decorators, Wright and Mansfield to refurbish in the Adam Revival style. The reception rooms are a far cry from the solid comfort of the tower houses. These well lit, elegant rooms are a perfect setting for the many family mementoes. From the ground floor entrance hall with its coffered ceiling the staircase leads up to the main apartments. The striking portrait halfway up is Pompeo Batoni's elegant presentation of *Lord Haddo* as the Grand Tourist. His son, the Prime Minister Earl, is commemorated by many souvenirs in the Ante-Room with its 18C panelling and carved overdoors. Alongside Sir Thomas Lawrence's Byronic portrait of the *4th Earl*, are portraits of one of his guardians, *Sir William Pitt the Younger* as well as other political contemporaries such as *Sir Robert Peel* and the *Duke of Wellington* (the 4th Earl, was Foreign Secretary to both). The bust of Queen Victoria was a personal gift to the former P.M. It was the 4th Earl who suggested the buying of the Balmoral estate. The Queen's Bedroom was in fact used by the sovereign on her 1857 visit to Haddo. In the Dining Room the group of family portraits include the *7th Earl* in his Thistle Robes and the 4th Earl's actor friend *John Philip Kemble.* Part of the 19C alterations included the transformation of a hay loft into the splendid cedar panelled library we see today. The creators of the Library, *We Twa* are depicted above the fireplaces. The architect of the London Law Courts, G.E. Street created another neo-Geothic work when designing the chapel with its Burne-Jones east window.

THE GROUNDS

Haddo House Country Park. – The 180 acres of parkland with its splendid trees are the result of the 4th Earl's planting programme. The landscaping includes two visitas, Victoria Avenue from the entrance front, and a second on the east side beyond the formal garden, reaching away to the lake, the focal point.

HAWICK (Borders)   Pop 16 697
Michelin map **401** fold 36 -L17

The largest Border burgh, Hawick, is an industrial centre with knitwear as the main industry, an agricultural market town, with one of the oldest auction marts and a busy shopping centre. Its main street is known as the "Oxford Street of the Borders". The town's history, like that of many Border towns, is a lengthy tale of raids, fire and destruction, the more notable events of which figure in the **Common Riding** ceremonies *(p 28)*, led by the Cornet.

Hosiery and knitwear industry. – Hawick is the undisputed centre of this industry. Hand knitting was the rule prior to the introduction of frame knitting in 1680 and it was 1771 before this activity was commercialized in Hawick. By 1816 the Hawick district had probably half the total number of frames operating in Scotland. Wool garments, fashioned hose and the new vogue tweeds all required high quality yarns and from the 1830s imported wool was increasingly used. Although spinning and carding were mechanized the rest was basically a cottage industry. In the second half of the 19C the emphasis shifted from the manufacture of stockings to woollen underwear. Introduced in 1858 the power or steam frame only became a general investment around 1880 and even then had little application in high quality wool work. In the 20C outerware has dominated the production, with swings from menswear to women's fashion goods. Since 1960, knitwear has proved to be the main growth area in the textile industry. Larger firms coexist with the smaller individualist producers, but colour, handle and styling remain of primary importance in an export dominated industry. Labour shortage has been the cause of the setting up of branch factories at Braemar, Inverness and Arbroath.
A few firms offer conducted tours round the mills. Apply to the tourist information office for addresses and times.

SIGHTS

The Equestrian Monument. – At the north end of the High Street the "Horse" commemorates the Hornshole Skirmish of 1514 which avenged the loss at Flodden the previous year of the entire Hawick contingent. The Cornet in top hat and green frock coat, atop a ladder, busses the monuments flag (ie ties on blue and gold ribbons).

The Motte. – A flat topped mound, once a pre-Roman site or Norman palisaded fort, and in all probability man-made, is the assembly point to greet the dawn on the Common Riding Saturday.

tc **Wilton Lodge Museum.** – Set in the public park of the same name, this mansion now houses a local museum with sections on the knitwear industry in Hawick, the town in the past, the Common Riding Ceremonies and natural history.

★ HERMITAGE CASTLE (Borders)

Michelin map **401** fold 40 - L18 - 16 miles south of Hawick

Access from Hawick by the A7 then the local road or directly by the B6399.

tc In an isolated moorland setting this louring pile gives an impression of massive impregnability and is highly evocative of the troubled times in the Borders. This was the stronghold of the Wardens of the March, strategically placed to guard the Hermitage Water and the old reiver's routes running from Hawick via Newcastleton into England.

Hermitage figures in the background of Raeburn's first version of the Scott portrait which is now at Bowhill *(qv)*.

Middle March Stronghold. – The remains of the hermitage which gave its name to the castle, lie upstream. Owned successively by the Soulis, Dacre, Douglas and Bothwell families the stronghold's turbulent and often cruel history gives it a prominent place in local ballads and legends. It is perhaps best known for Mary Queen of Scots lightning visit to her Warden of the Marches, the Earl of Bothwell in 1566 *(p 136)*.

Buildings. – Deceivingly uniform from the outside, this broad rectangular mass is in fact composed of various buildings and additions. The tall outer walls, some with a pronouced batter, have few windows, irregularly placed, loopholes, a crowning wallhead parapet and the two highly distinctive pointed arches. The earliest building, mid-14C, is distinguished by its red ashlar stonework and consists of an east and west range connected by walls, around a courtyard. The ruins of this fortified manorhouse were incorporated in a late 14C tower house, with the entrance to the west. Later additions were the four corner towers, linked by the masonry supported by the flying arches to give a seemingly rectangular form.

★★ HOPETOUN HOUSE (Lothian)

Michelin map **401** fold 31 – J 16 – 2 miles west of South Queensferry

tc Set on the south bank of the Forth, to the west of Edinburgh, this imposing monument stands in landscaped grounds enhanced by manicured lawns and great vistas. Here is the place to discover the contrasting exteriors of 17C Sir William Bruce and 18C William Adam and the vastly different interior styles of Bruce and the Adam sons, Robert and James, the whole highlighted by fine furniture and a notable collection of paintings.

The Hope family seat. – The Abercorn estate with Midhope Castle was purchased by John Hope in 1678. The original mansion (1699-1703) by **Sir William Bruce** was altered shortly afterwards by John's son, **Charles Hope**, 1st Earl of Hopetoun who commissioned **William Adam**, Bruce's onetime apprentice to enlarge his residence. The result was the east front in the Roman baroque manner which we see today. With William Adam's death in 1748 the sons **Robert** and **James**, continued the work, in particular the interior decoration of the State Apartments. It is interesting to note that Robert Adam embarked on his Grand Tour (1754-8) at the age of 26 in the entourage of Charles, Lord Hope and James later 3rd Earl. Many of Adam's ideas for Hopetoun were written instructions sent from Italy as were the slabs of marble etc.

Later earls continued to extend their lands with estates in Lanarkshire, West Lothian, East Lothian and Fife and were widely known as agricultural improvers. General Sir John Hope, 4th Earl (1765-1823) was a distinguished soldier assuming command at Corunna following Sir John Moore's death and fighting under Wellington in the Peninsular War. He was also a great art collector. The 4th Earl received George IV at Hopetoun during his 1822 state visit to Scotland which was stage managed by Sir Walter Scott, and occasioned the great revival of all things Scottish and the unspoken acceptance of Highland dress again.

In more recent times the 1st and 2nd Marquesses of Linlithgow were notable diplomats and statesmen, serving respectively as Govenor-General of Australia and Viceroy of India.

TOUR *1 hour*

Exterior. – The square from of Bruce's mansion in his mature Classical style, with two main storeys on a rusticated basement remains the centrepiece of the west front. Seven bays across, the central portion is slightly recessed. The angularity of straight headed windows, hood moulds, string courses and quoins contrasts with the segmental pediment enclosing an intricate tympanum. In sharp contrast, the more theatrical and certainly very splendid east front moves outward from a central unit through curved colonnades to the advanced pavilions and is surely one of William Adam's masterpieces. Strictly symmetrical, a roof top balustrade with urns unifies the whole while the cornice achieves a similar purpose at a lower level. The four-storey central block is given vertical emphasis by the use of a two storey Corinthian order, while the lower pavilions have triangular pedimented windows between twinned pilasters and are overlooked by lantern turrets. *(Resemblance with Buckingham House see London p 40.)*

Interior. – Again the more severe designs of Bruce, who used almost exclusively local materials, can be readily distinguished from the opulence of the Adam interiors of the State Apartments. Move straight through the hall to start with the Bruce rooms.

Library. – Two rooms were made into one to create this pine panelled room now lined with bookshelves. Above the Glen Tilt marble fireplace is David Allan's painting (*c*1782) of the two youngest daughters of the 3rd Earl. In the small library with carved and gilded oak wainscotting and a Portsoy *(qv)* marble fireplace is a portrait by Sir Nathaniel Dance of *Charles, Lord Hope* (1740-66) one of Adam's companions on the Grand Tour.

Garden Room. – Originally the entrance hall this is Bruce decoration at its best : handsome but sober oak panelling is enhanced by the gilded cornice, doorheads and pilaster capitals and a set of silver armorial candle sconces. Above the fireplace the *4th Earl* is shown in the uniform *(see museum)* of Captain of the Royal Company of Archers, the Sovereign's Bodyguard in Scotland. The 18C Dutch clock (Jan Henkels) opposite, regularly comes to life with its windmill and musicians.

Bruce Bedchamber. – The centrepiece of this sumptuously decorated room is the magnificent bed with red damask hangings by Mathias Lock. Painted decoration on a white background alternates with panels of red damask. Of the original suite the dressing room and closet have an exhibition on Sir William Bruce and his work and beyond is the fireproof Charter Room.

Bruce Staircase. – Octagonal pine wainscotting admirably carved by Alexander Eizat, echoes the form of the oak handrail and banisters round an octagonal well. The paintings (1967) are by William McLaren.

West Wainscot Bedchamber. – The room is hung with Antwerp tapestries (*c*1700).

Down to the ground floor again.

Entrance Hall. – The hall linking the Bruce house to the Adam State Apartments is a sober introduction for the splendours to come. A coved ceiling and plain pale green walls are set off by the white and gold detailing of the cornice and doorheads and inset marble medallions.

Yellow Drawing Room. – The proportions of the State Apartments, now reordered, are undoubtedly those of William Adam while the interior decoration has the definite imprint of Robert Adam. Above the yellow silk hung damask walls the coved ceiling is adorned with gold highlighted corner cartouches and a matching central motif. Details of the frieze, door pediments and cases are picked out in gold. The paintings include a Teniers and a contemporary copy of Rembrandt's portrait of *An Old Woman* and the *Adoration of the Shepherds* (school of Rubens). The Cullen pier glasses and console tables between the windows are part of the original 18C dining room furniture. The Cullen commodes on either side of the fireplace came from the State Bedroom. In this room, in 1822 George IV knighted the portrait painter Henry Raeburn and Capt. Adam Ferguson, the Keeper of the Regalia in Scotland.

Red Drawing Room. – The ceiling of this room, originally the Saloon, is a Rococo work of gilded plasterwork by Clayton and is one of Adam's earliest works. The James Cullen furniture was designed for the room and is arranged in typical parade fashion: mahogany arm and side chairs and the superb gilt console tables, with oval pier glasses above. The white marble fireplace with caryatids is a Michael Rysbrack work (1756). The paintings include two of the Hope brothers, *James later 3rd Earl* and *Charles, Lord Hope* during their Grand Tour.

State Dining Room. – Refurbished in 1820 this room is typical of the late Regency period with its decorative cornice, leatherised gold cloth on the walls, ornate curtains and pelmets and the ceiling sunburst. The chairs and the marble topped pier tables with an inlaid H are once again Cullen. Family portraits grace the walls.
A staircase leads up to the museum.

Museum. – The subjects covered are the crossing of the Forth from earliest times including the once proposed tunnel to join the Hopetoun estates, costumes, china and the Hope family.
Another staircase leads up to the **rooftop terrace** commanding good views of the grounds and the Firth of Forth.

HUNTLY (Grampian)   Pop 4 130

Michelin map **401** fold 16 – L11

Huntly is set in the heart of Strathbogie, a hilly countryside of farming and forestry. This busy market town was for long the seat of the house of Gordon, whose ancestral home stands on the banks of the Deveron.

Gay Gordons. – This powerful family became the leaders of the Catholic cause in the Counter Reformation struggles. Bruce originally granted these forfeited lands to Adam Gordon from Berwickshire. Successive Gordons built a stone tower, then a more commodious seat. George 4th Earl, rebuilt a palace having razed to the cellars the previous construction. Active in the defence of his religion, he died at the Battle of Corrichie when he took up arms against Mary Queen of Scots' royal troops. His son was beheaded in Aberdeen. His grandson the 6th Earl and 1st Marquess made the architectural embellishments to the castle. Following the Civil War the Duke moved to Fochabers *(qv)*.

SIGHTS

Leave from the spacious square dominated by a statue of the Duke of Richmond and follow Castle Street up to Huntly Academy. Better known as the Gordon Schools, the establishment was founded in 1839-41 in memory of the 5th Duke of Gordon. The building by Archibald Simpson marks the site of the outer gatehouse of the castle.

Continue on down the tree shaded avenue to the castle ruins.

tc **Huntly Castle.** – Strategically set commanding the confluence of the Bogie and Deveron rivers, the ruins of Huntly Castle are famous for the elaborate **heraldic carvings★★★**. The original motte and bailey structure was superseded by a 15C keep itself abandoned in favour of a more spacious palace on the south side. Z-plan in layout, it has a massive drum and staircase towers at diametrically opposite ends of the oblong block. The building we see today was built between 1551 and 1554 on an older basement. Like Slains, the castle was blown up in 1594 and it was during the rebuilding of the early 17C that the then Marquess embellished the upper parts. Before entering examine the **south front** with its three oriel windows and inscribed friezes.

George Gordon First Marquis of Huntlie 16
Henriette Stewart Marquesse of Huntlie 02

Moving round to the courtyard, the motte is on the left while the palace and other ruins are sited on the bailey to the right. Once inside the cobbled courtyard make for the entrance doorway in the staircase tower. Above the doorway is a magnificent piece of **heraldic sculpture**. Inside note the equally finely carved fireplaces of the principal rooms. One has medallion portraits of the embellishing Marquess and his wife, the second has their arms surmounted by the royal arms of the United Kingdom and is dated 1606, only three years after the Union.

EXCURSION

tc **Leith Hall.** – *7 miles south of Huntly by the A97 and B9002.*
For over 300 years Leith Hall was the home of the Leith family, later Leith-Hays. Originally the family is thought to have come to the British Isles with William the Conqueror, becoming shipowners at Leith, the port of Edinburgh, provosts of Aberdeen, and finally lairds at Leith Hall. The story of the house is the story of the family, and typical of many Scottish landowners. The original tower house built in 1650 is now the north wing. The house was extended by subsequent generations to give today's four wings around a central courtyard. The visitor arrives facing the west wing (1868 addition), with its arched entrance to the courtyard. The main entrance to the house is at the east wing which is reached by moving in an anti-clockwise direction via the charming south wing façade with its two Venetian windows. The tour of the house takes visitors through all four wings, in which are displayed family possessions over three centuries and reflecting the military traditions of the Leith-Hays. In particular, the library contains George III's pardon to the staunch Jacobite, Andrew Hay, the saviour of Leith Hall. It was to Andrew that Prince Charles Edward Stuart gave the prized shagreen writing case on the eve of the Battle of Culloden.

★★ INVERARAY (Strathclyde)   Pop 399

Michelin map 🔲 fold 26 – E 15

The delightful whitewashed town of Inveraray on the shores of Loch Fyne is a short distance from its castle, the seat of the chief of Clan Campbell.

18C planned village. – Neil Campbell, one of Bruce's most faithful supporters, acquired the forfeited MacDougall lands in the 14C. The family went from strength to strength and in the 15C they established their main seat at Inveraray. The medieval settlement arose at the mouth of the River Aray, around the Campbell stronghold. The town achieved royal burgh status in 1648 but it was almost a century later before the 3rd Duke envisaged his ambitious, scheme to rebuild the castle and settlement. Ambitious, as work started only a year after the unsettling 1745 rising, in an area where there were no roads. The military road from Dumbarton only arrived in 1745. Building work on the castle took 12 years (1746-58), with Roger Morris as architect and William Adam as clerk of works, although the town took the better part of 100 years to complete. The 5th Duke redecorated the interiors in the neo-classical style after the fashion of Calton House, the Prince of Wales' London establishment.

★★THE CASTLE *time : 1 hour*

tc **Exterior.** – Roger Morris' original Gothic Revival edifice was altered externally in the 19C with the additon of a range of dormers at battlement level and conical roofs to the corner towers. On the four fronts pointed Gothic windows predominate with a tiered central keep rising above the general roof line.

★★★**Interior.** – During the 5th Duke's late 18C redecorations the original long gallery was subdivided to give two main rooms on either side of a small entrance hall.

Dining Room. – This room is a masterpiece of delicately detailed decoration where roof and walls are perfectly matched. The compartmented plasterwork ceiling by a London craftsman is complemented by Clayton's frieze and cornice, and matches admirably the superb painted work of Girard and Guinand (grisaille roundels over doors and in wall panels). The 18C chairs are of Scottish fabrication after a French design and are covered with 18C Beauvais tapestry. Resplendent under the Waterford chandelier (1800) and on the Gillow table are several German silver gilt nefs (*c*1900).

Tapestry Drawing Room. – The outstanding set of 18C Beauvais tapestries and decorative panels and overdoors by Girard, rival the compartmented ceiling based on Robert Adam's design. Off this room the China Turret has an impressive display of porcelain, Worcester, Derby, Japanese, Meissen...

Armoury Hall. – The hall rises through several storeys to the armorial roof. The plain pastel coloured walls provide the ideal background for the impressive display of arms (pole-arms, Lochaber axes and broadswords). From one of these balconies the Duke's personal piper awakes the household with a medley of Campbell tunes.

Saloon. – The main family portraits hang here where the decoration is confined to an attractive frieze, curtain pelmets and girandoles on the end walls. The principal portraits face each other, namely Pompeo Batoni's *8th Duke of Hamilton* and Gainsborough's portrait of *Conway,* enlarged to match the former. Among the relics in the show cases are some belonging to the Duke who was Montrose's arch enemy.

North West Hall and Staircase. – Of the portraits note the builder *3rd Duke* by Allan Ramsay and the *5th Duke* (Gainsborough) and his Duchess Elizabeth Gunning.

★★THE TOWN

This tidy township has a showpiece waterfront facing the loch head. The parish church has a prominent site in the axis of the main street.

tc **Bell Tower.** – The 10th Duke conceived the idea of building the tower as a memorial to all Campbells who had fallen in war. Each of the 10 bells of the peal is named after a Celtic saint. St Mund the patron saint of Clan Campbell is number three. *(Regular bell ringing sessions)*. 176 steps lead to the top with a good view of Loch Fyne and the countryside for miles around.

The bridges. – Robert Mylne designed the bridge over the Aray close to the castle, and Roger Morris the single arch Garron bridge some two miles to the north of Inveraray.

EXCURSIONS

★★Oban hinterland. – *Description p 161.*

★Auchindrain. – *6 miles to the southwest by the A83.*

tc This open-air folklife museum evokes everyday life as it was for the ordinary people of the West Highlands. Communal-tenancy, where a group of tenants hold and work a farm, was the commonest kind of farm in Scotland. This system lasted the longest in the Highlands. Auchidrain is a very ancient settlement, with a history dating back over 1000 years.
Start the visit with the display centre which gives details on the way of life (field patterns, domestic interiors and occupations) then visit the township where houses, barns and byres are being restored and furnished as museum pieces.

tc **Castle Fisheries.** – *1 1/2 miles to the northwest by the A819.*
Follow the successive stages in the rearing of rainbow and brown trout on a fish farm. Visit the sick tank, feed the fish and fish (permits required) in one of two well stocked lochans.

★★★ INVEREWE GARDENS (Highland)

Michelin map **401** fold 10 – C 10 – Poolewe

tc These outstanding gardens in their magnificent west coast setting are at all seasons a real source of pleasure and enjoyment and unrivalled display of beauty. The gardens leave none indifferent and all will find satisfaction, either visual or intellectual as it deploys its unfailing charm. Here are combined luxuriance, exoticness and diversity of species, planned yet natural, tended with utmost care and well integrated with the natural landscape.

Barren headland to sub-tropical luxuriance. – In 1862 the founder **Osgood Mackenzie** (1843-1922) bought a Wester Ross estate including Am Ploc Ard, the high lump in Gaelic. The peninsula was a barren site, exposed to Atlantic gales and salt spray with an acid peaty soil devoid of vegetation. The initial work included rabbit fencing, the creation of a Corsican pine and Scots fir windbreak and the transportation of soil for bedding the plants. A lifetime of patient planning, judicious planting and careful tending aided by the tempering effects of the Gulf Stream, produced the delightfully informal garden of today. Osgood's cherished work was continued by his daughter Mrs Sawyer who in 1952 handed the gardens over to the National Trust for Scotland.

The gardens. – Visitors are free to wander at will but a suggested route is indicated by arrows and numbers. Each species is labelled and the guide book contains a list of the more interesting plants. Half of this 64 acre site is woodland. Here on a latitude, similar to that of Leningrad, flourish some 2 500 species many of which are

(National Trust for Scotland)

The garden in summer

exotic, but flourish in some sheltered corner. Colour is to be found in most seasons : mid-April to mid-May (rhododendrons), May (azaleas), June (rock garden, herbaceous and rose borders), early autumn (heathers) and November (maples).
The twisting paths give unexpected and ever changing vistas of garden, sea and mountain. The high viewpoint affords a view back towards Poolewe in its head of the loch setting with the Torridon peaks in the background.

Michelin map 🔲 fold 15 - H11
See the town plan in the current Michelin Red Guide Great Britain and Ireland

Inverness stands at the northern end of the Great Glen, astride the outlet of Loch Ness, and has long been known as the capital of the Highlands. At the very hub of the Highland communications system, the town makes an ideal touring centre for much of the Highlands.

Hub of the Highlands. – The strategic importance of this site has been appreciated from earliest times as testified by the existence in the vicinity of a variety of ancient sites and monuments. St Columba is said to have visited Brude, King of the Picts at his capital beside the Ness, although the exact site is unsure. By the 11C King Duncan (c1010-40) made famous by Shakespeare, had his castle in the town. The town's very strategic importance was its downfall in later times when it suffered variously at the hands of the English, Bruce himself, turbulent Highland clans, the Lord of the Isles, Mary Queen of Scots' supporters and Jacobites. The post '15 Rising, law and order policy for the Highlands enacted by General Wade included the creation of a citadel, as one of several strategic strongholds in the Highland fringes. Culloden (*see below*) and its tragic aftermath was the ultimate action of the '45 Rising. Such a troubled history means that Inverness has few historic buildings. The architecture of the town of today is largely that of the 19C, one of expansion due in large to Telford's construction of the Caledonian Canal (1803-22) and the arrival of the railway.

Inverness remains the administrative centre for both the district and region and in addition has the headquarters of the Highlands and Islands Development Board. Founded in 1965 this organization has as objective the promotion of the social and economic development of the aforementioned area through the financing of industry, tourism, agriculture and fishing.

The **Northern Meeting Piping Competitions** *(p 212)* are held annually in Eden Court Theatre and are the oldest of all piping contests dating back to 1781.

SIGHTS

Inverness Castle. – A series of earlier castles have preceded the present 19C building which serves as court house and administrative offices. The esplanade with the **statue** of Flora MacDonald, affords a good **view** of the Ness and the town.

★★**Museum and Art Gallery.** – *Castle Wynd.*

tc On the first floor an imaginative and well presented exhibition "Inverness, Hub of the Highlands" interprets the rich heritage of the Highlands. Topics of special local significance include the Great Glen, the vitrified fort Craig Phadrig (visible from the window), the Picts and their surviving works, to the engineering feats of more recent times, the military roads of General Wade, Telford's Caledonian Canal and the Kessock Bridge. The upper floor has exhibits on the Highland way of life and the silver producing centres of Inverness, Tain and Wick. The reception area of this level has a show case containing a presentation pair of **Doune pistols** *(qv)* by John Murdoch. Admire the exquisite craftsmanship of these guns dated *c* 1790.

Town House. – *At the foot of Castle Wynd.*

This Victorian replacement was the scene in 1921 of the first ever Cabinet Meeting outside London. The base of the mercat cross incorporates the Clach- na-Cuddain or stone of the tubs, used as a resting place by washerwomen on their way to and from the Ness. As long as the stone remains Inverness will continue to flourish.

tc **Abertarff House.** – *Church Street.*

Recently renovated this 16C house serves as the Highland Region Headquarters for the National Trust for Scotland.

Kessock Bridge. – Opened in 1982 this suspension bridge spanning the Beauly Firth carries the A9 north to the Black Isle. With a total length of 3451ft the bridge's main span has a clearance of 95ft above high water. It is planned to build a second bridge over the Dornoch Firth further to the north. There is a good **view**★ of Inverness as you cross the bridge.

St Andrew's Cathedral. – *Ardross Street.*

This imposing and richly decorated neo-Gothic edifice was built from 1866-9 for the Episcopal diocese of Moray, Ross and Caithness. The nave piers are monolithic columns of polished Peterhead granite, the reredos and pulpit of carved stone. Both the choir screen and rood cross are by Robert Lorimer.

Eden Court Theatre. – *Bishop's Road.*

The custom-built leisure centre completed in 1976 comprises a theatre, conference centre and art gallery.

Tomnahurich Cemetery. – From the 220ft – 67m summit there is a good **view** of Inverness.

EXCURSIONS

tc **Culloden.** – *6 miles east of Inverness by the A9 and B9006. NTS Visitors Centre.*

On the 16 April 1746 this bleak moor saw the end of the Jacobite Rising of 1745 *(p 108)* when Prince Charles Edward Stuart's army was defeated by a government army under the Duke of Cumberland, the younger son of King George II. His treatment of the injured and prisoners earned him the sobriquet "Butcher Cumberland". The prince himself, after months in hiding as a fugitive escaped to France and lifelong exile. The **visitor centre** has an audiovisual programme entitled *The Story of the Forty Five* and a historical display, which help to place the battle in its historical context. The **Old Leanach Cottage** has a variety of exhibits including a plan of the battlefield. Stones and monuments mark the various command posts and graves of the clans (Cairn, Clan Graves, Well of the Dead) while footpaths demarcate the front lines of the opposing armies.

★Clava Cairns. – *Same road out of Inverness as for Culloden. Turn right at the Cumberland Stone then continue for 1 mile.*
This impressive site includes three cairns, girdled by stone circles, and a small ring of boulders. The middle cairn was a ring-cairn with its centre always open to the sky. The two others had entrance passages leading to a burial chamber; they are now unroofed. Some of the stones of the cairns bear cupmarks. The complex is late Neolithic in date and each cairn and stone ring formed part of a single design.

Beauly. – *12 miles west of Inverness.*
In a sheltered position at the head of the Beauly Firth this delightful village takes its name *Beau Lieu* from the name given to the 13C priory by the Burgundian monks.

tc **Beauly Priory.** – The red sandstone priory was founded in 1230 like its two sister Valliscaulian houses, Pluscarden and Ardchattan. The remaining roofless church has a particularly elegant west front, unusual trefoil windows in the south wall of the nave and attractively framed windows in the chancel.

tc **Highland Craftpoint.** – The objective of this centre is to develop and promote the Scottish crafts industry by providing a range of professional services. The public is welcome to visit the complex : exhibitions, audiovisual presentation and information services.

The Black Isle. – *30 miles. Leave Inverness to the north by the Kessock Bridge and at the Tore roundabout take the A 832 to the right.*
In contradiction to its name this is a green peninsula, washed by the waters of the Beauly, Moray and Cromarty Firths, where fertile farmlands fringe the forested central ridge. The rural charm of the Black Isle remains unspoilt by the industrial developments on the northern shore of the Cromarty Firth.

Fortrose. – Pop 1 500 with Rosemarkie. This busy little town is the chief community of the Black Isle. David I founded the diocese of Ross in 1126 but it was more than 200 years later before the bishop and chapter moved from neighbouring Rosemarkie where there had been a Celtic settlement. Away from the bustle of the main street the remnant of the **cathedral church** makes an attractive picture in its peaceful **setting★** of green lawns enclosed by the charming red sandstone houses of the former close. The remaining south aisle has attractive vaulting and the damaged tomb of its builder Euphemia, Countess of Ross, widow of the Wolf of Badenoch. The detached two storeyed building may have served as a sacristy and chapter house.

Branch off to the right.

Chanonry Point. – This looks over to Fort George *(qv)* only three miles distant. A **monument** commemorates the ·Brahan Seer put to death for a prophecy which displeased his patron's wife, the Countess of Seaforth.

tc **Rosemarkie.** – This village has a popular beach. In the High Street, **Groam House Museum** has a very fine Pictish stone with elaborate interlaced designs and an audiovisual presentation on the Brahan Seer and the Black Isle countryside.

Cromarty. – Pop 680. On the tip of the Black Isle peninsula, this village stands on the south side of the narrows, guarded by the hills, the Sutors of Cromarty, facing Nigg Bay to the north with its platform construction yard. This now peaceful village popular as a holiday place, was a thriving port in the lifetime of its most famous son, the stonemason turned writer and geologist **Hugh Miller** (1802-56). His birthplace, **Hugh**
tc **Miller's Cottage,** is now a museum with geological specimens, documents and personal souvenirs of the man who wrote the classic work on the Old Red Sandstone.

tc **Cruises on Loch Ness.** – *Description p 123.*

INVERURIE (Grampian)   Pop 8 550

Michelin map 401 fold 20 – M 12

Inverurie is the chief town of the Garioch, an agricultural basin to the east of the Grampian foothills enclosed to the south by Bennachie and the Correen Hills. Known at one time for its locomotive works it is now the administrative centre for the Gordon District. The surrounding area is particularly rich in prehistoric monuments.

The Bass. – *Cemetery.*
The Garioch was granted to David Earl of Huntingdon (c1144-1219) a grandson of David I (and brother of Malcolm IV and William the Lion). Here at Inverurie he established a motte and bailey stronghold. The higher of the two mounds was the motte or bass, the lower the bailey.

Brandsbutt Stone. – *1/4 mile to the northwest in a housing estate.*
This reconstructed Pictish Symbol Stone is decorated with the crescent, V- rod, serpent and Z-rod symbols *(p 21)*. Down one side is a line of Ogams.

EXCURSIONS

Kinkell Church. – *2 1/2 miles southeast of Inverurie.*
The roofless ruin of this church has a decorated **sacrament house** dated 1524 and the grave slab (upright) of Gilbert de Greenlaw in full armour. This warrior lost his life at the Battle of Harlaw in 1411 *(see below)*.

Maiden Stone. – *5 miles from Inverurie off the A 96.*
On the way out notice up on the right the **tower** which commemorates the **Battle of Harlaw.** This ferocious and bloody battle was fought in 1411 to save Aberdeen from sacking at the hands of a Highland army led by Donald, Lord of the Isles. This was not the first battle in the area as some experts give Bennachie (1733ft-528m) straight ahead, as the site of Mons Graupius, Agricola's crushing victory over the Picts in AD 84.

Take the road to the left (signposted) after the picnic by-pass.

Maiden Stone. – Standing at the roadside this tall granite Pictish Symbol Stone bears a very faint cross on one side and elephant and Pictish symbols (Z-rod and mirror and comb) on the reverse.

Loanhead Recumbent Stone Circle. – *1/4 mile from Daviot to the north of Inverurie.* This Bronze Age monument, a stone circle with a recumbent, is a variation common to the Grampian area. The circle enclosing a low ring cairn was used for funerary purposes at a later date. Alongside is an area of cremation burials enclosed by low walls.

tc **Fyvie Castle.** – *13 miles north of Inverurie by the B 9170 and the A 947.*
This superb castle was owned successively by Prestons, Meldrums, Setons, Gordons and Forbes-Leiths. Alexander Seton (c1639-1719) the Lord Chancellor remodelled the castle incorporating the already existing towers (Preston and Meldrum). In the process he created the spectacular 150ft long front which is an outstanding example of 17C baronial architecture and the splendid wheel stair dated 1603.
In May 1984 the National Trust for Scotland acquired the castle and contents, which include a superb collection of portraits and in particular a fine group by Raeburn.

★ IONA, Isle of (Strathclyde) Pop 128

Michelin map 401 fold 25 – A 14 and 15
Access : see the current Michelin Red Guide Great Britain and Ireland

One of the most venerated places in Scotland is a remote and lonely windswept isle off the southwest tip of Mull. Over 1 400 years ago St Columba and his companions landed on the southern shore of this Inner Hebridean Isle to establish a monastic settlement. Today the island is an important place of pilgrimage although there are few tangible remains.

The Columban Settlement. – In 563 AD, 166 years after St Ninian's mission *(p 203)* **St Columba** (521-597) and a group of followers set off from Ireland. Their chosen site, this bare and somewhat inhospitable island, suited the tenets of their monastic traditions. The community flourished and was successful in converting the native people of the mainland. Even after the death of Columba in 597, and the decisions of the Synod of Whitby (664), the community went from strength to strength and was to become the mother house for the Columban monasteries. Although nothing remains of St Columba's monastery the period was one of great artistic achievement. Other than the intricately beautiful carved crosses and grave slabs it has been suggested that the sacred work of art, the *Book of Kells* was undertaken in whole or in part, by the scribes and illuminators of the Iona community. This period of artistic accomplishment was brought to an end by the Norse raids of the 8 and 9C. Some of the monks accepted refuge at Dunkeld which became the new centre of the Columban Church. Following a particularly savage raid in 803 AD when 68 monks lost their lives, the remaining members with the relics of St Columba and perhaps the *Book of Kells* returned to Kells in Ireland.

Medieval foundation. – At the beginning of the 13C Reginald son of Somerled, King of the Isles, founded a Benedictine monastery and a nunnery to be headed by his sister. With the forfeiture of the Lordship of the Isles, the principal source of patronage, the monastery lost its independence. For a short period in the 16C the church was elevated to cathedral status but by the Reformation, disrepair had already set in.

Rebirth. – Following the foundation in 1938 of the Iona Community, originally a Church of Scotland brotherhood and now an ecumenical community of women and men, a programme of restoration of the monastic buildings was undertaken, and completed in 1966. The Abbey is now open all year round as a place of hospitality, reflection and worship. Although the sacred precincts belong to the Church of Scotland Trust, the rest of the island is in keeping for the nation under the auspices of the National Trust for Scotland.

Access. – *No cars are allowed on the island. All sights on Iona are easily reached on foot from the pier at Baile Mór.*

SIGHTS

Take the road straight up from the pier continuing past the post office.

Nunnery. – The remains of the nunnery founded at the same time as the monastery were restored in the late 19C.
Beyond the main group is a simple rectangular building, St Ronan's Church, with narrow triangular headed windows.

Once through the gate continue along the road.

★Maclean's Cross. – Dating from the 15C this cross is a product of the local school of carvers. On the west face is a Crucifixion while on the reverse the intricately carved patterns maintain the Celtic traditions.

Follow the road round past St Columba Hotel.

Reilig Odhrian. – This early Christian burial ground is reputed to be the burial place of Scotland's kings from Kenneth MacAlpine to Malcolm III, the Lords of the Isles and other chieftains. The most notable medieval effigies and grave slabs are now in the Infirmary Museum *(see opposite).*

★St Oran's Chapel. – The chapel, the island's oldest surviving building, dates from the 12C (restored 20C). The simple rectangular structure has a worn but rather fine Norman west door with three arches of beak-head and chevron decoration.

Pass through to the abbey precincts.

Street of the Dead. – Part of the paved processional way, which led from the landing place to the abbey, is uncovered at this point.

Tor Abb. – This hillock is said to mark the site of St Columba's cell.

High Crosses. – Of the three standing crosses **St Martin's★** (8C), complete and original, displays figure scenes on the west face. Only the truncated shaft of St Matthew's (9-10C) remains. The third one is a replica of St John's Cross (8C). On the latter the decorative work is divided into panels.

The abbey. – The present church no doubt stands on the site of its Columban predecessor. The original 13C church was altered towards the end of the century and enlarged in the 15C. Conversion work included the adding of a tower at the crossing and a south aisle to the choir. Fragments of the 13C Benedictine church include the north transept, and arcade of the choir's north wall. The elaborate trefoil headed doorway below was inserted when the north aisle was converted into a sacristy in the 15C. Note the carved capitals of the arcade and the piers of the crossing. The pale creamy green communion table is of Iona marble.

A door in the north wall of the nave leads into the cloisters with the unusual twin columned arcade. There are two originals in the west side.

Return to the west front of the church.

The small building to the north of the west front is St Columba's Shrine and is said to be the original burial place of the saint. The exact whereabouts of the saint's relics remain a mystery.

Go right round the far side of the buildings to the back.

★Infirmary Museum. – The museum houses an outstanding collection of early Christian and medieval stones. The early Christian works (nos 1-49) dating from 563 AD to the second half of the 12C include incised crosses (nos 3-33) and ring crosses (nos 23-33 and 38-48). The medieval section (nos 50-110) has examples of the Iona school of carving (14-15C). Their work included grave slabs, effigies and free standing crosses (see Maclean's Cross). The group (nos 71-83) of grave slabs includes human figures and the distinctive West Highland galleys. Nos 98-101 show the armour of the period.

Michael Chapel. – This small chapel is used for public worship in the winter months.

★ JEDBURGH (Borders)   Pop 4 168

Michelin map **401** fold 36 – M17

The historic royal burgh of Jedburgh, lying astride the Jed Water, is on one of the main routes into Scotland, as taken by the Roman Dere Street and the present A68. At one time the site of a castle and abbey the town was granted royal burgh status in 1165 by William the Lion. However, it remained vulnerable in this troubled border region and its history reflects that of the area. Now a peaceful market town, with some attractive buildings in the native tradition, new light industries have been introduced to broaden the industrial base.

The local speciality is a mint flavoured boiling sweet, **Jehart Snails.** The Common Riding or **Jethart Callant's Festival** *(p 28)* comprises a series of ride outs to historic places, led by the Callant. Another local event is the mid-February Ba' Game when those born above the mercat cross, the Uppies, oppose the Downies with the respective goals or hails being the Castle Jail grounds and Townfoot.

★★JEDBURGH ABBEY   *time : 1/2 hour*

One of the famous Border abbeys it was founded by **David I** in 1138 as a priory for Augustinian canons from Beauvais in France and elevated to abbey status 14 years later (1152). Work started at the church's east end in 1140 and continued for 75 years, before the cloister buildings were commenced. A majestic building it witnessed in its early days such royal events as the coronation of the founder's grandson, Malcolm IV (1153-65) and the marriage of Alexander III (1249-86) to his second wife Yolande de Dreux. Constant attack and plundering were the fate of many of the great buildings in the region. The destruction of the 1545 raid ended abbey life although the church continued to be used as a place of worship until 1875.

Abbey Church. – The mellow toned stone building is roofless but otherwise comparatively complete. Seen from Abbey Close, the late 12C, transitional **west front** is a powerful and most original feature. The main section with a deeply recessed, round headed doorway crowned by three pedimented gables, has above a tall fairly narrow window rising through the upper two sections to a rose adorned gable, the whole being flanked by solid buttresses. Strength, originality and soaring height are its chief characteristics. The rhythm and regularity of the **nave** display the assurance of an art well mastered. The increasing number of elements per bay pulls the eye upwards from the pointed arches on solid clustered columns, through the triforium section of round headed arches, subdivided by two smaller lancets, to the clerestory and the serried ranks of lancets in groups of four.

The tower above the crossing is trimmed with a delicate balustrade.

Beyond, the mid-12C east end, the earliest part of the church, is highly unorthodox. Massive round pillars rise upwards to the clerestory, buttressing the truncated arches of the main arcade. Distinctive features of the Norman style include the rounded arches, and chevron decoration.

Cloister buildings. – On a sloping site and now reduced to the foundations, these follow the usual pattern around the cloister, with,in the east range, the parlour, chapter house and treasury below, and dormitory above. The refectory, cellars and kitchens border the south side and offer a good view of the south elevation. Compare the Norman doorway giving access from the south aisle to the cloister, weathered but with a variety of sculptural motifs still discernible, to the replica on the left, resplendent with the full wealth of detail.

ADDITIONAL SIGHTS

★Mary Queen of Scots
tc **House.** – This is an attractive 16C L-shaped tower house in the vernacular style which stands in its own well tended garden. Originally the property of the Kers of nearby Ferniehirst, it took its present name following Mary Queen of Scots' visit in 1566 when she lodged here. Her stay was prolonged by ill health (to the point of fearing for her death) after her famous ride to visit the injured Earl of Bothwell, her future husband, at Hermitage Castle (qv) at least twenty miles distant.

Ground floor. – The kitchen, on the left is cobbled and barrel vaulted. The thickness of the walls can be appreciated by the width of the window embrasures.

First floor. – The larger banqueting hall has a variety of interesting historic relics associated with Mary Queen of Scots : Private Communion Service, watch, thimblecase, seal and death mask. Portraits of this hapless Queen include a copy of Clouet's Le Deuil Blanc and Hilliard's The Morton Portrait. The niche to the side of the fireplace was reserved for the bucket of salt, a rare commodity in those days. The adjoining chamber has facsimile documents including Elizabeth's warrant to execute Mary, the Geneva or "Breeches Bible" and a series of portraits of personalities of the period including the contentious Breadalbane Portrait by George Jamesone.

As in all Ker houses the spiral staircase is left handed to allow this Kerry-fisted family to use their sword hands.

Second floor. – In the small Queen's Bedroom is a 16C tapestry which is believed to be the original hanging. The larger Guard Room, hung with the onetime front door, has a variety of local exhibits. Jethard Jug and Billiyard, old weights and measures standards, the Dead Bell and an unusual Hangman's Ladle along with a replica of the much treasured flag captured at Bannockburn (1314) by the men of Jedburgh.

tc **Jedburgh Castle Jail and Museum.** – Built in the 1820s this Georgian prison was the site of the original Jedburgh Castle, a favourite residence of royalty in the 12C and practical for hunting parties in the ancient Jed Forest. In the 15C the castle was pulled down by the townsfolk to prevent it falling into English hands.

In 1823 the present building, a Howard Reform Prison, was considered one of the most modern of its time in Scotland.

The buildings. – Three prison blocks arranged around the central governor's block were linked to the latter by first floor gangways. The top floor terrace of the central block served as point of surveillance and was expediently provided with a bell to sound the alarm in times of escape.

The three cell blocks had a similar disposition with cells leading off a central passage. Inmates cells included two windows, a wooden bed and central heating – the grate at floor level covered the hot air ducts which were supplied by a stove in the windowless cell on the ground floor.

Exhibits in the main block show life of the period, the architect's plans and his other works and notables connected with Jedburgh.

JEDBURGH

Abbey Bridge End	2
Abbey Close	3
Bongate	5
The Bow	6
Bridge Street	7
Old Bridge End	13

Castlegate. – Leading downhill to Market Place, the way to the castle is bordered by some attractive houses (restored). On the left nos **65** and **67 (A)** have incorporated into their walls two sculptures, one of which may well represent the Turnbull bull. Abbey Close **(3)**, leading off down to the right to the abbey is where in 1803 the Wordsworths received Scott who read them part of his *Lay of the Last Minstrel* (plaque nos **6** and **7, B**).

Continuing down Castlegate, no **11 (D)** on the left is where Bonnie Prince Charlie lodged in 1745 when leading his Jacobite army into England.

Market Place. – A plaque in the road marks the original site of the mercat cross around which clustered the stalls. The plaque on the County Buildings **(H)** commemorates Sir Walter Scott's first appearance as an advocate in 1793.

The Canongate continues down to the A 68 which borders the Jed Water, bridged at this point by the **Canongate Bridge★** a mid-12C triple arched bridge. Stout piers with pointed cutwaters, support the narrow bridge provided with occasional pedestrian recesses.

EXCURSION

Waterloo Monument. – *3 miles to the north of Jedburgh by the A 68 and then the B 6400. A path leads from the Lothian Estates Woodland Centre (tree exhibition) to the base of the monument.*

tc

Standing on the summit of Peniel Heugh (744ft-227m) the Waterloo Monument *(no access to viewing platform)* was built to commemorate Wellington's Victory of 1815 and it is one of the Border's most prominent landmarks. Formerly the site of pre-Roman camps, with Dere Street on its western flank, the craggy eminence offers a splendid **panorama★★** of the surrounding countryside : fertile Teviot valley to the Cheviots in the south and east, great stretches of arable land, Smailholm Tower due north and the Eildons to the northwest.

★ KELLIE CASTLE (Fife)

Michelin map **401** fold 28 – L15 – 10 miles south of St Andrews.

tc

One of the chief charms of this laird's house is the chance to appreciate an example of unspoilt 16 and 17C Scottish traditional architecture. Originally the home of the Oliphants, it passed in 1613 to the Erskines or Earls of Mar and Kellie. The castle and lands were dissociated in the late 18C and a period of neglect and ruin followed from 1830 until a lease was granted in 1876 to Professor James Lorimer, an Edinburgh jurist. Gradually restored to its former glory, with the help of the talented Lorimer family, namely **Sir Robert Lorimer** (1864-1929), architect and restorer, famous for his Thistle Chapel in St Giles and the Scottish National War Memorial at Edinburgh Castle, John his painter brother, and in the next generation, Hew Lorimer the sculptor and his wife.

The castle. – Built of rubble sandstone, the plan is T-shaped with each wing of the T forming a tower. The northwest tower, the original 14C keep, was subsequently heightened to 5 storeys. About 1573 a second quite separate tower, was added to the east. Finally between 1573 and 1605 an L-shaped addition completed the T-plan. The southwest tower, containing the entrance door, is splendid with corbelled and conical roofed angle turrets and crow stepped gables.

Walk round the outside to the garden to discover the fascinating array of domestic architectural features – corbelled turrets with conical roofs, pedimented dormers, crow stepped gables, chimney stacks, varyingly pitched roofs and string courses. The impression is one of spontaneous, rather than planned growth, the result of the masons art of solving each problem as it arose.

Interior. – There is an audiovisual presentation of the Lorimer family and their restoration of the castle. The late 17C plasterwork ceilings are notable, in particular the **Vine Room** ceiling with its delicate trailing vine branches on the coving and painted central panel, *Mount Olympus* by Jacob de Wet. The ceiling of the Earl's Room is simpler and the unifying simplicity of that in the Great Hall is also strikingly fine. Also typical of the period is the Memel pine panelling in the Withdrawing Room painted with over 60 romantic landscapes.

★ KELSO (Borders)   Pop 4 852

Michelin map **410** fold 36 – M 17

Standing at the confluence of the Tweed and its main tributary, the Teviot, Kelso, a handsome market town remarkable for its Georgian architecture, serves a rich agricultural hinterland. Although arable farming predominates in the rich **Merse** *(qv)*, the outlying hill regions maintain the tradition of hill sheep farming, however, the area is also known as horse country – be it for riding, trekking, jumping, hunting or breeding. Kelso inherited Roxburgh's St James' Fair and the tradition is maintained by the famous Ram Sales *(July)*, the Horse and Pony Sales *(April and September)*, an agricultural show, the Border Union Show *(July)*. Kelso is also busy on race meeting days with Kelso races organized to the north at Berrymoss and the point-to-point races across the river at Friarshaugh *(February and March)*.

The other great annual event is the Kelso Civic Week *(p 28)* with its varied programme of events including the Kelso Laddie leading his supporters on the Whipman's Ride. Also popular is the Tweed Raft Race from Kelso to Carham.

A good **view** of the town in its riverside setting, can be had from the Maxwellheugh road.

HISTORICAL NOTES

The original settlement grew up at a fording point, the first west of Berwick and then developed round the abbey here in 1128. Kelso flourished when the nearby prosperous royal burgh of Roxburgh was destroyed in 1460 and her prosperity increased with the abbey's although she also suffered the fate of the abbey in 1545 when Hertford attacked. The town was raised to a burgh of barony in 1614 in favour of Robert Ker, 1st Earl of Roxburghe.

SIGHTS

Kelso Bridge (Z). – The attractive five arched bridge, built (1800-3) by John Rennie served as a model for his Waterloo Bridge. The lamp standards at the south end came from its London version when it was replaced in the 19C.
The bridge offers a splendid **view★** upstream over the lazy flowing Tweed, of Kelso on the right with Floors in its fine setting and the mound of Roxburgh Castle on the left. An elegant toll house (Z **A**) still stands on the north bank.

Abbey Close (Z **2**). – The previous bridge opened onto this close which is dominated by a church on the left and the white harled outline of **Turret House** (Z **B**) probably 17C and one of the oldest if not the oldest, standing, in Kelso.

Abbey (Z). – The abbey was founded in 1128, the monks having moved from two previous sites at Selkirk and Roxburgh before finally settling here. With royal patronage the abbey grew and acquired extensive lands to become the richest in the land and the abbot claimed seniority amongst the Scottish clergy. The building itself, a vast edifice, took 84 years to complete. Following the death of James II while besieging Roxburgh Castle, the infant **James III** was crowned in the abbey. Time and again the abbey suffered from invading forces, the most destructive being that of Hertford's "Rough Wooing" in 1545 despite a desperate fight by the monks. By 1587 the abbey was officially defunct and in 1592 James VI granted it and the lands to Robert Ker of Cessford, 1st Earl of Roxburghe. From 1649 to 1771 the roofed over transept served as parish church till the Rhymer's prediction proved true, then the ruins were pillaged for dressed stone. In 1919 the abbey was presented to the nation by the Duke of Roxburghe.

The **ruins,** date from the last quarter of the 12C. This once mighty abbey with its grandiose double transept plan was undoubtedly the largest and the most unusual of the Border group.

A 6089 EDINBURGH

KELSO
200 m
200 yards

A 698 HAWICK, JEDBURGH

On entering, only part of the south recessed doorway is visible, with a variety of sculpture on the arches, while rising above is the west transept tower, again massive in construction. Moving through to the abbey churchyard, turn around to admire the elevation. Three sections with round headed openings rise above very attractively carved intersecting arcading.
The modern partial cloister (1933) by Reginald Fairlie is the Roxburghe family vault. The sculpture is interesting for the use of Celtic designs.
The **west front** and **tower** are best seen from the churchyard outside the abbey grounds. This is by far the most imposing part with its unique ordinance. In the transitional style, the recessed round headed doorway with its pediment is surmounted by successive horizontal sections, each adorned with varying architectural elements. The whole is flanked by stout buttresses crowned with round turrets. The overall impression of this unique composition is one of soaring strength.

Pass through the churchyard to the car park. In the far corner is the house, adorned with a statue of a dog, Waverley Cottage (Z **D**) where Walter Scott spent some of his time while attending Kelso Grammar School.

The Border Abbeys were part of King David's main achievement, the widespread development of monasticism in 12C Scotland. Kelso 1128 (original foundation 1113), Melrose 1136, Jedburgh 1138, Dryburgh 1150.

tc **Old Parish Church** (Z). – The highly unusual but controversial octagonal-shaped church was built in 1773 by a local man James Nisbet. The ground floor straight headed windows and the above round headed ones are all equipped with hood moulds, a common architectural feature of the region. The eight sided roof is topped by a lantern.

Return to cobbled, Bridge Street where you pass, set back on the left, **Ednam House** (**Z E**) now a hotel. This fine Georgian mansion dates from 1761.

★★**Market Square** (Z). – Spacious and elegant, this vast square is dominated by the 19C **Town Hall** (**Z H**) which was built by public subscription and surrounded by a selection of 18 and 19C town buildings : three storeyed, parapeted hipped roofs with dormers, straight headed windows some with straight hoods on scroll brackets, some in colourful harling, others of dressed stone, all a delight in summer with colourful hanging baskets and window box displays. On the west side **Cross Keys Hotel** (**YZ F**) was one of the staging points on the Edinburgh – London coaching route. The names of the adjoining streets – Horsemarket (**Y 13**), Woodmarket (**Z 24**) – are reminders of the original role of the square as the market place, as is the bull ring (**Z G**) embedded at the centre of a star formation in the cobbles.

The dilapidated Tudor building with oriel windows in Woodmarket (now a furniture storage premises) was built in 1885 as the corn exchange.

Roxburgh Street (Y). – Leading off down towards the river is an alley which gives access to the **Cobby Riverside Walk**, affording pleasant views of the river, the weir, the eminence and onetime site of Roxburgh castle, Floors Castle magnificently set, and the backs of a series of town houses. Climb back up to Roxburgh Street where on the left is the majestic entrance to Floors built in 1929 by Reginald Fairlie. Two cupolaed lodges (**Y K**) are linked by grandly gilded gates.

Return to the town centre by Roxburgh Street passing on the way no 138, **Walton Hall** (**Y L**) behind massive wooden gates, the onetime home of James Ballantyne a school-fellow of Scott's and later business partner in his printing business. **Falcon Hall** (**Y P**) is also noteworthy.

EXCURSIONS

★★**Tower houses and stately homes.** – *25 miles. Round tour in the area to the northwest of Kelso.*

> *Leave Kelso by the A 6089 which follows the Floors estate wall.*

★**Floors Castle.** – *Description p 106.*

> *Take the B 6397 to the left, crossing rich arable farmland then turn left onto the B 6404. Take the road signposted Sandyknowe farm up to the right then branch left towards the steading. Continue through the steading and over the cattle grid up to the car park at the foot of the tower.*

★**Smailholm Tower.** – Standing like a sentinel 57ft tall, this lone tower house captures the
tc history of the Borders when the marches were controlled from such peel towers, where a day and night watch was kept. This 16C example is highly attractive with its rubble masonry and contrasting red standstone trims. Restored in the 1980s the interior houses an exhibition of beautifully detailed dolls representing characters from the Border ballads. Sandyknowe was where the young Walter Scott spent his childhood years with his grand parents. The rousing tales of the Border ballads caught the small boy's imagination.

The rocky outcrop at the base of the tower commands a **panoramic view**★★ of the Border countryside over a patchwork of rich arable farmland with, in the distance other local landmarks : the Waterloo Monument on Peniel Heugh due south and two of the Eildons to the west.

> *Make for Smailholm village and then on to Mellerstain by the B 6397 and back entrance.*

★★★**Mellerstain.** – *Description p 154.*

> *Make for the A 6089, turning left towards Gordon and at the road junction take the A 6105 to the left, continue for about 1 mile.*

tc **Greenknowe Tower.** – In an elevated site, surrounded by marshland, this lovely 16C L-shaped tower house, now a roofless ruin, still stands sentinel. Traditional forms are in evidence – rubble stonework of varying colours, corbelled squinch supported turrets, crow stepped gables and the iron yett. Over the entrance the lintel comprises the owner's arms and the date 1581.

Internally the disposition although showing a greater concern for comfort, is typical of such a building with cellar and kitchen on the ground floor, the laird's hall on the first and bedchambers above.

> *Return to Gordon and continue out to the east by the A 6105 in the direction of Greenlaw. Turn sharp right onto the B 6364.*

Greenknowe Tower

The imposing edifice high on the right is **Hume Castle** *(no admittance, danger from falling stones)*. The earliest stronghold on the site dated from the 13C and like all Border peels suffered attack at regular intervals. In this case it was Hertford in 1547 and Cromwell's troops in 1651 when the Governor Cockburn penned the following verse

"I Willie o'the Wastle,
Stand fast in my castle;
An a'the dogs in your toun,
Sanna gar me gang doon"

The present structure dates from the 18C. From its foot there are splendid views of the Merse.

Continue on the A 6089 to Kelso.

Roxburgh Castle. – *1 mile west of Kelso, by the A 699.*
The original site of Roxburgh Castle of Marchmount was the mound on the peninsula between the Tweed and Teviot, only slightly upstream from Kelso. In all probability a royal burgh in 1124, the town was one of the exclusive parliament, the "Court of the Four Burghs" along with Berwick, Edinburgh and Stirling. The prosperous burgh which grew up around its stronghold, was endowed with an abbey (1126-28) and even a Mint but proximity to the Border meant it was in English hands from the beginning of the 14C to the taking of the castle in 1460 when **James II** lost his life *(p 107)*. His widow Mary of Gueldres gave orders to dismantle both castle and town Today there are no visible signs, other than the mound.

Cheviot foothills. – *19 miles round trip. Leave Kelso to the south by the A 698 and then the B 6352 to reach the lower foothills of the Cheviots.*
Yetholm. – The twin villages of **Town Yetholm** (pop 475) and **Kirk Yetholm** (pop 131) are separated by the Bowmont Water. Kirk Yetholm known as the gipsy village still has a cottage named "The Palace", the home of Esther Faa Blyth, the last elected ruler. The 250 mile long Pennine Way, following the spine of England from Derby, ends here.

Take the B 6401 south out of town Yetholm and continue till the bridge over the Kale Water then turn right.

Linton. – The small parish church standing high on a hillock has a unique Norman tympanum known as the **"Somerville Stone"**.

Return to the B 6401 passing through Morebattle and continuing alongside the course of the Kale Water.

Up on the left are the remains of the once redoubtable Ker stronghold of Cessford Castle, a strategic point in the Marches defensive system.

At the A 698 turn right to return to Kelso.

★ KILDRUMMY CASTLE (Grampian)

Michelin map 401 fold 19 – L 12 – 38 miles west of Aberdeen – Local map p 37

tc The extensive ruins of this 13C courtyard castle, the most northerly in Scotland, rank high amongst 13C strongholds along with Bothwell and Dirleton. The defensive design is unusual in that it combines two different concepts, that of the keep with that of the gatehouse. The former was French in origin the latter English.

"Queen of Highland Castles". – The earliest place of strength in Mar, the Doune of Invernochty, was ten miles upstream. With the incorporation of the Celtic province of Moravia into the Scottish state during the reign (1214-49) of Alexander II it became necessary to control the approaches to the new territory. A stone castle was built in the 13C, to serve both local and national ends. Bruce considered the castle sure enough in 1306 to serve as refuge for his Queen and her ladies. Besieged by the future Edward II of England the castle fell to treachery. Firing and dismantling followed. Rebuilt the castle suffered a second siege in 1335 when it was held by Bruce's sister. Annexed by the Crown in 1435 the fate of this fine stronghold was sealed in 1715 when it served as headquarters for organizing the rising of 1715 by the last Mar proprietor, Bobbing John. Forfeiture and dismantling followed.

Castle. – Although some parts of the castle are no more than foundations, in particular the gatehouse and keep, the layout is still visible. The massive curtain wall is defended by a series of round towers with the key point, the keep in the northwest corner. Approach from the south and enter by the late 13-14C gatehouse, with its twin drum towers, which so closely resembles the one at Harlech. The gatehouse as the pre-eminent point of defence was an English concept, much favoured by Edward II when building his Welsh strongholds. In the northwest corner little also remains of the **keep** or Snow Tower, the original strongpoint traditionally withdrawn from the entrance. This originally five storey tall tower, with its own water supply, closely resembled the one at Coucy in France, the home of Alexander II's wife Marie de Coucy. Also to the rear of the enclosure are the domestic buildings, the great hall flanked by the solar and kitchen. To the east is the gable of a mid-13C chapel with an attractive triple lancet window.

The main shopping streets are indicated at the beginning of the list of streets, which accompany town plans.

KILMARNOCK (Strathclyde)   Pop 48 787

Michelin map 401 fold 34 – G17

Lying in the heart of the Ayrshire countryside, Kilmarnock is the area's premier shopping town. Main industries include whisky blending and carpet making.

SIGHTS

tc **Dean Castle.** – *Off Glasgow Road.*
The grounds are now a country park. The castle was for long the seat of the Boyd family. Following a fire in the 18C it stood empty prior to a complete restoration in the 20C. In the 14C **keep**, the main halls, hung with 15-16C Flemish tapestries, are the setting for two small but exceptionally rich medieval collections. In the great hall, the mainly 16C **arms and armour★** display includes pieces of outstanding craftsmanship, all finely decorated. Upstairs in the solar are early **musical instruments★** of Italian, French and German origin, all decoratively painted, inlaid or carved. Outstanding is the 17C Italian spinet supported by its gilt figure and the 16C and early 17C lutes and guitars.

tc **Dick Institute.** – *Elmbank Avenue.*
The library, museum and art gallery are under one roof. On the first floor the museum includes extensive geological and natural history sections. Note the Lochlea Crannog (lake dwelling) exhibit. The more specialized collection of **basket-hilted swords** has examples of both Scottish and foreign craftsmanship. Great skill and artistry were lavished on the elaboration of the openwork baskets. The paintings of the permanent collection are displayed in rotation and include works by Corot, Teniers, Constable, Millais and the Scottish School.

tc **Burns Monument.** – *Kay Park.*
The 80ft tower was erected in 1879 to commemorate Burns. His Kilmarnock Edition printed in the town in 1786, put him on the road to fame and caused him to change his mind about emigrating to the West Indies. There is a small Burns museum.

KINTYRE (Strathclyde)

Michelin map 401 folds 30 and 34 – D 16 and 17

Kintyre is the southern part of that long West Coast peninsula. The western shores are pounded by the great Atlantic rollers while the east coast looks over the sheltered Kilbrannan Sound to Arran. Kintyre with its varying scenery and seascapes affords a pleasant drive. The western (A 83) road is the wider and faster with good views of Ireland, while the eastern one is single track with passing places. The points of interest are described below in alphabetical order, leaving the tourist free to decide his own route.

SIGHTS

★Carradale. – Pop 262. This small village has a pleasant site, fringing the tiny harbour, a haven for a busy fishing fleet.

Campbeltown. – Pop 6 133. The main market and shopping town of the peninsula, Campbeltown is also a holiday centre. In the 19C the town boasted a large fleet based on the Loch Fyne herring fishery and over thirty distilleries producing a variety of malt whiskies. Both sectors have declined drastically, although the industries are still represented. The cross near the pier is 15C.

Clachan. – At nearby Ronachan Point grey seals may be seen basking on the offshore rocks.

tc **Claonaig.** – Pier for the ferry to Lochranza on Arran *(summer only).*

tc **Kennacraig.** – Ferry port for Islay and Jura.

Machrihanish. – Pop 219. This west coast town is known for its six mile long sandy beach and 18 hole golf course. The town had a colliery which closed in 1967. A nearby farm was the home of **William McTaggart** (1835-1910) who was inspired by local landscapes. Many of his canvases including *The Herring Fishers, The Golden Grain* and *Dawn at Sea* (Kelvingrove) were innovatory in that they captured the fleeting sparkle of light.

Mull of Kintyre. – Campbeltown Pipe Band and Paul McCartney with the song *Mull of Kintyre* brought worldwide publicity to this headland only 13 miles distant from Ireland.

Saddell. – Overgrown ruins are all that remain of this once important West Highland abbey founded *c*1207 by Reginald, the son of Somerled, Lord of the Isles. Reginald who was the ruler of Kintyre and Islay, is said to be buried here. In the churchyard a **collection★** of 14-16C grave slabs displays the unusual panoply of West Highland subjects : warriors, weapons, galleys and interlacing. The black galley with its sails furled symbolizes the end of a voyage.

tc **Skipness Castle.** – *Leave the car at the entrance to the grounds.*
This vast courtyard fortress incorporates within its curtain wall an early 13C hall house and 16C tower house. Red sandstone door and window trims add a decorative touch to this imposing stronghold which marked the southern limit of Campbell territory. There are good views across the Kilbrannan Sound to Arran.

tc **Tayinloan.** – Ferry port for Gigha, celebrated for its cheese and the gardens at Achamore.

Tarbert. – Pop 1 391. At the head of East Loch Tarbert, this small town marks the isthmus dividing Kintyre from Knapdale to the north. The houses fringe the harbour and bay lively with fishing boats and yachts in summer. There are only scant overgrown remnants of Bruce's castle. History recalls that the same warrior king, in imitation of the 11C Magnus Barefoot, King of Norway, dragged his boats across the isthmus on his way to attack Castle Sween in 1315.

Michelin map 四 fold 31 – K 15

The "Lang Town" combines the roles of holiday resort and industrial town. In the 19C the town was famous as the great centre of linoleum making, an industry which is still represented in the highly diversified industrial base of today.

The promenade, over a mile long is the site of the annual Links Market *(p 212)* a fair which dates back to 1305. Today it is a funfair.

Famous sons. – These include the 13C wizard **Michael Scott** *(p 156)*, the economist author of *The Wealth of Nations*, **Adam Smith** (1723-90) and the architect **Robert Adam** (1728-92). The latter were both leading members of that circle of great men which contributed to Edinburgh's Enlightenment.

SIGHTS

tc **Ravenscraig Castle.** – *Enter from Ravenscraig Park (car park) and follow signposts.* The ruins of Ravenscraig Castle stand on a rocky promontory overlooking Kirkcaldy Bay. The castle, started in 1460, was intended for James II's Queen, Mary of Gueldres who was widowed later in the same year *(p 140)*. During the Wars of the Roses, Mary had offered refuge to the Lancastrian Queen and fearing reprisals she took refuge in the east tower, where she was conveniently near to her ally, Bishop Kennedy of St Andrews. Following the dowager queen's death in 1463 the castle was part of an exchange between James III and William Sinclair and remained in that family until 1896.

This castle is important as an early example of artillery fortification, a fitting achievement for James II, that firearms enthusiast. Note in particular the design of the main front facing the vulnerable landward side across a deep ditch. Here windows are replaced by gunports. The main front, a formidable battery, comprises two towers flanking a central block. The left tower was built as an independent unit.

tc **Museum and Art Gallery.** – *War Memorial Gardens. Start upstairs with the art gallery.*

Art Gallery. – Although a relatively small collection the gallery has two outstanding holdings by William McTaggart and S.J. Peploe. The works *(room 4)* by **William McTaggart** (1835-1910), who as early as the 1870s was working out-of-doors, display a feeling for light and bold brushwork. Typical of his exploratory spirit are *Corn in the Ear* (1887) with its rich colours and the drama of *The Storm* (1883). Continuing the tradition of powerful brushwork and bold colour, a generation later, are the canvases *(room 6)* of the Colourist **S.J. Peploe** (1871-1935). The *Still life with Japanese Background* retains the black outlines and Cubist influences so characteristic of this artist's work.

Museum. – The ground floor rooms include an exhibition on Kirkcaldy district past and present and an interesting display on local potteries, in particular the delicately handpainted Wemyss Ware.

tc **Industrial Museum.** – *Abbotshall Road.* Of particular interest is the section on linoleum making. The first factory (Nairn's Folly, Pathhead) producing floor cloth opened in 1847 to compensate for the decline in demand for ships sail canvas. The industry went from strength to strength.

★ **KIRKCUDBRIGHT** (Dumfries and Galloway)   Pop 2 502

Michelin map 四 fold 43 – H 19

Kirkcudbright (pronounced Kirkcoobrie), set on the east bank of the Dee, now derives its livelihood from farming, fishing and tourism. The open waterfront was once a bustling port and the town itself a royal burgh and county town for the Stewartry. The latter was originally a general term for crown territory administered by a Steward, and this is the last remaining example.

In the late 19C the town had an active artists colony, which included such names as E.A. Hornel and his firm friend Charles Oppenheimer, E. A. Taylor and Jessie M King, Phyllis Bone and Bessie McNicol.

SIGHTS

tc **Broughton House.** – At the beginning of the century this 17C house became the home of the artist, **Edward Atkinson Hornel** (1864-1933), whose portrait by Bessie McNicol hangs in the Dining Room. Although Australian by birth Hornel was known for his Galloway scenes. He owed his prominence on the 19C Scottish art scene, and in particular the Glasgow School to the originality of his bold and colourful style. The works on display include some of his Japanese paintings the result of an extended visit to that country with his fellow artist George Henry. These firm friends formed the nucleus of an important local art colony. His splendid **Japanese garden** was another by- product of his fascination for that country.

Barrhill Road 2	St Mary's Place 6
Beaconsfield Place 3	Silver Craigs Road 7
Bridge Street 5	Victoria Park 9

tc **MacLellan's Castle.** – In 1582 the onetime provost of the town, **Sir Thomas MacLellan** quarried the adjoining ruined monastery to build his town residence, which is impressive for its sheer size. A spacious staircase, with straight flights, leads from the ground floor cellars and kitchen to the great hall where the massive fireplace is equipped with a **laird's lug** or spy hole. By 1752 the mansion was roofless.

Greyfriars Kirk. – Formerly part of a 15C monastery, the kirk shelters the memorial of MacLellan, the castle builder, who is portrayed as a knight in full armour.

High Street. – The west and south sides of this L-shaped street provide a mixture of styles some with a vernacular flavour and others with a Georgian sophistication, interrupted by cobbled closes or pends. No **14 (A)** was the home of the artist, Charles Oppenheimer, who took to landscape painting under his next door neighbour's influence, while the mosaic on no **44 (B)** announces the presence of two more artists, the husband and wife team of EA Taylor and Jessie M King. At the angle the 16-17C **tolbooth (D)** and 1610 mercat cross are symbols of past burghal status. The former complete with jougs is where John Paul Jones *(p 74)* was imprisoned.

tc **Stewartry Museum.** – A small local museum, bursting with items, has particularly interesting exhibits on curling (album) and quoiting, an old game played with iron rings resembling horseshoes, which used to be popular in every parish, and local personalities such as Thomas Telford, Old Mortality, John Paul Jones, Jessie Marion King and the 5th Earl of Selkirk. Here also are to be found such mysteries as a luggie, raunhels and a coggie.

EXCURSIONS

★Dundrennan Abbey. – *5 miles. Leave Kirkcudbright by the A 711.*
tc This Cistercian abbey was founded in 1142 by King David with the concurrence of Fergus, Lord of Galloway his childhood friend, in a typically remote but fertile site. Monastic foundations were David's way of subduing and governing, ensuring peace and prosperity as well as evangelizing. The monastery prospered but by the time it passed into secular hands at the Reformation it was in a precarious state. In 1568 Mary Queen of Scots halted here on her flight into England.
The ruins have a grandeur and austere simplicity true to the Cistercian tradition and are in direct contrast to the more compelling and gentler beauty of its daughter house Sweetheart *(qv)*. The parts still standing include a section of the south wall, the transepts, chapter house and some outbuildings. As an early example of the Gothic style the 12C transepts combine the use of the pointed arch (main arcade and triforium level) with the round arch of the clerestory. The remains of the chapter house rebuilt in the 13C already show a more decorative Gothic style. See in particular the charming group of entrance doorway flanked by windows, in the façade overlooking the cloister.

> *Continue on the A 711 for a further 9 miles. At the junction with the B 736 to Castle Douglas, take the single track road to the right.*

tc **Orchardton Tower.** – This unusual and attractive tower house dates from the mid-15C. Although only two storeys tall the tower is complete with turnpike, cap-house and crenellations.

tc **Tongland Power Station.** – *2 miles north of Kirkcudbright.*
Following the creation of a national grid system in 1926, Tongland was built between 1931-6 as headquarters for the Galloway Hydro-Electric Scheme. The tour includes the turbine hall with the original turbo generators, the arch and gravity dam (984ft along its crest and 66ft above the river bed), the overflow spillway, flood gates and ever popular **fish ladder**. Twenty nine stepped pools and four resting ones allow salmon to move upstream to spawn. An average of 4000 pass through annually.

Coastal drive to Creetown. – *20 miles – 2 hours 40 mins. Leave Kirkcudbright by the A 755, the Gatehouse of Fleet road.*

Gatehouse of Fleet. – Pop 837. This tidy and picturesque town is an example of late 18C town planning. Tourism is now the main source of income. Gatehouse became the centre for a group of artists including the local Faed brothers. **John Faed** (1820-1902) is known for his Scottish historical subjects *The Wappenschaw, Tam O'Shanter* and *The Warning before Flodden.*

> *Take the A 75 Newton Stewart road, which follows the coast.*

tc **Cardoness Castle.** – This mid-15C tower house is prominently set on a rocky outcrop overlooking the tidal Fleet. The oblong tower is typical of the period when more attention was lavished on the refinement of decorative detail (jambs, capitals and mouldings). A turnpike, linking the different floors, leads to the parapet *(79 steps)* which affords a view across the Fleet to Cally Palace Hotel, the onetime home of 'Mr Evidence' Murray, and the estuary with Wigtown peninsula on the horizon.

> *Six miles further on, turn right off the main road to the Cairn Holy site.*

Cairn Holy. – *1/2 mile from the main road. Bear left twice up a farm road. Park at the first monument.*
As was usual with the burial monuments of the Neolithic settlers these are in a commanding site with a good outlook over the Solway.
The Cairn Holy chambered cairns are two of a group in the vicinity. At the first site, **Cairn Holy I**, a forecourt precedes the burial chamber which is clearly visible, while the second, **Cairn Holy II** *(2 minutes further up the road)* has a double chamber.
One mile further along the main road stands **Carsluith Castle**. This 15C tower house with a later staircase tower belonged to the Brown family, whose most famous member was Gilbert Brown, the last abbot of Sweetheart Abbey.

> *The road moves down to the haughlands of the estuary before reaching Creetown.*

Creetown. – Pop 780. This delightful village, famous in the past for its granite quarries
tc has a **gem and rock museum** with a dazzling collection of Scottish and worldwide specimens.

KIRRIEMUIR (Tayside)

The small town of Kirriemuir, with its narrow winding streets lined by red sandstone houses, has a certain charm. Set on the slopes of the Highland rim overlooking the great sweep of Strathmore, Kirriemuir is at the heart of the rasp growing country. This was the birthplace of the playwright J.M. Barrie and the Thrums of his books.

tc **J.M. Barrie's Birthplace.** – *No 9 Brechin Road.*
The four roomed cottage was where **James Barrie** (1860-1937) the playwright and author of *Peter Pan* was born in 1860. Start upstairs in the right hand room where there is a recorded commentary on the contents and Barrie. The exhibits include a suede Peter Pan costume equipped with its detachable "kiss" and a painting of the St Bernard, Porthos, the model for Nana. The room downstairs with the albums provides an interesting insight into this rather private man, but a master of stagecraft *(Dear Brutus, the Admirable Crichton)*.
The small wash house outside, served as a makeshift theatre and no doubt provided the inspiration for the Wendy House built by the Lost Boys in Never Never Land.

Cemetery. – *Turn left off Brechin Road to take Cemetery Road right to the top.*
Barrie's grave is signposted. The short walk has good views of the agricultural patchwork of Strathmore below.

tc **Camera Obscura.** – *Barrie Pavilion, Kirriemuir Hill.*
The camera obscura provides excellent views of the Highland glens to the north and south over Strathmore to Dundee.

KNAPDALE (Strathclyde)

Knapdale is the northern part of the Kintyre peninsula, stretching from the Crinan Canal in the north to West Loch Tarbert. The sea lochs, Sween and Coalisport, bite deeply into this area of parallel ridges where hills, forest and water are all basic components of the landscape.

> *The roads go nowhere in particular and most are narrow with passing places.*

Crinan to Kilmory Knap *12 miles – 1/2 hour*

★**Crinan.** – This delightful hamlet stands at the western end of the nine mile long **Crinan Canal** which links the Sound of Jura and Loch Fyne. The canal with its fifteen locks was opened in 1801 to save fishing boats the long sail round the Mull of Kintyre. Today yachts and pleasure craft make a colourful spectacle as they manoeuvre and jostle for position in the holding pool and locks.

> *Take the Cairnbaan road which follows the canal then turn sharp right at Bellanoch. Fork left in the direction of Achnamara a forestry village.*

Castle Sween. – *In the grounds of the caravan site. View from the outside only.*
On the east shore of Loch Sween stand the ruins of this four square castle on its rocky outcrop. It was built by Somerled in the 12C and it is reputed to be one of the earliest mainland stone castles.

> *Continue south.*

tc **Kilmory Knap.** – The ruined chapel with its perspex roof shelters a good **collection** of West Highland sculptured monuments. The free standing **Macmillan's Cross**★ is an excellent example. The figure of Christ Crucified is accompanied by John and Mary, interlacing and a claymore. On the other face more interlacing accompanies a hunting scene. The cross commemorates Alasdair Macmillan a member of the clan which held sway over Knapdale. The grave slabs around the wall portray warriors in martial finery, intricate interlace patterns incorporating affronting beasts and claymores *(illustration p 22)*.

KYLE OF LOCHALSH (Highland)

First and foremost this is the ferry port for Skye and is in consequence a very busy place in summer. The community developed around the railhead once the line had been extended westwards from Strome Ferry in the 1890s.
Kyle of Lochalsh makes a good excursion point for discovering Torridon and Applecross to the north or Kintail to the east. The areas to the south remain remote and secluded.

EXCURSIONS

★★★**Northwards to Ullapool via Gairloch.** – *Description p 202.*

★**Eilean Donan Castle.** – *9 miles to the east by the A 87.*
tc The castle has an idyllic island **site**★★ (today linked by a bridge) with a superb mountain and loch setting. Following the abortive Jacobite rising of 1719 the ruins were abandoned for 200 years, until the 20C when a complete reconstruction was undertaken. The two rooms open to the public (Billeting Room and Banqueting Hall) have a variety of MacRae mementoes. For long the MacRaes were guardians of the castle for, and bodyguards to, the MacKenzies and hence known as "MacKenzie's Shirt of Mail". The vantage point of the outer ramparts offers excellent **views** of the three lochs.
Beyond at the head of Loch Duich is Glen Shiel.

Glen Shiel. – This grandiose V-shaped valley passes from the head of Loch Duich through to Loch Cluanie. Stretching six miles down the left side of the Glen are the **Five Sisters of Kintail.** Rising abruptly from the lochside some of the peaks top 3 000ft. The valley was the site of the Battle of Glen Shiel (10 June) which ended the Jacobite rising of 1719. A Jacobite expedition with Spanish troops had landed two months earlier and occupied Eilean Donan. The troops had been forced to surrender to the bombardment from three English frigates and the battle was the concluding action in this short lived episode.

LANARK (Strathclyde)   Pop 8 700

Michelin map **401** fold 35 – I 16

This busy market town has one of the biggest livestock markets in Scotland. The town has William Wallace associations and what is supposedly the oldest racing trophy, The Silver Bell. Festivals include the Lanimer Festival *(p 212)* with the traditional riding of the marches and the more unusual "Whuppity Scourie" ceremony *(p 212)* when winter is banished.

★NEW LANARK *time : 1 hour*

New Lanark down on the floor of the deep gorge of the River Clyde, is a good example of an 18C planned industrial village.

When the Glasgow tobacco trade collapsed due to the American War of Independence (1776-83) cotton manufacturing was quick to take its place exploiting a workforce skilled in linen making. In 1783, a Glasgow manufacturer and banker **David Dale** (1736-1806) brought Richard Arkwright, inventor of the spinning power frame, to the area to prospect suitable sites for a new factory. The present site was chosen and the smallest of the Falls of Clyde harnessed to provide water power for the mills. Building started in 1785 and by 1799 the four mills and associated housing comprised Scotland's largest cotton mill supporting a village population of over 2 000. In 1800 Dale sold the mills to his future son-in-law, **Robert Owen** (1771-1858) the social reformer, who took over as managing partner and was to remain for 25 years. The mills were a commercial success enabling Owen to put a series of social experiments into practice. He created the Nursery Buildings, the Institute for the Formation of Character, the village store and school. Owenism was widely acclaimed in that age of increasing industrialization but was ecclipsed by government and employer resistance. Cotton continued to be manufactured here until 1968. A major restoration programme is now in progress.

tc **The village.** – The centrepiece, **New Buildings** (1798), pinpointed by the bell tower is prolonged to the right by the **Nursery Buildings** (1809) to house the pauper apprentices who worked and usually lived in the mills, and then the co-operative **store** (1810). The bow ended **counting house** terminates a line of restored tenements which took its name, **Caithness Row**, from the storm bound Highlanders on their way to America who were accommodated and subsequently settled here. At the other end of the village, beyond Dale and Owen's houses, is more tenement housing, while between the river and the lade stands the massive **mill** comprising three units. The fourth mill was destroyed by fire in 1883. Looking from the main road the mill on the right was reduced in height for security reasons while no 2 mill was extended at a later period. The most handsome of all, no 3 the only mill building to have been rebuilt by Owen in 1826. Beyond these are the Institute, a sort of community centre, and the school.

The **Dyeworks**, by the river, serve as a Scottish Wildlife Trust visitor centre with an audiovisual show and displays illustrating the varied wildlife of the Falls of Clyde Reserve.

tc **Falls of Clyde.** – *From New Lanark a riverside path leads upstream to the gorge section of the Clyde with its series of falls, now harnessed by a hydro-electric scheme.*

This stretch of river with the three sets of falls, was once one of Scotland's most visited beauty spots. The Falls were portrayed variously by Turner, Paul Sandby and Jacob More and described by Wordsworth, Coleridge and Scott.

In spite of a lack of bathing naiads, and even water at times, this wooded stretch of the Clyde retains a certain charm which was much appreciated by the Romantics. A viewpoint beyond Bonnington Power Station provides an excellent **view** of the highest falls, **Corra Linn** where the drop is 60ft. These become spectacular on open days when the water is turned on and thunders over the rocky lips, down to a boiling rushing mass below with a pall of vapour hanging above.

EXCURSION

tc **Craignethan Castle.** – *5 miles northwest of Lanark by the A 72. Turn left on the far side of Crossford.*

Sir James Hamilton of Finnart (1512-71) Master of Works to James V and natural son of the 1st Earl of Arran built this attractive biscuit coloured tower house with its double courtyard. The original stronghold stands on a promontory with steep slopes on three sides while the vulnerable fourth side, overlooked by high ground is protected by a dry ditch then an outer courtyard. Built between 1530 and 1540 this ruin *(restoration work in progress)* has the distinction of being designed for defence against artillery. In the right hand corner of the first courtyard is a 17C dwelling (curator's house) built by the Covenanter **Andrew Hay.** On the floor of the dry ditch, separating the two courtyards is a unique defensive feature, a **caponier** or vaulted gallery. A tall 5ft thick curtain wall originally rose behind the ditch and access to the inner courtyard was by a gateway round to the left. The tower house with its two storeys is squat by normal standards, probably not rising above the curtain which preceded it. Attractive corbelling supports the parapet.

LARGS (Strathclyde)   Pop 9 771

Michelin map 401 fold 30 – F 16

Largs is a popular Ayrshire coast resort, much frequented by Glaswegians, with ample
accommodation and the usual range of amenities.
The town, was the site of the **Battle of Largs** (1263) an inconclusive affair during the
reign of Alexander III. The Norwegian, King Haakon was on a summer expedition to
his foreign territories of the Western Isles and Isle of Man when his fleet was blown
ashore at Largs, with the ensuing battle. Haakon died at Kirkwall on the return journey.
A monument on the shore to the south of the town and the **Viking Festival** *(p 212)* both
commemorate this battle. Three years later by the Treaty of Perth, the Norwegians
renounced all claims to the Western Isles, although retaining Orkney and Shetland.
Relations so improved between the two nations that Alexander's daughter, Margaret
married King Eric in 1281.

★Skelmorlie Aisle. – *Old Kirkyard, back off Main Street.*

tc Originally the north transept of a larger church the aisle was transformed into a
mausoleum by Sir Robert Montgomery in 1636. The refined but stark simplicity of
the exterior gives no hint of the inner splendours. The elegant canopied **Renaissance
monument★** is a mass of fine sculptural detail akin to the decorative work at Argyll's
Lodging, Stirling. The coffered design of the **painted ceiling★** frames heraldic devices,
signs of the Zodiac, the seasons and ornate Italianate patterns. In the winter scene
note the players of golf or kolf.

EXCURSIONS

tc **Great Cumbrae.** – The island's main town, **Millport,** strung out round the head of Millport
tc Bay is much favoured by Glasgow holidaymakers. One mile out of town is the **University
Marine Biological Station.** This scientific research centre has a small but interesting
exhibition explaining the geology and marine conformation of the Clyde Sea Area and
work of the station. Specimens of the various local species are to be found in the
adjoining **aquarium** (13 tanks).
The island affords the best view of the industrial complex on the mainland at
Hunterston Sands. The massive buildings of Hunterston Nuclear Power Sation, are
near to the British Steel Corporation's iron ore terminal for Ravenscraig.

tc **Hunterston Nuclear Power Station.** – *5 miles south of Largs by the A 78.*
This is part of an industrial zone south of Largs, beyond the residential and now
flourishing holiday resort of **Fairlie,** world famous for its yacht building yards. Famous
examples included the various *Shamrock* yachts built for the founder of the tea-empire
and enthusiast yachtsman Sir Thomas Lipton (1850-1931). Lipton was runner-up
five times in his bid to win the America's Cup.
Hunterston sits on a promontory, sheltered by the Cumbraes. Hunterston A was
Scotland's first commercial nuclear power station after the experimental one at
Dounreay *(qv)*. Opened in 1964 this was one of the first generation Magnox Reactors.
Three years later work started on Hunterston B, an advanced gas-cooled reactor (AGR),
and power was first produced in 1976. Together these nuclear stations play a vital
role in supplying Scotland's electricity.

LAUDER (Borders)   Pop 604

Michelin map 401 fold 36 – L 16

Lauder, a royal burgh, is a quiet town on the A 68 main road north to Edinburgh. The
town is remembered in history for the episode that gave the name 'Bell-the-Cat' Angus
to the 5th Earl, Archibald Douglas. In 1482 a group of nobles, jealous of James III's
low born advisors, took revenge by hanging six of the favourites from the bridge that
once stood in the grounds of Thirlestane Castle.
The Common Riding *(p 28)* is one of the Border's original ceremonies and still rides
the bounds, as at its inception.

THIRLESTANE CASTLE *time : 3/4 hour*

tc The castle has been the home of the Maitland family from the 16C to the present
day. The original tower, on an ancient fortified site, was transformed into a residence
by William Maitland, Secretary to Mary Queen of Scots. His brother, John Maitland
was Lord High Chancellor to James VI and his grandson, the 1st and only Duke of
Lauderdale, a member of Charles II's Cabal and virtual ruler of Scotland from 1660
to 1678. The Duke, with Sir William Bruce as architect, enlarged and refurbished the
castle. For much of its subsequent history Thirlestane was the seat of the Earls of
Lauderdale, and was further extended in the 1840s with the addition of the Victorian
wings and courtyard.

Exterior. – The splendid main front is an imposing composition, the result of several
additions. The original 16C oblong tower house, quartered by round towers, was
extended by Sir William Bruce when he flanked the west end with two massive square
towers. In Victorian times David Bryce again extended outwards by adding further
wings in a slightly darker stonework. The harmonious massing of the different parts
is enhanced by the varied roofscape deployed around the central ogee, and decorative
effect of the red sandstone trims, corbelling and balustrades. The entrance is
particularly imposing.

Interior. – Most of the interior decoration dates from the 1840 refurbishing and the
furniture is mainly 19C as the original pieces were removed by the cartload to Ham
(see the Michelin Green Guide London). Upstairs the glory of the State Rooms is the
series of 17C **plasterwork ceilings★★** each more ornate and decorative than the last.

Amidst the wealth of detail look for the splendid Lauderdale eagles with each feather done individually. The ceilings were the work of George Dunsterfield who was also employed at Holyroodhouse, another Bruce project. In the Duke's Room note the *Duke,* his first wife *Anne Home* and her successor the notorious *Elizabeth Countess of Dysart.*

tc **The Border Country Life Museum.** – The museum in the courtyard wing provides displays illustrating all aspects of rural life in the Borders from prehistoric times to the present.

ADDITIONAL SIGHTS

Tolbooth. – Overlooking the market place the tolbooth consisted of the prison on the ground floor with the council chamber above.

Parish Church. – Standing near the tolbooth, the church, in the form of a Greek cross, was built in 1673 by William Bruce. Inside the gallery fronts are decorated with tinctured coats of arms.

★ LENNOXLOVE (Lothian)

Michelin map **401** fold 32 – L 16 – 1 mile south of Haddington

tc Historic associations and rich collections, some from Hamilton Palace, make this historic house an interesting outing.

A Maitland seat. – Originally known as Lethington, the oldest part was built *c*1345 by the Maitlands. The best known was **William Maitland** (1525-73), Secretary to Mary Queen of Scots, described by Queen Elizabeth of England as "The Flower of the Wits of Scotland". His brother John became Lord High Chancellor to James VI. The 1st Duke of Lauderdale, was a member of Charles II's Cabal. His second wife was Elizabeth, widowed Countess of Dysart. The enlargement of the old tower was started by the 1st Earl of Lauderdale, and completed by his son, the Duke. Their other houses included Thirlestane Castle *(see opposite)* and Ham House. The improvements at both Thirlestane and Lethington were planned by Elizabeth's relative, Sir William Bruce of Kinross. On the death of the Duke of Lauderdale, Lethington passed to the Duchess's son, Lord Huntingtower, and was purchased by the Trustees of Frances Teresa Stewart, Duchess of Lennox, known as "La Belle Stewart" (1647-1702), a favourite at the Court of Charles II and subsequently immortalised as Britannia on British coins. Lethington then formed a bequest to Walter Stewart, Master of Blantyre, the Duchess of Lennox's cousin, later 4th Lord Blantyre. The house was renamed Lennoxlove as a condition of the bequest, and to signify the love of the Duchess for the Duke of Lennox. The house remained the property of the Lords Blantyre until 1900 and of their descendants the Baird family until purchased in 1946 by the 14th Duke of Hamilton. It now contains many of the treasures from the Hamilton Palace Collection.

TOUR *3/4 hour*

Interior – The portraits bring to life the story of this historic home and its many famous owners. Of special interest in the **Front Hall** are the portraits attributed to Mytens of *James, 2nd Marquess of Hamilton* who accompanied James VI to England in 1603. Portrayed by Ponsford is the *Marquess of Huntly* Cock o' the North, uncle of Susan Beckford who married the 10th Duke of Hamilton. There is also a portrait believed to be of *John Knox*. On the first floor landing are portraits by Kneller of *William Douglas,* Earl of Selkirk, who became 3rd Duke of Hamilton, and of his wife *Anne,* Duchess in her own right. There are also portraits of *Sir William Hamilton,* the celebrated art collector and diplomat, and of his wife *Emma,* mistress of Lord Nelson, who figures in a triple portrait by Angelica Kauffman.

The wall cabinets of the **China Hall** display 18 to 20C armorial porcelain. In the **Blue Room,** William Beckford, collector, eccentric and author, is pictured as a boy. He was the father of the 10th Duchess. There is also a portrait by David Wilkie of the *10th Duke of Hamilton* (1767- 1852), known as "Il Magnifico" who enlarged Hamilton Palace, added to the collections of furniture and paintings and built his own mausoleum at Hamilton. There are also portraits by Henry Raeburn of the *8th* and *11th Dukes,* the latter as a child. The former is portrayed riding from Edinburgh to Hamilton in under three hours in fulfillment of a wager. Several French items include furniture by Courtois, a piano by Pleyel, Napoleon's bedside table, and a portrait of the *Marquis of Marigny,* brother of Madame de Pompadour.

The **Petit Point Room** is dominated by the inlaid tortoiseshell writing cabinet, a gift from Charles II to La Belle Stewart. The damask wall hangings are appliqued with older petit point embroideries. In the **Yellow Room** a double portrait of the *2nd Duke of Hamilton* and the *Duke of Lauderdale* establishes the link between the original and present owners of Lennoxlove. There are also portraits by Lely of the *Duke and Duchess of Lennox*. The Duke was drowned while on a diplomatic mission in Elsinor. The **Great Hall,** which represented the whole living portion of the original tower, was remodelled in 1911-2 by Robert Lorimer. It contains the Death Mask of Mary Queen of Scots, and also her silver casket, a betrothal gift from her first husband, François II of France.

For travelling in Scotland

   the *Green Guide Scotland,*

   the *Michelin Map no* **401** *, scale 1 : 400 000,*

   the *Red Guide Great Britain and Ireland* (hotels and restaurants)

are complementary.

Michelin map **401** folds 2, 5, 6 and 9
Access : see the current Michelin Red Guide Great Britain and Ireland.

Although one island, Lewis and Harris, are part of the 130 mile chain of islands the Outer Hebrides. Buffeted by the Atlantic waves, treeless and windswept, their isolation has in fact preserved their cultural identity. Gaelic is widely spoken and many are bilingual. The Free Church is the Island's main denomination and they hold by a strict observance of the sabbath. One of the surprising features of the island is to see two fairly sizeable churches standing side by side.

Landscapes. – Moorlands, glistening lochans, superb sandy beaches and crystal clear water are common features of the island's landscapes. Although joined Lewis and Harris are physically very disparate. The landscapes of Lewis are essentially rolling moorlands scattered with lochans. Harris is altogether more rugged and mountainous.

Peat working. – A common feature is the many peat workings lining the moorland roadsides. The blanket peat cover averaging a depth of 5ft is the universal soil. It is readily exploited as a domestic fuel. In March the peats are cut, thrown up then stacked in fours and left to dry. In summer they are bagged for collection and driven home. Nearly every house has the inevitable peat stack.

Harris Tweed. – The orb trademark guarantees that this fine quality cloth is handwoven by the islanders in their homes. Weaving tweed originated in Harris but it was later commercialized in Lewis where today all processes after weaving are done in the mills of Stornoway and Shawbost.
It is still common to see bundles of tweed awaiting collection at road ends.

Midges. – The uncommonly present midge has no common antidote.

SIGHTS

The following sights are described in alphabetical order.

tc **Arnol Black House.** – *Signposted off the main A 858.*
This straw thatched house shelters under one roof the sleeping area with box beds, the living area, byre and stable cum barn. This type of dwelling known as the Black House, due to its open hearth, was common up until 40 to 60 years ago. Housing grants have been responsible for the conversion of many.

★★**Callanish Standing Stones.** – *Well signposted off the A 858.*
This group of stones (locals maintain you never get the same number twice) forms a circle with alignments radiating outwards at the compass points. The site is in fact one of a series in the vicinity and it is generally assumed they were used for astronomical observations. The site dates from the late Stone Age and early Bronze Age (3000-1500BC), making it over 4000 years old and roughly contemporary with Stonehenge *(see the Michelin Guide, The West Country)*. The stones are Lewisian gneiss and were once partially buried under peat. The central cairn or burial chamber was a later addition by the Neolithic people (2500-2000BC).

★**Carloway Broch.** – *Signposted off the A 858.*
Although not a complete example of a broch *(p 183)*, enough remains of this structure to intrigue. Admire the skill of the stonemason as the sides swell out at the bottom. The galleried walls and entrance guard chamber are still visible.

Eye Peninsula. – To the northeast of Stornoway the peninsula has some fine sandy beaches.

Leverburgh. – The township of Obboe was renamed by the English soap magnate, Lord Leverhulme in 1923. He had acquired Harris in 1919 and Lewis later the same year and dreamed of developing the islands. None of the schemes flourished including the project to make Leverburgh an important fishing port. All was abandoned when Lord Leverhulme died in 1925.
The An Clochan, cafe cum tweed shop, has a good Harris Tweed Exhibition.

tc **St Clement's Church.** – In the township of Rodel near the southern tip of Harris is a church with, the outstanding **tomb**★ of the 16C builder, Alexander MacLeod (d 1546). Carvings decorate the arch and back of the recess above the effigy of the 8th Chief of MacLeod. The Twelve Apostles are portrayed on the arch. The other carvings include the Virgin and Child, flanked by two bishops, a hunting scene, a castle and the galley emblem of the Lords of the Isles.

tc **Shawbost Museum.** – This folk museum gives an insight into the life and customs of the past. Many of the explanatory notices are in Gaelic.

Stornoway. – Pop 5 152. The capital and only town of any size lies on a narrow neck of the Eye Peninsula. The main shopping area fronts the landlocked harbour which is also overlooked by the 19C castle (now a technical college) and its wooded grounds. A good view of the town can be had from the foot of the War Memorial on the hill behind the hospital. Stornoway makes a good excursion centre for visiting Lewis and Harris. As hotels and petrol pumps are scarce, take a picnic lunch and keep your petrol tank filled up.

Tarbert. – Pop 479. The main community of Harris sits on the isthmus between West and East Lochs Tarbert. The town is the ferry terminal for Skye and North Uist.

Uig. – This township is famed on two counts as the home of the Brahan Seer *(p 133)* and as the place where the Lewis Chessmen were found in a sandbank in 1813.

Passing places
are provided to allow vehicles to pass one another,
but also to permit overtaking.
Do not park in passing places. Do not hold up a following vehicle.

Michelin map 401 fold 31 – J 16

The now quiet residential town of Linlithgow gives little hint of its dramatic past which centred on the royal palace. Today the town remains little altered in plan. Linlithgow stands on the south bank of the loch, away from the busy M 9 motorway.

Royal burgh. – The history of the town is essentially that of its palace. The royal burgh grew up around the manor house and as early as Edward I's time its strategic role controlling the east west route was appreciated. The burgh with its port at Blackness flourished and in 1368 its importance was such that it was included in the Court of the Four Burghs. With the rebuilding of both the palace and St Michael's the 15 and 16C was a time of great prosperity, which ended with the Union of the Crowns. Despite the introduction of the leather industry during the Commonwealth, the smaller landward burghs like Linlithgow declined in the face of competition from the great industrial centres of the west coast flourishing on Atlantic trade. In 1822 the Union Canal was opened and prospered for 20 years. Regular day and overnight, services of "Hoolets" or "Wee Owls" plied the canal, but the barges were eclipsed with the coming of the railway in 1842, reviving the town's fortunes. In 1972 the new motorway M 9 relieved the town of much of the heavy traffic.

★★LINLITHGOW PALACE *time : 3/4 hour*

tc The formidably bare and vast form of this onetime royal residence dominates the town and loch of Linlithgow from its promontory site. Now roofless, the layout of this 15 to 17C building with its many staircases and corridors is typical of a search for comfort and a more logical disposition. The palace was the favourite residence of several Stewart monarchs.

Manor house. – Originally an island site it was appreciated for its strategic location and for the good hunting in the surrounding countryside. The original manor house accompanied by a conveniently near place of worship, was encircled by a wooden palisade by Edward I on his 1301-2 winter campaign. David II rebuilt the manor and it was his edifice which was gutted by a fire which ravaged the town, church and manor in 1424. On the return of the third Stewart King, James I, from 18 years captivity in England, he undertook the first phase of construction from 1425 to 1435.

Favourite royal residence. – However it was during the reigns of James IV and V that Linlithgow became a favoured royal residence. **James IV** was responsible for another period of building and alterations (1490-1530) probably partly in preparation for his new bride Margaret Tudor whom he married in 1503 and who spent most of her married life here. This was Scotland's Golden Age and their court was a merry glittering one with Linlithgow Palace fully participating in the round of merry pursuits. James IV was an active sportsman who liked both hunting and hawking but he also loved the indoor entertainments provided by jugglers, acrobats, rope dancers, minstrels and poets. On 10 April 1512 the future James V was born here, a year before that fateful date in 1513 when the flower of Scotland's knighthood died alongside their King at Flodden *(qv)*. Following this the Dowager Queen left with her children for Stirling. **James V** had his father's same love for Linlithgow Palace and often resided here. It was his second wife Mary of Guise who declared "she had never seen such a princely palace". The palace was the venue for an open air performance of James V's onetime tutor, Sir David Lindsay's *Satire of the Three Estates.* Having lost two sons, Mary of Guise gave birth to the future Mary Queen of Scots on 8 December 1542 only days before the king died of a broken heart. As Regent, Mary of Guise, continued to visit the great palace as did Mary Queen of Scots on several occasions but its heyday was past and decline set in during the reign of James VI with the removal of the court to London following the Union of the Crowns (1603). The north wing was rebuilt, after the roof collapsed, from 1618-20 however later occupants included Cromwell and troops for 9 years (1650-9). There was a fleeting visit by Bonnie Prince Charlie in 1745 and subsequently by the Duke of Cumberland's troops after whose stay fire gutted the palace leaving it the roofless ruin we see today.

★Gateway. – The one storey gateway at the head of the Kirkgate (5) gives access to the Royal Park wherein stand the palace and St Michael's Church. Built by James V *c*1535 the town side of the gateway is adorned with 4 gaily painted orders, 19C representations of the originals, showing from left to right The Garter, The Thistle, The Golden Fleece and St Michael.

The Courtyard. – The centrepiece of the inner close is the magnificently intricate stone **fountain★★** built by James V in the 1530s. Octagonal in shape the three basins decreasing in size are adorned by figures, buttresses, roundels, arms and various bearers.
The courtyard elevations present a variety of styles, openings and decorative devices. Of the four ranges three are 15-16C while the north one is 17C. On the east side above the round headed arch of the former entrance, three canopied niches with angels above, are surmounted by an elaborate moulding. The more strictly symmetrical north elevation (1618-20) with its regular string courses has window pediments sporting some of the national emblems.
Take the northeast spiral staircase to reach the main apartments on the first floor.

Interior at first floor level. – To the left of the Screens Passage is the kitchen with its vast fireplace. The **Great Hall** of impressive dimensions runs the full length of the east range. At the dais end is a superb **hooded fireplace★★** with delicately carved ornamentation. Beyond the corner solar, the **chapel** retains four elaborately carved, but statueless, canopied niches between the windows. The remaining part of this wing is occupied by a hall followed by a corner chamber. Both of these ranges have the innovative feature of a corridor running along the courtyard side.

The apartments of the west range include the King's Hall, the Presence Chamber with an unusual window and at the end, the King's Bed Chamber.

The adjoining **King's** and **Queen's Oratories** have beautifully carved bosses figuring the unicorn. A wooden gangway leads through the shell of the range, remodelled by William Wallace in the early 17C. The new style is clearly visible in the decoration of the remaining fireplaces.

The visitor should then discover the various ground floor cellars and guardrooms and take one of the turnpikes (northwest) for an overall view of the palace and its setting.

Exterior. – The striking feature of the entrance façade is the group of five closely set lancet windows indicating the chapel. Moving round to the east façade, the original entrance is flanked by elongated canopied niches with above the royal coat of arms. The Great Hall is positioned by the great window and six fairly large windows slightly higher up. The openings of the 17C north front are more numerous and regular while on the plainer west face the corner towers are more easily distinguished.

★ST MICHAEL'S

tc The building we see today is essentially the 15C reconstruction of an earlier one destroyed by fire. This burgh church is one of the largest pre-Reformation ecclesiastic buildings. Taking over a century to complete, construction started with the nave progressing to the choir (1497), the tower and finally the apse *c*1531. Gothic, in the more Scottish Decorated style the church has a strong resemblance to Stirling's Church of the Holy Rude.

Exterior. – The most striking external feature of this aisled cruciform building with transeptal chapels and a polygonal apse is the west end tower with its **spire**, which however controversial, maintains the medieval tradition that any addition to a church should be in the style of the period to emphasize that it is both ancient and modern. The Geoffrey Clarke laminated timber and aluminium spire was erected in 1964 to replace an earlier crown spire. Also original is the south porch with the unusual oriel window above, flanked by a turret staircase, and further round on the southwest buttress the only statue to survive the "cleansing" by the Lords of the Congregation in 1559 is a weathered, bewinged and armoured St Michael.

Interior. – Pleasingly plain with little sculptural ornament, the pointed arcades and clustered piers of the five bay nave continue for three bays into the chancel, separated only by the great chancel arch, and terminate with the tall windows of the three sided apse. The elevation in both parts is similar excepting the blind triforium in the chancel. The nave, chancel and apse are roofed with a 19C plaster ceiling (replacing an 1812 oak roof) while the original rib vaulting still covers the aisles and transept chapels. Particularly worthy of attention are the tracery and stained glass. Perpendicular tracery fills the three tall apse windows while the stained glass of the central one (8 lights) portrays Psalm 104 (The Creation). The window overlooking the war memorial in the chancel's south aisle recounts the history of the church and depicts three sovereigns James IV, David I and Queen Victoria. Note above the stonemasons at work. Just before the transept chapel is a lovely Burne-Jones design (1899) in muted colours. The jewel of the church is the Flamboyant window in the south transept chapel with highly decorative and unusual tracery above the six lights. It was in this chapel that James IV was said to have seen the ghost forewarning him of impending doom at Flodden. A Herbert Hendrie (1936) window in the southwest wall overlooks the font (ie west end of the south aisle). Finally comes the west window again, in more muted colours with The Transfiguration (1898) effectively highlighted. Stone carvings in the vestry include fragments of a pre-Reformation retable : The Agony in the Garden and The Betrayal.

★THE TOWN

The town has conserved its medieval layout, with a long main street backed by its burgess plots widening at the market place and closed by its ports. The arrival of the railway destroyed the town wall to the north.

The Cross. – This, the onetime market place, has in the centre the **cross well** a 19C replica of its predecessor. On the north side is the grandly imposing **Town Hall (H)** which dates from the 17C. Cromwell des-

LINLITHGOW

200 m
0
200 yards

BO' NESS
A 706
St Ninian's Road
M.9. STIRLING FALKIRK
A 803 LANARK
A 706 LANARK

LOCH

PALACE
The Peel
ST MICHAEL'S
GATEWAY
5
H 7
The Cross
High Street
High
POL.
West Port House
9
Royal
Terrace
Union Canal

A 803 SOUTH QUEENSFERRY
M.9. EDINBURGH SOUTH QUEENSFERRY

A
B
C
2
10
6
3

13

7

Back Station Road	2	Preston Road	7
Friarsbrae	3	St John's Avenue	9
Kirkgate	5	Strawbery Bank	10
Manse Road	6	West Port	13

troyed the original. The present divided staircase is a 20C replacement for a wrought iron loggia.

High Street. – In East High Street **nos 40-48 (A)** are known as Hamilton Lands *(not open to the public)*. These rubblework, crow stepped and gable ended dwellings are typical of the late 16C early 17C when Linlithgow was still at the height of its mercantile prosperity. The narrow frontages corresponded to the width of the burghal lot (rig) and the round arched pend was a typical feature of such layouts. There are more in West High Street.

A plaque on the wall of the Sheriff Court (**B**) marks the approximate site of Archbishop Hamilton's house, from which the Regent Moray was shot in 1570. The latter died and the archbishop was later hanged for suspected complicity in this incident and the Darnley murder. **West Port House**, as the name suggests, marked the site of the west gate. The three storey L-plan house dating from 1600 retains a turret staircase.

EXCURSIONS

tc **Blackness Castle.** – *4 miles northeast of Linlithgow.*
The now peaceful village of Blackness was once the flourishing seaport for Linlithgow. Likewise its castle, standing on a rocky promontory, jutting out into the Firth of Forth, was formerly one of the most important in the kingdom. Following the Union of 1707 it was one of four Scottish strongholds (Edinburgh, Stirling and Dumbarton) to be garrisoned.
Serving as a royal castle, prison for Covenanters, ordnance depot and youth hostel this stronghold is in the shape of a ship. The south or "stern" tower is 16C with curtain walls of the same period, enclosing a 15C central tower and meeting at the north or "bow" tower, reduced to serve as a gun platform. The latter affords a fine **view** across the Firth of Forth and of the bridges to the right.

tc **Kinneil House.** – *4 miles to the northwest. Leave Linlithgow by the A 706, at the first major crossroads in Bo' Ness turn left onto Dean Road. The entrance is on the left in a wide bend.*
This semi-ruin consists of the original fortified tower house and adjoining wing, the Palace. James Hamilton 2rd Earl of Arran (*c*1516-75) Protector and Governor during Mary Queen of Scots' minority started to build the tower house (1546-50) while work on the Palace commenced in 1553. The 1st Duke of Hamilton added end pavilions, one of which connects the two buildings. Disrepair ensued and during demolition in 1936, 16 and 17C tempera **paintings** were discovered in the Palace block. The barrel vaulted Arbour Room has a floral pattern with roundels overpainted with a compartmented design dating from 1621-4. Note the Hamilton arms on a window vault and the 1570 Samson and Delilah medallion. The paintings in The Parable Room, above, depict the story of The Good Samaritan. The timber compartmented ceiling is 17C.
It was in an outhouse that **James Watt** (1736-1819) conducted experiments on his steam engine, financed by the founder of the Carron Works and the then owner of Kinneil House.

LIVINGSTON (Lothian)   New Town – Pop 39 000
Michelin map **401** fold 31 – J 16

Between the Pentland and the Bathgate Hills Scotland's 4th New Town, Livingston astride the M 8 Motorway and the River Almond was designated in April 1962 as part of a programme for development and growth in Central Scotland. A major factor in its choice as an industrial growth point was its excellent location at the heart of Scotland's communications network with easy road and rail access to other major towns, airports and ports.

The master plan. – Prior to designation the local population of 2 000 was concentrated in two areas, the oil shale mining community of Livingston Station and Livingston Village, the historical associations of which go back to the 17C. The 1981 figure of approximately 39 000 is expected to reach 70 000 early in the 21C.
Communications have been planned on a grid system with a two tier road network separated from the pedestrian ways. Housing, in the eleven to twelve housing districts, is varied in both technique and type of accommodation and is interspersed with ample play facilities. The main town centre, Almondville, regroups a shopping centre, office and public buildings and certain recreational facilities, while five main industrial areas are used by 200 companies with a strong emphasis on electronics (30 companies) and offshore developments. A science park provides liason with university research departments.
Livingston is also known for its Ecumenical Parish where congregations from different Protestant traditions share churches, have joint worship and team ministry.
Open spaces include the proposed town park centring on the green belt of the River Almond with its trim track and Howden Park Centre with its spacious grounds and community centre in the 18C mansion, Howden House, once associated with the family of Henry Raeburn the 18C portrait painter.

FOLLOW THE COUNTRY CODE

Guard against all risk of fire.
Fasten all gates.
Keep dogs under proper control.
Keep to the paths across farmland.
Avoid damaging fences, hedges and walls.
Leave no litter.
Safeguard water supplies.
Protect wildlife, wild plants and trees.
Go carefully on country roads.
Respect the life of the countryside.

★★ LOCH LOMOND (Strathclyde and Central)

Michelin map 🔢 folds 26 and 30 – F and G 15

The legendary beauty of the "Queen of Scottish Lochs", so often celebrated in song and verse, is one of blue waters flanked by shapely mountains or fringed by more pastoral wooded shores. The loch 23 miles long and 5 miles at its widest has a maximum depth of 653ft. The water discharges into the Firth of Clyde by the River Leven and up to the 13C was known by the same name. It was only later that it took the name of the prominent ben on its eastern shore.

(Scottish Tourist Board)

Loch Lomond

The ruggedly mountainous scenery of the narrow northern end changes in the south to a more pastoral setting of wooded islands and shores.

Only 20 miles from the centre of Glasgow the shores are popular for day outings. It is advisable to avoid the weekends, as traffic on the busy west shore road is often nose to tail. For the energetic, part of the West Highland Way *(p 11)* from Glasgow to Fort William follows the east shore.

tc **Boat trip.** – By far the best way to discover the charms of Loch Lomond is to take a pleasure steamer *(Countess Fiona* or *The Maid of the Loch),* which leaves from Balloch pier, and calls at Luss, Rowardennan, Tarbet and Inversnaid.

SITES AND TOWNS

Balloch. – Pop 5 771. The boat trips leave from this resort.

Inchmurrin. – The largest of the 30 or so islands spangling the wider southern part of the loch. At the southern tip are the ruins of what was once a Lennox stronghold.

Inchcailloch. – Nature Reserve.

Balmaha marks the passage of the Highland Boundary Fault where mountains suddenly rise out of lowlands.

★**Luss.** – Pop 256. A highly attractive village with mellow coloured stone cottages.

Beyond Luss the loch narrows and the mountains close in.

Rowardennan. – The loch's eastern road ends at Rowardennan, now a youth hostel. A path leads from the pier to the summit of Ben Lomond.

★★**Ben Lomond.** – The shapely form of this 3 192ft-974m peak rises on the east shore behind Rowardennan. This is the most southerly of the Highland Munros *(p 16).*

On a level with Tarbet the dramatic pile of Ben Arthur (2 891ft-881m) better known as the Cobbler rises in the distance.

Tarbet. – Pop 257. Tarbet lies at the head of a short valley which leads southwestwards to Arrochar. The Vikings are said to have hauled their galleys over this neck of land to claim sovereignty over the peninsula.

Inversnaid. – *Description p 199.*

From here there is a splendid **view**, across the loch, of the mountains on the far shore : left to right the craggy shaped **Cobbler,** then a group of four, A'Chrois, Beinn Ime (3 318ft-1 011m) and Chorranach further back with Ben Vane rising from the lochside.

*The thistle sign which waymarks
the Scottish Long Distance Footpaths*

★★ LOCH TAY (Tayside)

Michelin map 401 folds 23 and 27 – H 14

Loch Tay is an attractive freshwater loch in a mountain setting with Ben Lawers rising to majestic heights on the north shore. Over 14 miles long from Killin to Kenmore and never more than a mile wide the loch is fed by the Dochart and Lochay while at the east end the River Tay appears for the first time.

Roads run along both shores. The northern, the faster of the two, gives access to Ben Lawers while the narrower and more winding southern road affords splendid views across to the mountain.

North Shore Killin to Kenmore *17 miles – 1/2 hour*

Killin. – Pop 600. At the head of Loch Tay this village is busy with passing trade in summer. To the west of Killin (best seen from the bridge) the River Dochart tumbles over as rapids, the **Falls of Dochart,** towards the loch. On a rocky outcrop overlooking the loch stand the tree sheltered and overgrown ruins of Finlarig Castle, seat of Black Duncan of the Cowl, the ruthless chief of Clan Campbell. Finlarig was notorious for its beheading pit.

★★**Ben Lawers.** – 3 984ft-1 214m. *Take the road to the left signposted Ben Lawers Visitors Centre (NTS). 2 1/2 miles by single track road.*

tc The **Visitor Centre** at a height of 1 300ft provides an excellent audiovisual programme on the mountain, its formation and the rare alpine flora. The climb to the summit of Ben Lawers is only for the suitably equipped.

On the way down the road provides good **views** of Loch Tay.

Isle of Loch Tay. – *No access.* When Alexander I's Queen Sybilla died in 1122 the king granted her burialplace, the isle, to the monks of Scone. A nunnery succeeded the monastery until the late 15C when it became the Campbells penultimate stepping stone from their original home on Loch Awe to the present site of Taymouth Castle.

★**Kenmore.** – Pop 211. The village stands at the east end where the Tay issues from the loch. Nearby this model village, the Campbells of Glenorchy built their principal seat, Taymouth Castle *(private),* in the early 19C. From here, and the earlier Balloch Castle, the Breadalbane line held sway.

★ MANDERSTON (Borders)

Michelin map 401 fold 32 – N 16 – 2 miles east of Duns

tc Manderston is a splendid Edwardian country house, in immaculate grounds, where the hallmark of extravagant splendour applies throughout, from the great function rooms through the domestic quarters and even out to the farm buildings.

Exterior. – The long low, two storeyed building beneath a balustraded roof is interrupted on the south or garden front by two gracefully curved, projections and a great porticoed entrance on the main front.

Interior. – The supreme craftsmanship of plasterwork ceilings, doors, fireplaces and furnishings are matched by the quality of the materials – marble, rosewood, mahogany, alabaster, brass, silver... and the refinement of the objets d'art. John Kinross' interior designs are in the manner of Robert Adam.

Ground floor. – From the impressively spacious Hall heightened by the dome, fringed by delicate plasterwork, pass through the Ante-Room with effective alabaster panels on the right, to the Dining Room. Completed in 1905 the highly elaborate compartmented ceiling is set off by plain walls the perfect background for the paintings, furniture and unique Blue John collection.

The Library now doubling as a billiard room, is hung with crimson silk damask and was one of the first to be redecorated. Compare this ceiling with the previous one. Double doors (find the light switches) lead through to the richly munificent Ballroom with the embossed silk and velvet wall hangings, and the curtains woven with gold or silver threads, all now over 80 years old. The ceiling paintings were by a local Coldstream man, Robert Hope. The Morning Room almost certainly has the original fireplace and ceiling. In the Tea Room a Lutyens painting shows the Miller children grouped round a dog by Landseer. Sir James, who was responsible for the house as we see it today, is on the left.

Leading up to the first floor the staircase with a silver baluster and brass banister, is a replica of one in the Petit Trianon in Versailles.

First Floor. – The same munificence and attention to detail has been lavished on the suite of bedrooms and bathrooms.

Basement. – Down the backstairs. One of the more fascinating aspects of the visit is the vast domain of kitchen, scullery, five larders, housekeeper's room, linen store and servants' hall, a highly organized realm, where the housekeeper and the butler reigned supreme over an impressive army of domestic staff. Even the courtyard doors are all appropriately marked – baggage, breeches, kitchen...

Grounds, gardens and outbuildings. – The south front overlooks terraced gardens and grassy slopes down to the lake with on the far side, the Woodland Garden (rhododendrons and azaleas) and on a clear day the Cheviots as backdrop.

On the entrance front, manicured lawns and majestically spreading trees precede gates to formal gardens. Beyond the Marble Dairy, in the form of a chapter house, has an oak panelled tea room above. Standing nearby is the head gardener's house with its attractive walled garden.

The refinement of the **stables★**, arranged around two courtyards, is all the more striking for being unexpected. Teak and brass predominate while in the mahogany panelled harness room, both the floor and the central table are of marble.

★★★ MELLERSTAIN (Borders)

Michelin map **401** fold 36 – M 17 – 6 miles northwest of Kelso

tc Mellerstain is the amazing detail and delicacy of Robert Adam interiors, gracing a house of homely proportions – a testimony to the genius of one man.

History. – The Mellerstain estate was purchased in 1642 by a Lanarkshire man and passed in 1646 to his son Robert Baillie, a staunch Covenanter. Imprisoned in Edinburgh's Tolbooth he was visited by his friend's daughter, Grisell Hume, who on that occasion met for the first time her future husband, the young **George Baillie** (1664-1738). Several years were to pass, including exile and hardship in Holland for both families, before a return in 1688 to their native Borders and the marriage of Grisell to George Baillie in 1692. **Lady Grisell Baillie** (1665-1746), a remarkable woman of many parts was Mellerstain's heroine and mistress, ruling her household with efficiency, unbounded energy and gentleness. She lived to see the completion of the William Adam wings but on her death the estate passed to her grandson George Baillie who engaged **Robert Adam** (1728-92) to bridge the gap between the two wings.

Exterior. – Rarely did Robert Adam plan a house from beginning to end, and added to this the fact that his father designed the wings, makes a visit to Mellerstain a must. Imposingly plain the exterior comprises the yellow stone castellated centre by Robert Adam flanked at right angles by the two earlier wings by his father William. Although only 45 years separate the constructions, the contrast in architectural styles is striking and best seen from the courtyard front. The wings of 1725 have a certain vernacular charm compared with the severity and plainness of the castellated Gothic centre.

THE HOUSE *time : 1 hour*

Interior. – Less grandiose than elsewhere (Culzean, Osterley, Syon) but nonetheless so typically Adam, it boasts a series of remarkable **ceilings★★★**, often with matching fireplaces, woodwork and furniture.

Stone Hall. – Part of the William Adam wing this room has a Delft tile adorned fireplace. On display in the east corridor is an original copy of the National Covenant subscribed by the 2nd Earl of Haddington.

In the eastern section of the main corridor are several portraits including *Lady Murray*, Grisell's daughter and Allan Ramsay's *Dr Torriano* (1738) one of the first paintings executed by the artist while in Italy.

Sitting Room. – Adam designed a Gothic ceiling and a fireplace with Dutch tiles for this room. The furniture is principally from the Queen Anne period and among the paintings, there is a beautiful conversation piece by Nasmyth.

(Lord Binning)

The Library

★★★The Library. – An initial impression of colour – pale green, ivory white, pink, blue-grey and of an overall grand design with the delicately detailed ceiling as centrepiece, slowly gives way to a perception of constituent components, the Zucci roundels – *Minerva, Learning* and *Teaching* – vases, medallions, trophies and figure panels and recesses, with the unifying pattern echoed in the bookcases, frieze, fireplace, superbly carved doors and mirror cupboards of the window wall. The Roubiliac busts of Lady Grisell Baillie and her daughter face each other above the end wall doors.

Music Room. – Designed as the Dining Room, the plain claret-coloured walls provide a sharp contrast to the highly decorative ceiling with plaster reliefs of urns, eagles, sphinxes, medallions, rinceaux and fan ornaments surrounding the central medallion. The end wall pier glasses are to Adam's designs while above the fireplace is *Patrick Hume* by William Aikman with, to the left and right, his granddaughters by Maria Varelst, *Grisell, Lady Murray* and *Rachel, Lady Binning* respectively.

Drawing Room. – Rich and ornate, heavily patterned silk brocade wall hangings and Aubusson carpet, ormolu mounted furniture, the overall effect is again in sharp contrast to the two preceding rooms. The ceiling colour scheme is subdued and includes a griffen and vase pattern which repeats itself in the frieze. The Adam design on the satinwood side table is echoed in the marble fireplace.

Of the portraits, several are by Allan Ramsay, or Old Mumpy as Adam called him, including *Lady Murray*. Gainsborough portrayed *Hon. Mrs George Baillie,* the builder's wife and above the fireplace is a Van Dyck of *Prince d'Angri.*

Small Drawing Room. – Originally a bed chamber, the Adam imprint is everywhere, in the octagon designed ceiling, frieze, fireplace and massive mirror. Allan Ramsay's portrait of *Hon George Baillie* hangs above the fireplace.

Small Library. – This small room, originally two dressing rooms, has the distinction of having two different Adam ceilings.

Main Corridor. – The ceiling design again differs from that of the eastern section and is decidedly Gothic in inspiration.

Main Staircase. – A majestic double staircase climbs and unites to rise as a single flight to the first floor, where an early 16C Flemish tapestry is displayed. Several bedrooms are open and note in particular in the Manchineel Bedroom, the 19C carpet, handwoven in Alloa.

Great Gallery. – The final surprise, on the second floor, is a noble apartment with screens of Ionc columns at either end, alas unfinished. Adam's proposed design is on display, as is his father's project for the central block. *Lady Grisell Baillie* and *George Baillie* are portrayed by Medina. The enigma remains – what was the function of this gallery and why was it never completed?

Returning to the Inner Hall, the mirror and table are Adam works while the canvases are by Veronese and Van Dyck.

Front Hall. – The apsidal ended room with deep frieze allows for the development of a compartmented ceiling. The portrait of *Lady Grisell Baillie*, aged 60, is by Maria Varelst.

★ MELROSE (Borders)   Pop 2 185

Michelin map ▩▩▩ fold 36 – L 17

Grouped round its beautiful abbey ruins, in the middle reaches of the Tweed, Melrose is overshadowed by the triple peaks of the Eildons. This attractive town bustles in the summer with visitors and makes an ideal touring centre for exploring the surrounding countryside.

The town's Summer Festival *(p 28)* and the day of the Melrose Sevens are lively occasions.

★★MELROSE ABBEY *time : 1 hour*

tc Traditionally the site of early settlers with forts on the Eildons and the great Roman camp of Trimontium, beyond Newstead, the Cistercian monks who settled **David I's** 1136 foundation proved no exception in choosing the fertile Tweed haughlands as the site of their new abbey. The monks from Rievaulx built an original 12C church which was damaged by 14C raids in particular Edward II's retreating army of 1322. Robert the Bruce ensured the rebuilding of the abbey and it was here that his heart was buried, when the Good Sir James Douglas, was killed in Spain. (Exact position unsure.) The ruins date from the late 14 early 16C and are in a pure Gothic. The community, grew and prospered becoming probably the richest abbey in Scotland, a fact which was not to save it the fate of most Scottish abbeys, passing into secular hands, decline of the community and subsequent decay of the buildings. It was Sir Walter Scott who initiated repairs between 1822 and 1826 securing for posterity some of the loveliest ruins and establishing them as a must for travellers in the mid-19C.

> "If thou woulds't view fair Melrose aright
> Go visit it by the pale moonlight
> For the gay beams of lightsome day
> Gild, but to flout the ruins grey".

Abbey Church. – The harmony of the stone with tints varying from ochre to red, the profusion of decorative sculptural work, so uncharacteristic of the Cistercian order, and the purity of the Gothic style make for an extremely impressive and attractive group of ruins.

Exterior. – To fully appreciate the **decorative sculpture**★★★ walk round the outside. The chapels of the south side are lit by a series of large pointed windows with elegant tracery, separated by pinnacled buttresses. The south transept gable is a profusion of detailed sculptural work. The pointed arched, moulded doorway is surmounted by the great south window with its elegant infilling framed by an ogee arch and a series of intricate canopied niches the whole being flanked by pinnacled and niched buttresses. The east gable with the great oriel and its fragile tracery is crowned at the apex with the *Coronation of the Virgin.*

Interior. – The layout is probably similar to the early 12C church with only a low wall and doorway remaining of the latter at the west end. A pulpitum divides the lay brother's choir from the monk's choir. On the nave's south side the clustered piers support moulded pointed arches which open onto eight chapels. The choir beyond the pulpitum has later buttressing work and barrel vaulting, as this once served as parish church. The north transept contained the night stair and still has statues of Sts Peter and Paul, above the west clerestory windows. The south transept frames the impressive window. The presbytery is distinguished by intricate vaulting where the bosses represent The Trinity.

Conventual buildings. – The layout of this once vast ensemble is indicated by the foundations.

Cloister. – Conforming to usual practice buildings border the garth and walks on all sides. The east range housed the chapter house in the centre and dormitory above, the north the kitchens and refectory, the west the early frater with the lay brothers' cloister beyond. The arcading on the east wall and north processional doorway with a highly ornamental accolade to the right are the main features.

Commendator's House. – *Across the road and over the Great Drain.* The museum in this restored building contains sculptural fragments, explanations on construction methods, in addition to exhibits on Trimontium, Sir Walter Scott's associations with Melrose, paving similarities with Rievaulx and Byland and the Cistercian colonization of Britain.

ADDITIONAL SIGHTS

tc **Priorwood Garden.** – *Entrance Abbey Street.*
Next to the abbey precincts this small garden specializes in flowers for drying. The roadside wall has attractive ironwork by Luytens.

High Street. – The street is bordered by some fine 18C buildings in the vicinity of the Market Square, with its 17C mercat cross. The narrowing at the Jedburgh road exit marks the site of the East Port.

EXCURSIONS

Eildon Hills. – *Leave Melrose by the Lilliesleaf B 6359 road turning left at the signpost Eildon Walk, cross the bridge then follow, the path taking you up to the saddle between the two summits. Time 1 1/4 hours. Strong shoes if wet, for the grassy slopes.*
The Eildons are of volcanic origin, but legend has it that this triple peaked hill was the work of the 13C wizard **Michael Scott** who is buried in Melrose Abbey. Scott was in fact a mathematician, philosopher, doctor of theology and friend of the Emperor Frederick II. He figures in Dante's *Inferno* as Michele Scotto. The peaks are a conspicuous landmark in the region and the Eildon Hill North (1 325ft-404 m) which was successively an Iron Age hill fortress and Roman signal station now provides a magnificent **panorama★★★** : Melrose and its abbey, with Gattonside on the far side of the Tweed, the Leaderfoot viaduct, Smailholm Tower, east and south to the Cheviots, Peniel Heugh with its monument round to the Tweed again and the Gala Water Valley with Galashiels, a linear settlement.

★★Scott's View. – *Leave Melrose by the B 6361 running close to the Tweed. Continue down towards the river passing the impressive red sandstone viaduct turn left onto the A 68, then right once over the river to climb down towards the river at Leaderfoot taking the local road to climb up the flank of Bemersyde Hill. Turn right into the B 6356.*

★★Scott's View. – Automobile Association viewfinder 593ft-181m. This wide view of typical Border scenery encompasses from the right the Tweed Valley with Melrose and Galashiels, the inevitable Eildons ahead sloping down to Newtown St Boswells then round to Minto, Rubers and Black Laws. In the near foreground is Bemersyde House the home presented in 1921 by a grateful nation to Earl Haig who is buried in Dryburgh Abbey. Down on the Tweed meander is Old Melrose, the original site of the Cistercian settlement.

Continue by the local road to Dryburgh Abbey in its fine setting.

★★Dryburgh Abbey. – *Description p 69.*

Return to Leaderfoot and take the B 6360 under the A 68 overpass and viaduct to follow the north bank of the Tweed.

This stretch of road has most attractive views over the valley and Melrose, before reaching Gattonside, once the site of the abbey orchards.

Turn left over the Tweed and left again back into Melrose.

Newstead. – Pop 195. East of Melrose this attractive hamlet was the home of the stonemasons who built Melrose Abbey and is reputedly the oldest inhabited place in Scotland.
A memorial by the roadside just out of Newstead marks the site of Trimontium the largest Roman Fort in southern Scotland. It was built by the troops of Agricola in the 1C AD, on the line of Dere Street.

MOFFAT (Dumfries and Galloway) Pop 2 031

Michelin map **401** fold 35 – J 17

A small town at the head of Annandale, Moffat is set in the heart of scenically beautiful countryside. Once a flourishing spa in the 18C, the town is principally a market town for the surrounding hill sheep farming area and a tourist centre with ample excursions into the hills around.

Moffat House Hotel. – *High Street.*
John Adam built this 18C mansion as a residence for the 2nd Earl of Hopetoun. The severity of the design is relieved by the contrasting colours and textures of the building materials. It was during his stay as a tutor that James Macpherson (1738-96) 'translated' the Ossian Fragments.

Colvin Fountain. – *High Street.*
The bronze ram on the fountain testifies to the importance of sheep farming in the area.

Churchyard. – *Off High Street.*
This is the final resting place of the road engineer John Loudon McAdam (1756-1836), the inventor of the macadam road surface.

tc **Museum.** – *The Neuk.*
The museum tells the story of Moffat through the centuries touching on such topics as clan warfare, Covenanting times and its heyday as a spa.

EXCURSION

Tweedsmuir Hills. – *Round tour of 44 miles – 2 hours. Take the Selkirk road the A 708.*
This climbs out of the Annan Valley over into the wilder scenery of the Moffat Water Valley, a classic U-shaped glacially deepened valley.

★★**Grey Mare's Tail.** – The Tail Burn forms this spectacular waterfall as it plunges 200ft from the hanging valley to join the Moffat Water in its heavily glaciated valley. A sheep pen near the roadside car park provides explanatory notes on the geological history of the site. Two paths lead to the waterfall. The one on the left, the easier leads to the bottom of the waterfall, while the one on the right, much steeper and stonier climbs up to the valley and moraine dammed Loch Skeen. Stout footwear is needed for the second.

The road moves up the now narrow V-shaped valley to cross the pass and descend into another glacially overdeepened valley of the Little Yarrow Water. Between the Loch of the Lowes and St Mary's Loch, originally one, stands Tibbie Sheil's Inn, the meeting place of James Hogg and his friends, made famous by Christopher North's *(p 169)* accounts. On the slope beyond the souvenir shop and cafe is the seated figure of **James Hogg** (1770-1835), "the Ettrick Shepherd".

St Mary's Loch. – The admirable hill setting reflects in the waters of the loch which provides good sailing and trout fishing.

Take to the left the road signposted Tweedsmuir (11 miles) following the Megget Water. No buses or caravans are allowed on this narrow road with passing places.

Megget Dam and Reservoir. – This recently completed dam with its curved embankment and grassy cover, blends well with the landscape. This scheme parallels the Upper Tweed one. There are good viewing points on the road running along the north shore of the reservoir.

The road descending, suddenly affords a splendid view of the Talla Reservoir – source of Edinburgh's water supply – in its hill setting.

Turn left onto the A 701.
Pass on the left the source of the Tweed on the northern side of the Tweedsmuir Hills.

Devil's Beef Tub. – The steep sided depression between the Tweedsmuir and Lowther Hills was so named, as it served as a refuge for stolen cattle in reiving days. (See Scott's Red Gauntlet).

Continue down Annandale where the valley is wider and the scene, one of a smiling arable landscape, with in the far distance Moffat nestling on the valley floor.

MONTROSE (Tayside) Pop 9 959

Michelin map 401 fold 24 – M13

The East Coast town of Montrose sits on a peninsula between a tidal basin and the sea. The steeple of the parish church pinpoints the town from afar. Ever popular with summer visitors the town has a vast stretch of golden sand, several golf courses and scenic countryside nearby to explore. Montrose has always been a busy shopping centre and market town for the rich agricultural hinterland and a thriving port. Increased prosperity has accrued from North Sea Oil with the establishment of an oil base on the Ferryden side of the River South Esk.

Heretics and martyrs. – In the difficult times leading up to the Reformation, Montrose had more than its fair share of martyrs. Namely David Straton (d 1534) and **George Wishart** whose execution at St Andrews in February 1546 sparked off reprisals which resulted in the stabbing of Cardinal Beaton *(p 177)*. Protestant connections continued with John Knox who was a regular visitor to John Erskine of nearby Dun House. Erskine was the town's provost and one of the first Moderators. The tradition continued with Knox's follower, the scholar and linguist **Andrew Melville** (1554-1622) and his nephew James who led a determined fight against James VI's policy to introduce Episcopacy. The former is remembered for his admonition to James VI that he was but "God's silly vassal".

SIGHTS

High Street. – The elongated triangular layout is medieval and many of the original wynds and closes between the burgess plots still remain. Interspersed between the substantial 17 and 18C buildings are a number of gable ended houses from which the Montrosians acquired their nickname "gable endies". This feature is a relic of trading days with the Low Countries.

Old Town House. – This 18C building, with a 19C addition, has an elegant arcade on the High Street side, facing the statue of Joseph Hume, the politician and reformer.

Old Church and Steeple. – The 220ft Gothic steeple, a notable landmark, was added to this 18C church by Gillespie Graham in the 19C. The famous Paniter Panels in the Museum of Antiquities came from the earlier church on this site.

MONTROSE

Castlestead. – At the south end of the High Street this castellated building is now used as offices. It was the site of a 13C castle which later became the town house of the Graham family. The Marquess of Montrose was no doubt born at the family seat, Old Montrose, to the south of the Basin.

tc **Museum.** – *Panmure Place.*
The collection includes sections on the town's activities in the past (salmon fishing, 18C tobacco trade and whaling), natural history dioramas and biographical sections on famous citizens from the Marquess of Montrose leader of the Royalist party, the politician and reformer Joseph Hume to William Lamb, the 20C sculptor. Note in particular the bust of his contemporary Hugh McDiarmid, who was editor of the local paper in the 1920s.

tc **William Lamb Memorial Studio.** – *Market Street.*
In this small studio is a display of sculptures, paintings and sketches by the relatively unknown but talented artist **William Lamb** (1893-1951). The bronzes have a verve and sureness of touch which is amazing for one who, following a war wound to his right hand, taught himself to work with the left. The furniture of the panelled sitting room upstairs is reminiscent of Mackintosh's work. One of his life-size works *The Seafarer*, cast posthumously, stands down by the harbour.

EXCURSION

★Glen Esk. – *29 miles via Brechin and Edzell. Leave Montrose to the west by the A935.*

Brechin. – *Description p 50.*

Take the B9667 north out of Brechin to cross the A94 and reach Edzell.

Edzell. – Pop 658. This attractive village was resited here in the 19C. The original settlement was in the vicinity of the castle.

Follow the Fettercairn road out of Edzell, the B966 and once across the river North Esk turn left.

tc **Folk Museum (The Retreat).** – This local museum gives a fascinating account of life in the glen, of the closeknit community, the people, their occupations and hobbies.

The road continues up to just before the ruin of Invermark Castle, another Lindsay stronghold. There is then a footpath up past Loch Lee, the reservoir for Dundee.

★ MULL, Isle of (Strathclyde) Pop 1569

Michelin map **401** folds 21, 22, 25 and 26 – B and C14
Access. : see the current Michelin Red Guide Great Britain and Ireland

The Inner Hebridean island of Mull with its varied scenery and peacefulness is an ideal holiday centre and the stepping stone for Iona.

Scenery. – The sheltered Sound of Mull separates the 24 mile long and 26 mile wide island from the mainland. The 300 miles of deeply indented coastline alternates from the rocky cliffs of the Ross of Mull with offshore skerries, to the small creeks and sheltered sandy beaches like Calgary Bay. Inland the scenery can be desolate and dramatic like the moorlands which rise to the island's highest peak, **Ben More** (3169ft-966m) or peaceful and pastoral, dotted with crofting townships. As with all the Hebridean Islands the seaward vistas are superb.

Traditional. – The **Mull Music Festival** *(p 212)* reflects the island's rich musical heritage, with concerts for accordians, fiddles, pipes and gaelic choirs. At other times ceilidhs give summer visitors a chance to hear this traditional music. The **Tobermory Highland Games** *(p 28)* are known for the piping and clan march.

tc The **Mull Little Theatre**, in the grounds of Druimard House near Dervaig has a summer season with plays adapted for a cast of two. There are only 37 seats, so it is advisable to book in advance.

SIGHTS

The island roads are twisting and narrow - with the exception of the new stretch from Craignure to Fionnphort - but perfectly suited to a leisurely discovery of Mull's charms. The sights are listed alphabetically.
Petrol stations are widely scattered. Keep your tank topped up.
Do not park in the passing places.

★★Calgary Bay. – This unspoilt west coast bay with its strand of white shell sand is an ideal spot for bathing.

Craignure. – This is one of the two terminal points for the Oban ferry. The island's two castles are nearby.

tc **Duart Castle.** – *3 miles from Craignure.*
Duart, home of the chief of **Clan Maclean**, is on a strategic site perched on a rocky crag, guarding the Sound of Mull. The earliest keep built *c*1250, was extended, only to be stormed in the 17C, garrisoned by Redcoats in the 18C then abandoned to fall into a ruinous condition. The 26th clan chief restored the stronghold to its present day appearance. Clan and family mementoes are on show. On the upper floor a Scouting Exhibition recalls Lord Maclean, 27th clan chief and his lifetime devotion to the movement and his role as Chief Scout. The ramparts have good views across to the mainland.

★Isle of Iona. – *Description p 134. Access from Fionnphort on the Ross of Mull.*

Loch na Keal. – West coast sea loch.

tc **Staffa.** – This basaltic island, lying on the western seaboard of Mull, owes its fame to Mendelssohn's overture *Fingal's Cave* composed following his 1829 visit.

Tobermory. – Pop 641. The main town and ferry port of Tobermory attractively fringes its island sheltered anchorage, Tobermory Bay. A popular yachting centre, the harbour is often a mass of bobbing and clinking yachts. The bay is also known as the last resting place of a galleon from Ragusa, then part of the Venetian Empire. The galleon had sailed with the Spanish Armada (1588) and tales of treasure have always been part of her mystery.

tc **Torosay Castle.** – *1 1/2 miles from Craignure.*
Torosay (1856) is an example of David Bryce's fluency in the Scottish baronial style. Inside are mementoes of the

(BTA)

Tobermory

Guthrie family, owners since the early 19C. Murray Guthrie (Sargent sketch in the library) commissioned Robert Lorimer to lay out the delightful **gardens★**. There are the fountain and lion terraces, the water and Japanese gardens and the statue walk. These unexpected Italian terraced gardens, have far reaching **views★**, with Duart Castle *(two mile footpath to Duart Castle)* in the foreground and the mountains of the mainland on the horizon. Ben Nevis may be seen on a clear day.

NAIRN (Highland)   Pop 8 037

Michelin map 401 fold 15 – I11

This favourite seaside resort, on the southern shore of the Moray Firth, owes its popularity to a combination of sun, sea and sand. Nairn with its excellent facilities, in particular for golf, makes an ideal touring centre.

EXCURSIONS

★Cawdor Castle. – *Description p 54.*

tc **Fort George.** – *10 miles to the west by the A96 and then the B9006 to the right.* Set on a peninsula jutting into the Moray Firth this fortress was built between 1748 and 1769 to replace the medieval castle in Inverness, reconstructed by Wade, and blown up in 1746 by the Jacobites. The fort is impressive for its size and the
tc elaboration of its defences. The chapel and **Regimental Museum of the Queen's Own Highlanders** are open to the public.

Auldearn. – *2 miles to the east by the A96. Turn left following the signs to Boath Dovecot.*
The village was the scene of a battle on 9 May 1645 when the Marquess of Montrose defeated a Convenanting army. A plan of the battle is provided at the viewpoint. The 17C **Boath Dovecot** *(illustration p 25)* marks the site of a 12C royal castle.

NORTH BERWICK (Lothian)   Pop 5 162

Michelin map 401 fold 32 – L15

On the southern shore of the Firth of Forth this ancient royal burgh is a popular holiday and golfing resort and provides a complete range of amenities - vast sandy beaches, golf courses and putting greens, the famous heated outdoor swimming pool, sailing and sea angling facilities. The town is also favoured by commuters with the railway giving rapid access to Edinburgh.
North Berwick and its vicinity are evoked by **Robert Louis Stevenson** (1850-94) in *The Lantern Bearers* as he brings to life the area where he spent some of his boyhood summers.

SIGHTS

Auld Kirk. – On the harbour promontory, dividing the two sandy beaches, are the scant remains of the town's first parish church (12C), the one so notoriously associated with the gathering of witches of 1590 and James VI. Burial place for the Lauder and Douglas families the church was abandoned in 1680-2, the upkeep of the connecting bridge to what was then an island promontory proving too onerous.

Old Parish Church. – *Kirk Port.*
Now also a ruin this was the 17C replacement for the Auld Kirk. In the churchyard is a headstone commemorating John Blackadder, the Covenanting divine and martyr of the Bass.

The Lodge. – The 18C white harled building was the town house of the Dalrymple family. Now divided into flats, the grounds form a public park.

Town House. – At the corner of Quality and High Streets stands an attractive 18C building with outside stairs and clock tower. The upper chamber still serves as a meeting place for committees and community councils.

tc **Museum.** – *School Road.*
This local museum with sections on history, archaeology and natural history also has particularly interesting exhibits on golf and its origins and the seabirds which haunt the rocky coasts and islands of the area.

North Berwick Law. – 612ft-187m. *1 mile to the south of the town centre by Law Road. Signposted path with occasional seats.*
Another of East Lothian's volcanic hills and distinguishing landmarks, the Law has a commanding **panorama**★★★ *(view indicator)* with the town spread out at its feet to St Abb's Head, then inland to the Lammermuir Hills, Traprain and the Garleton Hills backed by the Moorfoots and Pentlands and even as far as Ben Lomond on a clear day, then the Forth, the Ochils and the Grampians with the East Neuk of Fife on the northern shore of the Firth. The Law is the scene of an annual hill race in August.

EXCURSIONS

tc **The Bass Rock.** – At the entrance to the Firth of Forth, 3 miles from North Berwick, the rounded form of this volcanic hill rises to 350ft-107m above sea level. Now equipped with a lighthouse and foghorn for Forth shipping, its role has varied throughout history from that of retreat for St Baldred ; to fortress ; Covenanters' prison (Peden, John Blackadder and Trail) ; last stronghold of the Stuart monarchy's cause to surrender (1691-4) ; to the present day sanctuary of a myriad of seabirds. There is a boat trip which makes it possible to observe this wildlife at fairly close quarters depending on the weather. Every conceivable crevice and ledge of the vertical cliffs is the domain of some seabird be it guillemot, razorbill, cormorant, puffin, tern, eider duck, gull or the famous **Solan Goose** or **Gannet** which takes its latin name *Sula Bassana* from this island. Only thirteen gannetries exist in the United Kingdom, the most famous being the Bass Rock and St Kilda. This unusual bird comes to land during the breeding season only (February-May) leaving in August when the chick is 2 months old. Having fed the chick till its departure the deserted young are driven by hunger down to the sea where they usually float and flounder, protected by their excess fat, for about 3 weeks before learning to fly. The single egg is protected in turn by the parents who cover it with first one then the other webbed foot. The birds are excellent divers going down at least 50ft for their prey. They may live from 20 to 38 years.

★**The coastal road from North Berwick to Port Seton.** – *16miles. Leave North Berwick to the west by the A198.*
Dirleton. – *Description p 65.*
Gullane. – Pop 1 701. With five golf courses, this golfer's paradise is known for the famous Muirfield Course, home of the Honourable Company of Edinburgh Golfers (f 1744) and one of the regular venues for the British Open Golf Championship. Growing as a commuter's haven from Edinburgh, the village with its fine sandy beach has always been popular for day outings from the capital.
Once over the Peffer Burn take the local road to the left.
tc **Myreton Motor Museum.** – This privately owned museum presents in cramped and unpretentious surroundings a panorama of roadworthy vehicles, motorcycles and bicycles, a far cry from the spit and polish image of the more traditional motor museums. The cars, each with their individual case histories, tell a story of misfortune and neglect or loving care and attention. Admire the Galloway with its thistle adorned footplates, an exhibit at the 1926 Scottish Motor Show, a 14 seat charabanc from Ford, the Citroen Kegresse with its six forward and two reverse gears, the Standard Beaverette looking like something out of science fiction and the Bollee Motor Tricycle *c*1896, which once belonged to the Hon.C.S.Rolls.
Continue along the A198 which follows the policies of Luffness Castle. The tower house stands on the left.
Aberlady. – Pop 884. Now a golfing and growing commuting centre this village, in the 12C was the port for the royal burgh of Haddington *(qv).* Linear in layout there are some striking rows of 19C estate cottages in the neo-Gothic style.
Once out of Aberlady the road follows the estate wall of Gosford House on the left, backed by the strangely wind sculptured trees, with Gosford Bay on the right (several car parks give access to the sands - Ferry Ness free ranging car park). Continue by the B 1348 to follow the coast, with fine views across the Firth to the Fife coastline and Edinburgh with its distinctive landmarks of the Castle and Arthur's Seat.
Cockenzie and Port Seton. – Of the original industries, salt panning, fishing and coal mining, the latter two are still thriving with the seine fishing fleet operating out of Port Seton. Cockenzie harbour was built for exporting coal from the Tranent mine, brought to the coast by one of the earliest railways. The dominating features of this coastal stretch are the twin towers of the Cockenzie Power Station.
Return inland to join the A198, taking the North Berwick direction.
Seton Collegiate Church. – *Description p 182.*

Circular tour from North Berwick. – *21 miles. Leave North Berwick to the east by the A198.*

★★**Tantallon Castle.** – *Description p 193.*

Whitekirk. – Pop 70. The parish church of St Mary's, a 15C mellow red sandstone building with typical crow steps and a squat tower with corbelled parapet, originally belonged to Holyrood Abbey. The presence of a Holy Well made this a great pilgrimage centre, which was visited in 1435 by the Papal Legate, Aeneas Sylvius Piccolomini later Pope Pius II. Burnt by sufragettes in 1914 the church was restored by Robert Lorimer.

In the field behind, the 16C three storeyed building may have served as the tithe barn for the storage of grain.

★**Tyninghame.** – Pop 186. This is an extremely attractive estate village . Most of the houses have only one storey in pink sandstone with pantiled roofs. The original village situated in the grounds of Tyninghame House was removed in 1761.

tc **Tyninghame Gardens.** – The grounds of Tyninghame House *(private)* include the walled garden, an apple walk with espalier apple trees, a woodland wilderness leading to the secret garden with roses in profusion and a terrace garden with a path down to the remains of the 12C St Baldred's Church. Originally part of a monastery, two arches have typical Norman motifs : chevrons, billets and overlapping scales.

Take the B1407 through the village of Tyninghame

★**Preston Mill.** – A picturesque landmark in its riverside setting, 16C **Preston Mill** with its
tc red pantiled roofs and rubble masonry is one of Scotland's rare working water mills and is believed to be of Dutch design. In the cone shaped kiln, damp oats were dried on perforated metal plates before being transferred by chute to the mill for sieving, bruising, grinding, shelling ... The great water wheel was made in the Carron works in 1760.

In a field beyond *(5 mins walk)* is the oddly truncated beehive shaped **Phantassie Dovecot** *(illustration p 25)*. Circular with two string courses – to prevent rats climbing up – the south facing side has a sloping roof and two sets of flight holes. Inside the 500 nests are reached by a revolving ladder.

Take the A1 in the direction of Haddington. Turn right onto the B1347.

★**Museum of Flight.** – *East Fortune Airfield.* In a vast hangar, an outstation of the Royal
tc Scottish Museum, there is a collection of aircraft ranging from a 1930 Puss Moth monoplane, a PH Dragon wooden frame and fabric covered passenger biplane, to a German Komet rocket powered fighter (1944), as well as a 1945 Spitfire, a supersonic Lightning fighter and a 1975 hang glider.

In the hangar, side exhibits include trainer cockpits, aero engines, a flight deck, a complete Blue Streak Rocket, scale models and a section on the development of fighter aircraft from 1914-40 culminating in the Battle of Britain, with such evocative names as Spitfires, Hurricanes, Heinkels and Messerschmitts. The airship on show is Tiny, otherwise known as **H.M. Airship R 34**. It is particularly appropriate as it was from this airfield that she set out on her historic maiden double Atlantic crossing in 1919.

The B1377 then the B1347 lead back to North Berwick.

★ **OBAN** (Strathclyde)   Pop 6 897

Michelin map **401** fold 26 – D14

The busy tourist centre of Oban is built round the bay of the same name and is backed by a ring of low hills. Much of the town's activity is concentrated in and around the harbour, where fishing vessels, ferries, excursion steamers and a variety of pleasure craft find refuge in this haven protected by the island of Kerrera.

Although a service centre (livestock market and fishing port) for the outlying area and islands, the town's whole economy is geared to tourism. Hotels and boarding houses line the seafront, a far cry from the situation in 1773 when Dr Johnson had to content himself with "a tolerable inn".

Becoming a fishing port in the 18C the town only really developed a century later with the arrival of the steamboats and then the railway, giving Oban its very Victorian aspect.

Oban makes an ideal touring centre for excursions by both land and sea. Numerous ferries and buses leave from the harbour. Enquire locally.

During the **Argyllshire Highland Gathering** *(p 28)* there is an important piping competition on the first day with the traditional games on the second.

The outstanding landmark is McCaig's Tower, high on the hill, a replica of the Colosseum. The project was initiated in 1897 by an Oban banker to relieve unemployment and act as a family memorial. The building has remained incomplete since the banker died.

EXCURSIONS

★★**The hinterland.** – *83 miles. Leave by the A85. Turn left at Dunbeg and continue for a mile.*

tc **Dunstaffnage.** – This impressive 13C castle, one of the principal seats of the MacDougalls, rises out of a rocky outcrop on a promontory commanding the entrance to Loch Etive. The thick curtain walls of this stronghold are punctuated by three towers and a 17C tower house. It is claimed that Dunstaffnage was the home of the Scots Court prior to Kenneth MacAlpine's unification and removal of the seat of power to Scone *(qv)*. Flora MacDonald was held prisoner here on her way to The Tower in 1746.

On the main road turn left in the village of Taynuilt.

★Bonawe Furnace. – This charcoal fuelled furnace started iron smelting in 1753 and
tc continued until the 1870s using iron-ore from Cumbria, brought by sea, and locally
supplied charcoal. Still visible on site are the furnace with water wheel to activate
the bellows, and the vast charcoal and iron-ore sheds.

Return to the main road, the A85.

Pass of Brander. – This narrow treeless defile leading from Loch Etive to Loch Awe is
bordered to the north by the lower slopes of **Ben Cruachan** (3689ft-1126m), a mountain
with several peaks. It was here, aided by swirling mists, that Bruce gained a decisive
victory (1308) over the MacDougalls of Lorn. The pass is the post glacial outlet of
Loch Awe, which originally drained away to the southwest at Ford.

★Cruachan Power Station. – Part of the Awe scheme, the Cruachan power station, opened
tc in 1965, has a total installed capacity of 400 Megawatts and an annual output of
450 million units of electricity. The power station is an engineering feat on two counts.
Firstly the pump turbines are reversible and are used to pump water from Loch Awe
to the high level reservoir in the corrie on Ben Cruachan, which in turn feeds by means
of two shafts an underground power station in the heart of the mountain. Secondly a
mile long road tunnel leads to the Machine Hall, impressively excavated out of solid rock.

The road then follows Loch Awe still skirting the lower slopes of Ben Cruachan.

★★Loch Awe. – Over 25 miles long this is Scotland's longest loch. In pre-glacial times the
loch had its outlet by Ford. Today the loch drains via the River Awe and the Pass of
Brander where the former is harnessed for HEP. It is in the heart of Campbell country
with the family seat situated successively on Innischonnail Island then at Kilchurn,
at the head of Loch Awe.

Turn right onto the A819.

tc From this road there are good views of the ruins of **Kilchurn Castle** *(illustration p 13)*,
the 15C stronghold built by Sir Colin Campbell, on a spit of land jutting out into the
headwaters of Loch Awe. Extensions were made to the castle in 1693 by John
Campbell, 1st Earl of Breadalbane, but by the middle of the following century the castle
was abandoned. The Breadalbane Campbells had by then reached the eastern end
of Loch Tay *(qv)*.

The road on this side provides views of the 2 mile wide loch with Ben Cruachan as
backdrop and over to the Pass of Brander.

The road rises to moorland country, following Glen Aray before descending to
Inveraray on the edge of Loch Fyne.

Castle Fisheries. – *Description p 131.*

★★Inveraray. – *Description p 130.*

★★Loch Fyne. – This great sea loch stretches from the heart of the Argyll mountains down
past the arm of Loch Gilp where it turns due south to reach the open sea north of
Arran. In the 19C this magnificent loch was the scene of a highly successful herring
fishery. Five to six hundred boats fished the loch working from the many fishing villages
which developed on the lochside. In the 1880s the most common type of boat was
the Loch Fyne Skiff.

★Auchindrain. – *Description p 131.*

tc **Crarae Woodland Garden.** – The 50 acres of the delightful woodland garden occupy a
sloping site overlooking Loch Fyne. The natural setting in a small glen with its rushing
burn and waterfalls is complemented by man's judicious planting of trees, shrubs and
plants. The garden is best in spring (rhododendrons) or in autumn when the leaf colours
are a blaze of russet shades. The winding and climbing paths afford occasional
glimpses of the loch and mountains.

Lochgilphead. – Pop 1 184. This small but busy town set at the head of Loch Gilp, an
arm of Loch Fyne, developed with the completion of the Crinan Canal *(qv)*.

★Crinan. – *Description p 144.*

Dunadd Fort. – *Access by the farm road to the left.*
The rocky eminence rising abruptly out of the flat lands of the Great Moss was a Dark
Age fortification. The site was one of three capitals of the Scots Kingdom of Dalriada
between 498 and 843 AD. On a slab of rock near the top, look for the footprint and
boar sculpture said to be associated with kingship rituals.

The road then enters Kilmartin Glen, leading through a pass to reach the southern
end of Loch Awe its pre-glacial outlet.

Kilmartin. – In the churchyard is a good collection of **sculptured stones** *(one of the two
groups is under cover)*. Mostly grave slabs, these monuments are peculiar to the
Western Isles and Highlands and date in general from the 14 to 16C. The carvings
include the usual delicate celtic designs and effigies of warrior chiefs in their finest
tc armour. Inside the **church cross no 3** is outstanding. On one face is a finely executed
and most moving Christ Crucified, with on the reverse, Christ in Majesty. The cross
is attributed to the 16C.

tc **Carnasserie Castle.** – Carnasserie stands on a strategic site commanding the route
northwards to Loch Awe. This 16C castle is remarkable for its carved detail and
mouldings, which reveal the influence of the Renaissance. Its fireplaces are particulary
fine. It was the seat of Superintendent and Bishop John Carswell from 1566 to 1572
and it was here that he translated John Knox's *Book of Common Prayer* into Gaelic,
the first printed book in that language. Subsequently owned by the Campbells, it has
fine armorial panels over its entrance.

Follow the A816 back to Oban.

★Sea Life Centre. – *11 miles north of Oban, just off the A828.*
tc Discover the living creatures of the marine world in this original aquarium. Walk
around, over and under the tanks to view the occupants. The touch tank with its sea
urchins, starfish and crabs is always a firm favourite. In addition there is a fish farming
exhibit and, outside, a seal pool.

Michelin map 🔲 – inset folds 4 and 8 – K, L 6 and 7
Access : see the current Michelin Red Guide Great Britain and Ireland

The archipelago of the Orkney Islands is made up of 67 islands, less than 30 of which are uninhabited. The islands along with Shetland and the Western Isles have special status as the Islands Area. The capital Kirkwall is centrally situated on Mainland.

HISTORICAL NOTES

Prehistory. – The first settlers were established on the islands by the 4th millenium BC and the island has a great wealth of impressive prehistoric remains. Among the most remarkable are the Neolithic settlement at Skara Brae, the outstanding tomb of Maes Howe, the Bronze Age stone circle of Brodgar, the Iron Age brochs of Birsay and Gurness and the Pictish earthhouses.

The Golden Age. – With the arrival of the Norsemen in the 8 and 9C this Pictish land became Scandinavian. The Norse settlement was a peaceful and gradual process and in due course Orkney as part of a Norse earldom became the pivot of Viking Britain. The history of the earls of Orkney, who ruled as sovereigns, is traced in *The Orkneyinga Saga*. They include such notable figures as Thorfinn the Mighty, Saint Magnus the martyr and the crusader Rognvald. It is this Norse heritage which differentiates the Orkney and Shetland Islands from the rest of Scotland. Even today the imprint is clear in place names, in the form of a magnificent cathedral, or in literature so influenced by the sagas, as well as in artistic designs and in time honoured traditions. As late as the 19C Norn – a form of Norse – was the language spoken and not Gaelic.

Surety for a dowry. – The late medieval period brought Scottish rule when the islands were given in security (1468) for the dowry of Margaret of Denmark, future bride of James III. The period is often associated with misrule and the despoiling of Orkney lands by Scottish overlords, and more particularly with tyranny, in the case of the Stewart Earls of Orkney. The 18C saw another era of prosperity with the making of **kelp**. Seaweed was burned to obtain an ash residue rich in potash and soda which was in demand for the glass and soap manufacturing industries. The kelp industry (1780-1830) brought great prosperity to the local lairds who were nicknamed Kelp Lairds. Many of the fine mansions, especially on the outlying islands, belong to this period.

Today. – In these low lying and fertile islands agriculture is the main source of income with the rearing of beef cattle and dairying as the main activities. Distilling and tourism follow. The traditional crafts such as knitwear and straw-backed Orkney chairs continue to flourish. A new element in the economy is oil with the creation of the oil handling terminal at Flotta on Scapa Flow.

Literature. – With their rich heritage of the sagas it is not surprising that Orkney in the 20C should lay claim to authors of calibre such as poet and critic **Edwin Muir** (1887-1959), novelist and playwright **Eric Linklater** (1899-1974) and prose writer **George Mackay Brown** (b 1921). All have been influenced by the great heritage of their native islands.

Orkney and the visitor. – The islands have a wealth to offer the unhurried visitor, from peaceful, pastoral landscapes to the more dramatic splendours of the coastal scenery, and from the mysteries and treasures of prehistory to a wide range of present day cultural activities, often deeply rooted in the past. The cliffs provide ideal nesting grounds for fascinating seabird colonies, where every ledge, nook and crannie is the home of some feathered creature. Seals and otters are also common to the islands.

Admission charges, when given at the end of the guide, are for adults.
Reductions are often available for children, OAPs, students and groups.

*BROUGH OF BIRSAY (Island)

tc This tidal island lying just offshore from the northwestern point of Mainland has important remains of Pictish and Norse settlements.

Access. – *The island can be reached on foot at low tide across a causeway. For times of low tide apply to the local tourist offices in Stromness or Kirkwall.*

Pictish metalworkers. – The earliest remains are houses and metalworking debris of the Pictish period. Recent archaeological excavations have thrown much doubt on the original interpretation of the remains as a monastery. The site includes a fine Pictish symbol stone replica.

Norse occupation. – In the 10C and 11C Norsemen lived on the Brough and a group of farmsteads marks this period. The Norse Earls (Jarls) of Orkney, made Birsay one of their principal seats in Orkney. **Earl Thorfinn the Mighty** (*c*1009-65), on his return from a pilgrimage to Rome, built a church *c*1050 either on the Brough or in Birsay village. Was the church on the Brough the Christchurch of the *Orkneyinga Saga* ? In the early 12C it is likely there was a Norse monastery on the Brough. Thorfinn's church became the cathedral of Orkney and this was the initial resting place of St Magnus (*p 164*). His holy relics remained enshrined here for over twenty years before Bishop William finally had them translated to Kirkwall. In the mid-12C the new church in Kirkwall took over the functions of cathedral. The church on the Brough continued to be visited throughout the medieval period but eventually fell into ruin. That in Birsay village now lies under the parish church.

VISIT

Excavations have uncovered evidence of the above periods and the result is somewhat confusing. Take your bearings from the most prominent feature, the church.

Norse Cathedral. – The church on the Brough has a small oblong nave, short narrow choir and rounded apse. It is unlikely to date from before the early 12C. The church is set within an enclosure representing the **Norse graveyard**. Both Pictish and Norse graves have been uncovered. An important example of the former is the **Birsay Stone** (replica) portraying three armed warriors. On the far side (to the north) of the church are the domestic buildings of the priests, in three ranges enclosing a courtyard.

Norse long houses. – To the southwest and higher up the slope are typical Norse houses with the living quarters at the upper end and byre lower down. The walls had cores of turf. Between the church and the cliff (to the east) are the complex remains of Norse buildings of various periods, some of which have been thought to represent Earl Thorfinn's palace.

Site museum. – Display of objects found during excavations.

★★KIRKWALL (Mainland) Michelin map **401** fold 4   Pop 4 617

Kirkwall stands on the northern end of the Kirkwall-Scapa isthmus which divides Mainland into eastern and western parts. The town dominated by its splendid 800 year old cathedral spreads up the hillside from the harbour. Historically Kirkwall has been the main island centre since it was a Norse trading centre and today it combines its role of capital with that of shopping and business centre.

Notable events include the Christmas and New Year's Day Ba' Games when the Uppies play the Downies, symbolizing the ancient rivalry between the bishop's ecclesiastical town and the secular authority represented by the now vanished castle.

Touring Mainland. – The central situation of Kirkwall makes it an ideal touring centre with easy access to all parts of Mainland. In the summer season bus tours take in all the major sites. Bicycle hire is also popular for those with more time.

★★★ST MAGNUS CATHEDRAL

tc The founder, Earl Rognvald, started to build his new cathedral in 1137 with the intention of dedicating it to his murdered kinsman, **Earl Magnus**. Building operations supervised by the earl's father Kol were terminated rapidly in 1152. Two years later the Orkney See became part of the Norwegian diocese centred on Trondheim, an arrangement which was to continue until 1472. The cathedral is Norman in character and contemporary with two other masterpieces of this style, Durham and the nave of Dunfermline Abbey *(qv)*. The exterior, severe and quite plain, is dominated by the tower and steeple. The three west front doorways added later, are very beautiful, although much weathered, and show originality in the alternate use of red and yellow sandstone.

St Magnus Cathedral – doorway

Interior. – The initial impression is one of vastness although the dimensions of this cruciform church are relatively small. Although massive and somewhat severe, the admirable proportions, strong sense of unity, and warm tones of the red stone make for a most pleasing result. The view is best from the west end. The design of the nave elevation moves eastwards in seven bays as slowly as its moves upwards through the triforium and clerestory, where there is no quickening of the rhythm. Ornamental detail is confined to decorative mouldings on the recessed arches of the main nave arcade, the interlaced wall arcading of the nave aisles and transepts and the grotesque heads of the choir consoles. The square pillars on either side of the organ screen enshrine the relics of St Magnus (right) slain in 1115, and his nephew Earl Rognvald, the builder (left).

SIGHTS

The other main sights stand within what must have been the cathedral precinct.

★Earl's Palace. – Although ruined this early 17C palace still displays much architectural
tc sophistication and beauty. The refinement is all the more surprising in that the builder was the villainous despot, **Patrick Stewart**, Earl of Orkney (d1615). He displayed that strange combination of splendour and infamy, so typical of many Italian Renaissance potentates. Like his father he was executed, but only when the final hour had been postponed to allow the condemned man time to learn the Lord's Prayer.

The palace, built between 1600-7, is an early example of the Renaissance style. Details of interest on the exterior include the corbelling - ornate and varied - of the windows, chimney breast and corbel course, the sculptured panel above the main entrance and the oriel windows.

Inside a splendidly spacious staircase with straight flights rises to the Great Hall and the other principal apartments. The vaulted chambers on the ground floor have exhibits on Orkney's other notable historic monuments and prehistoric sites.

tc **Bishop's Palace.** – A new episcopal palace was built in the 12C alongside the new cathedral, the original seat having been at Birsay *(p 163)*. It was in the original palace that the Norwegian King Haakon died in December 1263 after the Battle of Largs *(qv)*. His death and the palace are described in one of the Sagas. Two rebuildings followed in the 16 and 17C, the latter by Earl Patrick as part of his scheme to create a vast lordly residence incorporating his new palace across the road. The round tower on the corner is part of Bishop Reid's 16C remodelling. The yellow sandstone figure of a bishop in a red niche is 13C.

★Tankerness House Museum. – This rather fine 16C town mansion houses a
tc well-presented museum portraying life in Orkney from its prehistoric beginnings to the present day. The island's many outstanding prehistoric sites are described chronologically and accompanied by artifacts. This makes an ideal introduction prior to exploring the islands. Do not miss the St Magnus Reliquary, a simple wooden casket. Upstairs the exhibits portraying domestic life include an example of the straw backed Orkney chairs, excellent draught excluders.

The main street. – Stroll along the town's main thoroughfare, a narrow stone flagged way which incorporates, **Broad, Albert** and **Bridge Streets,** and ends at the harbour. Onetime town houses of country lairds, now occupied by shops and sometimes still emblazoned, provide the main points of interest, along with the pends leading to attractive paved courtyards.

EXCURSIONS

1 **Eastern Mainland.** – *23 miles to Burwick.*

This excursion is an excellent opportunity to visit some of the Orkney Islands (Lamb Holm, Glims Holm, Burray and South Ronaldsay) without taking a boat or plane. The road passes through some of Orkney's finest agricultural land.

Take the airport road out of Kirkwall then fork right to the A961, South Ronaldsay road.

The early stretch has a good view of **Scapa Flow**, the naval base where on 21 June 1919 the entrapped German Grand Fleet was scuttled. Activity has returned with the Island of Flotta being used as a pipeline landfall and tanker terminal for gas and oil from the Piper and Claymore Fields. Lyness on Hoy serves as a supply base.

After St Mary's follow signposts to St Margaret's Hope.

Beyond is the first of the **Churchill Barriers** linking Mainland to three outlying islands. These concrete causeways were built during World War II after the torpedoing of the battleship HMS *Royal Oak*, to protect the eastern entrances to Scapa Flow. The work was undertaken by Italian prisoners who completed the four sections totalling one and a half miles in length.

Turn left immediately after crossing the first causeway.

★**Italian Chapel.** – *Lamb Holm.*
tc Two nissen huts were converted into a chapel with the materials to hand, by the prisoners working on the construction of the causeways between 1943-5. With its rood screen and fresco paintings, it stands 40 years later as a testimony of faith in adversity.

On either side of the following two causeways there are rusting hulks esteemed as scallop breeding grounds.

On the island of South Ronaldsay a roadside viewpoint with indicator offers **views**★ across the Pentland Firth of Dunnet Head and John o'Groats on the Scottish mainland.

tc **Burwick.** – In summer a passenger ferry operates between Burwick and John o'Groats *(qv)*.

★★ 2 **Western Mainland.** – *53 miles. Allow a day.*

This tour combines important prehistoric sites with the tranquil agricultural landscape of the interior and the more dramatic coastal scenery. The tour may be taken in either direction and started from either Kirkwall or Stromness.

Leave Kirkwall by the Stromness road, the A965.

Rennibister Earth House. – *Leave the car on the road up to the farm. The site is behind the farmhouse. Access by a trap door and ladder down into the chamber.*
This earth-house or souterrain consists of an oval chamber with five wall recesses and an entrance passage. Human bones were found in the chamber, but its original purpose is uncertain. Souterrains are Iron Age in date ; some belong to the period of the brochs, but both earlier and later examples are known. They are usually found under or by round houses of stone or timber.

Turn left twice following the HBM signposts to Wideford Cairn.

Wideford Hill Cairn. – *One mile on foot from the road. The site is on the flank of the hill, follow the path. Access by a trap door and ladder.*
Dating from between 3500 and 2500 BC this chambered tomb, within its cairn, has a main chamber with side cells. From the hillside there is a lovely **view** northwards over the Bay of Firth.

Return to the main road, the A965 and at Finstown turn right onto the A966 in the direction of Georth (Evie). Gurness Broch is signposted to the right.

tc **Gurness Broch**. – *A carworthy sandy track continues beyond the first car park round the shore to the beach, the Sands of Evie.*

At the point of Akerness promontory are the remains of a broch *(p 183)* altered by subsequent phases of occupation. The result is a cluttered complex of later settlements inside and beyond the broch.

The A966 has good **views** across the Eynhallow Sound of Rousay and the smaller island of Eynhallow.

Continue round the north coast to the village of Birsay, turn right.

There are good **views**★ of Marwick Head.

★**Brough of Birsay**. – *Description p 163.*

Return to the village.

Earl's Palace. – In the village of Birsay are the ruins of a residence built, around three sides of a courtyard, by the late 16C earls of Orkney. This once sumptuous building is another example of the outstanding architectural heritage from these builder earls *(p 164)*.

Take the A967 then turn right onto the B9056 to the Bay of Skaill.

The prominent headland pinpointed by the Kitchener Memorial is Marwick Head, known for its sea bird colony.

★★**Skara Brae**. – *Description p 167.*

Continue by the B9056 then turn right onto the A967 and right again towards Stromness.

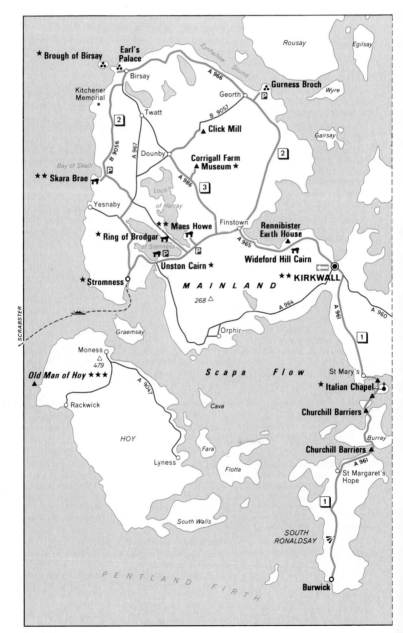

★Stromness. – *Description p 168.*

Leave by the A965 and once over the outlet of the Loch of Stenness take the farm road to the left.

★Unston Cairn. – *Park in front of the house. The key hangs in a box at the back door.* The cairn on the edge of the Loch of Stenness contains an excellent example of a communal chambered tomb typical of Stone Age times. The main chamber is divided by upright slabs into compartments. The pottery found here gave rise to the name Unstan ware which dates from the mid-fourth millenium BC.

Turn left onto the B9055.

Pass on the right the Stones of Stenness with its few remaining stones.

★Ring of Brodgar. – The Bronze Age stone circle stands in an impressive site on a neck of land between the lochs of Stenness and Harray. Of the original 60 stones 27 remain upright. Two entrance causeways interrupt the encircling ditch.

Once back onto the main road continue only for a short distance. Park beside Tormiston Mill.

★★Maes Howe. – *Description below.*

Return to Kirkwall.

★ ③ Corrigall Farm Museum. – *14 miles from Kirkwall by the A965 and A986.*

tc A most delightful and successful museum of farming and rural life. The group of 18C buildings has been restored to its mid-19C appearance. The stone buildings have flagstone floors and fittings. The flagstone roofs are heather thatched and turfed. The

original 'firehouse' has been subdivided by a gable fireplace into 'in-by' and 'oot-by'.The out-by (1a) had pig stalls and recessed goose nests. The in-by (1b) was the family room with sleeping area beyond. The present exhibition area (3) was the byre, which was later replaced by a separate building (4) with its ingenious flagstone stalls, drain and angle nooks for hens' nests. The following building contains the stable for the working Clydesdales (6) with a small lean-to for the ponies (7) and a barn with threshing floor (note position of doors for winnowing), kiln (9) and peat store (10).

Continue along the A986 to Dounby and then turn right for 2 miles by the B9057 to reach Click Mill.

Click Mill. – This is the last working example in Orkney of a horizontal water mill.

★★MAES HOWE (Mainland)

tc This Neolithic chambered cairn is an outstanding piece of skill and craftsmanship in an age when the only tools were of flint or stone. Built without the use of mortar prior to 2700 BC (Stonehenge 2800-1560 BC) the ingenuity of construction and quality of workmanship are such that it has been suggested this was the tomb of a chieftain or ruling family. The whole is covered by a mound (Maes Howe means great mound) 26ft high and 115ft in diameter and encircled by a ditch.

Interior. – A 39ft long passage leads to the 15ft square inner chamber off which open three burial cells. The tomb was pillaged in the 12C by Norsemen who removed all the treasure, taking three nights to accomplish the feat! This tale is told by the rich collection of runic inscriptions to be found within the tomb itself.

★★SKARA BRAE (Mainland)

tc On the west coast of Mainland, overlooking the Bay of Skaill, clusters a group of Stone Age dwellings. Long protected by sand, the site is well preserved and provides a vivid picture of life in Neolithic times.

Period of occupation. – Most of our knowledge of this best preserved of all Northwest European Neolithic villages comes from the excavations of Professor Childe in 1928-9, and smaller but more detailed excavations in 1972-3. Radiocarbon dating shows the two main periods of settlement belong between about 3100 BC and 2500 BC.

The inhabitants and their activities. – The first inhabitants grew grain and kept cattle, sheep and pigs. They fished in the sea which at that time

Plan of typical house

was much further than now from the village. To supplement their diet they hunted deer. Their tools were of wood, stone, bone and horn. They dressed in skin clothing, and had shell and bone necklaces and ornaments. Their pottery, heavily decorated, ranges from small fine cups to large coarse storage vessels. They belonged to a culture which buried its dead in tombs like Quoyness on Sanday and Maes Howe.

The settlement. – *Half mile walk from the roadside car park.*
Today several dwellings (nos 1-10) remain, linked by once covered passageways (A, B and F). Seven are well preserved, remains of several others are less prominent. Only drift wood and scrubby trees were available for timber and even the furniture was built of stone. Rectangular in shape with rounded corners the huts had regularly coursed flagstone walls. Each dwelling had a short entrance passage guarded by a door at the inner end. The hearth for the fire was in the middle and smoke was allowed to escape by a hole in the roof. Stone slabs were used to fashion the beds against the walls, the shelved dressers and wall cupboards. Privies were connected to an underground sewer system. The boxes lined with clay, which are let into the floor, may have served as tanks for bait. The best preserved house (no 7) has been roofed over. Some of the artifacts found on the site are displayed in the small museum (custodian's office) while the others are in the National Museum of Antiquities, Edinburgh.

★**STROMNESS** (Mainland) Michelin map **401** fold 4   Pop 1 646

The second Mainland centre and principal fishing port, Stromness is often the visitors first view of the islands as it is the terminal for the boat service from the Scottish mainland *(see the current Michelin Red Guide Great Britain and Ireland under Thurso)*. Although used as a haven by the Norsemen, the settlement only really developed in the 18C as a trading centre and the last port of call for the Hudson Bay Company's ships *(see Michelin Green Guide Canada)*. Whaling and herring fishing then took over as the principal activities. The dominance of the sea in the past is reflected in the physical layout. A long winding and paved main street is overlooked on the seaward side by gable ended dwellings each with their own jetties.
The P. & O. Ferry Terminal Building has a seasonal tourist office with a small introductory display on the island.

SIGHTS

tc **Pier Arts Centre.** – The gallery has a permanent **collection of abstract art★** highlighted by some of the greatest works of the 1929-63 period when St Ives was a leading centre *(see Michelin Green Guide The West Country)*. Ben Nicholson and Barbara Hepworth are represented by some of their early works, together with canvases of other St Ives painters (Peter Lanyon, Patrick Heron, Naum Gabo ...).

tc **Museum.** – Orkney's natural history and maritime museum includes displays on whaling, fishing, the Hudson Bay Company and the scuttled German Fleet in Scapa Flow *(p 165)*.

EXCURSIONS

★★**Western Mainland.** – This tour described under the excursions of Kirkwall may be undertaken starting from Stromness.

tc **Pentland Firth Crossing.** – This is a two hour journey for the roll-on, roll-off car ferry operating between Stromness and Scrabster *(for further details see the current Michelin Red Guide Great Britain and Ireland)*. The crossing is an ideal way of seeing the outstanding cliff scenery of Hoy (the name means high island). The only mountains are to be found here, and where these meet the sea the result is the sheer cliffs of St John's Head (1 140ft-347m). Even more breathtaking is the sight of the 450ft-137m sea stack, **The Old Man of Hoy★★★**, rising sheer out of turbulent waters. This red sandstone stack was climbed for the first time in 1966 but it is more usually the domain of a myriad of screeching and hovering seabirds.

PAISLEY (Strathclyde)

Michelin map **401** folds 30 and 31 – G16

The industrial town of Paisley, long famed for its Paisley Shawls and thread production, now has a more highly diversified industrial sector although thread production still plays an important role. The village which grew up around the 12C monastic establishment expanded, in the 18C due to linen manufacturing.

Cradle of the Stewarts. – David I granted lands and the hereditary position of High Steward to Walter Fitzalan. **Walter Stewart (1292-1326)** the 6th High Steward married Marjory Bruce who died giving birth to their son, the future Robert II, the first Stewart king. The **Royal House of Stewart** (later Stuart), despite James V's prophecy (*p 105*), did not end with Mary Queen of Scots but continued to rule until the 17C. Twelve Stuarts reigned for over 300 years and four occupied the English throne. The male line ceased in 1807 with the death of Prince Henry Benedict, Cardinal York. HRH The Prince Charles is the 29th Lord High Steward of Scotland.

(Paisley Museum)

Paisley Pattern Shawl – detail

Paisley Shawls. – When the fashion for imitation Kashmir shawls developed in 18C Europe, Paisley was not one of the initial centres (Edinburgh and Norwich) to manufacture such goods. It was 1805 before an Edinburgh manufacturer introduced the art to Paisley, where it prospered, initially as a cottage industry. Such was the success that all patterned shawls with the traditional "pine" motif came to be known as **Paisley Shawls**. In early examples decorated end pieces and borders with two or three colours were sewn onto plain centres, which were later covered with a small motif. With the introduction of the Jacquard loom (1820s) the industry became more factory based, and intricate overall patterns with as many as ten colours were popular. Printed shawls were introduced in the 1840s and were followed in the 1860s by the reversible shawl which never gained any real popularity.

The local museum has an excellent collection, demonstrating all the beauty and intricacy of these multicoloured, fine garments which were appreciated equally for their warmth, lightness and softness.

Famous sons. – **John Wilson (1785-1854)** alias Christopher North the poet, essayist, contributor to the *Blackwood Magazine* and Professor of Moral Philosophy at Edinburgh, was a contemporary of Scott and firm friend of "the Ettrick Shepherd" and Thomas de Quincey. The latter figures in his masterpiece *Noctes Ambrosianae*, a series of imaginary colloquies in an Edinburgh tavern. Paisley was also the birthplace of the poet weaver, **Robert Tannahill (1774-1810)** and the ornithologist and poet **Alexander Wilson (1766-1813)**. Originally a weaver also, Wilson emigrated to America where his work on North American birds influenced America's own John J Audubon.

SIGHTS

tc **Paisley Abbey.** – Walter Fitzalan founded a priory in 1163 bringing monks from the Cluniac establishment at Wenlock. Elevated to abbey in 1245 the monastery became one of the most powerful and richest.

Although the priory was a 12C foundation, the church we see today is mostly 15C and the result of many rebuildings and extensive restorations. In the heart of Paisley, the church is an impressive sight as it stands unencumbered by encroaching buildings. The deeply recessed west front doorway is 13C Early Pointed Gothic. Inside, the corbelled galleries at the clerestory level of the nave are unusual in that they go round the outside of the pillars. The St Mirin Chapel, in the south transept, commemorates St Columba's friend and contemporary. The long choir, a 19 and 20C restoration, has Robert Lorimer furnishings. Here also is the tomb reputed to be that of Marjory Bruce, wife of the 6th High Steward of Scotland *(see above)*.

The Place of Paisley *(Place and Tower, 197 steps)* is all that remains of the monastic buildings which were appropriated as the commendator's residence.

tc **Paisley Museum and Art Gallery.** – *High Street.*

This 19C building, another of the Coats bequests, houses a series of well displayed collections. The comprehensive **Paisley Shawl Section★**, outlines the development of this specialised local activity and includes examples of its varied products *(see above for more details)*. The art gallery has a number of works by the Scottish School (Gillies, Walton and George Henry). Other sections include a good pottery collection, local and *tc* natural history exhibits. The **observatory** has displays on astronomy, meteorology and space flight.

EXCURSION

tc **Kilbarchan Weaver's Cottage.** – *5 miles west of Paisley, off the A737.*
This 18C weaver's cottage with its typical interior of the period, is a reminder of the local cottage industry which still reigned supreme at the turn of the last century. Displayed throughout the cottage are examples of locally woven work including tartan which was produced more recently. The handlooms in the basement are still used for demonstration purposes. The attractive cottage garden has an interesting collection of herbs and local historical artifacts.

★ **PERTH** (Tayside)   Pop 43 030

Michelin map **401** fold 27 – J14

Perth, the Fair City on the Tay, has conserved few historic buildings. Pleasantly situated in its riverside setting between two vast parklands, this onetime royal burgh has succeeded better than most in retaining an atmosphere of a county town. It is an ideal touring centre.

HISTORICAL NOTES

Although Roman camps were known to the north at Bertha and south at Carpow, the earliest community at this point grew up around the inland port, at the end of the present High Street, using water-borne transport. The town achieved royal burgh status in the 12C and both William the Lion and Robert the Bruce gave confirming charters. During the reign of James I, in his attempt to create an efficient system of government, Perth bacame the meeting place on several occasions for Parliament. The town would no doubt have become the centre of government or capital had not James I lost his life *(p 171)* in one of the town's monasteries. By the 16C the walled town was a prosperous burgh and the various trades and crafts are perpetuated today by street names : Cow, Meal, Flesher's, Cutlog, Baxter's (Bakers) Vennels and Ropemakers Close, Mercer Terrace, Glover Street and Skinnergate.

"The rascal multitude". – Among the contributing factors to the Reformation were the laxity of monastic houses and increasing dissatisfaction and estrangement with the established church, thus providing a growing number of reformers. In those disturbed times events such as John Knox's fiery sermon of 11 May 1559 roused the mob to a wave of destruction which in Perth alone resulted in the loss of all four monastic houses. The Lords of the Congregation left from Perth on their subsequent campaign.

The 17C was a period of decline due to a change in foreign trading patterns. Along with other East Coast towns Perth was subjugated as part of Monck's pacification campaign. In the latter half of the century Perth prepared to welcome the University of St Andrews, which was then in conflict with the citizens of that town. The site proposed was that of Gowrie House, scene of the Gowrie Conspiracy. However the move was never made. Prosperity returned in the 18C with the agricultural improvements and the town expanded beyond its medieval limits.

Inland port. – From earliest times the Tay was important in bringing trade to the town and river traffic included both foreign and coastwise vessels. Between 1814 and the 1930s a steamboat service plied between Dundee and Perth. Today Perth's port, situated downstream, handles fertilisers as imports, with grain, timber, malt and potatoes as the main exports.

With its reputation as an excellent salmon river, the Tay also boasts pearl fishing. The gems obtained from freshwater mussels range in colour from white and grey, to gold and lilac.

Perth today. – The town has an important role as a communications centre at the junction of natural routes, the motorway connection and new Friarton Bridge, a motorail terminal and a busy port. Still important as a market town for the agricultural hinterland, Perth is famous for its Aberdeen Angus Shows and sales *(February and October)*, the Perthshire Agricultural Show *(August)* and is the home of both the Aberdeen Angus and Highland Cattle Societies. The industrial sector includes two famous whisky distillers and glass making. The town is also the home of the General Accident Insurance Company, with their new headquarters at Cherrybank.

Notable events in the year's calender include five race meetings *(April, May, August, September and October)* as well as Perth Horse Show, a Carriage Driving Championship *(May)* at Scone racecourse, the Perth Highland Games *(August)* and Curling Championships.

SIGHTS

tc **★Black Watch Regimental Museum** (Y). – Balhousie Castle, the former home of the Earls of Kinnoull, is the setting for the regimental headquarters and museum. The origins of the regiment date back to the early 18C when General Wade was given the task of bringing peace, law and order to the Highlands. During his subsequent programme of road and bridge building, Wade enlisted and armed, groups of Highlanders to keep the peace. These companies were known as **The Black Watch** for the watch they kept on the Highlands and for their dark tartan, a direct contrast to the Red of the Government troops. The Regiment was formed in 1739 *(p 38)*. This well presented museum is organized chronologically to unfold the Regimental history through its battles and campaigns with paintings, silver, Colours and uniforms.

North Inch (Y). – The 100 acres of this park, extending northwards along the west bank of the Tay are mainly given over to sports facilities. The outstanding feature is the domed form of Bell's Sports Centre (Y) built in 1978. It was on the North Inch that the great **Clan Combat** took place in 1396 between thirty champions from clans Chattan and Kay. There were few survivors in this event which Scott describes in his novel *The Fair Maid of Perth*. Robert III and his Queen were spectators from the nearby Blackfriars Monastery, which once stood at the south end of the park.

★Georgian terraces. – On the completion of Smeaton's bridge in 1772 the town began to spread beyond the medieval limits. Entire streets were built in the new Georgian style, such as Barossa Place with its substantial villas, and **Rose Terrace** (Y) dominated by its centrepiece, the Old Perth Academy (**Y A**) (1807). John Ruskin (1819-1900) spent much of his childhood at no 10 (**Y B**). Continue round to the delightful curve of **Atholl Crescent** (**Y 2**) the first extension in the new town development. A plaque on the southwest corner of Blackfriars Street (**Y 6**) marks the site of Blackfriars Monastery. Founded in 1231 the monastery was the scene of James I's assassination (1437). 1559 brought destruction, as with all Perth's other monastic establishments.

North Port (**Y 27**) leads to **The Fair Maid's House**, the home of Scott's heroine, Catherine Glover which is now a Scottish Crafts Shop. Charlotte Street leading round to Tay Street is backed by a short Georgian row, the last house of which has an attractive fire plaque. Smeaton's elegant nine-arched **Perth Bridge** bestrides the Tay, still fairly wide at this point.

Take George Street (**YZ 17**) which is overlooked on the right by the Museum and Art Gallery.

tc **★Museum and Art Gallery** (Y). – The building is marked by an imposing portico and dome. In addition to displays on natural history and furniture there are particularly interesting sections on the local glass (Monart and Vasart ware), silver and clock making industries.

The British section of the art gallery has one of **John Millais's** (1829- 96) large Scottish landscapes. Millais owed his Perthshire connections to his wife Effie Gray. An enthusiastic shooter and fisher, he has captured well the autumnal feel and tints of a Tayside scene in *Chill October* (1870). *Loch Katrine* (1866) is a canvas by that specialist of Highland scenes Horatio McCulloch (1805-67). Alongside are works by Cadell, Henry and David Wilkie. In the adjoining foreign section Ribera's (1591-1652) *St Andrew* is an example of his robust and uncompromisingly realistic style.

George Street, one of the main shopping streets, leads to High Street.

tc **St John's Kirk** (Z). – Pinpointed by its unusual steepled tower, the church is another example of the great burgh kirks. Founded in the 12C, this mainly 15C church was restored in 1925-6 to house a war memorial. It was probably from this church that Perth took its early name of St John's toun, perpetuated today by the name of the local football team.

At the junction with South Street, a plaque (Z **D**) on the building on the left, marks the onetime site of the Bishops of Dunkeld's house. The Salutation Hotel (Z **E**) (1699) with its Venetian window was used by Bonnie Prince Charlie.

Continue down South Street towards the Tay and turn right onto Tay Street.

From here there is a good view of Perth Bridge.

Tay Street. – The imposing colonnaded frontage of the **Sheriff Court** (1820) is characteristic of Robert Smirke's Greek inspired work. A plaque to the left commemorates and represents the once magnificent Gowrie House (1520-1807). It was the scene of the mystery shrouded **Gowrie Conspiracy** (5 August 1600) when the descendants of the lst Earl of Gowrie were murdered. The question remains, was it attempted regicide or a vengeful counterplot on the part of James VI? The versions are various.

Water Works (Z). – *Tourist Information Centre.* This handsome circular building is girdled by a balustrade, crowned by an elegant dome and guarded by an urn topped tower. The town's water supply was planned and the building designed in 1810 by the Rector of the Academy and finished *c*1930-1.

Marshall Place, another terrace of Georgian buildings, is interrupted by the crown spire of the 19C St Leonard's-in-the-Fields, and overlooks the green swards of South Inch.

King James VI Hospital (Z). – In 1429 James I founded the only **Carthusian Monastery** in Scotland on this site. The murdered founder, his Queen Joan Beaufort and Margaret Tudor, James IV's Queen, were all buried within its walls. The monastery was destroyed in 1559. The present four storeyed, H-plan building, now divided into flats, was founded by James VI in 1587 originally as a hospital. The façade overlooking Hospital Street is crowned by an unusual cupola which originally came from Nairne House.

OUTSKIRTS

tc **Caithness Glass**. – *Two miles north of Perth just off the A9* (Y) *in the Inveralmond Industrial Estate.*

Opened in 1979 this factory produces beautiful hand made paperweights. A visitor's gallery with windows onto the workshop allows the visitor to observe all the production processes.

★Branklyn Garden. – *Signposted off the A85* (Z).

tc The saying, "Small is beautiful" aptly applies to this garden on sloping ground on the east bank of the Tay, overlooking Perth. Begun in 1922 as a private garden these two acres have a wide variety of plants. It is a profusion of colour, scent and shape and perfect for those who like to study individual plants.

Kinnoull Hill. – 792ft-241m *Take Bowerswell Road* (Y **7**). *20 minute walk up from the Braes Road car park to the view indicator.*

The summit commands an extensive view★, away from the Highland rim, round over Perth which is superbly spread out below, to the New Friarton Bridge then follows the Tay round into the Carse of Gowrie with the Ochils and Lomonds in the distance. The craggy cliffs of Kinnoull towering 700ft above the Tay are dominated by the follies of Kinnoull Watch Tower and its counterpart a mile further to the east on Binn Hill, both in imitation of Rhineland castles.

EXCURSIONS

★★Scone Palace. – *2 miles northeast of Perth by the A93* (Y).

★Huntingtower Castle. – *3 miles northwest of Perth by the A9* (Y) *and then the A85.*

tc Originally known as the Castle of Ruthven it was the hunting seat of the family of the same name and scene of the **Raid of Ruthven** (1582). William, 4th Lord Ruthven, created Earl of Gowrie the previous year, invited the 16 year old James VI to the castle, where he was sequestered for 10 months by a group of nobles resentful of the influence the Earl of Arran and Duke of Lennox exercised over the young monarch. Although officially pardoned, the Earl of Gowrie was beheaded in 1584 at Stirling, on charges connected with an attack on Stirling Castle. Revenge was to follow with the counterplot, the Gowrie Conspiracy *(see above)* in 1600. The castle was confiscated, its name changed to Huntingtower and the family name of Methven proscribed. In 1643 the castle passed into the hands of William Dysart "whipping-boy" for Charles I and father of Elizabeth Dysart, Duchess of Lauderdale.

This typical 15-16C tower house consists of two towers, which were joined in the 17C to provide more commodious accommodation. Both towers have three storeys plus a garret served by turnpikes. Note in particular the roofline with corbelled wall walk, corner turrets, punctuated by chimneys and crow stepped gable ends. The **painted timber ceiling** on the first floor of the eastern tower is one of the earliest of its kind (*c*1540). An unusual feature is the dovecot in the garret of the western tower.

★Elcho Castle. – *Leave Perth by the A912* (Z), *before the motorway turn left into a* *tc* *local road in the direction of Rhynd. HBM signposting leads down to the castle by a farm road and through the steading.*

Overlooking the Tay, the Earls of Wemyss' family seat is reputedly on or near the site of an earlier stronghold and onetime retreat of Wallace. Built in the second half of the 16C, the main body of the castle has an accretion of towers with jambs in an attempt to provide more ample living accommodation. Above the plain walls, pierced by windows with wrought iron grills and gun ports, the wallhead is an intriguing composition of decorative elements : pediments, roll moulded window surrounds, corbelled turrets, crow stepped gables and chimney stacks. The north and west fronts are good examples of the improvisatorial Scottish masons at their best in producing a building which literally seems to grow.

The southwest tower has an unusually elegant and spacious **staircase** leading up from the ground floor. The main apartments on the first floor have vaulted kitchen and cellar space below, and two floors of well lit apartments above, many of which have their own fireplace. Three turnpikes serve the different levels.

Abernethy. – Pop 889. *8 miles southeast of Perth by the A912 (Z) and A913.*
Happily the main road by-passes the old centre of this peaceful village on the lower slopes of the Ochils. Lying as it did at the heart of the Pictish kingdom some claimed this was the early capital. Later it was the site of a Celtic settlement and the only
tc relic of its ancient past is an **11C Round Tower★**. This Irish type tower served the dual purpose of place of refuge and belfry. Standing alone at the kirkyard gate this 74ft tall tower tapers slightly. Two periods of construction are clearly visible. Note the elevated position of the door, a defensive feature, the jougs attached to the wall and the Pictish symbol stone at its foot.

Glenshee. – *40 miles. Leave Perth to the north by the A93 (Y).*
★★Scone Palace. – *Description p 180.*
Meikleour Beech Hedge. – The beech trees forming this 100ft high hedge were planted in 1746.

Blairgowrie. – Pop 6 122. In the heart of the soft-fruit growing countryside, the town becomes the main ski centre for Glenshee in winter.
The road follows the Black Water up Glenshee, a typical Angus Glen, as far as the Spittal of Glenshee. The final ascent to the Cairnwell Pass (2199ft-665m) was famous for the zig- zag bend, the **Devil's Elbow**, now by-passed by a new stretch of the A93.

Glenshee. – The Glenshee ski area is on both sides of the valley and in particular the slopes of the Cairnwell. A comprehensive lift system (12 lifts and two chairlifts) gives access to ski runs ranging from easy to expert. Facilities include a plastic slope. The
tc Cairnwell Chairlift takes summer visitors to the summit (3059ft-933m). The **panorama★★** encompasses Ben Macdui, Beinn à Bhuird, Lochnagar and Glas Maol on the far side of the valley, all Munros. In summer it is also a centre for hang gliding.

The A93 continues for a further 12 miles to Braemar.

Take your time on Highland roads.
The scenery can only be enjoyed at leisure.

PETERHEAD (Grampian)   Pop 17 015
Michelin map **401** fold 16 – 011.

The busy shopping centre of Peterhead has an active harbour with both fishing and oil supply vessels. The original burgh was founded in 1593 by George Keith the 5th Earl Marischal and by the end of the 17C it had become a fashionable spa. Peterhead then became the premier whaling port before losing this position to Dundee and itself becoming a flourishing herring port.
Many of the buildings are built of the local pink or Peterhead granite.

tc **Arbuthnot Museum.** – *St Peter Street.* The displays illustrate Peterhead's maritime past : whaling, herring fishing and the ancillary trades, model ships and the harbour.

EXCURSION

South to Collieston. – *14 miles. Leave Peterhead by the A952. Branch left to take the A975. Park in the lay-by.*

Bullers of Buchan. – *Care is needed on the clifftop paths.* This rock chasm makes an awesome sight in rough weather. In the words of Boswell the Pot or Buller is 'a monstrous cauldron'.

Continue on the main road passing Cruden Bay with its sandy beach and golf course on the links. Slains Castle is signposted to the left (poor road surface).

Slains Castle. – The pink granite ruins on the cliff edge are the remains of a castle built by Francis Hay, the 9th Earl of Erroll on his return from exile. The earl had conspired with Huntly in a counter Reformation plot. James VI personally supervised the destruction of both family seats. The Hays are hereditary Lord High Constables of Scotland. Robert the Bruce gave the original seat, confiscated from the Red Comyn, to Gilbert Hay for his faithful services.

Return to the A975. The B9003 leads to Collieston.

Collieston. – This former fishing village with its small sandy bay is now a popular summer resort. Inland is the visitor centre for the Sands of Forvie and Ythan Estuary Nature Reserve. The reserve with the large dune system and inter-tidal mud flats is important for wintering wildfowl and as a breeding ground.

Michelin map **401** – fold 23 – I 13

Set in the lovely Tummel Valley, this holiday resort makes an ideal touring centre for the magnificent scenery of the surrounding countryside. The busy main street is a succession of hotels, guest houses, restaurants, cafes, tweed and Highland craft shops. One of the main drove roads from the north followed the alignment of the valley and **General Wade** (1673-1748) in the 1720s and 30s built one of his first military roads from Dunkeld to Inverness. Prior to this the main settlement was Moulin, and as late as the 1880s Pitlochry itself numbered barely 300 people. The town's growth was due in large part to its popularity as a health resort in Victorian times, and more recently as a tourist centre ideally situated astride the Great North Road. Today the by-pass relieves the summer congestion caused by through traffic.

The **Pitlochry Highland Games** feature competitions for top pipe bands and traditional heavyweight sports.

SIGHTS

tc **Pitlochry Power Station.** – Part of the North of Scotland Hydro-Electric Board's Tummel Valley Scheme, the 54ft high and 457ft long dam retains Loch Faskally to even out the flow of water. There is an exhibition which includes two videos on the Tummel Scheme and the life cycle of the salmon. The main attraction is the **salmon ladder** permitting salmon to move upstream to their spawning grounds, between April and October. 34 pools, 3 of which are resting ones, rise up in steps to the level of the loch. The salmon can be observed at close quarters through windows in the fish observation room.

The three mile long artificial Loch Faskally is stocked with salmon and trout. It provides good angling and boating facilities and a pleasant walk *(1 hour)* around the shores.

tc **Festival Theatre.** – *At Port-Na-Craig, on the same bank of the Tummel as the salmon ladder.*

Founded in 1951 the original tented theatre known as "the theatre in the hills" has been replaced by a splendid all-purpose building incorporating a 540 seat theatre, restaurant and exhibition facilities. The repertory company presents a summer season of drama, music and art with a changing programme.

EXCURSIONS

Rannoch Moor. – *38 miles to Rannoch Station from Pitlochry*

The B8019 follows the nothern shore of Lochs Tummel and Rannoch.

The scenery is as fine as any in the Central Highlands with excellent prospects of mountains and lochs. The run ends with the desolation of Rannoch Moor.

★★**Queen's View.** – *Access from the Forestry Commission car park and information centre.* This famous viewpoint, named after Queen Victoria's 1866 visit, has a truly royal vista up Loch Tummel, which is dominated by the cone shape of Schiehallion (3547ft-1083m) on the left.

Loch Tummel. – Hydro electric works in the vicinity have been responsible for increasing the size of the original loch from 2 3/4 miles in length to 7 miles and its depth by 17ft. The power station at the Tummel Bridge end is powered by water from the Loch Errochty reservoir, high in the mountains to the north and which arrives by 6 miles of tunnel.

Loch Rannoch. – The larger of the two lochs is almost 10 miles long and an average 3/4 mile wide.

The road remains close to the loch side. On the south shore are the remains of the native pine forest, the Black Wood of Rannoch.

Beyond the head of Loch Rannoch the B846 continues a further 6 miles to Rannoch Station, on the West Highland Railway (Glasgow-Fort William). The terrain is hummocky with glacial debris and erratics all around. The Gaur is a typical Highland river with a boulder strewn course.

Once over the watershed, Rannoch Moor stretches away to the horizon.

Rannoch Moor. – The fastness of this desolate wilderness is legendary. At an average height of 1000ft-305m the granite floor is mainly covered with blanket bog and occasional lochans with the peat in places reaching a depth of 20ft. The moor was a centre of ice dispersal during the Ice Age, with glaciers radiating outwards and gouging, amongst others, the troughs of the Rannoch - Tummel Valley and Glen Coe in the west.

Killiecrankie. – *Leave Pitlochry to the north to join the A 9.*

Beyond Garry Bridge leading to Lochs Tummel and Rannoch, the river, road and railway run parallel to negotiate the narrow defile of the Pass of Killiecrankie.

tc **Killiecrankie Visitor Centre.** – *NTS Visitors Centre.* The centre commemorates the scene of the **Battle of Killiecrankie** (27 July 1689) which was fought on higher ground to the north of the pass (the battlefield is on private land). When William and Mary landed, with the subsequent flight of James VII, those who remained faithful to James (Jacobite) and the Stuart cause were rallied by **John Graham of Claverhouse, Viscount Dundee** (*c*1649-89). The mainly Highlander Jacobite army having seized Blair Castle, moved south to meet the government troops under Mackay. The encounter was brief, and a decisive victory for Dundee who was mortally wounded in the fray. A month later the leaderless Highlanders were beaten at Dunkeld *(qv)*. The final Jacobite saga ended in 1746 with Culloden.

From the Visitors Centre a path (signposted) leads to the **Soldier's Leap** where a fleeing government soldier is said to have jumped to escape from his Jacobite pursuers. A second path leads down through the wooded Pass of Killiecrankie to the car park beside Garry Bridge.

★★ PITMEDDEN GARDEN (Grampian)

Michelin map 401 fold 16 – N 11 – 14 miles north of Aberdeen

tc The formal Great Garden at Pitmedden is a rare jewel in this "'cold shoulder'" of the northeast.

The creator. – In the early 17C the Pitmedden estate was acquired by the Setons. When John the 3rd laird was killed at the Battle of Brig o'Dee (1639) his two young sons were entrusted to a relative George Seton, 3rd Earl of Winton. An improving laird and man of advanced tastes he had established gardens at Winton and Pinkie. It was **Sir Alexander Seton** (*c* 1639- 1719), the younger brother, and lawyer by profession, who when in disagreement with King James VII's religious policy retired to his estate and set about the creation of a formal garden. Having spent time in exile it is possible that Alexander Seton may have admired the masterpiece of Le Notre at Vaux-le-Vicomte, or nearer home have been influenced by the gardens of Sir William Bruce at Holyroodhouse and Balcaskie. In this treeless and stony area he created a garden unparalleled in Scotland, except by the Lindsays at Edzell.

Recreation. – Time had effaced the formal designs and in 1951 when the donation was made to the National Trust for Scotland the lower area was a productive vegetable garden. The original plans had been lost along with family papers when Pitmedden Castle was burnt in 1818. New designs were established based on Charles II's garden at Holyroodhouse.

The gardens today. – Although open all the year the gardens are seen at their very best in July and August when the 30/40 000 annuals are in bloom. The initial impression of immaculately tended gardens where neatly clipped yews, trim boxwood hedges, shaven lawns edge masses of colour and contrast with the more natural exuberance of the harbaceous borders. The walled garden is planned on two levels. An upper western half mostly lawns and hedges with a newly laid out herb garden, overlooks the lower formal garden area. The belvedere provides the best viewing point. Trim boxwood hedges provide the geometric designs and outlines of the four parterres. The colour is provided by annuals, coloured gravels and green turf paths. Three of the designs are geometric while the fourth represents the armorial display of Sir Alexander Seton. Also part of the original plan are two gazebos with their ogee shaped roofs, the central fountain (rebuilt) and the entrance staircase linking the two levels.

The grounds. – In the surrounding policies a woodland walk and nature trail allow the visitor to discover some rare breeds of livestock or endangered species. The
tc outbuildings house a **Museum of Farming Life** with implements and artifacts from the age of the horse.

IN THE VICINITY

tc **Tolquhon Castle.** – The original tower house belonged to the Prestons of Craigmillar *(qv)* before passing by marriage to the Forbeses in 1420. A cultured and enlightened 7th laird **William Forbes** (d1596) employed Thomas Leiper the local mason to add a quadrangular mansion to the original tower house between 1584-9. Many local contemporaries, with the exception of Lindsay at Edzell and Keith at Dunnottar, were still building tower houses. The castle remained occupied until the mid-19C.
Tolquhon is a most attractive ruin with its mellow stonework enhanced by the well tended lawns. A double courtyard edifice, the main buildings are arranged around the inner court. The inner entrance front incorporates on the left the original 15C tower, now ruined, a twin drum gatehouse adorned with heraldic panels and curious sculptured figures and projecting round tower to the right. The main apartments are at first floor level in the wings to the right and straight ahead. Note in particular the main staircase leading to the hall, with its attractively flagged floor, and the long gallery with book cupboards, the pit prison and the drainage system.

Tarves. – Pop 850. In the kirkyard of this neat village, arranged around its square, is the **Forbes monument** to the builder of nearby Tolquhon Castle. A basically Gothic structure it is resplendent with Renaissance details and statuettes of William and his wife. This is also the work of Thomas Leiper.

★★ ROSSLYN CHAPEL (Lothian)

Michelin map 401 fold 31 – K 16 – 7 miles south of Edinburgh

tc Set on the edge of the Esk valley, the 15C Rosslyn Chapel famous for its stone carvings, is unique in style and a masterpiece of craftsmanship. The beauty, intricacy and richness have to be seen to be believed.

History. – The founder **Sir William St Clair,** third and last Prince of Orkney (1396-1484) and lord of nearby Rosslyn Castle, with the intention of creating a unique work, assembled workmen from various European countries. Work started in 1446 and came to a halt in 1486 two years after Sir William's death. Of the planned cruciform collegiate church only the choir was completed. Damaged in 1592, used as a stable for the horses of Monck's troops in 1650 it was restored in 1861 and still serves as an Episcopalian place of worship.

Exterior. – A foretaste of the richness to come, the pinnacled flying buttresses, window hood moulds, heraldic roof cornice, corbels and canopies of niches are covered with decorative sculpture.

Interior. – A five bay choir with clerestory above is bordered by north, south and east aisles, the latter being prolonged by a Lady Chapel stretching the full width of the building and raised by one step. The five compartments of the vaulted choir, spangled with stars, roses and other decorative paterae are separated by sculptured ribs. In the side aisles, architraves between the pillars and outer walls separate pointed vaulting, with the apex running in a north-south direction, while the Lady Chapel has groined vaulting with pendants. Amidst this wealth of detail the outstanding feature is the **Apprentice Pillar★★★** *(illustration p 25)*. Legend has it that while the master mason was on a tour abroad prior to executing this work, the apprentice produced the pillar we see today. On his return the enraged master mason in a fit of jealously killed the apprentice (see 30, 29 and 27). From the base with eight intertwined dragons, foliage winds up the column to the carved capital. The Stafford Knot is visible on the south side. Such is the wealth and richness of the carvings that they defy description. Some of the scenes from this Bible of Stone are listed below and pinpointed on the accompanying plan.

North Aisle. – (1) wall pillar to the right of the door : Crucifixion ; (2) wall pillar : plaited crown of thorns ;(3) pillar : imp ; (4) pillar : lion's head ; (5) wall pillar : shield ; (6) wall pillar : shield displaying the arms of the founder and his wife ; (7) architrave, east side : Our Blessed Lord seated in Glory ; (8) windows : two of the Twelve Apostles ; (9) arch : Samson pulling down the pillars of the House of Dagon.

Lady Chapel. – (10) and (11) roof ribs : the Dance of Death is portrayed by a series of 16 figures ; (12) pendant : Star of Bethlehem with 8 figures evoking the Birth of Christ ; (13) pillars : angels ; (14) **Apprentice Pillar★★★** ; carvings above include Isaac on the altar and a ram caught in a thicket ; (15) and (16) roof ribs : series of eight figures.

South Aisle. – (17) architrave : inscription in Lomardic letters : Wine is strong, the King is stronger, Women are stronger but above all truth conquers ; (18) window : two of the Twelve Apostles ; (19) architrave ; east side : The Virtues ; west side : The Vices ; (20) window arch : Nine Orders of the Angelic Hierarchy.

Choir. – (21) niche : modern Virgin and Child replacing the statue destroyed at the Reformation ; (22) floor : founder's burial slab ; (23) pillar : human figures and animals ; (24) pillar : Anna the Prophetess ; (25) arch : Twelve Apostles and Four Martyrs each with the instruments of their martyrdom ; (26) pillar : Jesus as the Carpenter of Nazareth, 2 men wrestling and Samson or David with a lion ; (27) under niche : the widowed mother ; (28) pillar : crowned figure ; (29) cornice level : the master mason ; (30) cornice level : the apprentice with the scar on his left temple ; (31) pillar : Prodigal son feeding the swine ; (32) pillar : three figures looking north to (1).

★★ ST ANDREWS (Fife)   Pop 11 630

Michelin map 401 fold 28 – L14

St Andrews on the Fife coast is famous as a seat of learning and the home of golf. As the onetime metropolitan see of Scotland, the city was in the mainstream of Scottish history and its rich heritage includes a 12C cathedral, 13C castle and 15C university. Today the town has a charm all its own and is a busy holiday resort in summer, reverting to the role of a university town in term time with an active cultural life.

HISTORICAL NOTES

An early ecclesiastical settlement associated with relics of St Andrew, it grew in importance with the founding of the St Regulus Church, a priory in the 12C and finally a grandiose cathedral, all of which eclipsed the Celtic settlement of St Mary on the Rock. The monastic establishment renowned as a seat of learning was the precursor of the university.

With a growing university attracting scholars and students of a high calibre, 15C St Andrews was an active and prosperous burgh well meriting the attribution of a national role as ecclesiastical capital of Scotland in 1472.

Prosperity and the population declined in the 17C, due in part to the loss of the archbishopric (1689 Revolution), the changing trading patterns now with the American colonies as well as the political changes after the 1707 Act of Union. The 18C was also one of general decline.

The 19C was the beginning of the growth of golf as a sport and by the turn of the century the town had achieved renown as a Mecca of golf. The popularity as a holiday and golfing resort has gone from strength to strength.

St Andrews University. – Founded in 1410 (1413 Papal Bull) by **Henry Wardlaw**, Bishop of St Andrews, it was the first in Scotland and third in Great Britain after Oxford and Cambridge. Typical of medieval colleges there were no buildings until the Pedagogy was built in 1430, followed by the Colleges of St Salvator's (1450), St Leonard's (1512) and St Mary's (1537). Three of Scotland's 15C poets, William Dunbar, Gavin Douglas and Sir David Lindsay all studied here. By the 16C St Leonard's was already associated with reformist doctrines and university associations with leading figures of the Reformation are numerous, Patrick Hamilton, Alexander Alane (Alesius), Henry Scrimger as well as Andrew and James Melville. The resultant struggles with the established ecclesiastical hierarchy and the crown are well known historical events *(p 178)*. Towards the end of the 17C decline had set in and although the proposal to transfer the University to Perth fell through, it continued into the 18C when St Leonard's and St Salvator's were amalgamated to form United College in 1747. The 19C was a period of reforms and reorganization and the student population reached its lowest ebb in the 1870s with a total of 130. By the end of the 19C, and the 1897 union with Dundee, numbers were in constant progression. Despite the loss of Queen's in 1967, the present student population of 3 672 has greatly enlarged premises, and is once again largely residential.

Golf a Royal and Ancient Game. – St Andrew's links - with swards of springy turf and sand bunkers - have, since the 15C, been a place for playing golf or the early ball and stick version of this sport. So popular was the game that by 1457 an Act of Scottish Parliament was passed requiring that "futeball and the golfe be utterly cryit down" in favour of kirk attendance and archery practice. Mary Queen of Scots was an occasional player, her son James VI popularized the game in England and both James Melville and the Marquess of Montrose played here as students. Founded in 1754, the Society of St Andrews Golfers had the title **Royal and Ancient** conferred on it by William IV in 1834 and is now recognized as the ruling body. Equipment developed as featheries were replaced by guttas, guttas by rubber-cores, and wooden shafts by steel, which revolutionized the game. To meet the increasing popularity of the sport, new courses (New 1895, Jubilee 1897, Eden 1912) were laid out supplementing the **Old Course,** established several centuries ago. By the beginning of the 20C St Andrews was firmly established as the Golfing Mecca and the town now regularly hosts the British Open and Amateur Championships, Walker Cup Matches and a variety of other big money tournaments which draw the stars of the professional circuit, bringing record breaking crowds of 193 000 (1984 Open) despite television coverage. Two of the greatest names in golfing history are immortalized by hole names on the Old Course : Tom Morris (18th) and Bobby Jones (10th).

★THE CATHEDRAL (B)

tc The 16C precinct wall encloses the cathedral ruins and church of St Regulus. The imposing **St Regulus Church (B B)** with its lofty western tower may well have been the shrine built to shelter St Andrew's relics. Queen Margaret's son, Alexander I nominated Robert Prior of Scone as Bishop of St Andrews, and it was he who built the church between 1127 and 1144. The tower *(151 steps)* has a magnificent **panorama★★** of St Andrews and its main monuments. Bishop Robert founded the priory *c*1159 and his successor Bishop Arnold began work on the new cathedral, which was consecrated in 1318 by Lamberton in the presence of Robert the Bruce. Only the 12C east and late 13C west gables and the south wall of the nave remain of this once immense building with its 10 bay nave. Following the depredations of the Reformation, subsequent neglect and 17C quarrying for stone, this once noble building was reduced to the ruin we see today. To the south were the buildings of what must have been one of the most powerful monastic establishments. Foundations indicate the layout.

tc The **museum (B M)** has a good collection of early Christian sculptured stones – fragments of 8-9C cross slabs – from St Mary of the Rock and a superb 8 or 10C **sarcophagus.**

THE CASTLE (B)

tc Overlooking the foreshore, the ruins once formed part of the palace and stronghold of the Bishops and Archbishops of St Andrews. Founded *c*1200 the castle suffered greatly during the Wars of Independence. Bishop Henry Wardlaw, founder of the university, was tutor to James I and it is possible that his young charge spent time here prior to his captivity in England. Bishop Kennedy taught James II how to break the power of his nobles by comparing them to a bundle of arrows, with the suggestion he snap each one individually.

Many reformers suffered imprisonment here, including George Wishart whom Cardinal Beaton had burnt at the stake in front of his palace, and Patrick Hamilton another martyr. Following the martyrdom of Wishart a group of Protestants seeking revenge gained admission to the castle disguised as stonemasons and murdered Cardinal Beaton (1494-1546). They held the castle for a year and were joined at intervals by others such as John Knox, and the siege was only lifted when the garrison capitulated to the French fleet. The besieged were taken to France and Knox was sent to the galleys.

The late 16C entrance range with the central Fore Tower, originally flanked by two round towers, was the work of Archbishop Hamilton and it was supposedly from this façade, the exact spot is contested, that the body of Cardinal Beaton was displayed to the crowd. The buildings were arranged around a courtyard. In what remains of the northwest or Sea Tower is the grim **Bottle Dungeon** of late 14C construction. 24ft deep it is hewn out of solid rock. The other interesting items are a **mine** and **counter mine** *(enter from the ditch in front of the entrance building)* excavated during the 1546-7 siege.

In the pavement in front of the castle are the initials of George Wishart marking the spot where he was burnt at the stake in 1546.

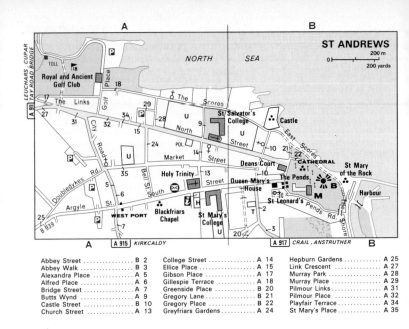

tc THE UNIVERSITY

St Salvator's College (AB). – Now the centre of United College, St Salvator's was founded in 1450 by Bishop James Kennedy. The chapel and tower, above the entrance archway, form the North Street frontage and are a good example of 15C Gothic ecclesiastical style. The two ranges around the quadrangle are 19C reconstructions. **St Salvator's Chapel** was, according to Dr Johnson, "the neatest place of worship he had seen". The collegiate church was restored in the 19 and 20C. Inside is the **founder's tomb** an amazingly intricate 15C work of art in the Gothic style. The pulpit opposite, with the preacher's hour glass, is supposedly the one used by John Knox.
The initials PH laid in the pavement before the entrance, mark the spot where **Patrick Hamilton** (1504-28), one of the early reformers, was burned on the 29 February 1528.

tc **St Leonard's Chapel** (B). – The chapel belonged to the college of the same name. The original buildings were a hospital for pilgrims to St Andrew's shrine, then a nunnery, before being acquired to form the nucleus of the new college of St Leonard's. When St Leonard's and St Salvator's were united in 1747, the chapel was neglected while the buildings and grounds were eventually taken over by St Leonard's girls school. The 1950s restoration recreated the medieval layout with a screen and organ loft dividing the building in two.

St Mary's College (A). – In the early days of the university, classes were held in the priory buildings until Bishop Henry Wardlaw provided the Pedagogy (1430). This was superseded one hundred years later when Archbishop James Beaton founded St Mary's College (1537). The college became a theological College in 1579. The buildings on the west side of the quadrangle are 16C. On the ground floor College Hall has portraits of past principals including Cardinal Beaton. Up two flights of stairs is one of the original student chambers with box beds. On the north side is the old **University Library**, on the site of the original Pedagogy, which is now refurbished as the Psychology Department. On the street front there are a series of arms of University Chancellors. The first floor Senate Room is part of a 19C extension. The two Joseph Knibb longcase clocks flanking the fireplace were part of Gregory's equipment *(see below)*. Both Archbishop Sharp and Cardinal Beaton are portrayed amongst the notables.
The Upper Hall (1612-43), "Elegant and luminous" according to Johnson, is a galleried room panelled with pale Baltic pine. This was where **Gregory** the Astronomer (1638-75) and inventor of the reflecting telescope worked. The ground floor Parliament Hall completed in 1643 is where the Scottish Parliament sat from 1645-6 following Philiphaugh *(qv)*.

ADDITIONAL SIGHTS

The town has retained its original layout with three main streets – South, Market and North Streets – converging on the cathedral.

★West Port (A). – The main entrance to the old town, it was built in 1589 and opens onto South Street.

Blackfriars Chapel (A). – This is all that remains of a mid-15C foundation for Dominican Friars. Dating from the 16C, note the three sided termination. The imposing building behind is part of Madras College.

tc **Holy Trinity Church** (A). – This burgh church, rebuilt in 1410, was modified in the late 18C and restored in the 20C. Only the corbelled tower with the stone steeple is 15C. Inside Archbishop Sharp's monument graphically records his death in 1679 on Magus Muir *(see opposite)*.

Queen Mary's House (B). – A 16C house in attractive rubble stonework with a pantile roof.

Deans Court (B). – This 16C building is now a post-graduate students residence.

The Pends (B). – A 14C vaulted gatehouse which was the main entrance to the priory. The road follows the precinct wall down to the harbour.

Harbour (B). – Rebuilt in the 17C with stone from the castle and cathedral.

Church of St Mary of the Rock (B). – This was the site of the 12C Celtic settlement which was gradually superseded by St Regulus and the new cathedral and priory.

Royal and Ancient Golf Club (A). – *For club members only*. The imposing 1854 clubhouse overlooks the Ist and 18th holes of the Old Course and is the headquarters of the Royal and Ancient Golf Club.

EXCURSIONS

★★The East Neuk. – *Description p 82.*

★Inland Fife. – *30 miles*. This excursion through the agricultural hinterland of St Andrews has a varied selection of places of interest to visit.

> *Leave St Andrews to the northwest by the Cupar road, the A91. Once over the Eden turn right in the direction of Guardbridge.*

Guardbridge. – Small village with an important paper mill and narrow 15C bridge, which was built by Bishop Wardlaw.

★Leuchars Parish Church. – Pop 2 500. The fame of the village of Leuchars derives in part from its RAF station and Leuchars Junction, the railway station for St Andrews. However pride of place is taken by the **parish church** which dominates the village from its elevated position. The 12C chancel and semicircular east end are exceptional examples of **Norman work**. On the external walls, under the cornice of grotesque heads are two fine bands of arcades. The tower and lantern are 17C. Inside, the perspective towards the apse is framed by the richly moulded chancel and apse arches. Corbels carved with grotesque heads are similar to those in Dalmeny Church *(qv)*.

> *Take the road to the right behind Leuchars Parish Church.*

tc **Earlshall Castle.** – Sir William Bruce built Earlshall in 1546 and Robert Lorimer was responsible for the 1891 restoration. The painted ceiling of the 2nd floor gallery is outstanding. Executed between 1617-20 the black and white design incorporates Bruce, royal and Scottish nobles' coats of arms, and a variety of truly fabulous beasts all linked together by geometric patterns. The topiary garden represents chessmen.

> *Return to the main road going in the direction of Cupar.*

Cupar. – Pop 7 370. Busy market town for central Fife.

> *Take the A92, the Kirkcaldy road to the southeast then fork second left to the A916.*

tc **Hill of Tarvit.** – Hill of Tarvit is an Edwardian country house designed by Robert Lorimer. It was commissioned by Mr Frederick Bower Sharp (d1932), a jute manufacturer and financier from Dundee. In 1904 Frederick Sharp purchased the estate which included the original house, Wemysshall (1996) attributed to Sir William Bruce, and the 16th century Scotstarvit Tower. Frederick Sharp was an art collector of note and his family residence was designed as a suitable setting for his important collection of fine furniture, Old Masters, tapestries, Chinese porcelain and bronzes.
One can enjoy the complete "Upstairs, Downstairs" situation of the elegant Edwardian period, the grandeur and charm of the main rooms and the fascination of the kitchen premises, with the laundry in the garden.
A nature trail leads through the wild garden to the hilltop (692ft-211m) viewpoint indicator with a panoramic view of Fife and beyond.

tc **Scotstarvit Tower.** – *Leave car on roadside of A916.*
A notable landmark, this L-shaped tower house dates from *c*1579 and rises through five storeys. The vertical accommodation, consisting of six chambers with a well lit main hall on the first floor, is reached by a turnpike stair. The cap-house is of an unusual variety. This was the home of **Sir John Scot** (1585-1670) lawyer, author, part-time cartographer and brother-in-law to William Drummond of Hawthornden. Ben Jonson walked to Midlothian to visit both men in the 17C.

> *Once through Craigrothie turn sharp left onto the B939 to St Andrews.*

★Ceres. – Pop 970. This picturesque village with its arched bridge and village green is
tc the home of the **Fife Folk Museum** with comprehensive displays of everyday items, a cottar's living room and tool and agricultural section.

> *Continue along the B939 in the direction of Pitscottie. At the Strathkinness junction turn right. Once up the hill a signpost to the right indicates the footpath to follow (5 min walk).*

Magus Muir. – When level with the railed enclosure in the field, veer right towards the pyramid shaped monument. This marks the spot where Archbishop Sharp of St Andrews was ambushed and murdered on 3 May 1679.

tc **Craigtoun Country Park.** – This attractive country park has a variety of children's amusements and pleasant gardens.

> *The local road leads back to St Andrews.*

In addition to those described in the guide there are other castles which are open to the public by appointment only.
Enquire locally for further details.

tc On the east bank of the Tay two miles out of Perth, Scone Palace has within its grounds Moot Hill, one of Scotland's most hallowed historic sites. The Palace itself is a treasure house with superb collections of French furniture, ivories and porcelain.

Heartland of a Scoto – Pictish Kingdom. – Although the exact role of the site in Pictish times is unsure its considerable importance is in no doubt. The tradition was perpetuated by Kenneth MacAlpine in the mid-9C when he made Scone the centre of his new Scoto-Pictish Kingdom, a counterpart to his recently created ecclesiastical centre at Dunkeld to the north. From this time on Scottish Kings were ceremonially enthroned on the **Stone of Destiny** (Stone of Scone) which MacAlpine had brought in 838 from Dunstaffnage.

Robert the Bruce was the first of many Scottish Kings to be crowned here, right up to James VI, the last being Charles II in 1651. Such was the stone's importance that Edward I in 1296, following his defeat of the Scots and imprisonment of King John Balliol, had the Stone of Destiny and other regalia carried off to Westminster Abbey where it has been part of the Coronation Chair ever since, except for a six month interlude in 1950-1.

Religious Centre. – The original Celtic community was superseded when Alexander I founded an Augustinian priory *c*1120, the first of that Order in Scotland. The priory was colonized by canons from Nostell in Yorkshire. The first prior, Robert was chosen by the same monarch to be Bishop of St Andrews in 1124 (St Regulus) and canons were called on in 1164 to go St Andrew's Abbey. The abbey and abbot's palace, as was the custom, served as a royal residence and during the reign of Robert III (1390-1406), St Giles, Edinburgh was attached to the abbey as a means of providing revenues for this recent foundation.

The abbey was sacked in the 1559 wave of destruction following John Knox's inflamatory sermon in Perth *(p 171)*, and together with its lands it subsequently (1580) became the property of the Earls of Gowrie who built a 16C house, Gowrie Palace, using the old palace stones. Following the Gowrie Conspiracy *(qv)* and the forfeiture of their property in 1600, James VI bestowed the estate on the Murray family, later the Earls of Mansfield. The 3rd Earl commissioned William Atkinson, a pupil of James Wyatt of Fonthill Abbey fame, to build the neo-Gothic palatial mansion (1802-8) we see today.

VISIT *time : 1 hour*

Interior. – Throughout this suite of richly furnished apartments in the neo-Gothic style are superb pieces of French furniture and a series of unusual and interesting timepieces. Outstanding in the **Dining Room** is the collection of **European ivories** (17-19C), a wonder of delicate carving. Arranged around the table, set with an armorial damask cloth and service, are locally made chairs in the Chippendale style. His Grace the **Hon William Murray** (1701-79), the eminent lawyer, politician and embellisher of Kenwood House *(see Michelin Green Guide London)* is portrayed here as is the lst Earl. In the adjoining **Ante-Room** Sir David Murray, the Cup Bearer to James VI, was the lucky recipient of the forfeited Gowrie lands and palace. In the **Drawing Room**, against the 18C figured Lyons silk hung walls, are a series of portraits including Allan Ramsay's pair of royal portraits (1765) of *King George II* and *Queen Charlotte,* and Reynold's portrait of *the lst Earl of Mansfield,* William Murray as Lord Chief Justice of England (1776). One of the greatest lawyers, noted for his eloquence, he was known as "Silver tongued Murray" and was the lifelong opponent of William Pitt the Elder. The Pierre Bara set of French fauteuils with fine needlework are dated 1756, while flanking the fireplace are two Boulle commodes. However the finest piece is Marie Antoinette's exquisite Reisener (1734-1806) **writing table.** The magnificent array of fine **porcelain** in the **Library** was collected by the lst and 2nd Earls. The lst Earl's portrait shows his prized possession, Bernini's bust of Homer which the Pope had given him, and flanking this is Rysbrack's bust of the Lord Chief Justice. The **Ambassador's Room** named after the 2nd Earl, politician, statesman and ambassador, who served in Dresden, Vienna and subsequently Paris, where he became the confidante of Louis XVI and Marie-Antoinette and acquired much of the fine French furniture now in the house. The bed was a royal piece commissioned for his *Grace the Ambassador,* who is portrayed here by Pompeo Batoni. Zoffany's portrait of the Ambassador's daughter, *Lady Elizabeth Murray* shows her in the grounds of Kenwood, the Earl's English country house and permanent home when rioting crowds destroyed his Bloomsbury residence. With a length of 168ft the appropriately named **Long Gallery** retains its original oak and bog oak flooring but sadly has lost its painted ceiling. Outstanding amidst the paintings and fine furniture is a unique collection of **Vernis Martin** objets d'art all made of *papier mâché.* David Wilkie's. *The Village Politicians* hangs here.

The grounds. – Facing the palace is **Moot Hill,** now occupied by a 19C chapel. Explanations for the name Moot are various. The Gaelic derivation *(Tom-a-mhoid)* would have it as a place where justice was administered, while the Boot version, more incredible, is the more appealing. It was said that when the earls, chieftains and other men of consequence came to swear fealty to the Lord High Ardh, they carried earth in their boots from their own lands, since fealty could only be sworn for their land while standing on it. Having taken the oath they then emptied the contents on the spot, hence Boot Hill.

The avenue opposite the main entrance leads down to the **Old Gateway,** emblazoned with the arms of James VI and the lst Viscount. Beyond was the original site of the village of Scone, before it was moved during 19C alterations to the palace. The 50 acre **pinetum** has some of the oldest firs including the Douglas species. The first such tree was sent by its namesake the celebrated botanist, David Douglas (1798-1834) who was born and worked on the estate.

The onetime royal and ancient burgh of Selkirk, a proud and handsome little town, is set high up on the southern flank of the Ettrick Water valley. The town's name is associated with the famous **Selkirk bannock**, a round fruit loaf.

The souter town. – The burgh was the royal hunting seat for the Ettrick Forest. It was here that David I established the monks from France in 1113, but finding the site uncongenial they moved on to Roxburgh, only to move again, two years later, to Kelso. Initially known for its "souters" or shoemakers (who supplied Bonnie Prince Charlie's army), prosperity grew with the introduction of weaving in the 17C and the early 19C growth of tweed mills down on the valley floor. Today Selkirk is a busy market centre.

Famous sons. – The most notable is the great African explorer **Mungo Park** (1771-1806) who was born at Foulshiels *(see below)*. Trained as a doctor he served his medical apprenticeship in Selkirk with a local practitioner. Many Border museums and houses have examples of the work of the watercolourist, **Tom Scott** (1854-1927).

Selkirk Common Riding. – On the second Friday in June the Burgh Standard Bearer and mounted followers ride the boundaries of Selkirk's Common Lands before Casting the Colours in Market Place, followed by the playing of the *Lilting*, Selkirk's lament for its Flodden dead.
Outside the Victoria Hall stands a forceful bronze statue of the warrior **Fletcher** (1913) by Thomas J. Clapperton. The statue commemorates the legend of the Selkirk contingent which fought at Flodden with James IV's army, when only one man returned at the end of the day, a certain Fletcher with a captured English banner which he cast on the cobbles in despair.

SIGHTS

tc **Halliwell's House Museum.** – *Halliwell's Close, off Market Place.*
The museum presents the intriguing display of an ironmonger's shop with objects and articles from the not so distant past. Upstairs there is a graphic presentation of the history of the royal burgh.

Market Place. – In the centre is the statue of **Sir Walter Scott,** sheriff of Selkirk for 33 years, which marks the site of the original courtroom in the old tolbooth. The present courtroom behind, contains his bench and chair and other items of interest.

Parish Church. – *Kirk Wynd.* The view from the churchyard extends over the Ettrick valley. The ruins are on the site of the Kirk o'The Forest where **William Wallace** was proclaimed Guardian of Scotland in 1298. In the Murray Aisle lie the maternal ancestors of Franklin D Roosevelt.
Higher up Kirk Wynd, at the crossroads, note the statue of a souter placed in the wall of the house on the left.

High Street. – The County Hotel on the left is a good example of a coaching inn, on the main Carlisle route. The bust at first floor level of no 49 (on the left) is the Border artist, Tom Scott. The statue standing to the right is Mungo Park.

EXCURSION

Yarrow Valley. – *20 miles. Leave Selkirk to the west.*

New Bridge. – Two previous bridges were destroyed by the roaring autumn floods of the Ettrick Water. The earliest was situated slightly downstream in 1777 and 200 years later, in October 1977, the second, Philiphaugh Bridge was similarly swept away, to be replaced by the present concrete structure.

    Take the A708 to the left.

Philiphaugh. – The haughlands of the Ettrick, were the site of the **Battle of Philiphaugh** in 1645 when the Covenanting Army under David Leslie routed the Royalist forces led by James Graham, the Marquess of Montrose.

The road then runs close to the Yarrow Water, just after its confluence with the Ettrick Water, both tributaries of the Tweed. The bridge on the left leads to Bowhill.

★★**Bowhill.** – *Description p 49.*

On the right is Foulshiels, the birthplace of the African explorer **Mungo Park** where he wrote *Travels in the Interior of Africa.*

tc **Newark Castle.** – *Usually visited from Bowhill, to which it is connected by a riverside walk.* This fine 15C tower within a bailey wall was once the royal hunting lodge for the Ettrick Forest and scene of the massacre of Montrose's infantry after the Battle of Philiphaugh in 1645.

The road continues up the valley into sheep farming country with small hill farms. At Yarrow a road leads off to the left to cross the spur and descend into the Ettrick Water valley. Once part of the great Ettrick Forest, the now bare hillsides are being reafforested by the Forestry Commission.

The B709 on the right at the Gordon Arms Hotel, makes a pleasant run through typical upland Border country passing by Traquair *(qv)* to the Tweed Valley at Innerleithen.

The valley opens out and soon St Mary's Loch comes into view in a most attractive hill setting.
A stile to the right leads up to St Mary's Kirk where **James Hogg** (1770- 1835) "the Ettrick Shepherd" is buried. Hogg the poet shepherd had Scott as friend and patron and his best known work is *Confessions of a Justified Sinner.* The site is the venue for an annual open-air service to commemorate the many conventicles held in the area by the Covenanters.

St Mary's Loch. – *Description p 157.*

SETON COLLEGIATE CHURCH (Lothian)

Michelin map 401 fold 31 – L 16 – 1 1/2 miles southeast of Cockenzie

tc Seton collegiate church is a good example of Scottish late Gothic architecture. Of the external features note in particular the stone slab roofing and originally pinnacled buttresses with statueless dais and canopies. The undersides of some of the dais are emblazoned with the Seton arms. The whole is dominated by the squat tower with its truncated broach spire.

Interior. – Inside, this well lit building has typical late medieval pointed barrel vaulting. At the polygonal east end, the earliest part of the building, moulded ribs fall onto carved corbels. There is a sedilia in the south wall and a delicate 15C piscina with a 15C tomb recess and recumbent effigies opposite.

The rib vaulting of the transept crossing descends onto piers with carved capitals showing vine, palm leaf and thistle motifs.

The 16C transepts, again with pointed barrel vaulting, have tomb recesses at either end. In addition the south transept has an ornate piscina.

The ruins of the living quarters lie in the southwest corner of the grounds, extending under the dividing wall of nearby Seton House *(private)*, one of Robert Adam's 18C castellated mansions. This was built on the site of Seton Palace, a magnificent 16C building and seat of the Setons, in particular the 6th Lord Seton, Mary Queen of Scots' staunch supporter. Lord Seton's sister was one of the four Marys. Some sculptural fragments from the palace are exhibited in the northeast corner of the grounds.

★ SHETLAND ISLANDS (Islands Area)   Pop 17 327

Michelin map 401 – inset folds 4 and 8
Access : see the current Michelin Red Guide Great Britain and Ireland.

This group, the most northerly of Scotland's islands, comprises 100 isles of which less than 20 are inhabited. The capital Lerwick is on the east coast of Mainland which is 50 miles long from end to end and 20 miles at its widest point. Shetland is some 60 miles to the north of Orkney.

HISTORICAL NOTES *(See Orkney Islands p 163)*

Shetland by contrast with Orkney has few tracts of flat land, is deeply penetrated by the sea and until recently had an economy dominated by fishing and crofting. The oil boom of the 1970s led to the disruption of this traditional and well balanced economy. Today with the largest European oil port sited at Sullom Voe, the oil industry comes second after fishing. It is planned to use oil revenues to bolster the traditional industries (crofting, fishing, fish processing and knitwear).

Shetland and the visitor. – The oil-related industrialization is limited to Sullom Voe. Elsewhere the islands retain the attractions of wild beauty, solitude and empty spaces. Mainland with all its coastal indentations means the sea is ever present. The long coastline is varied and of outstanding beauty, be it rocky and rugged or sandy and smooth. Again the wildlife is varied and plentiful.

★★Up Helly Aa. – This colourful and rousing fire festival is the most spectacular reminder of the Viking heritage. Explanations for the pageant held on the last Tuesday in January are various, from spring rites to placating the Norse gods, or up ending of the holy days. The principal figure the **Guizer Jarl** (earl) and his warriors, all clad in the finery of Viking war dress, head the great torch lit procession in their Viking longship. A thundering rendering of the *Galley Song* precedes the burning of the galley and the final song, *The Norseman's Home*. Celebrations continue throughout the night.

★★JARLSHOF (Mainland) 25 miles from Lerwick

tc Set on the seashore not far from one of the more recent constructions, Sumburgh airport, is the prehistoric site of Jarlshof. Here the sequence of occupation is clearly distinguished and covers a span of over 3 thousand years from the mid-2nd millenium BC to the 17C.

Visit the site in chronological sequence. The numbers are those used on the official plan.

Stone Age. – Only fragments remain of the earliest settlers' village, contemporary with Skara Brae *(qv)*, on the landward side of the site.

Bronze Age. – Dating from this period are six oval shaped houses with cubicles built into the walls Dwelling III is the best preserved. Note the trough quern and rubber. Later settlement of the early Iron Age period brought about the alteration of the original plan including the addition of earth houses.

Late Iron Age. – Corresponding to the first centuries of our era this settlement is clustered around the ruins of a broch, partly eroded by the sea. The broch itself is equipped with a well. The plan is confused by post-broch dwellings (wheelhouses 1-4) in and outside the main structure. W2 is the most completely preserved example of a wheelhouse or circular hut divided radially.

Viking era. – The remains include numerous long houses (1-8) the layout of which is complex reflecting various centuries of occupation.

Medieval farmstead. – Only parts of the original house and barn, dating from the 13 to 16C, are preserved.

Jarlshof. – The 16C New Hall was built for Earl Robert Stewart. It was converted into kitchens when a new Laird's House was added in the early 17C.

Museum. – This has finds from excavations and a plan of the entire Jarlshof site.

LERWICK (Mainland) Michelin map 🔟🔟🔟 fold 8   Pop 6 127

The port capital of Lerwick is set on a promontory overlooking the natural harbour, sheltered by the Island of Bressay. Always important as a fishing port, the oil boom has brought new activities to the town.

A port par excellence. – As a haven, Lerwick provided shelter for King Haakon's and other Viking fleets, Dutch fishing vessels in the 17C, the German and British navies in this century and now has an assorted flottila of oil vessels.

Commercial Street. – Known affectionately as The Street, this paved and twisting thoroughfare wins its way along the shore. Steep lanes lead off uphill.

Fort Charlotte. – From the walls of this 17C fort, rebuilt in the 18C, there is a good view of Bressay Sound and island of the same name.

Town Hall. – Stained glass windows depict Viking history.

tc **Shetland Museum.** – The exhibits illustrate Shetland history from the Stone Age.

★Clickhimin Broch. – The broch *(see below)* is the outstanding structural feature of *tc* this islet, which gives evidence of successive occupations. Although only 17ft high the characteristic layout of this defensive structure with its mural chambers and staircase, can still be seen.

EXCURSION

★Lerwick to Jarlshof. – *20 miles*. This run takes in various aspects of Shetland. Discover the more desolate moorland scenery, at times interrupted by peat cutting, the varied and attractive shoreline with crofting townships down by the sea and the numerous vestiges of man's occupation in the past.

Leave Lerwick by the A970.

The main road, before the turn off for Scalloway, provides a good view★ of the inlet of Gulber Wick. Deeply penetrating arms of the sea or *voes* are typical of Shetland.

Take the B9076 to the right to join the A970

On the way down pass on the right the valley which is the setting for Tingwall Loch. The head of the loch is reputed to be the site of the Law Ting Holm or meeting place of the old Norse Parliament.

Scalloway. – Pop 896. Attractively set round its bay, this the onetime capital, is *tc* dominated by the ruin of **Scalloway Castle**. As the principal island seat of Patrick Earl of Orkney *(p 164)* it is no less splendid than his other residences. Attractive details include the corbelling of the corner turrets, sculptured panel above the entrance doorway and sandstone window, door and angle trims.

Return to the A970.

The A970 provides a succession of attractive views of the east coast all the way down. Mousa Broch can be espied on its island site.

Turn right to take the B9122 and right again in Bigton.

St Ninian's Isle. – An attractive tombolo beach links this idyllic island to the mainland. It was in the ruins of an early Christian church that one of the most important treasure troves of silverware was found. The originals of St Ninian's Treasure are in the National Museum of Antiquities while the Shetland Museum has replicas.

The B9122 offers views of a succession of small sandy bays sheltered by headlands.

Return to the A970

★Shetland Croft House Museum. – This croft in the typical crofting township of Boddam gives *tc* an accurate picture of rural life in the mid-19C. The croft steading itself comprises kitchen, sleeping accommodation and byre with the barn behind and a small horizontal water mill down by the stream. Note the roofing of cured turf with straw on top.

Return to the main road, making south again towards the site of Sumburgh Airport on its isthmus separating the waters of the Atlantic and North Sea.

★★Jarlshof. – *Description opposite.*

★★★MOUSA BROCH (Mousa Island) 12 miles from Lerwick

tc This is an outstanding example of a broch, a structure unique to Scotland and the north in particular.

On this uninhabited island the visitor may glimpse seals basking on the shore and a small group of Shetland ponies.

Broch period. – Brochs are the culmination of a tradition of small stone fortified farms stretching back to 500 BC. Mousa itself probably dates to the first two centuries of our era. Mousa may have been more strongly built than the other 500 known brochs in Scotland, most of which are found in the Highlands and Islands. Many have been reduced to rubble.

The Broch. – Impressive from the outside it is awesome and fascinating inside. Ingeniously constructed, the tower is 43ft 6in high with a 50ft diameter at the base. The shape, not unlike a bottle kiln, swells out at the base. Enter by the 16ft long passage which had a door midway along. The courtyard with central hearth was surrounded by lean-to timber structures supported by the scarcements (ledges) still visible on the inner faces of the walls. Three doorways lead to mural chambers, a fourth opens into a staircase, again mural, which leads to the wallhead. Above the uppermost scarcement the hollow wall is divided by stone slabs into galleries, which open onto the courtyard by means of three sets of ladder-like openings.

SULLOM VOE (Mainland) 35 miles from Lerwick

From the main A970 the only indication of Europe's number one oil terminal is the eternal flame on the flare stack. The decisive factors in siting an oil terminal and accompanying port facilities at Sullom Voe were the presence of a deep sheltered inlet and its proximity to the oilfields in the East Shetland Basin. The port with its four specialized jetties can handle ships of up to 300 000 tons, and the terminal 1 400 000 barrels of oil per day. The oil arrives via two pipelines from 11 offshore oilfields 100 miles to the northeast. The gases (propane and butane) are separated from the oil and then stored prior to shipment. The terminal has no refining facilities. Calback Ness peninsula is the site for sixteen huge storage tanks.

★★ SKYE, Isle of (Highland)   Pop 7 364

Michelin map **401** folds 9, 10, 13, 14, 17 and 18 – A, B, 11 and 12.
Access : see the current Michelin Red Guide Great Britain and Ireland.

Skye, as a tourist attraction, evokes the mystery and enchantment of a Hebridean isle reputed for its spectacular scenery and wealth of legends. An aura of mysticism remains which had its origins in Norse and Gaelic times when the isle was known variously as the cloud island, misty isle or winged isle. The enchantment derives in part from the isle's rapidly changing moods. How not to be spellbound when a heavy mist is pierced by fingers of sunshine prior to rolling away, or when persistent rain clears to reveal a landscape of purest colours and streaming sunshine. Skye, 48 miles long and 3 to 25 miles in breadth, the largest of the Inner Hebrides group, is celebrated for its impressive mountains the, Cuillin Hills. Although treeless and bare, the scenery is an attractive combination of mountain and sea.

Crofting, tourism, and forestry are the main occupations. Skye is one of the strongholds of Gaelic which is spoken by 58 % of the island's population. Ostaig has a Gaelic College, Sabhal Mór Ostaíg a centre of Gaelic learning in the tradition of the Columban monks at Iona.

★★★THE CUILLINS

These dramatic often harsh mountains figure largely in most views of Skye. The **Black Cuillins** are a horse-shoe shaped range encircling the glacial trough of Loch Coruisk. Gabbro rocks form over twenty sharp peaks, all over 3000ft with the highest point being Sgurr Alasdair (3309ft-993m). This ridge intersected by ravines and vertical gulleys, provides a real challenge for climbers. Facing these across Glen Sligachan are the conical summits of the **Red Cuillins.** The pink granite here has weathered to more rounded forms. The Cuillins are a favourite haunt for climbers, geologists and holidaymakers, however treacherous weather, scree slopes, steep ascents and descents require skill and experience.

(Scottish Tourist Board)
The Cuillins

DUNVEGAN CASTLE

tc Famous as the seat of the MacLeods, this Hebridean fortress is set on a rocky platform commanding Loch Dunvegan. The visit reveals a fascinating story, a mixture of personalities, clan legends and mementoes. The castle enshrines several priceless heirlooms, notably the **Fairy Flag.** According to legend this was the parting gift to Iain the 4th Chief from his fairy wife with whom he had lived for twenty years. The Flag has the power of warding off disaster to the clan and has twice been invoked. Other prized possessions are the Dunvegan Cup and Horn of Sir Rory Mor the 15th Chief. Tradition requires that the heir, on coming of age, quaffs the horn filled with claret without falling down! Family portraits include canvases by Zoffany, Raeburn and Ramsay.

ADDITIONAL SIGHTS

★**Duirinish Peninsula.** – This westernmost wing spreads out into the Little Minch.
Dunvegan Castle. – *Description above.*
Dunvegan. – Pop 301. Main settlement on the west coast.
    From beyond Dunvegan the B884 crosses the peninsula to Glendale.
Looming large on the horizon are MacLeod's Tables, two flat topped mountains where a chief is said to have entertained the Scottish King to a torchlit banquet.

tc **Colbost Folk Museum.** – The Black House shows a typical abode of the 19C, with the family quarters and byre under one roof. Behind is an interesting example of an illicit whisky still. Documents on display recall how an uprising of local crofters highlighted the problems of 19C crofting. The resultant Croft Act accorded amongst other things the much sought after security of tenure.

A road forks to the right at Totaig, going in the direction of Dunvegan Head.

Monument. – A cairn monument overlooking Loch Dunvegan marks the site of a piping school of the MacCrimmons, the hereditary pipers to the MacLeods. A piping centre was re-established nearby in 1976.

Return to the main road.

Glendale Water Mill. – Beyond Glendale township, a typically scattered crofting community, there is a mill down in the bay. Over two hundred years ago, crofters came with their grain and a supply of peat, some even from the Outer Hebrides, to mill their grain here. The kiln was used to reduce the moisture content prior to grinding.

★★Trotternish Peninsula. – This 20 mile long peninsula to the north of Portree is known for its unusual rock formations. A coastal road circles it with lovely seascapes over the Sound of Raasay and Loch Snizort.

★Portree. – Pop 1 374. Set around a bay sheltered by two headlands, the isle's capital is a popular yachting centre.

The Storr. – A ten mile long ridge rising to 3 000ft-914m, the Storr is a succession of jagged rock shapes. Rising to 160ft-49m on the northeastern flank is the rock pinnacle **The Old Man of Storr.**

Kilt Rock. – *Leave the car at the picnic area and walk along the clifftop.*
There are interesting cliff formations of basaltic columns.

Quiraing. – From Staffin Bay, this great ridge with its numerous rocky bastions is clearly visible. At the northern end towers the 100ft-30m tall Needle.

Duntulm. – The jagged tooth of an ancient MacDonald stronghold stands on its cliff top site commanding the sea route to the Outer Hebrides.

Kilmuir. – In the churchyard is a Celtic cross monument to **Flora MacDonald** (1722-90) commemorating her bravery when she organized Prince Charles Edward Stuart's escape from the Outer Hebrides dressed as her maid. The Prince was soon to arrive in France and lifelong exile, having spent months wandering the Highlands, a hunted fugitive with £ 30 000 on his head. A quarter of a century later Dr Johnson and Boswell visited Flora at her nearby home.

★Skye Croft Museum. – The museum regroups a late 19C crofter house, a weaver's house,
tc a smithy and a ceilidh house. The latter has an interesting display of photographs and documents including newspaper cuttings, which give an idea of crofting life in the late 19C.

Uig. – Pop 103. Ferry port for Lewis and Uist.

Sleat Peninsula. – The moorland of the north gives way to a much greener and more fertile area, especially on the west coast, known as the Garden of Skye.

tc **Clan Donald Centre.** – This restored stable block serves as a visitor arrival point. One end of Armadale Castle houses a museum cum exhibition featuring the 'Sea Kingdom', the story of the Lords of the Isles and the Gaelic culture. The former grounds offer a selection of woodland walks, nature trails, the arboretum and scenic viewpoints overlooking the Sound of Sleat.

Do not underestimate distances.
Single track and winding lochside roads need time and care.

SOUTH QUEENSFERRY (Lothian)   Pop 7 540

Michelin map **401** fold 31 – J16

Former royal burgh and once a traffic congested ferry port, this now quiet small town nestles on the south shore of the Firth of Forth overshadowed by the two Forth Bridges. Constricted by a steep hillside the old part overlooks the foreshore while the newer housing developments spread over the top.
The unusual tradition of the **Burry Man Festival** *(p 212)* centres around an ungainly figure clad from head to toe with green burrs from the burdock plant. The exact origins of this popular event are shrouded in mystery.

Forth Crossing. – Being the narrowest point of the Forth, this has been the natural crossing point from earliest times. The first ferry instituted by **Queen Margaret** – hence the town's name – for pilgrims travelling north to Dunfermline, was operated by the Dunfermline monks and then local seamen. By the 17C it was one of the busiest ferry crossings in Scotland and was linked to the capital by one of the first turnpike roads. The fares current in 1650 were "Each Duke, Earl or Viscount 3s 4d ; Each Lord 1s 4d ; any other for each man or womane 1d ; Horse, cow or ox 2d and Each twenty sheep 4d". As early as the 18C when there was still no regular service, a tunnel was proposed to link the Hopetoun estates on either side of the Forth and also a chain bridge. Steam ferry ships were introduced in 1821 and in 1850-1 in the wake of the railway age both the Forth and the Tay saw the inauguration of the first railway ferries in the world for goods traffic only. This service continued to operate until the building of the Tay Bridge in 1878 and the Forth Bridge in 1890. Throughout the Queen's ferry continued to ply between North and South Queensferry until 1964 when Queen Elizabeth II made the last crossing, in the electric paddle ferry *Queen Margaret,* after opening the New Road Bridge.

(Wolfgang Meier/ZEFA)

Forth Railway Bridge

★★FORTH BRIDGES

The esplanade is an excellent **viewing point** for the Forth Bridges, in particular the Rail Bridge. The service area at the south end of the Road Bridge has a viewing terrace and commemorative plaque. It has a particularly good view of the road bridge.

Forth Rail Bridge. – Widely acclaimed as a great engineering achievement in its day the familiar outline of this cantilever bridge is well known. Built between 1883 and 1890 at a total coast of £ 3 177 206 it was an intrepid endeavour so soon after the great Tay Bridge Disaster of 1879 and was achieved not without injury and loss of life. The 135 acres of steel surface representing 50 000 tons of girders, take at least three years and 7 000 gallons of a special paint to respray from end to end.

	ROAD BRIDGE	RAIL BRIDGE	
MAIN SPAN	3 300ft	1 710ft	CENTRAL SPANS EACH
TOTAL LENGTH	1 1/2 miles	1 1/2 miles	TOTAL LENGTH
HEIGHT OF TOWERS	512ft	361ft	HEIGHT OF TOWERS
CLEARANCE	150ft	158ft	RAIL LEVEL ABOVE H.W.

tc **Forth Road Bridge.** – Upstream stands the counterpart to the rail bridge, the slim elegant form of the suspension bridge with its ever amazing "curve". With two 24ft wide carriageways, cycle tracks and pathways, the bridge took 6 years (1958-64) to complete using 39 000 tons of steel and 405 000 cubic feet of concrete at a total cost of £ 20 000 000.

ADDITIONAL SIGHTS

Hawes Inn. – At the east end of the esplanade, part of this building dates from the 17C. The Inn probably stands on the site of one of Queen Margaret's pilgrims' hospices and it figures in novels by Scott and R.L. Stevenson.

Main Street. – The elevated terraces, West, Mid and East are lined on the south side by houses, which belonged to the flourishing merchant community. Note in particular Black Castle with its pedimented dormer windows, one of which bears the date 1626, a heart, loveknot and initials. The 17C tolbooth tower has several public clocks.

EXCURSIONS

tc **Boat trip to Inchcolm Island.** – Known as the "Iona of the East", Inchcolm Island lies 1 1/2 miles due south of Aberdour and is famous for its abbey. The outward journey gives a good view of the south shore and Hound Point, an oil terminal for processed North Sea oil from Grangemouth, with a handling capacity for ships up to 280 000 tons. Beyond, on the foreshore, is the 12C Barnbougle Castle *(private)*, the first Rosebery seat *(p 64)* which was restored in 1880 and is said to be haunted by a hound in search of his master, hence the name of the point mentioned earlier.

Visible on the north shore are the remaining wings of Donibristle House, home of the Earls of Moray, one of whom was killed on the beach.

Braefoot Bay is a shipping terminal for gas products from the **Mossmorran** separation plant. Natural liquid gas arriving from St Fergus is separated into its four components (ethane, propane, butane and natural gasoline). Ethane is sent to a chemical plant while the other products are piped to the shipping terminal.

Cormorants and seals can be seen on some of the skerries and on Inchcolm itself.

Inchcolm Abbey. – In 1123 Alexander I was stormbound on the island and in thankfulness for the hospitality he received from a hermit he founded a monastery for Augustinian canons. The priory was later raised to abbatial status. Despite many English raids the abbey flourished up to the Reformation when it passed to the Stewarts as commendators and finally the Earls of Moray. The conventual buildings are well preserved and include one of Scotland's rare 13C octagonal chapter houses and 14C cloisters. What remains of the church, includes parts of the 13 and 15C buildings.

Port Edgar. – *To the west of South Queensferry, continuation of Hopetoun Road.* This is said to have been the original landing place of the storm swept Saxon prince, Edgar Atheling and his sister Princess Margaret, hence the name. The harbour built in the 19C as a terminus for the rail ferry *(p 185)* was later used as an Admiralty harbour and since 1978 has been developed as a marine leisure centre. All visitors are welcome.

In the fertile carselands of the Forth the modern town of Stirling spreads out around the rocky crag on which perches the historic nucleus of castle and old town. Strategically important from time immemorial as focal point for all Scotland, the long and eventful history of the town has been essentially that of its famous stronghold and onetime royal residence.

Stirling makes an excellent touring centre with a wealth of possible day excursions into the surrounding countryside. There is the splendid scenery of the Trossachs, Rob Roy countryside and Lochearnhead, the rolling pastoral Strathearn leading to Perth, the more rugged Ochils and further on, Fife with its East Neuk, and then St Andrews, or down to Edinburgh to mention only a few.

HISTORICAL NOTES

Strategic location. – The site of Stirling has always been of paramount strategic importance controlling as it does a crossing of the Forth at its tidal limit, a passage northwards between the Ochils and Gargunnock Hills, and being fortuitously doted with a superb and nigh impregnable strongpoint, the crag. This has been proved by the numerous battles fought in the vicinity : Stirling Bridge 1297, Falkirk 1298 and 1766, Bannockburn 1314, Sauchieburn 1488, Kilsyth 1645 and the indecisive fray at Sheriffmuir 1715.

Early royal connections. – Few facts have come to light of early life on the crag. The royal associations began in 1124 with the death of Alexander I. In 1126 his brother, David I, granted the settlement royal status and the ensuing privileges ensured the town's subsequent prosperity and growth, becoming in the 12C one of the "Court of the Four Burghs" along with Berwick, Edinburgh and Roxburgh. It was from here that David I no doubt supervised the building of his abbey at Cambuskenneth (f1147) down on the carselands of the Forth.

Wars of Independence (1296-1305). – Due to its vital strategic importance the castle was attacked and counterattacked by both the English and Scots during this turbulent period which figures largely in the castle's own history and features two of Scotland's most famous heroes, Wallace and Bruce. The castle was recaptured from Edward I's garrison following **William Wallace's** *(p 190)* victory at the **Battle of Stirling Bridge** (1297) which was no doubt fought upstream from the present bridge. In 1304 the castle was the last Scottish stronghold in Wallace's hands and after capitulation there followed 10 years of English occupation. The castle again became the centre of a struggle in 1313, and the **Battle of Bannockburn** *(qv)* the following year was fought in the short term for possession of Stirling Castle with as long term aim the achieving of independence from the English.

Royal abode of the House of Stewart. – With the accession of the Stewarts, Stirling Castle became a permanent royal residence. James III (1451-88) strengthened the defences and built the gatehouse to the castle of his birth, as well as building the Great Hall as a meeting place for Parliament and other state occasions. Stirling's Golden Age corresponded with the reigns of James IV and V (1488-1542). **James IV**, a true Renaissance prince and contemporary of Henry VIII and François I, initiated the building of the Palace Block and the merry round of festivities of his court included the exploits of a certain Damian. Winged with cocks' feathers he surprisingly survived his flying escapade from the battlements, a feat recorded by William Dunbar in his satirical work *Fenyeit Freir of Tungaland*. On James' death at Flodden his Queen, Margaret brought her son to Stirling where he was crowned in the chapel (21 September 1513). James V continued his father's programme of building works and finished the Palace, one of Scotland's greatest Renaissance treasures. His daughter **Mary Queen of Scots** (1542-87) was crowned in the old Chapel Royal on 9 September 1543. Her infant son James was baptised in 1566, with the absent Elizabeth I as royal godmother, although the Queen was already estranged from her husband, Darnley. The following year, prior to his mother's abdication, the 13 month old prince was crowned in the parish church and it was here that he lived under the stern tutorship of George Buchanan. James rebuilt the Chapel Royal (1594) for the baptism of his own son, Prince Henry, in the same year. With the departure of James VI to Whitehall, Stirling's role as a royal residence ceased.

A prosperous royal burgh. – This royal burgh, with its exclusive trading privileges and the stimulus of the court, greatly prospered in the 15 and 16C, with the town itself spreading downhill from its august neighbour. The first half of the 15C saw the construction of a burgh church as well as the royal building projects. Courtiers and noblemen eager to be near the court, built town houses (Mar's Wark, Argyll's Lodging) and merchants followed suit. By the time the court had left, the town had acquired a trading impetus of its own.

Stirling was once again to play its military role of garrison town during the Covenanting troubles and the Commonwealth. Associations with the Jacobite rebellion included the Battle of Sheriffmuir which, although indecisive, ended the 1715 campaign, while the '45 links are even more numerous since Bonnie Prince Charlie wintered in the area prior to his final defeat at Culloden *(qv)*.

The 19C saw the growth of textile, coal mining and agricultural engineering industries. The town's central location and the coming of the railway contributed to its growth as a communications centre. In 1967 this historic town, with its thriving shopping centre and expanding industrial base was chosen as the site for a new university *(p 190)*. Stirling is well placed to take full advantage of any future growth in the electronics industry which is now so firmly established in the Central Belt that it has acquired the nickname, Silicon Glen. The town is also a leading agricultural market centre with a modern mart

187

★★STIRLING CASTLE

An important programme of restoration work is currently in progress and some parts of the castle may be closed.

tc With a magnificent site★★★, high on a crag dominating the Forth carselands, Stirling Castle was one of the strongest and most impregnable fortresses. The castle is approached, up the tail formation of the crag, through the old town. Standing sentinel on the esplanade *(car park)* is Bruce's statue.

tc **Castle Visitor Centre.** – An audiovisual presentation illustrates the castle's history through seven centuries.

Having crossed the ditch and first gateway continue upwards passing through the Inner Gateway. Take the ramp on the left up to the terrace which leads to the **Queen Anne Garden**, once a bowling green.

The 15C **Entry and Portcullis House**, the work of James IV, opens onto the Lower Square.

Lower Square. – This is overlooked on the left by the ornate façade of the Palace, with the Great Hall straight ahead and the Grand Battery to the right.

The Palace. – Begun in 1496 by James IV it was completed by 1540 in the reign of his son. A masterpiece of Renaissance ornamentation,

THE CASTLE

STIRLING CASTLE VISITOR CENTRE

Stirling, along with the other royal residences of Falkland and Linlithgow remain isloated examples of the then current European Renaissance ideas and were to have little direct effect on Scottish architecture in general.

★★★**External elevations.** – The outstanding feature of the palace, which is simple in plan with four buildings round a courtyard, is the elaborate design of the external elevations *(for further details see under Upper Square).*

Take the covered passageway to the left, passing the entrance to the Lion's Den (1).

Lady's Hole (2). – This terrace has good **views** to the west and in particular of the **King's Knot** below. Now all grass, the outlines of this garden can still be distinguished as laid out in 1627 by William Watt within the confines of the royal park. Away to the left the flagstaff of the rotunda at Bannockburn *(qv)* pinpoints another historic site.

Royal Apartments. – The Palace Block has cellars below with the royal apartments on the main floor and accommodation for the courtiers above. The Queen's Outer and Own Halls are two nobly proportioned chambers where examples of the famous 16C **Stirling Heads★★** are now on display. This series of oak medallions is an extremely fine and rare example of Scottish Renaissance wood carving. The medallions were originally set into a compartmented ceiling in the King's Presence Chamber (Own Hall). Of the original 56, roughly a quarter are missing, three are in the National Museum of Antiquities and the rest are at Stirling awaiting reinstatement. Set in circular frames the medallions portray kings and queens, courtiers of the period, mythical and Biblical figures. The carving is both lively and vigorous. Both the Queen's and King's Bedchambers are currently under restoration.

The Great Hall. – This free standing building was sadly much altered when used as a barracks in the 18C. An important programme of restoration is currently underway to recreate the former splendour of this apartment, a good example of late Gothic domestic architecture described by Defoe as "the noblest I ever saw in Europe". The original arrangement of the Gothic chamber included a dais at the south end flanked by magnificent oriel windows, with the screens and minstrel gallery at the opposite end. The hall with its oak hammerbeam roof was lit by paired windows.

Upper Square. – This courtyard provides a good vantage point for comparing the façades of the Great Hall (1460-88), the Palace (1496-1540) and Chapel (1594) showing clearly how styles changed in under 150 years.

The original front of the Great Hall had four pairs of deeply embrasured windows with below a lean - to roof protecting outside stairs leading up to the main chamber. Above the cornice was a crenellated parapet with wall walk. The **palace façade** by contrast has a variety of unusual sculptured decoration : between the windows, recessed and cusped arches are the setting for carved figures (left to right : James V ; young man holding cup ; Stirling Venus ; bearded man ; woman in flowing drapery) which are on the baluster wall shafts. Above an intricately carved cornice is the base for more pedestals set against the crenellated parapet. The façade of the Chapel Royal is staidly sober by comparison.

Chapel Royal. – The present church was hurriedly erected on the site of an earlier chapel by James VI for the baptism of Prince Henry. In the early classic Renaissance style, the courtyard front is most pleasing with 3 pairs of round headed windows on either side of the elaborate doorway. The chapel now serves as memorial hall for the regiment.

★**Argyll and Sutherland Highlanders Regimental Museum.** – Battle Honours, *tc* Colours, medals, peace and wartime uniforms, documents and pictures, all tell the story of nearly 200 years of regimental history and its heroic moments : The Thin Red Line at Balaclava 1854 and the Relief of Lucknow. The regiment is the proud possessor of an outstanding **collection of silver.**

Pass through to the Douglas Garden. It was in the building (Douglas Room) on the left that Black Douglas was treacherously murdered in 1452 by James II.

The wall walk round the battlements on the east side, has good views of the Forth carselands. From the **viewpoint** at the Grand Battery, pick out below the medieval Stirling Bridge bestriding the Forth with, in the middle distance, the tower of Cambuskenneth, the Wallace Monument and the Ochils on the horizon.

OLD TOWN

Explore the old town on foot starting from the esplanade.

The medieval town with its steep streets and narrow wynds spills downhill from the castle to the new centre of present-day Stirling. A 1960s restoration programme has brought to life an area of architectural and historic interest.

★**Argyll's Lodging.** – *Castle* *tc Wynd SYHA.* This splendid town mansion was built in 1632 by Sir William Alexander *(p 191)* founder of Nova Scotia. On his death the property passed to the Argyll family when alterations and extensions were made. The street side of this courtyard mansion is enclosed by a screen wall pierced by a fine rusticated Renaissance gateway. The courtyard façades are rich with Scottish **Renaissance decoration★** : strapwork on dormer and window heads, and an armorial panel above the entrance porch.

Mar's Wark. – *Top of Broad Street.*

Ruined but nonetheless impressive, this façade is all that remains of a palace started in 1570, but never completed for John Erskine (1510-72), Regent and 1st Earl of Mar. As Hereditary Keeper of the castle and guardian of Prince James it was only appropriate that his Grace have a private residence at hand. It is said that Cambuskenneth *(qv)* was quarried for stone. Ornamental sculpture and heraldic panels adorn the street front.

★**Church of the Holy Rude.** – This burgh church was built in stages on the site of *tc* an earlier church destroyed by fire. The oldest parts, the nave and lower part of the tower, date from the first half of the 15C. Of interest in the nave, with its round piers supporting pointed arches, is the original 15C oak **timberwork roof.** Almost a century older, (1507-1546) the choir and pentagonal apse were partitioned off from the rest between 1656 and the 1936-40 restoration. The **east end** is most impressive when seen from St John's Street, looming up massively with sloped intake buttresses between the great windows, characteristic of the Scottish Gothic style. It was here that the infant James VI was crowned in 1567 and John Knox preached the sermon.

tc **Guildhall.** – Originally known as Cowane's Hospital this E-shaped building was founded by **John Cowane** (*c*1570-1633) as an almshouse to accommodate twelve 'decayed' brethren. Built between 1633 and 1639 the premises included a refectory with sleeping accommodation above. The donator, a member of the Council of Royal Burghs and Scots Parliament, a man of some substance, stands jauntily above the doorway. Known affectionately as "stany breeks" he is said to come to life at Hogmanay.

At no 39 St John Street is **Bothwell House (A)** a three storey rubble stonework house with a projecting tower.

Broad Street. – Once the centre of burgh life, Broad Steet with its mercat cross **(D)**, marks the site of the market and place of execution. Sir William Bruce designed the elegant **tolbooth (B)** (1701-4), shortly after his release from Stirling Castle where he had been held for Jacobite sympathies. The design is unusual in that the stairs climb internally over the cells and up to the panelled rooms. The crowning feature of the six-storey tower is an unusual pavilion with delicate crestings. Across the street at no 16 **(E)** the narrow gable ended house has inscribed window pediments. At the bottom of Broad Street is **Darnley's House (F)** a four storeyed town house where he is supposed to have stayed when his son, the future James VI was being crowned.

tc Further down in St Mary's Wynd is the now roofless **John Cowane's House (G)**.

ADDITIONAL SIGHT

tc **Smith Museum and Art Gallery** (M). – *Via St John Street.*
The main exhibition relates the history of this royal burgh.

EXCURSIONS

Northeast of Stirling. – *8 miles. Leave Stirling to the north by the A9 and at the Causewayhead roundabout take the B998.*

★★**Panorama from the Wallace Monument.** – *10 minute walk uphill from the car park.* A well
tc known landmark, this 19C monument standing sentinel on Abbey Craig (362ft-110m) commemorates the patriot **Sir William Wallace** (1270-1305), responsible for rallying Scottish forces against English rule in the period 1297-1305. Hero of the hour at the Battle of Stirling Bridge (1297) he became Guardian, prior to the instauration of a collective system. Following the Scots submission in 1304, Wallace, hunted and captured, died a traitor's death in London the year after. There is an audiovisual presentation of the patriot and his place in Scottish history. Another room within the Monument, the Hall of Heroes, has a *Son et Lumière* highlighting the importance of such figures as Sir Walter Scott, Robert the Bruce, and Robert Burns. The viewing platform (*242 steps*) has a tremendous **panorama**★★ of Stirling in the flat carselands of the Forth.

Also visible is the **University of Stirling** (f 1967) in its lake and parkland setting, with the Ochils as backdrop. The baronialized Airthrey Castle, another of Adam's castle houses, serves as administrative centre while the MacRobert Centre is the focus of cultural activity for both town and gown.

> *Return to the Causewayhead roundabout take the Alloa road or the A91. The abbey is signposted to the right shortly afterwards.*

tc **Cambuskenneth Abbey.** – The remains of this once great abbey lie within a loop on the flat and fertile carselands of the Forth. About 1147 David founded an Augustinian monastery which grew to become one of the most prosperous and influential houses, whose abbots were often statesmen of note. Proximity to Stirling meant royal patronage and the abbey was used for meetings of the Scottish Parliament, in particular the 1326 one when the burghs were represented for the first time. The remains include an attractive, free standing 13C **belfry** which rises through three storeys to a height of 79ft. The 19C restoration replaced a saddle back roof with a parapeted terrace (*98 steps*) providing a good view of the abbey's layout and of the castle and Wallace Monument on their respective crags. The rest of the monastic buildings consist only of foundations. Within the church there is a 19C monument marking the graves of **James III** (1451-88), victim of the rebel lords after the Battle of Sauchieburn (1488) and his Queen Margaret of Denmark.

> *Return to the A91 and turn right. At the roundabout turn left to follow the A91.*

tc **Menstrie Castle.** – *Signposted off the main street.*

16C Menstrie Castle (converted into flats) has a heraldic display in the commemoration room (public library), a reminder that Nova Scotia was an early Scottish colony. Menstrie was the birthplace of the colony's founder **Sir William Alexander,** 1st Earl of Stirling (1567-1640). The baronetage was created to further the development of the colony and replenish impoverished royal coffers. In return for a payment each baronet was granted land in Eastern Canada. The project ceased when Nova Scotia was returned to the French in 1631 although charters continued to be granted until 1637 !

tc **Bannockburn Heritage Centre.** – *2 miles south of Stirling. Leave Stirling to the south by the A9.*

The equestrian statue (1964) of King **Robert the Bruce** (1274-1329) within the Rotunda marks Bruce's command post on the eve of the historic **Battle of Bannockburn,** 24 June 1314. Although numerically superior, the English forces, led by Edward II in person, were routed and Bannockburn was a turning point in the Wars of Independence. Since his coronation at Scone in 1306 and Edward I's death in 1307, the Bruce had been steadily regaining his kingdom and by 1314 Stirling Castle was the most important stronghold still in English hands. This decisive victory did much to achieve independence for Scotland although it was 1320 and 1328 before this was formalized in The Declaration of Arbroath *(qv)* and the Treaty of Northampton respectively.

tc **Scotland's Safari Park, Blair Drummond.** – *5 miles. Leave Stirling to the west by the A84.*

Exotic cattle, tigers, lions, yak, zebras, deer, monkeys, giraffes and camels roam the wild animal reserves in the parkland setting of Blair Drummond *(private)*. Other attractions include a boat safari to Chimpanzee Island with an aquatic show and pets corner.

STONEHAVEN (Grampian)   Pop 4 730

Michelin **401** fold 20 – N13

Stonehaven lies spread out at the head of a bay, sheltered by two rocky headlands, Downie Point to the south and Garron Point to the north. This seaside resort with its many amenities, including an indoor pool and wide curve of shingle beach, is popular with holidaymakers.

The townspeople bring in the New Year with the **Swinging Fireball Ceremony** *(p 212)* in the old town's High Street. The tradition is said to originate from a pagan custom for warding off evil spirits.

The town has one of the country's few surviving **quoiting** clubs in Dunnottar Quoiting Club (f 1890). The sport consists of slinging heavy metal rings or quoits (kites in the Mearns vernacular) with a handgrip, to land as near as possible to a metal pin. The game is sometimes played in the dark with the aim of extinguishing a candle's flickering flame. The main pitches are at Smiddymuir and the Mill Lade.

SIGHTS

Old Town. – Centred round the harbour this town was founded in the 17C by George Keith (1553-1623) 5th Earl Marischal. Although there are still a few fishing vessels the harbour today is busy with pleasure-craft. A new role is that of base for the Rescue Section of the Offshore Survival Centre of Robert Gordon's Institute of Technology, which develops new maritime systems. The oldest building, the **tolbooth,** was built in the late 16C by the 5th earl to serve as a storehouse for Dunnottar Castle's supplies.
tc Inside is a small **museum** covering fishing and coopering. In the High Street are the mercat cross and 18C town steeple.

New Town. – In the second half of the 18C a local laird, Robert Barclay of Ury, who had made his fortune in Jamaica, planned a new settlement to the north of the river Carron. The spacious square is still dominated by the market buildings and steeple. A plaque at no 9 Market Square (south side) commemorates **Robert William Thomson** (1822-73) inventor in 1845 of the Pneumatic Tyre, known then as "aerial wheels".

EXCURSIONS

tc **Muchalls Castle.** – *5 miles north of Stonehaven and 3/4 mile off the north bound carriageway of the A92.*

This small laird's house was built from 1619 to 1627by the Burnetts of Crathes. Crow stepped gables, corner turrets and attractive corbelling give a certain charm to the L-shaped house which overlooks the courtyard. Gun loops pierce the enclosing wall. Inside the magnificent **plasterwork ceilings★★** are outstanding. That of the great hall low enough to be examined in detail - combines coats of arms, portrait medallions and pendants within an elaborate design of ribs. The brightly tinctured overmantel (1624) portrays the post-Union (1603) Scottish coat of arms flanked by unusual paired caryatids supporting the ceiling. This chimney is equipped with a laird's lug and hidden staircase. In addition, to two other plasterwork ceilings, the house boasts a secret tunnel to the coast and a ghost, the Green Lady !

The coast road south to Gourdon. – *12 miles south of Stonehaven by the A92.*

★★Dunnottar Castle. – *Description p 80.*

Catterline. – Pop 619. This tiny fishing village with its row of cottages clinging to the clifftops and jagged rocky outcrops on the seashore, has been made famous by the atmospheric canvases of **Joan Eardley** (1921-63) of which no two are alike. From 1950 to her death she portrayed this coastline through the changing seasons with a vigour and freedom of brushwork which matched the rugged nature of the landscape and fierceness of the sea.

tc **Kinneff Old Church.** – *1 mile off the A92, well signposted.*
It was under the floorboads of an earlier church on this site, that the Scottish Regalia was concealed from 1652 to 1660 *(p 80)*.

> *Return to the A92 before taking the B967 to the right. A local road to the left leads down to the church.*

Arbuthnott Church. – This parish church has a lovely example of late Scottish Gothic in the Arbuthnott Aisle. Both the aisle and west end bell tower are 15C. In the churchyard to the left of the entrance, is a memorial stone to James Leslie Mitchell (1901-35), author of the trilogy *A Scots Quair*. Writing under the pen name Lewis Grassic Gibbon, he gave a vivid description of life in the Mearns in the early part of the 20C.

> *Return to the A92 and continue through Inverbervie.*

Gourdon. – Pop 600. Down by the shore this picturesque fishing village is known for long line fishing for haddock and cod.

STRANRAER (Dumfries and Galloway)   Pop 9 853

Michelin map 401 fold 42 – E19

At the head of Loch Ryan, the agricultural market town of Stranraer depends ever increasingly on the ferry service to Larne with two to eight sailings daily. The town is a good base from which to visit the Rhinns.

EXCURSIONS

tc **Castle Kennedy Gardens.** – *3 miles east of Stranraer, on the A75, Dumfries road.*
The natural beauty of the site, a peninsula between two lochs, is an essential part of these gardens where vistas, sweeping lawns and tree-lined avenues are a delight, the more so for their unexpectedness. The ruins are those of Castle Kennedy, onetime seat of the powerful Ayrshire family of the same name. The stronghold had passed in the 17C into the hands of the Ist Earl of Stair or "Curse of Scotland" and it was the **2nd Earl** who created the gardens following the castle's destruction by fire (1716). The earl commissioned **William Adam** to create a formal design for Newliston, his West Lothian seat, but at Castle Kennedy Adam advocated an informal garden to harmonize with the setting. In the words of Samuel Boyse, secretary to Sir John Clerk another contemporary exponent of the natural, the gardens are "Too form'd for Nature - yet too wild for Art". In 1842 following a period of neglect, Loudon restored the gardens to their original aspect, which we see today with the Castle Kennedy ruins, the 19C baronial Lochinch Castle (present seat of the Earls of Stair) and several water features (Round Pond, canal and lochs) all forming the focal points of a vista or an avenue. Different in conception, this garden is undoubtedly at its best during the rhododendron and azalea season.

tc **Glenluce Abbey.** – *10 miles from Stranraer by the Dumfries road the A75. After 9 miles on the A75 turn sharp left at the railway viaduct up a farm road.*

tc **Castle of Park.** – This tower house rising tall in a commanding site overlooking Luce Bay and glen, was built in 1590 by Thomas Hay, son of the last abbot of Glenluce. The door has an inscribed lintel.

> *On the main road again turn left after crossing the river and continue for a mile up the valley.*

Glenluce Abbey. – The abbey was founded in the late 12C by Roland, Lord of Galloway, on a beautiful site in the Water of Luce Valley, befitting a Cistercian establishment. The outstanding features of the ruins are the 15C **chapter house** with some fine sculptural work and the drainage stystem with some of the original earthenware pipes still in place *(see also the display in the custodian's office)*. The abbey has associations with Michael Scott, the 13C wizard. On the north side of the church is Lochinvar's last resting place.

Mull of Galloway. – *48 miles round tour. Leave Stranraer to the south by the A77.*
This drive along quiet back roads explores the southern arm of the Rhinns of Galloway right down to the extremity, the Mull of Galloway. The coutryside is more rugged where small fields are enclosed by stone dykes and where gorse and whin abound. This is dairy country where the Frisian reigns supreme. The splendid coastline is the real attraction where sandy beaches alternate with stretches of rugged cliffs and occasional bays harbour peaceful villages and ports. Bathing in the warmth of the Gulf Stream, the region enjoys Scotland's mildest climate.

Sandhead. – Pop 250. Typical seaside village with great stretches of sandy beach overlooking Luce Bay.

> *Beyond Sandhead take the local road inland to Kirkmadrine Church.*

Kirkmadrine Church. – The porch has been glazed in, to shelter some of Scotland's earliest existing **Christian monuments**. Three of the tombstones bear Latin inscriptions and the Chi-Rho monogram. They date from the 5 and 6C. These stones are reminders of the early Christian mission established at Whithorn *(qv)* and are typical examples of work by the resultant Whithorn School.

tc **Ardwell House Garden.** – Visit when the daffodils are out or the rhododendrons and azaleas are in bloom.

> *Continue to the small village of Drummore from where the B7041 leads to the southernmost tip. The last part of the road is single track with passing places.*

Mull of Galloway. – *Short walk from car park.* Lying on a level with Belfast and Hartlepool, this rugged headland is fringed with 200-250ft cliffs. The waters offshore are notorious for strong tides. Good views of Cumberland and Ireland can be had on a clear day.

> *Continue on the B road to Port Logan.*

Port Logan. – The chief attraction of this small community sheltering behind its
tc embankment, is the **Logan Fish Pond** on the far side of the bay. This 30ft deep rock pool,
once a fish larder for Logan House, is now stocked mostly with cod, tame enough
to be hand fed.

★**Logan Botanic Garden.** – This annexe of the Royal Botanic Garden has a large variety of
tc exotic plants which flourish in the warmth of the Gulf Stream. Impeccably kept with
something to delight everyone, the garden has two main parts, walled and woodland.
Outstanding among the many plants (all well labelled) from warm temperate regions
of the world, are the Cabbage Palms, in reality members of the lily family, and the
Tree Ferns of which two different species are grown.

At Ardwell take the B road to Portpatrick.

Portpatrick. – Pop 540. On the west coast, the peninsula's most important community
is this popular seaside village. The houses climbing the slopes at the back of the bay
overlook the small harbour which in pre-steam days was the terminal for the Irish
crossing. The Southern Upland Way *(p 12)* links Portpatrick to Cockburnspath on the
east coast.

The A77 returns to Stranraer.

★★ TANTALLON CASTLE (Lothian)

Michelin map **401** fold 32 – M 15 – 3 miles east of North Berwick

tc The formidable ruin of Tantallon in its splendid **clifftop site**★★★ facing the Bass,
continues to defy the pounding waves and howling easterly winds, so aptly described
by Scott in his narrative poem *Marmion*.

"... Tantallon vast
Broad, massive, high and stretching far,
And held impregnable in war
On a projecting rock it rose,
And round three sides the ocean flows,
The fourth did battled walls enclose ...".

A Douglas Stronghold. – Although originally the property of the Earls of Fife, it is
renowned in Scottish history as a stronghold of the great house of **Douglas**. It is probable
that William, lst Earl of Douglas was the builder. Other closely associated Douglases
include Archibald the 5th Earl of Angus better known as "Bell the Cat" *(p 146)* and
Archibald 6th Earl of Angus both of whom were besieged by their respective kings
in this stronghold, the latter in his absence. The stronghold fell, following 12 days
of bombardment, to General Monck in February 1651.
Dating from the late 14C, with 16C alterations, Tantallon is one of the great castles
of enclosure. The massive 50ft tall curtain wall links the gatehouse and flanking
circular towers and cuts off the impregnable promontory site. The attractively
weathered red sandstone enhances this rather foreboding, stark ruin.
Two ditches and earthen ramparts defend the landward side and access to the bailey
is by the now ruined Outer Gate. The lectern type dovecot is 17C. The inner ditch
stretches right across the headland at the foot of the curtain walls.

Mid Tower. – In the late 14C a barbican, distinguished by green stone with red string
courses, was added to the gatehouse and followed by an outwork in the 16C. The
Earl of Angus' coat of arms is high up on the forework. Pass through the passage
to the original doorway. To the right is a guardroom and to the left a passage leading
to a turnpike which gives access to the four floors above, each consisting of a single
apartment with garderobe and small adjacent chambers.
The **well** in the close goes down to a depth of 106ft.

East Tower. – The five storeys are reached by a turnpike. At each level there are
apartments with fireplaces, stone benches and mural garderobes.

Douglas Tower. – Above the pit prison with a bedrock floor, are 6 storeys of apartments
similar to those in the East Tower.

Curtain Walls. – Over 12ft thick and 50ft high, they connect the towers by a wall walk
and originally had their own independent stairways with mural chambers. The wall
walk was once roofed over and edged by a parapet wall.

Northern Courtyard Range. – The western part included the Laigh and Long Halls and was
contemporary with the towers and curtain walls. It was altered in the 16C when the
eastern part comprising the ground floor kitchen and bakehouse was added.

THORNHILL (Dumfries and Galloway)   Pop 1 510

Michelin map **401** fold 39 – I18

The wide tree-lined main street of this ducal village is dominated by the Queensberry
Column, crowned by the winged horse of the Queensberrys whose ancestral home
Drumlanrig Castle stands nearby. Thornhill in Mid-Nithsdale is a good base for
exploring the Lowther Hills.

EXCURSION

Lowther Hills. – *41 miles.* This run crosses the Lowthers, an area of scenic grandeur,
once active lead mining country and now hill sheep country.
On leaving Thornhill, Drumlanrig can be glimpsed in its commanding situation away
to the left.
★★**Drumlanrig Castle.** – *Description p 68.*

At Carronbridge, fork right to follow the A702 until the signpost to Durisdeer.

Durisdeer. – Set at the foot of the Lowther Hills this hamlet is pinpointed by its church tower. In the Queensberry Aisle *(enter from round the back)* are the **Queensberry Marbles,** an elaborate monument to the Union Duke *(p 69).* **John Nost** (fl 1686-1729) has portrayed with amazing delicacy, in white marble, the nonchalantly reclining figure of the 2nd Duke and the recumbent Duchess in all their magnificent elegance.

> *Return to the A702 which makes straight for the hill mass of the Lowthers with the mast on Lowther Hill (2 379ft-725m) pinpointing one of the highest summits.*

Strategically important in the past as a route to the north for armies, raiders and cattle, the **Dalveen Pass** (1 140ft-347m) is today negotiated with ease by road. From the flat valley floor, steep, treeless slopes rise to heights of 1 800ft. Once in the Daer Water Valley the slopes are gentler and the summits lower.

> *At Elvanfoot branch left onto the Leadhills road, the B7040.*

On either side of this steadily rising road can be seen the scars of lead mining.

Leadhills. – Pop 331. At an altitude of 1 350ft-411m lead mining was the mainstay of this village, where rows of miner's cottages face one another across the valley. This village is known for its miner's library founded in 1741 and as the birthplace of **Allan Ramsay** (1686-1758) author of *The Gentle Shepherd,* a pioneer poet in his use of the Scots language and father of the portrait painter.

Wanlockhead. – Pop 130. This scattered village was the centre of a thriving lead mining industry. Known in all probability by the Romans, it is reputed that local gold was used in James V's crown and for his "bonnet pieces". *(illustration p 117).* Between 1680 and 1934 lead ore was mined and smelted locally with a period of renewed activity *tc* in the 1950s. The **Scottish Lead Mining Museum** in its mines' forge museum presents the history of Scottish lead mining and displays on local mining and social relics. The open-air section includes a mining trail with a unique wooden beam engine and conducted tours of an 18C lead mine.

The road follows the Mennock Pass, a narrow wooded glen to reach the A76.

> *Turn left towards Thornhill.*

THURSO (Highland) Pop 9 060

Michelin map **401** fold 3 – J8

A busy resort in summer Thurso, astride the river of the same name, overlooks Thurso Bay. The town makes a good centre for visiting the north coast from Durness to Duncansby Head and even for a trip to the Orkneys.

tc **Folk Museum.** – *High Street.* Local collection.

EXCURSION

North coast from Thurso to Durness. – *74 miles by the A836 then the A838.* Bleak moorland scenery gives way to the glories of coastal scenery beyond, composed of an ever changing pattern of sandy bays, lochs and headlands.

Scrabster. – Terminal port for the car ferry to Stromness in the Orkneys *(see the current Michelin Red Guide to Great Britain and Ireland).* Flagstone fencing can still be seen in the vicinity.

tc **Dounreay.** – The Dounreay Exhibition Area comprises a picnic area and an explanatory exhibition. Tours to the Prototype Fast Reactor leave from the exhibition area. The Dounreay Fast Reactor (DFR) with its large pale green globe, operated from 1959 to 1977 when it was de-commissioned. Alongside is the Prototype Fast Reactor (PFR) an experimental station for the development of future commercial fast reactors. The reactor uses a fuel mixture of uranium and plutonium with liquid sodium metal as a medium to transfer heat from the reactor core.

(P Lorne/Explorer)

The coast near Durness

Melvich Bay. – From the War Memorial behind the hotel in the crofting community of Melvich there is a splendid **view** over Melvich Bay with the sand bar. The island of Hoy is visible in the distance.

The road beyond Melvich is single track with passing places.

Cross the River Strathy which opens into another sandy estuary, Strathy Bay.

★**Strathy Point.** – *15 min walk from the car park to the point.*
There are excellent **views**★★★ along the coast to the east of Strathy Bay in the foreground, with further out Dounreay and Hoy in the distance.

The landscape then becomes scoured and hummocky with the stately outline of the granite peaks of **Ben Loyal**★★ (2 504ft-764m) ahead, rising above the plateau surface.

Bettyhill. – Pop 177. This is one of the crofting communities which originated at the time of the clearances when crofters were evicted, in this case from Strathnaver, to make way for sheep. Many emigrated while others tried to eke out an existence in seashore communities. The story of the clearances is the subject of an exhibition in *tc* **Farr Church.**

The road then follows the sandy estuary of **Torrisdale Bay**★, crosses the river, then climbs out of Strathnaver to ascend to the scoured plateau surface dotted with reed choked lochs. Go round Cnoc an Fhreiceadain and just before reaching Coldbackie there are excellent **views**★★ of the great sea loch, the Kyle of Tongue, with Rabbit Islands in the middle.

Tongue. – Pop 129. Small village on the shores of the sea loch.
The Kyle of Tongue is bridged by a causeway which offers a new view inland towards Ben Loyal and ahead the ruined Mackay stronghold perched on an eminence.

The road is double track beyond Tongue.

The more regular outline of Ben Hope appears on the horizon. Peat banks are visible from time to time. On the descent there are glimpses of Loch Hope stretching away to the left. From the west side of Loch Hope there are fine views of the loch stretching away to **Ben Hope**★ (3 040ft-927m) in the background. Only slightly further on a magnificent **view**★★★ unfolds of Loch Eriboll, another deeply penetrating sea loch.

The road becomes single track on the east side.
Do not impede the flow of traffic by parking in passing places.

Go round the loch.
Sangobeg has a lovely sandy beach.

Durness. – *Description p 81.*

Smoo Cave. – An outcrop of well jointed limestones in the Durness vicinity accounts for the presence of this cave and the sandy beaches. The waters of the Allt Smoo plunge down a sink hole to reappear at sea level at the mouth of the outer cave. The two inner caves are accessible only to equipped potholers.

TORPHICHEN (Lothian)   Pop 615

Michelin map **401** fold 31 – J16

In the village of Torphichen there are the remains of the Knights Hospitallers principal Scottish seat.

The Order in Scotland. – The earliest foundation was made by David I in 1153 at Torphichen. In that turbulent age "The Privilege of St John" or Right of Sanctuary delimited by a central stone, in the neighbouring churchyard, and four boundary stones, was frequently invoked. 1554 saw the suppression of the Order and the creation of a temporal lordship which was granted to the last prior. The Sovereign Order of Malta was re-established in England in 1831, as was St John's as a Protestant Order by Royal Charter in 1888. A Scottish Priory followed in 1947.

tc **Preceptory.** – Of the original 12C building , the transepts and central tower remain, adjoining an 18C parish church which occupies the site of the nave. Externally the bell tower and transept gables are crow stepped, the result of 15C alterations. The foundations of the domestic buildings lie to the north.
Inside, rib vaulting covers the transepts and built into the walled up west arch is a monument to Sir George Dundas. A turnpike staircase *(45 steps)* leads to the upper chambers (exhibition on the Hospitallers and some sculptural fragments) and the bell tower.

EXCURSION

★**Cairnpapple Hill.** – 1000ft-305m. *1 1/2 miles from Torphichen. The narrow*
tc winding road is well signposted.
This site, now clearly marked out since excavations in 1947, is unique in that five distinct phases are evident (a model and descriptive noticeboards are inside the custodian's hut). The earliest monument of the Late Neolithic period (2500-2000 BC) delimited by a series of holes with associated cremations, was altered in the Copper Age (2000-1650 BC) with the addition of an outer bank, ditch and other stone holes in an oval formation, ie the stone circle (1-24).
The central part of the monument is under a cement dome and a ladder leads down into the interior. The early Bronze Age 1 (1650-1500 BC) is represented by a large burial cairn bounded by a kerb of twenty-one stones with two cists in the middle. The Middle Bronze Age 1 (1400-1200 BC) is an enlargement of the kerb with 2 related burials, while the final phase consisting of four graves on the eastern side orientated east-west is probably Early Iron Age.
An extensive **view** stretches from the Bass Rock in the east to the mountains of Arran in the west.

tc The white mass of Traquair peeps out from its tree cover, on the south bank of the Tweed. The long and peaceful history of house and family is vividly illustrated by a wealth of relics, treasures, traditions and legends.

Royal hunting lodge. – As early as 1107 Alexander I stayed at Traquair which remained a royal residence up to the 13C, used initially as a hunting seat for the surrounding forests. The favourite residence of William the Lion, it was transformed during the Wars of Independence into a Border peel or fortified tower, becoming one of a series of strategically placed strongholds such as Neidpath and Elibank. In the late 13C the tower was in English hands and both Edward I and II stayed here, but it was returned to the Scottish Crown in the early 14C. James III gave Traquair to two of his favourites, firstly Robert Lord Boyd and then his Master of Music, William Rogers but not before the latter, in turn, had sold the property to James Earl of Buchan uncle to the King.

Tower house to mansion. – The Earl's son **James Stuart** inherited in 1491 and the present owners are direct descendants. James' plans to extend were cut short by his untimely death at Flodden in 1513 and it was not until the 16 and 17C centuries that the original peel was transformed into a mansion house. James' grandson **Sir John Stuart**, 4th Laird of Traquair was Captain of Mary Queen of Scots' Bodyguard and even played host to his Queen and Lord Darnley in 1566 thus explaining the many personal belongings and associations with this period.

Another notable figure was **John Stuart, 1st Earl of Traquair** (1600-59) who rose to the high office of Lord High Treasurer, but misfortune befell him and loss of office followed, obliging the earl to return to his estate and preoccupy himself with home affairs. He changed the course of the Tweed and added a storey to the house. It was during his son, John's lifetime that the Catholic faith was adopted by the family, a tradition which has been maintained and was to make Traquair an active centre for the Jacobite cause in the 18C. **Charles, 4th Earl** (1659-1741) a staunch Jacobite sympathiser married Lady Mary Maxwell uniting the Maxwell and Stuart estates. One of the Maxwell seats was the now demolished Terregles House in Dumfriesshire and many of its treasures are at Traquair. Charles commissioned James Smith to make certain alterations (1695-9). The side wings were remodelled, a wrought iron screen erected in the forecourt, a formal garden was created and given two attractive pavilions with ogee shaped roofs. Since then the exterior of Traquair has remained unaltered.

VISIT *time : 1 1/2 hours*

Ground floor. – The oak armorial in the hall displaying Scotland's royal arms dates from Mary Queen of Scots' 1566 visit. The corner cupboards in the panelled still room contain Chinese and English porcelain. The elm chairs are part of a Scottish made set dating from around 1750.

The main staircase leads off the hall. Note at the bottom the vigorously carved oak door from Terregles House, a second is in the National Museum of Antiquities.

First floor. – The width of the drawing room gives some indication of the narrowness of the building. Other noteworthy features include the fragments of 18C painted beams, the 1651 Andreas Ruckers harpsichord, and portraits of the *4th Earl*, *Dryden* and another by George Jamesone (*c* 1620). Pass through the dressing room to reach the King's Room, dominated by the splendidly ornate yellow State Bed, again from Terregles and said to be the one used by Mary Queen of Scots. The bedspread was the work of Mary and her four Marys, and the cradle was used by her son, King James VI. Beside the powder closet is the door giving access to the unevenly stepped, steep narrow stairs of the original 12C tower and the secret stairs.

Second floor. – This may be reached by the secret or main stairs. The Museum Room display includes a variety of historical documents, mementoes and other interesting items such as the 1530 fragment of wall painting and a collection of Amen glass.

Return to the main stairs and go up another flight.

Third floor. – The Library remains almost intact as formed in 1700-40 with books still bearing the mark of their shelf number and place. Adjoining is a second library with 19C works. At the end of the corridor the Priest's Room originally served as the chapel and it was in these cramped quarters that the chaplain lived his furtive existence as testified by the hidden stairs, with the false cupboard entrance.

Return to the ground floor.

Take the passage to the left to see the vaulted chamber of the original construction. This is where the cattle used to be herded in times of raids.

South wing. – In the dining room there is another group of family portraits, with Medina's one of the *4th Earl and Countess of Traquair* who had 17 children, and another of the Jacobite, *Charles 5th Earl*. Above the fireplace is the *1st Earl* with the rod of office as Lord High Treasurer.

North wing. – Following the Catholic Emancipation Act of 1829 the chapel replaced the priest's room as the place of worship. The set of twelve 16C carved wood panels depicts episodes from the Life of Christ.

Outbuildings. – Next to the chapel is the reception centre and shop while above is a fully equipped wash house. The brew house below the chapel, is adjoined by the stables and a grain loft. The site of the Well Pool marks the former bed of the Tweed and the grounds include a choice of woodland walks.

The Steekit Yetts. – This famous entrance otherwise known as the Bear Gates (1737-8) lies at the end of a grassy tree-lined avenue. Tradition has it that the gates were closed by the 5th Earl on the departure of Bonnie Prince Charlie with a vow to reopen them only on the Restoration of a Stuart.

Michelin map **401** folds 26 and 27 – G15

One of Scotland's most famous beauty spots, the Trossachs conjures up an idyllic landscape of great scenic beauty where rugged, but not so lofty mountains, and their wooded slopes are reflected in the sparkling waters of the lochs.

"So wondrous and wild, the whole might seem
The scenery of a fairy dream".

The Trossachs proper are delimited by the head of Loch Achray in the east, the foot of Loch Katrine to the west, Ben An (1750ft-533m) to the north and Ben Venue (2 393ft-727m) to the south. The term is now more generally taken to cover a wider area reaching from Loch Venachar in the east to the shores of Loch Lomond.

Proximity to the great urban populations of Edinburgh, Glasgow and the Central Valley, combined with ease of accessibility, make this a most popular area with locals and tourists alike. To appreciate to the full the solitude and scenic splendours it is advisable to visit early in the morning when the coaches are not yet about and driving on the narrow roads is still a pleasure.

The Fairy Folk. – Local folklore includes such supernatural creatures as the Water Bull of Loch Katrine and the Water Horse of Loch Venacher. An Aberfoyle minister, the Reverend Robert Kirk, committed to print their secrets in *The Secret Commonwealth of Elfs, Fawns and Fairies* (1691) following a prolonged stay with the fairies. Another more humorous tale is that of the first commercial venture to ply the waters of Loch Katrine with a steamboat, *The Water Witch*. The offending boat sank to tales of goblins and monsters, and the Highlanders' oared-galley trade continued to flourish.

Rob Roy MacGregor. – An altogther more substantial figure was that of **Rob Roy** (1671-1734) outlaw and leader of the MacGregors. Much of this rugged terrain was MacGregor country and is closely associated with his exploits, which Sir Walter Scott recounted in *Rob Roy* (1818). Sir Walter was instrumental in popularizing the Trossachs with his romantic poem *The Lady of the Lake*. Such was the public desire to follow in the footsteps of Scott's fictional characters that the Duke of Montrose built **Duke's Road** in 1820, a connecting road north from Aberfoyle. Other famous visitors included the Wordsworths and Coleridge in 1830 following which Wordsworth wrote *To a Highland Girl.*

Queen Elizabeth Forest Park. – As early as 1794 planned forestry was being practised in the vicinity of Lochs Ard and Chon with tanning, building materials and fuel as the main products. In 1928 the Forestry Commission purchased land south of Loch Ard, the initial step in the creation of the Queen Elizabeth Forest Park. Designated as such in 1953 the park has 32 000 acres of plantations out of its total 41 973 acres. Loch Ard, Archray and Rowardennan forests stretch from the Trossachs proper to the eastern shore of Loch Lomond. The great tourist popularity of the area emphasizes the importance of the Forestry Commission's role in maintaining a balance between recreation and conservation. For amenities provided within the Forest Park's boundaries see the Forest Park Visitor Centre *(p 198)*.

Excursions. – The area described here under the heading Trossachs has been intentionally extended towards Loch Lomond in the west and in the south to the Lake of Menteith for the convenience of the round tour described below, which has Callander as its starting point. An alternative day tour combining boat and bus trips covers the western part of the area, starting from Balloch.

ROUND TOUR STARTING FROM CALLANDER
59 miles – allow a day including visits and boat trip – local map p 198

★**Callander.** – *Description p 53.*

> *Leave Callander by the A84 in the direction of Crianlarich (Lochearnhead). After one mile branch left to take The Trossachs road, the A821.*

This road climbs up with the great shoulder of **Ben Ledi** (2 882ft-879m) on the right. On looking backwards Callander can be seen nestling in the valley floor. As the road moves round the lower slopes of Ben Ledi, it approaches the 4 mile-long, **Loch Venachar** *(parking and picnic places).*

Brig o'Turk. – This widely scattered village at the mouth of Glen Finglas is closely associated with the Ruskins and Millais who spent an extended holiday in the area in 1853. Brig o'Turk was one of the early summer haunts of the Glasgow Boys *(qv)*. Games Guthrie's *Highland Funeral (Art Gallery and Museum Kelvingrove)* depicts an episode of the period.

Once across the Finglas Water the road enters the **Achray Forest** part of the Queen Elizabeth Forest Park. After the initial discovery of a smaller loch, Loch Achray only passing glimpses can be had of this, while the second great peak of the area, **Ben Venue** (2 393ft-727m) stands out in the distance with the white form of Loch Achray Hotel at its feet. Pass on the right the castellated 20C reconstruction of the Trossachs Hotel, originally named Drunkie Hotel and changed due to a visit of Queen Victoria. At the end of the Loch the road continues on to Loch Katrine (dead end).

★★**Loch Katrine.** – *1 mile from the A821 to the pier and car park which is reserved for boat passengers. No access round loch for vehicles.*

Other than hill walking the only but very rewarding way to discover this famous loch *tc* is to take a **boat trip** on the *SS Sir Walter Scott*.

The loch 10 miles long and 2 at its widest has been Glasgow's water supply since 1859, when Queen Victoria officiated at the inauguration. On the north eastern slopes of the twin peaked Ben Venue are Corrie na Urisgean (Goblin's Cave) the traditional meeting place of Scotland's goblins, and Bealach nam Bo (Pass of the Cattle), a route much favoured by the drover Rob Roy when returning home with cattle. Ellen's Isle (Eilean Molach) figures in Scott's *The Lady of the Lake.* The boat turns about at Stronachlachar from where a road leads westwards to Inversnaid on the shores of

197

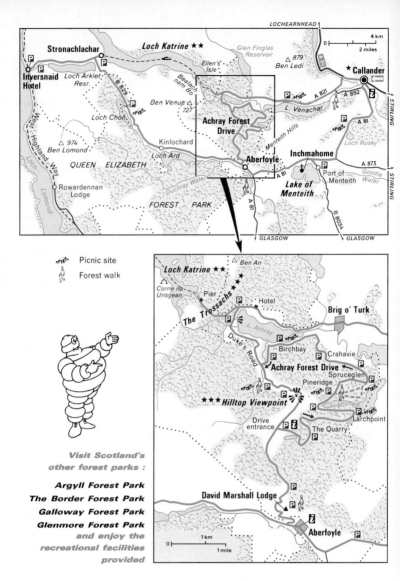

Picnic site

Forest walk

Visit Scotland's
other forest parks :

Argyll Forest Park
The Border Forest Park
Galloway Forest Park
Glenmore Forest Park
and enjoy the
recreational facilities
provided

Loch Lomond. Glen Gyle at the head of Loch Katrine was the birthplace of Rob Roy
(p 197) and on the north shore is a MacGregor burial place. Factor's Isle, another Rob
Roy haunt is where the outlaw held the Duke of Montrose's factor, Baillie Nicol Jarvie,
in reprisal for having evicted Rob Roy's family.

> *Return to the junction with the A821 and take Duke's Road, in the Aberfoyle*
> *direction to pass round the head of Loch Achray.*

From level with the **car park** there is a good view up the loch. Once round to the south
side the road climbs with good views over Loch Achray.

★★★**Hilltop viewpoint.** – *Park at the roadside ; 5 min climb to viewfinder.*
There is an excellent **panorama★★★** of the Trossachs, encompasing Ben Venue, Loch
Katrine with its mountain ring, Ben An, Finglas Reservoir, Ben Ledi with Brig o'Turk
at its feet, Loch Venachar and due east round to the Menteith Hills. In the immediate
foreground is Loch Drunkie in the heart of Achray Forest.

tc **Achray Forest Drive.** – This seven mile long forest road makes an excellent outing for
those wanting an afternoon away from it all *(ample parking and picnic places with
a choice of walks)* but since it is through forested countryside it has few views of the
surrounding countryside.
Away on the right can be seen scars of now disused slate quarries.

tc **David Marshall Lodge.** – A Forest Park Visitor Centre *(exhibition on the park and famous
people associated with it ; information centre for park amenities open to the public).*
A variety of trails are open to the public including the Fairy Trail centred on Doon
Hill, the site from where the Rev Robert Kirk was spirited away by the fairy folk.
The road then descends into Aberfoyle leaving behind the mountainous rim of the
Central Highlands.

Aberfoyle. – Pop 593. A clachan in the time of Rob Roy, Aberfoyle was made famous
as the meeting place of Rob and Nicol Jarvie. Today the village is busy with tourists
in summer.

> *Leave Aberfoyle to the west by the B829, a single track road.*

This scenic road, ending beside Inversnaid Hotel on Loch Lomond, makes a pleasant
drive through the southwestern part of the Queen Elizabeth Forest Park.

Loch Ard. – The road along the north shore runs close to the water's edge of Loch Ard described by Queen Victoria in 1869 as "a fine long loch with trees of all kinds overhanging the road, heather making all pink, bracken, rocks, high hills of such fine shape and trees growing up them as in Switzerland. Altogether the whole view was lovely". The scenery has lost none of its attraction with the southern shore clothed with the trees of Loch Ard Forest. The prominent outline of Ben Lomond looms large on the horizon. There is a fine view of Loch Chon, backed by the 'Arrochar Alps' in the distance.

Loch Chon. – This is the smaller of the two lochs.

At the road junction the branch to the right leads to Stronachlachar.

Stronachlachar. – On the south shore of Loch Katrine. The *SS Sir Walter Scott* makes a stop at this point.

Return to the junction and carry straight on.

Loch Arklet. – *Reservoir, no access to the water's edge.* This artificial loch lies in a glacially created hanging valley.
The ruins to the right are those of Inversnaid barracks built in the early 18C to curb the MacGregors.

Inversnaid. – On Loch Lomondside, the hotel overlooks the pier, one of the stopping
tc places of the steamer cruises *(p 152)*. The far side of Loch Lomond is dominated by the peaks of the Cobbler, Bens Vorlich, Vane and Ime. The West Highland Way follows this shore of Loch Lomond, on its way north to Fort William.

Return towards Aberfoyle, leaving to the east. At the junction with the A81 turn left.

The road skirts the great rounded spine of the Menteith Hills.

Lake of Menteith. – On the northern edge of Flanders Moss the lake is one of the venues for the national bonspiel, the Grand Match between north and south, organized by the Royal Caledonian Curling Club.

Pass the lake and then turn right in the direction of Arnprior. The car park is half a mile down the road.

tc **Inchmahome Priory.** – *This is an island monastery. To attract the ferryman's attention when he is on the island, turn the white board on the jetty.*
The mid-13C ruins include the church of the Augustinian priory, with its deeply recessed west doorway strongly resembling the one at Dunblane and the chapter house which shelters an unusual **double effigy★** tomb monument. Mary Queen of Scots spent some time here in 1547 prior to embarking for France.

Return to Callander by the A81.

The main car parks are indicated on the town plans.

★★ The TWEED Valley (Borders)

Michelin map **401** folds 35 and 36 – K, L and M17

This Border river is one of Scotland's longest and certainly one of the most beautiful, and the finest landscapes are those it adorns with its long vistas and graceful curves. Added to this is the presence of a series of famous landmarks on its banks which make it a first class attraction for tourists.
The **Glorious Tweed Festival** *(p 212)* is a varied programme of events celebrating the Borders heritage.

HISTORICAL AND GEOGRAPHICAL NOTES

River and landscapes. – The Tweed, third longest after the Tay and Clyde, rises in the Tweedsmuir Hills and ends in England, having served as frontier for part of the way. The Tweed basin is ringed by hills with the Cheviots to the south, Southern Uplands to the west and Lammermuir Hills to the north. Tributaries include the Yarrow, Ettrick, Gala, Leader and Teviot.
In its upper reaches the Tweed cuts discordantly across the major structures and its valley is constricted and irregular. In its middle reaches, between the uplands and the Merse, it is broad with majestic curves, overlooked by ruined abbeys and prosperous Border towns.

In the past. – From earliest times the region was favoured as an area of settlement. Iron Age and Roman forts testify to this. Monastic houses chose its fertile haughlands as ideal sites. The area is best known for the troubled times of Border raids and reiving as recounted in the ballads. The Border Laws accepted by both kingdoms were enforced by Wardens of the March, three for each country. It was the responsibility of these officers, often hereditary, to repel invasion and keep the peace. The Tweed valley has a rich heritage from this period with the traditional Border peels or fortified tower houses. Outstanding examples are Neidpath, Smailholm and Greenknowe. The memory of these times is also kept alive by the common ridings *(p 28)* when groups of citizens ride the burgh boundaries.

The Tweed today. – The valley is noted primarily for its agriculture with hill sheep farming on the uplands and mixed arable farms on the flatter and richer till soils of the Merse *(qv)*. The traditional woollen and knitwear industries are of paramount importance to the Tweed towns. The Tweed, Queen of the Salmon rivers, and its tributaries provide several hundred miles of freshwater fishing with a possible catch of 16 different species of fish, and stillwater or loch fishing for trout, pike and perch.

THE MIDDLE TWEED from Kelso to Neidpath Castle
40 miles – allow a day

★**Kelso**. – *Description p 137.*

> *Leave Kelso by the A699 which follows the south bank.*

Floors Castle can be seen in its attractive terraced setting on the north bank. Pass on the left the site of Roxburgh Castle.

St Boswells. – Pop 1 002. The village was once the site of an important livestock fair.

> *Take the local road B6404 to the northeast to cross the Tweed and visit one of the Border monasteries.*

★★**Dryburgh Abbey.** – *Description p 69.*

> *Continue by the local road B6356 which skirts Bemersyde Hill.*

★★**Scott's View.** – *Description p 156.*

> *Turn left onto the local road and once under the main road cross the river to take the B6361.*

Pass the 19-span Leaderfoot Viaduct. Further on a monument, to the left of the road, marks the site of the Roman settlement of Trimontium.

★**Melrose.** – *Description p 155.*

> *Leave to the west by the A7 and at the second roundabout follow signs to Abbotsford.*

★★**Abbotsford.** – *Description p 32.*

> *Once back to the A7 cross the Tweed.*

Galashiels. – Pop 13 314. On the narrow floor of the Gala Water this busy tweed and knitwear manufacturing and shopping centre is one of the largest Border towns. The **Braw Lad's Gathering** *(p 28)* is another of the common ridings.

> *Continue by the A72 to rise out of the constricted valley of the Gala Water to go round Meigle Hill.*

Clovenfords. – Pop 270. The hotel, once a coaching inn, was patronised by Scott who came to fish the Tweed. This hamlet was the site of the Tweed Vineries, where the Duke of Buccleuch's gardeners produced the famous Clovenford Tweed grapes.

> *The A72 then follows the north bank quite closely as the forested valley sides move in.*

The valley is still quite wide and pastoral at this point.

tc **Walkerburn.** – Pop 842. This small mill town is the home of the **Scottish Museum of Woollen Textiles.** The history of textiles is traced from the cottage industry through the Industrial Revolution to the present day. Around the room of the weaver's cottage are a series of hand and power operated machines, exhibits on how fields and hedgerows provided the old dyes, the evolution of cloth from single colours, the first black and white mixtures including the black and white shepherd check adopted by Sir Walter Scott as the Scott tartan, and other tartans.

Innerleithen. – Pop 2 533. In a lovely setting at the meeting of Leithen Water with the River Tweed, wide and meandering at this point, the small woollen-textile town of Innerleithen prospered from a modest rural village, following the opening of the first mill in 1790 by Alexander Brodie. The medicinal merits of the waters although known were popularized by Sir Walter Scott, in *St Ronan's Well.*

> *Take the B709 to the left in Innerleithen to reach Traquair on the south bank.*

★★**Traquair House.** – *Description p 196.*

The ruined form of Cardrona Tower can be seen on the far side.

Peebles. – Pop 5 884. This pleasant and peaceful town makes a good excursion centre for exploring the Tweeddale countryside. It was a flourishing spa in the 19C.

tc The **Tweeddale Museum** *(Chambers Institution first floor)* is a small local museum presenting a number of temporary displays throughout the year.

tc **Neidpath Castle.** – This 14C tower house is dramatically situated on a rocky outcrop overlooking the Tweed. It is of the traditional Scottish L-plan and an interesting example of the adaptation of a medieval tower house to 17C requirements.

★ ULLAPOOL (Highland)   Pop 807
Michelin map **401** fold 10 – E10

The white houses of the fishing port and resort of Ullapool make a most attractive picture, set on the shore of Loch Broom. In summer the waterfront is a lively throng of yachters and holidaymakers. Ullapool makes an ideal touring centre for the Wester Ross coast and is an unrivalled centre for sea angling.

The village was laid out in the late 18C by the British Fisheries Society and flourished as a fishing port during the herring boom. Fishing is still an important activity, based on the Minch fishery and in season the trawlers anchor in the loch while a fleet of factory ships can usually be seen in attendance at the mouth of Loch Broom. The port is also terminal for the car ferry to Stornoway *(access : see the current Michelin Red Guide Great Britain and Ireland)*, and a haven for many small pleasure craft in summer.

EXCURSIONS

tc **Boat trips to the Summer Isles.** – Various boats sail to this group of offshore islands where seals and seabirds are the principal attractions. For further details apply to the tourist information office in the car ferry terminal or to the various huts on the waterfront.

★★Falls of Measach. – *11 miles by the A835.*
The road follows the northern shore of **Loch Broom★★** in its most pleasantly attractive mountain setting. The loch sides are dotted with houses and traces of former field patterns are visible on the south side. From a point near the head of the loch there are particularly attractive views both up and down this 21 mile long loch.

★★Falls of Measach. – In the wooded cleft of the mile long **Corrieshalloch Gorge★** the waters of the River Droma make a spectacular sight as they drop over 150 feet. The bridge over the chasm and a viewing platform provide excellent vantage points.

★★Northwards to Lochinver. – *37 miles.* Although the run follows the main road it passes through splendid scenery punctuated by some of the most impressive peaks.

Take the A835 to the north, out of Ullapool.

Just before Morefield there is a very fine **view★★** of Ullapool below in its lochside setting with beyond the blue waters of Loch Broom stretching away to its mountain fringe. From the lay-by on the top of the rise a path *(7 mins)* leads out to the point of a craggy promontory from where there is a **view★** of Loch Broom, the outer bay of Loch Broom, the anchorage for factory ships in season, and the Summer Isles in the distance.

Ardmair. – Hamlet on the shore of Loch Kanaird.
Before entering the small valley look back to the view over Isle Martin in Loch Kanaird, and out to sea. The road crosses Strath Kanaird, and Ben More Coigach (2 438ft-743m) rises to the left as sheer as a cliff wall.

tc **Knockan Information Centre.** – The centre is on the edge of the Inverpolly National Nature Reserve covering an area of 26 827 acres. This glacially scoured countryside with its many lochs and lochans, the largest of which is Loch Stonascaig, has three important landmarks, the peaks of **Cul Mor** (2786ft-849m), **Cul Beag** (2523ft-769m) and **Stac Pollaidh** (2010ft-613m). These upstanding masses of Torridonian Sandstone lie on a base of Lewisian gneiss. The geological sequence exposed at Knockan Cliff is explained on the nature cum geological trail from the centre. From the centre there is a view across the main road of the main peaks, with from left to right Cul Beag, Stac Pollaidh and Cul Mor with its whitish quartzite summit.
Before reaching Ledmore junction there is a view to the left over the waters of Cam Loch to the sheer slopes of **Suilven** (2399ft-731m), a twin peaked mountain when seen from the north or south.

Turn left at Ledmore junction to take the A837.

The road passes Loch Awe and its outlet the river Loanan with to left and right the majestic forms of **Canisp** (2779ft-846m) and the rounded outliers of **Ben More Assynt** (3273ft-998m). The Inchnadamph area at the head of Loch Assynt is a Cambrian limestone outcrop noted for its underground features. To visit

(P Roy/Explorer)

Highland farm

tc the **Inchnadamph Nature Reserve** visitors must obtain prior permission from Assynt Estate Office. Prior to the forking of the lochside road there is a splendid view of the ruins of Ardvreck Castle, a 16C MacLeod stronghold. Following his capture in 1650 the Marquess of Montrose was imprisoned here before being taken to Edinburgh and executed.

★★Loch Assynt. – The road along this 6 mile long loch is particularly scenic. The waters are flanked to the left by Beinn Gharbh, with at times Canisp peeping from behind, and to the right the lofty peak of **Quinag** (2654ft-808m).
The road follows the loch's abrupt change of direction and then the winding River Inver across a hummocky, loch dotted landscape to come out at Lochinver.

★Lochinver. – Pop 283. Set round the head of a sea loch, this attractive village with its mountainous backdrop is best seen from the sea. It is a busy holiday centre, in particular for the outstandingly beautiful scenery of the Stoer Peninsula, with its many charming crofting communities and sandy coves. The port is a haven for a busy fishing fleet and pleasure boats.

Join us in our never ending task of keeping up to date.
Send us your comments and suggestions, please.

Michelin Tyre Public Limited Company,
Tourism Department,
DAVY HOUSE – Lyon Road – HARROW
MIDDLESEX HA1 2 DQ.

Michelin map 🔢 – folds 10 and 14 – D 11

The Atlantic seabord of Wester Ross includes such notable areas of Highland scenery as Applecross, Torridon and Gairloch. The scenery is wild and dramatic with magnificent mountains and placid lochs as the basic elements of the landscape. Explore the area from any one of the main touring centres, Kyle of Lochalsh, Gairloch or Ullapool. Discover the rugged beauty of a wild and rocky landscape, the splendour of majestic mountains (Beinn Eighe, Liathach, Slioch and An Teallach), the beauty of Lochs Maree, Torridon, Broom and Ewe and the charm of small isolated communities like Plockton, Poolewe, Kinlochewe and Applecross. Take the time to walk or climb, and sail or fish, to enjoy to the full this glorious area.

★★★From Kyle of Lochalsh to Gairloch

102 miles – allow a day

The itinerary described covers 102 miles although there are alternatives which reduce the mileage to 74. This route covers some of the finest Wester Ross scenery namely the shores of Loch Maree, the Torridon area and the fastness of the Applecross peninsula. This is a land of incomparable mountains, of lochs and seashore, of woods and moorland, where all come together in nearly perfect proportions. Parts of the route are busy roads in the tourist season but other stretches still permit the luxury of enjoying it all in solitude. Keep the petrol tank well topped up.

Kyle of Lochalsh. – *Description p 144.*

> *Leave Kyle to the north by the coast road which has good views seawards to Skye with the Cuillins prominent on the skyline.*

★**Plockton.** – Pop 425. This most attractive village, with its palm tree-lined main street has an ideal site facing east overlooking a sheltered bay. Originally a refugee settlement at the time of the clearances, it is now a holiday centre popular for yachting and windsurfing.

> *At Achmore take the A890 to the left.*

Pass, down on the shore, Stromeferry a former rail head and ferry point. The lochside road on the southern shore has fine views of the loch.

Loch Carron. – This sea loch has two branches, Loch Kishorn and Upper Loch Carron, backed by the glen of the same name.

> *At the junction take the A896 to the left.*

Loch Carron. – Pop 204. Small linear settlement down on the loch shore.

> *Follow the A896 as it branches to the right beyond Lochcarron and rises to cross moorland and then take a narrow valley down to the shore of Loch Kishorn.*

On the far side are the Applecross mountains, from left to right, are Meal Gorm (2 328ft-710m), Sgurr a' Chaorachain (2539ft-776m), forming the sides of the valley to be ascended, and Beinn Bhàn (2938ft-896m). Once round the head of Loch Kishorn, an arm of Loch Carron, the oil platform construction site is on the right.

> *The A896 is a possible short cut to Shieldaig. The itinerary follows the narrow road to the left to cross the Applecross Peninsula via Bealach-na Bo.*

The route has hairpin bends and 1 : 4 gradients and is not recommended for learner drivers, caravans or heavy vehicles. The pass is impassable in wintry conditions. The splendour of the views well rewards those prepared to make the journey.

Bealach-na Bo. – 2 053ft-626m. The road winds upwards then rises gradually following the east flank. Striated rock and scree slopes are overlooked by rocky overhangs. Hairpin bends allow the final ascent of the back wall of the corrie. The **vista★★** framed by the hanging valley is spectacular with below, Lochs Kishorn, Carron and Alsh and Skye in the distance.

The rocky moorland surface is dotted with lochans. From the car park there are superb **views★★★**westwards of Skye, the Cuillins and the fringing islands.

The descent to Applecross and the coast is more gradual.

Applecross. – Pop 235. On a bay with a popular red sandy beach. This was the site in the 7C of St Maelrubha's monastery.

The coastal road has good views across the Inner Sound to Raasay and Rona with Skye beyond.

> *Continue round the south shore of Lochs Torridon, Sheildaig and Upper Loch Torridon.*

Torridon. – The village lies at the foot of Liathach at the head of Upper Loch Torridon.

tc **Torridon Countryside Centre.** – The centre has an audiovisual introduction to the Torridon area. Nearby is a small deer museum. In addition, information is available on climbing and walking routes. Remember these mountains can be dangerous and are only for the experienced, fit and properly equipped. Changeable weather makes them treacherous. Always leave behind a detail of routes and objectives with an estimated time of return.

> *The A896 is single track with passing places.*

Glen Torridon. – The glen leads through a flat bottomed glacial valley. The lower part of the glen is overlooked on the left by **Liathach** (3 456ft-1 054m) meaning Grey One, with its seven tops, another mountain of impressive dimensions. The valley on the right, containing Loch Clair, leads through to Glen Carron *(no through road for cars).* The imposing range of **Beinn Eighe** (3 309ft-1 010m) to the left is a long ridge of seven peaks, the most easterly ones have a whitish quartizite capping.

Kinlochewe. – Pop 85. The village has retained the loch's original name and is today known as a good centre for climbing, hill walking and fishing.

> *Take the A832 to the left.*

tc **Aultroy Visitor Centre.** – The centre has an excellent three dimensional model of the area between Lochs Alsh and Broom. Discover the main points of interest of the Beinn Eighe National Nature Reserve, Britain's first ever. Of particular interest within its total area of 11 757 acres is the imposing mountain ridge of Beinn Eighe (visible from a window in the centre), as well as one of the few remaining fragments of the native Scots Pine Forest.
The roadside picnic area makes an ideal vantage point for viewing the loch and Slioch (the Spear) on the far side. This is also the starting point of a 4 mile nature and mountain trail on the lower slopes of Beinn Eighe. A 4/5 hour hike, wear boots.

★★★**Loch Maree.** – This magnificent loch epitomizes the rugged scenic grandeur of the west coast. 12 miles long and 3 miles wide the loch is ensconced between the towering form of **Ben Slioch** (3 217ft-980m) to the north and a shoulder of Beinn Eighe. At its widest part the loch is studded with isles and it was on the Isle Maree that St Maelrubha set up his cell in the 7C. The isle became a popular place of pilgrimage and Loch Ewe was rechristened Maree, a corruption of Maelrubha. In the 17C the well forested lochside slopes were the site of iron smelting.

★**Victoria Falls.** – *Car park off the main road.* A viewing platform and riverside path have good views of these falls as they drop in two stages over great slabs of rock. The falls are named after Queen Victoria who visited the area in 1877.
A roadside viewing point overlooks the dammed Loch Bad an Sgalaig. The surrounding country is hummocky and dotted with small lochs.

> *Pass the bay of Charlestown.*

Gairloch. – Pop 125. As a holiday centre Gairloch lies at close proximity to the majestic mountain scenery of the Torridon area and the splendid sandy beaches of the immediate coastline. At the head of Loch Gairloch the pier still has the lively bustle
tc of a fishing port. The **Gairloch Heritage Museum** is a local museum dealing with life in the past in the parish of Gairloch. There is a realistic reconstruction of a croft interior of 100 years ago. Other topics of interest include the Loch Maree ironworks of the 17C, illicit whisky distilling and Queen Victoria's 1877 visit to the area.

★★From Gairloch to Ullapool

56 miles – about 4 hours

The run reveals to full advantage the scenic coastline to the north where bays, beaches and headlands succeed one another backed, inland, by breathtaking mountain scenery. The A832 leads northeastwards across the rock and moorland neck of the Rudhe Reidh peninsula.

> *Stop before descending to the River Ewe.*

The roadside viewpoint has a superb **view**★★★ of Loch Maree with its forested islands and majestic mountain flanks.
Loch Ewe stretches ahead enclosed by the peninsulas of Rudhe Reidh and Rubha Mor.

Poolewe. – Small village at the head of Loch Ewe.

★★★**Inverewe Gardens.** – *Description p 131.*

View indicator. – This vantage point has a lovely **view**★ of Loch Thurnaig in the foreground, the Inverewe Gardens promontory behind, then Loch Ewe backed by Rudhe Reidh, and the Isle of Ewe to the right.

Second viewpoint. – The Isle of Ewe lies straight ahead while Aultbea shelters down in a bay to the right.

> *The road rises up and over Rubha Mor Peninsula.*

The descent offers a wide **view** over Gruinard Bay and Island of the same name, once the scene of an anthrax experiment *(the public is strictly forbidden to land).*
As the road follows the southern shore, straight ahead is **An Teallach** (3 484ft-1 062m) with away to the left the twin peaks of Beinn Ghobhlach, the Forked Mountain.
At the head of the loch the road follows the wooded Strath Beag up to the moors of Dundonnell Forest. This stretch of the road, known as Destitution Road, was made during the potato famine of 1851 to give work to starving men.
There is an excellent roadside vantage point with a **view**★ over the farmland and woodland of Strath More at the head of Loch Broom.

> *Turn left at Braemore Junction.*

★★**Falls of Measach.** – *Description p 201.*

★★**Loch Broom.** – *Description p 201.*

★**Ullapool.** – *Description p 200.*

WHITHORN (Dumfries and Galloway)   Pop 990

Michelin map ▨ fold 42 – G19

Whithorn, as the cradle of Scottish Christianity, predates Iona by over 150 years. This unassuming town with its wide main street serves the surrounding dairy farming community of the Machars.

Candida Casa. – In the year 397 when the Roman legions were still in Britain, St Ninian established the first Christian mission beyond Hadrian's Wall. Reputedly a local man, **St Ninian** (*c*360-*c*432) was educated and consecrated bishop in Rome. On his return he built a small stone church daubed with light coloured plaster known as **Candida Casa**, the White House (in Anglo-Saxon *huit aern*) the first Christian church in Scotland. The bishop's influence was widespread but tended to be overshadowed by the later Celtic Columban mission. The saint's tomb became a place of pilgrimage which was to remain popular until the beginning of the 16C. The bishopric lapsed however, during a period of Viking rule which ended after 1100. In 1128 Fergus, Lord of Galloway built a priory cathedral over the ruins of *Candida Casa* which was served by Premonstratensians, reviving the original see, which remained under the sway of York. Severance from York came in 1472 when the see of St Andrews was raised to a Bishopric. Twenty years later Galloway was put under the jurisdiction of Glasgow which had recently acquired episcopal status.

SIGHTS

From the main street a pend leads through the former priory gatehouse, built in the 15C by Bishop George Vaus, and emblazoned with the pre-Union Scottish coat of arms supported by two unicorns. Beyond in one of the cottages on the right is the museum.

tc **Museum.** – The museum gives a short history of the priory and houses a notable collection of **early Christian crosses**★★. These standing crosses or headstones denoted individual graves and date from the Christian period in Whithorn. The earliest Christian memorial in Scotland is the **Latinus Stone** (no 1) dated AD 450 and inscribed with the name of the relative who erected it. Two more exist at Kirkmadrine. Typical of the more decorative Whithorn School is no 7. Later stones (nos 3 and 5) show a Northumberland influence (eg Ruthwell). St Peter's Stone (no 2) is 7C or early 8C.

tc **Priory.** – The ruins (nave, south and Lady Chapels) set on a knoll are scanty and belong mainly to the medieval cathedral. The building to the left, originally the nave, served as a parish church until 1822. Note the reset Norman doorway in the south wall. The rest of the structure is mainly 13C, much altered. To the right, the paved area and low walls mark the east end with crypts underneath. The probable site of *Candida Casa* is beyond.

BRUCE STREET ┼ **Museum**

EXCURSION

Isle of Whithorn. – *4 miles. Leave Whithorn by the A750.*

Isle of Whithorn. – Pop 222. The village, a popular yachting centre, is known for the ruined **St Ninian's Chapel** which stands on the rocky foreshore. *(5min walk from pier).* At onetime thought to be the site of *Candida Casa*, this 13C chapel with its enclosure wall may well mark the site where St Ninian himself landed, or else was for the convenience of pilgrims coming by sea.

Take the Port William road the A750 then the A747.

St Ninian's Cave. – This cave, with some crosses carved in the rock, is said to be St Ninian's place of retreat.

Continue on the A747.

Monreith. – At Monreith the road to the left, signposted St Medan's Golf Course, leads to the wide sandy sweep of Monreith Bay.
On the way down, perched on a clifftop to the right of the road, is the bronze otter, a memorial to the naturalist **Gavin Maxwell** (1914-69) author of the best seller *Ring of Bright Water*.

WICK (Highland)   Pop 7 617
Michelin map 401 fold 7 – K8

Wick, standing on the river of the same name, is called after the Norse term Vik meaning bay. A small fishing fleet dealing mainly in white fish operates out of the harbour and is a reminder of greater things in the past.

The "silver darlings". – Wick was one of the first towns to develop the herring fishery on a large scale and by the early 19C was the largest herring fishing port. In its heyday over 1 000 boats operated out of the harbour and the neighbouring port of **Pulteneytown** on the south bank. The British Fisheries Society commissioned Telford to draw up the plans for this new fishing settlement. In those days it was a common sight to see the harbours a jumble of undecked boats and mass of masts, and the quays and all available dockside space spilling over with the paraphenalia of the curing industry. Curing, to be done imperatively within 24 hours, entailed gutting, packing in barrels and salting, and involved large squads of itinerant workers, mostly women.

SIGHTS

tc **Wick Heritage Centre.** – A series of tableaux reconstitute the town's history and heritage : a model of 20C Wick when it was one of the premier herring ports, cooper's shop, a fish kiln, working lighthouse and interiors.

tc **Caithness Glass.** – *Harrowhill.*
The present factory was founded in 1960. The glassware is known for its high quality workmanship, subtle colours, fine design and engraving. Visitors are welcome to the factory where the glass making process can be followed *(see also Perth p 172).*

EXCURSIONS

Prehistoric and 20C Caithness. – *30 miles to the south by the A9.* This run takes the visitor through flat, moorland countryside to two prehistoric sites and a 20C crofting museum.

★**The Hill o'Many Stanes.** – *Right off the main road.*
This site with its 22 rows of small stones is a Bronze Age monument (c1850 BC). The purpose of this fan shaped arrangement may have been astronomical. Other settings exist in the north but the most famous examples are those of Carnac in Brittany *(see the Michelin Green Guide Brittany).*

★**Grey Cairns of Camster.** – *5 miles off the main road by a narrow road with passing places.*
This is typical crofting country - a bleak expanse of moorland dotted with small cultivated areas and crofts. The first of the two cairns is the **Round Cairn** with its 20ft long entrance passage *(to be negotiated on hands and knees)* and chamber. The much larger second one, the **Long Cairn**★★ is 200ft long by 65ft wide. This longhorned structure incorporates two earlier beehive cairns. The main chamber *(of relatively easy access)* is tripartite, subdivided by large slabs. The chambered cairns of the area date from the Neolithic period (4400-2000 BC).

tc **Laidhay Croft Museum.** – Long white washed crofts like this one are typical of the Caithness area. Under one roof there are the living quarters subdivided by box beds, into kitchen, parlour and sleeping area, with the byre and stables at either end. Furnished as it would have been in the 1930s this museum gives a real insight into life at the time. The barn, beside the car park, is an interesting example of **cruck construction** using drift wood in an area where timber was scarce.

★**Duncansby Head.** – *21 miles including detours to the north by the A9.*
This excursion takes you to the northeastern tip of the Scottish mainland and is notable for its magnificent coastal scenery. Sheltered coves and sandy bays alternate with giddily steep cliffs and such associated features as rock stacks, natural arches and bridges, and narrow inlets known locally as goes. The rock ledges are the home of guillemots, shags, fulmars, kittiwakes and a variety of gulls and other species.

Leave Wick to the north by the road signposted Noss Head. Leave the car in the car park then take the path through the fields ; 15 minute walk.

Girnigoe and Sinclair Castles. – *Ruins in a dangerous condition.* The jagged ruins of two adjacent castles are dramatically set on a peninsula, overlooking the great sandy sweep of Sinclair's Bay on one side and a typical geo on the other. Nearest to the point of the peninsula is the late 15C Castle Girnigoe with its evil dungeon. The part known as Castle Sinclair, an early 17C addition, stands to the left beyond a ditch. Both were the seat of the Sinclair Earls of Caithness.

Return to the outskirts of Wick to take the John o'Groats road, the A9.

Pass on the way the tall ruined form of Keiss Castle and standing nearby the white form of its successor *(private).*

tc **John Nicolson Museum.** – Auckengill. The artifacts on display were found by John Nicolson during a lifetime of excavating local brochs. Caithness has over 100 of these Iron Age brochs *(p 183).*

The road climbs and once over the rise the southernmost isle of the Orkney Islands can be seen in the distance.

tc **John o' Groats.** – 876 miles from Land's End, this scattered community takes its name from a Dutchman, Jan de Groot who started a regular ferry service to the Orkney Islands in the 16C. The octagonal tower of the hotel recalls the story of the ferryman, who to settle problems amongst his seven descendants, built an eight sided house with eight doors and an octagonal table. A passenger boat service still operates from the harbour to Burwick on South Ronaldsay.

Take the road to the east to Duncansby Head 2 miles away.

★**Duncansby Head.** – From around the lighthouse, which commands this northeastern headland of mainland Scotland, there is a good view across the Pentland Firth, a seven mile wide channel notorious for its treacherous tides. A path leads to another clifftop viewpoint overlooking the **Stacks of Duncansby**★★. Standing offshore these pointed sea-stacks rise to a spectacular height of 210ft-64 m.

Index

Practical information

The following chapter regroups the addresses and telephone numbers of the main organizations and associations, a calendar of events and a section on times and charges for admission. The addresses given below are listed in the same order as the organizations are mentioned in the introduction *(pp 11-29)*

PLANNING YOUR HOLIDAY AND LEISURE TIME

Tourist Information Centres. – Scottish Tourist Board, 23 Ravelston Terrace, Edinburgh EH4 3EU, ☎ 031 332 2433. The addresses of the 34 area tourist boards may be obtained from the STB.

National Trust for Scotland (NTS). – 5 Charlotte Square, Edinburgh EH2 4DU, ☎ 031 226 5922.

Historic Buildings and Monuments (HBM). – Scottish Development Department, 3-11 Melville Street, Edinburgh EH3 7QD, ☎ 031 226 2570.

ACCESS TO SCOTLAND'S WIDE OPEN SPACES

Country Parks. – Countryside Commission for Scotland, Battleby, Redgorton, Perth PH1 3EW, ☎ 0738 27921.

National Nature Reserves. – Nature Conservancy Council, 12 Hope Terrace, Edinburgh EH9 2A5, ☎ 031 447 4784

National Forest Parks. – Forestry Commission (Scotland), 231 Corstorphine Road, Edinburgh EH12 7AT, ☎ 031 334 0303.

Long Distance Footpaths. – Countryside Commission for Scotland *(see above)*.

SPORTS AND OUTDOOR ACTIVITIES

Scottish Sports Council. – 1-3 St Colme Street, Edinburgh EH3 6AA, ☎ 031 225 8411.

Scottish Federation of Sea Anglers. – 8 Frederick Street, Edinburgh.

Mountaineering Council of Scotland. – Hon Secretary, Mr C.J. Eatough, South Tillysole Cottage, Kinnaird Park, Brechin, Angus DD9 6TX.

Gardens

Scotland's Gardens Scheme. – The General Organizer, 31 Castle Terrace, Edinburgh EH1 2EL, ☎ 031 229 1870.

Wildlife

Nature Conservancy Council. – *See above.*

Scottish Wildlife Trust. – 25 Johnston Terrace, Edinburgh EH1 2NH, ☎ 031 226 4602.

TRADITIONAL SCOTLAND

Tartans

The Scottish Tartans Society. – Museum of Scottish Tartans, Comrie, Perthshire PH6 2DW, ☎ Comrie (0764) 70779.

Scotland's Clan Tartan Centre. – 70-74 Bangor Road, Leith, Edinburgh, ☎ 031 553 5100.

Heraldic displays

Lord Lyon King of Arms. – The Court of the Lord Lyon, HM New Register House, Edinburgh EH1 3YT, ☎ 031 556 7255.

Tracing your ancestors

The National Library of Scotland. – George IV Bridge, Edinburgh EH1 IEW, ☎ 031 226 4531.

General Register Office. – New Register House, Edinburgh EH1 3YT, ☎ 031 556 3952.

Scottish Record Office. – HM General Register House, Edinburgh EH1 3YY, ☎ 031 556 6585.

Scottish Ancestry Research Society. – 3 Albany Street, Edinburgh EH1 3PY, ☎ 031 556 4220

Gaelic

An Comunn Gaidhealach. – 109 Church Street, Inverness IVI IEY.

Crafts

Scottish Craft Centre. – Acheson House, 140 Canongate, Edinburgh EH8 8DD, ℡ 031 556 8136/7370.

Highland Craftpoint. – Beauly, Inverness-shire IV4 7EH, ℡ Beauly (0463) 782 578.

Whisky

The Scotch Whisky Association. – 17 Half Moon Street, London W1Y 7RB, ℡ 01 629 4384.

Principal Office. – 20 Atholl Crescent, Edinburgh EH3 8HF, ℡ 031 229 4383.

CALENDAR OF EVENTS

Listed below are a few of the most popular annual events. These are a sampling of some of Scotland's most colourful customs and traditions. For more details on these and others contact the Scottish Tourist Board, 23 Ravelston Terrace, Edinburgh, EH4 3EU or local Tourist Information Centres.

DATE AND PLACE	DESCRIPTION OF EVENT
JANUARY	Burns Night : Burns Suppers to celebrate the birthday of the national poet with haggis as the main dish.
Lerwick, Shetland	Up-Helly-Aa : torchlight procession followed by burning of Viking warship, singing and all night dancing.
FEBRUARY . . . . **Jedburgh, Borders**	Ba'Game
Venue changes annually	Scottish Curling Championship
MARCH . . . . . . **Lanark, Strathclyde**	Whuppity Scourie : banishing winter
Edinburgh, Lothian	Edinburgh Folk Festival
MARCH-APRIL . **Glenshee, Tayside**	Glenshee, Snow Fun Week
APRIL . . . . **Kirkcaldy, Fife**	Links Market : funfair
Ayr, Strathclyde	Scottish Grand National
Mull, Strathclyde	Mull Music Festival
APRIL-SEPT . . . . **Pitlochry, Tayside**	Pitlochry Festival Theatre Season
MAY . . . . **Lerwick, Shetland**	Shetland Folk Festival
Blair Castle, Tayside	Atholl Highlanders' Parade
JUNE . . . . **Lanark, Strathclyde**	Lanark Lanimer Festival
Kirkwall and Stromness, Orkney	St Magnus Festival
Doune, Central	Motor Racing Hill Climb
Ingliston, near Edinburgh	Royal Highland Agricultural Show
Venue changes annually	Scottish Pipe Band Championship
JULY . . . . . . **Glamis Castle, Tayside**	Scottish Transport Extravaganza
Eyemouth, Borders	Herring Queen Festival
Glasgow, Strathclyde	Glasgow International Folk Festival
AUGUST . . . . **Aberdeen, Grampian**	International Youth Festival of Music and the Arts
Venue changes annually	World Pipe Band Championship
South Queensferry, Lothian	Burry Man Festival : Burry man clad in sticky burrs tours the town collecting for charity, on the last day of fair week
Edinburgh, Lothian	Edinburgh International Festival, Military Tattoo and Festival Fringe
Fort William, Highland	Glen Nevis River Race
SEPTEMBER **Fort William, Highland**	Ben Nevis Race
Largs, Strathclyde	Largs Viking Festival
Inverness, Highland	Northern Meeting Piping Competition
Doune, Central	Motor Racing Hill Climb
OCTOBER **Venue changes annually**	The National Mod
Tweed Valley, Borders	Glorious Tweed Festival
Blair Castle, Tayside	Grants' World Piping Championship
NOVEMBER . . . **Aviemore, Highland**	Scotland's Whisky Festival
DECEMBER . . . . . **Kirkwall, Orkney**	The Ba' Games
Stonehaven, Grampian	Swinging Fireball Ceremony

Times and charges for admission

Times and charges for admission are liable to alteration without prior notice. Due to the fluctuations in the cost of living and the constant change in the opening times, the information below is given only as a general indication.

The prices quoted apply to individual adults ; where a property belongs to the National Trust for Scotland or the Historic Buildings and Monuments, the letters NTS or HBM appear after the charge. Many places offer reduced rates for children and OAPs.

Groups should apply in advance in writing or at least phone ahead - some houses and museums are small and have limited space and facilities, limited parking space etc. Many places have special days for groups ; many offer special rates for advance bookings. Several gardens raise plants for sale in adjoining plant centres ; houses have restaurants providing light refreshments, often home-made and delicious.

Last admission. – The times quoted are those of opening and closure ; heritage, ruined and small sights are liable to closure at midday. Most places do not admit visitors in the last hour or half hour - arrive, therefore, with plenty of time to spare.

a

ABBOTSFORD HOUSE

House. – Open late March-end October 10am-5pm ; Sundays 2-5pm ; ℡ Innerleithen (0896) 2043 ; £1.30.

ABERDEEN

King's College Chapel. – Open 9am-5pm ; to visit apply to the buildings officer, left of entrance to the quadrangle ; 50p.

Cruickshank Botanic Gardens. – Open weekdays 9am-4.30pm ; weekends 2-5pm.

St Machar's Cathedral. – Open May-September 9am-5pm ; October-April 9am-5pm.

Fish Market. – Mondays – Fridays from 7am.

Maritime Museum. – Open Mondays-Saturdays 10am-5pm ; closed Christmas and New Year holidays ; ℡ Aberdeen (0224) 585 788. NTS Visitor Centre : May-September, Mondays-Saturdays 10am-5pm.

Town House. – Tours by arrangement Monday-Friday 9am-5pm ; contact the Town Sergeant's Office in the Town House ; ℡ Abedeen (0224) 642 121.

Provost Skene's House. – Open Mondays-Saturdays 10am-5pm ; closed Christmas and New Year holidays ; ℡ Aberdeen (0224) 641 086.

Anthropological Museum (Marischal College). – Open Mondays-Fridays 10am–5pm ; Sundays 2-5pm ; closed 25 December-3 January ; ℡ Aberdeen (0224) 40 241 (ext. 243).

St Nicholas Kirk. – Open Mondays, Tuesdays and Fridays 12 noon-4pm ; Saturdays 10am-12noon.

St Mary's Chapel. – Thursdays 2-7pm ; Fridays and Saturdays 10am-12noon.

James Dun's House. – Open Mondays-Saturdays 10am-5pm ; closed Christmas and New Year holidays ; ℡ Aberdeen (0224) 646 333.

Art Gallery. – Open Mondays – Saturdays 10am-5pm (8pm Thursdays); Sundays 2-5pm ; closed Christmas and New Year holidays; ℡ Aberdeen (0224) 646 333.

ABERDOUR

Aberdour Castle. – Open April-September weekdays 9.30am-7pm ; Sundays 2-7pm ; October-March 9.30am-4pm ; Sundays 2-4pm ; closed Thursday pm and Fridays ; 50p HBM.

Boat trip to Inchcolm Island. – June-mid September daily 10.30 and 11.30am (except Sundays) 1.30, 2.30 and 3.30pm ; April, May and late September confirm sailing times with Dougal Barrie, Hawkcraig House, Aberdour ; ℡ Aberdour (0383) 860 335 ; Rtn fare £ 2 excluding abbey admission charge : 60p HBM.

ABERFELDY

Castle Menzies. – Open April-September weekdays 10.30am-5pm : Sundays 2-5pm ; £1.00.

St Mary's Church. – Open at all reasonable times ; HBM.

ALFORD

Grampian Transport Museum. – Open April-September daily 10.30am-5pm ; ℡ Alford (0336) 2 292 ; £1.10 includes entry to Railway Museum.

Alford Valley Railway Museum. – Open April-September daily 10.30am-5pm ; £1.10 includes entry to Transport Museum. Trains operate at peak weekends ; Adult 70p ; children : 50p.

Kildrummy Castle Garden. – Open April-October daily 9am-5pm ; gardens 30p ; car park 10p.

Glenbuchat Castle. – Open at all reasonable times ; HBM.

Corgarff Castle. – Open April to September weekdays 9.30am-7pm ; Sundays 2-7pm; keykeeper in winter ; 50p HBM.

ARBROATH

Abbey. – Open April-September weekdays 9.30am-7pm ; Sundays 2-7pm ; October-March weekdays 9.30am-4pm ; Sundays 2-4pm ; 50p HBM.

Signal Tower Museum. – Open April-September Mondays-Saturdays 10.30am- 1pm, 2-5pm ; Sundays in July and August 2-5pm ; November-March Mondays-Fridays 2-5pm ; Saturdays 10.30am-1pm, 2-5pm ; closed public holidays ; ☏ Montrose (0674) 73 232.

St Vigeans Museum. – Open April-September 9.30am-7pm ; Sundays 2-7pm ; October-March weekdays 9.30am-4pm ; Sundays 2-4pm ; HBM.

ARRAN, Isle of

Brodick Castle. – Open Easter weekend then May-September daily 1-5pm ; ☏ Brodick (0770) 2 202 ; castle and garden £1.25 NTS.

Country park and gardens. – All year daily 10am-5pm : garden only 80p.

Rosaburn Heritage Museum. – Open May-September, Mondays-Fridays 10.30am-1pm, 2-4.30pm ; Sundays and holidays 2-4.30pm ; ☏ Brodick (0770) 83 278 ; 60p.

Lochranza Castle. – Open at all reasonable times, apply to Mr Kerr of Croftbank HBM.

AVIEMORE

Strathspey Railway. – Steam train serice : late June-late August Mondays-Thursdays and weekends Easter-October ; for time-table telephone : ☏ Boat of Garten (047 938) 692. Adult Rtn 3rd class £2 : family ticket £5 ; time : 20 min single journey.

Osprey Hide. – Open mid May-August daily 10am-8.30pm ; mid April-mid May 10am-6.30pm ; ☏ Boat of Garten (047 983) 694 or 648.

Landmark Visitor Centre. – Open June-August 9.30am-9.30pm ; April, May, September, October 9.30am-6pm ; November-March 9.30am-5pm ; closed Christmas Day ; ☏ Carrbridge (047 984) 614 ; £1.75 inclusive ticket.

Highland Wildlife Park. – Open April-October 10am-6pm ; ☏ Kincraig (054 04) 270 ; £5.50 per car.

Highland Folk Museum. – Open April-October 10am-6pm ; Sundays 2-6pm ; November-March, Mondays-Fridays 10am-3pm ; ☏ Kingussie (054 02) 307 ; £1.

Ruthven Barracks. – Open April-October weekdays 9.30am-7pm, Sundays 2-7pm ; November-March weekdays 9.30am-4pm : Sundays 2-4pm ;

Clan Macpherson Museum. – Open May-September. Mondays-Saturdays 10am-5.30pm ; Sundays 2.30-5.30pm ; ☏ Newtonmore (054 03) 332 ; by donation.

AYR

Tam o'Shanter Museum. – Open April-September, 9.30am-5.30pm ; June-August Sundays 2.30-5pm ; October-March 12noon to 4pm ; ☏ Ayr (0292) 269 794 ; 35p.

Burns Cottage and Museum. – Open June-August 9am-7pm ; Sundays 10am-7pm ; April, May, September, October 10am-5pm ; Sundays 10-5pm ; November-March 10am-4pm ; closed Christmas and New Year holidays ; ☏ Ayr (0292) 41 215 ; 80p including Burns Monument and Gardens.

Land o'Burns. – Open July-August 10am-9pm ; June and September 10am-6pm ; October-May 10am-5pm ; closed Christmas and New Year Holidays.

Burns Monument and Gardens. – As Burns Cottage and Museum, see above.

Bachelors' Club. – Open April-October daily 10am-6pm ; other times by appointment ; ☏ Tarbolton (541) 424 ; 55p NTS.

Burns House Museum. – Open Easter-September 11.30am-5.30pm : Sundays 2-5pm ; other times by special arrangement, ☏ Mauchline (0290) 50 045 ; 15p.

Crossraguel Abbey. – Open April-September 9.30am-7pm ; Sundays 2-7pm ; October-March 9.30am-4pm ; Sundays 2-4pm ; closed Thursday pm and Fridays ; 50p HBM.

Souter Johnnies's Cottage. – Open April-September daily 12noon-5pm except Fridays ; other times by appointment ☏ Kirkoswald (065 56) 603 or 274 ; 60p NTS.

b

BANFF ·

Duff House. – Open April-September 9.30am-7pm ; Sundays 2-7pm ; keykeeper in winter ; 50p HBM.

BIGGAR

Gladstone Court Museum. – Open April-October 10am-12.30pm, 2-5pm ; Sundays 2-5pm ; evenings by appointment ☏ Biggar (0899) 21 050 ; 80p ; reduced charge for joint ticket with Greenhill.

Greenhill Covenanting Museum. – Open April-mid October, daily 2-5pm ; evenings by appointment ☏ Biggar (0899) 21 050 ; 60p.

John Buchan Centre. – Open April-mid October, daily 2-5pm ; other times by appointment ℡ Biggar (0899) 21 050 ; 50p.

Broughton Place. – Open April-September, daily, except Wednesdays, 10.30am-6pm ; ℡ Broughton (089 94) 234 ; gallery free : garden 40p.

The BINNS

The House. – Guided tours Easter weekend then May-September daily, except Fridays, 2-5pm ℡ Philpstoun (050 683) 4 255 ; time : 40 minutes ; £1.10 inclusive ticket, NTS. Parkland all year daily 10am-7pm.

BLAIR ATHOLL

The Mill. – Open April-October weekdays 10am-6pm ; Sundays 12noon to 6pm.

Atholl Country Collection. – Open July-August weekdays 9.30am-5.30pm ; weekends 1.30-5.30pm ; late May, June, September daily 1.30-5.30pm ; ℡ Blair Atholl (079 681) 232 ; 50p.

Clan Donnachaidh Museum. – Open April-October.

BLAIR CASTLE

The Castle. – Open Easter week, Sundays and Mondays in April then everyday from the third Sunday in April to the second Sunday in October, weekdays 10am-6pm ; Sundays 2-6pm, 12 noon in July and August ; ℡ Blair Atholl (079 681) 207 ; £1.80.

BOTHWELL CASTLE

The Castle ruins. – Open April-September weekdays 9.30am-7pm ; Sundays 2-7pm ; October-March weekdays 9.30am-4pm ; Sundays 2-4pm ; closed Thursday pm and Fridays in winter ; 50p HBM.

Parish Church. – Key from nearby house.

David Livingstone Centre. – Open daily 10am-6pm ; Sundays 2-6pm ; £1.

BOWHILL

The House. – Open 6 July-11 August, weekdays, 11am-5pm ; Sundays 2-6pm ; ℡ Selkirk (0750) 20 732 ; £1.50 inclusive ticket.

BRECHIN

The Aberlemno Stones. – The stones are boarded up between November and April.

Fasque. – Open May-September daily, except Fridays, 1.30-5.30pm ; ℡ Fettercairn (056 14) 201 ; £1.25.

BRODIE CASTLE

The Castle. – Open Easter and then May-September weekdays 11am-6pm ; Sundays 2-6pm ; ℡ Brodie (030 94) 371 ; £1.30. Grounds open all year daily 9.30-sunset ; by donation

C

CAERLAVEROCK CASTLE

The Castle ruins. – Open April-September weekdays 9.30am-7pm ; Sundays 2-7pm ; October-March weekdays 9.30am-4pm ; Sundays 2-4pm ; 50p HBM.

The CAIRNGORMS

The Cairn Gorm Chairlift. – The chairlift leaving form the Coire Cas car park operates all the year round weather permitting : 9am-4pm ; 5pm July and August. Two stages : adult Rtn £2.60, partial and family tickets available.

CASTLE DOUGLAS

Threave Garden. – Open all year 9am-sunset ; walled garden and glasshouses 9am-5pm ; ℡ Castle Douglas (0556) 2 575 ; £1.10, NTS.

NTS Visitor Centre. – Open April-October daily 9am-6pm.

Threave Castle. – Open April-September weekdays 9.30am-7pm ; Sundays 2-7pm ; October-March weekdays 9.30am-4pm ; Sundays 2-4pm ; 50p HBM including the ferry which stops 45 minutes before closing time.

CASTLE FRASER

The Castle. – Open May-September daily 2-6pm ; £1.10, NTS.

Garden and Grounds. – Open all year, daily 9.30am-sunset, by donation.

CAWDOR CASTLE

The Castle. – Open May-6 October, daily, 10am-5.30pm ; ℡ Cawdor (066 77) 615 ; £1.80.

COCKBURNSPATH

Dunglass Collegiate Church. – Open April-September weekdays 9.30am-7pm ; Sundays 2-7pm ; October-March weekdays 9.30am-4pm ; Sundays 2-4pm ; 50p HBM.

COLDSTREAM

Coldstream Museum. – Open Whitsun-September, Tuesdays-Fridays 2-5pm ; Saturdays 10am-1pm ; ℻ Coldstream (0890) 2 630 ; 35p.

The Hirsel. – The estate is open daily during daylight hours ; ℻ Coldstream (0890) 2 834 ; by donation. (House not open).

CRAIGIEVAR CASTLE

The Castle. – Guided tours May-September daily except Fridays, 2-6pm ; ℻ Lumphanan (033 983) 635 ; £1.30 NTS.

The Grounds. – Open all year daily 9.30-sunset ; by donation.

CRATHES CASTLE

The Castle. – Open Easter then May-September, weekdays 11am-6pm ; Sundays 2-6pm ; ℻ Crathes (033 044) 525 ; £1.70 inclusive ticket, NTS.

Gardens and Grounds. – Open daily 9.30-sunset ; Garden only : 60p ; Grounds only ; 30p.

CRICHTON CASTLE

The Castle ruins. – Open April-September, weekdays 9.30am-7pm ; Sundays 2-7pm ; closed Mondays-Fridays in winter ; 50p HBM.

CRIEFF

Crieff Visitors Centre. – Open all year. Factories Monday-Friday. Showroom open all the time ; ℻ Crieff (0764) 2 141.

Stuart Strathearn. – Open June-September 9am-8pm ; Sundays 10am-8pm ; October-May 9am-5pm ; Sundays 11am-5pm ; closed the week between Christmas and New Year ; ℻ Crieff (0764) 4 004.

Glenturret Distillery. – Open July and August, Mondays-Saturdays, 9.45am-4pm ; March-June, September, October, Mondays-Fridays, 10am-12noon, 1.30pm-3.30pm ; November and December, Mondays-Fridays tours at 2pm, 2.45pm and 3.30pm ; ℻ Crieff (0764) 2 424 ; Guided tour and taste free ; heritage centre 80p.

Drummond Castle Gardens. – Open 6 May-1 September, daily, 2-6pm ; 3 April-5 May and 4-29 September, Wednesdays and Sundays only 2-6pm ; ℻ Muthill (076 4 81) 257 ; £1.00.

Tullibardine Chapel. – Open at all reasonable times ; apply to the nearby farmhouse for the key HBM.

Strathallan Aero Park. – Open April-October, 10am-6pm ; ℻ (076 46) 2 545 ; £1.80.

Innerpeffray Library and Chapel. – Open weekdays 10am-12.45pm, 2-4.45pm ; Sundays 2-4pm ; closed Christmas and New Year holidays ; ℻ Crieff (0764) 2 819 ; 50p.

Museum of Scottish Tartans. – Open Easter - September weekdays 9am-5pm ; Sundays 2-4pm ; rest of the year Mondays-Fridays 10am-4pm ; Saturdays 10am-1pm, closed Sundays ; ℻ Comrie (0764) 70 779 ; 70p.

CULLEN

Cullen Auld Kirk. – Open April-September 9.30am-6.30pm.

CULROSS

The Palace. – Open April-September weekdays 9.30am-7pm ; Sundays 2-7pm ; October-March 9.30am-4pm ; Sunday 2-4pm ; £1 HBM.

Tolbooth. – Open May-September, daily except Fridays, 9.30am-12.30pm and 2-5pm ; Sundays 2-5pm ; ℻ Culross (0383) 880 359 ; 35p NTS ; 65p inclusive ticket with the Study.

The Study. – Open April and October, Saturdays 9.30am-12.30pm, 2-4pm ; Sundays 2-4pm ; ℻ Culross (0383) 880 359 ; 30p NTS.

Culross Abbey. – Open April-September weekdays 9.30am-7pm ; Sundays 2-7pm ; October-March weekdays 9-30am-4pm ; Sundays 2-4pm ; £1.00 HBM.

Parish Church. – Key at the manse, adjoining.

CULZEAN CASTLE

The Castle. – Open April-September, daily 10am-6pm ; October, daily 12noon-5pm ; ℻ Kirkoswald (065 56) 274 ; £1.60 NTS.

The Country Park. – Open all year ; April-September 10am-6pm ; October-March 10am-4pm ; Limited facilities available out of season.

DALKEITH

St Nicholas Buccleuch Church. – Key from Church Officer's House, adjacent, or from manse.

Dalkeith House Country Park. – Open April-October daily 11am-6pm ; November at weekends only ; ℻ Edinburgh 031 663 4178 ; 65p.

Newbattle Abbey. – To visit apply in writing to the warden.

DALMENY

Dalmeny House. – Guided tours, May-September, Sundays-Thursdays, 2-5.30pm ; closed Fridays and Saturdays ; ☎ Edinburgh 031 331 1888 ; £1.50.

DEESIDE

Drum Castle. – Open May-September daily 2-6pm ; ☎ Drumoak (033 08) 204 ; £1.10 NTS.

The Grounds. – Open all year, daily 9.30am-sunset ; by donation.

Balmoral Castle. – Grounds open May, June and July when the royal family is not in residence.

Braemar Castle. – Open May-7 October, daily 10am-6pm ; closed for the Braemar Gathering ; ☎ Braemar (033 83) 219 ; £1.10.

DIRLETON

Dirleton Castle. – Open April-September weekdays 9.30am-7pm ; Sundays 2-7pm ; October-March weekdays 9.30am-4pm ; Sundays 2-4pm ; £1 HBM.

DOLLAR

Castle Campbell. – Open April-September weekdays 9.30am-7pm ; Sundays 2-7pm ; October-March weekdays 9.30am-4pm ; Sundays 2-4pm ; closed Thursday pm and Fridays in winter ; ☎ Dollar (025 94) 2 408 ; 50p HBM.

DORNOCH

Dunrobin Castle. – Open mid June-mid September, weekdays 10.30am-5.30pm ; Sundays 1-5.30pm ; ☎ Golspie (040 83) 3177 ; £1.80.

DOUGLAS

St Bride's Church. – Key from Mrs G. Gowan, No 2 Clyde Road, behind the inn. HBM.

DOUNE

Doune Castle. – Open June-August daily 10am-6pm, April, May, September and October 10am-4.30pm ; closed Thursdays in April and October ; £1.00 HBM.

Doune Motor Museum. – Open April-October, daily 10am-5pm ; ☎ Doune (0786 84) 1203 ; £1.50.

DRUMLANRIG CASTLE

The Castle. – Open July-August, weekdays 11am-5pm ; Sundays 2-6pm ; Easter, May and June, weekdays 1.30-5pm ; Sundays 2-6pm ; ☎ Thornhill (0848) 30 248 ; £2.00.

DRYBURGH ABBEY

The Abbey. – Open April-September weekdays 9.30am-7pm ; Sundays 2-7pm ; October-March weekdays 9.30am-4pm ; Sundays 2-4pm ; £1.00 HBM.

DUFFTOWN

Glenfiddich Distillery. – Guided tours, all year except Christmas and New Year holidays 9.30am-4.30pm ; weekends mid May-mid October : Saturdays 9.30am-4.30pm : Sundays 12noon-4.30pm ; time : 1-1 1/4 hours includes audiovisual presentation ; ☎ Dufftown (0340) 20 373.

Balvenie Castle. – Open April-September weekdays 9.30am-7pm ; Sundays 2-7pm ; closed in winter ; 50p HBM.

The Glenlivet. – Open April-October, Mondays-Fridays, 11am-4pm ; ☎ (080 73) 427.

Glenfarclas. – Open Mondays-Fridays, 9am-4.30pm : closed Christmas and New Year holidays : ☎ (080 72) 257.

Tamdhu. – Open Easter-September, Mondays-Fridays, 10am-4pm ; ☎ (034 06) 221.

Glen Grant. – Open mid April-September, Mondays-Fridays, 10am-4pm ; ☎ Rothes (034 03) 494.

Strathisla. – Open June-early September, Mondays-Fridays, 9am-4.30pm ; ☎ (054 22) 7471.

DUMFRIES

Burns' House. – Open April-August weekdays 10am-5pm ; Sundays 2-5pm September-March weekdays 10am-5pm, closed Sundays and Mondays ; ☎ Dumfries (0387) 53 374 ; 30p.

Dumfries Museum and Old Bridge House. – Open April-September weekdays 10am-1pm ; 2-5pm, Sundays 2-5pm ; October-March 10am-1pm, 2-5pm ; closed Sundays and Mondays ; ☎ Dumfries (0387) 53 374 ; camera obscura : 50p.

Lincluden College. – Open April-September weekdays 9.30am-7pm ; Sundays 2-7pm ; October-March weekdays 9.30am-4pm ; Sundays 2-4pm ; closed Thursday pm and Fridays ; 50p HBM.

Shambellie House Museum of Costume. – Open mid May-mid September Thursdays to Mondays 10am-5.30pm ; Sundays 12noon-5.30pm ; to New Abbey (038 785) 375.

Sweetheart Abbey. – Open April to September weekdays 9.30am-7pm ; Sundays 2-7pm ; October-March weekdays 9.30am-4pm ; Sundays 2-4pm ; 50p HBM.

Duncan Savings Bank Museum. – Open April-September daily 10am-6pm ; October-March 10am-4pm ; ☎ Clarencefield (038 787) 640.

Ruthwell Cross. – Key to church from Mrs Coultard at the new bungalow on the B 724 or from the old manse (now a small country hotel).

Ellisland Farm. – Open at all reasonable times, all year round, 7 days a week. Interior of farmhouse and museum room may only be viewed when curator is present ; intending visitors should phone in advance ℡ (0387 74) 426.

Rammerscales. – Usually open 2-5pm in May and August ; for further details ℡ Lochmaben (038 781) 361

DUNBAR

John Muir's Birthplace. – Open May-September daily except Wednesdays and Sundays, 10am-12.30pm, 1.30-4.30pm ; ℡ Dunbar (0368) 63 353 ; 40p.

DUNBLANE

Dunblane Cathedral. – Open April-September weekdays 9.30am-7pm ; Sundays 2-5.30pm ; October-March 9.30am-4pm ; Sundays 2-4pm ; ℡ Dunblane (0786) 82 33 88.

Cathedral Museum. – Open daily in summer, by request at other times.

DUNDEE

McManus Galleries and Barrack Street Museum. – Open Mondays-Saturdays 10am-5pm ; closed December and New Year holidays ; ℡ Dundee (0382) 23 141 (ext 136).

Tay Road Bridge. – Toll, cars : 30p.

The Frigate Unicorn. – Open 5 April-7 October 11am-1pm, 2-5pm ; Sundays 2-5pm ; closed Tuesdays ; ℡ Dundee (0382) 21 555 ; 50p.

Mills Observatory. – Open April-September 10am-5pm, Saturdays 2-5pm ; October to March 3-10pm ; Saturdays 2-5pm ; closed Sundays and public holidays ; ℡ Dundee (0382) 67 138.

Broughty Castle Museum. – Open Mondays-Saturdays 10am-5pm ; closed December and New Year holidays ; ℡ Dundee (0382) 23 141 (ext 136).

Claypotts Castle. – Open April-September weekdays 9.30am-7pm ; Sundays 2-7pm ; closed in winter ; 50p HBM.

DUNFERMLINE

Abbey Church. – Open April-September 9.30am-12noon, 1 to 7pm ; Sundays 2-6pm ; October-March 9.30am-12noon, 1 to 4pm ; Sundays 2-4pm ; HBM.

Pittencrieff House Museum. – 5 May-7 September, daily except Tuesdays, 11am-5pm ; ℡ Dunfermline (0383) 721 814.

Andrew Carnegie Birthplace. – Open April-November 11am-5pm ; Sundays 2-5pm ; 8pm Wednesdays ; December-March 2-4pm ; ℡ Dunfermline (0383) 724 302.

Dunfermline District Museum. – Open Mondays-Saturdays 11am-5pm ; closed Sundays and local pulic holidays ; ℡ Dunfermline (0383) 26 914.

Loch Leven Castle. – Open Mondays-Saturdays 10am-6pm ; Sundays 2-6pm ; closed in winter ; 50p HBM.

DUNKELD

Dunkeld Cathedral. – Open April-September 9.30am-7pm ; Sundays 2-7pm ; October-March 9.30am-4pm ; Sundays 2-4pm ; ℡ Dunkeld (035 02) 601 ; HBM.

Scottish Horse Regimental Museum. – Open Easter-September 10.30am- 12.30pm, 2-4.45pm.

Loch of the Lowes Nature Reserve. – Open June-August 9am-8.30pm ; April, May and September 9am-7pm ; ℡ Dunkeld (035 02) 337 ; by donation.

DUNNOTTAR CASTLE

The Castle ruins. – Open April-October, Mondays-Saturdays 9am-6pm ; Sundays 2-5pm ; closed Saturdays November-March ; 75p.

DUNS

Jim Clark Memorial Room. – Open Easter - September 10am-6pm ; Sundays 2-6pm ; ℡ Duns (0361) 82 600 : 40p.

Polwarth Church. – Key obtainable from either Mrs M. Tait, Polwarth Mill or Mrs J. Boyd, St Leonards, Polwarth.

DURNESS

Balnakeil Craft VIllage. – Centre open April-September Mondays-Saturdays 10am-6pm. ℡ Durness (097 181) 242.

Cape Wrath. – Ferry and minibus service : mid May-mid September seven days per week ; ferry at least two return trips daily 11.00am and 2.30pm ; in the high season approx eight return trips per day between 9.30am and 6.30pm ; crossing time : 10 mins ; Fare £1.00 Rtn. ℡ Durness (097 181) 376. Connecting minibus service with all ferries ; time : 40 mins ; Fare £3.00 Rtn. ℡ Durness (097 181) 287.

e

The EAST NEUK

Crail Museum. – Open Easter, June-late September, 10am-12.30pm, 2-5pm ; Sundays 2-5pm ; ☏ Crail (0333) 50 869 ; 40p NTS.

Scottish Fisheries Museum. – Anstruther. Open April-October, 10am-5.30pm ; Sundays 2-5pm ; November-March 2-5pm, closed Tuesdays, Sundays 2-5pm ; ☏ Anstruther (0333) 310 628 ; 85p.

Boat Trips to the Isle of May. – The M/B *Hilda Ross* sails from Anstruther to the Isle of May daily from May-September, including Sundays. Minimum time spent on the isle is 2 hours. Sailing times vary according to tide and weather. Rtn fare £6.

St Fillan's Cave. – Pittenweem. Open Easter-Christmas 10am-5.30pm ; Sundays 2.30-5.30pm ; the rest of the year closed Mondays-Wednesdays ; key available from the Gingerbread Horse. 9 High Street. ☏ Pittenweem (0333) 311 495 ; 25p.

ECCLEFECHAN

Arched House. – Open Easter-October Mondays-Saturdays, 10am-6pm ; ☏ Ecclefechan (057 63) 666 ; 45p NTS.

EDINBURGH

Conducted coach tours. – Transport Information Centre on Waverley Bridge. ☏ 031 556 5656 or in writing to Lothian Region Transport Head Office, 14 Queen Street, Edinburgh EH21JL ; ☏ 031 554 4494.

The Festival : programme, bookings and tickets. – The Festival : available from Edinburgh Festival Society/Ticket Office, 21 Market Street ; Office ☏ 031 226 4001 ; bookings ; ☏ 031 225 5756 ; Festival Club, Senior Staff Club of Edinburgh University 9-15 Chambers Street.
The Military Tattoo : available from Ticket Office, 31-33 Waverley Bridge, ☏ 031 225 1188.
The Fringe : available from Edinburgh Festival Fringe Society, 170 High Street ; ☏ 031 226 5257 ; Fringe Club, Edinburgh University Union, Bristo Square.
Folk Festival : available from Folk Festival, 170 High Street ☏ 031 226 3645.

Tourist Information Centre. – Waverley Market ; ☏ 031 557 2727.

Edinburgh Castle. – Open April-September, 9.30am-5.05pm (last admission) ; Sundays 11am-5.05pm October-March 9.30am-4.20pm (last admission). Sundays 12.30pm-3.35pm : closed Christmas and New Year holidays ; ☏ 031 225 9846 ; £2.00 HBM. Opening hours may be altered during the Tattoo, state and military events.

Royal Scots Regimental Museum. – Open May-September 9.30am-4.30pm ; Sundays 11am-4.30pm ; October-April 9.30am-4pm : closed weekends and the week between Christmas and New Year. ☏ 031 336 1761 Ext 4265.

Palace of Holyroodhouse. – Guided tours leave about every 10 minutes ; time : 40 mins ; ticket office open late March-late October, weekdays 9.30am- 5.15pm, Sundays 10.30am-4.30pm ; late October-March weekdays 9.30am-3.45pm : closed on Sundays ; ☏ 031 556 7371 ; £1.30 Closed during Royal and State visits, especially in May and early June, check in advance.

The Abbey of Holyroodhouse. – Same opening times as the palace. see above. Visitors are free to visit on their own. at the end of the guided tours.

Outlook Tower. – Open April-September 9.30am-5.30pm ; Sundays 10am-6pm ; October-March 9.30am-4pm ; Sundays 10am-4pm ; closed Christmas and New Year holidays ; ☏ 031 226 3709 ; £1.25.

Gladstone's Land. – Open April-Oct. weekdays 10am-5pm ; Sundays 2-5pm ; 90p NTS.

Lady Stair's House. – Open June-September, Mondays-Saturdays, 10am-6pm ; 5pm the rest of the year.

St Giles Cathedral. – Open April-September 9am-7pm ; Sundays 7.30am-9pm ; October-March 9am-5pm ; Sundays 7.30am-9pm ; ☏ 031-225-4363 ; Thistle Chapel 30p.

Parliament Hall. – Open Tuesdays-Fridays 10am-4pm ; closed on public holidays.

Wax Museum. – Open April-September daily 10am-7pm ; October-March 10am-5pm ; closed Christmas and New Year holidays ; ☏ 031 226 4445.

Museum of Childhood. – Closed during the building of an extension ; normal opening hours June-September weekdays 10am-6pm ; October-April 10am-5pm ; ☏ 031 225 2424. Temporary exhibition of items from the collection is being staged in the Canongate Tolbooth. See below.

John Knox House. – Open April-October weekdays 10am-5pm ; November-March 10am-4pm ; closed Christmas and New Year holidays ; ☏ 031 556 6961 ; 70p.

Canongate Tolbooth. – Open June-September Mondays-Saturdays 10am-6pm ; October-May 10am-5pm ; closed Christmas and New Year holidays ; ☏ 031 225 2424 (ext 6638).

Huntly House. – Open June-September, Mondays-Saturdays, 10am-6pm ; 5pm the rest of the year.

Acheson House. – Open Mondays-Saturdays 10am-5.30pm : closed public and local holidays ; ☏ 031 556 8136/7370.

Greyfriars Church. – Open Mondays-Fridays 10am-12noon, 2-4pm.

Talbot Rice Art Gallery. – Open Mondays-Saturdays 10am-5pm.

Royal Scottish Museum. – Open Mondays-Saturdays 10am-5pm ; Sundays 2-5pm ; closed Christmas and New Year holidays and a day in May ; ☏ 031 225 7534.

New Town Conservation Committee. – 13 A Dundas Street, ☏ 031 556 7054. The committee organizes from June-August, Sunday forenoon and Wednesday evening walks, tickets and information from the headquarters at the above address.

National Trust for Scotland. – Headquarters, 5 Charlotte Square, Edinburgh EH2 404. Open Mondays-Fridays 9am-5.30pm ; ☏ 031 226 5922.

The Georgian House. – Open April-October, weekdays 10am-5pm ; Sundays 2-5pm ; November 10am-4.30pm ; Sundays 2-4.30pm ; £1.10, NTS.

West Register House. – Open Mondays-Fridays, 10am-4pm.

National Portrait Gallery. – Open Mondays-Saturdays 10am-5pm ; Sundays 2-5pm ; in winter closed from 12.30-1.30pm ; ☏ 031-556 8921.

National Museum of Antiquities. – Open Mondays-Saturdays 10am-5pm, Sundays 2-5pm ; closed Christmas and New Year holidays.

General Register House. – Open Mondays-Fridays 10am-4pm.

Scott Monument. – Open April-September 9am-6pm ; October-March 9am-3pm ; 40p.

National Gallery of Scotland. – Open Mondays-Saturdays, 10am-5pm, Sundays 2-5pm ; Prints and drawings weekdays 10am-12.30pm, 2-4pm ; in winter certain rooms are closed between 12noon and 2pm ; closed Christmas and New Year holidays and May Day ; ☏ 031 556 8921.

Royal Scottish Academy. – Open Mondays-Saturdays 10am-5pm ; Sundays 2-5pm.

Nelson's Monument. – Open April-September, Mondays 1-6pm ; Tuesdays- Saturdays 10am-6pm ; October-March Mondays-Saturdays 10am-3pm ; 40p.

Royal Botanic Garden. – Open daily summer (BST) 9am-1 hour before sunset ; from 11am on Sundays ; winter (GMT) 9am-sunset, from 11am on Sundays ; closed Christmas and New Year holidays ; ☏ 031 552 7171.

Edinburgh Zoo. – Open April-September 9am-6pm ; Sundays 9.30am-6pm ; October-March 9am-dusk ; Sundays 9.30am-dusk ; ☏ 031 334 9171 ; £2.40.

Lauriston Castle. – Open April-October, daily except Fridays, 11am-5pm ; the rest of the year weekends only 2-4pm ; ☏ 031 336 2060 ; 80p.

Scottish Agricultural Museum. – Open May-September, Mondays-Fridays, 10am-4pm ; Sundays 12noon-5pm.

St Mary's Cathedral. – Open 7.30am-6pm ; 5.30pm on Saturdays.

Scottish National Gallery of Modern Art. – Open Mondays-Saturdays 10am-5pm ; Sundays 2-5pm ; ☏ 031 556 8921.

Royal Observatory. – Open Mondays-Fridays 10am-4pm ; weekends 12noon-5pm ; closed for week between Christmas and New Year ; holidays open afternoons only ; ☏ 031 667 3321 ; 65p.

Craigmillar Castle. – Open April-September weekdays 10am-7pm ; Sundays 2-7pm ; October-March weekdays 10am-4pm ; Sundays 2-4pm ; closed Thursday pm and Fridays ; 50p HBM. Restoration work in progress.

Hillend Ski Centre. – Open all the year round 9.30am-9pm ; closes 5pm at weekends May-August : the chairlift of the main slope is available to sightseers and hill walkers on the Pentlands ; 70p Rtn.

CastleLaw Hill Fort. – Key available from Crosshouse Farm on the main road, at all reasonable times, HBM.

Malleny House Garden. – Open May-September daily 10am-dusk. (House not open) ; 55p NTS.

EDZELL CASTLE

The castle and gardens. – Open April-September weekdays 9.30am-7pm ; Sundays 2-7pm ; October-March 9.30-4pm ; Sundays 2-4pm ; closed Tuesdays and Thursday am ; 50p HBM.

ELGIN

The Cathedral. – Open April-September weekdays 9.30am-7pm ; Sundays 2-7pm ; October-March weekdays 9.30am-4pm ; Sundays 2-4pm ; 50p HBM.

Elgin Museum. – Open April-mid September Mondays to Fridays 10am-4pm ; Saturdays 10am-12noon ; the rest of the year Saturdays only 10am-12noon ; ☏ Elgin (0343) 3675 ; 25p.

Spynie Palace. – View from the outside only HBM.

Duffus Castle. – Open April-September weekdays 9.30am-7pm ; Sundays 2-7pm ; October-March 9.30am-4pm ; Sundays 2-4pm ; 50p HBM.

Burghead Well. – Open at all reasonable times. Key and information board available from the house next door.

Pluscarden Abbey. – Open every day of the year 5am-8.45pm ; ☏ Dallas (034 389) 257.

EYEMOUTH

Eyemouth Museum. – Open July-August, Mondays-Saturdays 10am-7pm ; Sundays 2-7pm ; April-June, September-October, weekdays, 10am-6pm ; Sundays 2-6pm ; ☏ Eyemouth (0390) 50 678 ; 70p.

Coldingham Priory. – Open at all reasonable times.

St Abb's Head. – Pedestrians free, Parking at main car park (by donation) or at lighthouse (limited space £1.00).

f

FALKLAND

The Palace of Falkland. – Open April-September Mondays-Saturdays 10am-6pm ; Sundays 2-6pm ; October : Saturdays 10am-6pm ; Sundays 2-6pm ; ℡ Falkland (0337) 57 397 ; £1.30. Garden only : 80p NTS.

FLOORS CASTLE

The Castle. – Open Easter weekend and end April-end September, 11am-5.30pm ; closed Saturdays in July and August ; closed Fridays and Saturdays in May, June and September ; ℡ Kelso (0573) 23 333 ; £1.60.

FOCHABERS

Tugnet Ice House. – Open June-September daily 10am-4pm ; ℡ Elgin (0343) 451 21.
Baxters – Open April-October, Mondays-Fridays, 10am-4pm ; ℡ Fochabers (0343) 820 393.

FORRES

Falconer Museum. – Open July and August 9.30am-1pm, 2-6.30pm ; mid May-June, September 9.30am-1.30pm, 2-5.30pm ; October-mid May 10am-12.30pm, 1.30- 4.30pm ; ℡ Forres (0309) 73 701.
Culbin Forest. – Forest walks and picnic places ; access is controlled by the Forestry Commission.

FORT WILLIAM

West Highland Museum. – Open Mondays-Saturdays, July-August 9.30am-9pm ; June and September 9.30-5.30pm ; October-May 10am-1pm, 2-5pm ; closed Christmas and New Year holidays ; ℡ Fort William (0397) 2169 ; 30p.
Ben Nevis Exhibition. – Open mid March-October, daily 9am-10pm ; Sundays 11am-9pm ; in winter 9am-5.30pm and closed on Sundays ; Fort William (0397) 4406 ; 10p.
Glenfinnan NTS Visitor Centre. – Open July, August daily 9.30am-7pm ; April, June, September, October daily 10am-5.30pm ; ℡ Kinlocheil (039 783) 250 ; 50p NTS.
Boat trips from Arisaig. – Regular sailings, May-September, to Skye, Mull, Rhum, Eigg, Muck, Canna. All enquiries to Murdo Grant, Station Road, Arisaig (06 875) 219 or 224.

g

GALLOWAY FOREST PARK

Raider's Road. – Open end May-October 9am to dusk ; one 50p piece for toll machine.
Newton Stewart Museum. – Open April-September, Mondays-Saturdays, 2-5.30pm ; Sundays from July 2-5pm ; ℡ Newton Stewart (0671) 2106 ; 50p.

GLAMIS

Angus Folk Museum. – Open May-September 12noon-5pm ; 80p NTS.
Meigle Museum. – Open April-September weekdays 9.30am-7pm ; October-March weekdays 9.30am-4pm ; closed Sundays ; 50p HBM.

GLAMIS CASTLE

The Castle. – Guided tours May-September, daily except Saturdays ; 1-5pm ; ℡ Glamis (030 784) 242/3 ; £1.80.

GLASGOW

Tourist Information Centre. – 35-39 St Vincent Place, Glasgow Gl 2ER, ℡ 041 227 4894.
The Travel Centre. – St Enoch Square, Glasgow ℡ 041 226 4826.
Glasgow Cathedral. – Open Mondays-Saturdays 9.30am-7pm (4pm the rest of the year) ; Sundays 2-5pm.
The Burrell Collection. – Open, Mondays-Saturdays, 10am-5pm ; Sundays 2- 5pm : closed Christmas and New Year's Days, ℡ 041 649 7151. There are guided lecture tours at 11am and 2pm ; time : 1 1/4 hours.
Provand's Lordship. – Open Mondays to Saturdays 10am-5pm ; Sundays 2-5pm.
People's Palace. – Open weekdays 10am-5pm ; Sundays 2-5pm ; closed Christmas and New Year's Days : ℡ 041 554 0223.
The Barras. – Weekend market, open 9am-5pm.
Hunterian Museum. – Open Mondays-Fridays 10am-5pm ; Saturdays 9.30am-1pm ; closed public holidays ; ℡ 041 339 8855 (ext 221).
Hunterian Art Gallery. – Open Mondays-Fridays, 10am-12.30pm ; 1.30-3pm, 3.30-5pm ; Saturdays 9.30-11am ; 11.30-1pm. The Mackintosh House : Mondays-Fridays 10-11.30am ; 12.30-5pm : Saturdays 9.30am-1pm ; 50p for Mackintosh House on weekday afternoons and Saturdays. ℡ 041 339 8855/7431.
Art Gallery and Museum Kelvingrove. – Open Mondays-Saturdays 10am-5pm ; Sundays 2-5pm ; closed Christmas and New Year's Days.

Botanic Gardens. – Gardens : daily 7am-dusk ; Kibble Palace : 10am-4.45pm (4.15pm in winter) ; Main range : 1-4.45pm (4.15pm in winter) Sundays 12noon-4.45pm (4.15pm in winter) ; ℡ 041 334 2422.

City Chambers. – Guided tours, Mondays-Fridays, at 10.30am and 2.30pm ; closed public holidays and for certain functions and visits : ℡ 041 227 4017/4018.

Hutchesons' Hall. – NTS Visitor Centre. Shop and reception area open Mondays-Fridays 9am-5pm ; Saturdays 10am-4pm ; closed public holidays ; ℡ 041 552 8391.

Royal Exchange. – Open Mondays-Fridays, except Wednesdays, 9.30am-8pm : Saturdays 9am-1pm, 2-5pm ; ℡ 041 221 1876.

Glasgow School of Art. – Guided tours, 7 January-15 December, Mondays-Fridays, 10am-12noon ; 2-4pm ; ℡ 041 332 9797.

The Tenement House. – Open April-October daily 2-5pm : the rest of the year weekends only 2-4pm ; ℡ 041 333 0183 ; 85p NTS. Due to the smallness of the flat, admission is by application in advance.

Museum of Transport. – Open weekdays 10am-5pm ; Sundays 2-5pm ; closed Christmas and New Year's Days ; ℡ 041 423 8000.

Pollok House. – Open weekdays 10am-5pm ; Sundays 2-5pm ; closed Christmas and New Year's Days ; ℡ 041 632 0274.

Clyde Estuary : boat trips. – During July and August the paddle steamer *Waverley* visits the Firth of Clyde resorts with departures from Glasgow, Helensburgh, Dunoon, Rothesay, Largs, Millport and Ayr. Further details from Waverley Excursions Ltd, Anderston Quay, Glasgow ; ℡ 041 221 8152.

Dumbarton Castle. – Open April-September, Mondays-Saturdays 9.30am-7pm : Sundays 2-7pm ; October-March Mondays-Saturdays 9.30am-4pm ; Sundays 2-4pm ; 50p HBM.

Hill House. – Helensburgh. Open all year, daily 1-5pm ; 90p NTS.

Younger Botanic Garden. – Benmore. Open April-October daily 10am-6pm ; ℡ Dunoon (0369) 6261 ; 20p.

Newark Castle. – Open April-September weekdays 9.30am-7pm ; Sundays 2-7pm ; keykeeper in winter, 50p HBM.

Rothesay Castle. – Open April-September weekdays 9.30am-7pm ; Sundays 2-7pm ; October-March 9.30am-4pm ; Sundays 2-4pm ; closed Thursdays and Fridays winter ; 50p HBM.

Glasgow Zoological Gardens. – Open June-September daily 10am-6pm ; 5pm October-May ; ℡ 041 771 1185 ; £1.60.

NTS Visitor Centre. – Open June-August, daily 9.30am-7pm ; April-May, September-October daily 10-5.30pm ; 25p NTS.

North Lorn Folk Museum. – Open mid May-September, Mondays-Saturdays, 10am-5.30pm ; 30p.

Boat trips. – For cruises on Loch Ness apply to Abbey Cruisers Fort Augustus ; ℡ Fort Augustus (0320) 6316. See also under Inverness.

Great Glen Exhibition. – Open April-October daily 9.30am-5.30pm.

Fort Augustus Abbey. – Church open all day (7.30am-8.30pm) Building operations may compromise guided tours. Telephone in advance to Fort Augustus (0320) 6232.

Urquhart Castle. – Open April-September weekdays 9.30am-7pm ; Sundays 2-7pm ; October-March 9.30am-4pm ; Sundays 2-4pm ; £1.00 HBM.

Loch Ness Monster Exhibition. – Open April-October daily 9.30am-9.30pm ; ℡ (0320) 6341.

h

St Mary's Parish Church. – Open Mondays-Saturdays 10am-4pm.

Hailes Castle. – Open April-September weekdays 9.30am-7pm ; Sundays 2-7pm ; October-March weekdays 9.30am-4pm ; Sundays 2-4pm ; 50p HBM.

The House. – Guided tours May-September, daily, 2-6pm ; closed 18/19 May ; £1.30 NTS.

The Garden and Country Park. – Open all year, daily 9.30am-8pm or sunset ; by donation.

Wilton Lodge Museum. – Open April-September 10am-12noon, 1-5pm ; Sundays 2-5pm ; October-March weekdays, except Saturdays, 1-4pm ; Sundays 2-4pm ; ℡ Hawick (0450) 73 457. 45p.

The Castle. – Open April-September weekdays 10am-7pm ; Sundays 2-7pm ; October-March, weekdays, 9.30am-4pm ; Sundays 2-4pm ; 50p HBM.

HOPETOUN HOUSE

The House. – Open Easter, May-late September, daily 11am-5.30pm ; ℡ 031 331 2451 ; £1.90.

HUNTLY

Huntly Castle. – Open April-September weekdays 10am-7pm ; Sundays 2-7pm ; October-March, weekdays, 9.30am-4pm ; Sundays 2-4pm ; 50p HBM.

Leith Hall. – Guided tours May-September daily 2-6pm ; ℡ (046) 43 216 ; £1.10 NTS. The garden and grounds open all year daily 9.30am-sunset ; by donation.

i

INVERARAY

Inveraray Castle. – Open July, August weekdays, 10am-6pm ; Sundays 1-6pm ; April, September-October weekdays except Fridays 10am-1pm ; Sundays 1-6pm ; ℡ Inveraray (0499) 2203 ; £1.80.

Bell Tower. – Open Late May-late September weekdays 10am-1pm ; 2-5pm ; Sundays 3-6pm ; ℡ Inveraray (0499) 2433 ; small fee to ascend tower.

Auchindrain. – Open June-August daily, 10am-5pm ; April, May, September daily, except Saturdays, 11am-4pm ; ℡ Inveraray (0499) 5235 ; £1.00.

Castle Fisheries. – Open April-October, daily, 10am-6pm ; ℡ Inveraray (0499) 2233 ; 90p.

INVEREWE GARDENS

The Gardens. – Open early May-early September weekdays 10am-6.30pm ; Sundays 12noon-6.30pm ; April-early May, early September-mid October 10.30am-5.30pm. Sundays 12noon-5.30pm ; the rest the year 9am-4pm ; ℡ Poolewe (044 586) 229 ; £1.50 NTS.

INVERNESS

Museum and Art Gallery. – Open Mondays-Saturdays, 9am-5pm, closed Christmas and New Year ; ℡ Inverness (0463) 237 114.

Abertarff House. – NTS information centre and shop. Open weekdays 9am-5.30pm.

Culloden. – Site : open all year ; NTS Visitor Centre : open June-October daily 9.30am-8pm ; April-May, September-October daily 10am-6pm ; £1.05 NTS.

Beauly Priory. – Open April-September weekdays 9.30am-7pm ; Sundays 2-7pm ; October-March weekdays 9.30am-4pm ; Sundays 2-4pm ; closed Mondays and Tuesday am in winter ; 50p HBM.

Highland Craftpoint. – Open end May-mid September, Mondays-Fridays 10am-5pm ; ℡ Beauly (0463) 782 578.

Groam House Museum. – Open June-mid September, weekdays 10.30am-12.30pm, 2.30-4.30pm ; Sundays 2.30-4.30pm ; ℡ Fortrose (0381) 20 924 ; 30p.

Hugh Miller's Cottage. – Open May-September, weekdays 10am-12noon, 1-5pm ; Sundays June-September 2-5pm ; ℡ Cromarty (03 817) 245 ; 65p.

Cruises on Loch Ness. – Apply to Scott II, Clachnaharry ; ℡ Inverness (0463) 33140 or Jacobite Cruises, Canal Bridge, Loch Ness Road ; ℡ Inverness (0463) 33999.

INVERURIE

Fyvie Castle. – Not to be opened to the public until 1 May 1986-NTS.

IONA ; Isle of

Infirmary Museum. – Open all year 9am-5.30pm ; by donation ; ℡ Iona (068 17) 404.

j

JEDBURGH

Jedburgh Abbey. – Open April-September, weekdays, 9.30am-7pm ; Sundays 2-7pm ; October-March weekdays 9.30am-4pm ; closed Thursday pm and Fridays in winter ; 50p HBM.

Mary Queen of Scots House. – Open, April-September, weekdays 10am-12noon, 1-5pm ; Sundays 1-5pm ; ℡ Jedburgh (0835) 63 331 ; 50p.

Jedburgh Castle Jail and Museum. – Open, April-September, weekdays 10am-12noon, 1-5pm ; Sundays 1-5pm ; ℡ Jedburgh (0835) 63 254 ; 40p.

The Woodland Centre. – Open July-August, daily except Fridays and Saturdays 1-5pm ; Easter-June September-October Wednesdays and Sundays only 1-5pm ; ℡ Jedburgh (0835) 62 201 ; 80p.

k

KELLIE CASTLE

The Castle. – Open May-September daily except Fridays 2-6pm ; Weekends in April and October 2-6pm ; £.1.10 NTS.

KELSO

Old Parish Church. – Open weekdays 10am-4pm.

Smailholm Tower. – Open April-September weekdays 9.30am-7pm ; Sundays 2-7pm ; keykeeper in winter ; 50p HBM.

Greenknowe Tower. – Apply to the custodian.

KILDRUMMY CASTLE

The Castle ruins. – Open April-September weekdays 9.30am-7pm ; Sundays 2-7pm ; October-March weekdays 9.30am-4pm ; Sundays 2-4pm ; 50p HBM.

KILMARNOCK

Dean Castle. – Guided tours mid May-late September, 2-5pm ; Saturdays 12noon-5pm ; ℡ Kilmarnock (0563) 26 401 ; 50p.

Dick Institute. – Open April-September Mondays, Tuesdays, Fridays 10am-8pm ; 5pm on Wednesdays and Saturdays ; the rest of the year 10am-5pm ; ℡ Kilmarnock (0563) 26 401.

Burns Monument. – Temporarily closed except an application to the curator of the Dick Institute.

KINTYRE

Claonaig. – Ferry to Lochranza (Isle of Arran) summer only 6-7 daily ; 30 minutes.

Kennacraig. – Ferry to Port Ellen (Isle of Islay) 1-2 daily ; 2 hours, Ferry to Port Askaig (Isle of Islay) Mondays-Saturdays 1 daily; 1h 45 minutes. Ferry service from Port Askaig to Jura.

Skipness Castle. – View from the outside.

Tayinloan. – Ferry to Ardminish (Isle of Gigha) daily ; 20 minutes.

KIRKCALDY

Ravenscraig Castle. – Open April-October, weekdays, 10am-12.30pm, 1.30-6pm ; Sundays 2-6pm ; 50p HBM.

Museum and Art Gallery. – Open weekdays 11am-5pm, Sundays 2-5pm ; ℡ Kirkcaldy (0592) 260 732.

Industrial Museum. – Open May-August, weekdays 2-5pm ; ℡ Kirkcaldy (0592) 260 732.

KIRKCUDBRIGHT

Broughton House. – Open April-October, Mondays-Saturdays, 11am-1pm, 2-5pm ; November-March Tuesdays and Thursdays 2-5pm ; ℡ Kirkcudbright (0557) 30 437 ; 50p.

MacLellan's Castle. – Open April-September weekdays 9.30am-12noon, 2-7pm ; Sundays 2-7pm ; October-March Saturdays 9.30am-12noon, 2-4pm ; Sundays 2-4pm ; 50p HBM.

Stewartry Museum. – Open Easter-October, Mondays-Saturdays, 11am-1pm, 2-4pm (5pm in July and August) ; ℡ Kirkcudbright (0557) 30 797 ; 50p.

Dundrennan Abbey. – Open April-September, weekdays, 9.30am-7pm ; Sundays 2-7pm ; October-March weekdays 9.30am-4pm ; Sundays 2-4pm ; 50p HBM.

Tongland Power Station. – Guided tours May-September, Mondays-Saturdays 10am-3.30pm ; time : 2 hours ; book in advance by telephoning Kirkcudbright (0557) 30 114. Transport leaves from the Tourist Information Office.

Cardoness Castle. – Open April-September, weekdays 9.30am-7pm ; Sundays 2-7pm ; October-March weekdays 9.30am-4pm ; Sundays 2-4pm ; 50p HBM.

Gem and Rock Museum. – Open April-October, daily 9.30am-7pm ; November-March 9.30am-5pm, ℡ Newton Stewart (0671) 82 357 ; 60p.

KIRRIEMUIR

J. M. Barrie's Birthplace. – Open May-September, Mondays-Saturdays 10am-12.30pm ; 2-6pm ; Sundays 2-6pm ; ℡ Kirriemuir (0575) 72 646 ; 60p NTS.

Camera Obscura. – Open during summer at weekends weather permitting.

KNAPDALE

Kilmory Knap. – Key chained to the door. HBM.

KYLE OF LOCHALSH

Eilean Donan Castle. – Open early April-September, daily 10am-12noon, 2-6pm ; ℡ Dornie (059 985) 291 202 ; £1.00.

l

LANARK

New Lanark. – The village is open at all times. Access to mill area 9am-5pm ; Only on specific days do certain volunter householders open their doors to visitors.

Falls of Clyde. – Nature Reserve visitor centre open daily 9am-5pm. The waterfalls are in full flow four times a year when a change-over at the power station permits.

Craignethan Castle. – Open April-September daily 9.30am-7pm ; Sundays 2-7pm ; October-March daily 9.30am-4pm ; Sundays 2-4pm ; 50p HBM.

LARGS

Skelmorlie Aisle. – Open, April-September, weekdays 9.30am-7pm ; Sundays 2-7pm : keykeeper in winter : 50p HBM.

Great Cumbrae. – Caledonian MacBrayne Ferries : to Cumbrae Slip, vehicles and passengers : time : 10 mins ; to Millport, summer only 4-7 daily (30 mins). Buses run between Cumbrae Slip and Millport. Bicycles can be hired in Millport.

University Marine Biological Station. – Open Mondays-Fridays, 9.30am-12.30pm, 2-5pm ; Saturdays 9.30am-12.30pm ; June to September 2-5pm on Saturdays ; 30p.

Hunterston Nuclear Power Station. – Free guided tours are available of Hunterston B in the summer months. Bookings are by telephone, to West Kilbride (0294) 823 668. Children over 11 are welcome, but must be accompanied by an adult.

LAUDER

Thirlestane Castle. – Open July-August daily except Fridays, 2-5pm ; May, June, September, Wednesdays and Sundays only 2-5pm ; ☎ Lauder (057 82) 254 ; £2.00 inclusive ticket.

Border Country Life Museum. – Same opening period as the castle 12noon- 6pm.

LENNOXLOVE

The Castle. – Guided tours, April-September Wednesdays and weekends, 2-5pm ; ☎ Haddington (062 082) 3 720 ; £1.25.

LEWIS and HARRIS, Isle of

Arnol Black House. – Open April-September 9.30am-7pm ; October-March 9.30am-4pm ; closed Sundays ;

St Clement's Church. – Open at all reasonable times.

Shawbost Museum. – Open April-September Mondays-Saturdays 10am-6pm.

LINLITHGOW

Linlithgow Palace. – Open April-September, weekdays, 9.30am-7pm ; Sundays 2-7pm ; October-March weekdays 9.30am-4pm ; Sundays 2-4pm ; £1.00 HBM.

St Michael's. – Open June-September, Mondays-Saturdays, 10-12noon, 2-4pm ; Sundays 2-4pm ; October-May Mondays-Fridays 10am-12noon, 2-4pm. Vestry, enter from the north aisle, apply to the caretaker to open.

Blackness Castle. – Open April-September, weekdays 9.30am-7pm ; Sundays 2-7pm ; October-March weekdays 9.30am-4pm ; Sundays 2-4pm ; closed Monday pm and Tuesdays in winter ; 50p HBM.

Kinneil House. – Open April-September, weekdays 9.30am-7pm ; Sundays 2-7pm ; October-March weekdays 9.30am-4pm ; 2-4pm ; closed Tuesday pm and Fridays ; 50p HBM.

LOCH LOMOND

Boat trip. – Mid July-beginning of September two sailings daily 10.15am and 3.45pm ; 1 April-9July and September one daily 10.15am. No sailings on Mondays : round trip £6. Apply to Alloa Brewery Co Ltd, Anderston House, 389 Argyle Street, Glasgow ☎ 041 226 4271 ; recorded message 041 248 2699.

LOCH TAY

Ben Lawers Visitor Centre. – Open June-August, 10am-5pm ; April-May, September 11am-4pm ; 60p NTS.

m

MANDERSTON

The House. – Open mid May-September, Thursdays and Sundays only 2-5.30pm ; ☎ Duns (0361) 83 450 ; £2.00.

MELLERSTAIN

The House. – Open May-September, daily except Saturdays, 12.30-5pm ; ☎ Gordon (057 381) 225 ; £1.70.

MELROSE

The Abbey. – Open April-September, Mondays-Saturdays 9.30am-7pm ; Sundays 2-7pm ; October-March weekdays 9.30am-4pm, Sundays 2-4pm ; ☎ Melrose (089 682) 2 562 ; £1.00 HBM.

Priorwood Garden. – Open July-September weekdays 10am-6pm ; Sundays 1.30-5.30pm ; May-June, October weekdays 10am-5.30pm ; Sundays 1.30-5.30pm ; November-December weekdays only 10am-1pm, 2-5.30pm ; ☎ Melrose (089 682) 2555 NTS. 30p.

MOFFAT

Museum. – Open Easter-September, weekdays 10.30am-1pm, 2.30pm-5pm ; Sundays 2.30am-5pm ; ☎ Moffat (0683) 20868 ; 30p.

MONTROSE

Museum. – Open April-October weekdays 10.30am-1pm, 2-5pm (2-5pm Sundays in July and August) ; November to March weekdays 2-5pm ; ☎ Montrose (0674) 732 32.

William Lamb Memorial Studio. – Open June-September Sundays 2-5pm ; Wednesdays also in July and August 2-5pm.

Glen Esk Folk Museum. – Open Easter and Sundays, June-September daily 2-6pm : 30p.

MULL, Isle of

Mull Little Theatre. – Summer season late May-late September.

Duart Castle. – Open May-September daily, 10.30am-6pm ; ☎ Craignure (068 02) 309 ; £1.50.

Staffa. – Boat trips from Ulva Ferry, Fionnphort and Iona ; enquire locally.

Torosay Castle. – Open April-October, daily, 10am-5pm ; ☎ Craignure (068 02) 421 ; £1.50 inclusive ticket ; Gardens only : sunrise-sunset ; 80p.

n

NAIRN

Fort George. – Open April-September 10am-6pm, Sundays 2-2.30pm ; October-March weekdays 10am-4pm ; 50p HBM.

Regimental Museum of the Queen's Own Highlanders. – Open April-September Mondays-Fridays 10am-6.30pm ; Sundays 2-6.30pm ; closed Saturdays ; October-March, Mondays-Fridays 10am-4pm ; closed weekends ; ☎ Inverness (0463) 224 380.

NORTH BERWICK

Museum. – Open July-September weekdays 10am-1pm, 2-5pm ; Sundays 2-5pm ; ☎ North Berwick (06 20) 3470.

Boat trips to the Bass Rock. – Daily trips round Bass Rock (weather permitting) May-September ; 1 hour ; £1.50.

Myreton Motor Museum. – Open Easter, May-October, daily 10am-6pm ; 5pm the rest of the year ; ☎ Aberlady (087 57) 288 ; 75p.

Tyninghame Gardens. – Open June-September, Mondays-Fridays, 10.30am-4.30pm ; ☎ (0620) 860 330 ; 70p.

Preston Mill. – Open April-September, Mondays-Saturdays 10am-12.30pm, 2-5.30pm ; Sundays 2-5.30pm ; October : Mondays-Saturdays 10am-12.30pm, 2-4.30pm ; Sundays 2-4.30pm ; November-March Saturdays 10am-12.30pm, 2-4.30pm, Sundays 2-4.30pm ; 80p NTS.

Museum of Flight. – Open July-August daily 10am-4pm and on certain local holidays.

o

OBAN

Dunstaffnage. – Open April-September weekdays 9.30am-7pm : Sundays 2-7pm : October-March weekdays 9.30am-4pm ; Sundays 2-4pm ; closed Thursday pm and Fridays in winter ; 50p HBM.

Bonawe Furnace. – Open April-September, weekdays, 9.30am-7pm ; Sundays 2-7pm ; closed in winter ; 50p HBM.

Cruachan Power Station. – Open April-October daily 9am-4.30pm ; Short audiovisual ; presentation ; 20 min guided tour in minibus into the heart of the mountain ; £1.00. Preferably book in advance.

Kilchurn Castle. – Restoration work in progress but part of castle is open to the public HBM.

Crarae Woodland Garden. – Open March-October 9am-6pm ; admission charge.

Kilmartin Church. – Open April-September 9.30am-7pm ; the rest of the year apply to Mrs Fraser at no 2.

Carnasserie Castle. – Open April-September weekdays 9.30am-7pm ; Sundays 2-7pm ; October-March weekdays 9.30am-4pm ; Sundays 2-4pm ; HBM.

Sea Life Centre. – Open July-August daily 9am-8pm ; April-June, September-October daily 9am-6pm ; ☎ 0631 72 386 ; £1.50.

ORKNEY ISLANDS

Brough of Birsay. – Open April-September weekdays 9.30am-7pm ; Sundays 2-7pm ; October-March weekdays 9.30am-4pm ; Sundays 2-4pm ; closed Mondays and Tuesday am in winter ; 50p HBM.

St Magnus Cathedral. – Open 9am-1pm, 2-5pm ; closed Sundays and holidays.

Earl's Palace. – Open April-September weekdays 9.30am-7pm ; Sundays 2-7pm ; October-March weekdays 9.30am-4pm ; Sundays 2-4pm ; closed Friday pm and Saturdays in winter ; 50p HBM combined ticket with Bishop's Palace.

Bishop's Palace. – Combined ticket with Earl's Palace, see above. HBM.

Tankerness House Museum. – Open Mondays-Fridays, 10.30am-12.30pm and 1.30-5pm ; Sundays 2-5pm April-September only.

Italian Chapel. – Open at all times.

Burwick. – In summer a passenger ferry operates between Burwick and John o'Groats.

Gurness Broch. – Open April-September weekdays 9.30am-7pm ; Sundays 2-7pm ; October-March weekdays 9.30am-4pm : Sundays 2-4pm : 50p HBM.

Corrigall Farm Museum. – Open April-September weekdays 10.30am-1pm, 2-5pm : Sundays 2-7pm.

Maes Howe. – Open April-September weekdays 9.30am-7pm ; Sundays 2-7pm ; October-March weekdays 9.30am-4pm, Sundays 2-4pm ; £1.00 HBM.

Skara Brae. – Open April-September weekdays 9.30am-7pm ; Sundays 2-7pm ; October-March weekdays 9.30am-4pm ; Sundays 2-4pm ; £1.00 HBM.

Pier Arts Centre. – Open, Tuesdays-Saturdays, 10.30am-12.30pm, 1.30-5pm ; Sundays 2-5pm in summer.

Stromness Museum. – Open summer 10.30am-12.30pm, 1.30-5pm ; winter 11am-12.30pm, 1.30-5pm ; closed 3 weeks in February ; 20p.

Pentland Firth Crossing. – See the current Michelin Red Guide under Thurso (Scrabster) or Stromness (Orkney Islands) for the P & O ferries ; time : 2 hours.

PAISLEY

Paisley Abbey. – Open daily 10am-3pm, by donation, Place of Paisley : open once a month 1-5pm.

Paisley Museum and Art Gallery. – Open Mondays-Saturdays, 10am-5pm, closed local and national holidays ; ☏ Paisley (041) 889 3151.

The Observatory. – Open Mondays-Fridays 2-5pm, Saturdays 10am-1pm, 2-5pm ; ☏ Paisley (041) 889 3151.

Kilbarchan Weaver's Cottage. – Open June-August daily 2-5pm ; April-May, September-October Tuesdays, Thursdays and weekends 2-5pm ; ☏ Glasgow 041 552 8391, 60p NTS. Weaver at work Tuesdays and Saturdays.

PERTH

Black Watch Regimental Museum. – Open Easter-September weekdays only 10am-3.30pm ; ☏ Perth (0738) 71 781 (ext 30).

Museum and Art Gallery. – Open Mondays-Saturdays 10am-1pm, 2-5pm ; ☏ Perth (0738) 32 488.

St John's Kirk. – Open 10am-12noon, 2-4pm ; closed January-mid March.

Caithness Glass. – Open Mondays-Saturdays, 9am-5pm, Sundays 1-5pm ; ☏ Perth (0738) 37 373. Glass making Mondays-Fridays only, 9am-4.30pm.

Branklyn Garden. – Open March-October daily 10am-sunset ; 75p NTS.

Huntingtower Castle. – Open April-September weekdays 9.30am-7pm, Sundays 2-7pm ; October-March weekdays 9.30am-4pm, Sundays 2-4pm ; 50p HBM.

Elcho Castle. – Open April-September weekdays 9.30am-7pm, Sundays 2-7pm ; October-March weekdays 9.30am-4pm, Sundays 2-4pm ; 50p HBM.

Abernethy Round Tower. – Apply to the custodian at all reasonable times. HBM.

Glenshee. – Cairnwell Chairlift : open all the year round 9am-4.30pm ; charge.

PETERHEAD

Arbuthnot Museum. – Open Mondays-Fridays 10am-12noon, 2-5pm ; Saturdays 2-5pm.

PITLOCHRY

Pitlochry Power Station. – Open April-October daily 9.40am-5.30pm ;

Festival Theatre. – Summer season : April-October.

Killiecrankie Visitor Centre. – Open July and August daily 9.30am-6pm ; April-June and September-October daily 10am-6pm ; 10p NTS.

PITMEDDEN GARDEN

The Garden. – Open all year daily 9.30am-sunset ; £1.05 inclusive ticket NTS.

Museum of Farming Life. – Open May-September, daily 11am-6pm.

Tolquhon Castle. – Open April-September weekdays 9.30am-7pm, Sundays 2-7pm ; October-March weekdays 9.30am-4pm ; Sundays 2-4pm ; Sundays 2-4pm ; 50p HBM Lunch hour 12.30-1.30pm.

r-s

ROSSLYN CHAPEL

The Chapel. – Open April-October, weekdays 10am-5pm, Sundays 12-4.45pm ; outwith these hours by arrangement ℘ 031 440 2159 ; 50p.

ST ANDREWS

The Cathedral. – Open April-September weekdays 9.30am-7pm ; Sundays 2-7pm : October-March weekdays 9.30am-4pm ; Sundays 2-4pm ; HBM.

St Regulus Tower and Museum. – Combined ticket ; 50p.

The Castle. – Open April-September weekdays 9.30am-7pm, Sundays 2-7pm ; October-March weekdays 9.30am-4pm ; Sundays 2-4pm ; 50p HBM.

The University. – Guided tours of the university 1 July-15 September, daily 10.30am and 2.30pm ; 50p. Starting point Porter's Lodge, St Salvator's Quadrangle.

St Leonard's Chapel. – Open 10am-4pm.

Holy Trinity Church. – Opening hours as intimated on notice board.

Earlshall Castle. – Open Easter-September, Thursdays-Sundays 2-6pm ; ℘ Leuchars (0334 83) 205 ; £1.50.

Hill of Tarvit. – Open May-September, daily except Fridays, 2-6pm ; weekends only 2-6pm during April and October : ℘ Cupar (0334) 53 127 ; £1.10 NTS. Gardens and grounds open all year 10am-dusk ; 55p.

Scotstarvit Tower. – Same opening times as Hill of Tarvit, see above. Key available from Hill of Tarvit.

Fife Folk Museum. – Open April-October, daily except Tuesdays 2-5pm ; Sundays 2.30-5.30pm ; ℘ Ceres (033 482) 380 ; 50p.

Craigtoun Country Park. – Open April-September, daily 10.30am-6pm, £1.00.

SCONE PALACE

The Palace. – Open early April-mid October daily 10am-5.30pm ; Sundays 2-5.30pm but in July and August Sunday opening is 11am-5.30pm ; mid October-March by arrangement ; ℘ Perth (0738) 52 300 ; £1.90.

SELKIRK

Halliwell's House Museum. – Open April-October weekdays 10am-5pm ; Sundays 2-5pm ; November-December Mondays-Fridays 2-4.30pm ; ℘ Selkirk (0750) 20 096 ; 50p.

Newark Castle. – Tower closed due to danger from falling stones.

SETON COLLEGIATE CHURCH

The Church. – Open April-September, weekdays 9.30am-7pm ; Sundays 2-7pm ; October-March weekdays 9.30am-4pm ; Sundays ; 2-4pm ; closed Tuesday pm and Wednesdays ; 50p HBM.

SHETLAND ISLANDS

Jarlshof. – Open April-September weekdays 9.30am-7.30pm ; October-March 9.30am-4pm ; Sundays 2-4pm ; closed Wednesday pm and Tuesdays in winter ; 50p HBM.

Shetland Museum, Lerwick. – Open Mondays Wednesdays and Fridays 10am-1pm : 2.30-5pm, 6-8pm Tuesdays and Saturdays 10am-1pm ; 2.30-5pm ; Thursday 10am- 1pm.

Clickhimin Broch. – Open Mondays-Saturdays 9.30am-7pm : Sundays 2-7pm. If closed enquire at garage opposite. HBM.

Scalloway Castle. – Open Mondays-Saturdays 9.30am-7pm ; Sundays 2-7pm : HBM.

Shetland Croft House Museum. – Open May-September daily except Mondays 10am-1pm, 2-5pm ;

Mousa Broch. – Via motor boat from Sandwick by arrangement with the proprietor Tom Jamieson. Leebitton, to Sandwick (95) 367 ; charge, 10 minute boat trip from Sandwick jetty.

SKYE, Isle of

Dunvegan Castle. – Open mid May-September, Mondays-Saturdays, 10.30am-5pm : April-mid May and first two weeks in October, 2-5pm ; closed Sundays ℘ Dunvegan (047 022) 206 ; £1.80.

Colbost Folk Museum. – Open daily 10am-7pm ; 45p.

Skye Croft Museum. – Open April-October, Mondays-Saturdays 9am-6pm ; closed Sundays ; ℘ 047 052 279 ; 50p.

Clan Donald Centre. – Open April-mid October Mondays-Saturdays 10am-5.30pm ; Sundays June-September 1-5.30pm ; ℘ 047 14 227 ; £1.00.

SOUTH QUEENSFERRY

Forth Road Bridge. – Toll bridge : 30p. foot and cycle tracks : free.

Boat trip to Inchcolm Island. – *The Maid of the Forth* operates from Hawes Pier at weekends from Easter-mid September and on weekdays from July-early September. See notice board at Hawes Pier, Tourist Information Centres or Hotel Receptions for sailing schedules. Round trip : 2 hours giving over an hour on the island : Adults £3.25.

STIRLING

Castle Visitor Centre. – Open, April-September, weekdays 9.30am-6pm ; Sundays 10.30am-5.30pm ; October-March weekdays 9.30am-5.05pm ; Sundays 12.30pm-4.20pm ; closed January.

Stirling Castle. – Open June-August weekdays 10am-8pm, Sundays 11am-8pm ; April, May September weekdays 10am-6.45pm, Sundays 11am-6pm ; October-March weekdays 10am-4pm ; Sundays 1-4pm ; £1.30, guided tour optional. Tickets from the Castle Visitor Centre £1.20 HBM.

Argyll and Sutherland Highlanders Regimental Museum. – Open April-September weekdays 10am-5.30pm ; Sundays 11am-5pm ; October weekdays only 10am-4pm : ☎ Stirling (0786) 75165 ; by donation.

Argyll's Lodging. – Not at present open to the public.

Church of the Holy Rude. – Open April-October 9.30am-5.30pm ; when closed during summer apply to the caretaker of the Guildhall opposite.

Guildhall. – Open all the year, apply to the caretaker.

John Cowane's House. – Open May-September, Tuesdays and Thursdays 10am-12noon, 2-4pm.

Smith Museum and Art Gallery. – Open Wednesdays, Thursdays, Fridays and Sundays 2-5pm, Saturdays 10.30am-5pm ; ☎ Stirling (0786) 71 917.

Wallace Monument. – Open daily May-August 10am-6.30pm ; 5.30pm April, September ; 4.30pm February, March, October and closed Wednesdays and Thursdays ; ☎ Stirling (0786) 72140 ; 50p.

Cambuskenneth Abbey. – Belfry open April-September only, weekdays 9.30am-7pm ; Sundays 2-7pm ; closed in winter ; grounds open all the year round ; 50p HBM.

Menstrie Castle. – Commemoration Room : May-September, Wednesdays, and weekends only 2-5.30pm ; 20p NTS.

Bannockburn Heritage Centre. – Site open all year. The visitor centre (open 1 March-31 October 10am-6pm ; 10p) includes ST B and NTS information centres shop and snack bar. An audiovisual presentation (10 mins : 50p) every 20 minutes outlines events leading up to Bannockburn and the battle itself.

Scotland's Safari Park. – Open late March-early October daily, 10am-4.30pm ; ☎ Stirling (0786) 841 456 ; £3 all inclusive.

STONEHAVEN

Tolbooth museum. – Open June-September daily 2-5pm ; Mondays, Thursdays and weekends also 10am-12noon, closed Tuesdays.

Muchalls Castle. – Guided tours, May-September, Tuesdays and Sundays 3-5pm ; ☎ Newtonhill 302 17 ; 30p.

Kinneff Old Church. – Open at all reasonable times.

STRANRAER

Castle Kennedy Gardens. – Open April-September, daily 10am-5pm ; ☎ Stranraer (0776) 2024 ; £1.00.

Castle of Park. – Visible from the outside only HBM.

Glenluce Abbey. – Open April-September weekdays 9.30am-7pm ; Sundays 2-7pm ; October-March Saturdays 9.30am-4pm ; Sundays 2-4pm ; 50p HBM.

Ardwell House Garden. – Open March-October daily 10am-6pm ; ☎ 077 686 227 ; 50p.

Logan Fish Pond. – Open late May-mid September, Mondays, Wednesdays, Fridays and Sundays 10am-12noon, 2-5.30pm ; 20p.

Logan Botanic Garden. – Open April-September, daily 10am-5pm ; ☎ 077 686 231 ; 50p per car admits all passengers.

TANTALLON CASTLE

The castle ruins. – Open April-September weekdays 9.30am-7pm, Sundays 2-7pm ; October-March 9.30am-4pm ; Sundays 2-4pm ; £1.00 HBM.

THORNILL

Scottish Lead Mining Museum. – Open Easter-September, daily, 11am-4pm ; ☎ Wanlockhead (065 94) 387 ; Museum 50p ; Mine 50p.

THURSO

Folk Museum. – Open Mondays-Saturdays, 10.30am-1pm, 2-5pm ; nominal charge.

Dounreay. – Exhibition Area : open May-September, daily, 9am-4pm.

Farr Church. – Open 2-5pm : 50p.

TORPHICHEN

Preceptory. – Open April-September weekdays 9.30am-7pm, Sundays 2-7pm ; October-March weekdays 9.30am-4pm ; Sundays 2-4pm ; closed alternate Wednesdays and every Friday ; 50p HBM.

Cairnpapple Hill. – Open April-September weekdays 9.30am-7pm ; Sundays 2-7pm ; closed in winter also Monday am and Fridays in summer ; 50p HBM.

TRAQUAIR HOUSE

The House. – Open July-mid September daily 10.30am-5.30pm ; April-June and 3 weeks in October 1.30-5.30pm ; ☎ Innerleithen (0896) 830/323 ; £1.80.

The TROSSACHS

Boat trips on Loch Katrine. – Car park (30p) reserved for boat passengers. No access round the loch for vehicles. *SS Sir Walter Scott* two trips daily, at 11am and 2.30pm ; time 1 hour 40 mins Rtn including a 10 min stop at Stronachlachar ; capacity 350-400 but be early as this is a favourite trip with bus parties which are booked in advance ; £1.75 Rtn ; steamer enquiries ☎ 041 336 5333.

Achray Forest Drive. – Open Easter-September daily 10am-6pm ; all vehicles must be out by 7pm ; two 50p pieces for the ticket machine ; 30 mins, maximum speed 15mph.

David Marshall Lodge. – Admission charge : 20p per car.

Inversnaid. – For cruises on Loch Lomond, see under the entry of that name.

Inchmahome Priory. – Open April-September daily 9.30am-7pm ; October-March, daily 9.30am-4pm ; closed Thursdays and Fridays in winter ; £1.00 inclusive of ferry HBM. To attract the ferryman's attention when he is on the island, turn the white board on the jetty.

The TWEED Valley

Scottish Museum of Woollen Textiles. – Open Mondays-Saturdays 9.30am-5pm ; Sundays 12.30-4pm ; ☎ Walkerburn (089 687) 281 ; 25p.

Tweeddale Museum. – Open Mondays-Fridays, 9am-7pm ; 5.30pm Wednesdays ; ☎ Peebles (0721) 201 23.

Neidpath Castle. – Open early April-mid October, daily, 10am-6pm ; 50p.

U

ULLAPOOL

Boat trips to the Summer Isles. – For further details apply to the tourist information office in the car ferry terminal or to the various huts on the waterfront.

Knockan Information Centre. – Open May-mid September, Mondays-Fridays 10am-6pm.

Inchnadamph Nature Reserve. – Prior permission must be obtained from Assynt Estate Office ; ☎ Lochinver (057 14) 203.

W

WESTER ROSS

Torridon Countryside Centre. – Open June-October weekdays 10am-6pm ; Sundays 2-6pm ; ☎ Torridon (044 587) 221, audiovisual presentation by donation. Deer museum : 30p. Guided walks June-September only.

Aultroy Visitor Centre. – Open in summer.

Gairloch Heritage Museum. – Open Easter-September, Mondays-Saturdays 10am-6pm ; ☎ Gairloch (044 5) 83 243 ; 30p.

WHITHORN

Museum. – Open April-September weekdays 9.30am-7pm ; Sundays 2-7pm ; October-March weekdays 9.30am-4pm ; Sundays 2-4pm ; 50p HBM.

Priory. – Key and torch for crypts from the museum, see above. HBM.

WICK

Wick Heritage Centre. – Open April-September, Tuesdays-Saturdays, 10.30am-5pm ; October-December Saturdays only 2-5pm ☎ Wick (0955) 3268.

Caithness Glass. – Open Mondays-Fridays 9am-5pm ; Saturdays 9am-4pm (1pm in winter) ; ☎ Wick (0955) 2286.

Laidhay Croft Museum. – Open April-September, daily 10am-6pm ; ☎ Lybster (059 32) 357 ; 50p.

John Nicolson Museum. – Open daily 2-5pm : 50p.

John o' Groats. – Passenger boat service to Burwick on South Ronaldsay : 4 times daily : time 45 minutes.

MANUFACTURE FRANÇAISE DES PNEUMATIQUES MICHELIN

Société en commandite par actions au capital de 700 000 000 de francs

Place des Carmes-Déchaux – 63 Clermont-Ferrand (France)

R.C.S. Clermont-Fd B 855 200 507

© Michelin et Cie, Propriétaires-Éditeurs 1985

Dépôt légal 12.85 – ISBN 2.06.015.715-X – ISSN 0763-1383

Printed in France – 12-85-60

Photocomposition et impression : MAURY Imprimeur S.A., Malesherbes, n° B 85-16216